Designing the User Interface

Strategies for Effective Human–Computer Interaction

Second Edition

Ben Shneiderman
The University of Maryland

 Addison-Wesley Publishing Company

Reading, Massachusetts • Menlo Park, California • New York
Don Mills, Ontario • Wokingham, England • Amsterdam
Bonn • Sydney • Singapore • Tokyo • Madrid
San Juan • Milan • Paris

Many of the designations used by manufacturers and sellers to distinguish their products are claimed as trademarks. Where those designations appear in this book, and Addison-Wesley was aware of a trademark claim, the designations have been printed in initial caps or all caps.

The programs and applications presented in this book have been included for their instructional value. They have been tested with care, but are not guaranteed for any particular purpose. The publisher does not offer any warranties or representations, nor does it accept any liabilities with respect to the programs or applications.

Library of Congress Cataloging-in-Publication Data

Shneiderman, Ben.
    Designing the user interface : strategies for effective human
-computer interaction / Ben Shneiderman. -- 2nd ed.
        p.   cm.
    Includes bibliographical references and index.
    ISBN 0-201-57286-9
    1. Human-computer interaction. 2. User interfaces (Computer
systems) 3. System design.   I. Title.
QA76.9.I58S47 1992
004.6--dc20   91-35589
                                                                    CIP

Chapter opener illustrations © Paul S. Hoffman; chapter opener outlines © Teresa Casey.

3 4 5 6 7 8 9 10 DO 959493

Preface to the First Edition

FIGHTING FOR THE USER

Frustration and anxiety are a part of daily life for many users of computerized information systems. They struggle to learn command language or menu selection systems that are supposed to help them do their job. Some people encounter such serious cases of computer shock, terminal terror, or network neurosis that they avoid using computerized systems. These electronic-age maladies are growing more common; but help is on the way!

Researchers have shown that redesign of the human–computer interface can make a substantial difference in learning time, performance speed, error rates, and user satisfaction. Information and computer scientists have been testing design alternatives for their impact on these human performance measures. Commercial designers recognize that systems that are easier to use will have a competitive edge in information retrieval, office automation, and personal computing.

Programmers and quality assurance teams are becoming more cautious and paying greater attention to the implementation issues that guarantee high-quality user interfaces. Computer center managers are realizing that they must play an active role in ensuring that the software and hardware facilities provide high-quality service to their users.

In short, the diverse use of computers in homes, offices, factories, hospitals, electric power control centers, hotels, banks, etc. is stimulating widespread interest in human factors issues. Human engineering, which was seen as the paint put on at the end of a project, is now understood to be the steel frame on which the structure is built.

However, an awareness of the problems and a desire to do well are not sufficient. Designers, managers, and programmers must be willing to step forward and fight for the user. The enemies include inconsistent command languages, confusing operation sequences, chaotic display formats, inconsistent terminology, incomplete instructions, complex error recovery procedures, and misleading or threatening error messages.

I believe that progress in serving users will be rapid because as examples of excellence proliferate, users' expectations will rise. The designers, managers, and researchers who are dedicated to quality and to nurturing the user community will have the satisfaction of doing a good job and the appreciation of the users they serve.

The battle will not be won by angry argumentation over the "user friendliness" of competing systems or by biased claims that "my design is more natural than your design." Victory will come to people who take a disciplined, iterative, and empirical approach to the study of human performance in the use of interactive systems. More and more, system developers, maintainers, and managers are collecting performance data from users, distributing subjective satisfaction surveys, inviting users to participate in design teams, conducting repeated field trials for novel proposals, and using field study data to support organization decision making.

Marshall McLuhan observed that "the medium is the message." Designers send a message to the users by the design of interactive systems. In the past, the message was often an unfriendly and unpleasant one. I believe, however, that it is possible to send a much more positive message that conveys the genuine concern a designer has for the users. If the users feel competent in using the system, can easily correct errors, and can accomplish their tasks, then they will pass on the message of quality to the people they serve, to their colleagues, and to their friends and families. In this way, each designer has the possibility of making the world a little warmer, wiser, safer, and more compassionate.

My goals are to encourage greater attention to the user interface and to help develop a more rigorous science of user interface design. *Designing the User Interface* presents design issues, offers experimental evidence where available, and makes reasonable recommendations where suitable.

Designing the User Interface was written primarily for designers, managers, and evaluators of interactive systems. It presents a broad survey of the issues in designing, implementing, managing, maintaining, training, and refining the user interface of interactive systems. The book's second audience is researchers in human performance with interactive systems. These researchers may have their background in computer science, psychology, human factors, ergonomics, education, management information systems, information science, or industrial engineering, but they all share a desire to understand the complex interaction of people and machines. Students in these fields will also benefit from the contents of this book. It is my hope that this book will stimulate the introduction of courses on user interface design in all of these disciplines. Finally, serious users of interactive systems may benefit by a more thorough understanding of the design questions for user interfaces.

An author's work is highly personal and sometimes lonely. That isolation is softened by family and friends who must put up with the author's struggle. In this connection, I thank my wife, Nancy, and children, Sara and Anna, for cheering me on, accepting my intense involvement in writing, and showing me the beauty in living and loving.

Preface to the Second Edition

Writing a second edition is like restoring a Persian rug. Every knot must be examined to determine if its color and tone are still good for another decade. Then, if a section needs repair, each new knot must be made to match the local color and the global pattern. The tension, length, color, and glow have to be in harmony with the neighboring knots. Extensions and new fringes must blend with and preserve the unity of the entire work. It is a tedious job, but the final results are satisfying.

I have tried to respond to the many comments and suggestions I have received over the past five years and the unusually thoughtful, extensive, and supportive reviews that 11 people provided last year when the second edition proposal was circulated. Reading reviews that were published when the first edition came out also helped to guide my work. Major topics have been added and many refinements have been made. Significance levels have been removed, references to obscure and student projects have been nearly eliminated, and references have been updated extensively, while the older, foundational references have been retained. The technology, development processes, applications, and theory have advanced since I wrote the first edition, and I have tried to keep up. My goal here, however, is not to record what is happening at every research frontier, but rather to give a balanced and thorough presentation of our steadily growing discipline. I hope to have written a book that is comprehensible to practitioners as well as senior and graduate students. My orientation is from computer science, but I hope that professionals and students with backgrounds in software engineering, psychology, business, library and information science, education, and design will also be served well.

Chapter 1 has been expanded to cover internationalization, and to include the needs of disabled and elderly users. At the end of Chapter 1, after the specific references for that chapter, I have included an extensive set of information resources for newcomers to user-interface design. Chapter 2 expands the coverage of several theories, but I wish we had more potent and widely accepted theories to talk about. Chapter 3, on menus, has been updated throughout. On the other hand, there was not too much to add to Chapter 4, on command languages, although some readers may be surprised to see how much I had to say in the much expanded section on natural language. Chapter 5, on direct manipulation, was the most enjoyable to revise because so many interesting developments have occurred and so many productive opportunities are opening up. I had great fun writing the section on virtual reality, and I hope readers will tolerate the colorful language in that section. Much of the previous lengthy discussion of our DMDOS software has been cut, but our recent work on teleoperation is an important addition (partially derived from Keil-Slawik, Reinhard, Plaisant,

Catherine, and Shneiderman, Ben, Remote direct manipulation: A case study of a tele-pathology workstation, in Bullinger, H.-J. (Editor) *Human Aspects of Computing: Design and Use of Interactive Systems and Information Management*, Elsevier, Amsterdam, The Netherlands, *Proc. HCI '91 International*, Stuttgart, Germany (1991), 1006–1011).

Chapter 6, on input/output devices, has been updated and now includes a discussion of Fitts's law. Chapter 7, on response time, has been shortened in response to the recommendation of several reviewers. Chapter 8, on messages and screen design, has been revised modestly throughout. The section on window management has grown into a full Chapter 9. I feel that I have made a useful contribution in sorting out the complex issues in window design.

Reviewers encouraged me to put in a complete Chapter 10, on computer-supported cooperative work. I have blended several suggestions about what to write about hypertext and have added a new Chapter 11, on information exploration tools, that combines hypertext, some background on information retrieval, and several interesting developments in data visualization (partially derived from Shneiderman, Ben, Visual user interfaces for information exploration, Keynote address, *Proc. American Society for Information Science Conference*, Washington, D.C. (October 1991), 378–385).

Chapter 12, on manuals and online help, has been extensively revised, and Chapter 13, on evaluation methods, now covers usability testing more thoroughly, as many reviewers recommended. Chapter 14 covers specification methods, software-prototyping tools, programmer toolkits, and user-interface management systems. The Afterword includes a portion of my keynote talk from the ACM SIGCAS (Human values and the future of technology: A declaration of empowerment, Keynote address, ACM SIGCAS Conference on Computers and the Quality of Life (September 1990); reprinted in *ACM SIGCHI Bulletin* (January 1991)) and discussions of ethical and social issues. The Afterword has brought the broadest range of responses—from enthusiasts who want more to critics who want it cut.

Writing this book was a great opportunity to catch up on what my colleagues are doing and to think seriously about what I am doing. It has been intense and exhausting, but was a useful experience that I hope will contribute to increasing interest in user-interface design.

Writing is a lonely process, but feedback I received from close colleagues and anonymous reviewers helped guide me and keep me going. My thanks for their comments on various chapters goes to: Maryam Alavi, University of Maryland; Al Badre, Georgia Institute of Technology; Richard Bellaver, Ball State University; David Brown, Worcester Polytechnic Institute; Rick Chimera, University of Maryland; Vitaly Dubrovsky, Clarkson University; James Foley, Georgia Institute of Technology; Rex Hartson, Virginia Polytechnic Institute; Thomas Hewett, Drexel University; Susanne Humphrey,

National Library of Medicine; Rob Jacob, Naval Research Laboratories; Charles Kreitzberg, Cognetics Corporation; James Larson, Portland State University and Intel; Gary Marchionini, University of Maryland; Brad Myers, Carnegie-Mellon University ; Anthony Norcio, University of Maryland, Baltimore County; Kent Norman, University of Maryland; Randy Pausch, University of Virginia; Catherine Plaisant, University of Maryland; C. Ray Russell, Appalachian State University; Michael Spring, University of Pittsburgh; and Craig Wills, Worcester Polytechnic Institute.

I am grateful to my colleagues, especially, Catherine Plaisant, Rick Chimera, Kent Norman, and Gary Marchionini, and the graduate students, especially, David Carr, Brian Johnson, Richard Potter, and Andrew Sears, at the Human–Computer Interaction Laboratory at the University of Maryland for helping to create new ideas, making each day a satisfying challenge, enriching me with their insights, and offering suggestions to improve this book.

Paul Hoffman's chapter opening artwork interprets the message of each chapter in an elegant, thoughtful, and creative manner. Teresa Casey prepared the 15 chapter opening graphics of icons zooming out to become windows containing each chapter's table of contents. Her creative ideas and artistic skill have refined my rough sketches into provocative designs that demonstrate some of the possibilities available to user-interface architects. Mildred Johnson's heroic efforts in collecting the figures and gaining permissions enabled me to show user-interface designs from a variety of sources. She has been my secretary for more than 12 years and has contributed to my work in many constructive ways.

Peter Gordon's encouragement was vital in making this book a reality. He, Helen Goldstein, and Patsy DuMoulin at Addison-Wesley were important contributors to the book's form and content.

I hope that this book will contribute to making future technologies more humane and to making the human experience a bit more intimate, wiser, safer, kinder, and more joyous.

Ben Shneiderman
Department of Computer Science
University of Maryland
College Park, MD 20742
ben@cs.umd.edu

Credits

Chapter 1: *The Home Computer Revolution* by Theodore Holm Nelson, © 1977 by Theodore Holm Nelson. Reprinted with permission. *The Home Computer Revolution* is available from The Distributors, South Bend, Indiana.

Chapter 3: *A Certain World* by W.H. Auden, © 1970 by W.H. Auden. Reprinted by permission of Curtis Brown, Ltd., and Faber and Faber Limited, London.

Chapter 5: "Leibniz," by Frederick Kreiling, is from *Scientific American*, May, 1968, p. 94.

Chapter 8: *On Shame and the Search for Identity*, © 1958 by Helen Merrell Lynd and renewed 1986 by Staughton Lynd and Andrea Nold. Reprinted by permission of Harcourt Brace Jovanovich, Inc.

Chapter 11: *Drumming at the Edge of Magic: A Journey Into the Spirit of Percussion*, © 1990 by Mickey Hart. Reprinted by permission of HarperCollins Publishers.

"Visualization in Scientific Computing," by B. McCormick, T. De Fanti, and K. Brown, Eds., is from *Computer Graphics 21*, 6 (November 1987), published by ACM SIGGRAPH, New York.

Chapter 13: *Principles in Design*, by W.H. Mayall, Van Nostrand Reinhold, New York, 1979, is reprinted with permission of The Design Council, London.

Chapter 14: *The Natural House* by Frank Lloyd Wright, © The Frank Lloyd Wright Foundation 1954, is reprinted courtesy of the Frank Lloyd Wright Archives.

Afterword: *The Myth of the Machine: Technics and Human Development*, © 1967 by Lewis Mumford, reprinted by permission of Harcourt Brace Jovanovich, Inc.

Technics and Civilization by Lewis Mumford, © 1934 and renewed 1962 by Lewis Mumford, reprinted by permission of the publisher.

Megatrends: Ten New Directions Transforming Our Lives, by John Naisbitt, is © 1982 by John Naisbitt, and reprinted with the permission of Warner Books, Inc., New York.

Thomas J. Watson, Jr., as cited by Jin, Gregory K., in "On A Positive MIS Ideology," appearing in *Human Factors in Information Systems: An Organizational Perspective* by Jane Carey, Ablex Publishing Company, Norwood, New Jersey, 1991. Reprinted with permission.

Arno Penzias, *Ideas and Information*. Reprinted with permission of W.W. Norton and Company, Inc, New York.

Contents

Designing the User Interface

Strategies for Effective Human–Computer Interaction

Second Edition

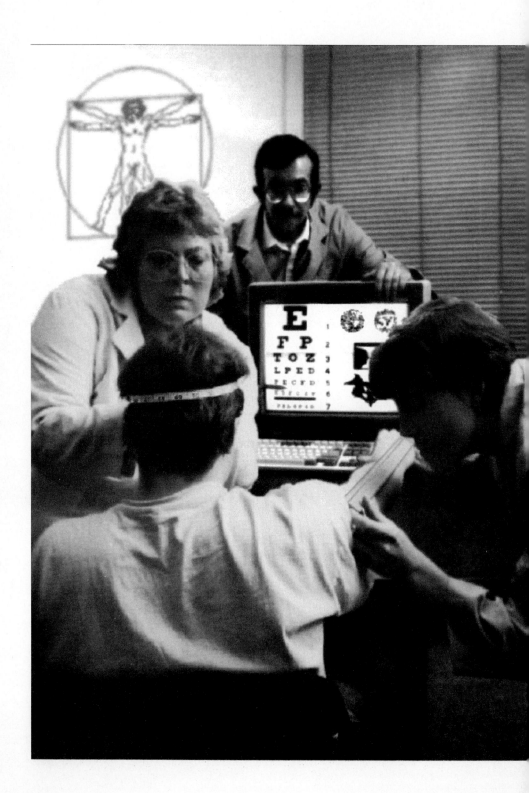

CHAPTER 1

Human Factors of Interactive Software

Designing an object to be simple and clear takes at least twice as long as the usual way. It requires concentration at the outset on how a clear and simple system would work, followed by the steps required to make it come out that way—steps which are often much harder and more complex than the ordinary ones. It also requires relentless pursuit of that simplicity even when obstacles appear which would seem to stand in the way of that simplicity.

T. H. Nelson, *The Home Computer Revolution*, 1977

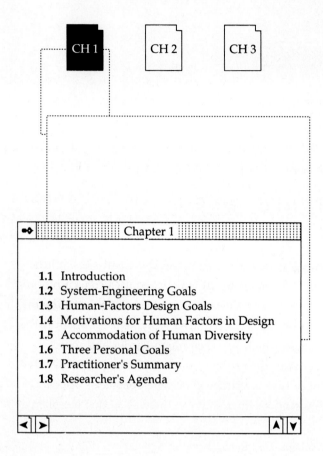

1.1   Introduction

New technologies provide extraordinary—almost supernatural—powers to those who master them. Computer systems are a new technology in the early stages of dissemination and refinement. Great excitement now exists as designers provide remarkable functions in carefully crafted interactive systems. The opportunities for system builders and entrepreneurs are substantial, since only a fraction of the potential functions and market has been explored.

Like early photography equipment or automobiles, computers are available only to people who are willing to devote effort to mastering the technology. Harnessing the computer's power is a task for designers who understand the technology and are sensitive to human capacities and needs.

Human performance in the use of computer and information systems will remain a rapidly expanding research and development topic in the coming decades. This interdisciplinary journey of discovery combines the data-gathering methods and intellectual framework of experimental psychology with the powerful and widely used tools developed from computer science. Contributions also accrue from educational and industrial psychologists, instructional designers, graphic artists, technical writers, and experts in the traditional areas of human factors or ergonomics.

Applications developers who apply human-factors principles and processes are producing exciting interactive systems. Provocative ideas emerge in the pages of the numerous thick computer magazines, the shelves of the proliferating computer stores, and the menus of the expanding computer networks. User interfaces also produce corporate success stories, intense competition, copyright-infringement suits, mega-mergers and takeovers, and international recognition. At an individual level, doctors can make a more accurate diagnosis, children can learn more effectively, graphic artists can explore more creative possibilities, and pilots can fly airplanes more safely. Nonetheless, we still must cope with the frustration, fear, and failure that results when a user faces excessive complexity, incomprehensible terminology, or chaotic layouts in a system.

The steadily growing interest in user-interface design spans remarkably diverse systems (Figures 1.1a through 1.1f and Color Plates 1 through 9). Text editors, word processors, and document formatters are used routinely in many offices, and some businesses now use painting, drawing, desktop publishing, and graphics systems. Electronic mail, bulletin boards, and computer conferencing have provided new communication media. Image processing, storage, and retrieval are used in applications from medicine to space exploration. Scientific visualization and simulator workstations allow safe, inexpensive training and experimentation. Electronic spreadsheets are in common use. Decision-support systems serve as tools for analysts from many disciplines. Computers are often used for job training and education. Home automation and environmental control are areas of active research. Public-access information, from museum kiosks to bibliographic retrieval, is widely used. Commercial systems include inventory, personnel, reservations, air traffic, and electric-utility control. Computer-assisted software-engineering tools and programming environments allow rapid prototyping, as do computer-assisted design, manufacturing, and engineering workstations. Most of us use various consumer electronics, such as VCRs, telephones, cameras, and appliances. Art, music, sports, and entertainment all are assisted or enhanced by computer systems.

Practitioners and researchers in many fields are making vital contributions. Academic and industrial theorists in computer science, psychology, and hu-

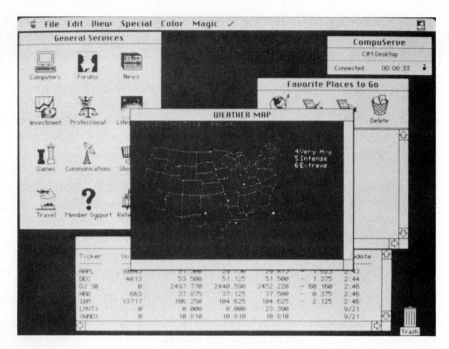

Figure 1.1(a)

By incorporating pull-down menus, dialog boxes, and several other features, the CompuServe Information Manager enables subscribers to the CompuServe Information Service to access, sort, and utilize information more efficiently. With more than 1500 databases, the CompuServe Information Service provides hourly updates on national, world, and political news as well as current weather. (Courtesy of CompuServe Incorporated, Columbus, OH.)

man factors are developing perceptual, cognitive, and motor theories and models of human performance; experimenters are collecting empirical data.

Software designers are exploring how best to present menu selection and form fillin. They are developing command, parametric, and query languages, as well as natural language facilities for input, search, and output. They are using sound (such as music and voice), graphics, animation, and color displays, still images, and video to improve the information content of the interface. Error messages and error prevention guide users in efficient interactions. And techniques such as direct manipulation, telepresence, and virtual realities may change the way we interact with and think about computers.

Hardware developers and system builders are offering novel keyboard designs and pointing devices, as well as large, high-resolution color displays. They are designing systems that provide rapid response times for

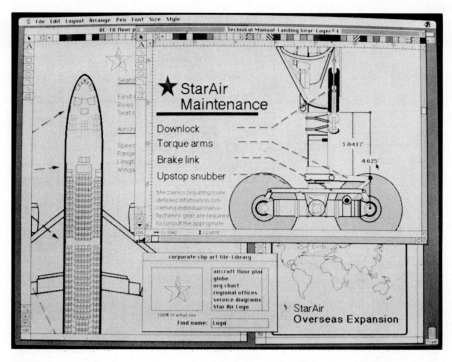

Figure 1.1(b)

MacPaint 2 provides color painting and powerful tools on the Macintosh computers. This example shows aircraft-maintenance diagrams. (Courtesy of Claris Corp., Santa Clara, CA.)

increasingly complex tasks, and that have fast display rates and smooth transitions for increasingly high-resolution displays. Parallel architectures, for example, support rapid interaction. Technologies that allow speech input and output, and gestural input and tactile or force-feedback output, increase ease of use, as do input devices such as the touchscreen and stylus.

Developers with an orientation toward educational psychology, instructional design, and technical writing are creating engaging online tutorials, training, reference manuals, demonstrations and sales materials, and are exploring novel approaches to group lectures, personalized experiential training, and video presentations.

Graphic designers are actively engaged in visual layout, color selection, and animation. Each chapter opener of this book contains a strategy for icons that open into windows to show the chapter table of contents.

Sociologists, anthropologists, philosophers, policy makers, and managers are dealing with organizational impact, computer anxiety, job redesign,

Figure 1.1(c)

PRODIGY Information System has thousands of services, including a U.S. national weather map that is updated regularly. (Courtesy of Prodigy Services Company, White Plains, NY.)

retraining, distributed teamwork, computer-supported cooperation strategies, work-at-home schemes, and long-term societal changes.

This is an exciting time for developers of user interfaces. The hardware and software foundations for the bridges and tunnels have been built. Now, the roadway can be laid and the stripes painted to make way for the heavy traffic of eager users.

The rapid growth of interest in user-interface design is international in scope. In the United States, the Association for Computing Machinery (ACM) Special Interest Group in Computer Human Interaction (SIGCHI) had more than 5000 members in 1991 and was the fastest growing of the 35 SIGs. The annual CHI conferences draw almost 2500 people. The Human Factors Society and other professional groups also devote increasing attention to human–computer interaction. In Europe, the ESPRIT project devotes approximately 150 person-years of effort per year to the topic. In 1988 in Japan, the Ministry of International Trade and Industry created the FRIEND21 project, conducted by Institute for Per-

Figure 1.1(d)

"Where in Time is Carmen Sandiego?" is one of the most popular educational
games in the home market. It is part of a series that includes U.S. national and
world travel facts. (Courtesy of Brøderbund Software, Inc., Novato, CA.
© Brøderbund Software, Inc. 1991. All rights reserved.)

sonalized Information Environment (Nonogaki and Ueda, 1991; specialized references for this chapter appear on page 36; general information
resources begin on page 38). This consortium of 14 major computing,
home-electronics, and publishing companies is conducting basic human-
interface research.

1.2   System-Engineering Goals

High-level goals of making the quality of life better (see Afterword) are
important to keep in mind, but designers have more specific goals. Every
designer wants to build a high-quality interactive system that is admired by
colleagues, celebrated by users, circulated widely, and imitated frequently.
Appreciation comes, not from flamboyant promises or stylish advertising
brochures, but rather from inherent quality features that are achieved by
thoughtful planning, sensitivity to user needs, careful attention to detail in
design and development, and diligent testing.

Figure 1.1(e)

SONY Palmtop uses a stylus to allow pointing to text/icons and creating graphics. Handwritten character recognition uses stroke sequence information to improve accuracy. (Courtesy of SONY Corp., Tokyo, Japan.)

Managers can promote attention to user-interface issues by selection of personnel, preparation of schedules and milestones, construction and application of guidelines documents, and commitment to testing. Designers then propose multiple design alternatives for consideration, and the leading contenders are subjected to further development and testing (see Chapter 13). User-interface management systems (UIMSs) and other software tools (see Chapter 14) enable rapid implementation and easy revision. Evaluation of designs refines the understanding of appropriateness for each choice.

Successful designers go beyond the vague notion of "user friendliness" and probe deeper than simply making a checklist of subjective guidelines. They must have a thorough understanding of the diverse community of users and the tasks that must be accomplished. Moreover, they must have a deep commitment to serving the users, which strengthens their resolve when they face the pressures of short deadlines, tight budgets, and weak-willed compromisers.

Effective systems generate positive feelings of success, competence, mastery, and clarity in the user community. The users are not encumbered by the

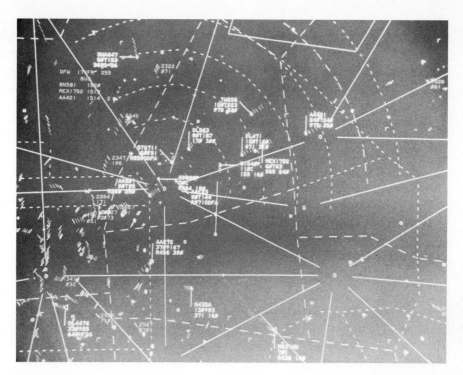

Figure 1.1(f)

Air-traffic control information for the Fort Worth, Texas ARTCC radar showing sequencing of Dallas–Fort Worth arrivals over the Blue Ridge VOR, prior to handoff to DFW. (FAA photograph by S. Michael McKean.)

computer and can predict what will happen in response to each of their actions. When an interactive system is well designed, the interface almost disappears, enabling users to concentrate on their work, exploration, or pleasure. Creating an environment in which tasks are carried out almost effortlessly and users are "in the flow" requires a great deal of hard work from the designer.

Setting explicit goals helps designers to achieve them. In getting beyond the vague quest for user-friendly systems, managers and designers can focus on specific goals that include well-defined system-engineering issues and measurable human-factors issues. The U. S. Military Standard for Human Engineering Design Criteria (1989) states these purposes:

- Achieve required performance by operator, control, and maintenance personnel
- Minimize skill and personnel requirements and training time
- Achieve required reliability of personnel–equipment combinations
- Foster design standardization within and among systems

1.2.1   Proper functionality

The first step is to ascertain the necessary functionality—what tasks and subtasks must be carried out. The frequent tasks are easy to determine, but the occasional tasks, the exceptional tasks for emergency conditions, and the repair tasks to cope with errors in use of the system are more difficult to discover. Task analysis is central, because systems with inadequate functionality frustrate the user and are often rejected or underutilized (Bailey, 1989). If the functionality is inadequate, it does not matter how well the human interface is designed. Excessive functionality is also a danger, and probably the more common mistake of designers, because the clutter and complexity make implementation, maintenance, learning, and usage more difficult.

1.2.2   Reliability, availability, security, and data integrity

A vital second step is ensuring proper system reliability: commands must function as specified, displayed data must reflect the database contents, and updates must be applied correctly. Users' trust of systems is fragile; one experience with unexpected results will undermine a person's willingness to use a system for a long time. The software architecture, hardware components, and network support must ensure high availability. If the system is not available or introduces errors, then it does not matter how well the human interface is designed. Attention must also be paid to ensuring privacy, security, and data integrity. Protection must be provided from unwarranted access, inadvertent destruction of data, or malicious tampering.

1.2.3   Standardization, integration, consistency, and portability

As the number of users and software packages increases, the pressures for and benefits of standardization grow. Slight differences among systems not only increase learning times, but can lead to annoying and dangerous errors. Gross differences among systems require substantial retraining and burden the users in many ways. Incompatible storage formats, hardware, and software versions cause frustration, inefficiency, and delay. Designers must decide whether the improvements they offer are useful enough to offset the disruption to the users.

   Standardization refers to common user-interface features across multiple applications. Apple Computers (1987) successfully developed an early standard that was widely applied by thousands of developers, enabling users to learn multiple applications quickly. IBM's Common User Access

(1989, 1991) specifications came later; it will take many years for their benefits to emerge.

In the UNIX environment, the command language was standard from the beginning (with some divergences), but there are now several competing standards for graphic user interfaces. UNIX was a leader and inspiration in standardizing data formats to enable integration across the numerous application packages and software tools, and to allow portability across hardware platforms.

Consistency primarily refers to common action sequences, terms, units, layouts, color, typography, and so on within an application program; it is naturally extended to include compatibility across application programs and compatibility with paper or non–computer-based systems. International standards are emerging that may have a profound influence on designers.

Portability refers to the potential to convert data and to share user interfaces across multiple software and hardware environments. Arranging for portability is a challenge for designers who must contend with different display sizes and resolutions, color capabilities, pointing devices, data formats, and so on. Some UIMSs help by generating code for Macintosh, IBM PC, UNIX, and other environments so that the interfaces are similar in each environment. Standard text files (in ASCII) can be moved easily across environments, but graphic images, spreadsheets, video images, and so on are far more difficult to convert.

1.2.4   Schedules and budgets

Careful planning and courageous management are needed if a project is to be on schedule and within budget. Delayed delivery or cost overruns can threaten a system because of the confrontational political atmosphere in a company, or because the competitive market environment contains potentially overwhelming forces. If an in-house system is delivered late, then other projects are affected, and the disruption may cause managers to choose to install an alternative system. If a commercial system is too costly, customer resistance may emerge to prevent widespread acceptance, allowing competitors to capture the market.

Proper attention to human-factors principles and rigorous testing often leads to reduced cost and rapid development. A carefully tested design generates fewer changes during implementation and avoids costly updates after release of new systems. The business case for human factors in computer and information systems is strong (Klemmer, 1989; Chapanis, 1991), as demonstrated by many successful products whose advantage lay in their superior user interfaces.

1.3   Human-Factors Design Goals

If adequate functionality has been chosen, reliability is ensured, standardization addressed, and schedule plus budgetary planning is complete, then developers can focus their attention on the design and testing process. The multiple design alternatives must be evaluated for specific user communities and for specific benchmark sets of tasks. A clever design for one community of users may be inappropriate for another community. An efficient design for one class of tasks may be inefficient for another class.

1.3.1   The Library of Congress experience

The relativity of design played a central role in the evolution of information services at the Library of Congress. Two of the major uses of computer systems were cataloging new books and searching the online book catalog. Separate systems for these tasks were created that optimized the design for one task and made the complementary task difficult. It would be impossible to say which was better, because they were both fine systems, but they were serving different needs. Posing such a question would be like asking whether the New York Philharmonic Orchestra was better than the New York Yankees baseball team.

The bibliographic search system, SCORPIO (Figure 1.2), was successfully used by the staffs of the Library of Congress, the Congressional Research Service (CRS), and the Senate and the House of Representatives. They could do bibliographic searching and also could use the same system to locate and read CRS reports, to view events recorded in the bill-status system, and much more. The professional staff members took a 3- to 6-hour training course and then could use terminals in their office, where more experienced colleagues could help them with problems and where adequate consultants were usually available.

Then, in January 1981, the Library of Congress stopped entering new book information in the manual card catalogs, thus requiring the general public to use one of the 18 terminals in the main reading room to locate new books. For even a computer-knowledgeable individual, learning to use the commands, understanding the cataloging rules, and formulating a search strategy would be a challenging task. The reference librarians claimed that they could teach a willing adult the basic features in 15 minutes. But 15 minutes per patron would overwhelm the staff; more important, most people are not interested in investing even 15 minutes in learning to use a computer system for this purpose. Library patrons have work to do and often perceive the computer as an intrusion in or interference with their

```
E272 SIGNED ON LOC - CICS/VS, 10/08/91 19.50.28
 bgns lccc


TUESDAY, 10/08/91  07:50 P.M.
***LCCC- THE LIBRARY OF CONGRESS COMPUTERIZED CATALOG
             is now available for your search.
             The Term Index was updated on 10/07/91.


   CONTENTS:   Books, some microforms
                      English                    1968-
                      French                     1973-
                        German/Portuguese/Spanish   1975-
                      Other European             1976-1977-
                      Non European               1978-1979-


   TO START     BROWSE first words of         EXAMPLES
      SEARCH:       subject ------->           browse solar energy
                    author --------->            browse faulkner, william
                    title ------->              browse megatrends
                    call # (partial) ----->     browse call QA76.9
                    LC card number ------>      lccc 80-14332


   FOR HELP:    Type the word HELP, and press the ENTER key.


      READY FOR NEW COMMAND:
browse pirsig


To choose from list, see examples at bottom.
FILE: LCCC
Terms alphabetically close to:PIRSIG


B01 PIRSCHEL, OTTO//(AUTH=1)
B02 PIRSCHEN IM DSCHUNGEL//(TITL=1)
B03 PIRSCHGANGE IM SPRACHREVIER//(TITL=1)
B04 PIRSEIN, ROBERT WILLIAM//(AUTH=1)
B05 PIRSICH, VOLKER//(AUTH=3)
B06+PIRSIG ON MINNESOTA PLEADING//(TITL=1)
B07 PIRSIG, MAYNARD E//(AUTH=8)
B08 PIRSIG, ROBERT M//(AUTH=4; INDX=3)
B09 PIRSL, EMIL//(AUTH=1)
B10 PIRSON-DE CLERCQ, JACQUELINE//(AUTH=1)
B11 PIRSON, A//(AUTH=2)
B12 PIRSON, JEAN-FRANCOIS//(AUTH=1)
```

Figure 1.2

Users of the Library of Congress's SCORPIO can access many databases, including the Computerized Card Catalog. User-typed commands are underscored. Abbreviated forms of the command are available. This search shows a browse command for the author "pirsig," a select command to choose the set of books by the author, and a display command to view the catalog entries.

```
—EXAMPLES:  s b6                    (SELECTs line b6; creates a SET for
                                     each term type)
                 f b6-b8/b10      (FINDs b6-b8 and b10; combines sets,
                                     displays result)
                 r b6                  (RETRIEVEs term on b6; searches text
                                     in some files)
                 r subj=b6          (RETRIEVEs term type specified;
                                     e.g., SUBJ, TITL)


     Next page of BROWSE list, press ENTER key.   More info,
     type HELP BROWSE.
     READY:
select b8


SET   1               4: SLCT AUTH/PIRSIG, ROBERT M
SET   2               3: SLCT INDX/PIRSIG, ROBERT M
READY FOR NEW COMMAND:
display 1


ITEMS 1-4 OF 4                      SET 1: BRIEF DISPLAY              FILE: LCCC
                                       (ASCENDING ORDER)
1. 73-12275:Pirsig, Robert M.   Zen and the art of
       motorcycle maintenance.   New York, Morrow, 1974.   412 p, 21 cm.
     LC CALL NUMBER: CT275.P648 A33
2. 83-25026:Pirsig, Robert M.   Zen and the art of
       motorcycle maintenance.   New York, Morrow, 1984, c1974.
       412 p., 22 cm.
     LC CALL NUMBER: CT275.P648 A33 1984
3. 90-37374:DiSanto, Ronald L.   Guidebook to Zen and the art
       of motorcycle maintenance /.   New York, W. Morrow, 1990.
       407 p, ill., map, 25 cm.
     LC CALL NUMBER: CT275.P6483 D57 1990
4. 91-16417:Pirsig, Robert M.   Lila.   New York, Bantam Books,
       1991.   409 p., 25 cm.
     LC CALL NUMBER: PS3566.I66 L54 1991


     READY:
   ends


THIS SEARCH REQUIRED 7.69 MINUTES.   THANK YOU.
'SCORPIO' IS A SERVICE OF THE LIBRARY OF CONGRESS.
```

Figure 1.2

(Con't.)

work. The SCORPIO system that worked so well for one community of users was inappropriate for this new community.

The system designers revised the online messages to provide more supportive and constructive feedback, offered extensive online tutorial material, and began to explore the use of menu-selection approaches for the novice users. In short, adapting the system to serve a new community of users demanded substantial redesign of the human interface.

As the years passed, incremental improvements were applied. Regular users took courses, read the manuals, and received personal assistance from the devoted reference librarians. However, the goal of providing excellent service to first-time users was still unfulfilled. Guided by a team from the University of Maryland and from Cognetics Corp., the staff of the Library of Congress Information Technology Service, led by Maryle Ashley, created a completely new touchscreen system called ACCESS. Two years of planning, user surveys, design, testing, and redesign generated a new front end to the existing system. The new Computer Catalog Center, just steps away from the elegant domed main reading room in the classic Jefferson Building, opened in June 1991 with 18 actively used ACCESS touchscreens (Figures 1.3a through 1.3f) and 30 command-oriented terminals.

1.3.2   Measurable human-factors goals

Once a determination has been made of the user community and of the benchmark set of tasks, then the human-factors goals can be examined. For each user and each task, precise measurable objectives guide the designer, evaluator, purchaser, or manager. These five measurable human factors are

Figure 1.3(a)

The new ACCESS (Figure 1.3a–f) system simplifies use for first-time users by providing touchscreen selection, and information about possible actions.

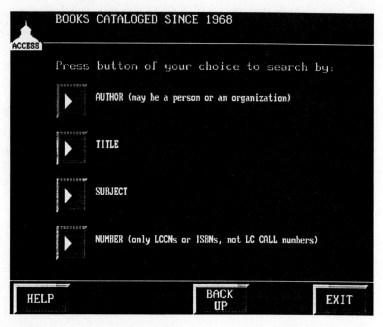

Figure 1.3(b)

(Con't.)

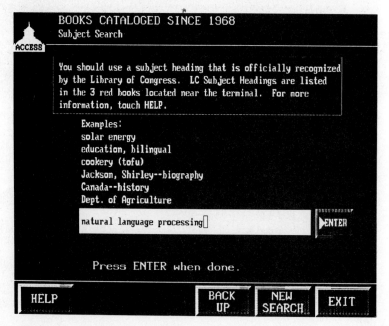

Figure 1.3(c)

(Con't.)

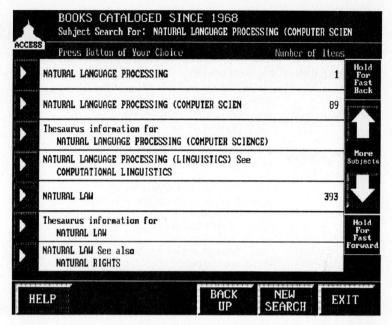

Figure 1.3(d)

(Con't.)

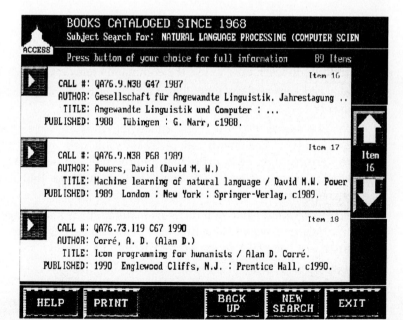

Figure 1.3(e)

(Con't.)

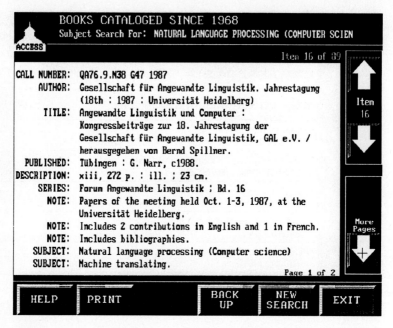

Figure 1.3(f)

(Con't.)

central to evaluation:

1. *Time to learn:* How long does it take for typical members of the user community to learn how to use the commands relevant to a set of tasks?

2. *Speed of performance:* How long does it take to carry out the benchmark set of tasks?

3. *Rate of errors by users:* How many and what kinds of errors are made in carrying out the benchmark set of tasks? Although time to make and correct errors might be incorporated into the speed of performance, error making is such a critical component of system usage that it deserves extensive study.

4. *Retention over time:* How well do users maintain their knowledge after an hour, a day, or a week? Retention may be linked closely to time to learn; frequency of use plays an important role.

5. *Subjective satisfaction:* How much did users like using various aspects of the system? The answer can be ascertained by interview or by written surveys that include satisfaction scales and space for free-form comments.

Every designer would like to succeed in every category, but there are often forced tradeoffs. If lengthy learning is permitted, then task-performance speed may be reduced by use of complex abbreviations, macros, and shortcuts. If the rate of errors is to be kept extremely low, then speed of performance may have to be sacrificed. In some applications, subjective satisfaction may be the key determinant of success; in others, short learning times or rapid performance may be paramount. Project managers and designers must be aware of the tradeoffs, and must make their choices explicit and public. Requirements documents and marketing brochures should make clear which goals are primary.

After multiple design alternatives are raised, the leading possibilities should be reviewed by designers and users. Paper mockups are useful, but online prototypes of the system create a more realistic environment for review. Design teams negotiate the guidelines document to make explicit the permissible formats, sequences, terminology, and so on. Then, the full design is created with suitable software tools, and testing can begin to ensure that the user-interface design goals are met. The user manual and the technical reference manual can be written before the implementation to provide another review and perspective on the design. Next, the implementation can be carried out with proper software tools; this task should be a modest one if the design is complete and precise. Finally, the acceptance test certifies that the delivered system meets the goals of the designers and customers. The development and evaluation process is described in greater detail in Chapter 13.

1.4   Motivations for Human Factors in Design

The enormous interest in human factors of interactive systems arises from the complementary recognition of how poorly designed many current systems are and of how genuinely developers desire to create elegant systems that serve the users effectively. This increased concern emanates from four primary sources: life-critical systems; industrial and commercial uses; office, home, and entertainment applications; and exploratory, creative, and collaborative systems.

1.4.1   Life-critical systems

Life-critical systems include those that control air traffic, nuclear reactors, power utilities, manned spacecraft, police or fire dispatch, military operations, and monitoring and instruments in medical settings. In these applications, high costs are expected, but they should yield high reliability and effectiveness. Lengthy training periods are acceptable to obtain rapid, error-free performance even when the user is under stress. Subjective satisfaction is less of an issue, because the users are well motivated. Retention is obtained by frequent use of common functions and practice sessions for emergency actions.

1.4.2   Industrial and commercial uses

Typical industrial and commercial uses include banking, insurance, order entry, inventory management, airline and hotel reservations, car rentals, utility billing, credit-card management, and point-of-sales terminals. In these cases, costs shape many judgments; lower cost may be preferred even if there is some sacrifice in reliability. Operator training time is expensive, so ease of learning is important. The tradeoffs for speed of performance and error rates are decided by the total cost over the system's lifetime. Subjective satisfaction is of modest importance; retention is obtained by frequent use. Speed of performance becomes central for most of these applications because of the high volume of transactions, but operator fatigue or burnout is a legitimate concern. Trimming 10 percent off the mean transaction time means 10 percent fewer operators, 10 percent fewer terminal workstations, and possibly a 10-percent reduction in hardware costs. A 1988 study by developers of a system to manage telephone directory assistance indicated that a 0.8-second reduction in the 15-second mean time per call would save $40 million per year (Springer, 1987).

1.4.3   Office, home, and entertainment applications

The rapid expansion of office, home, and entertainment applications is the third source of interest in human factors. Personal-computing applications include word processing, automated transaction machines, video games, educational packages, information retrieval, electronic mail, computer conferencing, and small-business management. For these systems, ease of learning, low error rates, and subjective satisfaction are paramount because use is frequently discretionary and competition is fierce. If the users cannot succeed quickly, they will abandon the use of a computer or try a competing package. In cases where use is intermittent, retention is likely to be faulty, so online assistance becomes important.

Choosing the right functionality is difficult. Novices are best served by a constrained simple set of actions; but, as users' experience increases, so does their desire for more extensive functionality and rapid performance. A layered or level structured design is one approach to graceful evolution from novice to expert usage. Low cost is important because of lively competition, but extensive design and testing can be amortized over the large number of users.

1.4.4   Exploratory, creative, and cooperative systems

An increasing fraction of computer use is dedicated to supporting human intellectual and creative enterprises. Electronic encyclopedias, database browsing, collaborative writing, statistical hypothesis formation, business decision making, and graphical presentation of scientific simulation results are examples of exploratory environments. Creative environments include writer's toolkits or workbenches, architecture or automobile design systems, artist or programmer workstations, and music-composition systems. Expert systems aid knowledgeable users in medical diagnosis, financial decision making, oil-well log data analysis, satellite-orbit maneuvering, and military advising. Cooperative systems enable two or more people to work together even if the users are separated by time and space, through use of electronic text, voice, and video mail; through electronic meeting systems that facilitate face-to-face meetings; or through groupware that enables remote collaborators to work on a document, spreadsheet, or image concurrently.

In these systems, the users may be knowledgeable in the task domain but novices in the underlying computer concepts. Their motivation is often high, but so are their expectations. Benchmark tasks are more difficult to describe because of the exploratory nature of these applications. Usage can range from occasional to frequent. In short, it is difficult to design and evaluate these systems. At best, designers can pursue the goal of having the computer vanish as users become completely absorbed in their task domain. This goal seems to be met most effectively when the computer provides a direct-manipulation representation of the world of action. Then tasks are carried out by rapid familiar selections or gestures, with immediate feedback and a new set of choices.

1.5   Accommodation of Human Diversity

The remarkable diversity of human abilities, backgrounds, motivations, personalities, and workstyles challenges interactive system designers. A right-handed male designer with computer training and a desire for rapid interaction using densely packed screens may have a hard time developing a successful workstation for left-handed women artists with a more leisurely and free-form work style. Understanding the physical, intellectual, and personality differences among users is vital.

1.5.1   Physical abilities and physical workplaces

Accommodating the diverse human perceptual, cognitive, and motor abilities is a challenge to every designer. Fortunately, there is much literature reporting research and experience from design projects with automobiles, aircraft, typewriters, home appliances, and so on that can be applied to the design of interactive computer systems (Van Cott and Kinkade, 1972; Tichauer, 1978). In a sense, the presence of a computer is only incidental to the design; human needs and abilities are the guiding forces.

Basic data about human dimensions comes from research in *anthropometry* (Dreyfus, 1967; Roebuck et al., 1975). Thousands of measures of hundreds of features of males and females, children and adults, Europeans and Asians, underweight and overweight, and tall and short individuals provide data to construct means and 5 to 95 percentile groupings. Head, mouth, nose, neck, shoulder, chest, arm, hand, finger, leg, and foot sizes have been carefully cataloged for a variety of populations. The great diversity in these static measures reminds us that there can be no image of an "average" user, and that compromises must be made or multiple versions of a system must be constructed.

The choice of keyboard design parameters (see Section 6.2) evolved to meet the physical abilities of users in terms of distance between keys, size of keys, and required pressure. People with especially large or small hands may have difficulty in using standard keyboards, but a substantial fraction of the population is well served by one design. On the other hand, since screen-brightness preferences vary substantially, designers must provide a knob to enable user control. Controls for chair heights and backs or for display-screen angles also allow individual adjustment. When a single design cannot accommodate a large fraction of the population, then multiple versions or adjustment controls are helpful.

Physical measures of static human dimensions are not enough. Measures of dynamic actions—such as reach distances while seated, speed of finger presses, or strength of lifting—are also necessary (Bailey, 1982; Kantowitz and Sorkin, 1983).

Since so much of work is related to perception, designers need to be aware of the ranges of human perceptual abilities (Schiff, 1980). Vision is especially important and has been thoroughly studied (Wickens, 1984). For example, researchers consider human response time to varying visual stimuli, or time to adapt to low or bright light. They examine human capacity to identify an object in context, or to determine velocity or direction of a moving point. The visual system responds differently to various colors, and some people are color blind. People's spectral range and sensitivity vary. Peripheral vision is quite different from perception of images in the fovea. Flicker, contrast, and motion sensitivity must be considered, as must the impact of glare and of visual fatigue. Depth perception, which allows three-dimensional viewing, is based on several cues. Some viewing angles and distances make the screen easier to read. Finally, designers must consider the needs of people who have eye disorders, damage, or disease, or who wear corrective lenses.

Other senses are also important: touch for keyboard or touchscreen entry, and hearing for audible cues, tones, and speech input or output (see Chapter 6). Pain, temperature sensitivity, taste, and smell are rarely used for input or output in interactive systems, but there is room for imaginative applications.

These physical abilities influence elements of the interactive system design. They also play a prominent role in the design of the workplace or workstation (or playstation). The American National Standard for Human Factors Engineering of Visual Display Terminal Workstations (1988) lists these concerns:

- Work-surface and display support height
- Clearance under work surface for legs
- Work-surface width and depth
- Adjustability of heights and angles for chairs and work surfaces
- Posture—seating depth and angle; back-rest height and lumbar support
- Availability of armrests, foot rests, and palm rests
- Use of chair casters

Workplace design is important in ensuring job satisfaction, high performance, and low error rates. Incorrect table heights, uncomfortable chairs, or inadequate space to place documents can substantially impede work. The Standard document also addresses such issues as illumination levels (200 to 500 lux), glare reduction (antiglare coatings, baffles, mesh, positioning), luminance balance and flicker, equipment reflectivity, acoustic noise and vibration, air temperature, and movement, and humidity, and equipment temperature.

The most elegant screen design or command language can be compromised by a noisy environment, poor lighting, or a stuffy room, which will eventually lower performance, raises error rates, and discourage even motivated users.

Another physical-environment consideration involves room layout and the sociology of human interaction. With multiple workstations for a classroom or office, alternate layouts can encourage or limit social interaction, cooperative work, and assistance with problems. Because users can often quickly help one another with minor problems, there may be an advantage to layouts that group several terminals closely together or that enable supervisors or teachers to view all screens at once from behind. On the other hand, programmers, reservations clerks, or artists may appreciate the quiet and privacy of their own workspace.

The physical design of workplaces is often discussed under the term *ergonomics*. Anthropometry, sociology, industrial psychology, organizational behavior, and anthropology may offer useful insights in this area.

1.5.2   Cognitive and perceptual abilities

A vital foundation for interactive systems designers is an understanding of the cognitive and perceptual abilities of the users (Kantowitz and Sorkin, 1983; Wickens, 1984). The human ability to interpret sensory input rapidly and to initiate complex actions makes modern computer systems possible. In milliseconds, users recognize slight changes on their displays and begin to issue a stream of commands. The journal *Ergonomics Abstracts* offers this classification of human *central processes*:

- Short-term memory
- Long-term memory and learning
- Problem solving
- Decision making
- Attention and set
- Search and scanning
- Time perception

They also suggest this set of *factors affecting perceptual motor performance*:

- Arousal and vigilance
- Fatigue
- Perceptual (mental) load
- Knowledge of results
- Monotony and boredom
- Sensory deprivation
- Sleep deprivation
- Anxiety and fear
- Isolation
- Aging
- Drugs and alcohol
- Circadian rhythm

These vital issues are not discussed in depth in this book, but they have a profound influence on the design of most interactive systems. The term *intelligence* is not included in this list, because of its controversial nature and the difficulty of measuring pure intelligence.

In any application, background experience and knowledge in the task domain and the computer domain (see Section 2.2) play a key role in learning and performance. Task or computer skill inventories can be helpful in predicting performance.

1.5.3   Personality differences

Some people dislike or are made anxious by computers; others are attracted to or are eager to use computers. Often, members of these divergent groups disapprove or are suspicious of members of the other community. Even people who enjoy using computers may have very different preferences for interaction styles, pace of interaction, graphics versus tabular presentations, dense versus sparse data presentation, step-by-step work versus all-at-once work, and so on. These differences are important. A clear understanding of personality and cognitive styles can be helpful in designing systems for a specific community of users.

A fundamental difference is one between men and women, but no clear pattern of preferences has been documented. It is often pointed out that the preponderance of video-arcade game players are young males, and so are the designers. Women will play any game, but popular choices are Pacman and its variants plus a few other games such as Donkey Kong or Centipede. We have only speculations regarding why women prefer these games. One female commentator labeled Pacman "oral aggressive" and could appreciate the female style of play. Other women have identified the compulsive cleaning up of every dot as an attraction. These games are distinguished by their less violent action and sound track. Also, the board is fully visible, characters have personality, softer color patterns are used, and there is a sense of closure and completeness. Can these informal conjectures be converted to measurable criteria and then validated? Can designers become aware of the needs and desires of women, and create video games that will be more attractive to women than to men?

Turning from games to office automation, the largely male designers may not realize the effect on women users when the command names require the users to KILL a file or ABORT a program. These and other potential unfortunate mismatches between the user interface and the user might be avoided by more thoughtful attention to individual differences among users. Huff (1987) found a bias when he asked teachers to design educational games for boys or girls. The designers created gamelike challenges when they expected boys as users, and used more conversational dialogs when they expected girls as users. When told to design for students, the designers produced boy-style games.

Unfortunately, there is no simple taxonomy of user personality types. An increasingly popular technique is to use the Myers–Briggs Type Indicator (MBTI) (Shneiderman, 1980), which is based on Carl Jung's theories of personality types. Jung conjectured that there were four dichotomies:

- *Extroversion versus introversion*: Extroverts focus on external stimuli and like variety and action, whereas introverts prefer familiar patterns, rely on their inner ideas, and work alone contentedly.

- *Sensing versus intuition*: Sensing types are attracted to established routines, are good at precise work, and enjoy applying known skills, whereas intuitive types like solving new problems and discovering new relations, but dislike taking time for precision.
- *Perceptive versus judging*: Perceptive types like to learn about new situations, but may have trouble making decisions, whereas judging types like to make a careful plan, and will seek to carry through the plan even if new facts change the goal.
- *Feeling versus thinking*: Feeling types are aware of other people's feelings, seek to please others, and relate well to most people, whereas thinking types are unemotional, may treat people impersonally, and like to put things in logical order.

The theory behind the MBTI provides portraits of the relationships between professions and personality types and between people of different personality types. It has been applied to testing user communities and to provide guidance to designers.

Many hundreds of psychological scales have been developed, including risk taking versus risk avoidance; internal versus external locus of control; reflective versus impulsive behavior; convergent versus divergent thinking; high versus low anxiety, tolerance for stress, tolerance for ambiguity, motivation, or compulsiveness; field dependence versus independence; assertive versus passive personality; and left- versus right-brain orientation. As designers explore computer applications for home, education, art, music, and entertainment, they will greatly benefit from paying greater attention to personality types.

1.5.4   Cultural and international diversity

Another perspective on individual differences has to do with cultural, ethnic, racial, or linguistic background. It seems obvious that users who were raised learning Japanese or Chinese will scan a screen differently from users who were raised learning English or French. Users from cultures that have a more reflective style or respect for ancestral traditions may prefer different interfaces from users from cultures that are more action-oriented or novelty-based.

Little is known about computer users from different cultures, but designers are regularly called on to make designs for other languages and cultures. The growth of a worldwide computer market (many U. S. companies have more than half their sales in overseas markets) means that designers must prepare for internationalization. Software architectures that facilitate making local versions of user interfaces should be emphasized. For example, all text (instructions, help, error messages, labels) might be stored in files, so that versions in other languages could be generated with no or little additional programming. Hardware concerns include character sets, keyboards, and special input devices. User-interface design concerns for internationalization include:

Characters, numerals, special characters, and diacriticals

Left-to-right versus right-to-left versus vertical input and reading

Date and time formats

Numeric and currency formats

Telephone numbers and addresses

Names and titles (Mr., Ms., Mme.)

Social-security, national identification, and passport numbers

Capitalization and punctuation

Sorting sequences

Icons, buttons, colors

Pluralization, grammar, spelling

Etiquette, policies, tone, formality, metaphors

The list is long, and yet is incomplete. Whereas early designers were often excused from cultural and linguistic slips, the current highly competitive atmosphere means that more effective localization will often produce a strong advantage. To promote effective designs, usability studies should be run with users from each country, culture, and language community (Nielsen, 1990).

1.5.5   Users with disabilities

The flexibility of computer software makes it possible for designers to provide special services to users who have disabilities (McWilliams, 1984). The U. S. General Services Administration's (GSA) guide, *Managing End User Computing for Users with Disabilities* (1989), describes effective accommodations for users who have low vision or are blind, users with hearing impairments, and users with mobility impairments. Enlarging the text presented on a display (Glinert and Ladner, 1984) or converting displays to braille or voice (Durre and Durre, 1986; Durre and Glander, 1991) output can be done with hardware and software supplied by many vendors. Text-to-speech conversion can help blind users to receive electronic mail or to read text files, and speech-recognition devices permit voice-controlled operation of some software. Users with hearing impairments often can use computers without change (conversion of tones to visual signals is often easy to accomplish), and can benefit from office environments that depend on electronic mail and facsimile transmission (FAX). Telecommunications devices for the deaf (TDD) enable telephone access to information (such as train or airplane schedules) and services (federal agencies and many companies offer TDD access). Special input devices for users with physical disabilities will depend on the user's specific impairment; numerous assisting devices are available. Speech recognition, eye-gaze control, head-mounted optical mouse, and many other innovative devices (even the telephone) were pioneered for the needs of disabled users (see Chapter 6).

Designers can benefit by planning early to accommodate users with disabilities, since substantial improvements can be made at low or no cost. The term *computer curbcuts* brings up the image of sidewalk cutouts to permit wheelchair access that are cheaper to build than step-down side-walks, if they are planned rather than added later. Similarly, moving the on–off switch to the front of a computer costs little or nothing (if planned in advance) and helps mobility-impaired users, as well as other users. The motivation to accommodate users who have disabilities has increased since the enactment of U. S. Public Laws 99-506 and 100-542, which require U. S. government agencies to establish accessible information environments that accommodate employees and citizens who have disabilities. Any company wishing to sell products to the U. S. government should adhere to the GSA recommendations (1989). Further information about accommodation in workplaces, schools, and the home is available from many sources:

- Private foundations (for example, the American Foundation for the Blind)
- Associations (for example, the Alexander Graham Bell Association for the Deaf, the National Association for the Deaf, and the Blinded Veterans Association)
- Government agencies (for example, the National Library Service for the Blind and Physically Handicapped of the Library of Congress and the Center for Technology in Human Disabilities at the Maryland Rehabili-tation Center)
- University groups (for example, the Trace Research and Development Center on Communications and the Control and Computer Access for Handicapped Individuals at the University of Wisconsin)
- Manufacturers (for example, Apple, AT&T, DEC, and IBM)

Learning-disabled children account for 2 percent of the school-age popu-lation in the United States. Their education can be positively influenced by design of special courseware with limits on lengthy textual instructions, confusing graphics, extensive typing, and difficult presentation formats (Neuman, 1991). Based on observations of 62 students using 26 packages over 5.5 months, Neuman's advice to designers of courseware for learning-disabled students is applicable to all users:

1. Present procedures, directions, and verbal content at levels and in formats that make them accessible even to poor readers.
2. Ensure that response requirements do not allow students to complete programs without engaging with target concepts.
3. Design feedback sequences that explain the reasons for students' errors and that lead students through the processes necessary for responding correctly.
4. Incorporate reinforcement techniques that capitalize on students' sophistication with out-of-school electronic materials.

Our studies with minimally learning-disabled fourth, fifth, and sixth graders learning to use word processors reinforce the need for direct manipulation (see Chapter 5) of visible objects of interest (MacArthur and Shneiderman, 1986). The potential for great benefit to people with disabilities is one of the unfolding gifts of computing. The Association for Computing Machinery (ACM) Special Interest Group on Computers and the Physically Handicapped (SIGCAPH) publishes a quarterly newsletter of interest to workers in this area.

1.5.6   Elderly users

If they are fortunate, all people grow old. There can be many pleasures and satisfactions to seniority, but there are also negative physical, cognitive, and social consequences of aging. Understanding the human factors of aging can lead us to computer designs that will facilitate access by the elderly. The benefits to the elderly include practical needs for writing, accounting, and the full range of computer tools, plus the satisfactions of education, entertainment, social interaction, communication, and challenge (Furlong and Kearsley, 1990). Other benefits include increased access of the society to the elderly for their experience, increased participation of the elderly in society through communication networks, and improved chances for productive employment of the elderly.

The National Research Council's report on Human Factors Research Needs for an Aging Population describes aging as

A nonuniform set of progressive changes in physiological and psychological functioning.... Average visual and auditory acuity decline considerably with age, as do average strength and speed of response.... [People experience] loss of at least some kinds of memory function, declines in perceptual flexibility, slowing of "stimulus encoding," and increased difficulty in the acquisition of complex mental skills,...visual functions such as static visual acuity, dark adaptation, accommodation, contrast sensitivity, and peripheral vision decline, on average, with age. (Czaja, 1987)

This list has its discouraging side, but many people experience only modest effects and continue participating in many activities, even through their nineties.

The further good news is that computer-systems designers can do much to accommodate elderly users, and thus to give the elderly access to the beneficial aspects of computing and network communication. How many young people's lives might be enriched by electronic-mail access to grand-parents or great-grandparents? How many businesses might benefit from electronic consultations with experienced senior citizens? How many gov-ernment agencies, universities, medical centers, or law firms could advance their goals by better contact with knowledgeable elderly citizens? As a society, how might we all benefit from the continued creative work of senior citizens in literature, art, music, science, or philosophy?

As the U.S. population grows older, designers in many fields are adapting to the elderly. Larger street signs, brighter traffic lights, and better night-time lighting can make driving safer for drivers and pedestrians. Similarly, larger fonts, higher display contrast, easier-to-use pointing de-vices, louder audio tones, and simpler command languages are just a few of the steps that user-interface designers can take to improve access for the elderly (Tobias, 1987; Christiansen et al., 1989). Many of these adjustments can be made through software-based control panels that enable users to tailor the system to their changing personal needs. System developers have yet to venture actively into the potentially profitable world of golden-age software, in parallel to the growing market in kidware. Let's do it *before* Bill Gates turns 65!

Electronic-networking projects, such as the San Francisco–based SeniorNet, are exploring the needs of elderly users (anyone over 55 years of age may join) for computing services, networking, and training. Computer games are also attractive for the elderly because they stimulate social interaction, provide practice in sensorimotor skills such as eye–hand coordi-nation, enhance dexterity, and improve reaction time. In addition, meeting a challenge and gaining a sense of accomplishment and mastery are helpful in improving self-image (Whitcomb, 1990).

In our research group's brief experiences in bringing computing to two residences for elderly people, we also found that the user's widespread fear of computers and belief that they were incapable of using computers gave way rather quickly with some positive experiences. These elderly users, who explored video games, word processors, and educational games, felt quite satisfied with themselves, were eager to learn more, and transferred their new-found enthusiasm to trying automated bank machines or supermarket touchscreen computers. Suggestions for redesign to meet the needs of elderly users (and possibly other users) emerged, such as the appeal of high-precision touchscreens compared with the mouse (see Chapter 6).

In summary, computing for elderly users provides an opportunity for the elderly, for system developers, and for all society. The Human Factors Society has a Technical Group on Aging that publishes a newsletter at least twice per year and organizes sessions at conferences.

1.6   Three Personal Goals

Clear goals are useful, not only for system development, but also for educational and professional enterprises. Over the past 20 years, I have pursued three broad goals: (1) influencing academic and industrial researchers; (2) providing tools, techniques, and knowledge for commercial systems implementors; and (3) raising the computer consciousness of the general public.

1.6.1   Influencing academic and industrial researchers

Early research in human–computer interaction was done largely by introspection and intuition, but this approach suffered from lack of validity, generality, and precision. The techniques of controlled psychologically oriented experimentation can lead to a deeper understanding of the fundamental principles of human interaction with computers.

The reductionist scientific method has this basic outline:

- Understand practical problem and related theory
- Lucid statement of a testable hypothesis
- Manipulation of a small number of independent variables
- Measurement of specific dependent variables
- Careful selection and assignment of subjects
- Control for biasing in subjects, procedures, and materials
- Application of statistical tests
- Interpretation of results, refinement of theory, and guidance for experimenters

Materials and methods must be tested by pilot experiments, and results must be validated by replication in variant situations.

Of course, the highly developed and structured method of controlled experimentation has its weaknesses. It may be difficult or expensive to find adequate subjects, and laboratory conditions may distort the situation so much that the conclusions have no application. When we arrive at results for large groups of subjects by statistical aggregation, extremely good or poor performance by individuals may be overlooked. Furthermore, anecdotal evidence or individual insights may be given too little emphasis because of the authoritative influence of statistics.

In spite of these concerns, controlled experimentation provides a productive basis that can be modified to suit the situation. Anecdotal experiences and subjective reactions should be recorded, thinking aloud or protocol approaches should be employed, field or case studies with extensive performance data collection should be carried out, and the individual insights of researchers, designers, and experimental participants should be captured.

Within computer science, there is a growing awareness of the need for greater attention to human-factors issues. Researchers who propose new programming languages or data-structure constructs are more aware of the need to match human cognitive skills. Developers of advanced graphics systems, robots, computer-assisted design systems, or artificial-intelligence applications increasingly recognize that the success of their proposals depends on the construction of a suitable human interface. Researchers in these and other areas are making efforts to understand and measure human performance.

There is a grand opportunity to apply the knowledge and techniques of traditional psychology, and of recent subfields such as cognitive psychology, to the study of human–computer interaction. Psychologists are investigating human problem solving with computers to gain an understanding of cognitive processes and memory structures. The benefit to psychology is great, but psychologists also have the golden opportunity to influence dramatically an important and widely used technology.

Researchers in information science, business and management, education, sociology, anthropology, and other disciplines are benefiting and contributing by their study of human–computer interaction (National Research Council, 1983; Marchionini and Sibert, 1991). There are so many fruitful directions for research that any list can be only a provocative starting point. We shall examine just a few.

Reducing anxiety and fear of computer usage Although computers are widely used, they still serve only a fraction of the population. Many competent business executives resist use of computers. The elderly often avoid using helpful computer-based devices, such as bank terminals or word processors, because they are anxious about, or even fearful of, breaking the computer, making an embarrassing mistake, or being incapable of succeeding. Interviews with nonusers of computers would help us to determine the sources of this anxiety and to formulate design guidelines for alleviating the fear. Tests could be run to determine the effectiveness of the redesigned systems and of improved training procedures.

Graceful evolution Although novices may begin their interactions with a computer by using menu selection, they may wish to evolve to faster or more powerful facilities. Methods are needed to smooth the transition from novice to knowledgeable user to expert. The differing requirements of novice and experts in prompting, error messages, online assistance, display complexity, locus of control, pacing, and informative feedback all need investigation. The design of user-adjustable control panels to support adaptation and evolution is also an open topic.

Menu selection and form fillin The content, number, placement, and phrasing of menu choices could be studied with attention to titling of menu frames, effectiveness of instructions, availability of typeahead strategies or menu shortcuts, backtracking, and graphic design to show hierarchical organization (Chapter 3). Much progress could be made in this area with only modest experimental effort. An opportunity also exists to develop software architectures for menu-management systems and graphical user interfaces that dramatically reduce the amount of code while permitting end users to develop and maintain their own menus, forms, or dialog boxes.

Command languages Command languages, a traditional style of inter-action, are excellent candidates for research to understand the importance of consistency in syntactic format, congruent pairings of commands, hierarchical structure, choice of familiar command names and parameters, suitable abbreviated forms, automatic command completion, and interfaces for command entry (Chapter 4). Opportunities still exist for designing advanced macro languages, specialized notations for programmers, and software tools.

Direct manipulation Visual interfaces in which the user operates on a representation of the objects of interest are extremely attractive (Chapter 5). Empirical studies would refine our understanding of what is an appropriate analogical or metaphorical representation and what is the role of rapid, incremental, reversible operations. Newer forms of direct manipulation—such as visual languages, spatial visualization, remote control, telepresence, and virtual reality—are further topics for research.

Input devices The plethora of input devices presents opportunities and challenges to system designers (Chapter 6). There are heated discussions about the relative merits of high-precision touchscreens; styli, pen, and gestural input; the mouse; voice input; eye-gaze input; datagloves; or force-feedback joysticks. Such conflicts could be resolved through extensive experimentation with multiple tasks and user communities. Underlying issues include speed, accuracy, fatigue, error correction, and subjective satisfaction.

Information exploration As navigation, browsing, and searching of hypermedia or multimedia databases become more common, the pressure for more effective strategies and tools will increase (Chapter 11). Users will want to filter, select, and restructure their information rapidly and with minimum effort, without fear of disorientation or of getting lost. Large databases of text, images, graphics, sound, and scientific data will become easier to explore with emerging data-visualization tools.

Online assistance Although many systems offer some help or tutorial information online, we have only limited understanding of what constitutes effective design for novices, knowledgeable users, and experts (Chapter 12). The role of these aids and of online user consultants could be studied to assess the effect on user success and satisfaction. The goal of *just in time* (JIT) training is elusive, but appealing.

Specification and implementation of interaction UIMSs (Chapter 14) reduce implementation times by an order of magnitude, when they match the task. There are still many situations in which extensive coding in procedural languages must be added. Specification languages have been proposed, but these are still a long way from being complete and useful. Advanced research on tools to aid interactive-systems designers and implementers might have substantial payoff in reducing costs and improving quality.

1.6.2   Providing tools, techniques, and knowledge for systems implementers

User-interface design and development is one of the hot topics for the 1990s, and international competition is lively. There is a great thirst for knowledge, software tools, design guidelines, and testing techniques. New UIMSs (see Chapter 14) provide support for rapid prototyping and system development while aiding design consistency and simplifying evolutionary refinement.

Guidelines documents are being written for general audiences and for specific applications. Many projects are taking the productive route of writing their own guidelines, which are specifically tied to the problems of their application environment. These guidelines are constructed from experimental results, experience with existing non–computer-based systems, review of related computer-based systems, and some knowledgeable guesswork.

Iterative usability studies and acceptance testing are appropriate during system development. Once the initial system is available, refinements can be made on the basis of online or printed surveys, individual or group interviews, or more controlled empirical tests of novel strategies (see Chapter 13).

Feedback from users during the development process and for evolutionary refinement can provide useful insights and guidance. Online electronic-mail facilities may allow users to send comments directly to the designers. Online user consultants and telephone hot-line workers can provide not only prompt assistance, but also much information about the activities and problems of the user community.

1.6.3   Raising the computer consciousness of the general public

The media are so filled with stories about computers that raising public consciousness of these tools may seem unnecessary. In fact, however, many people are still uncomfortable with computers. When they do finally use a bank terminal or word processor, they may be fearful of making mistakes, anxious about damaging the equipment, worried about feeling incompetent, or threatened by the computer "being smarter than I am." These fears are generated, in part, by poor designs that have complex commands, hostile and vague error messages, tortuous and unfamiliar sequences of actions, or a deceptive anthropomorphic style.

One of my goals is to encourage users to translate their internal fears into action. Instead of feeling guilty when they get a message such as SYNTAX ERROR, they should express their anger at the system designer who was so inconsiderate and thoughtless. Instead of feeling inadequate or foolish because they cannot remember a complex sequence of commands, they should complain to the designer who did not provide a more convenient mechanism, or should seek another product that does.

As examples of successful and satisfying systems become more visible, the crude designs will appear increasingly archaic and will become commercial failures. As designers improve interactive systems, some of these fears will recede and the positive experiences of competence, mastery, and satisfaction will flow in. Then, the images of computer scientists and of data-processing professionals will change in the public's view. The machine-oriented and technical image will give way to one of personal warmth, sensitivity, and concern for the user.

1.7   Practitioner's Summary

If you are designing an interactive system, a thorough task analysis can provide the information for a proper functional design. You should pay attention to reliability, availability, security, integrity, standardization, portability, integration, and the administrative issues of schedules and budgets.

As design alternatives are proposed, they can be evaluated for their role in providing short learning times, rapid task performance, low error rates, ease of retention, and high user satisfaction. As the design is refined and implemented, you can test for accomplishment of these goals with pilot studies, usability tests, and acceptance tests. The rapidly growing literature and sets of design guidelines may be of assistance in developing your project standards and practices, and in accommodating the increasingly diverse and growing community of users.

1.8   Researcher's Agenda

The opportunities for researchers are unlimited. There are so many interesting, important, and doable projects that it may be hard to choose a direction. Each experiment has two parents: the practical problems facing designers, and the fundamental theories based on psychological principles of human behavior. Begin by proposing a lucid, testable hypothesis. Then, consider the appropriate research methodology, conduct the experiment, collect the data, and analyze the results. Each experiment also has three children: specific recommendations for the practical problem, refinements of your theory of human performance, and guidance to future experimenters. Each chapter of this book ends with specific research proposals.

References

Specialized references for this chapter appear here; general information resources are in the section that follows immediately.

Chapanis, Alphonse, The business case for human factors in informatics. In Shackel, Brian and Richardson, Simon (Editors), *Human Factors for Informatics Usability*, Cambridge University Press, Cambridge, UK (1991), 39–71.

Christiansen, M., Chaudhary, S., Gottshall, R., Hartman, J., and Yatcilla, D., EASE: A user interface for the elderly. In Salvendy, G. and Smith, M. J. (Editors), *Designing and Using Human-Computer Interfaces and Knowledge Based Systems*, Elsevier Science Publishers B.V., Amsterdam, The Netherlands (1989), 428–435.

Czaja, Sara J., (Editor), *Human Factors Research Needs for an Aging Population*, National Academy Press, Washington, DC (1990).

Durre, Karl and Durre, Ingeborg, Electronic paper for blind children, *Education and Computing 2* (1986), 101–106.

Durre, Karl P. and Glander, Karl W., Design considerations for microcomputer based applications for the blind. In Nurminen, M. I., Jarvinen, P., and Weir, G. (Editors), *Human Jobs and Computer Interfaces*, North-Holland, Amsterdam, The Netherlands (1991).

Furlong, Mary and Kearsley, Greg, *Computers for Kids Over 60*, SeniorNet, San Francisco, CA, (1990).

Glinert, Ephraim and Ladner, Richard, A large font virtual terminal interface, *Communications of the ACM 27*, 6 (June 1984), 567–572.

General Services Administration, Information Resources Management Services (GSI, IRMS), *Managing End User Computing for Users with Disabilities*, GSI, IRMS, Washington, DC (1989).

Huff, C. W. and Cooper, J., Sex bias in educational software: The effect of designers' stereotypes on the software they design, *Journal of Applied Social Psychology 17*, 6 (June 1987), 519–532.

MacArthur, Charles and Shneiderman, Ben, Learning disabled students' difficulties in learning to use a word processor: Implications for instruction and software evaluation, *Journal of Learning Disabilities 19*, 4 (April 1986), 248–253.

Marchionini, Gary and Sibert, John (Editors), An agenda for human–computer interaction: Science and engineering serving human needs, *ACM SIGCHI Bulletin* (October 1991).

McWilliams, Peter A., *Personal Computers and the Disabled*, Quantum Press/ Doubleday, Garden City, NY (1984).

National Research Council Committee on Human Factors, *Research Needs in Human Factors*, National Academy Press, Washington, DC (1983).

Neuman, Delia, Learning disabled students' interactions with commercial courseware: A naturalistic study, *Educational Technology Research and Development 39*, 1 (1991), 31–49.

Nonogaki, Hajime and Ueda, Hirotada, FRIEND21 Project: A construction of the twenty-first century human interface, *Proc. CHI' 91 Human Factors in Computer Systems*, ACM, New York (1991), 407–414.

Springer, Carla J., Retrieval of information from complex alphanumeric displays: Screen formatting variables' effect on target identification time. In Salvendy, Gavriel (Editor), *Cognitive Engineering in the Design of Human–Computer Interaction and Expert Systems*, Elsevier, Amsterdam (1987), 375–382.

Tobias, Cynthia L., Computers and the elderly: A review of the literature and directions for future research, *Proc. Human Factors Society Thirty-First Annual Meeting*, Santa Monica, CA (1987), 866–870.

Whitcomb, G. Robert, Computer games for the elderly, *Proc. Conference on Computers and the Quality of Life '90*, ACM SIGCAS/, New York (1990), 112–115.

General information resources

Primary journals include:

Behaviour and Information Technology (BIT), Six issues per year, Taylor and Francis Ltd, London.

Human–Computer Interaction, Four issues per year, Lawrence Erlbaum Associates, Inc., Hillsdale, N. J.

Interacting with Computers, Three issues per year, Butterworth Scientific Limited, Westbury House, Guildford, Surrey.

International Journal of Man–Machine Studies , Twelve issues per year, Academic Press, London.

International Journal of Human–Computer Interaction, Four issues per year, Ablex Publishing Corp., Norwood, N. J.

Abstracts in Human–Computer Interaction, Four issues per year, abstracting journal, Ergosyst Associates, Inc., Lawrence, KS.

Other journals that regularly carry articles of interest are these:

ACM Computing Surveys
Communications of the ACM (CACM)
ACM Transactions of Graphics
ACM Transactions on Information System
Computers and Human Behavior
Cognitive Science
Ergonomics
Human Factors (HF)
IBM Systems Journal
IEEE Computer
IEEE Computer Graphics and Applications
IEEE Software
IEEE Transactions on Systems, Man, and Cybernetics (IEEE SMC)
Journal of Applied Psychology
Journal of Visual Languages and Computing

The Association for Computing Machinery (ACM) has a Special Interest Group on Computer and Human Interaction (SIGCHI) that publishes an excellent quarterly newsletter and holds regularly scheduled conferences. The ACM Special Interest Group on Graphics (SIGGRAPH) also covers this topic in its conferences and quarterly newsletter. The Human Factors Society has a Computer Systems Group, which publishes a quarterly newsletter. The American Society for Information Science (ASIS) has a Special Interest Group on Human–Computer Interaction (SIGHCI) that publishes a quarterly newsletter and participates by organizing sessions at the annual ASIS convention. The International Federation for Information Processing has a working group, WG 6.3, on human–computer interaction.

Conferences, such as the ones held by the ACM (SIGCHI and SIGGRAPH especially), IEEE, ASIS, Human Factors Society, and IFIP, often have relevant papers presented and later published in the proceedings. The INTERACT, the Human–Computer Interaction International, and the Work with Display Units series of conferences (held approximately every other year) are also important resources with broad coverage of user-interface issues. Several newer, more specialized conferences may be of interest to some people: User Interfaces Software and Technology 1, 2, 3, and 4; Hypertext 87, 89, and 91; and Computer Supported Collaborative Work 86, 88, and 90.

The list of guidelines documents and books is a starting point to investigate the large and growing literature in this area. Gerald Weinberg's 1971 book, *The Psychology of Computer Programming*, is a continuing inspiration to thinking about how people interact with computers. James Martin provided a thoughtful and useful survey of interactive systems in his 1973 book, *Design of Man–Computer Dialogues*. My 1980 book, *Software Psychology: Human Factors in Computer and Information Systems*, promotes the use of controlled experimental techniques and the reductionist scientific method. Richard Rubinstein and Harry Hersh's *The Human Factor: Designing Computer Systems for People* (1984) offers an appealing introduction and many useful guidelines.

Don Norman's 1988 book *The Psychology of Everyday Things* is a refreshing look at the psychological issues in the design of the everyday technology that surrounds us. As a reader, I was provoked equally by the sections dealing with doors or showers and those discussing computers or calculators. This book has a wonderful blend of levity and great depth of thinking, practical wisdom, and thoughtful theory.

Readers looking for a fresh perspective might enjoy the novel approach taken by Harold Thimbleby in *User Interface Design*, from ACM Press, 1990. A lively collection of essays was assembled by Brenda Laurel in close collaboration with Apple, under the title *The Art of Human–Computer Interface Design*, published by Addison-Wesley, 1990.

Guidelines documents

General guidelines

American National Standard for Human Factors Engineering of Visual Display Terminal Workstations, ANSI/HFS Standard No. 100-1988, Human Factors Society, Santa Monica, CA (February 1988).

— Carefully considered standards for the design, installation, and use of visual display terminals. Emphasizes ergonomics and anthropometrics.

Banks, William W., Gertman, David I., and Petersen, Rohn J., *Human Engineering Design Considerations for Cathode Ray Tube–Generated Displays*, NUREG/CR-2496, U. S. Nuclear Regulatory Commission, Washington, DC (April 1982).

— Detailed information and extensive references emphasizing perceptual issues and physical devices. Cites other guidelines documents and contains extensive appendices with experimental data about human visual performance.

Banks, William W., Gilmore, Walter E., Blackman, Harold S., and Gertman, David I., *Human Engineering Design Considerations for Cathode Ray Tube–Generated Displays*, Volume II, NUREG/CR-3003, U. S. Nuclear Regulatory Commission, Washington, DC (July 1983).

— Thoughtful set of screen-design guidelines with examples from graphic displays. Covers screen layout, symbol selection, and font design.

Engel, Stephen E. and Granda, Richard E., *Guidelines for Man/Display Interfaces*, Technical Report TR 00.2720, IBM, Poughkeepsie, NY (December 1975).

— An early and influential document that is the basis for several of the other guidelines documents.

Human Engineering Design Criteria for Military Systems, Equipment and Facilities, Military Standard MIL-STD-1472D, U.S. Government Printing Office, Washington, DC (March 14, 1989, and later changes).

— Almost 300 pages (plus a 100-page index); covers traditional ergonometric or anthropometric issues. Later editions pay increasing attention to user–computer interfaces. Interesting and thought provoking, but sometimes outdated and difficult to read due to a six-level organization.

Lockheed Missiles and Space Company Human Factors Review of Electric Power Dispatch Control Centers, Volume 2: *Detailed Survey Results*, Electric Power Research Institute, Palo Alto, CA (1981).

— Well-researched and thoughtful comments about electric-power control centers, with many generally applicable conclusions.

Human Factors of Work Stations with Display Terminals, IBM Document G320-6102-1, San Jose, CA (1979).

— Informative and readable discussion about terminal design.

Human Factors Engineering Criteria for Information Processing Systems, Lockheed Missiles and Space Co., Inc., Sunnyvale, CA (September 1982).

— Well-written and precise guidelines, with numerous examples on display format, data entry, language and coding, interaction sequence control, error-handling procedures, online guidance, and color displays.

Guidelines for Control Room Reviews, NUREG-0700, U. S. Nuclear Regulatory Commission, Washington, DC (September 1981).

— Detailed checklist and issues for evaluating nuclear-reactor control rooms, with many items of interest to other control-room or workstation designers.

NASA Space Station Freedom Program: Human–Computer Interface Guide, Version 2.1, Johnson Space Center, Houston, TX (December 1988).

— Specific guidelines for designers of space-station user interfaces.

Smith, Sid L. and Mosier, Jane N., *Guidelines for Designing User Interface Software*, Report ESD-TR-86-278, Electronic Systems Division, the MITRE Corporation, Bedford, MA (August 1986). Available from National Technical Information Service, Springfield, VA. Also available on disk in an interesting hypertext format called NaviText SAM from Northern Lights Software Corp., Westford, MA (508) 692-3600.

— This thorough document, which has undergone several revisions, begins with a good discussion of human-factors issues in design. It then covers data entry, data display, and sequence control. Guidelines are offered with comments, examples, exceptions, and references. This is *the* place to start if you are creating your own guidelines.

Specific guidelines

Apple Human Interface Guidelines: The Apple Desktop Interface, Addison-Wesley, Reading, MA (1987), 144 pages.

— The Human Interface Group and the Technical Publications Group teamed up to produce this readable, example-filled book that starts with a thoughtful philosophy and then delves into precise details. Required reading for anyone developing Macintosh software. An inspiration to those who may be designing their own guidelines document; stimulates interesting reflections for researchers.

IBM Systems Application Architecture: Common User Access Guide to User Interface Design, IBM Document SC34-4289-00, (October 1991), 163 pages.

— This readable introduction to user-interface design is a textbook for software and user-interface designers that covers principles, components, and techniques.

IBM Systems Application Architecture: Common User Access Advanced Interface Design Reference, IBM Document SC34-4290-00, (October 1991), 401 pages.

— This volume is the latest version of IBM's Guide for application programmers who wish to adhere to the CUA design.   It identifies what the interface components are and when to use them.

IBM System Application Architecture: Common User Access, Advanced Interface Design Guide, IBM Document SC26-4582-0, Boca Raton, FL (June 1989), 195 pages.

— This now-outdated version of IBM standards shows progress over the 1987 document. It has heavy emphasis on graphic interaction, use of pointing devices, and windows. International standards for multiple languages are also given attention.

IBM System Application Architecture: Common User Access, Panel Design and User Interaction, IBM Document SC26-4351-0, Boca Raton, FL (December 1987), 328 pages.

— This older version of IBM's standards took years to prepare. It has been highly influential in the development of all IBM products and therefore in many corporate standards.

Open Software Foundation, *OSF/Motif Style Guide* and *OSF/Motif User's Guide*, Prentice-Hall, Englewood Cliffs, NJ (1990).

— Readable explanations for designers and for users to create or use applications under the OSF/Motif environment. Covers menus, windows, dialog boxes, and help facilities.

Sun Microsystems, Inc., *OPEN LOOK Graphical User Interface: Functional Specifications* and *OPEN LOOK Graphical User Interface: Application Style Guidelines*, Addison-Wesley, Reading, MA (1989).

— Detailed specifications for designers of toolkits and applications that adhere to the OPEN LOOK User Interface developed by Sun Microsystems in partnership with AT&T. The design principles and the examples are presented in a quite readable form.

Books

Classic books

Bolt, Richard A., *The Human Interface: Where People and Computers Meet*, Lifelong Learning Publications, Belmont, CA (1984), 113 pages.

Cakir, A., Hart, D. J., and Stewart, T. F. M., *Visual Display Terminals: A Manual Covering Ergonomics, Workplace Design, Health and Safety, Task Organization*, John Wiley and Sons, New York (1980).

Card, Stuart K., Moran, Thomas P., and Newell, Allen, *The Psychology of Human–Computer Interaction*, Lawrence Erlbaum Associates, Hillsdale, NJ (1983), 469 pages.

Crawford, Chris, *The Art of Computer Game Design: Reflections of a Master Game Designer*, Osborne/McGraw-Hill, Berkeley, CA (1984), 113 pages.

Dreyfus, W., *The Measure of Man: Human Factors in Design (Second Edition)*, Whitney Library of Design, New York (1967).

Galitz, Wilbert O., *Human Factors in Office Automation*, Life Office Management Association, Atlanta, GA (1980), 237 pages.

Hiltz, Starr Roxanne, *Online Communities: A Case Study of the Office of the Future*, Ablex, Norwood, NJ (1984), 261 pages.

Hiltz, Starr Roxanne and Turoff, Murray, *The Network Nation: Human Communication via Computer*, Addison-Wesley, Reading, MA (1978).

Kantowitz, Barry H. and Sorkin, Robert D., *Human Factors: Understanding People-System Relationships*, John Wiley and Sons, New York (1983), 699 pages.

Martin, James, *Design of Man–Computer Dialogues*, Prentice-Hall, Englewood Cliffs, NJ (1973). 509 pages.

McCormick, Ernest J. and Sanders, M. S., *Human Factors in Engineering and Design*, McGraw-Hill, New York (1982).

Mehlmann, Marilyn, *When People Use Computers: An Approach to Developing an Interface*, Prentice-Hall, Englewood Cliffs, NJ (1981).

Mumford, Enid, *Designing Human Systems for New Technology*, Manchester Business School, Manchester, England (1983) 108 pages.

National Research Council, Committee on Human Factors, *Research Needs for Human Factors*, National Academy Press, Washington, DC (1983), 160 pages.

Roebuck, J. A., Kroemer, K. H. E., and Thomson, W. G., *Engineering Anthropometry Methods*, Wiley, New York (1975).

Rubinstein, Richard and Hersh, Harry, *The Human Factor: Designing Computer Systems for People*, Digital Press, Maynard, MA (1984), 249 pages.

Schiff, W., *Perception: An Applied Approach*, Houghton Mifflin, New York (1980).

Sheridan, T. B. and Ferrel, W. R., *Man–Machine Systems: Information, Control, and Decision Models of Human Performance*, MIT Press, Cambridge, MA (1974).

Shneiderman, Ben, *Software Psychology: Human Factors in Computer and Information Systems*, Little, Brown, Boston (1980), 320 pages.

Tichauer, E. R., *The Mechanical Basis of Ergonomics*, John Wiley and Sons, New York (1978).

Turkle, Sherry, *The Second Self: Computers and the Human Spirit*, Simon and Schuster, New York (1984).

Weinberg, Gerald M., *The Psychology of Computer Programming*, Van Nostrand Reinhold, New York (1971), 288 pages.

Weizenbaum, Joseph, *Computer Power and Human Reason: From Judgment to Calculation*, W. H. Freeman, San Francisco (1976), 300 pages.

Wickens, Christopher D., *Engineering Psychology and Human Performance*, Charles E. Merrill, Columbus, OH (1984), 513 pages.

Recent publications

Bailey, Robert W., *Human Performance Engineering: Using Human Factors/Ergonomics to Achieve Computer Usability* (Second Edition), Prentice-Hall, Englewood Cliffs, NJ (1989), 563 pages.

Bass, Len and Coutaz, Joelle, *Developing Software for the User Interface*, Addison-Wesley, Reading, MA (1991), 256 pages.

Brown, C. Marlin "Lin", *Human-Computer Interface Design Guidelines*, Ablex, Norwood, NJ (1988), 236 pages.

Brown, Judith R. and Cunningham, Steve, *Programming the User Interface: Principles and Examples*, John Wiley and Sons, New York (1989), 371 pages.

Carroll, John M., *The Nurnberg Funnel: Designing Minimalist Instruction for Practical Computer Skill*, MIT Press, Cambridge, MA (1990), 340 pages.

Coats, R. B. and Vlaeminke, I., *Man–Computer Interfaces: An Introduction to Software Design and Implementation*, Blackwell Scientific Publications, Oxford, UK (1987), 381 pages.

Dumas, Joseph S., *Designing User Interfaces for Software*, Prentice-Hall, Englewood Cliffs, NJ (1988), 174 pages.

Ehrich, R. W. and Williges, R. C., *Human–Computer Dialogue Design*, Elsevier Science Publishers B.V., Amsterdam, The Netherlands (1986).

Foley, James D., van Dam, Andries, Feiner, Steven K., and Hughes, John F., *Computer Graphics: Principles and Practice* (Second Edition), Addison-Wesley, Reading, MA (1990), 1174 pages.

Galitz, Wilbert O., *Handbook of Screen Format Design* (Third Edition), Q. E. D. Information Sciences, Inc., Wellesley, MA (1989), 307 pages.

Gilmore, Walter E., Gertman, David I., and Blackman, Harold S., *User–Computer Interface in Process Control: A Human Factors Engineering Handbook*, Academic Press, San Diego, CA (1989) 436 pages.

Heckel, Paul, *The Elements of Friendly Software Design (The New Edition)*, SYBEX, San Francisco, CA (1991), 319 pages.

Kearsley, Greg, *Online Help Systems: Design and Implementation*, Ablex, Norwood, NJ (1988), 115 pages.

Kobara, Shiz, *Visual Design with OSF/Motif*, Addison-Wesley, Reading, MA (1991), 260 pages.

Krueger, Myron, *Artificial Reality II*, Addison-Wesley, Reading, MA (1991), 304 pages.

Laurel, Brenda, *Computers as Theater*, Addison-Wesley, Reading, MA (1991), 211 pages.

Marcus, Aaron, *Graphic Design for Electronic Documents and User Interfaces*, ACM Press, New York (1992), 266 pages.

Myers, Brad, *Creating User Interfaces by Demonstration*, Academic Press, New York (1988), 320 pages.

Nickerson, Raymond S., *Using Computers: Human Factors in Information Systems*, MIT Press, Cambridge, MA (1986), 434 pages.

Nielsen, Jakob, *Designing User Interfaces for International Use*, Elsevier Science Publishers, Amsterdam, The Netherlands (1990).

Nielsen, Jakob, *Hypertext & Hypermedia*, Academic Press, San Diego, CA (1990), 263 pages.

Norman, Donald A., *The Psychology of Everyday Things*, Basic Books, New York (1988), 257 pages.

Norman, Kent, *The Psychology of Menu Selection: Designing Cognitive Control at the Human/Computer Interface*, Ablex, Norwood, NJ (1991), 350 pages.

Oborne, David J., *Computers at Work: A Behavioural Approach*, John Wiley and Sons, Chichester, England (1985), 420 pages.

Ravden, Susannah and Johnson, Graham, *Evaluating Usability of Human-Computer Interfaces*, Halsted Press Division of John Wiley and Sons, New York (1989), 126 pages.

Shneiderman, Ben and Kearsley, Greg, *Hypertext Hands-On! An Introduction to a New Way of Organizing and Accessing Information*, Addison-Wesley, Reading, MA (1989), 165 pages and 2 disks.

Thimbleby, Harold, *User Interface Design*, ACM Press, New York (1990), 470 pages.

Thorell, L. G. and Smith, W. J., *Using Computer Color Effectively*, Prentice-Hall, Englewood Cliffs, NJ (1990), 258 pages.

Vaske, Jerry and Grantham, Charles, *Socializing the Human–Computer Environment*, Ablex, Norwood, NJ (1990), 290 pages.

Winograd, Terry and Flores, Fernando, *Understanding Computers and Cognition*, Ablex, Norwood, NJ (1986), 207 pages.

Zuboff, Shoshanna, *In the Age of the Smart Machine: The Future of Work and Power*, Basic Books, New York (1988), 468 pages.

Documentation

Brockman, R. John, *Writing Better Computer User Documentation: From Paper to Hypertext: Version 2.0*, John Wiley and Sons, New York (1990), 365 pages.

Horton, William K., *Designing and Writing Online Documentation: Help Files to Hypertext*, John Wiley and Sons, New York (1990), 372 pages.

Price, Jonathan, *How to Write a Computer Manual*, Benjamin/Cummings, Menlo Park, CA (1984), 295 pages.

Weiss, Edmond H., *How to Write a Usable User Manual*, ISI Press, Philadelphia (1985), 197 pages.

Reference resource

ACM, *Resources in Human–Computer Interaction*, ACM Press, New York (1990) 1197 pages.

Collections

Proceedings Human Factors in Computer Systems, Washington, DC, ACM (March 15–17, 1982), 399 pages.

The following volumes are available from ACM Order Dept., P. O. Box 64145, Baltimore, MD 21264, or from Addison-Wesley Publishing Co., Reading, MA 01867.

Proceedings ACM CHI '83 Conference: Human Factors in Computing Systems, Ann Janda (Editor), Boston, MA (December 12–15, 1983) .

Proceedings ACM CHI '85 Conference: Human Factors in Computing Systems, Lorraine Borman and Bill Curtis (Editors), San Francisco (April 14–18, 1985).

Proceedings ACM CHI '86 Conference: Human Factors in Computing Systems, Marilyn Mantei and Peter Orbeton (Editors), Boston (April 13–17, 1986).

Proceedings AGM CHI + GI '87 Conference: Human Factors in Computing Systems, John M. Carroll and Peter P. Tanner (Editors), Toronto, Canada (April 5–9, 1987).

Proceedings ACM CHI '88 Conference: Human Factors in Computing Systems, Elliot Soloway, Douglas Frye, and Sylvia B. Sheppard (Editors), Washington, DC (May 15–19, 1988).

Proceedings ACM CHI '89 Conference: Human Factors in Computing Systems, Ken Bice and Clayton Lewis (Editors), Austin, TX (April 30–May 4, 1989).

Proceedings ACM CHI '90 Conference: Human Factors in Computing Systems, Jane Carrasco Chew and John Whiteside (Editors), Seattle (April 1–5, 1990).

Proceedings ACM CHI '91 Conference: Human Factors in Computing Systems, Scott P. Robertson, Gary M. Olson, and Judith S. Olson (Editors), New Orleans, LA (April 27–May 2, 1991).

INTERACT '84: First IFIP International Conference on Human–Computer Interaction, North-Holland, Amsterdam, The Netherlands (September 1984).

INTERACT '87: Second IFIP International Conference on Human–Computer Interaction, North-Holland, Amsterdam, The Netherlands (1987).

INTERACT '90: Human–Computer Interaction, North-Holland, Amsterdam, The Netherlands (1990).

Classic collections

Badre, Albert and Shneiderman, Ben (Editors), *Directions in Human–Computer Interaction*, Ablex, Norwood, NJ (1980), 225 pages.

Blaser, A. and Zoeppritz, M. (Editors), *Enduser Systems and Their Human Factors*, Springer-Verlag, Berlin (1983), 138 pages.

Coombs, M. J. and Alty, J. L. (Editors), *Computing Skills and the User Interface*, Academic Press, New York (1981).

Curtis, Bill (Editor), *Tutorial: Human Factors in Software Development*, IEEE Computer Society, Los Angeles (1981), 641 pages.

Guedj, R. A., Hagen, P. J. W., Hopgood, F. R. A., Tucker, H. A., and Duce, D. A. (Editors), *Methodology of Interaction*, North-Holland, Amsterdam, The Netherlands (1980), 408 pages.

Hartson, H. Rex (Editor), *Advances in Human–Computer Interaction*, Volume 1, Ablex, Norwood, NJ (1985), 290 pages.

Larson, James A. (Editor), *Tutorial: End User Facilities in the 1980's*, IEEE Computer Society Press (EHO 198-2), New York (1982).

Monk, Andrew (Editor), *Fundamentals of Human–Computer Interaction*, Academic Press, London, U.K. (1984), 293 pages.

Muckler, Frederick A. (Editor), *Human Factors Review: 1984*, Human Factors Society, Santa Monica, CA (1984), 345 pages.

Salvendy, Gavriel (Editor), *Human–Computer Interaction, Proceedings of the First USA–Japan Conference on Human–Computer Interaction*, Elsevier Science Publishers, Amsterdam, The Netherlands (1984), 470 pages.

Shackel, Brian (Editor), *Man-Computer Interaction: Human Factors Aspects of Computers and People*. Sijthoff and Noordhoof Publishers, The Netherlands (1981), 560 pages.

Sime, M. and Coombs, M. (Editors), *Designing for Human–Computer Communication*, Academic Press, New York (1983), 332 pages.

Smith, H. T. and Green, T. R. G. (Editors), *Human Interaction with Computers*, Academic Press, New York (1980).

Thomas, John C. and Schneider, Michael L. (Editors), *Human Factors in Computer Systems*, Ablex, Norwood, NJ (1984), 276 pages.

Van Cott, H. P. and Kinkade, R. G. (Editors), *Human Engineering Guide to Equipment Design*, U. S. Superintendent of Documents, Washington, DC (1972), 752 pages.

Vassiliou, Yannis (Editor), *Human Factors and Interactive Computer Systems*, Ablex, Norwood, NJ (1984), 287 pages.

Recent collections

Baecker, Ronald, and Buxton, William (Editors), *Readings in Human–Computer Interaction: A Multidisciplinary Approach*, Morgan-Kaufmann Publishers, Los Altos, CA (1987), 738 pages.

Carey, Jane M. (Editor), *Human Factors in Management Information Systems*, Ablex, Norwood, NJ (1988), 289 pages.

Carey, Jane M. (Editor), *Human Factors in Information Systems: An Organizational Perspective*, Ablex, Norwood, NJ (1991), 376 pages.

Carroll, John M. (Editor), *Interfacing Thought: Cognitive Aspects of Human–Computer Interaction*, MIT Press, Cambridge, MA (1987), 324 pages.

Carroll, John M. (Editor), *Designing Interaction: Psychology at the Human-Computer Interface*, Cambridge University Press, Cambridge, U.K. (1991), 333 pages.

Durrett, H. John (Editor), *Color and the Computer*, Academic Press, New York (1987), 299 pages.

Hartson, H. Rex and Hix, Deborah (Editors), *Advances in Human–Computer Interaction*, Volume 2, Ablex, Norwood, NJ (1988), 380 pages.

Helander, Martin (Editor), *Handbook of Human–Computer Interaction*, Elsevier Science Publishers, Amsterdam, The Netherlands (1988), 1167 pages.

Hendler, James A. (Editor), *Expert Systems: The User Interface*, Ablex, Norwood, NJ (1987), 336 pages.

Klemmer, Edmund T. (Editor), *Ergonomics: Harness the Power of Human Factors in Your Business*, Ablex, Norwood, NJ (1989), 218 pages.

Laurel, Brenda (Editor), *The Art of Human–Computer Interface Design*, Addison–Wesley, Reading, MA (1990), 523 pages.

Nielsen, Jakob (Editor), *Coordinating User Interfaces for Consistency*, Academic Press, San Diego, CA (1989), 142 pages.

Norman, Donald A., and Draper, Stephen W. (Editors), *User Centered System Design: New Perspectives on Human–Computer Interaction*, Lawrence Erlbaum Associates, Hillsdale, NJ (1986), 526 pages.

Salvendy, Gavriel (Editor), *Handbook of Human Factors*, John Wiley and Sons, New York (1987), 1874 pages.

Salvendy, Gavriel (Editor), *Cognitive Engineering in the Design of Human–Computer Interaction and Expert Systems*, Elsevier, Amsterdam, The Netherlands (1987), 592 pages.

Salvendy, Gavriel, Sauter, Steven L., and Hurrell, Jr., Joseph J. (Editors), *Social, Ergonomic and Stress Aspects of Work with Computers*, Elsevier, Amsterdam, The Netherlands(1987), 373 pages.

Salvendy, Gavriel and Smith, Michael J. (Editors), *Designing and Using Human–Computer Interfaces and Knowledge Based Systems*, Elsevier, Amsterdam, The Netherlands (1989), 990 pages.

Shackel, Brian and Richardson, Simon (Editors), *Human Factors for Informatics Usability*, Cambridge University Press, Cambridge, U.K. (1991), 438 pages.

Sherr, Sol (Editor), *Input Devices*, Academic Press, San Diego, CA (1988), 301 pages.

Smith, Michael J. and Salvendy, Gavriel (Editors), *Work with Computers: Organizational, Management, Stress and Health Aspects*, Elsevier Science Publishers B. V., Amsterdam, The Netherlands, (1989), 698 pages.

Sullivan, Joseph W., and Tyler, Sherman W., *Intelligent User Interfaces*, Addison-Wesley, Reading, MA (1991).

Wiener, Earl L. and Nagel, David C. (Editors), *Human Factors in Aviation*, Academic Press, New York (1988), 684 pages.

Videotapes

Video is an effective medium for presenting the dynamic, graphical, interactive nature of modern user interfaces. Drawn from the Technical Video Program of the ACM SIGCHI conferences, the SIGGRAPH Video Review (SVR) makes it possible to see excellent demonstrations of often-cited but seldom-seen systems. SVR tapes are available in 1/2-inch VHS and 3/4-inch U-matic formats. Contact the Association for Computing Machinery (ACM), located in New York City, for more information.

Volume	Year	Conference Location
12/13	CHI'83	Boston, MA
18/19	CHI'85	San Francisco, CA
26/27	CHI'86	Boston, MA
33/34	CHI+GI'87	Toronto, Canada
45/46	CHI'89	Austin, TX
47/48	CHI'89	Austin, TX
55/56	CHI'90	Seattle, WA
57	CHI'90	All the Widgets (Special Instructional Issue)
58/59	CHI'88	Washington, DC
63/64	CHI'91	New Orleans, LA

The University of Maryland Instructional Television produces a live satellite television program and sells the tapes. Telephone (301) 405-4905.

Shneiderman, Ben, *Designing the User Interface*, Instructional Television, University of Maryland, College Park, MD (1987), 5 hours.

Shneiderman, Ben, Malone, Tom, Norman, Don, and Foley, James, *User Interface Strategies '88*, Instructional Television, University of Maryland, College Park, MD (1988), 10 hours.

Shneiderman, Ben, Marcus, Aaron, Carroll, John, and Mountford, Joy, *User Interface Strategies '90*, Instructional Television, University of Maryland, College Park, MD (1989), 5 hours.

Shneiderman, Ben, van Dam, Andries, Soloway, Elliot, and Curtis, Bill, *User Interface Strategies '91*, Instructional Television, University of Maryland, College Park, MD (1990), 5 hours.

Shneiderman, Ben, Landauer, Thomas K., Myers, Brad, Laurel, Brenda, *User Interface Strategies '92*, Instructional Television, University of Maryland, College Park, MD (1991), 5 hours.

Consulting and design companies

American Institutes for Research, Washington, DC.

Ergo Research Group, Inc., Norwalk, CT.

Cognetics Corp., Princeton Junction, NJ; Washington, DC.

Aaron Marcus and Associates, Emeryville, CA.

Preface User Interface Design, Burbank, CA.

INTERFACE ISLAND

Your guide to avoiding the pitfalls
at every of this dangerous, tricky
and treacherous terrain.

MURKY MTS.

CONSISTENCY FOREST

CLARITY CLEARING

LOGIC TREE

THE GR...

CHAPTER 2

Theories, Principles, and Guidelines

We want principles, not only developed—the work of the closet,—but applied, which is the work of life.

Horace Mann, *Thoughts*, 1867

2.1 Introduction

Successful designers of interactive systems know that they can and must go beyond intuitive judgments made hastily when a design problem emerges. Fortunately, guidance for designers is beginning to emerge in the form of (1) high-level theories or models, (2) middle-level principles, (3) specific and practical guidelines, and (4) strategies for testing. The theories or models offer a framework or language to discuss issues that are application independent, whereas the middle-level principles are useful in weighing more specific design alternatives. The practical guidelines provide helpful reminders of rules uncovered by previous designers. Early prototype evaluation encourages exploration and enables iterative testing and redesign to correct inappropriate decisions. Acceptance testing is the trial-by-fire to determine whether a system is ready for distribution; its presence may be seen as a challenge, but it is also a gift to designers since it establishes clear measures of success.

In many contemporary systems, there is a grand opportunity to improve the human interface. The cluttered displays, complex and tedious procedures, inadequate command languages, inconsistent sequences of actions, and insufficient informative feedback can generate debilitating stress and anxiety that lead to poor performance, frequent minor and occasional serious errors, and job dissatisfaction.

This chapter begins with a review of several theories, concentrating on the syntactic–semantic object–action model. Section 2.4 then deals with frequency of use, task profiles, and interaction styles. Eight principles of interaction are offered in Section 2.5. Strategies for preventing errors are described in Section 2.6. Specific guidelines for data entry and display appear in Sections 2.7 and 2.8. Testing strategies are introduced in Section 2.9; they are covered in detail in Chapter 13. In Sections 2.10 and 2.11, we address the difficult question of how to balance automation and human control. Section 2.12 covers some legal issues.

2.2 High-Level Theories

Many theories are needed to describe the multiple aspects of interactive systems. Some theories are *explanatory*: They are helpful in observing behavior, describing activity, conceiving of designs, comparing high-level concepts of two designs, and training. Other theories are *predictive*: They enable designers to compare proposed designs for execution time or error rates. Some theories may focus on perceptual or cognitive subtasks (time to find an item on a display, or time to plan the conversion of a bold-faced character to an italic one), whereas others concentrate on motor-task performance times. Motor-task predictions are the most well established and are accurate for predicting keystroking or pointing times (see Fitts' Law, Section 6.3.5). Perceptual theories have been successful in predicting reading times for free text, lists, or formatted displays. Predicting performance on complex cognitive tasks (combinations of subtasks) is especially difficult because of the many strategies that might be employed. The ratio for times to perform complex task between novices and experts or between first-time and frequent users can be as high as 100 to 1. Actually, the contrast is even more dramatic because novices and first-time users often are unable to complete the tasks.

A *taxonomy* is a kind of theory. A taxonomy is the result of someone trying to put order on a complex set of phenomena; for example, a taxonomy might be created for input devices (direct versus indirect, linear versus rotary)

(Card et al., 1990), tasks (structured versus unstructured, controllable versus immutable) (Norman, 1991), personality styles (convergent versus divergent, field dependent versus independent), technical aptitudes (spatial visualization, reasoning) (Egan, 1988), user experience levels (novice, knowledgeable, expert), or user-interfaces styles (menus, form fillin, commands). Taxonomies facilitate useful comparisons, enable education, guide designers, and often indicate opportunities for novel products.

Any theory that could help designers to predict performance even for a limited range of users, tasks, or designs would be a contribution (Card, 1989). For the moment, the field is filled with hundreds of theories competing for attention while being refined by their promoters, extended by critics, and applied by eager and hopeful—but skeptical—designers. This development is healthy for the emerging discipline of human–computer interaction, but it means that practitioners must keep up with the rapid developments, not only in software tools, but also in theories.

Another direction for theoreticians would be to try to predict subjective satisfaction or emotional reactions. Researchers in media and advertising have recognized the difficulty in predicting emotional reactions, so they complement theoretical predictions with their intuitive judgments and extensive market testing. Broader theories of small-group behavior, organizational dynamics, sociology of knowledge, and technology adoption may prove to be useful. Similarly, the methods of anthropology or social psychology may be helpful in understanding and overcoming barriers to new technology and resistance to change.

There may be "nothing so practical as a good theory," but coming up with an effective theory is often difficult. By definition, a theory, taxonomy, or model is an abstraction of reality and therefore must be incomplete. However, a good theory should at least be understandable, produce similar conclusions for all who use it, and help to solve specific practical problems.

2.2.1 Conceptual, semantic, syntactic, and lexical model

An appealing and easily comprehensible model is the four-level approach that Foley and van Dam developed in the late 1970s (Foley et al., 1990):

1. The *conceptual level* is the user's mental model of the interactive system. Two conceptual models for text editing are line editors and screen editors.
2. The *semantic level* describes the meanings conveyed by the user's command input and by the computer's output display.
3. The *syntactic level* defines how the units (words) that convey semantics are assembled into a complete sentence that instructs the computer to perform a certain task.
4. The *lexical level* deals with device dependencies and with the precise mechanisms by which a user specifies the syntax.

   This approach is convenient for designers because its top-down nature is easy to explain, matches the software architecture, and allows for useful modularity during design. Designers are expected to move from conceptual to lexical, and to record carefully the mappings between levels.

2.2.2   GOMS and the keystroke-level model

Card, Moran, and Newell (1980, 1983) proposed the *goals, operators, methods, and selection rules* (GOMS) model and the *keystroke-level model*. They postulated that users formulate goals (edit document) and subgoals (insert word) that they achieve by using methods or procedures for accomplishing each goal (move cursor to desired location by following a sequence of arrow keys). The operators are "elementary perceptual, motor, or cognitive acts, whose execution is necessary to change any aspect of the user's mental state or to affect the task environment" (Card, et al. 1983, p. 144) (press up-arrow key, move hand to mouse, recall file name, verify cursor is at end-of-file). The selection rules are the control structures for choosing among the several methods available for accomplishing a goal (delete by repeated backspace versus delete by placing markers at beginning and end of region and pressing delete button).
   The keystroke-level model is an attempt to predict performance times for error-free expert performance of tasks by summing up the time for keystroking, pointing, homing, drawing, thinking, and waiting for the system to respond. These models concentrate on expert users and error-free performance, with less emphasis on learning, problem solving, error handling, subjective satisfaction, and retention.
   Kieras and Polson (1985) built on the GOMS approach, and used production rules to describe the conditions and actions in an interactive text editor. The number and complexity of production rules gave accurate predictions of learning and performance times for five text-editing operations: insert, delete, copy, move, and transpose. Other strategies for modeling interactive-system usage involve transition diagrams (Kieras and Polson, 1985) (Figure 2.1). These diagrams are helpful during design, for instruction, and as a predictor of learning time, performance time, and errors.
   Kieras (1988), however, complains that the Card, Moran, and Newell presentation "does not explain in any detail how the notation works, and it seems somewhat clumsy to use. Furthermore, the notation has only a weak connection to the underlying cognitive theory." Kieras offers a refinement with his *Natural GOMS Language* (NGOMSL) and an analysis method for writing down GOMS models. He tries to clarify the situations in which the GOMS task analyst must make a *judgment call*, must make assumptions about how users view the system, must bypass a complex hard-to-analyze task (choosing wording of a sentence, finding a bug in a program), or must check for consistency. Applying NGOMSL to guide the process of creating

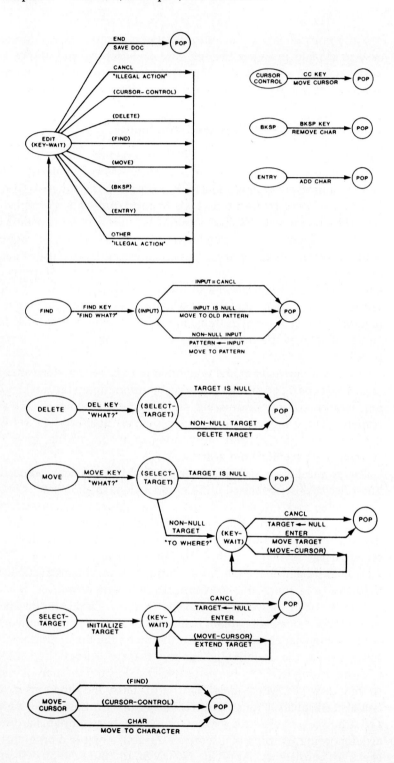

◀ **Figure 2.1**
_____

This generalized transition network for the Displaywriter shows the sequence of permissible actions. If the users begin at the EDIT state and issue a FIND command, they follow the paths in the FIND subdiagram. (Kieras, David and Polson, Peter, "An approach to the formal analysis of user complexity," *International Journal of Man-Machine Studies 22* (1985), 365–394. Used by permission of Academic Press, Inc. [London] Limited.)

online help, Elkerton and Palmiter (1991) created *method descriptions*, in which the actions necessary to accomplish a goal are broken down into steps. They also developed *selection rules*, by which a user can choose among alternative methods. For example, there may be several methods to delete fields.

Method to accomplish the goal of deleting the field:
   Step 1: Decide: If necessary, then accomplish the goal of selecting the field
   Step 2: Accomplish the goal of using a specific field delete method
   Step 3: Report goal accomplished
Method to accomplish the goal of deleting the field:
   Step 1: Decide: If necessary, then use the Browse tool to go to the card with the field
   Step 2: Choose the field tool in the Tools menu
   Step 3: Note that the fields on the card an background are displayed
   Step 4: Click on the field to be selected
   Step 5: Report goal accomplished
Selection rule set for goal of using a specific field delete method
   If you may want to paste the field somewhere else,
         then choose "Cut Field" from the Edit menu
   If you want to permanently delete the field,
         then choose "Clear Field" from the Edit menu
   Report goal accomplished.

The empirical evaluation with 28 subjects demonstrated that the NGOMSL version of help halved the time users took to complete information searches in the first of four trial blocks.

2.2.3   Seven stages of action

Norman (1988) offers *seven stages of action* as a model of human–computer interaction:

1. Forming the goal
2. Forming the intention

3. Specifying the action
4. Executing the action
5. Perceiving the system state
6. Interpreting the system state
7. Evaluating the outcome

Some of Norman's stages correspond roughly to Foley and van Dam's separation of concerns; that is, the user forms a conceptual intention, reformulates it into the semantics of several commands, constructs the required syntax, and eventually produces the lexical token by the action of moving the mouse to select a point on the screen. Norman makes a contribution by placing his stages in the context of *cycles of action* and *evaluation*. This dynamic process of action distinguishes Norman's approach from the other models, which deal mainly with the knowledge that must be in the users's mind. Furthermore, the seven-stages model leads naturally to identification of the *gulf of execution* (the mismatch between the users's intentions and the allowable actions) and the *gulf of evaluation* (the mismatch between the system's representation and the users' expectations).

This model leads Norman to suggest four principles of good design. First, the state and the action alternatives should be visible. Second, there should be a good conceptual model with a consistent system image. Third, the interface should include good mappings that reveal the relationships between stages. Fourth, the user should receive continuous feedback. Norman places a heavy emphasis on studying errors. He describes how errors often occur in moving from goals to intentions to actions and to executions.

2.2.4   Consistency through grammars

An important goal for designers is a *consistent* user interface. However, the definition of consistency is elusive and has multiple levels that are sometimes in conflict; also, it is sometimes advantageous to be inconsistent. The argument for consistency is that a command language or set of actions should be orderly, predictable, describable by a few rules, and therefore easy to learn and retain. These overlapping concepts are conveyed by an example that shows two kinds of inconsistency (A illustrates lack of any attempt at consistency, and B shows consistency except for a single violation):

Consistent	Inconsistent A	Inconsistent B
delete/insert character	delete/insert character	delete/insert character
delete/insert word	remove/bring word	remove/insert word
delete/insert line	destroy/create line	delete/insert line
delete/insert paragraph	kill/birth paragraph	delete/insert paragraph

Each of the actions in the consistent version is the same, whereas the actions vary for the inconsistent version A. The inconsistent action verbs are all acceptable, but their variety suggests that they will take longer to learn, will cause more errors, will slow down users, and will be harder for users to remember. Inconsistent version B is somehow more malicious because there is a single unpredictable inconsistency that stands out so dramatically that this language is likely to be remembered for its peculiar inconsistency.

To capture these notions, Reisner (1981) proposed an *action grammar* to describe two versions of a graphics-system interface. She demonstrated that the version that had a simpler grammar was easier to learn. Payne and Green (1986) expanded her work by addressing the multiple levels of consistency (lexical, syntactic, and semantic) through a notational structure they call *task–action grammars* (TAGs). They also address some aspects of completeness of a language by trying to characterize a complete set of tasks; for example, *up*, *down*, and *left* comprise an incomplete set of arrow-cursor movement tasks, because *right* is missing. Once the full set of task–action mappings is written down, the grammar of the command language can be tested against it to demonstrate completeness. Of course, a designer might leave out something from the task–action mapping and then the grammar could not be checked accurately, but it does seem useful to have an approach to checking for completeness and consistency. For example, a TAG definition of cursor control would have a dictionary of tasks:

move-cursor-one-character-forward   [Direction = forward,   Unit = char]
move-cursor-one-character-backward [Direction = backward, Unit = char]
move-cursor-one-word-forward   [Direction = forward,   Unit = word]
move-cursor-one-word-backward   [Direction = backward, Unit = word]

Then, the high-level rule schemas that describe the syntax of the commands are as follows:

1. task [Direction, Unit] —> symbol [Direction] + letter [Unit]
2. symbol [Direction = forward] —> "CTRL"
3. symbol [Direction = backward] —> "ESC"
4. letter [Unit = word] —> "W"
5. letter [Unit = char] —> "C"

These schemas will generate a consistent grammar:

move cursor one character forward   CTRL-C
move cursor one character backward   ESC-C
move cursor one word forward   CTRL-W
move cursor one word backward   ESC-W

Payne and Green are careful to state that their notation and approach are flexible and extensible, and they provide appealing examples in which their approach sharpened the thinking of designers.

Reisner (1990) extends this work by defining consistency more formally, but Grudin (1989) points out flaws in some arguments for consistency. Certainly, consistency is subtle and has multiple levels; there are conflicting forms of consistency, and sometimes inconsistency is a virtue (for example, to draw attention to a dangerous operation). Nonetheless, understanding consistency is an important goal for designers and researchers.

2.2.5   Widget-level theories

Many of the theories and predictive models that have been developed follow an extreme reductionist approach. It is hard to accept the low level of detail, the precise numbers that are sometimes attached to subtasks, and the assumptions of simple summations of time periods. Furthermore, many of the detailed models take an extremely long time to write, and many judgment calls plus assumptions must be made, so there is little trust that several analysts would come up with the same results.

An alternative approach is to follow the simplifications made in the higher-level UIMSs (Chapter 14). Instead of dealing with individual buttons and fields, why not create a model based on the widgets (interface components) supported in the UIMS? Once a scrolling-list widget was tested to determine user performance as a function of the number of items and the size of the window, then future widget users would have automatic generation of performance prediction. The prediction would have to be derived from some declaration of the task frequencies, but the description of the interface would emerge from the process of designing the interface.

A measure of layout appropriateness (frequently used pairs of widgets should be adjacent, and the left-to-right sequence should be in harmony with the task sequence description) would also be produced to guide the designer in a possible redesign. Estimates of the perceptual and cognitive complexity plus the motor load would be generated automatically (Sears, 1992). As widgets become more sophisticated and more widely used, the investment in determining the complexity of each widget will be amortized over the many designers and projects.

2.3   Syntactic–Semantic Model of User Knowledge

Distinctions between syntax and semantics have long been made by compiler writers who sought to separate out the parsing of input text from the operations that were invoked by the text. Interactive system designers can benefit from a syntactic–semantic model of user knowledge. In outline, this explanatory model suggests that users have syntactic knowledge about device-dependent details, and semantic knowledge about concepts. The semantic knowledge is separated into task concepts (objects and actions) and computer concepts (objects and actions) (Figure 2.2). A person can be an expert in the computer concepts, but a novice in the task concepts, and vice versa.

The *syntactic–semantic object–action* (SSOA) *model* of user behavior was originated to describe programming (Shneiderman, 1980) and has been applied to database-manipulation facilities (Shneiderman, 1981), as well as to direct manipulation (Shneiderman, 1983).

2.3.1   Syntactic knowledge

When using a computer system, users must maintain a profusion of device-dependent details in their human memory. These low-level syntactic details include the knowledge of which action erases a character (delete, backspace, CTRL-H, rightmost mouse button, crossing gesture, or ESCAPE), which action inserts a new line after the third line of a text file (CTRL-I, INSERT

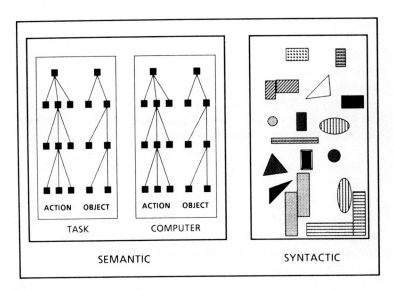

Figure 2.2

Syntactic–semantic model of objects and actions (SSOA model); a representation of the user's knowledge in long-term memory. The syntactic knowledge is varied, device dependent, acquired by rote memorization, and easily forgotten. The semantic knowledge is separated into the computer and task domains. Within these domains, knowledge is divided into actions and objects. Semantic knowledge is structured, device independent, acquired by meaningful learning, and stable in memory.

key, insert gesture between lines three and four, I3, I 3, or 3I), which icon scrolls text forward, which abbreviations are permissible, and which of the numbered function keys produces the previous screen.

The learning, use, and retention of this knowledge is hampered by two problems. First, these details vary across systems in an unpredictable manner. Second, acquiring syntactic knowledge is often a struggle because the arbitrariness of these minor design features greatly reduces the effectiveness of paired-associate learning. Rote memorization requires repeated rehearsals to reach competence, and retention over time is poor unless the knowledge is applied frequently. Syntactic knowledge is usually conveyed by example and repeated usage. Formal notations, such as Backus–Naur form, are useful for knowledgeable computer scientists but are confusing to most users.

A further problem with syntactic knowledge, in some cases, lies in the difficulty of providing a hierarchical structure or even a modular structure to cope with the complexity. For example, how is a user to remember these details of using an electronic-mail system: press RETURN to terminate a paragraph, CTRL-D to terminate a letter, Q to quit the electronic mail subsystem, and logout to terminate the session. The knowledgeable computer user understands these four forms of termination as commands in the context of the full system, but the novice may be confused by four seemingly similar situations that have radically different syntactic forms.

A final difficulty is that syntactic knowledge is system dependent. A user who switches from one machine to another may face different keyboard layouts, commands, function-key usage, and sequences of actions. Certainly, there may be some overlap. For example, arithmetic expressions might be the same in two languages; unfortunately, however, the small differences can be the most annoying. One system uses K to keep a file and another uses K to kill the file, or S to save versus S to send.

Expert frequent users can overcome these difficulties, and they are less troubled by syntactic knowledge problems. Novices and knowledgeable users, however, are especially troubled by syntactic irregularities. Their burden can be lightened by use of menus (see Chapter 3), a reduction in the arbitrariness of the keypresses, use of consistent patterns of commands, meaningful command names and labels on keys, and fewer details that must be memorized (see Chapter 4).

In summary, within the SSOA model, syntactic knowledge is arbitrary, system dependent, and ill structured. It must be acquired by rote memorization and repetition. Unless it is used regularly, it fades from memory.

2.3.2   Semantic knowledge—computer concepts

Semantic knowledge in human long-term memory has two components: computer concepts and task concepts (see Figure 2.2). Semantic knowledge has a hierarchical structure ranging from low-level actions to middle-level strategies to high-level goals (Shneiderman, 1980; Card et al., 1983). This presentation enhances the earlier SSOA model and other models by decoupling computer concepts from task concepts. This enhancement accommodates the two most common forms of expertness: task experts who may be novice computer users, and computer experts who may be new to a task. Different training materials are suggested for task or computer experts. Novices in both domains need yet a third form of training.

Semantic knowledge is conveyed by showing examples of use, offering a general theory or pattern, relating the concepts to previous knowledge by analogy, describing a concrete or abstract model, and indicating examples of incorrect use. There is an attraction to showing incorrect use to indicate clearly the bounds of a concept, but there is also a danger, since the learner may confuse correct and incorrect use. Pictures are often helpful in showing the relationships among semantic-knowledge concepts.

Computer concepts include *objects* and *actions* at high and low levels. For example, a central set of *computer-object* concepts deals with storage. Users come to understand the high-level concept that computers store information. The concept of stored information can be refined into the object concepts of the directory and the files of information. In turn, the directory object is refined into a set of directory entries that each have a name, length, date of creation, owner, access control, and so on. Each file is an object that has a lower-level structure consisting of lines, fields, characters, fonts, pointers, binary numbers, and so on.

The *computer actions* also are decomposable into lower-level actions. The high-level actions or goals, such as creating a text data file, may require load, insertion, and save actions. The midlevel action of saving a file is refined into the actions of storing a file and backup file on one of many disks, of applying access-control rights, of overwriting previous versions, of assigning a name to the file, and so on. Then, there are many low-level details about permissible file types or sizes, error conditions such as shortage of storage space, or responses to hardware or software errors. Finally, there is the low-level action of issuing a specific command, carried out by the syntactic detail of pressing the RETURN key.

These computer concepts were designed by highly trained experts in the hope that they were logical, or at least "made sense" to the designers. Unfortunately, the logic may be a complex product of underlying hardware, software, or performance constraints, or it might be just poorly chosen. Users are often confronted with computer concepts that they have great difficulty absorbing; but we have reason to hope that designers are improving and computer-literacy training is raising knowledge levels. For example, the action terminating a command by pressing RETURN is more and more widely known.

Users can learn computer concepts by seeing a demonstration of commands, hearing an explanation of features, or conducting trial-and-error sessions. A common practice is to create a model of concepts—abstract, concrete, or analogical—to convey the computer action. For example, with the file-saving concept, an instructor might draw a picture of a disk drive and a directory to show where the file goes and how the directory references the file. Alternatively, the instructor might make a library analogy or metaphor and describe how the card catalog acts as a directory for books saved in the library.

Since semantic knowledge about computer concepts has a logical structure and since it can be anchored to familiar concepts, we expect it to be relatively stable in memory. If you remember the high-level concept of saving a file, you will be able to conclude that the file must have a name, a size, and a storage location. The linkage to other objects and the potential for a visual presentation support the memorability of this knowledge.

These computer concepts were once novel, and were known to only a small number of scientists, engineers, and data-processing professionals. Now, these concepts are taught at the elementary-school level, argued over during coffee breaks in the office, and exchanged in the aisles of corporate jets. When educators talk of computer literacy, part of their plans cover these computer concepts.

In summary, according to the SSOA model, users must acquire semantic knowledge about computer concepts. These concepts are organized hierarchically, are acquired by meaningful learning or analogy, are independent of the syntactic details, should be transferable across different computer systems, and are relatively stable in memory. Computer concepts can be usefully subdivided into objects and actions.

2.3.3   Semantic knowledge—task concepts

The primary method that people use to deal with large and complex problems is to decompose them into several smaller problems in a hierarchical manner until each subproblem is manageable. Thus, a book is decomposed into the task objects of chapters, the chapters into sections, the sections into paragraphs, and the paragraphs into sentences. Each sentence is approximately one unit of thought for both the author and the reader. Most designed objects have similar decompositions: computer programs, buildings, television sets, cities, paintings, and plays, for example. Some objects are more neatly and easily decomposed than are others; some objects are easier to understand than are others.

Similarly, task actions can be decomposed into smaller actions. A construction plan can be reduced to a series of steps; a baseball game has innings, outs, and pitches; and a business letter comprises an address, date, addressee, body, signature, and so on.

In writing a business letter using computer software, users have to integrate smoothly the three forms of knowledge. They must have the high-level concept of writing (task action) a letter (task object), recognize that the letter will be stored as a file (computer object), and know the details of the `save` command (computer action and syntactic knowledge). Users must be fluent with the middle-level concept of composing a sentence and must recognize the mechanism for beginning, writing, and ending a sentence. Finally, users must know the proper low-level details of spelling each word (task), comprehend the motion of the cursor on the screen (computer concept), and know which keys to press for each letter (syntactic knowledge). The goal of minimizing syntactic knowledge and computer concepts while presenting a visual representation of the task objects and actions is the heart of the direct-manipulation approach to design (see Chapter 5).

Integrating the three forms of knowledge, the objects and actions, and the multiple levels of semantic knowledge is a substantial challenge that requires great motivation and concentration. Educational materials that facilitate the acquisition of this knowledge are difficult to design, especially because of the diversity of background knowledge and motivation levels of typical learners. The SSOA model of user knowledge can provide a guide to educational designers by highlighting the different kinds of knowledge that users need to acquire (see Chapter 12).

Designers of interactive systems can apply the SSOA model to systematize their efforts. Where possible, the semantics of the task objects should be made explicit and the user's task actions should be laid out clearly. Then, the computer objects and actions can be identified, leaving the syntactic details to be worked out later. In this way, designs appear to be more comprehensible to users and more independent of specific hardware.

2.4   Principles: Recognize the Diversity

The remarkable diversity of human abilities, backgrounds, cognitive styles, and personalities challenges the interactive-system designer. When multiplied by the wide range of situations, tasks, and frequencies of use, the set of possibilities becomes enormous. The designer can respond by choosing from a spectrum of interaction styles.

A preschooler playing a graphic computer game is a long way from a reference librarian doing bibliographic searches for anxious and hurried patrons. Similarly, a professional programmer using a new operating system is a long way from a highly trained and experienced air-traffic controller. Finally, a student learning a computer-assisted instruction lesson is a long way from a hotel reservations clerk serving customers for many hours per day.

These sketches highlight the differences in users' background knowledge, training in the use of the system, frequency of use, and goals, as well as in the impact of a user error. No single design could satisfy all these users and situations, so before beginning a design, we must make the characterization of the users and the situation as precise and complete as possible.

2.4.1   Usage profiles

"Know the user" was the first principle in Hansen's (1971) list of user-engineering principles. It is a simple idea, but a difficult goal and, unfortunately, an often-undervalued goal. No one would argue against this principle, but many designers assume that they understand the users and users' tasks. Successful designers are aware that other people learn, think, and solve problems in very different ways (Section 1.5). Some users really do have an easier time with tables than graphs, with words instead of numbers, with slower rather than faster display rates, or with a rigid structure rather than an open-ended form.

It is difficult for most designers to know whether Boolean expressions are too difficult a concept for library patrons at a junior college, fourth graders learning programming, or professional controllers of electric power utilities.

All design should begin with an understanding of the intended users, including profiles of their age, gender, physical abilities, education, cultural or ethnic background, training, motivation, goals, and personality. There are often several communities of users for a system, so the design effort is multiplied. In addition to these profiles, users might be tested for such skills as comprehension of Boolean expressions, knowledge of set theory, fluency in a foreign language, or skills in human relationships. Other tests might cover such task-specific abilities as knowledge of airport city codes, stockbrokerage terminology, insurance-claims concepts, or map icons.

The process of knowing the user is never ending, because there is so much to know and because the users keep changing. Every step in understanding the users and in recognizing them as individuals whose outlook is different from the designer's own is likely to be a step closer to a successful design.

For example, a generic separation into novice or first-time, knowledge-able intermittent, and expert frequent users might lead to these differing design goals:

Novice or first-time users: The first user community is assumed to have no syntactic knowledge about using the system and probably little semantic knowledge of computer issues. Whereas first-time users know the task semantics, novices have shallow knowledge of the task and both may arrive with anxiety about using computers that inhibits learning. Overcoming these limitations is a serious challenge to the designer. Restricting vocabulary to a small number of familiar, consistently used terms is essential to begin developing the user's knowledge of the system. The number of possibilities should be kept small, and the novice user should be able to carry out a few simple tasks to build confidence, to reduce anxiety, and to gain positive reinforcement from success. Informative feedback about the accomplishment of each task is helpful, and constructive, specific error messages should be provided when errors do occur. Carefully designed paper manuals and step-by-step online tutorials may be effective. Users are attempting to relate their existing knowledge to the task objects and actions in the application, so distractions with computer concepts and the syntax are an extra burden.

Knowledgeable intermittent users: Many people will be knowledgeable but intermittent users of a variety of systems. They will be able to maintain the semantic knowledge of the task and the computer concepts, but they will have difficulty maintaining the syntactic knowledge. The burden of memory will be lightened by simple and consistent structure in the command language, menus, terminology, and so on, and by use of recognition rather than recall. Consistent sequences of actions, meaningful messages, and frequent prompts will all help to assure knowledgeable intermittent users that they are performing their tasks properly. Protection from danger is necessary to support relaxed exploration of features or attempts to invoke a partially forgotten command. These users will benefit from online help screens to fill in missing pieces of syntactic or computer semantic knowledge. Well-organized reference manuals will also be useful.

Expert frequent users: The expert "power" users are thoroughly familiar with the syntactic and semantic aspects of the system and seek to get their work done rapidly. They demand rapid response times, brief and less distracting feedback, and the capacity to carry out actions with just a few keystrokes or selections. When a sequence of three or four commands is performed regularly, the frequent user is eager to create a *macro* or other abbreviated form to reduce the number of steps. Strings of commands, shortcuts through menus, abbreviations, and other accelerators are requirements.

These characteristics of these three classes of usage must be refined for each environment. Designing for one class is easy; designing for several is much more difficult.

When multiple usage classes must be accommodated in one system, the basic strategy is to permit a *level-structured* (some times called *layered* or *spiral approach*) to learning. Novices can be taught a minimal subset of objects and actions with which to get started. After gaining confidence from hands-on experience, the users can progress to ever greater levels of semantic concepts and the accompanying syntax. The learning plan should be governed by the progress through the task semantics. For users with strong knowledge of the task and computer semantics, rapid presentation of syntactic details is possible.

For example, novice users of a bibliographic-search system might be taught author or title searches first, followed by subject searches that require Boolean combinations of queries. The progress is governed by the task domain, not by an alphabetical list of commands that are difficult to relate to the tasks. The level-structured approach must be carried out in the design of not only the software, but also the user manuals, help screens, error messages, and tutorials.

Another approach to accommodating different usage classes is to permit user control of the density of informative feedback that the system provides. Novices want more informative feedback to confirm their actions, whereas frequent users want less distracting feedback. Similarly, it seems that frequent users like displays to be more densely packed than do novices. Finally, the pace of interaction may be varied from slow for novices to fast for frequent users.

2.4.2   Task profiles

After carefully drawing the user profile, the developers must identify the tasks. Task analysis has a long, but mixed, history (Bailey, 1989). Every designer would agree that the set of tasks must be determined before design can proceed, but too often the task analysis is done informally or implicitly. If implementers find that another command can be added, the designer is often tempted to include the command in the hope that some users will find it helpful. Design or implementation convenience should not dictate system functionality or command features.

High-level task actions can be decomposed into multiple middle-level task actions that can be further refined into atomic actions that the user executes with a single command, menu selection, and so on. Choosing the most appropriate set of atomic actions is a difficult task. If the atomic actions are too small, the users will become frustrated by the large number of actions necessary to accomplish a higher-level task. If the atomic actions are too large and elaborate, the users will need many such actions with special options, or they will not be able to get exactly what they want from the system.

The relative task frequencies will be important in shaping, for example, a set of commands or a menu tree. Frequently performed tasks should be simple and quick to carry out, even at the expense of lengthening some infrequent tasks. Relative frequency of use is one of the bases for making architectural design decisions. For example, in a text editor,

- Frequent actions might be performed by special keys, such as the four cursor arrows, INSERT, and DELETE.
- Intermediately frequent actions might be performed by a single letter plus CTRL, or by a selection from a pull-down menu—examples include underscore, center, indent, subscript, or superscript.
- Less frequent actions might require going to a command mode and typing the command name—for example, MOVE BLOCK or SPELLING CHECK.
- Infrequent actions or complex actions might require going through a sequence of menu selections or form fillins—for example, to change the printing format or to revise network protocol parameters.

A matrix of users and tasks can help us to sort out these issues (Figure 2.3). In each box, the designer can put a check mark to indicate that this user carries out this task. A more precise analysis would lead to inclusion of frequencies, instead of simple check marks.

2.4.3   Interaction styles

When the task analysis is complete and the semantics of the task objects and actions can be identified, the designer can choose from these primary interaction styles: menu selection, form fillin, command language, natural language, direct manipulation (Table 2.1). Chapters 3 through 5

Frequency of Task by Job Title

Job title	Query by patient	Update data	Query across patients	Add relations	Evaluate system
Nurses	0.14	0.11			
Physicians	0.06	0.04			
Supervisors	0.01	0.01	0.04		
Appointments personnel	0.26				
Medical-record maintainers	0.07	0.04	0.04	0.01	
Clinical researchers			0.08		
Database programmers			0.02	0.02	0.05

Figure 2.3

Hypothetical frequency-of-use data for a medical clinic information system. Queries by patient from appointments personnel are the highest-frequency task.

Table 2.1

Advantages and disadvantages of the five primary interaction styles.

Interaction Style	
Advantages	*Disadvantages*
menu selection	
shortens learning	imposes danger of many menus
reduces keystrokes	may slow frequent users
structures decision making	consumes screen space
permits use of dialog-management tools	requires rapid display rate
allows easy support of error handling	
form fillin	
simplifies data entry	consumes screen space
requires modest training	
makes assistance convenient	
permits use of form-management tools	
command language	
is flexible	has poor error handling
appeals to "power" users	requires substantial training and memorization
supports user initiative	
is convenient for creating user-defined macros	
natural language	
relieves burden of learning syntax	requires clarification dialog
	may require more keystrokes
	may not show context
	is unpredictable
direct manipulation	
presents task concepts visually	may be hard to program
is easy to learn	may require graphics display and pointing devices
is easy to retain	
allows errors to be avoided	
encourages exploration	
permits high subjective satisfaction	

explore these styles in detail; here, we give a comparative overview to set the stage.

Menu selection In menu-selection systems, the users read a list of items, select the one most appropriate to their task, apply the syntax to indicate their selection, confirm the choice, initiate the action, and observe the effect. If the terminology and meaning of the items are understandable and distinct, then the users can accomplish their task with little learning or memorization and few keystrokes. The greatest benefit may be that there is a clear structure to decision making, since only a few choices are presented at a time. This interaction style is appropriate for novice and intermittent users and can be appealing to frequent users if the display and selection mechanisms are rapid.

For designers, menu-selection systems require careful task analysis to ensure that all functions are supported conveniently and that terminology is chosen carefully and used consistently. Dialog-management tools to support menu selection are an enormous benefit in ensuring consistent screen design, validating completeness, and supporting maintenance.

Form fillin When data entry is required, menu selection usually becomes cumbersome, and form fillin (also called *fill-in-the-blanks*) is appropriate. Users see a display of related fields, move a cursor among the fields, and enter data where desired. With the form fillin interaction style, the users must understand the field labels, know the permissible values and the data-entry method, and be capable of responding to error messages. Since knowledge of the keyboard, labels, and permissible fields is required, some training may be necessary. This interaction style is most appropriate for knowledgeable intermittent users or frequent users. Chapter 3 provides a thorough treatment of menus and form fillin.

Command language For frequent users, command languages provide a strong feeling of locus of control and initiative. The users learn the syntax and can often express complex possibilities rapidly, without having to read distracting prompts. However, error rates are typically high, training is necessary, and retention may be poor. Error messages and online assistance are hard to provide because of the diversity of possibilities plus the complexity of mapping from tasks to computer concepts and syntax. Command languages and lengthier query or programming languages are the domain of the expert frequent users who often derive great satisfaction from mastering a complex set of semantics and syntax. Chapter 4 covers command languages and natural language interaction in depth.

Natural language The hope that computers will respond properly to arbitrary natural-language sentences or phrases engages many researchers and system developers, in spite of limited success thus far. Natural-language interaction usually provides little context for issuing the next command, frequently requires *clarification dialog*, and may be slower and more cumbersome than the alternatives. Still, where users are knowledgeable about a task domain whose scope is limited and where intermittent use inhibits command-language training, there exist opportunities for natural-language interfaces (discussed at the end of Chapter 4).

Direct manipulation   When a clever designer can create a visual representation of the world of action, the users' tasks can be greatly simplified because direct manipulation of the objects of interest is possible. Examples of such systems include display editors, LOTUS 1-2-3, air-traffic control systems, and video games. By pointing at visual representations of objects and actions, users can carry out tasks rapidly and observe the results immediately. Keyboard entry of commands or menu choices is replaced by cursor-motion devices to select from a visible set of objects and actions. Direct manipulation is appealing to novices, is easy to remember for intermittent users, and, with careful design, can be rapid for frequent users. Chapter 5 describes direct manipulation and its applications.

Blending several interaction styles may be appropriate when the required tasks and users are diverse. Commands may lead the user to a form fillin where data entry is required or menus may be used to control a direct-manipulation environment when a suitable visualization of actions cannot be found.

2.5 Eight Golden Rules of Dialog Design

Later chapters cover constructive guidance for design of menu selection, command languages, and so on. This section presents underlying principles of design that are applicable in most interactive systems. These underlying principles of interface design, derived heuristically from experience, should be validated and refined:

1. *Strive for consistency.* This principle is the most frequently violated one, and yet is the easiest one to repair and avoid. Consistent sequences of actions should be required in similar situations; identical terminology should be used in prompts, menus, and help screens; and consistent commands should be employed throughout. Exceptions, such as no echoing of passwords or confirmation of the DELETE command, should be comprehensible and limited in number.

2. *Enable frequent users to use shortcuts.* As the frequency of use increases, so do the user's desires to reduce the number of interactions and to increase the pace of interaction. Abbreviations, special keys, hidden commands, and macro facilities are appreciated by frequent knowledgeable users. Shorter response times and faster display rates are other attractions for frequent users.

3. *Offer informative feedback.* For every operator action, there should be some system feedback. For frequent and minor actions, the response can be modest, whereas for infrequent and major actions, the response should be more substantial. Visual presentation of the objects of interest provides a convenient environment for showing changes explicitly (see discussion of direct manipulation in Chapter 5).

4. *Design dialogs to yield closure.* Sequences of actions should be organized into groups with a beginning, middle, and end. The informative feedback at the completion of a group of actions gives the operators the satisfaction of accomplishment, a sense of relief, the signal to drop contingency plans and options from their minds, and an indication that the way is clear to prepare for the next group of actions.

5. *Offer simple error handling.* As much as possible, design the system so the user cannot make a serious error. If an error is made, the system should detect the error and offer simple, comprehensible mechanisms for handling the error. The user should not have to retype the entire command, but rather should need to repair only the faulty part. Erroneous commands should leave the system state unchanged, or the system should give instructions about restoring the state.

6. *Permit easy reversal of actions.* As much as possible, actions should be reversible. This feature relieves anxiety, since the user knows that errors can be undone; it thus encourages exploration of unfamiliar options. The units of reversibility may be a single action, a data entry, or a complete group of actions.

7. *Support internal locus of control.* Experienced operators strongly desire the sense that they are in charge of the system and that the system responds to their actions. Surprising system actions, tedious sequences of data entries, incapacity or difficulty in obtaining necessary information, and the inability to produce the action desired all build anxiety and dissatisfaction. Gaines (1981) captured part of this principle with his rule *avoid acausality* and his encouragement to make users the *initiators* of actions rather than the *responders*.

8. *Reduce short-term memory load.* The limitation of human information processing in short-term memory (the rule of thumb is that humans can remember "seven plus or minus two chunks" of information) requires that displays be kept simple, multiple page displays be consolidated, window-motion frequency be reduced, and sufficient training time be allotted for codes, mnemonics, and sequences of actions. Where appropriate, online access to command-syntax forms, abbreviations, codes, and other information should be provided.

These underlying principles must be interpreted, refined, and extended for each environment. The principles presented in the ensuing sections focus on increasing the productivity of users by providing simplified data-entry procedures, comprehensible displays, and rapid informative feedback that increase feelings of competence, mastery, and control over the system.

2.6 Preventing Errors

There is no medicine against death, and against error no rule has been found.
Sigmund Freud, (Inscription he wrote on his portrait)

Users of word processors, spreadsheets, database-query facilities, air-traffic control systems, and other interactive systems make mistakes far more frequently than might be expected. Card et al. (1980) reported that experienced professional users of text editors and operating systems made mistakes or used inefficient strategies in 31 percent of the tasks assigned to them. Brown and Gould (1987) found that even experienced authors had some errors in almost half their spreadsheets. Other studies are beginning to reveal the magnitude of the problem and the loss of productivity due to user errors.

One direction for reducing the loss in productivity due to errors is to improve the error messages provided by the computer system. Shneiderman (1982) reported on five experiments in which changes to error messages led to improved success at repairing the errors, lower error rates, and increased subjective satisfaction. Superior error messages were more specific, positive in tone, and constructive (telling the user what to do, rather than merely reporting the problem). Rather than using vague and hostile messages, such as SYNTAX ERROR or ILLEGAL DATA, designers were encouraged to use informative messages, such as UNMATCHED LEFT PARENTHESIS or MENU CHOICES ARE IN THE RANGE OF 1 TO 6.

Improved error messages, however, are only helpful medicine. A more effective approach is to prevent the errors from occurring. This goal is more attainable than it may seem in many systems.

The first step is to understand the nature of errors. One perspective is that people make mistakes or "slips" (Norman, 1983) that designers can avoid by organizing screens and menus functionally, designing commands or menu choices to be distinctive, and making it difficult for users to do irreversible actions. Norman offers other guidelines such as do not have modes, offer feedback about the state of the system, and design for consistency of commands. Norman's analysis provides practical examples and a useful theory.

2.6.1   Techniques for ensuring correct actions

The ensuing sections refine his analysis and describe three specific techniques for reducing errors by ensuring complete and correct actions: correct matching pairs, complete sequences, and correct commands.

Correct matching pairs   A common problem is the lack of correct matching pairs. It has many manifestations, and several simple prevention strategies. An example is the failure to provide the right parenthesis to close an open left parenthesis. If a bibliographic-search system allowed Boolean expressions such as COMPUTERS AND (PSYCHOLOGY OR SOCIOLOGY) and the user failed to provide the right parenthesis at the end, the system would produce a SYNTAX ERROR message or, even better, a more meaningful message, such as UNMATCHED LEFT PARENTHESES.

Another error is failure to include the closing quotation mark (") to close a string in BASIC. The command 10 PRINT "HELLO" is in error if the rightmost quotation mark is missing.

Similarly, a @B or other marker is required to indicate the end of boldface, italic, or underscored text in word processors. If the text file contains @BThis is boldface@B, then the three words between the @B markers appear in boldface on the printer. If the rightmost @B is missing, then the remainder of the file is printed in boldface.

A final example is omitting termination of a centering command in a text formatter. Some text formatters have a pair of commands—such as .ON CENTER and .OFF CENTER—surrounding lines of text to be centered. The omission of the latter command causes the entire file to be centered.

In each of these cases, a matching pair of markers is necessary for operation to be complete and correct. The omission of the closing marker can be prevented by use of an editor, preferably screen-oriented, that puts both the beginning and ending components of the pair on the screen in one action. For example, typing a left parenthesis generates a left and right parenthesis and puts the cursor in between to allow creation of the contents. An attempt to delete one of the parentheses will cause the matching parenthesis (and possibly the contents as well) to be deleted. Thus, the text can never be in a syntactically incorrect form.

Some people find this rigid approach to be too restrictive and may prefer a milder form of protection. When the user types a left parenthesis, the screen displays in the lower-left corner a message indicating the need for a right parenthesis, until that character is typed.

Another approach is to replace the requirement for the ending marker. Many microcomputer versions of BASIC do not require an ending quotation mark to terminate a string; they use a carriage return to signal the closing of a string. Variants of this theme occur in line-oriented text editors that allow omission of the final / in a CHANGE/OLD STRING/NEW STRING/ command. Many versions of LISP offer a special character, usually a right square bracket (]), to terminate all open parentheses.

In each of these cases, the designers have recognized a frequently occurring error and have found a way to eliminate the error situation.

Complete sequences   Sometimes, an action requires several steps or commands to reach completion. Since people may forget to complete every step of an action, designers attempt to offer a sequence of steps as a single action. In an automobile, the driver does not have to set two switches to signal a left turn. A single switch causes both turn-signal lights (front and rear) on the left side of the car to flash. When a pilot lowers the landing gear, hundreds of steps and checks are invoked automatically.

This same concept can be applied to interactive uses of computers. For example, the sequence of dialing up, setting communication parameters, logging on, and loading files is frequently executed by many users. Fortunately, most communications-software packages enable users to specify these processes once, and then to execute them by simply selecting the appropriate name.

Programming-language loop constructs require a WHILE-DO-BEGIN-END or FOR-NEXT structure, but sometimes users forget to put the complete structure in, or they delete one component but not the other components. One solution would be for users to indicate that they want a loop, and for the system to supply the complete and correct syntax, which would be filled in by the user. This approach reduces typing and the possibility of making a typographical error or a slip, such as the omission of one component. Conditional constructs require an IF-THEN-ELSE or CASE-OF-END structure; but again, users may forget a component when creating or deleting.

Users of a text editor should be able to indicate that section titles are to be centered, set in upper-case letters, and underlined, without having to issue a series of commands each time they enter a section title. Then, if a change is made in style—for example, to eliminate underlining—a single command would guarantee that all section titles were revised consistently.

As a final example, air traffic controllers may formulate plans to change the altitude of a plane from 14,000 feet to 18,000 feet in two steps; after raising the plane to 16,000 feet, however, the controller may get distracted and fail to complete the action. The controller should be able to record the plan and then have the computer prompt for completion.

The notion of complete sequences of actions may be difficult to implement, because users may need to issue atomic actions as well as complete sequences. In this case, users should be allowed to define sequences of their own—the macro or subroutine concept should be available at every level of usage.

Designers can gather information about potential complete sequences by studying sequences of commands actually issued and the pattern of errors that people actually make.

Correct commands   Industrial designers recognize that successful products must be safe and must prevent the user from making incorrect use of the product. Airplane engines cannot be put into reverse until the landing gear have touched down, and cars cannot be put into reverse while traveling forward at faster than 5 miles per hour. Many simpler cameras prevent double exposures (even though the photographer may want to expose a frame twice), and appliances have interlocks to prevent tampering while the power is on (even though expert users occasionally need to perform diagnoses).

The same principles can be applied to interactive systems. Consider these typical errors made by the users of computer systems: They invoke commands that are not available, type menu selection choices that are not permitted, request files that do not exist, or enter data values that are not acceptable. These errors are often caused by annoying typographic errors, such as using an incorrect command abbreviation; pressing a pair of keys, rather than a desired single key; misspelling a file name; or making a minor error such as omitting, inserting, or transposing characters. Error messages range from the annoyingly brief ? or WHAT?, to the vague UNRECOGNIZED COMMAND or SYNTAX ERROR, to the condemning BAD FILE NAME or ILLEGAL COMMAND. The brief ? is suitable for expert users who have made a trivial error and can recognize it when they see the command line on the screen. But if an expert has ventured to use a new command and has misunderstood its operation, then the brief message is not helpful.

Whoever made the mistake and whatever were its causes, users must interrupt their planning to deal with correcting the problem—and with their frustration in not getting what they wanted. As long as a command must be made up of a series of keystrokes on a keyboard, there is a substantial chance of making an error in entering the sequence of keypresses. Some keypressing sequences are more error-prone than others—especially those that require shifting or unfamiliar patterns. Reducing the number of keypresses can help, but it may place a greater burden on learning and memory, since an entry with reduced keystrokes; for example, RM may be more difficult to remember than the full command name, REMOVE (see Chapter 4).

Some systems offer automatic command completion that allows the user to type just a few letters of a meaningful command. The user may request the computer to complete the command by pressing the space bar, or the computer may complete it as soon as the input is sufficient to distinguish the command from others. Automatic command completion can save keystrokes and is appreciated by many users, but it can also be disruptive because the user must consider how many characters to type for each command, and must verify that the computer has made the completion that was intended.

Another approach is to have the computer offer the permissible commands, menu choices, or file names on the screen, and to let the user select with a pointing device. This approach is effective if the screen has ample space, the display rate is rapid, and the pointing device is fast and accurate. When the list grows too long to fit on the available screen space, some approach to hierarchical decomposition must be used.

Imagine that the 20 commands of an operating system were constantly displayed on the screen. After users select the PRINT command (or icon), the system automatically offers the list of 30 files for selection. Users can make two lightpen, touchscreen, or mouse selections in less time and with higher accuracy than they could by typing the command PRINT JAN-JUNE-EXPENSES.

In principle, a programmer needs to type a variable name only once. After it has been typed, the programmer can select it, thus eliminating the chance of a misspelling and an UNDECLARED VARIABLE message.

It is not always easy to convert a complex command into a small number of selections and thus to reduce errors. Pointing at long lists can be visually demanding and annoying if users are competent typists.

2.7   Guidelines: Data Display

Guidelines for display of data are being developed by many organizations. A guidelines document can help by promoting consistency among multiple designers, recording practical experience, incorporating the results of empirical studies, and offering useful rules of thumb (see Chapters 8 and 13). The creation of a guidelines document engages the design community in a lively discussion of input or output formats, command sequences, terminology, and hardware devices (Rubinstein and Hersh, 1984; Brown, 1988; Galitz, 1989). Inspirations for design guidelines can also be taken from graphics designers (Tufte, 1983, 1990).

2.7.1   Organizing the display

Smith and Mosier (1986) offer five high-level objectives for data display:

1. *Consistency of data display:* This principle is frequently violated, but violations are easy to repair. During the design process, the terminology,

abbreviations, formats, and so on should all be standardized and controlled by use of a written (or computer-managed) dictionary of these items.

2. *Efficient information assimilation by the user:* The format should be familiar to the operator, and should be related to the tasks required to be performed with these data. This objective is served by rules for neat columns of data, left justification for alphanumeric data, right justification of integers, lining up of decimal points, proper spacing, use of comprehensible labels, and appropriate use of coded values.

3. *Minimal memory load on user:* Users should not be required to remember information from one screen for use on another screen. Tasks should be arranged such that completion occurs with few commands, minimizing the chance of forgetting to perform a step. Labels and common formats should be provided for novice or intermittent users.

4. *Compatibility of data display with data entry:* The format of displayed information should be linked clearly to the format of the data entry.

5. *Flexibility for user control of data display:* Users should be able to get the information from the display in the form most convenient for the task on which they are working.

This compact set of high-level objectives is a useful starting point, but each project needs to expand these into application-specific and hardware-dependent standards and practices. For example, these detailed comments for control-room design come from a report from the Electric Power Research Institute (Lockheed, 1981):

- Be consistent in labeling and graphic conventions.
- Standardize abbreviations.
- Use consistent format in all displays (headers, footers, paging, menus, and so on).
- Present a page number on each display page, and allow actions to call up a page via entry of a page number.
- Present data only if they assist the operator.
- Present information graphically, where appropriate, using widths of lines, positions of markers on scales, and other techniques that relieve the need to read and interpret alphanumeric data.
- Present digital values only when knowledge of numerical value is actually necessary and useful.
- Use high-resolution monitors, and maintain them to provide maximum display quality.

- Design a display in monochromatic form, using spacing and arrangement for organization, and then judiciously add color where it will aid the operator.
- Involve operators in the development of new displays and procedures.

Chapter 8 further discusses data-display issues.

2.7.2   Getting the user's attention

Since substantial information may be presented to users for the normal performance of their work, exceptional conditions or time-dependent information must be presented so as to attract attention. Multiple techniques exist for attention getting:

Intensity: Use two levels only.

Marking: Underline, enclose in a box, point to with an arrow, or use an indicator such as an asterisk, bullet, dash, or an X.

Size: Use up to four sizes.

Choice of fonts: Use up to three fonts.

Inverse video: Use inverse coloring.

Blinking: Use blinking displays (2 to 4 hertz).

Color: Use up to four standard colors, with additional colors reserved for occasional use.

Color blinking: Use changes in color (blinking from one color to another).

Audio: Use soft tones for regular positive feedback, harsh sounds for rare emergency conditions.

A few words of caution are necessary. There is a danger in creating cluttered displays by overusing these techniques. Novices need simple, logically organized, and well-labeled displays that guide their actions. Expert operators do not need extensive labels on fields; subtle highlighting or positional presentation is sufficient. Display formats must be tested with users for comprehensibility.

Similarly highlighted items will be perceived as being related. Color coding is especially powerful in linking related items, but this use makes it more difficult to cluster items across color codes. Operator control over highlighting—for example, allowing the operator in an air-traffic control environment to assign orange to images of aircraft above 18,000 feet—may provide a useful resolution to concerns about personal preferences. Highlighting can be accomplished by increased intensity, blinking, or other methods.

Audio tones can provide informative feedback about progress, such as the clicks in keyboards or ringing sounds in telephones. Alarms for emergency conditions do alert operators rapidly, but a mechanism to suppress alarms must be provided. Testing is necessary to ensure that operators can distinguish among alarm levels. Prerecorded or synthesized voice messages are an intriguing alternative, but since they may interfere with communications among operators, they should be used cautiously.

2.8   Guidelines: Data Entry

Data-entry tasks can occupy a substantial fraction of the operator's time and are the source of frustrating and potentially dangerous errors. Smith and Mosier (1986) offer five high-level objectives for data entry:

1. *Consistency of data-entry transactions:* Similar sequences of actions should be used under all conditions; similar delimiters, abbreviations, and so on should be used.

2. *Minimal input actions by user:* Fewer input actions mean greater operator productivity and, usually, fewer chances for error. Making a choice by a single keystroke, mouse selection, or finger press, rather than by typing in a lengthy string of characters, is potentially advantageous. Selecting from a list of choices eliminates the need for memorization, structures the decision-making task, and eliminates the possibility of typographic errors. However, if the operators must move their hands from a keyboard to a separate input device, the advantage is defeated, because home-row position is lost. Experienced operators often prefer to type six to eight characters, instead of moving to a lightpen, joystick, or other selection device.
   A second aspect of this guideline is that redundant data entry should be avoided. It is annoying for an operator to enter the same information in two locations, since the double entry is perceived as a waste of effort and an opportunity for error. When the same information is required in two places, the system should copy the information for the operator, who still has the option of overriding by retyping.

3. *Minimal memory load on user:* When doing data entry, the operator should not be required to remember lengthy lists of codes and complex syntactic command strings.

4. *Compatibility of data entry with data display:* The format of data entry information should be linked closely to the format of displayed information.

5. *Flexibility for user control of data entry:* Experienced data entry operators may prefer to enter information in a sequence they can control. For example, on some occasions in an air-traffic control environment, the arrival time is the prime field in the controller's mind; on other occasions, the altitude is the prime field. Flexibility should be used cautiously, since it goes against the consistency principle.

2.9 Prototyping and Acceptance Testing

A critical component of clear thinking about interactive system design is the replacement of the vague and misleading notion of "user friendliness" with the five measurable quality criteria:

- Time to learn
- Speed of performance
- Rate of errors by users
- Retention over time
- Subjective satisfaction

Once the decision about the relative importance of each of the human-factors quality criteria has been made, specific measurable objectives should be established to inform customers and users and to guide designers and implementers. The acceptance test plan for a system should be included in the requirements document and should be written before the design is made. Hardware and software test plans are regularly included in require-ments documents; extending the principle to human-interface development is natural (Chapter 13).

The requirements document for a word-processing system might include this acceptance test:

> The subjects will be 35 secretaries hired from an employment agency. They have no word-processing experience, but have typing skills in the range of 35 to 50 words per minute. They will be given 45 minutes of training on the basic features. At least 30 of the 35 secretaries should be able to complete, within 30 minutes, 80 percent of the typing and editing tasks in the enclosed benchmark test correctly.

Another testable requirement for the same system might be this:

> After 4 half-days of regular use of the system, 25 of these 35 secretaries should be able to carry out, within 20 minutes, the advanced editing tasks in the second benchmark test, and should make fewer than six errors.

This second acceptance test captures performance after regular use. The choice of the benchmark tests is critical and is highly system dependent. The test materials and procedures must also be refined by pilot testing before use.

A third item in the acceptance test plan might focus on retention:

> After 2 weeks, at least 15 of the test subjects should be recalled, and should perform the third benchmark test. In 40 minutes, at least 10 of the subjects should be able to complete 75 percent of the tasks correctly.

Such performance tests constitute the definition of "user friendly" for this system. By having an explicit definition, both the managers and the designers will gain a clearer understanding of the system goals and whether they have succeeded. The presence of a precise acceptance test plan will force greater attention to human-factors issues during the design, and will ensure that pilot studies are run to determine whether the project can meet the test plan goals.

In a programming-workstation project, this early requirement for performance helped shape the nature of the interface:

> New professional programmers should be able to sign on to create a short program, and to execute that program against a stored test data set, without assistance and within 10 minutes.

Specific goals in acceptance tests are useful, but competent test managers will notice and record anecdotal evidence, such as suggestions from participants, subjective reactions of displeasure or satisfaction, their own comments, and exceptional performance (both good and bad) by individuals. The precision of the acceptance test provides an environment in which unexpected events are most noticeable.

2.10   Balance of Automation and Human Control

The principles in the previous sections are in harmony with the goal of simplifying the user's task—eliminating human actions when no judgment is required. The users can then avoid the annoyance of handling routine, tedious, and error-prone tasks, and can concentrate on critical decisions, planning, and coping with unexpected situations. The computers should be used to keep track of and retrieve large volumes of data, to follow preset patterns, and to carry out complex mathematical or logical operations (Table 2.2 provides a detailed comparison of human and machine capabilities).

The degree of automation will increase over the years as procedures become more standardized, hardware reliability increases, and software

Table 2.2

Relative capabilities of humans and machines. (Compiled from Brown (1988); McCormick, E. J., *Human Factors Engineering*, McGraw-Hill, New York (1970), 20–21; and Estes, W. K., Is human memory obsolete? *American Scientist 68* (1980), 62–69.)

Humans Generally Better	Machines Generally Better
Sense low level stimuli	Sense stimuli outside human's range
Detect stimuli in noisy background	Count or measure physical quantities
Recognize constant patterns in varying situations	Store quantities of coded information accurately
Sense unusual and unexpected events	Monitor prespecified events, especially infrequent
	Make rapid and consistent responses to input signals
Remember principles and strategies	Recall quantities of detailed information accurately
Retrieve pertinent details without a priori connection	Process quantitative data in prespecified ways
Draw on experience and adapt decisions to situation	
Select alternatives if original approach fails	
Reason inductively: generalize from observations	Reason deductively: infer from a general principle
Act in unanticipated emergencies and novel situations	Perform repetitive preprogrammed actions reliably
	Exert great, highly controlled physical force
Apply principles to solve varied problems	
Make subjective evaluations	Perform several activities simultaneously
Develop new solutions	
Concentrate on important tasks when overload occurs	Maintain operations under heavy information load
Adapt physical response to changes in situation	Maintain performance over extended periods of time

verification and validation improves. With routine tasks, automation is preferred, since the potential for error may be reduced. However, I believe that there will always be a critical human role because the real world is an "open system" (there is a nondenumerable number of unpredictable events and system failures). By contrast, computers constitute a "closed system" (there is only a denumerable number of predictable normal and failure situations that can be accommodated in hardware and software). Human judgment is necessary for the unpredictable events in which some action must be taken to preserve safety, avoid expensive failures, or increase product quality.

For example, in air-traffic control, common actions include changes to altitude, heading, or speed. These actions are well understood and are potentially automatable by a scheduling and route-allocation algorithm, but the controllers must be present to deal with the highly variable and unpredictable emergency situations. An automated system might deal successfully with high volumes of traffic, but what would happen if the airport manager closed two runways because of turbulent weather? The controllers would have to reroute planes quickly. Now suppose one pilot called in to request special clearance to land because of a failed engine, while a second pilot reported a passenger with a potential heart attack. Human judgment is necessary to decide which plane should land first and how much costly and risky diversion of normal traffic is appropriate. Air-traffic controllers cannot just jump suddenly into the emergency; they must be intensely involved in the situation to make an informed, rapid, and optimal decision. In short, the real-world situation is so complex that it is impossible to anticipate and program for every contingency; human judgment and values are necessary in the decision-making process.

Another example of the complexity of real-world situations in air-traffic control emerges from an incident on an Air Canada Boeing 727. The jet had a fire on board, and the controller cleared other traffic from the flight paths and began to guide the plane in for a landing. The smoke was so bad that the pilot had trouble reading his instruments. Then, the onboard transponder burned out, so the air-traffic controller could no longer read the plane's altitude from the situation display. In spite of these multiple failures, the controller and the pilot managed to bring down the plane quickly enough to save the lives of many—but not all—of the passengers. A computer could not have been programmed to deal with this unexpected series of events.

The goal of system design in many applications is to give operators sufficient information about current status and activities that, when intervention is necessary, they have the knowledge and the capacity to perform correctly, even under partial failures. Increasingly, the human role will be to respond to unanticipated situations, equipment failure, improper human performance, and incomplete or erroneous data (Eason, 1980; Sheridan, 1988).

The entire system must be designed and tested, not only for normal situations, but also for as wide a range of anomalous situations as can be anticipated. An extensive set of test conditions might be included as part of the requirements document. Operators need to have enough information that they can take responsibility for their actions.

Beyond performance of productive decision-making tasks and handling of failures, the role of the human operator will be to improve the design of the system. In complex systems, an opportunity always exists for improvement, so systems that lend themselves to refinement will evolve via continual incremental redesign by the operator.

2.11   Adaptive Agents and User Models versus Control Panels

The balance of automation and human control also emerges as an issue in systems for home and office automation. Many designers promote the notion of anthropomorphic agents that would wisely carry out the users's intents and anticipate needs (Norcio, 1989). These scenarios often show a responsive, butlerlike human being to represent the agent (a bow-tied, helpful young man in Apple Computer's 1987 video on the *Knowledge Navigator*), or refer to the agent on a first-name basis (such as Sue or Bob in Hewlett-Packard's 1990 video on computing in 1995). Others have described "knowbots," agents that traverse networks and scan large databases seeking information that the user might find interesting.

These fantasies are appealing; most people are attracted to the idea that a powerful functionary is continuously carrying out their tasks and watching out for their needs. The wish to create an agent that knows people's likes and dislikes, makes proper inferences, responds to novel situations, and performs competently with little guidance is strong for some designers. However, human–human interaction is not necessarily a good model for human–computer interaction. Many users have a strong desire to be in control and to have a sense of mastery over the system, so that they can derive feelings of accomplishment. Users usually seek predictable systems and shy away from complex unpredictable behavior. Simple task domain concepts should mask the underlying computational complexity, in the same way that turning on an automobile ignition is simple to the user but invokes complex algorithms in the engine-control computer. These algorithms may adapt to varying engine temperatures or air pressures, but the action at the user-interface level remains unchanged.

A variant of the agent scenario, which does not include an anthropomorphic realization, is that the computer employs a "user model" to guide an adaptive system. For example, several proposals suggest that, as users make menu selections more rapidly, indicating proficiency, advanced menu items or a command-line interface can be introduced. Automatic adaptations have been proposed for response time, length of messages, density of feedback, content of menus, order of menu items (see Section 3.3 for evidence against this strategy), type of feedback (graphic or tabular), and content of help screens. Advocates point to video games that increase the speed or number of dangers as users progress though stages of the game. However, games are quite different from most work situations, where users have external goals and motivations to accomplish their tasks. There is much discussion of user models, but little empirical evidence of their efficacy.

There are some opportunities to tailor system responses as a function of context, but unexpected behavior is a serious negative side effect that discourages use. If adaptive systems make surprising changes, users must pause to see what has changed. Then, they may become anxious because they may not be able to predict the next change, to interpret what has happened, or to restore the system to the previous state. The agent metaphor and "active, adaptive, intelligent" systems seem to be more attractive to designers who believe that they are creating something lifelike and even magical, than they are to users who may feel anxious and unable to control the system.

An alternative to agents and user models may be to expand the control-panel metaphor. Current control panels are used to set physical parameters, such as the speed of cursor blinking, rate of mouse tracking, or loudness of a speaker, and to establish personal preferences such as time, date formats, placement and format of menus, or color schemes (Figure 2.4 and 2.5). Some software packages allow users to set parameters such as the speed in games or the usage level as in HyperCard (from browsing to editing buttons to writing scripts and creating graphics). Users start at level 1, and can then choose when to progress to higher levels. Often, users are content remaining experts at level 1 of a complex system, rather than dealing with the uncertainties of higher levels. More elaborate control panels exist in style

Figure 2.4

Control panel from the Apple Macintosh with scrolling list of specific controls. (Copyright Apple Computer, Inc., Cupertino, CA. Used with permission.)

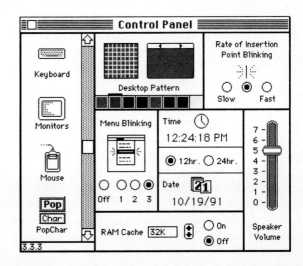

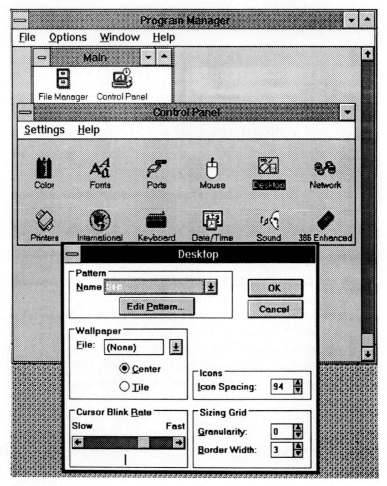

Figure 2.5

Control panel from Microsoft Windows graphical environment version 3.0. (Screen shot ©1985–1991 Microsoft Corporation. Reprinted with permission from Microsoft Corporation, Redmond, WA.)

sheets of word processors, specification boxes of query facilities, and scheduling software that carries out processes at regular intervals or when triggered by other processes.

Computer control panels, like cruise-control mechanisms in automobiles, are designed to convey the sense of control that users seem to expect. Increasingly, complex processes are specified by direct-manipulation programming (see Chapter 5) or by dialog-box specifications in graphical user interfaces. An effective design enables users to have a comprehensible task domain model of what the system does, and to make multiple choices rapidly.

2.12   Legal Issues

As user interfaces have become prominent, serious legal issues have emerged. Privacy issues are always a concern whenever computers are used to store data or to monitor activity. Medical, legal, financial, military, or other data often have to be protected to prevent unapproved access, illegal tampering, inadvertent loss, or malicious mischief. Physical security to prohibit access is fundamental; in addition, privacy protection can involve user-interface issues for encryption and decryption, password access, file-access control, identity checking, and data verification. Effective protection should provide a high degree of privacy with a minimum of interference.

A second issue is safety and reliability. User interfaces for aircraft, automobiles, medical equipment, military systems, or nuclear-reactor control rooms can affect life-or-death decisions. If an air-traffic controller is temporarily confused by the contents of the display, that could lead to disaster. If the user interface for such a system is demonstrated to be difficult to understand, it could leave the designer, developer, and operator open to a law suit alleging improper design. Designers should strive to make high-quality and well-tested interfaces that adhere to state-of-the-art design guidelines. Documentation of testing and usage should be maintained to provide accurate data on actual performance. Unlike architecture or engineering, user-interface design is not yet an established profession with clear standards.

A third issue is copyright protection for software and information (Clapes, 1989; Menell, 1989; Gilbert, 1990; NRC, 1991). Software developers who have spent time and money to develop a package are frustrated in attempting to recover their costs and make a profit if potential users pirate (make illegal copies of) the package, rather than buy it. Various technical schemes have been tried to prevent copying, but clever hackers can usually circumvent the barriers. It is unusual for a company to sue an individual for copying a program, but cases have been brought against corporations and universities. Site-license agreements are one solution, because they allow copying within a site once the fees have been paid. More complicated situations arise in the context of access to online information. If a customer of an online information service pays for time to access to the database, does the customer have the right to extract and store the retrieved information electronically for later use? Can the customer send an electronic copy to a colleague, or sell a bibliography carefully culled from a large commercial database? Do individuals, their employers, or network operators own the information contained in electronic-mail messages?

A fourth issue is freedom of speech in electronic environments. Is the right to make controversial statements through electronic mail or bulletin-board systems? Are such statements protected by the First Amendment? Are networks like street corners, where freedom of speech is guaranteed, or are networks like television broadcasting, where community standards must be protected? Should network operators be responsible for or prohibited from eliminating offensive or obscene jokes, stories, or images? Controversy has raged over whether a network operator can prohibit electronic-mail messages that were used to organize a rebellion against the network operators. Another controversy emerged over whether the network operator should suppress racist electronic-mail remarks or postings to a bulletin board. If libelous statements are transmitted, can a person sue the network as well as the source?

The most controversial issue for user-interface designers is that of copyright and patent protection for user interfaces. When user interfaces comprised coded commands in all-capital letters on a Teletype, there was little that could be protected. But the emergence of artistically designed graphic user interfaces with animations and extensive online help has led developers to file for copyright protection. This activity has led to many controversies:

- *What material is eligible for copyright?* Since fonts, lines, boxes, shading, and colors cannot usually be accorded copyrights, some people claim that most interfaces are not protectable. Advocates of strong protection claim that the ensemble of components is a creative work, just like a song that is composed of uncopyrightable notes or a poem of uncopyrightable words. Although standard arrangements, such as the rotated-L format of spreadsheets, are not copyrightable, collections of words, such as the Lotus 1-2-3 menu tree, have been accepted as copyrightable. Maybe the most confusing concept is the separation between ideas (not protectable) and expressions (protectable). Generations of judges and lawyers have wrestled with the issue; they agree only that there is "no bright shining line" between idea and expression, and that the distinction must be decided in each case. Most informed commentators would agree that the idea of working on multiple documents at once by showing multiple windows simultaneously is not protectable, but that specific expressions of windows (border decorations, animations for movement, and so on) might be protectable. A key point is that there should be a variety of ways to express a given idea. When there is only one way to express an idea—for example, a circle for the idea of a wedding ring—the expression is not protectable.

- *Are copyrights or patents more appropriate for user interfaces?* Traditionally, copyright is used for artistic, literary, and musical expressions, whereas patent is used for functional devices. There are interesting crossovers, such as copyrights for maps, engineering drawing, and decorations on teacups, and patents for software algorithms. Copyrights are easy to obtain (just put a copyright notice on the user interface and file a copyright application), are rapid, and are not verified. Patents are complex, slow, and costly to obtain, since they must be verified by the Patent and Trademark Office. Copyrights last 75 years for companies, and life plus 50 years for individuals. Patents last for only 17 years but are considered more enforceable. The strength of patent protection has raised concerns over patents that were granted for what appear to be fundamental algorithms for data compression and display management. Copyrights for printed user manuals and online help can also be obtained.

- *What constitutes copyright infringement?* If another developer copies your validly copyrighted user interface exactly, that is clearly a case of infringement. More subtle issues arise when a competitor makes a user interface that has elements strikingly similar, by your judgment, to your own. To win a copyright-infringement case, you must convince a jury of "ordinary observers" that the competitor actually saw your interface and that the other interface is "substantially similar" to yours.

- *Should user interfaces be copyrighted?* There are many respected commentators who believe that user interfaces should not be copyrighted. They contend that user interfaces should be shared and that it would impede progress if developers had to pay for permission for every user-interface feature that they saw and wanted to include in their interface. They claim also that copyrights interfere with beneficial standardization and that unnecessary artistic variations would create confusion and inconsistency. Advocates of copyrights for user interfaces wish to recognize creative accomplishments and, by allowing protection, to encourage innovation while ensuring that designers are rewarded for their works. Although ideas are not protectable, specific expressions would have to be licensed from the creator, presumably for a fee, in the same way that each photo in an art book must be licensed and acknowledged, or each use of a song, play, or quote must be granted permission. Concern over the complexity and cost of this process and the unwillingness of copyright owners to share is legitimate, but the alternative of providing no protection might slow innovation.

In the current legal climate, interface designers must respect existing expressions and would be wise to seek licenses or cooperative agreements to share user interfaces. Placing a copyright notice on the title screen of a system and in user manuals seems appropriate. Of course, proper legal counsel should be obtained.

2.13   Practitioner's Summary

Designing user interfaces is a complex and highly creative process that blends intuition, experience, and careful consideration of numerous technical issues. Designers are urged to begin with a thorough task analysis and a careful specification of the user communities. Explicit recording of task objects and actions based on a task analysis can lead to construction of useful metaphors or system images. Identification of computer objects and actions guides designers to develop simpler concepts that benefit novice and expert users. Next, designers create consistent and meaningful syntactic forms for input and display. Extensive testing and iterative refinement are necessary parts of every development project.

Design principles and guidelines are emerging from practical experience and empirical studies. Organizations can benefit by reviewing available guidelines documents and then constructing a local version. A guidelines document records organizational policies, supports consistency, aids the application of dialog-management tools, facilitates training of new designers, records results of practice and experimental testing, and stimulates discussion of user-interface issues.

2.14   Researcher's Agenda

The central problem for psychologists, human-factors professionals, and computer scientists is to develop adequate theories and models of the behavior of humans who use interactive systems. Traditional psychological theories must be extended and refined to accommodate the complex human learning, memory, and problem-solving required in these applications. Useful goals include descriptive taxonomies, explanatory theories, and predictive models.

A first step might be to investigate thoroughly a limited task for a single community, and to develop a formal notation for describing task actions and objects. Then, the mapping to computer actions and objects could be made precisely. Finally, the linkage with syntax would follow. This process would lead to predictions of learning times, performance speeds, error rates, subjective satisfaction, or human retention over time, for competing designs.

Next, the range of tasks and user communities could be expanded to domains of interest such as word processing, information retrieval, or data entry. More limited and applied research problems are connected with each of the hundreds of design principles or guidelines that have been proposed. Each validation of these principles and clarification of the breadth of applicability would be a small but useful contribution to the emerging mosaic of human performance with interactive systems.

References

Bailey, Robert W., *Human Performance Engineering: Using Human Factors/Ergonomics to Achieve Computer Usability* (Second Edition) Prentice-Hall, Englewood Cliffs, NJ (1989).

Brown, C. Marlin, *Human–Computer Interface Design Guidelines*, Ablex, Norwood, NJ (1988).

Brown, P., and Gould, J., How people create spreadsheets, *ACM Transactions on Office Information Systems 5* (1987), 258–272.

Card, Stuart K., Theory-driven design research, In McMillan, Grant R., Beevis, David, Salas, Eduardo, Strub, Michael H., Sutton, Robert, and Van Breda, Leo (Editors), *Applications of Human Performance Models to System Design*, Plenum Press, New York (1989), 501–509.

Card, Stuart K., Mackinlay, Jock D., and Robertson, George G., The design space of input devices, *Proc.CHI '90 Conference: Human Factors in Computing Systems*, ACM, New York (1990), 117–124.

Card, Stuart, Moran, Thomas P., and Newell, Allen, The keystroke-level model for user performance with interactive systems, *Communications of the ACM 23* (1980), 396–410.

Card, Stuart, Moran, Thomas P., and Newell, Allen, *The Psychology of Human–Computer Interaction*, Lawrence Erlbaum Associates, Hillsdale, NJ (1983).

Clapes, Anthony Lawrence, *Software, Copyright, and Competition: The "Look and Feel" of the Law*, Quorum, New York (1989).

Computer Science and Telecommunications Board National Research Council, *Intellectual Property Issues in Software*, National Academy Press, Washington, DC (1991).

Eason, K. D., Dialogue design implications of task allocation between man and computer, *Ergonomics 23*, 9 (1980), 881–891.

Egan, Dennis E., Individual differences in human–computer interaction. In Helander, Martin (Editor), *Handbook of Human–Computer Interaction*, Elsevier Science Publishers, Amsterdam, The Netherlands (1988), 543–568.

Elkerton, Jay and Palmiter, Susan L., Designing help using a GOMS model: An information retrieval evaluation, *Human Factors 33*, 2 (1991), 185–204.

Foley, James D., van Dam, Andries, Feiner, Steven K., and Hughes, John F., *Computer Graphics: Principles and Practice* (Second Edition), Addison-Wesley, Reading, MA (1990).

Gaines, Brian R., The technology of interaction—dialogue programming rules, *International Journal of Man–Machine Studies 14* (1981), 133–150.

Galitz, Wilbert O., *Handbook of Screen Format Design* (Third Edition), Q. E. D. Information Sciences, Wellesley, MA (1989).

Gilbert, Steven W., Information technology, intellectual property, and education, *EDUCOM Review 25* (1990), 14–20.

Grudin, Jonathan, The case against user interface consistency, *Communications of the ACM 32*, 10 (1989), 1164–1173.

Hansen, Wilfred J., User engineering principles for interactive systems, *Proc. Fall Joint Computer Conference 39*, AFIPS Press, Montvale, NJ (1971), 523–532.

Kieras, David, Towards a practical GOMS model methodology for user interface design. In Helander, Martin (Editor), *Handbook of Human–Computer Interaction*, Elsevier Science Publishers, Amsterdam, The Netherlands (1988), 135–157.

Kieras, David, and Polson, Peter G., An approach to the formal analysis of user complexity, *International Journal of Man–Machine Studies 22* (1985), 365–394.

Lockheed Missiles and Space Company, *Human Factors Review of Electric Power Dispatch Control Centers: Volume 2: Detailed Survey Results*, Prepared for Electric Power Research Institute, Palo Alto, CA (1981).

Menell, Peter S., An analysis of the scope of copyright protection for application programs, *Stanford Law Review 41* (1989), 1045–1104.

National Research Council, *Intellectual Property Issues in Software*, National Academy Press, Washington D.C. (1991).

Norcio, Anthony F. and Stanley, Jaki, Adaptive human–computer interfaces: A literature survey and perspective, *IEEE Transactions on Systems, Man, and Cybernetics 19* (1989), 399–408.

Norman, Donald A., Design rules based on analyses of human error, *Communications of the ACM 26*, 4 (1983), 254–258.

Norman, Donald A., *The Psychology of Everyday Things*, Basic Books, New York (1988).

Norman, Kent L., Models of the mind and machine: Information flow and control between humans and computers, *Advances in Computers 32* (1991), 119–172.

Payne, S. J. and Green, T. R. G., Task-Action Grammars: A model of the mental representation of task languages, *Human–Computer Interaction 2* (1986), 93–133.

Payne, S. J. and Green, T. R. G., The structure of command languages: An experiment on Task-Action Grammar, *International Journal of Man–Machine Studies 30* (1989), 213–234.

Reisner, Phyllis, Formal grammar and design of an interactive system, *IEEE Transactions on Software Engineering SE-5* (1981), 229–240.

Reisner, Phyllis, What is consistency? In Diaper et al. (Editors), *INTERACT '90: Human–Computer Interaction*, North-Holland, Amsterdam, The Netherlands (1990), 175–181.

Rubinstein, Richard, and Hersh, Harry, *The Human Factor: Designing Computer Systems for People*, Digital Press, Burlington, MA (1984).

Sears, Andrew, *Widget-Level Models of Human–Computer Interaction: Applying Simple Task Descriptions to Design and Evaluation*, PhD. Dissertation, Department of Computer Science, University of Maryland, College Park, MD (1992).

Sheridan, Thomas B., Task allocation and supervisory control. In Helander, M. (Editor), *Handbook of Human–Computer Interaction*, Elsevier Science Publishers, Amsterdam, The Netherlands (1988), 159–173.

Shneiderman, Ben, *Software Psychology: Human Factors in Computer and Information Systems*, Little, Brown, Boston, MA (1980).

Shneiderman, Ben, A note on the human factors issues of natural language interaction with database systems, *Information Systems 6*, 2 (1981), 125–129.

Shneiderman, Ben, System message design: Guidelines and experimental results. In *Directions in Human–Computer Interaction*, Badre, A. and Shneiderman, B. (Editors), Ablex, Norwood, NJ (1982), 55–78.

Shneiderman, Ben, Direct manipulation: A step beyond programming languages, *IEEE Computer 16*, 8 (1983), 57–69.

Smith, Sid L. and Mosier, Jane N., *Guidelines for Designing User Interface Software*, Report ESD-TR-86-278, Electronic Systems Division, the MITRE Corporation, Bedford, MA (1986). Available from National Technical Information Service, Springfield, VA.

Tufte, Edward, *The Visual Display of Quantitative Information*, Graphics Press, Cheshire, CT (1983).

Tufte, Edward, *Envisioning Information*, Graphics Press, Cheshire, CT (1990).

CHAPTER 3

Menu Selection and Form Fillin

A man is responsible for his choice and must accept the
consequences, whatever they may be.

W. H. Auden, *A Certain World*

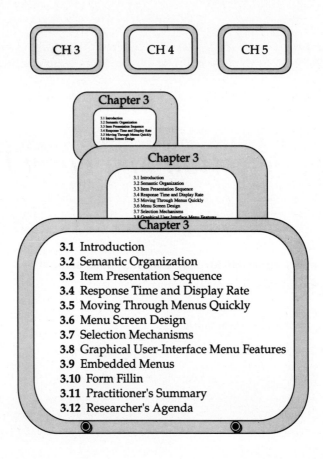

3.1 Introduction

Menu selection is attractive because it can eliminate training and memorization of complex command sequences. When the menu items are written using familiar terminology, users can select an item easily, and can indicate their choice with one or two keypresses or use of a pointing device. This simplified interaction style reduces the possibility of keying errors and structures the task to guide the novice and intermittent user. With careful design and high-speed interaction, menu selection can become appealing to expert frequent users, as well. The success of menu selection in the Macintosh, Microsoft Windows 3.0, or OSF/Motif is an indication of the widespread appeal of seeing choices and of selecting by pointing.

Menu selection is often contrasted with use of command language, but the distinctions are sometimes blurred. Typically, menu selection requires a single keystroke or mouse click, whereas commands may be lengthy; but how would you classify a menu in which users have to type a six- or eight-letter item? Typically, menu selection displays the choices, whereas commands must be memorized, but how would you classify a menu that offered four numbered choices and accepted 10 more generic commands that are not displayed? The command menu bar in LOTUS 1-2-3 is a success because is allows the duality that novices treat it as a menu and walk through the levels, whereas experienced users construct commands by typing ahead several levels of menu choices. If light can be a wave and a particle, then why should an interface not be a menu and a command?

Rather than debate terminology, it is more useful to maintain an awareness of how much information is on the display at the moment the selection is made, what are the form and content of item selection, and what task domain knowledge is necessary for users to succeed. Menu selection is especially effective when users have little training, use the system only intermittently, are unfamiliar with the terminology, and need help in structuring their decision-making process.

However, if a designer uses menu selection, this choice does not guarantee that the system will be appealing and easy to use. Effective menu-selection systems emerge only after careful consideration of and testing for numerous design issues, such as semantic organization, menu-system structure, number and sequence of menu items, titling, prompting format, graphic layout and design, phrasing of menu items, display rates, response time, shortcuts through the menus for knowledgeable frequent users, on-line help, and selection mechanisms (keyboard, pointing devices, touchscreen, voice, etc.) (Norman, 1991).

3.2   Semantic Organization

The primary goal for menu designers is to create a sensible, comprehensible, memorable, and convenient semantic organization relevant to the user's tasks. We can learn some lessons by following the semantic decomposition of a book into chapters, a program into modules, the animal kingdom into species, or a Sears catalog into sections. Hierarchical decompositions—natural and comprehensible to most people—are appealing because every item belongs to a single category. Unfortunately, in some applications, an item may be difficult to classify as belonging to one category, and the temptation to duplicate entries or to create a network increases. In spite of their limitations, tree structures have an elegance that should be appreciated.

Restaurant menus separate appetizers, soups, main dishes, desserts, and drinks to help customers organize their selections. Menu items should fit logically into categories and have readily understood meanings.

Restauranteurs who list dishes with idiosyncratic names such as "veal Monique," generic terms such as "house dressing," or unfamiliar labels such as "wor shu op" should expect that waiters will spend ample time explaining the alternatives, or should anticipate that customers will become anxious because of the unpredictability of their meals.

Similarly, for computer menus, the categories should be comprehensible and distinctive so that the users are confident in making their selections. Users should have a clear idea of what will happen when they make a selection. Computer menus are more difficult to design than are restaurant menus, because computer displays typically have less space than do printed menus; display space is a scarce resource. In addition, the number of choices and the complexity is greater in many computer applications, and computer users may not have helpful waiters to turn to for an explanation.

The importance of meaningful organization of menu items was demonstrated in a study with 48 novice users (Liebelt et al., 1982). Simple menu trees with three levels and 16 target items were constructed in both meaningfully organized and disorganized forms. Error rates were nearly halved and user think time (time from menu presentation to user's selection of an item) was reduced for the meaningfully organized form. In a later study, semantically meaningful categories—such as food, animals, minerals, and cities—led to shorter response times than did random or alphabetic organizations (McDonald et al., 1983). This experiment tested 109 novice users who worked through 10 blocks of 26 trials. The authors conclude that "these results demonstrate the superiority of a categorical menu organization over a pure alphabetical organization, particularly when there is some uncertainty about the terms." With larger menu structures, the effect is even more dramatic, as has been demonstrated by studies with extensive video-text databases (Lee and Latremouille, 1980; McEwen, 1981; Perlman, 1984).

These results and the SSOA model suggest that the key to menu-structure design is first to consider the semantic organization that results from the task. The task terms and structure come first; number of items on the display becomes a secondary issue.

Menu-selection applications range from trivial choices between two items to complex information systems with 300,000 displays. The simplest applications consist of a single menu, but even with this limitation, there are many variations (Figure 3.1). The second group of applications includes a linear sequence of menu selections; the progression of menus is independent of the user's choice. Strict tree structures make up the third and most common group. Acyclic (menus are reachable by more than one path) and cyclic (structures with meaningful paths that allow users to repeat menus) networks constitute the fourth group. These groupings describe the semantic organization; special traversal commands may enable users to jump around the branches of a tree, to go back to the previous menu, or to go to the beginning of a linear sequence.

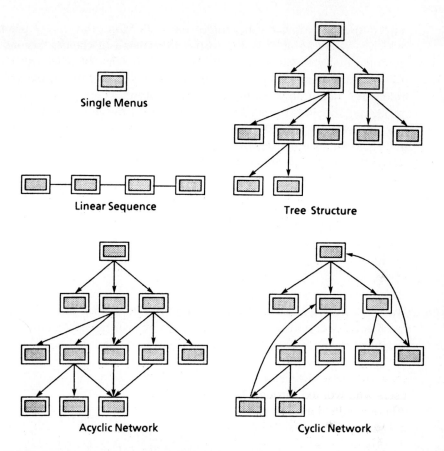

Single Menus

Linear Sequence

Tree Structure

Acyclic Network

Cyclic Network

Figure 3.1

Menu systems can use simple single or linear sequences of menus. Tree-structured menus are the most common structure. Traversing deep trees or more elaborate acylic or cyclic menu structures can become difficult for some users.

3.2.1 Single menus

In some situations, a single menu is sufficient to accomplish a task. Single menus may have two or more items, may require two or more screens, or may allow multiple selections. Single menus may pop up on the current work area or may be permanently available (in a separate window or on a data tablet) while the main display is changed. Different guidelines apply for each situation.

Binary menus The simplest case is a binary menu with yes–no or true–false choices, such as is found in many home computer games. An example is DO YOU WANT INSTRUCTIONS (Y,N)? Even this simple example can be

improved. First, novice users might not understand the (Y,N) prompt—
which is really an abbreviated form of the menu of choices. Second, this
common query leaves the user without a clear sense of what will happen
next. Typing Y might produce many pages of instructions, and the user
might not know how to stop a lengthy output. Typing N is also anxiety
producing, because users have no idea of what the program will do. Even
simple menus should offer clear and specific choices that are predicable and
thus give the user the sense of control:

```
Your choices are

    1 -- Get 12 lines of brief instructions.
    2 -- Get 89 lines of complete instructions.
    3 -- Go on to playing the game.

Type 1, 2, or 3, and press RETURN:
```

Since this version has three items, it is no longer a binary menu. It offers
more specific items, so the user knows what to expect, but it still has the
problem that users must take instructions now or never. Another strategy
might be this:

```
At any time, you may type

    ? -- Get 12 lines of brief instructions.
   ?? -- Get 89 lines of complete instructions.

Be sure to press RETURN after every command
Ready for game playing commands:
```

This example calls attention to the sometimes narrow distinction between
commands and menu selection; the menu choices have become more
command-like since the user must now recall the ? or ?? syntax.

Menu items can be identified by single-letter mnemonics, as in this photo-
library retrieval system:

```
Photos are indexed by film type
        B Black and white
        C Color
Type the letter of your choice
    and press RETURN:
```

The mnemonic letters in this menu are often preferred to numbered choices
(see Section 3.7). The mnemonic-letter approach requires additional caution
in avoiding collisions and increases the effort of translation to foreign
languages, but its clarity and memorability are an advantage in many
applications.

In graphic user interfaces, the user can point to selection buttons with a mouse or other cursor-control device. Choosing the orientation for output can be done with a pair of icons. The selected item is the darker one (inverted). In the following example, choosing between Cancel and OK can be by mouse click, but the thickened border on OK could indicate that this selection is the default, and that a RETURN keypress will select it.

These simple examples demonstrate alternative ways to identify menu items and to convey instructions to the user. No optimal format for menus has emerged, but consistency across menus in a system is extremely important.

Multiple-item menus and radio buttons Single menus may have more than two items. One example is an online quiz displayed on a touchscreen:

```
Who invented the telephone?
   Thomas Edison
   Alexander Graham Bell
   Lee De Forest
   George Westinghouse
Touch your answer.
```

Another example is a list of options in a document-processing system:

```
EXAMINE, PRINT, DROP, OR HOLD?
```

The quiz example has distinct, comprehensible items, but the document-processing example shows an implied menu selection that could be confusing to novice users. There are no explicit instructions, and it is not apparent that single-letter abbreviations are acceptable. Knowledgeable and expert users may prefer this short form of a menu selection, usually called a *prompt*, because of its speed and simplicity.

In graphic user interfaces, such selections are often called *radio buttons* since only one item can be selected at a time. This choice of paper size for printing shows US Letter as the selected item:

Paper:	● US Letter	○ A4 Letter
	○ US Legal	○ B5 Letter
	○ No. 10 Envelope	

```
SUPERDUPERWRITER MAIN MENU          SUPERDUPERWRITER MAIN MENU
                      PAGE 1                               PAGE 2
  1   Edit                             7   Alter line width
  2   Copy                             8   New character set
  3   CReate                           9   Search
  4   Delete                          10   Set passWord
  5   Print                           11   Set cursor Blink rate
  6   View index                      12   Set beep Volume

Type the number/letter              Type the number/letter
  or M for more choices.                 or P to go back to Page 1.
Then Press RETURN                   Then Press RETURN
```

Figure 3.2

This text-oriented extended menu operates in a traditional keyboard style with numeric selection and with mnemonic letters.

Extended menus Sometimes, the list of menu items may require more than one display but allow only one meaningful item to be chosen. One solution is to create a tree-structured menu, but sometimes the desire to limit the system to one conceptual menu is strong. The first portion of the menu is displayed with an additional menu item that leads to the next display in the extended menu sequence. A typical application is in word-processing systems, where common choices are displayed first, but infrequent or advanced features are kept on the second display (Figure 3.2). Sometimes, the extended screen menu will continue for many screens. Extended menus provide a justification for the more elaborate scrolling capabilities found in most graphical user interfaces (Figure 3.3).

Pull-down and pop-up menus *Pull-down menus* are constantly available to the user via selections along a top menu bar; *pop-up menus* appear on the display in response to a click with a pointing device such as a mouse. The Xerox Star, Apple Lisa, and Apple Macintosh (Figure 3.4) made these possibilities widely available, and their versions have become standardized (Windows 3.0, IBM CUA SAA, OSF/Motif). Common items in the menu bar are File, Edit, Search, Font, Format, View, and Help. The user can make a selection by moving the pointing device over the menu items, which respond by

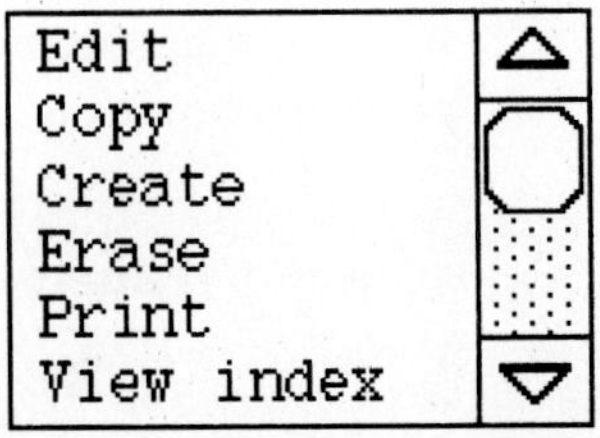

Figure 3.3

This graphical extended menu uses pointing and clicking to select an item, and scrolling to move among the items. Contrast to Figure 3.2.

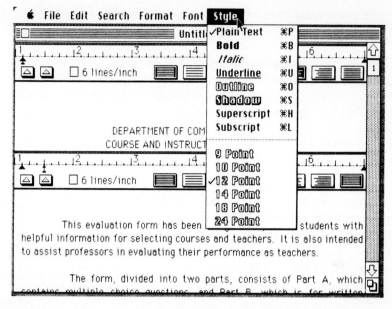

Figure 3.4

The pull-down menu on an early Apple Macintosh MacWrite program enabled users to select font variations and size. (Photo courtesy of Apple Computer, Inc.)

highlighting (reverse video, a box surrounding the item, and color all have been used). This Macintosh menu bar shows the available pull-down menus:

File   Edit   Font   Size   Style   Format   Spelling   View

The contents of the pop-up menu may depend on where the cursor is when the pointing device is clicked. Since the pop-up menu covers a portion of the display, there is strong motivation to keeping the menu text small. Hierarchical sequences of pop-up menus are also used. Pop-up menus can also be organized in a circle to form *pie menus* (Callahan et al., 1988):

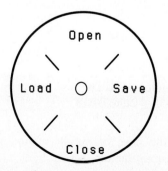

The pie menus are convenient because selection is more rapid and, with practice, can be done without visual attention.

Permanent menus Single menus can be used for permanently available commands that can be applied to a displayed object. For example, the Bank Street Writer, a word processor designed for children, always shows a fragment of the text and this menu:

```
ERASE     MOVE      FIND      TRANSFER
UNERASE   MOVEBACK  REPLACE   MENU
```

Moving the left and right arrow keys causes items to be highlighted sequentially in reverse video. When the desired command is highlighted, pressing the RETURN key initiates the action. Similarly, PRODIGY provides this menu on the bottom of the display:

```
NEXT BACK MENU PATH JUMP ACTION HELP EXIT
```

Only the permissible items are shown at any moment, however.

Other applications of permanent menus include paint programs, such as PC Paintbrush (Color Plate 1), PenPlay II (Figure 3.5 and Color Plate 2), computer-assisted design packages, or other graphics systems that display an elaborate menu of commands to the side of the object being manipulated. Mice, touchscreens, or other cursor-action devices allow users to make selections without keyboards.

Multiple-selection menus or check boxes A further variation on single menus is the capacity to make multiple selections from the choices offered. For example, a political-interest survey might allow multiple choice on one display (Figure 3.6). A multiple-selection menu with mouse clicks as the selection method is a convenient strategy for handling multiple binary choices, since the user is able to scan the full list of items while deciding. In the following Macintosh example, Bold and Underline have been selected; Superscript and UPPERCASE (grayed out) become available as a pop-up menu after the check box is selected:

Summary Even the case of single menus provides a rich domain for designers and human-factors researchers. Questions of wording, screen

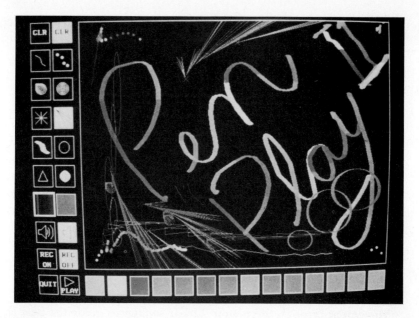

Figure 3.5

PenPlay II display shows menus of tool icons on the left and palette at bottom. Free-hand drawing on a touchscreen surface with a finger is accompanied by sounds. Gestures create varied patterns, including raindrops, snowflakes, needles, and colored circles, all of which can be recorded and replayed. (Implemented by Andrew Sears. Available from the University of Maryland Office of Technology Liaison, College Park, MD.)

Figure 3.6

This multiple-selection touchscreen menu enables users to make up to three selections of political issues.

layout, and selection mechanism all arise even in the simple case of choosing from one set of items. Still more challenging questions emerge during design of sequences and trees of menus.

3.2.2 Linear sequences and multiple menus

Often, a series of interdependent menus can be used to guide users through a series of choices in which they see the same sequence of menus no matter what choices they make. For example, a document-printing package might have a linear sequence of menus to choose print parameters, such as device, line spacing, and page numbering (Figure 3.7). Another familiar example is an online examination that has a sequence of multiple-choice test items, each made up as a menu.

With high-resolution screens and pointing devices, it is possible to include several menus on a single display, thereby simplifying the user interface and speeding usage (Figure 3.8).

Movement through the menus Linear sequences guide the user through a complex decision-making process by presenting one decision at a time. The document-printing example could be improved by offering the user several menus on the screen at once. If the menus do not fit on one screen, then there should be a mechanism for going back to previous screens to review or change choices made earlier. A second improvement is to display previous

```
Do you want the document printed at
 T - your Terminal
 P - the computer center line Printer
 L - the computer center Laser printer
Type your choice and press RETURN:

Do you want
 1 - single spacing
 2 - double spacing
 3 - triple spacing
Type your choice and press RETURN:

Do you want
 N - No page numbering
 T - page numbering on the Top, right justified
 B - page numbering at the Bottom, centered
Type your choice and press RETURN:
```

Figure 3.7

A linear sequence of menus allows the user to select three print parameters for a document: printing device, line spacing, and page numbering.

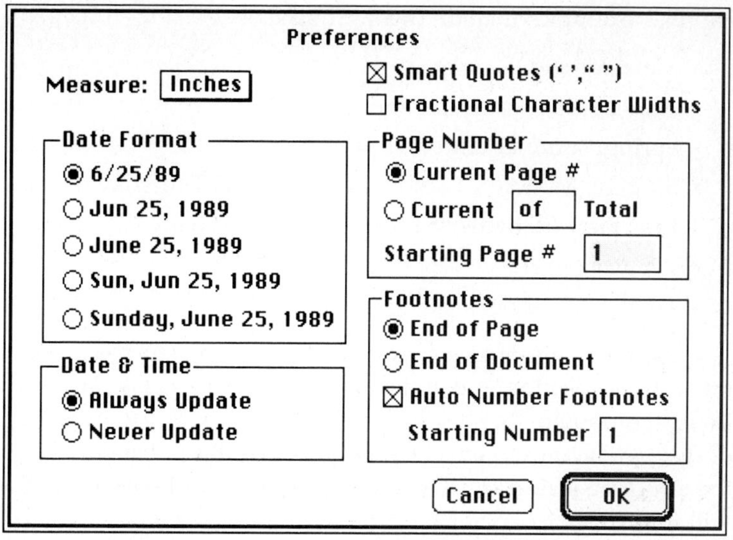

Figure 3.8

A set of independent menus collected on a single dialog box within Claris's MacWrite II. (Courtesy of Claris Corp., Santa Clara, CA.)

choices, so users can see what decisions they have made. A third improvement is to let the users know how many and which menus they have not yet seen.

Summary Linear sequences and multiple menus provide simple and effective means for guiding the user through and structuring a decision-making process. The user should be given a clear sense of progress or position within the menus, and the means for going backward to earlier choices (and possibly terminating or restarting the sequence).

Choosing the order and layout of menus in a linear sequence is often straightforward, but care must be taken to match user expectations. One strategy is to place the easy decisions first (or in the upper left in a multiple menu), to relieve users of simple concerns quickly, enabling them to concentrate on more difficult choices.

3.2.3 Tree-structured menus

When a collection of items grows and becomes difficult to maintain under intellectual control, people form categories of similar items, creating a tree structure (Clauer, 1972; Brown, 1982; Norman, 1991). Some collections can be partitioned easily into mutually exclusive groups with distinctive identifiers.

Familiar examples include these groupings:

- Male, female
- Animal, vegetable, mineral
- Spring, summer, autumn, winter
- Sunday, Monday, Tuesday, Wednesday, Thursday, Friday, Saturday
- Less than 10, between 10 and 25, greater than 25
- Percussion, string, woodwind, brass
- Fonts, size, style, spacing

Even these groupings may occasionally lead to confusion or disagreement. Classification and indexing are complex tasks, and, in many situations, there is no single solution that is acceptable to everyone. The initial design can be improved as a function of feedback from users. Over time, as the structure is improved and as users gain familiarity with it, success rates will improve.

In spite of the associated problems, tree-structured menu systems have the power to make large collections of data available to novice or intermittent users. If each menu has eight items, then a menu tree with four levels has the capacity to lead an untrained user to the correct frame out of a collection of 4096 frames.

If the groupings at each level are natural and comprehensible to users, and if users know for what they are looking, then the menu traversal can be accomplished in a few seconds—more quickly than flipping through a book. On the other hand, if the groupings are unfamiliar and users have only a vague notion for what they are looking, they may get lost in the tree menus for hours (Robertson et al., 1981; Norman and Chin, 1988).

Terminology from the user's task domain can orient the user. Instead of using a title, such as MAIN MENU OPTIONS, that is vague and emphasizes the computer domain, use terms such as FRIENDLIBANK SERVICES or simply GAMES.

Depth versus breadth The *depth*, or number of levels, of a menu tree depends, in part, on the *breadth*, or number of items per level. If more items are put into the main menu, then the tree spreads out and has fewer levels. This shape may be advantageous, but only if clarity is not compromised substantially and if a slow display rate does not consume the user's patience. Several authors have urged using four to eight items per menu, but, at the same time, they urge using no more than three to four levels. With large menu applications, one or both of these guidelines must be compromised.

Several empirical studies have dealt with the depth-breadth trade-off and the evidence is quite strong that breadth should be preferred over depth. In fact, there is reason to encourage menu trees to be limited to three levels;

when the depth goes to four or five there appears to be a greater chance of users becoming lost or disoriented.

Kiger (1984) grouped 64 items in these menu-tree forms:

8 x 2	Eight items on each of two levels
4 x 3	Four items on each of three levels
2 x 6	Two items on each of six levels
4 x 1 + 16 x 1	A four-item menu followed by a 16-item menu
16 x 1 + 4 x 1	A 16-item menu followed by a four-item menu

The deep narrow tree, 2 x 6, produced the slowest, least accurate, and least preferred version; the 8 x 2 was among those rated highest for speed, accuracy, and preference. The 22 subjects performed 16 searches on each of the five versions.

Landauer and Nachbar (1985) confirmed the advantage of breadth over depth and developed predictive equations for traversal times. They varied the number of items per level from 2, 4, 8, to 16 to reach 4096 target items of numbers or words (Figure 3.9). The times for the task with words ranged from 23.4 seconds down to 12.5 seconds as the breadth increased and the

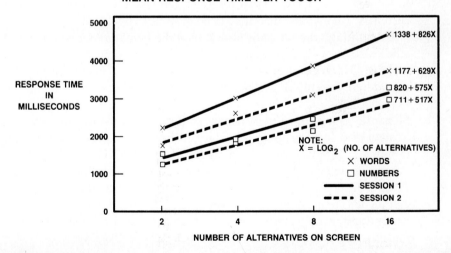

Figure 3.9

The advantage of broader shallower trees was demonstrated in a study with menus with branching factors of 2, 4, 8, and 16 items. (Adapted with courtesy of Bellcore, Morristown, NJ.)

number of levels decreased. Over the range studied, the authors suggest that a simple function of the number of items on the screen will predict the time, T, for a selection:

$$T = k + c^*\log b$$

where k and c are empirically determined constants for scanning the screen to make a choice, and b is the breadth at each level. Then, the total time to traverse the menu tree depends on only the depth, D, which is

$$D = \log_b N$$

where N is the total number of items in the tree. With $N = 4096$ target items and a branching factor of $b = 16$, the depth, $D = 3$, and the total time is $3^*(k + c^*\log 16)$.

Norman and Chin (1988) fixed the number of levels at four, with 256 target items, and varied the shape of the tree structure. They recommend greater breadth at the root and at the leaves, and added a further encouragement to minimize the total number of menu frames needed so as to increase familiarity. In an interesting variation, Wallace et al. (1987) confirmed that broader, shallower trees (4 x 3 versus 2 x 6) produced superior performance, and showed that, when users were stressed, they made 96 percent more errors and took 16 percent longer. The stressor was simply an instruction to work quickly ("It is imperative that you finish the task just as quickly as possible"); the control group received gentler verbal instruction to avoid rushing ("Take your time; there is no rush").

Even though the semantic structure of the items cannot be ignored, these studies suggest that the fewer the levels, the greater the ease of decision making. Of course, display rates, response time, and screen clutter must be considered, in addition to the semantic organization.

Semantic grouping in tree structures Rules for semantic validity are hard to state, and there is always the danger that some users may not grasp the designer's organizational framework. Young and Hull (1982) examined "cognitive mismatches" in the British Prestel Viewdata system (Martin, 1982). The problems that they identified included overlapping categories, extraneous items, conflicting classifications in the same menu, unfamiliar jargon, and generic terms. Based on this set of problems, the rules for forming menu trees might be these:

- *Create groups of logically similar items*: For example, a comprehensible menu would list countries at level 1, states or provinces at level 2, and cities at level 3.

- *Form groups that cover all possibilities*: For example, a menu with age ranges 0–9, 10–19, 20–29, and greater than 30 makes it easy for the user to select an item.
- *Make sure that items are nonoverlapping*: Lower-level items should be naturally associated with a single higher-level item. Young and Hull offered an example of a poorly designed screen with `Places in Britain` and `Regions of England` as overlapping items on the same menu.
- *Use familiar terminology, but ensure that items are distinct from one another*: Choosing the right terminology is a difficult task; feedback from sample users will be helpful during design and testing.

Menu maps As the depth of a menu tree grows, users find it increasingly difficult to maintain a sense of position in the tree, and their sense of disorientation, or of "getting lost," grows. To overcome this sense of disorientation, some menu systems come with a printed index of terms that is easier to scan than is a series of screen displays. The French Minitel system offers a detailed cross-referenced index that, in 1991, was 62 pages long and contained more than ten thousand entries. The CompuServe Information Service's 1991 index contained almost 3000 subjects; it included a diagram, or map, of the first three levels of the tree structure, which contained 43 menus. The PRODIGY information system uses a cascade approach to show its large menu tree (Figure 3.10a and b).

The relative merits of a map and an index were studied in a small menu structure with 18 animals as target items (Billingsley, 1982). In this case, users who had the chance to study an index did somewhat better than a control group that had no special navigation aids. The group with an overall map did substantially better than did both the index and control groups.

	Control	Index	Map
Number of subjects	10.0	8.0	8.0
Mean time per search	35.3	30.7	19.2
Mean choices per search	12.3	8.4	4.7

Menu learning for a three-level, three-item (3 x 3) menu was studied with four forms of training (Parton et al., 1985). The four forms were as follows:

1. *Online exploration*: Subjects could explore the menus online.
2. *Command sequences*: Subjects studied, on paper the 27 paths through the three levels; e.g., `Plans Division`, `Concepts`, `Systems Analyst`.

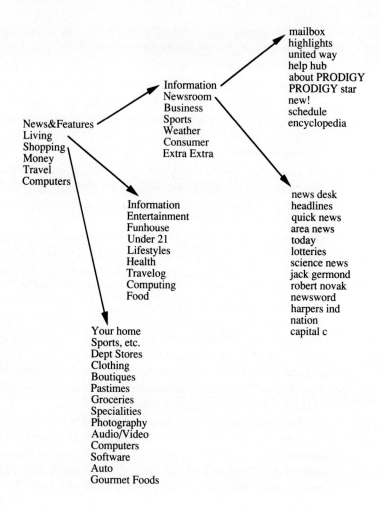

Figure 3.10(a)

The PRODIGY information system. (Figure 3.10a and b: Courtesy of Prodigy Services Company, White Plains, NY.) (a) Partial menu tree.

3. *Frames:* Subjects studied online the 13 menu frames, like this one:

```
Plans Division
Concepts
Designs
Proposals
```

4. *Menu map:* Subjects studied online a tree-structured layout of the 13 frames.

The 65 undergraduate subjects had a 12-minute training period followed by a 10-minute work period. The results indicate a strong advantage for those who had the menu map (Table 3.1).

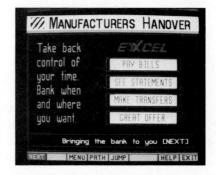

Figure 3.10(b)

Four displays.

Table 3.1

Scores on four dependent variables showed improved performance for subjects who had studied a graphical menu map for a three-level menu. (Source: Parton et al., 1985.)

Variable	Online Exploration	Command Sequences	Frames Map	Menu
Targets found	8.2	4.7	6.5	8.5 n.s.
Average number of menus visited	10.6	20.4	19.6	9.4 p<.10
Recall of tree (max = 27)	10.1	8.4	9.8	16.7 p<.05
Satisfaction (best = 5)	3.6	3.1	2.8	4.8 p<.01

As the tree structure grows, users have greater difficulty in maintaining an overall understanding of the semantic organization. Viewing the structure one menu at a time is like seeing the world through a cardboard tube; it is hard to grasp the overall pattern and to see relationships among categories. Offering a spatial map can help overcome users to this difficulty.

Summary There is no perfect menu structure that matches every person's knowledge of the application domain. Designers must use good judgment for the initial implementation, but then must be receptive to suggested improvements and empirical data. Users will gradually gain familiarity, even with extremely complex tree structures, and will be increasingly successful in locating required items.

3.2.4   Acyclic and cyclic menu networks

Although tree structures are appealing, sometimes network structures are more appropriate. For example, it might make sense to provide access to banking information from both the financial and consumer parts of a tree structure. A second motivation for using networks is that it may be desirable to permit paths between disparate sections of a tree, rather than requiring users to begin a new search from the main menu. These and other conditions lead to network structures in the form of acyclic, or even cyclic, graphs. As users move from trees, to acyclic networks, to cyclic networks, the potential for getting lost increases.

With a tree structure, the user can form a mental model of the structure and of the relationships among the menus. Developing this mental model may be more difficult with a network. With a tree structure, there is a single parent menu, so backward traversals toward the main menu are straightforward. In networks, a stack of visited menus must be kept to allow backward traversals. In a thorough study of 17 subjects using menu networks of 50 frames, Mantei (1982) concluded that "the structure of the user interface . . . causes disorientation if this structure is not obvious to the user."

If networks are used, it may be helpful to preserve a notion of "level," or distance from the main menu. Users may feel more comfortable if they have a sense of how far they are from the main menu.

3.3   Item Presentation Sequence

Once the items in a menu have been chosen, the designer is still confronted with the choice of presentation sequence. If the items have a natural sequence—such as days of the week, chapters in a book, or sizes of eggs—then the decision is trivial. Typical bases for sequencing items include these:

- *Time*: Chronological ordering
- *Numeric ordering*: Ascending or descending ordering
- *Physical properties*: Increasing or decreasing length, area, volume, temperature, weight, velocity, etc.

Many cases have no natural ordering, and the designer must choose from such possibilities as:

- *Alphabetic sequence of terms*
- *Grouping of related items* (with blank lines or other demarcation between groups)
- *Most frequently used items first*
- *Most important items first:* Importance may be difficult to decide and may vary among users

Card (1982) experimented with a single 18-item vertical permanent menu of text-editing commands such as INSERT, ITALIC, and CENTER. He presented subjects with a command, and they had to locate the command in the list, move a mouse-controlled cursor, and select the command by pressing a button on the mouse. The menu items were sequenced one of three ways: alphabetically, in functional groups, and randomly. Each of four subjects made 86 trials with each sequencing strategy. The mean times were as follows:

Strategy	Time per trial
alphabetic	0.81 seconds
functional	1.28 seconds
random	3.23 seconds

Since subjects were given the target item, they did best when merely scanning to match the menu items in an alphabetic sequence. The performance with the functional groupings was remarkably good, indicating that subjects began to remember the groupings and could go directly to a group. In menu applications where the users must make a decision about the most suitable menu item, the functional arrangement might be more appealing. Users' memory for the functionally grouped items would be likely to surpass their memory for the alphabetic or random sequences. The poor performance that Card observed with the random sequence confirms the importance of considering alternative item presentation sequences.

With a 64-item menu, the time for locating a target word was found to increase from just over 2 seconds for an alphabetic menu to more than 6 seconds for a random menu (McDonald et al., 1983). When the target word was replaced with a single-line definition, the 109 subjects could no longer scan for a simple match and had to consider each menu item carefully. The advantage of alphabetic ordering nearly vanished. User reaction time went up to about 7 seconds for the alphabetic and about 8 seconds for the random organization. Somberg and Picardi (1983) studied user reaction times in finding to which category a target word belonged in a five-item menu. Their three experiments revealed a significant and nearly linear relationship between the user's reaction time and the serial position of the correct category in the menu. Furthermore, there was a significant increase in reaction time if the target word was unfamiliar, rather than familiar.

If frequency of use is a potential guide to sequencing menu items, then it might make sense to vary the sequence adaptively to reflect the current pattern of use. Unfortunately, adaptations can be disruptive, increasing confusion and undermining the users's learning of menu structures. In addition, users might become anxious about other changes occurring at any moment. Evidence against such changes was found in a study in which a pull-down list of food items was resequenced to ensure that the most frequently selected items migrated toward the top (Mitchell and Shneiderman, 1988). Users were clearly unsettled by the changing menus, and their performance was better with static menus. Evidence in favor of adaptation was found in a study of a telephone book menu tree that had been restructured to make frequently used telephone numbers more easily accessible (Greenberg, 1985). However, this study did not deal with the issue of potentially disorientating changes to the menu during usage. To avoid disruption and unpredictable behavior, it is probably a wise policy to allow users to specify when they want the menu restructured.

3.4   Response Time and Display Rate

A critical variable that may determine the attractiveness of menu selection is the speed at which users can move through the menus. The two components of speed are system *response time*, the time it takes for the system to begin displaying information in response to a user selection, and *display rate*, the rate in characters per second at which the menus are displayed (see Chapter 7).

Deep menu trees or complex traversals become annoying to the user if system response time is slow, resulting in long and multiple delays. With slow display rates, lengthy menus become annoying because of the volume of text that must be displayed. In positive terms, if the response time is long, then designers should create menus with more items on each menu to reduce the number of menus necessary. If the display rate is slow, then designers should create menus with fewer items to reduce the display time.

If the response time is long and the display rate is low, menu selection is unappealing, and command-language strategies, in spite of the greater memory demands on the users, become more attractive.

With short response times and rapid display rates, menu selection becomes a lively medium that can be attractive even for frequent and knowledgeable users.

In five studies with 165 adult users of a videotext system, response-time delay pairs (0 versus 10 seconds, 10 versus 15 seconds, and 3 versus 7 seconds) did not yield a statistically significant difference in the preference or performance measures tested (Murray and Abrahamson, 1983). The authors' interpretation was that "inexperienced videotext users are relatively immune to a wide range of constant values of system delay." Other studies have also found that novice users are often pleased with slower response times. However, the large variations in individual performance may have obscured the usual preference for faster response times. Murray and Abrahamson found a significant effect that indicated that large variations in response time led to slower user-response rates.

3.5   Moving Through Menus Quickly

Even with short response times and high display rates, frequent menu users may become annoyed if they must make several menu selections to complete a task. There may be some advantage to reducing the number of menus by increasing the number of items per menu, where possible, but this strategy may not be sufficient. As response times lengthen and display rates decrease, the need for shortcuts through the menus increases.

Instead of creating a command language to accomplish the task with positional or keyword parameters, the menu approach can be refined to accommodate expert and frequent users. Three approaches have been used: allow typeahead for known menu choices, assign names to menus to allow direct access, and create menu macros that allows users to assign names to frequently used menu sequences.

3.5.1   Menus with typeahead—the BLT approach

A natural way to permit frequent menu users to speed through the menus is to allow *typeahead*. The user does not have to wait to see the menus before choosing the items, but can type a string of letters or numbers when presented with the main menu. For example, in the document-printing package in Section 3.2, the user could type T2N to get printing at the terminal, double spacing, and no page numbering. The IBM Interactive

System Productivity Facility (ISPF) has numbered choices and allows typeahead with a decimal point between choices (for example, 1.2.1). Typeahead becomes important when the menus are familiar and response time or display rates are slow, as in many voice-mail systems. Most telephone-inquiry and electronic-mail systems allow the experienced user to enter a string of keypresses at any point in the session.

If the menu items are identified with single letters, then the concatenation of menu selections in the typeahead scheme generates a command name that acquires mnemonic value. To users of a photo-library search system that offered menus with typeahead, a color slide portrait quickly became known as a CSP, and a black-and-white print of a landscape became known as a BPL. These mnemonics come to be remembered and chunked as a single concept. This strategy quickly became known as the *BLT approach*; after the abbreviation for a bacon, lettuce, and tomato sandwich.

The attraction of the BLT approach is that users can gracefully move from being novice menu users to being knowledgeable command users. There are no new commands to learn, and as soon as users become familiar with one branch of the tree, they can apply that knowledge to speed up their work. Learning can be incremental; users can apply one-, two-, or three-letter typeahead, and then explore the less familiar menus. If users forget part of the tree, they simply revert to menu usage.

The BLT approach requires a more elaborate parser for the user input, and handling nonexistent menu choices is a bit more problematic. It is also necessary to ensure distinct first letters for items within each menu, but not across menus. Still, the typeahead or BLT approach is attractive because it is powerful, is simple, and allows graceful evolution from novice to expert.

3.5.2   Menu names for direct access

A second approach to support frequent users is to use numbered menu items and to assign names to each menu frame. Users can follow the menus or, if they know the name of their destination, they can type it in and go there directly. The CompuServe Information Service has a three-letter identifier for major topics, followed by a dash and a page number. Rather than working their way through three levels of menus at 30 characters per second, users know that they can go directly to TWP-1, the start of the subtree containing today's edition of *The Washington Post*. Similarly, PRODIGY users can JUMP to the WEATHER by typing those words.

This strategy is useful if there is only a small number of destinations that each user needs to remember. If users need to access many different portions of the menu tree, they will have difficulty keeping track of the destination names. A list of the current destination names is necessary to ensure that designers create unique names for new entries.

An empirical comparison of the learnability of the typeahead and direct-access strategies demonstrated an advantage for the latter (Laverson et al., 1987). Thirty-two undergraduates had to learn either path names (typeahead) or destination names (direct access) for a four-level menu tree. The direct-access names proved to be significantly faster to learn and were preferred. Different tree structures or menu contents may influence the outcome of similar studies.

3.5.3 Menu macros

A third approach to serving frequent menu users is to allow regularly used paths to be recorded by users as *menu macros*. In other words, users can define their own commands. A user can invoke the macro facility, traverse the menu structure, and then assign a name. When the name is invoked, the traversal is executed automatically. This mechanism allows individual tailoring of the system and can provide a simplified access mechanism for users with limited needs.

3.6 Menu Screen Design

Little experimental research has been done on menu-system screen design. This section contains many subjective judgments, which are in need of empirical validation (Table 3.2).

Table 3.2

Menu selection guidelines that have been distilled from practice, but that still require validation and clarification.

Menu Selection Guidelines

- Use task semantics to organize menus (single, linear sequence, tree structure, acyclic and cyclic networks)
- Prefer broad and shallow to narrow and deep
- Show position by graphics, numbers, or titles
- Use item names as titles for trees
- Use meaningful groupings of items
- Use meaningful sequencing of items
- Make items brief, begin with keyword
- Use consistent grammar, layout, terminology
- Allow typeahead, jumpahead, or other shortcuts
- Allow jumps to previous and main menus
- Consider online help, novel selection mechanisms, response time, display rate, and screen size

3.6.1   Titles

Choosing the title for a book is a delicate matter for an author, editor, or publisher. A more descriptive or memorable title can make a big difference in reader responses. Similarly, choosing titles for menus is a complex matter that deserves serious thought.

For single menus, a simple descriptive title that identifies the situation is all that is necessary. With a linear sequence of menus, the titles should accurately represent the stages in the linear sequence. For the menus in the document-printing package (Section 3.2), the titles might be `Printing location`, `Spacing control`, and `Page numbering placement`. Consistent grammatical style can reduce confusion. If the third menu were titled `How do you want page numbering to be done?` or `Select page numbering placement options`, many users would be unsettled. Excess verbiage becomes a distraction. Brief noun phrases are often sufficient.

For tree-structured menus, choosing titles is more difficult. Such titles as `Main menu` or topic descriptions as `Bank transactions` for the root of the tree clearly indicate that the user is at the beginning of a session. One potentially helpful rule is to use the exact words in the high-level menu items as the titles for the next lower-level menu. It is reassuring to users to see an item such as `Business and financial services` and, after it has been selected, a screen that is titled `Business and financial services`. It might be unsettling to get a screen titled `Managing your money`, even though the intent is similar. Imagine looking in the table of contents of a book and seeing a chapter title such as "The American Revolution," but, when you turn to the indicated page, finding "Our early history"—you might worry about whether you had made a mistake, and your confidence might be undermined.

Using menu items as titles may encourage the menu author to choose items more carefully so that they are descriptive in two contexts.

A further concern is consistency in placement of titles and other features in a menu screen. Teitelbaum and Granda (1983) demonstrated that user think time nearly doubled when the position of information, such as titles or prompts, was varied on menu screens.

In networks of menus, titles become even more important as a guidepost because the potential for confusion is greater. If menu items are made to match the title, then several menus in a network may have the same items. It is satisfying to find the item `Electronic mail` in several menus, but unsettling to find menus with variant terms such as `Electronic mail`, `Sending a note to another user`, and `Communicating with your colleagues`.

3.6.2 Phrasing of menu items

Just because a system has menu choices written with English words, phrases, or sentences, it is not guaranteed to be comprehensible. Individual words may not be familiar to some users, and often two menu items may appear to satisfy the user's needs, whereas only one does. This enduring problem has no perfect solution. Designers can gather feedback from colleagues, users, pilot studies, acceptance tests, and user-performance monitoring. The following guidelines may seem obvious, but we state them because they are so often violated:

- *Use familiar and consistent terminology:* Carefully select terminology that is familiar to the designated user community, and keep a list of these terms to facilitate consistent use.

- *Ensure that items are distinct from one another*: Each item should be distinguished clearly from other items. For example, Slow tours of the countryside, Journeys with visits to parks, and Leisurely voyages are less distinctive than Bike tours, Train tours to national parks, and Cruise ship tours.

- *Use consistent and concise phrasing*: The collection of items should be reviewed to ensure consistency and conciseness. Users are likely to feel more comfortable and be more successful with Animal, Vegetable, and Mineral than with Information about animals, Vegetable choices you can make, and Viewing mineral categories.

- *Bring the keyword to the left:* Try to write menu items so that the first word aids the user in recognizing and discriminating among items. Users scan menu items from left to right; if the first word indicates that this item is not relevant, they can begin scanning the next item.

3.6.3 Graphic layout and design

The constraints of screen width and length, display rate, character set, and highlighting techniques strongly influence the graphic layout of menus. Presenting 50 states as menu items was natural for the Domestic Information Display System built by NASA on a large screen with rapid display rate. On the other hand, the CompuServe Information Service, which must accommodate microcomputer users with 40-column displays over 30-character-per-second telephone lines, used the main menu page shown in Figure 3.11. An improved menu with greater breadth and more distinctive terms was introduced in 1985 (Figure 3.12). As users move down the tree, they find the page numbers always displayed at the upper right, a title, numbered

Figure 3.11

Early version of CompuServe main menu. The items are not sufficiently distinctive; for example, users would have a hard time deciding where to look for programs to assist them with home checkbook management. (Courtesy of CompuServe, Incorporated, Columbus, OH.)

```
COMPUSERVE                    PAGE CIS-1

    COMPUSERVE INFORMATION SERVICE

1  HOME SERVICES
2  BUSINESS & FINANCIAL
3  PERSONAL COMPUTING
4  SERVICES FOR PROFESSIONALS

5  USER INFORMATION
6  INDEX


ENTER YOUR SELECTION NUMBER,
OR H FOR MORE INFORMATION.
```

choices, and instructions. This consistent pattern puts users at ease and helps them to sort out the contents. Menu designers should establish guidelines for consistency of at least these menu components:

- *Titles*: Some people prefer centered titles, but left justification is an acceptable approach, especially with slow display rates.

- *Item placement*: Typically items are left justified with the item number or letter preceding the item description. Blank lines may be used to separate meaningful groups of items. If multiple columns are used, a consistent pattern of numbering or lettering should be used (for example, down the columns).

Figure 3.12

Revised CompuServe main menu with more items and more distinctive separation among items. Compare to Figure 3.11. (Courtesy of CompuServe, Incorporated, Columbus, OH.)

```
CompuServe                              TOP

 1  Instructions/User Information
 2  Find a Topic
 3  Communications/Bulletin Bds.
 4  News/Weather/Sports
 5  Travel
 6  The Electronic MALL/Shopping
 7  Money Matters/Markets
 8  Entertainment/Games
 9  Home/Health/Family
10  Reference/Education
11  Computers/Technology
12  Business/Other Interests

Enter choice number !
```

- *Instructions*: The instructions should be identical in each menu, and should be placed in the same position. This rule includes instructions about traversals, help, or function-key usage.
- *Error messages*: If the users make an unacceptable choice, the message should appear in a consistent position.
- *Status reports*: Some systems indicate which portion of the menu structure is currently being searched, which page of the structure is currently being viewed, or which choices must be made to complete a task. This information should appear in a consistent position.

Consistent formats help users to locate necessary information, focus users' attention on relevant material, and reduce users' anxiety by offering predictability.

In addition, since disorientation is a potential problem, techniques to indicate position in the menu structure can be useful. In books, different fonts and typeface indicate chapter, section, and subsection organization. Similarly, in menu trees, as the user goes down the tree structure, the titles can be designed to indicate the level or distance from the main menu. If different fonts, typefaces, or highlighting techniques are available, they can be used beneficially. But even simple techniques with only upper case characters can be effective; for example,

```
***************************
*        MAIN MENU        *
***************************
```

followed by

```
* * * HOME SERVICES * * *
```

followed by

```
- - NEWSPAPERS - -
```

followed by

```
New York Times
```

gives a clear indication of progress down the tree. When traversal back up the tree or to an adjoining menu at the same level is done, the user has a feeling of confidence in the action.

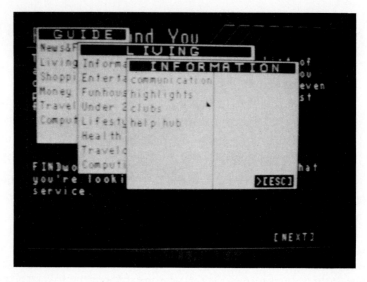

Figure 3.13

Cascade of menus from PRODIGY Information Service. (Courtesy of Prodigy
Services Company, White Plains, NY.)

With linear sequences of menus, the users can be given a simple visual
presentation of position in the sequence by the use of a *position marker*.
In a computer-assisted instruction sequence with 12 menu frames, a
position marker just below the menu items might show progress. In the
first frame, the position marker was +---------, in the second frame
it was   -+---------, and in the last frame it was -----------+. The
users can gauge their progress, and can see how much remains to be
done. The position marker served to separate the items from the instructions in a natural way, and the position was indicated in a nonobtrusive
manner.

With graphic user interfaces, many possibilities exist for showing successive levels of a tree-structured menu or progress through linear sequences. A
common approach is to show a cascade of successive menu boxes set slightly
lower than and slightly to the right of the previous items (Figure 3.13). For
pull-down menus, *walking menus* are perceptually meaningful, but can
present a motor challenge to move the cursor in the appropriate direction
(Figure 3.14).

With rapid high-resolution displays, more elegant visual representations
are possible. With enough screen space, it is possible to show a large portion
of the menu map, and to allow users to point at a menu anywhere in the tree.
Graphic designers or layout artists may be useful consultants in design
projects.

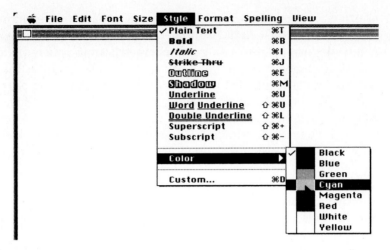

Figure 3.14

Walking menus are a motor challenge to users who must move the cursor down to the proper item and then carefully to the right to produce the submenu. This example from Claris's MacWrite II shows selection of colors for text. (Courtesy of Claris Corp., Santa Clara, CA.)

3.7   Selection Mechanisms

At first glance, choosing the menu-selection mechanism appears to be a minor design decision that can be made quickly, so that the design team can get on to more important matters. On the other hand, the selection mechanism is the central aspect of the menu system for most users (pointing devices, such as the mouse, are covered in Section 3.8). For keyboard-oriented systems this issue might be simplified to this question: Should the designer use numbers or letters for indicating menu items?

The arguments in favor of *numbered items* are that there is a clear sequencing of items, and that even nontypists can find the numbers on the keyboard. In some systems, numeric keypads are the only input device. Sequential numbering is satisfying because the user can see quickly how many items there are, and visual scanning is aided by the natural numeric ordering. As users scan down the items, they can use the numbers as a guide to make sure that they review each choice. When menu items have a natural numeric sequence—for example, the twelve months of the year, the chapters of a book, or the days of the week—numbered choices are appealing.

The disadvantage of numbers is that, when there are more than 10 items, two keypresses are required to make a selection. Another problem with using numbers only is that, if there are standard menu items such as HELP or

BACK TO MAIN MENU, then these items may have a different number on each screen. If there is no natural numbering of menu items, then the numbering may be misleading, somehow indicating preference for item 1. Attaching numbers to a group of colors or of bank-loan plans may mislead the user into believing that there is some hidden sequencing or preference.

If lettered items are used for menu items, then there is the choice between ABCDEF...lettering (sequential) and meaningful letter choices (mnemonic). Sequential lettering is similar to numbering, but 26 choices are available before two keypresses are required. There is some evidence that there is less likelihood of a keying error with letters than with numbers, because the letters are more spread out on the keyboard. It may be a bit more tricky for someone unfamiliar with a typewriter keyboard to locate the proper letter, but this problem does not appear to be a serious hindrance. Mnemonic lettering for menu items is appealing because the congruence between the description of the item and the keypress can build user confidence in the task. For example, it makes sense that T is for TRANSFER and W is for WITHDRAWAL.

Of course, there are mixed strategies. Some systems, such as CompuServe, use numbers for the primary menu items and letters for generic functions, such as M to get to the previous MENU and H to get to HELP information. This approach solves some problems and helps to clarify the grouping of menu items. Perlman (1984) found user think times to be lowest with mnemonic letter items and highest with sequential (and therefore nonmnemonic) letter items. Numbered items produced a middle level of user think time.

3.7.1   Typeahead selections

We cannot make the design decision without looking at the larger issue of tasks that require several menu selections. If a sequence of menus is to be viewed, the mnemonic-lettering approach gains substantially because the user can remember sequences such as TCS, for "Transfer from Checking to Saving," more easily than 253. If the user can type these selection letters before seeing the full menu, then the mnemonic-lettering approach becomes a command language for the frequent user. This typeahead approach (Section 3.5.1) is powerful, since it makes the same system appealing to novices and frequent users. Furthermore, it facilitates the graceful evolution from novice to expert—users type ahead only as much as they can remember, and then examine the next menu.

3.7.2   System evolution

Another advantage of mnemonic lettering is that, as items are added to menus, there is no need to renumber the other choices. Mnemonic lettering does have the problem of collisions—that is, of more than one choice with the same first letter. Collisions present a serious concern, but often an acceptable alternate term can be found. If not, then using more than one letter of the term may be necessary.

3.7.3   Mixed letters and numbers

If numeric data entry is to be made on some menu or data-entry screens, then the lettered-item approach will be advantageous since the typeahead command string may be more comprehensible. For example, the direction to deposit $40.00 in savings account 38847 might be entered as `D40.00S38847`, which is more appealing than `340.00638847`. On the other hand, if the data entry is for alphabetic strings, then the numbered approach might yield a more comprehensible command string. The alternation of letters and numbers helps to break a string into more meaningful chunks.

3.7.4   Arrow-key movement of highlight bar

Instead of typing a choice, users can move a highlight bar to the intended item. The cursor could be moved by the arrow keys, tab key, or space bar. This approach is appealing to novice users for single screen selections, even though there may be more keystrokes and the RETURN key must be pressed. There is a great sense of satisfaction in being able to move the highlight bar among the items. The menu item is highlighted clearly on the screen and in the user's mind, user confidence is high, and screen space is conserved since item labels are not needed. Brightness, underscoring, boxes, color, or reverse video can be used to indicate the item that has been selected. Of course, this approach does not lend itself to typeahead schemes.

3.8   Graphical User-Interface Menu Features

With modern graphical user interfaces, menu selection by mouse clicks becomes the common method of working with pull-down and pop-up menus plus the ubiquitous dialog boxes containing radio buttons, check boxes, text-entry fields, and scrollable lists of choices (Figure 3.15). The key issues are how to show where selection is possible (the *affordance*), which item has been selected (*highlighting*), whether *de-selection* is possible, and how *activation* is invoked. The mouse, touchscreen, or stylus for pointing at sets of buttons or on scrollable lists are widely appreciated for being rapid and direct (see Chapter 5). The graphical environment allows more information to be conveyed in the menu through use of, for example, the actual fonts in a font selection menu or the actual colors in a color-selection menu. Items

Figure 3.15

Dialog box from the PenPoint stylus-
based user interface shows typical
graphical user interface features:
scrolling menus for character font and
size, plus a set of six check boxes for the
style. Buttons on the bottom apply the
selections and close the dialog box.
Close triangle is in the upper left.
(Courtesy of GO Corp., Foster City, CA.)

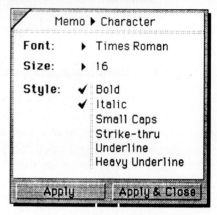

not available in the current context can be grayed out to hold their place in
the menu while showing their current unavailability. Spatial placement of
items can also be helpful in showing relationships among items and in
guiding users through a sequence of selections. Boxes around items, white
spaces, varying font sizes, and use of color can help to organize the display.
Iconic menus are discussed in Section 5.4.

Graphical approaches will continue to gain adherents where the available
technology supports this style of design. Three-dimensional affordances and
lighting models with shading are eye-catching and novel, but they risk being
distracting and taking more screen space (see Chapter 9).

3.9   Embedded Menus

All the menus discussed thus far might be characterized as *explicit menus* in
that there is an orderly enumeration of the menu items with little extraneous
information. In many situations, however, the menu items might be *embedded* in text or graphics and still be selectable.

When we designed a textual database about people, events, and places for
a museum application, it seemed natural to allow users to retrieve detailed
information by selecting a name in context (Koved and Shneiderman, 1986).
Selectable names were highlighted, and users could move a reverse-video
bar that jumped among highlighted names by pressing the four arrow keys
(Figure 3.16). They made selections by pressing ENTER, and they obtained a
new article title plus the option of returning to the previous article title. The
names, places, phrases, or foreign-language words were menu items embed-

```
WASHINGTON, DC: THE NATION'S CAPITAL    PAGE 2 OF 3

    Located between Maryland and Virginia,
Washington, DC embraces the White House and the
Capitol, a host of government offices as well
as the Smithsonian museums.
Designed by Pierre L'Enfant, Washington, DC is
a graceful city of broad boulevards, national
monuments, the rustic Rock Creek Park, and
the National Zoo.
    First-time visitors should begin at the mall
by walking from the Capitol towards the
Smithsonian museums and on
```

```
SMITHSONIAN MUSEUMS: In addition to the familiar
castle and popular Air & Space Museum there are 14
other major sites.
```
SEE ARTICLE ON "SMITHSONIAN MUSEUMS"

BACK PAGE   NEXT PAGE   RETURN TO "NEW YORK CITY"   EXTRA

Figure 3.16

Embedded menus in this early version of Hyperties improved comprehensibility over numbered menu lists and lowered anxiety for novice users. A reverse-video selector box initially covers the NEXT PAGE command. Users move the selector box over highlighted references or commands, and then select by pressing ENTER. A touchscreen version allows selection by merely touching the highlighted reference or command. (Created in 1983–1985 by Human–Computer Interaction Laboratory, University of Maryland, College Park, MD; distributed and refined by Cognetics Corporation, Princeton Junction, NJ.)

ded in meaningful text that informed users and helped to clarify the meaning of the items. Subsequent implementations used mouse selection or touchscreens.

Embedded menus have emerged in other applications. Air-traffic control systems allow selection of airplanes in the spatial layout of flight paths to provide more detailed information for controllers. Geographic display systems allow selection of cities or zooming in on specific regions to obtain more information (Herot, 1984). In these applications, the items are icons, text, or regions in a two-dimensional layout.

Hypertext (Section 11.4) program browsers allow software engineers to explore programs by simply pointing and clicking on variables to get the data declaration, or on function invocations to get the function definition (Seabrook and Shneiderman, 1989). Many spelling checkers use the embedded-menu concept by highlighting possibly misspelled words in the context of the words' use. The author of the text can move a cursor to a highlighted word and request alternate corrected spellings; or can type in the correctly spelled word.

Embedded menus permit items to be viewed in context and eliminate the need for a distracting and screen-wasting enumeration of items. Contextual display helps keep the users focused on their tasks and on the objects of interest. Items rewritten in list form may require longer descriptions (of the items) and may increase the difficulty of making selections because of confusion arising from cross-referencing between the menu and the context.

3.10   Form Fillin

Menu selection is effective for choosing an item from a list, but some tasks are cumbersome with menus. If data entry of personal names or numeric values is required, then keyboard typing becomes more attractive. The keyboard may be viewed as a continuous single menu from which multiple selections are made rapidly. When many fields of data are necessary, the appropriate interaction style might be called *form fillin*. For example, the user might be presented with a purchase-order form for ordering from a catalog, as in Figure 3.17.

The form-fillin approach is attractive because the full complement of information is visible, giving the users a feeling of being in control of the dialog. Few instructions are necessary, since this approach resembles famil-

```
Type in the information below, pressing TAB to move the cursor,
and press ENTER when done.

   Name:  _____    Phone:  (___) ___-____

Address:  _____

   City:  _____    State:  __   Zip Code:  _____

Charge Number:  ____  ____  ____  ____

      Catalog                              Catalog
      Number          Quantity             Number          Quantity


      _____        _____             _____        _____


      _____        _____             _____        _____


      _____        _____             _____        _____


      _____        _____             _____        _____
```

Figure 3.17

A form-fillin design for a department store.

iar paper forms. On the other hand, users must be familiar with keyboards, use of the TAB key to move the cursor, error correction by backspacing, field-label meanings, permissible field contents, and use of the ENTER key. Form fillin must be done on displays, not on hardcopy devices, and the display device must support cursor movement.

An experimental comparison of database update by form fillin and by a command-language strategy demonstrated a significant speed advantage for the former (Ogden and Boyle, 1982); eleven of the 12 subjects expressed a preference for the form-fillin approach.

3.10.1   Form-fillin design guidelines

There is a paucity of empirical work on form fillin, but a number of design guidelines have emerged from practitioners (Galitz, 1980; Pakin and Wray, 1982; Brown, 1986). Many companies offer form-fillin creation tools, such as Hewlett-Packard's VPLUS, IBM's ISPF, DEC's FMS, Ashton-Tate's dBASE, and Borland's Paradox. Software tools simplify design, help to ensure consistency, ease maintenance, and speed implementation. But even with excellent tools, the designer must still make many complex decisions (Table 3.3).

The elements of form fillin design include the following:

- *Meaningful title*: Identify the topic and avoid computer terminology.
- *Comprehensible instructions*: Describe the user's tasks in familiar terminology. Try to be brief; if more information is needed, make a set of help screens available to the novice user. In support of brevity, just

Table 3.3

Form fill-in guidelines distilled from practice, but in need of validation and clarification.

Form Fillin Design Guidelines
- Meaningful title
- Comprehensible instructions
- Logical grouping and sequencing of fields
- Visually appealing layout of the form
- Familiar field labels
- Consistent terminology and abbreviations
- Visible space and boundaries for data-entry fields
- Convenient cursor movement
- Error correction for individual characters and entire fields
- Error messages for unacceptable values
- Optional fields marked clearly
- Explanatory messages for fields

describe the necessary action (Type the address or simply address:) and avoid pronouns (You should type the address) or references to the user (The user of the form should type the address). Another useful rule is to use the word type for entering information and press for special keys such as the TAB, ENTER, cursor movement, or programmed function (PFK, PF, or F) keys. Since "ENTER" often refers to the special key, avoid using it in the instructions (for example, do not use Enter the address, instead stick to Type the address.) Once a grammatical style for instructions is developed, be careful to apply that style consistently.

- *Logical grouping and sequencing of fields:* Related fields should be adjacent, and should be aligned with blank space for separation between groups. The sequencing should reflect common patterns—for example, city followed by state followed by zip code

- *Visually appealing layout of the form*: Using a uniform distribution of fields is preferable to crowding one part of the screen and leaving other parts blank. Alignment creates a feeling of order and comprehensibility. For example, the field labels Name, Address, and City were right justified so that the data-entry fields would be vertically aligned. This layout allows the frequent user to concentrate on the entry fields and to ignore the labels. If users are working from hard copy, the screen should match the paper form.

- *Familiar field labels*: Common terms should be used. If Address were replaced by Domicile, many users would be uncertain or anxious about what to do.

- *Consistent terminology and abbreviations*: Prepare a list of terms and acceptable abbreviations and use the list diligently, making additions only after careful consideration. Instead of varying such terms as Address, Employee Address, ADDR., and Addr., stick to one term, such as Address.

- *Visible space and boundaries for data-entry fields*: Underscores or other markers indicate the number of characters available, so users will know when abbreviations or other trimming strategies are needed.

- *Convenient cursor movement*: A simple and visible mechanism is needed for moving the cursor, such as a TAB key or cursor-movement arrows.

- *Error correction for individual characters and entire fields*: A backspace key and overtyping should be allowed to enable easy repairs or changes to entire fields.

- *Error messages for unacceptable values*: If users enter an unacceptable value, the error message should appear on completion of the field. The message should indicate permissible values of the field; for example, if the zip code is entered as `28K21` or `2380`, the message might indicate that `Zip codes should have 5 digits`.

- *Optional fields clearly marked*: The word `Optional` or other indicators should be visible. Optional fields should follow required fields, whenever possible.

- *Explanatory messages for fields*: If possible, explanatory information about a field or its values should appear in a standard position, such as in a window on the bottom, whenever the cursor is in the field.

- *Completion signal*: It should be clear to the users what they must do when they are finished filling in the fields. Generally, designers should avoid automatic completion when the last field is filled, because users may wish to review or alter field entries.

These considerations may seem obvious, but often forms designers omit the title, or include unnecessary computer file names, strange codes, unintelligible instructions, unintuitive groupings of fields, cluttered layouts, obscure field labels, inconsistent abbreviations or field formats, awkward cursor movement, confusing error-correction procedures, hostile error messages, and no obvious way to signal completion.

Detailed design rules should reflect local terminology and abbreviations. They should specify field sequences familiar to the users; the width and height of the display device; highlighting features such as reverse video, underscoring, intensity levels, color, and fonts; the cursor movement keys; and coding of fields.

3.10.2 Coded fields

Columns of information require special treatment for data entry and for display. Alphabetic fields are customarily left justified on entry and on display. Numeric fields may be left justified on entry, but then become right justified on display. When possible, avoid entry and display of leftmost zeros in numeric fields. Numeric fields with decimal points should line up on the decimal points.

Special attention should be paid to such common fields as these:

- *Telephone numbers*: Offer a form to indicate the subfields:

  `Telephone: (_ _ _) _ _ _-_ _ _ _`

  Be alert to such special cases, such as addition of extensions or the need for nonstandard formats for foreign numbers.

- *Social-security numbers*: The pattern for Social-security numbers should appear on the screen as

  `Social-security number: _ _ _ - _ _ - _ _ _ _`

When the user has typed the first three digits, the cursor should jump to the leftmost position of the two-digit field.

- *Times*: Even though the 24 hour clock is convenient, many people find it confusing and prefer A.M. or P.M. designations. The form might appear as

  `_ _:_ _ _ _   (9:45 AM or PM)`

Seconds may or may not be included, adding to the variety of necessary formats.

- *Dates*: How to specify dates is one of the nastiest problems; no good solution exists. Different formats for dates are appropriate for different tasks, and European rules differ from American rules. It may take years before an acceptable standard emerges.

  When the display presents coded fields, the instructions might show an example of correct entry; for example,

  `Date: _ _/_ _/_ _   (04/22/93 indicates April 22, 1993)`

For many people, examples are more comprehensible than is an abstract description, such as `MM/DD/YY`.

- *Dollar amounts (or other currency)*: The dollar sign should appear on the screen, so users then type only the amount. If a large number of whole-dollar amounts is to be entered, users might be presented with a field such as

  `Deposit amount: $_ _ _ _ _.00`

with the cursor to the left of the decimal point. As the user types numbers, they shift left. To enter an occasional cents amount, the user must type the decimal point to reach the `00` field for overtyping.

Other considerations in form-fillin design include multiscreen forms, mixed menus and forms, use of graphics, relationship to paper forms, use of pointing devices, use of color, handling of special cases, and integration of a word processor to allow remarks.

3.11   Practitioner's Summary

Begin by understanding the semantic structure of your application within the vast range of menu-selection situations. Concentrate on organizing the sequence of menus to match the users' tasks, ensure that each menu is a meaningful semantic unit, and create items that are distinctive and comprehensible. If some users make frequent use of the system, then typeahead, shortcut, or macro strategies should be allowed. Permit simple traversals to the previously displayed menu and to the main menu. Finally, be sure to conduct human-factors tests and to involve human-factors specialists in the design process (Savage et al., 1982). When the system is implemented, collect usage data, error statistics, and subjective reactions to guide refinement.

Whenever possible, use a menu-builder or menu-driver system to produce and display the menus. Commercial menu-creation systems are available and should be used to reduce implementation time, to ensure consistent layout and instructions, and to simplify maintenance.

3.12   Researcher's Agenda

Experimental research could help us to refine the design guidelines concerning semantic organization and sequencing in single and linear sequences of menus. How can differing communities of users be satisfied with a common semantic organization when their information needs are very different? Should users be allowed to tailor the structure of the menus, or is there greater advantage in compelling everyone to use the same structure and terminology? Should a tree structure be preserved even if some redundancy is introduced? How can networks be made safe?

Research opportunities abound. Depth versus breadth tradeoffs under differing conditions need to be studied to provide guidance for designers. Layout strategies, wording of instructions, phrasing of menu items, use of color, response time, and display rate are all excellent candidates for experimentation. Exciting possibilities are becoming available with larger screens, graphic user interfaces, and novel selection devices.

Implementers would benefit from the development of software tools to support menu-system creation, management, usage-statistics gathering, and evolutionary refinement. Portability of *menuware* could be enhanced to facilitate transfer across systems.

References

Billingsley, P. A., Navigation through hierarchical menu structures: Does it help to have a map? *Proc. Human Factors Society, Twenty-Sixth Annual Meeting* (1982), 103–107.

Brown, C. Marlin, *Human-Computer Interface Design Guidelines*, Ablex, Norwood, NJ (1988).

Brown, James W., Controlling the complexity of menu networks, *Communications of the ACM 25*, 7 (July 1982), 412–418

Callahan, D., Hopkins, M., Weiser, M., and Shneiderman, B., An empirical comparison of pie versus linear menus, *Proc. CHI '88 Human Factors in Computer Systems*, ACM, New York (1988), 95–100.

Card, Stuart K., User perceptual mechanisms in the search of computer command menus, *Proc. Human Factors in Computer Systems* (March 1982), 190–196.

Clauer, Calvin Kingsley, An experimental evaluation of hierarchical decision-making for information retrieval, IBM Research Report RJ 1093, San Jose, CA (September 15, 1972).

Galitz, W. O., *Human Factors in Office Automation*, Life Office Managment Assn., Atlanta, GA (1980).

Greenberg, Saul and Witten, Ian H., Adaptive personalized interfaces: A question of viability, *Behaviour and Information Technology 4*, 1 (1985), 31–45.

Herot, Christopher F., Graphical user interfaces. In Vassiliou, Y. (Editor), *Human Factors and Interactive Computer Systems*, Ablex, Norwood, NJ (1984), 83–103.

Kiger, John I., The depth/breadth trade-off in the design of menu-driven user interfaces, *International Journal of Man–Machine Studies 20* (1984), 201–213.

Koved, Lawrence, and Shneiderman, Ben, Embedded menus: Menu selection in context, *Communications of the ACM 29* (1986), 312–318.

Landauer, T. K., and Nachbar, D. W., Selection from alphabetic and numeric menu trees using a touch screen: Breadth, depth, and width, *Proc. Human Factors in Computing Systems*, ACM SIGCHI, New York (April 1985), 73–78.

Laverson, Alan, Norman, Kent, and Shneiderman, Ben, An evaluation of jump-ahead techniques for frequent menu users, *Behaviour and Information Technology 6* (1987), 97–108.

Lee, E., and Latremouille, S., Evaluation of tree structured organization of information on Telidon, *Telidon Behavioral Research I*, Department of Communications, Ottawa, Canada (1980).

Liebelt, Linda S., McDonald, James E., Stone, Jim D., and Karat, John, The effect of organization on learning menu access, *Proc. Human Factors Society, Twenty-Sixth Annual Meeting* (1982), 546–550.

McDonald, James E., Stone, Jim D., and Liebelt, Linda S., Searching for items in menus: The effects of organization and type of target, *Proc. Human Factors Society, Twenty-Seventh Annual Meeting* (1983), 834–837.

McEwen, S. A., An investigation of user search performance on a Telidon information retrieval system, *Telidon Behavioral Research 2*, Ottawa, Canada (May 1981).

Mantei, Marilyn, Disorientation behavior in person–computer interaction, Ph. D. Dissertation, Department of Communications, University of Southern California, Pasadena, CA (August 1982).

Martin, James, *Viewdata and the Information Society*, Prentice-Hall, Englewood Cliffs, NJ (1982).

Mitchell, Jeffrey and Shneiderman, Ben, Dynamic versus static menus: An experimental comparison, *ACM SIGCHI Bulletin 20*, 4 (1989), 33–36.

Murray, Robert P., and Abrahamson, David S., The effect of system response delay and delay variability on inexperienced videotext users, *Behavior and Information Technology 2*, 3 (1983), 237–251.

Norman, Kent, *The Psychology of Menu Selection: Designing Cognitive Control at the Human/Computer Interface*, Ablex, Norwood, NJ (1991).

Norman, Kent L. and Chin, John P., The effect of tree structure on search in a hierarchical menu selection system, *Behaviour and Information Technology 7* (1988), 51–65.

Ogden, William C. and Boyle, James M., Evaluating human–computer dialog styles: Command versus form/fill-in for report modification, *Proc. Human Factors Society, Twenty-Sixth Annual Meeting,* Human Factors Society, Santa Monica, CA (1982), 542–545.

Pakin, Sherwin E. and Wray, Paul, Designing screens for people to use easily, *Data Management* (July 1982), 36–41.

Parton, Diana, Huffman, Keith, Pridgen, Patty, Norman, Kent, and Shneiderman, Ben, Learning a menu selection tree: Training methods compared, *Behaviour and Information Technology,* (1985), 81–91.

Perlman, Gary, Making the right choices with menus, *INTERACT '84,* First IFIP International Conference on Human–Computer Interaction, North-Holland, Amsterdam, The Netherlands (1984), 291–295.

Robertson, G., McCracken, D., and Newell, A., The ZOG approach to man–machine communication, *International Journal of Man–Machine Studies 14* (1981), 461–488.

Savage, Ricky E., Habinek, James K., and Barnhart, Thomas W., The design, simulation, and evaluation of a menu driven user interface, *Proc. Human Factors in Computer Systems* (1982), 36–40.

Seabrook, R., and Shneiderman, B., The user interface in a hypertext, multi-window browser, *Interacting with Computers 1* (1989), 299–337.

Shneiderman, Ben, Direct manipulation: A step beyond programming languages, *IEEE Computer 16,* 8 (1983), 57–69.

Somberg, Benjamin, and Picardi, Maria C., Locus of information familiarity effect in the search of computer menus, *Proc. Human Factors Society, Twenty-Seventh Annual Meeting* (1983), 826–830.

Teitelbaum, Richard C., and Granda, Richard, The effects of positional constancy on searching menus for information, *Proc. CHI '83, Human Factors in Computing Systems,* Available from ACM, Baltimore, MD (1983), 150–153.

Wallace, Daniel F., Anderson, Nancy S., and Shneiderman, Ben, Time stress effects on two menu selection systems, *Proc. Human Factors Society, Thirty-First Annual Meeting* (1987), 727–731.

Young, R. M., and Hull, A., Cognitive aspects of the selection of Viewdata options by casual users, *Pathways to the Information Society, Proc. Sixth International Conference on Computer Communication,* London, U.K. (September 1982), 571–576.

CHAPTER 4

Command Languages

I soon felt that the forms of ordinary language were far too diffuse . . . . I was not long in deciding that the most favorable path to pursue was to have recourse to the language of signs. It then became necessary to contrive a notation which ought, if possible, to be at once simple and expressive, easily understood at the commencement, and capable of being readily retained in the memory.

Charles Babbage, "On a method of expressing by signs the action of machinery," 1826

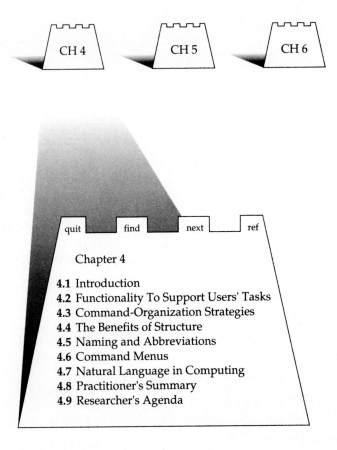

4.1 Introduction

The history of written language is rich and varied. Early tally marks and pictographs on cave walls existed for millennia before precise notations for numbers or other concepts appeared. The Egyptian hieroglyphs of 5000 years ago were a tremendous advance because standard notations facilitated communication across space and time. Eventually, languages with a small alphabet and rules of word and sentence formation dominated because of the relative ease of learning, writing, and reading. In addition to these natural languages, special languages for mathematics, music, and chemistry emerged because they facilitated communication and problem solving. In the twentieth century, novel notations were created for such diverse domains as dance, knitting, higher forms of mathematics, logic, and DNA molecules.

The basic goals of language design are

- Precision
- Compactness
- Ease in writing and reading
- Speed in learning
- Simplicity to reduce errors
- Ease of retention over time

Higher-level goals include

- Close correspondence between reality and the notation
- Convenience in carrying out manipulations relevant to users' tasks
- Compatibility with existing notations
- Flexibility to accommodate novice and expert users
- Expressiveness to encourage creativity
- Visual appeal

Constraints on a language include

- The capacity for human beings to record the notation
- The match between the recording and the display media (for example, clay tablets, paper, printing presses)
- The convenience in speaking (vocalizing)

Successful languages evolve to serve the goals within the constraints.

The printing press was a remarkable stimulus to language development because it made widespread dissemination of written work possible. The computer is another remarkable stimulus to language development, not only because widespread dissemination through networks is possible, but also because computers are a tool to manipulate languages and because languages are a tool for manipulating computers.

The computer has had only a modest influence on spoken natural languages, compared to its enormous impact as a stimulus to the development of numerous new formal written languages. Early computers were built to perform mathematical computations, so the first programming languages had a strong mathematical flavor. But computers were quickly found to be effective manipulators of logical expressions, business data, graphics, sound, and text. Increasingly, computers are used to operate on the real world: directing robots, issuing dollar bills at bank machines, controlling manufacturing, and guiding spacecraft. These newer applications encourage language designers to find convenient notations to direct the computer while preserving the needs of people to use the language for communication and problem solving.

Therefore, effective computer languages must not only represent the users' tasks and satisfy the human needs for communication, but also be in harmony with mechanisms for recording, manipulating, and displaying these languages in a computer.

Computer programming languages that were developed in the 1960s and early 1970s, such as FORTRAN, COBOL, ALGOL, PL/I, and Pascal, were designed for use in a noninteractive computer environment. Programmers would compose hundreds or thousands of lines of code, carefully check them over, and then *compile* or interpret by computer to produce a desired result. Incremental programming was one of the design considerations in BASIC and in advanced languages such as LISP, APL, and PROLOG. Programmers in these languages were expected to build smaller pieces online and interactively to execute and test the pieces. Still, the common goal was to create a large program that was preserved, studied, extended, and modified. The attraction of rapid compilation and execution led to the widespread success of the compact, but sometimes obscure, notation used in C. The pressures for team programming, organizational standards for sharing, and the increased demands for reusability promoted encapsulation and the development of object-oriented programming concepts in languages such as ADA and C++.

Scripting languages emphasizing screen presentation and mouse control became popular in the late 1980s, with the appearance of HyperCard, SuperCard, ToolBook, etc. These languages included novel operators, such as `ON MOUSE DOWN`, `BLINK`, or `IF FIRST CHARACTER OF THE MESSAGE BOX IS 'A'` (see Section 14.3.3).

Database query languages developed in the middle to late 1970s, such as SQL and QUEL, emphasized shorter segments of code (three to 20 lines) that could be written at a terminal and executed immediately. The goal of the user was more to create a result than a program.

Command languages, which originated with operating-systems commands, are distinguished by their immediacy and by their impact on devices or information. Users issue a command and watch what happens. If the result is correct, the next command is issued; if not, some other strategy is adopted. The commands are brief and their existence is transitory. Of course, command histories are sometimes kept and macros are created in some command languages, but the essence of command languages is that they have an ephemeral nature and that they produce an immediate result on some object of interest.

Command languages are distinguished from menu-selection systems in that their users must recall notation and initiate action. Menu selection users receive instructions and must recognize and choose among only a limited set of visible alternatives; they respond more than initiate. Command-language users are often called on to accomplish remarkable feats of memorization and typing. For example, this UNIX command, used to delete blank lines from a file, is not obvious:

```
GREP -V ^$ FILEA > FILEB
```

Similarly, to get printout on unlined paper with the IBM 3800 laser printer, a user at one installation was instructed to type

```
CP TAG DEV E VTSO LOCAL 2 OPTCD=J F=3871 X=GB12
```

The puzzled user was greeted with a shrug of the shoulders and the equally cryptic comment that "Sometimes, logic doesn't come into play; it's just getting the job done." This style of work may have been acceptable in the past, but user communities and their expectations are changing. The empirical studies described in this chapter are beginning to clarify guidelines for many command-language design issues.

Command languages may consist of single commands or have complex syntax (Section 4.2). The language may have only a few operations, or may have thousands. Commands may have a hierarchical structure or permit concatenation to form variations (Section 4.3). A typical form is a verb followed by a noun object with qualifiers or arguments for the verb or noun. Abbreviations may be permitted (Section 4.5). Feedback may be generated for acceptable commands, and error messages (Section 8.2) may result from unacceptable forms or typos. Command-language systems may offer the user brief prompts, or may be close to menu-selection systems (Section 4.6). Finally, natural-language interaction can be considered as a complex form of command language (Section 4.7).

4.2 Functionality to Support Users' Tasks

People use computers and command-language systems to accomplish a wide range of tasks, such as text editing, operating-system control, bibliographic retrieval, database manipulation, electronic mail, financial management, airline or hotel reservations, inventory, manufacturing process control, and adventure games.

The critical determinant of success is the *functionality* of the system. People will use a computer system if it gives them powers not otherwise available. If the power is attractive enough, people will use a system despite a poor user interface. Therefore, the first step for the designer is to determine the functionality of the system by assessing the users' task domain.

A common design error is excess functionality. In a misguided effort to add features, options, and commands, the designer can overwhelm the user.

Excess functionality means more code to maintain, potentially more bugs, possibly slower execution, and more help screens, error messages, and user manuals (see Chapters 8 and 12). For the user, excess functionality slows learning, increases the chance of error, and adds the confusion of longer manuals, more help screens, and less specific error messages. On the other hand, insufficient functionality leaves the user frustrated because an apparent function is not supported. For instance, the system might require the user to copy the contents of the screen by hand because there is no simple print command, or to reorder the output because there is no sort command.

Evidence of excessive functionality comes from a study of 17 secretaries at a scientific research center who used IBM's XEDIT editor for a median of 18 months for 50 to 360 minutes per day (Rosson, 1983). Their usage of XEDIT commands was monitored for 5 days. The average number of commands used was 26 per user, with a maximum of 34; the number of commands was correlated with experience ($r = 0.49$). XEDIT has 141 commands, so even the most experienced user dealt with less than a quarter of the commands. Users did not appear to employ idiosyncratic subsets of the language, but instead added commands to their repertoire in an orderly and similar pattern.

Careful task analysis might result in a table of user communities and tasks with each entry indicating expected frequency of use. The high-volume tasks should be made easy to carry out, and then the designer must decide which communities of users are the prime audience for the system. Users may differ in their position in an organization, their knowledge of computers, or their frequency of system usage. One difficulty in carrying out such a task analysis is predicting who the users might be and what tasks they might need to accomplish.

Inventing and supplying new functions are the major goals of many designers. They know that marketplace acceptance is often determined by the availability of functions that the competition does not provide. Word-processor designers continue to add such functions as boldface, footnotes, dual windows, mail merge, table editing, graphics, or spelling checks to entice customers. A feature-analysis list (Figure 4.1) can be helpful in comparing designs and in discovering novel functions (Roberts, 1980).

At an early stage, the destructive operations—such as deleting objects or changing formats—should be evaluated carefully to ensure that they are reversible, or at least are protected from accidental invocation. Designers should also identify error conditions and prepare error messages. A transition diagram showing how each command takes the user to another state is a highly beneficial aid to design, as well as to eventual training of users (Figure 4.2). If the diagram grows too complicated, it may signal the need for system redesign.

Major considerations for expert users are the possibilities of tailoring the language to suit personal work styles, and of creating named macros to

Text Editor Feature List

Estimated time to install (15 minutes to 2 hours)

Number of diskettes provided (1 to 7)
Right to make copies

On-screen tutorial
Textbook tutorial
Textbook reference guide
Online help
Meaningful error messages

Spelling checker built in to word processor
Thesaurus built in to word processor
Mail merge
Automatic table of contents generation
Automatic index generation

Menu, command, or function-key driven
Save block
Block defined by highlight or markers

Maximum size for block operation
Document size limit
Capacity to edit more than one file
Rename disk files
Copy disk files
Show disk directory

What you see is what you get
Preview print format
Editing allowed during printing
Print part of file
Chain documents for printing
Queue documents for printing
Automatic page numbering
Print multiple copies
Automatic file save
Save file without exiting
Automatic backup file
Create file without embedded codes

Subscript/superscript
Italics
Underscoring
Boldface
Multiple fonts

Multiple font sizes
Left and right justification
Centering
Tabbing
Proportional spacing
Multiple column output
Footnotes
Endnotes
Line-spacing options
Number of printers supported

Characters per line range (78-455)
Lines per screen
Change screen colors
Redefine key functions
Specify macros
Automatic hyphenization
Switch from insert to overwrite modes
Automatic indentation
Multiple indents/outdents
Change case command
Display ruler line to show tabs
Display column, line, and page number
Headers and footers
Math functions
Sort functions

Move cursor by character, word, sentence,
  paragraph
Move cursor by screen
Move cursor to left or right end of line
Move cursor to top or bottom of screen
Move cursor to top or bottom of document

Delete by character, word, line, sentence, or
  paragraph
Delete to end of document
Undelete

Search forward and backward
Search by patterns
Ignore case in searching
Leave and locate markers

Copy/move
Copy/move by columns

Figure 4.1

A feature-analysis list can be helpful in comparing designs and in discovering novel functions. This list was distilled from Roberts (1980) and Wiswell, Phil, Word processing: The latest word, *PC Magazine* (August 20, 1985), 110–134.

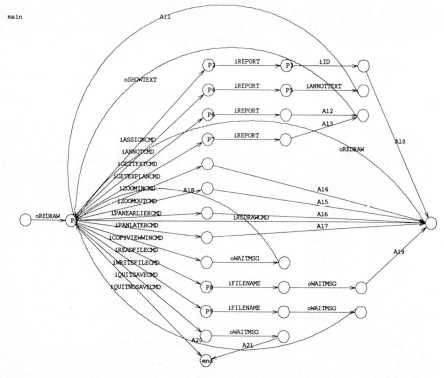

Figure 4.2

This transition diagram indicates user inputs with an "i" and computer outputs with an "o". This is a relatively simple diagram showing only a portion of the system. Complete transition diagrams may be many pages long. (Courtesy of Robert J. K. Jacob, Naval Research Laboratory, Washington, DC.)

permit several operations to be carried out with a single command. Macro facilities allow extensions that the designers could not foresee or that are beneficial to only a small fragment of the user community. A macro facility can be a full programming language that might include specification of arguments, conditionals, iteration, integers, strings, and screen-manipulation primitives, plus library and editing tools. Well-developed macro facilities are one of the strong attractions of command languages.

4.3   Command-Organization Strategies

Several strategies for command organization have emerged, but guidelines for choosing among these are only beginning to be discussed. A unifying concept, model, or metaphor is an aid to learning, problem solving, and retention

(Carroll and Thomas, 1982). Electronic-mail enthusiasts conduct lively discussions about the metaphoric merits of such task-related objects as file drawers, folders, documents, memos, notes, letters, or messages. They debate the appropriate task domain actions (CREATE, EDIT, COPY, MOVE, DELETE) and the choice of an action pair LOAD/SAVE (too much in the computer domain), READ/WRITE (acceptable for letters, but awkward for file drawers), or OPEN/CLOSE (acceptable for folders, but awkward for notes).

Similarly, debate continues over whether the commands should manipulate lines, as in program editors and older line-oriented editors, or words, sentences, and paragraphs, as in new word processors. Choosing one strategy over another is helpful. Designers who fail to choose, and instead attempt to support every possibility, risk overwhelming the users while missing the opportunity to optimize for one strategy. Designers often err by choosing a metaphor closer to the computer domain than to the user's task domain. Of course, metaphors can mislead the user, but careful design can reap the benefits while reducing the detriments.

Having adopted a concept, model, or metaphor for operations, the designer must now choose a strategy for the command structure. Mixed strategies are possible, but learning, problem solving, and retention may be aided by limitation of complexity.

4.3.1   Simple command list

Each command is chosen to carry out a single task, and the number of commands matches the number of tasks. With a small number of tasks, this approach can produce a system that is simple to learn and use. With a large number of commands, there is danger of confusion. The vi editor on UNIX systems offers many commands while attempting to keep the number of keystrokes low. The result is complex strategies employing single letters, shifted single letters, and CTRL key plus single letters (Figure 4.3). Furthermore, some commands stand alone, whereas others must be combined, often in irregular patterns.

4.3.2   Command plus arguments

Each command (COPY, DELETE, PRINT) is followed by one or more arguments (FILEA, FILEB, FILEC) that indicate objects to be manipulated:

```
COPY FILEA,FILEB
DELETE FILEA
PRINT FILEA,FILEB,FILEC
```

Commands may be separated from the arguments by a blank or other delimiter, and the arguments may have blanks or delimiters between them

vi Commands to Move the Cursor

Moving within a window

H	home position (upper left)
L	last line
M	middle line
(CR)	next line (carriage return)
+	next line
-	previous line
CTRL-P	previous line in same column
CTRL-N	next line in same column
(LF)	next line in same column (line feed)

Moving within a line

0	start of line
$	end of line
(space)	right one space
CRTL-H	left one space
h	left one space
w	forward one word
b	backward one word
e	end (rightmost) character of a word
)	forward one sentence
(	backward one sentence
}	forward one paragraph
{	backward one paragraph
W	blank out a delimited word
B	backwards blank out a delimited word
E	go to the end of a delimited word

Finding a character

fx	find the character x going forward
Fx	find the character x going backward
tx	go up to x going forward
Tx	go up to x going backward

Scrolling the window

CTRL-F	forward one screen
CTRL-B	backward one screen
CTRL-D	forward one half screen
CTRL-U	backward one half screen
G	go to line
/pat	go to line with pattern forward
pat	go to line with pattern backward

Figure 4.3

Commands to move the cursor. The profusion of commands in vi may enable expert users to get tasks done with just a few actions, but the number of commands can be overwhelming to novice and intermittent users.

(Schneider et al., 1984). Keyword labels for arguments may be helpful to some users; for example,

```
COPY FROM=FILEA TO=FILEB
```

The labels require extra typing and increase chances of a typo, but readability is improved and order dependence is eliminated.

4.3.3 Command plus options and arguments

Commands may have options (3, HQ, and so on) to indicate special cases. For example,

```
PRINT/3,HQ FILEA
PRINT (3,HQ) FILEA
PRINT FILEA -3,HQ
```

may produce three copies of FILEA at the printer in the headquarters building. As the number of options grows, the complexity can become overwhelming and the error messages less specific. The arguments may also have options, such as version numbers, privacy keys, or disk addresses.

The number of arguments, of options, and of permissible syntactic forms can grow rapidly. One airline-reservations system uses the following command to check the seat availability on a flight on August 21, from Washington's National Airport (DCA) to New York's La Guardia Airport (LGA) at about 3:00 P.M.:

```
A0821DCALGA0300P
```

Even with substantial training, error rates can be high with this approach, but frequent users seem to manage and even appreciate the compact form of this type of command.

The UNIX command-language system is widely used, in spite of the complexity of its command formats (Figure 4.4), which have been criticized severely (Norman, 1981). Here again, users will master complexity to benefit from the rich functionality in a system. Observed error rates with actual use of UNIX commands have ranged from 3 to 53 percent (Kraut et al., 1983; Hanson et al., 1984). Even common commands have generated high syntactic error rates: mv (18 percent), cp (30 percent), and awk (34 percent). Still, the complexity has a certain attraction for a portion of the potential user community. Users gain satisfaction in overcoming the difficulties and becoming one of the inner circle ("gurus" and "wizards") who are knowledgeable about system features—command-language macho.

at 2A Friday timehog
  at 2:00 a.m. Friday, run program
awk '{print $1 + $2}' file1
  print sum of first two fields of each line
cat − n file1
  print specified file to terminal, number output lines
cat file1 >> file2
  append file1 to end of file2
cc file.c
  compile C program, executable in a.out
cd /usr/lib
  change working directory to specified one
chmod g + rw file1 file2
  change mode of files, adding group read and write access
chmod 600 file
  change mode of file, allow only read and write by owner
cp file1 file2
  make a copy of file1 named file2
cp − r dir /tmp
  recursively copy dir and its subdirectories to /tmp
diff − l dir1 dir2
  summarize differences between files in dir1 and dir2
f77 file.f
  compile Fortran program, executable in a.out
f77 − o file file.f file.o
  compile Fortran program, link with file.o, executable in file
find $HOME − name '#*' − exec rm { } \;
  remove files with names beginning with a pound sign
finger name
  look up information on user's login or real name
grep '[Pp]hone' file
  print all lines in file containing Phone or phone
grep − l main *
  print names of files in current directory containing main
head − 6 file
  print first six lines of file
kill − 9 0
  send a KILL signal to processes started since login
ln − s file1 file2 /tmp
  make symbolic links to files in specified directory
lpq job user
  report print spooler status of user's job
lpr − p file
  paginate file and spool it to the line printer

ls
  print a list of the files in the current directory
ls − R /bin
  list files in specified directory and its subdirectories
mail molly tracey < file
  send a file to specified users as mail
man spell
  print Unix user's manual page for a command
mkdir /tmp/myjunk
  make a new directory
more + 50 file
  view file by screenful, starting at line 50
mv file1 file2 /tmp
  move files to specified directory
nroff file | more
  preview formatted file on terminal
pc file.p
  compile Pascal program, executable in a.out
pr file | lpr
  paginate a file with default header, spool output
ps l
  print long listing of current processes, PID's and status
pwd
  print current working directory
rlogin puter2
  login on remote computer
rm file
  remove (delete) a file
rm − i junk[0 − 9]
  remove files junk0 ... junk9, confirming first
sort + 3 − 4 file
  print file sorted only on fourth field
stty everything
  print all stty option settings
stty raw; prog; stty − raw
  set terminal to raw mode, run a program, and restore mode
style − p file
  print sentences in file containing a passive verb
vi file
  edit file using full screen editor
w
  list who's logged in, and what they're doing

Figure 4.4

Examples of common UNIX commands with brief explanations. (Courtesy of Specialized Systems Consultants, Inc., Seattle WA.)

4.3.4   Hierarchical command structure

The full set of commands is organized into a tree structure, like a menu tree. The first level might be the command action, the second might be an object argument, and the third might be a destination argument:

Action	Object	Destination
CREATE	File	File
DISPLAY	Process	Local printer
REMOVE	Directory	Screen
COPY		Laser printer
MOVE		

If a hierarchical structure can be found for a set of tasks, it offers a meaningful structure to a large number of commands. In this case, 5 x 3 x 4 = 60 tasks can be carried out with only five command names and one rule of formation. Another advantage is that a command-menu approach can be developed to aid the novice or intermittent user, as was done in VisiCalc and later Lotus 1-2-3 and Excel.

Several help systems allow a hierarchical command to retrieve text about subsystems and the letter's commands. For example, to get help on the editor command for deleting lines in a document, the user might type

```
HELP EDIT DELETE LINES
```

Of course, the difficulty comes in knowing what keywords are available. Users can type the first few elements of the command, and then receive a menu of items.

Many word processors, spreadsheets, and operating systems use a hierarchical command structure for the numerous commands that they support. For example, Figure 4.5 shows the command structure for MS-DOS 5.0.

File	Options	View
Open	Confirmation...	Single File List
Run...	File Display Options	Dual File Lists
Print	Select Across Directories	All Files
Associate	Show Information...	Program/File Lists
Search...	Enable Task Swapper	Program List
View File Contents	Display...	
	Colors...	Repaint Screen
Move...		Refresh
Copy...		
Delete...		
Rename...		
Change Attributes	Tree	Help
	Expand One Level	Index
Create Directory...	Expand Branch	Keyboard
	Expand All	Shell Basics
Select All	Collapse Branch	Commands
Deselect All		Procedures
		Using Help
Exit		
		About Shell

Figure 4.5

The tree structure of menus in Microsoft MS-DOS 5.0. (Screen shot ©1981–1991 Microsoft Corporation. Reprinted with permission from Microsoft Corporation, Redmond, WA.)

4.4   The Benefits of Structure

Human learning, problem solving, and memory are greatly facilitated by meaningful structure. If command languages are well designed, users can recognize the structure and can easily encode it in their semantic knowledge storage. For example, if users can uniformly edit such objects as characters, words, sentences, paragraphs, chapters, and documents, this meaningful pattern is easy to learn, apply, and recall. On the other hand, if they must overtype a character, change a word, revise a sentence, replace a paragraph, substitute a chapter, and alter a document, then the challenge grows substantially, no matter how elegant the syntax (Scapin, 1982).

Meaningful structure is beneficial for task concepts, computer concepts, and syntactic details of command languages. Yet, many systems fail to provide a meaningful structure. One widely used operating system displays various information as a result of forms of the LIST, QUERY, HELP, and TYPE commands, and moves objects as a result of the PRINT, TYPE, SPOOL, PUNCH, SEND, COPY, or MOVE commands. Defaults are inconsistent for different features, four different abbreviations for PRINT and LINECOUNT are required, binary choices vary between YES/NO and ON/OFF, and function-key usage is inconsistent. These flaws emerge from multiple uncoordinated design groups and insufficient attention by the managers, especially as features are added over time.

An explicit list of design conventions in a Guidelines Document can be an aid to designers and managers. Exceptions may be permitted, but only after thoughtful discussions. Users can learn systems with inconsistencies, but they do so more slowly and with greater chance of making mistakes. One difficulty is that there may be conflicting design conventions.

4.4.1   Consistent argument ordering

Choices among conventions can sometimes be resolved by experimentation with alternatives. A command language with six functions, each requiring two arguments, was developed for decoding messages (Barnard et al., 1981). One argument was always a message-identification number, and the other argument was a file number, code number, digit, and so on. In normal English usage, the message identification sometimes would be the direct object of an explanatory sentence, such as SAVE the MESSAGE ID with this REFERENCE NUMBER. So, one rule of consistent command formation was to follow English usage. The second consistency rule was to have the message identification always as the first or always as the second argument. The rules resulted in four possible command groups:

Direct object, argument first		Direct object, argument second	
SEARCH	file no,message id	SEARCH	message id,file no
TRIM	message id,segment size	TRIM	segment size,message id
REPLACE	message id,code no	REPLACE	code no,message id
INVERT	group size,message id	INVERT	message id,group size
DELETE	digit,message id	DELETE	message id,digit
SAVE	message id,reference no	SAVE	reference no,message id

Consistent, argument first		Consistent, argument second	
SEARCH	message id,file no	SEARCH	file no,message id
TRIM	message id,segment size	TRIM	segment size,message id
REPLACE	message id,code no	REPLACE	code no,message id
INVERT	message id,group size	INVERT	group size,message id
DELETE	message id,digit	DELETE	digit,message id
SAVE	message id,reference no	SAVE	reference no,message id

Forty-eight female subjects used one of these systems for 1 hour to decode messages. (Actually, one-half of the subjects had variant command names, such as SELECT instead of SEARCH, but this manipulation was a minor effect.) Time to perform tasks decreased during the 10 1-hour trials, but the speedup was consistent across command styles. The results strongly favored using consistent argument positions rather than the consistent direct-object positions, suggesting that English language rules of formation were not as effective as is the simpler positional rule. The shortest task times, fewest help requests, and fewest errors occurred with the consistent argument first. These results lead to the conjecture that command languages should allow users to express the simple, familiar, or well-understood features first, and then to consider the more varying aspects.

Follow-up studies by the same group (Barnard et al., 1981; Barnard et al., 1982) replicated the results about positional consistency and pursued several related issues. One frequent design consideration is whether the command verb or the object of interest should come first. Command-first form would be DISPLAY FILE or INSERT LIST; the object first form would be FILE DISPLAY or LIST INSERT. The evidence supports the command-first strategy used in most languages and the principle that there is a fixed order. Allowing users the freedom to put the command and object in either order generated more requests for help than did fixing the order. Subjects pressed function keys to initiate commands and to select objects, so a further replication is necessary to validate whether the results are consistent when users must remember and type commands. Factors influencing the results may be the relative number of commands and objects and the familiarity the user has with each.

Finally, pilot studies by James Foley at George Washington University suggest that object first may be more appropriate when using selection by pointing on graphic displays is used. Different thinking patterns may be engaged when users are faced with visually oriented interfaces (right brain) and when they use syntax-oriented command notations (left brain). The object-first approach also fits conveniently with the strategy of leaving an object selected (and highlighted) after an action is complete, so that, if the same object is used in the next action, it is already selected.

4.4.2 Symbols versus keywords

Further evidence that command structure affects performance comes from a comparison of 15 commands in a commercially used symbol-oriented text editor, and revised commands that had a more keyword-oriented style (Ledgard et al., 1980). Here are three sample commands:

Symbol editor	Keyword editor
`FIND:/TOOTH/;-1`	`BACKWARD TO "TOOTH"`
`LIST;10`	`LIST 10 LINES`
`RS:/KO/,/OK/;*`	`CHANGE ALL "KO" TO "OK"`

The revised commands performed the same functions. Single-letter abbreviations (`L;10` or `L 10 L`) were permitted in both editors, so the number of keystrokes was approximately the same. The difference in the revised commands was that keywords were used in an intuitively meaningful way, but there were no standard rules of formation. Eight subjects at three levels of text-editor experience used both versions in this counterbalanced order within-subjects design.

The results (Table 4.1) clearly favored the keyword editor, indicating that command-formation rules do make a difference. Unfortunately, no specific guidelines emerged except that we should avoid using unfamiliar symbols for new users of a given text editor, even if the users are experienced with other text editors. It is interesting that the difference in percentage of task completed between the symbol and keyword editor was small for the experienced users. One conjecture, supported in other studies, is that experienced computer users develop skill in dealing with strange notations and therefore are less affected by syntactic variations.

Table 4.1

Impact of revised text-editor commands on three levels of users. (Source: Ledgard et al., 1980.)

Users	Percentage of Task Completed		Percentage of Erroneous Commands	
	Symbol	Keyword	Symbol	Keyword
Inexperienced	28	42	19	11
Familiar	43	62	18	6.4
Experienced	74	84	9.9	5.6

4.4.3   Hierarchical structure and congruence

Carroll (1982) altered two design variables to produce four versions of a 16-command language for controlling a robot (Table 4.2). Commands could be hierarchical (verb–object–qualifier) or nonhierarchical (verb only) and congruent (for example, ADVANCE/RETREAT or RIGHT/LEFT) or noncongruent (GO/BACK or TURN/LEFT). Carroll uses *congruent* to refer to meaningful pairs of opposites (*symmetry* might be a better term). Hierarchical structure and congruence have been shown to be advantageous in psycholinguistic experiments. Thirty-two undergraduate subjects studied one of the four command sets in a written manual, gave subjective ratings, and then carried out paper-and-pencil tasks.

Subjective ratings prior to performing tasks showed that subjects disapproved of the nonhierarchical noncongruent form, and gave the highest rating for the nonhierarchical congruent form. Memory and problem-solving tasks showed that congruent forms were clearly superior, and that the hierarchical forms were superior for several dependent measures. Error rates were dramatically lower for the congruent hierarchical forms.

This study assessed performance of new users of a small command language. Congruence helped subjects to remember the natural pairs of concepts and terms. The hierarchical structure enabled subjects to master 16 commands with only one rule of formation and 12 keywords. With a larger command set—say, 60 or 160 commands—the advantage of hierarchical structure should increase, assuming that a hierarchical structure could be found to accommodate the full set of commands. Another conjecture is that retention should be facilitated by the hierarchical structure and congruence.

Carroll's study was conducted during a half-day period; with 1 week of regular use, differences probably would be reduced substantially. However, with intermittent users or with users under stress, the hierarchical congruent form might again prove superior. An online experiment might have been more realistic and would have brought out differences in command length

Table 4.2

Command sets and partial results. (Source: Carroll 1982.)

Congruent		Noncongruent	
Hierachical	Non-hierarchical	Hierachical	Non-hierarchical
MOVE ROBOT FORWARD	ADVANCE	MOVE ROBOT FORWARD	GO
MOVE ROBOT BACKWARD	RETREAT	CHANGE ROBOT BACKWARD	BACK
MOVE ROBOT RIGHT	RIGHT	CHANGE ROBOT RIGHT	TURN
MOVE ROBOT LEFT	LEFT	MOVE ROBOT LEFT	LEFT
MOVE ROBOT UP	STRAIGHTEN	CHANGE ROBOT UP	UP
MOVE ROBOT DOWN	BEND	MOVE ROBOT DOWN	BEND
MOVE ARM FORWARD	PUSH	CHANGE ARM FORWARD	POKE
MOVE ARM BACKWARD	PULL	MOVE ARM BACKWARD	PULL
MOVE ARM RIGHT	SWING OUT	CHANGE ARM RIGHT	PIVOT
MOVE ARM LEFT	SWING IN	MOVE ARM LEFT	SWEEP
MOVE ARM UP	RAISE	MOVE ARM UP	REACH
MOVE ARM DOWN	LOWER	CHANGE ARM DOWN	DOWN
CHANGE ARM OPEN	RELEASE	CHANGE ARM OPEN	UNHOOK
CHANGE ARM CLOSE	TAKE	MOVE ARM CLOSE	GRAB
CHANGE ARM RIGHT	SCREW	MOVE ARM RIGHT	SCREW
CHANGE ARM LEFT	UNSCREW	CHANGE ARM LEFT	TWIST
Subjective Ratings (1 = Best, 5 = Worst)			
	1.86	1.63	1.81	2.73
Test 1	14.88	14.63	7.25	11.00
Problem 1 errors	0.50	2.13	4.25	1.63
Problem 1 omissions	2.00	2.50	4.75	4.15

that would have been a disadvantage to the hierarchical forms because of the greater number of keystrokes required. However, the hierarchical forms could all be replaced with three-letter abbreviations (for example, MAL for MOVE ARM LEFT), thereby providing an advantage even in keystroke counts.

4.4.4   Consistency, congruence, and mnemonicity

An elegant demonstration of the importance of structuring principles comes from a study of four command languages for text editing (Green and Payne, 1984). Language L4 (Figure 4.6) is a subset of the commercial word processor based on the EMACS editor, but it uses several conflicting organizing principles. The authors simplified language L3 by using only the CTRL key, and using congruence and mnemonic naming where possible. Language L2 uses CTRL to mean *forward* and META to mean *backward*, but mnemonicity is sacrificed. Language L1 uses the same meaningful structure for CTRL and META, congruent pairs, and mnemonicity.

	L1	L2	L3	L4
move pointer forward a paragraph	CTRL-[	CTRL-A	CTRL-]	META-]
move pointer backward a paragraph	META-[	META-A	CTRL-[	META-[
move pointer forward a sentence	CTRL-S	CTRL-B	CTRL-)	META-E
move pointer backward a sentence	META-S	META-B	CTRL-(	META-A
view next screen	CTRL-V	CTRL-C	CTRL-V	CTRL-V
view previous screen	META-V	META-C	CTRL-~^	META-V
move pointer to next line	CTRL-<	CTRL-D	CTRL-N	CTRL-N
move pointer to previous line	META-<	META-D	CTRL-P	CTRL-P
move pointer forward a word	CTRL-W	CTRL-E	CTRL-}	META-F
move pointer backward a word	META-W	META-E	CTRL-{	META-B
redisplay screen	CTRL-R	CTRL-F	CTRL-Y	CTRL-L
undo last command	META-G	META-G	CTRL-U	CTRL-G
kill sentence forward	CTRL-Z	CTRL-H	CTRL-S	META-K
kill line	CTRL-K	CTRL-I	CTRL-K	CTRL-K
delete character forward	CTRL-D	CTRL-J	CTRL-D	CTRL-D
delete character backward	META-D	META-J	CTRL-DEL	CTRL-DEL
delete word forward	CTRL-DEL	CTRL-K	CTRL-X	META-D
delete word backward	META-D	META-K	CTRL-W	META-DEL
move pointer forward a character	CTRL-C	CTRL-L	CTRL-F	CTRL-F
move pointer backward a character	META-C	META-L	CTRL-B	CTRL-B
move pointer to end of file	CTRL-F	CTRL-M	CTRL-~>	META-~>
move pointer to beginning of file	META-F	META-M	CTRL-~<	META-~<
move pointer to end of line	CTRL-L	CTRL-N	CTRL-Z	CTRL-E
move pointer to beginning of line	META-L	META-N	CTRL-A	CTRL-A
forward string search	CTRL-X	CTRL-O	CTRL-S	CTRL-S
reverse string search	META-X	META-O	CTRL-R	CTRL-R

Figure 4.6

The four languages used in the study discussed in the text. (Green, T. R. G. and Payne, S. J., "Organization and learnability in computer languages," *International Journal of Man–Machine Studies 21* (1984) 7–18. Used by permission of Academic Press Inc. [London] Limited.)

Forty undergraduate subjects with no word-processing experience were given 12 minutes to study one of the four languages (Figure 4.6). Then, they were asked to recall and write on paper as many of the commands as possible. This step was followed by presentation of the command descriptions, after which they were asked to write down the associated command syntax. The free-recall and prompted-recall tasks were both repeated. The results showed a statistically significant difference for languages, with subjects using L4 demonstrating the worst performance. The best performance was attained with L1, which has the most structure. An online test would have been a useful followup to demonstrate the advantage obtained with practice and over a longer period.

In summary, sources of structure that have proven advantageous include these:

- Positional consistency
- Grammatical consistency
- Congruent pairing
- Hierarchical form

In addition, as discussed in the next section, a mixture of meaningfulness, mnemonicity, and distinctiveness is helpful.

One remaining form of structure is *visual* or *perceptual form*. The up- and down-arrows are highly suggestive of function, as are characters such as right- and left-angle brackets, the plus sign, and the ampersand. WORDSTAR takes advantage of a perceptual clue embedded in the QWERTY keyboard layout:

```
    E
A S D F
    X
```

CTRL-E moves the cursor up one line, CTRL-X moves the cursor down one line, CTRL-S moves the cursor one character left, CTRL-D moves the cursor one character right, CTRL-A moves the cursor one word left, and CTRL-F moves the cursor one word right. Other word processors use a similar principle with the CTRL-W, A, S, and Z keys or the CTRL-I, J, K, and M keys.

4.5 Naming and Abbreviations

In discussing command-language names, Schneider (1984) takes a delightful quote from Shakespeare's *Romeo and Juliet*: "A rose by any other name would smell as sweet." As Schneider points out, the lively debates in design circles suggest that this concept does not apply to command-language names. Indeed, the command names are the most visible part of a system and are likely to provoke complaints from disgruntled users.

Critics (Norman, 1981, for example) focus on the strange names in UNIX, such as MKDIR (make directory), CD (change directory), LS (list directory), RM (remove file), and PWD (print working directory); or in IBM's CMS, such as SO (temporarily suspend recording of trace information), LKED (link edit), NUCXMAP (identify nucleus extensions), and GENDIRT (generate directory). Part of the concern is the inconsistent abbreviation strategies that may take the first few letters, first few consonants, first and last letter, or first letter of each word in a phrase. Worse still are abbreviations with no perceivable pattern.

4.5.1   Specificity versus generality

Names are important for learning, problem solving, and retention over time. With only a few names, a command set is relatively easy to master; but with hundreds of names, the choice of meaningful, organized sets of names becomes more important. Similar results were found for programming tasks, where variable name choices were less important in small modules with from 10 to 20 names than in longer modules with dozens or hundreds of names.

In a word-processing training session (Landauer et al., 1983), 121 students learned one of three command sets containing only three commands: the old set (`delete`, `append`, `substitute`), a new supposedly improved set (`omit`, `add`, `change`), and a random set designed to be confusing (`allege`, `cipher`, `deliberate`). Task performance times were essentially the same across the three command sets, although subjective ratings indicated a preference for the old set. The random names were highly distinctive and the mismatch with function may have been so disconcerting as to become memorable. These results apply to only small command sets.

With larger command sets, the names do make a difference, especially if they support congruence or some other meaningful structure. One naming-rule debate revolves around the question of *specificity versus generality* (Rosenberg, 1982). Specific terms can be more descriptive, and if they are more distinctive, they may be more memorable. General terms may be more familiar and therefore easier to accept. Two weeks after a training session with 12 commands, subjects were more likely to recall and recognize the meaning of specific commands than of general commands (Barnard et al., 1982).

In a paper-and-pencil test, 84 subjects studied one of seven sets of eight commands (Black and Moran, 1982). Two of the eight commands—the commands for inserting and deleting text—are shown here in all seven versions:

Infrequent, discriminating words	`insert`	`delete`
Frequent, discriminating words	`add`	`remove`
Infrequent, nondiscriminating words	`amble`	`perceive`
Frequent, nondiscriminating words	`walk`	`view`
General words (frequent, nondiscriminating)	`alter`	`correct`
Nondiscriminating nonwords (nonsense)	`GAC`	`MIK`
Discriminating nonwords (icons)	`abc-adbc`	`abc-ac`

The "infrequent, discriminating" command set resulted in faster learning and superior recall than did other command sets. The general words were correlated with the lowest performance on all three measures. The nonsense words did surprisingly well, supporting the possibility that, with small command sets, distinctive names are helpful even if they are not meaningful.

4.5.2   Abbreviation strategies

Even though command names should be meaningful for human learning, problem solving, and retention, they must satisfy another important criterion. They must be in harmony with the mechanism for expressing the commands to the computer. The traditional and widely used command-entry mechanism is the keyboard, which indicates that commands should use brief and kinesthetically easy codes. Commands requiring shifted keys or CTRL keys, special characters, or difficult sequences are likely to cause higher error rates. For text editing, when many commands are applied and speed is appreciated, single-letter approaches are attractive. Overall, brevity is a worthy goal since it can speed entry and reduce error rates. Many word-processor designers have pursued this approach, even when mnemonicity was sacrificed, thereby making use more difficult for novice and intermittent users.

In less demanding applications, designers have used longer command abbreviations, hoping that the gains in recognizability would be appreciated over the reduction in key strokes. Novice users may actually prefer typing the full name of a command because they have a greater confidence in its success (Landauer et al., 1983). Novices who were required to use full command names before being taught two-letter abbreviations made fewer errors with the abbreviations than those who were taught the abbreviations from the start and than did those who could create their own abbreviations (Grudin and Barnard, 1985).

The phenomenon of preferring the full name at first appeared in our study of bibliographic retrieval with the Library of Congress's SCORPIO system. Novices preferred typing the full name, such as BROWSE or SELECT, rather than the traditional four-letter abbreviations BRWS or SLCT, or the single-letter abbreviations B or S. After five to seven uses of the command, their confidence increased and they attempted the single-letter abbreviations. A designer of a text adventure game recognized this principle and instructs novice users to type EAST, WEST, NORTH, or SOUTH; after five full-length commands, the system tells the user about the single-letter abbreviations. A related report comes from some users of IBM's CMS, who find that the minimal length abbreviations are too difficult to learn; they stick with the full form of the command.

With experience and frequent use, abbreviations become attractive for, and even necessary to satisfy, the "power" user. Efforts have been made to find optimal abbreviation strategies. Several studies support the notion that abbreviation should be made by a consistent strategy (Ehrenreich and Porcu, 1982; Benbasat and Wand, 1984; Schneider, 1984). Here are six potential strategies:

1. *Simple truncation*: Use the first, second, third, etc. letters of each command. This strategy requires that each command be distinguishable by the leading string of characters. Abbreviations can be all of the same length or of different lengths.

2. *Vowel drop with simple truncation*: Eliminate vowels and use some of what remains. If the first letter is a vowel, it may or may not be retained. H, Y, and W may or may not be considered as vowels.

3. *First and last letter*: Since the first and last letters are highly visible, use them; for example, use ST for SORT.

4. *First letter of each word in a phrase*: Use this popular technique, for example, with a hierarchical design plan.

5. *Standard abbreviations from other contexts*: Use familiar abbreviations such as QTY for QUANTITY, XTALK for CROSSTALK (a software package), PRT for PRINT, or BAK for BACKUP.

6. *Phonics*: Focus attention on the sound; for example, use XQT for execute.

Truncation appears to be the most effective mechanism overall, but it has its problems. Conflicting abbreviations appear often, and decoding of an unfamiliar abbreviation is not as easy as when vowel dropping is used (Schneider, 1984).

4.5.3 Guidelines for using abbreviations

Ehrenreich and Porcu (1982) offer this compromise set of guidelines:

1. A *simple*, primary rule should be used to generate abbreviations for most items; a *simple* secondary rule should be used for those items where there is a conflict.

2. Abbreviations generated by the secondary rule should have a marker (for example, an asterisk) incorporated in them.

3. The number of words abbreviated by the secondary rule should be kept to a minimum.

4. Users should be familiar with the rules used to generate abbreviations.

5. Truncation is an easy rule for users to comprehend, but it may also produce a large number of identical abbreviations for different words.

6. Use fixed-length abbreviations in preference to variable-length ones.

7. Abbreviations should not be designed to incorporate endings (e.g., ING, ED, S).

8. Unless there is a critical space problem, abbreviations should not be used in messages generated by the computer and read by the user.

Abbreviations are an important part of system design and they are appreciated by experienced users. Users are more likely to use abbreviations if they are confident in their knowledge of the abbreviations and if the benefit is a savings of more than one to two characters (Benbasat and Wand, 1984). The appearance of new input devices and strategies (for example, selecting by pointing) will change the criteria for abbreviations. Each situation has its idiosyncrasies and should be evaluated carefully by the designer, applying empirical tests where necessary.

4.6   Command Menus

To relieve the burden of memorization of commands, some designers offer users brief prompts of available commands. The early online version of the *Official Airline Guide* used such prompts as this:

```
ENTER +,L#,X#,S#,R#,M,RF (#=LINE NUMBER)
```

This prompt reminds users of the commands related to fares that have been displayed, and the related flight schedules:

+	move forward one screen
L#	limitations on airfares
X#	detailed information on a listed flight
S#	schedule information for the listed fare
R#	return flight information for this route
M	main menu
RF	return fares

Experienced users come to know the commands and do not need to read the prompt or the help screens. Intermittent users know the concepts and refer to the prompt to jog their memory and to get help in retaining the syntax for future uses. Novice users do not benefit as much from the prompt and must take a training course or consult the online help.

The prompting approach emphasizes syntax and serves frequent users. It is closer to but more compact than a standard numbered menu, and preserves screen space for task-related information. The early WORDSTAR

```
        A:GETTYS  PAGE 1 LINE 9 COL 62               INSERT ON
              < < <      M A I N    M E N U    > > >
     --Cursor Movement--    : -Delete- :   -Miscellaneous-  :  -Other  Menus-
^S char left ^D char right :^G  char  : ^I Tab   ^B Reform  : (from Main only)
^A word left ^F word right :DEL chr lf: ^V INSERT ON/OFF    :^J Help  ^K Block
^E line  up  ^X line down  :^T word rt:^L Find/Replce again:^Q Quick ^P Print
     --Scrolling--         :^Y  line   :RETURN End paragraph:^O Onscreen
^Z line down ^W line up    :          :  ^N Insert a RETURN :
^C screen up ^R screen down:          :  ^U Stop a command  :
L----!----!----!----!----!----!----!----!----!----!--------R
     Fourscore  and seven years ago our fathers brought forth on
this continent a new nation conceived in liberty and dedicated to
the  proposition  that  all men are created equal.   Now  we  are
engaged in a great civil war testing whether that nation,  or any
nation so conceived and so dedicated, can long endure.

     We are met on a great battlefield of that war.  We have come
to dedicate a portion of that field as a final resting-place  for
those  who here gave their lives that that nation might live.
```

Figure 4.7

The early Wordstar offered the novice and intermittent users help menus containing commands with one- or two-word descriptions.

editor offered the novice and intermittent user help menus containing commands with one- or two-word descriptions (Figure 4.7). Frequent users could turn off the display of help menus, thereby gaining screen space for additional text.

Several interactive systems on personal computers have another, still more attractive form of prompts called *command menus*. Users are shown a list of descriptive words and make a selection by pressing the left and right arrow keys to move a light bar. When the desired command word is highlighted, the user presses the return key to carry out the command. Often, the command menu is a hierarchical structure that branches to a second- or third-level menu.

Even though arrow-key movement is relatively slow and is not preferred by frequent users, command-menu items can be selected by single-letter keypresses. This strategy becomes a hierarchical command language; it is identical to the typeahead (BLT) approach of menu selection. Novice users can use the arrow keys to highlight their choice, or can type single-letter choices, but frequent users do not even look at the menus as they type sequences of two, three, four, or more single letters that come to be thought of as a command (Figure 4.5).

The Lotus 1-2-3 (Figure 4.8) implementation is especially fast and elegant. As command words are selected, a brief description appears on the line below, providing further assistance for novice users without distracting experts from their concentration on the task. Experienced users appear to work as fast as touch typists, making three to six keystrokes per second.

Pop-up or pull-down menus that use mouse selection constitute another form of command menu. Frequent users can work extremely quickly, and novices can take the time to read the choices before selecting a command.

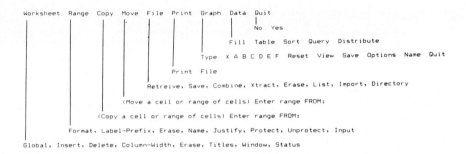

```
Worksheet  Range  Copy  Move  File  Print  Graph  Data  Quit
                                                   │
                                                   No  Yes

                                          Fill  Table  Sort  Query  Distribute

                                   Type  X A B C D E F  Reset  View  Save  Options  Name  Quit

                        Print  File

              Retrieve, Save, Combine, Xtract, Erase, List, Import, Directory

         (Move a cell or range of cells) Enter range FROM:

     (Copy a cell or range of cells) Enter range FROM:

  Format, Label-Prefix, Erase, Name, Justify, Protect, Unprotect, Input

Global, Insert, Delete, Column-Width, Erase, Titles, Window, Status
```

Figure 4.8

The first two levels of command menus from LOTUS 1-2-3 reveal the rich function available to users. At the third level, users may receive another menu or enter values. (Printed with permission of Lotus Development Corporation, Cambridge, MA.)

With a fast display, command menus blur the boundaries between commands and menus.

4.7   Natural Language in Computing

Even before there were computers, people dreamed about creating machines that would accept *natural language*. It is a wonderful fantasy, and the success of word-manipulation devices such as word processors, printing presses, tape recorders, and telephones may give encouragement to some people. Although there has been some progress in machine translation from one natural language to another (for example, Japanese to English), most effective systems require constrained or preprocessed input, or postprocessing of output. Undoubtedly, improvements will continue and constraints will be reduced, but high-quality reliable translations of complete documents without human intervention seems difficult to attain. Structured texts such as weather reports are translatable; technical papers are marginally translatable; novels or poems are not translatable. Language is subtle; there are many special cases, meaning is not easily programmed into machines, and context has a powerful and pervasive effect.

Although full comprehension and generation of language seems inaccessible, there are still many ways that computers can be used in dealing with natural language, such as for interaction, queries, database searching, text generation, and adventure games. So much research has been invested in natural-language systems that undoubtedly some successes will emerge, but widespread use may not develop because the alternatives may be more appealing. More rapid progress can be made if carefully controlled experimental tests are used to discover the designs, users, and tasks for which natural-language applications are most beneficial.

4.7.1   Natural-language interaction

Researchers hope that someday computers will respond easily to commands users issue by typing or speaking in natural language. *Natural-language interaction* (NLI) might be defined as the operation of computers by people using a familiar natural language (such as English) to give instructions and receive responses. Users do not have to learn a command syntax or to select from menus. Early attempts at generalized "automatic programming" have faded, but there are continuing efforts to provide domain-specific assistance.

The problems with NLI lie in not only implementation on the computer, but also desirability for large numbers of users for a wide variety of tasks. People are different from computers, and human–human interaction is not necessarily an appropriate model for human operation of computers. Since computers can display information 1000 times faster than people can enter commands, it seems advantageous to use the computer to display large amounts of information, and to allow novice and intermittent users simply to choose among the items. Selection helps to guide the user by making clear what functions are available. For knowledgeable and frequent users, who are thoroughly aware of the available functions, a precise, concise command language is usually preferred.

In fact, the metaphors of artificial intelligence (smart machines, intelligent agents, and expert systems) may prove to be mind-limiting distractions that inhibit designers from creating the powerful tools that become commercially successful. Spreadsheets, WYSIWYG word processors, and direct-manipulation graphics tools emerged from a recognition of what users were using effectively, rather than from the misleading notions of intelligent machines. Similarly, the next generation of groupware to support collaboration, visualization and simulation packages, tele-operated devices, and hypermedia stem from user-centered scenarios, rather than the machine-centered artificial-intelligence fantasies.

The SSOA model can help us to sort out the issues. NLI does not provide information about actions and objects in the task domain; users are usually presented with a simple prompt that invites a natural-language query. But the user may be knowledgeable about the task domain—for example, about the meaning of database objects and permissible actions. NLI also does not necessarily convey knowledge of the computer concepts—for example, tree-structuring of information, implications of a deletion, Boolean operations, or query strategies. NLI does relieve the user of learning new syntactic rules, since it presumably will accept familiar English language requests. Therefore, NLI can be effective for the user who is knowledgeable about some task domain and computer concepts but who is an intermittent user who cannot retain the syntactic details. Lately, some members of the artificial-intelligence community have understood the power of direct manipulation for conveying the system state and suggesting possible actions, and have attempted to blend visual presentation of status with natural-language input.

NLI might apply to checkbook maintenance (Shneiderman, 1980), where the users recognize that there is an ascending sequence of integer-numbered checks, and that each check has a single payee field, single amount, single date, and one or more signatures. Checks can be issued, voided, searched, and printed. In fact, following this suggestion, Ford (1981) created and tested an NLI system for this purpose. Subjects were paid to maintain their checkbook registers by computer using an APL-based program that was incrementally refined to account for unanticipated entries. The final system successfully handled 91 percent of users' requests, such as these:

```
Pay to Safeway on 3/24/86 $29.75.
June 10 $33.00 to Madonna.
Show me all the checks paid to George Bush.
Which checks were written on October 29?
```

Users reported satisfaction with the system and were eager to use the system even after completing the several months of experimentation. This study can be seen as a success for NLI, but alternatives might be even more attractive. Showing a full screen of checkbook entries with a blank line for new entries might accomplish most tasks without any commands and with minimal typing (similar to what is used in Quicken from Intuit). Users could do searches by entering partial information (for example, George Bush in the payee field) and then pressing a query key.

There have been numerous informal tests of NLI systems, but only a few have been experimental comparisons against some other design. Researchers seeking to demonstrate the advantage of NLI over command-language and menu approaches for creating business graphics were surprised to find no significant differences for time, errors, or attitude (Hauptmann and Green, 1983).

A more positive result was found with users of HAL, the restricted natural-language addition to Lotus 1-2-3 (Napier et al., 1989). HAL users could avoid the command-menu /WEY (for Worksheet Erase Yes), and could type requests such as \erase worksheet, \insert row, or \total all columns, starting with any of the 180 permissible verbs. In an empirical study, after 1.5 days of training, 19 HAL users and 22 Lotus 1-2-3 users worked on three substantial problem sets for another 1.5 days. Performance and preference strongly favored the restricted natural language version, but the experimenters had difficulty identifying the features that made a difference: "It is not clear whether Lotus HAL was better because it is more like English or because it takes advantage of context, but we suspect the latter is more important." By context, the authors meant features such as the cursor position or meaningful variable names that indicate cell ranges.

Some NLI work has turned to automatic speech recognition and speech generation to reduce the barriers to acceptance. There is some advantage to use of these technologies, but the results are still meager. A promising application is the selection of painting tools by discrete-word recognition (see Section 6.4.1), thus eliminating the frustration and delay of moving the cursor from the object to the tool menu on the border and back again (Pausch, 1991). Selections are voiced but feedback is visual. Users of the mouse plus the voice commands performed their tasks 21-percent faster than did the users who had only the mouse. Alternatives to voice, such as keyboard or touchscreen, were not tested.

There is some portion of the user spectrum that can benefit from NLI, but it may not be as large as promoters believe. Computer users usually seek predictable responses and are discouraged if they must engage in clarification dialogs frequently. Since NLI has such varied forms, the users must constantly be aware of the computer's response, to verify that their actions were recognized. Finally, visually oriented interactions, embracing the notions of direct manipulation (see Chapter 5), make more effective use of the computer's capacity for rapid display. In short, pointing and selecting in context is often more attractive than typing or even speaking an English sentence.

It is surprising that designers of expert systems have attempted to embed NLI. Expert systems already tax the user with complexity, lack of visibility of the underlying processes, and confusion about what functions the system can and cannot handle. A precise, concise notation or selection in context from a list of alternatives seems far more suitable in providing users with predictable and comprehensible behavior (Hayes-Roth, 1984) (Figure 4.9).

4.7.2   Natural-language queries

Since general interaction is difficult to support, some designers have pursued a more limited goal of *natural-language queries* (NLQ) against relational databases. The *relational schema* contains attribute names, and the database contains attribute values, both of which are helpful in disambiguating queries. A simulated query system was used to compare a subset of the structured SQL database facility to a natural-language system (Small and Weldon, 1983). The SQL simulation resulted in faster performance on a benchmark set of tasks. Similarly, a field trial with a real system, users, and queries pointed to the advantages of SQL over the natural-language alternative (Jarke et al., 1985). Believers in NLQ may claim that more research and system development is

---

Sample Session from an Expert System for Oil Drilling Advisor

What is the name of WELL–159?
  AGF7–93E

What is the profile of AGF7–93E?
  DEVIATED

Please enter information about FORMATION–1:

upper-limit meters	lower-limit meters	main-rock-type	homogenous/ interbedded
747	806	SHALE	HOMOGENOUS

Please enter information on PROBLEM–1:

problem-type	prior-action	total-depth	casting-shoe depth
STICKING	REAMING	1111 METERS	747 METERS

Please enter the composition of the drill-string starting from
the bit (type ? for assistance):?
  BIT 9"5/8 STAPB"5/8 SHORTDC7"3/4STA9"5/8...NDP5

What was the drilling method employed when the problem occurred:
  ROTARY

What is the depth of the freepoint?
  UNKNOWN

Figure 4.9

This extract demonstrates one designer's attempt at an expert-system dialog. User
input is shown in upper-case letters. Users must type in values even when
selection from a menu would be more meaningful, more rapid, and less error-
prone. Furthermore, there does not appear to be any way to go back to change
values, to view values, or to reuse values from previous sessions. (F. Hayes-Roth,
The knowledge-based expert system: A tutorial, *IEEE Computer 17*, 9 (September
1984), 11–28. Copyright 1984 IEEE.)

needed before NLQ, can be excluded, but improvements in menus, command languages, and direct manipulation seem equally likely.

Supporters of NLQ can point with some pride at the modest success of
the commercially available INTELLECT system, which has approximately
400 installations on large mainframe computers (Figure 4.10); the system's
appeal has faded in recent years, however, as users turn to other approaches. Business executives, sales representatives, and other people use
INTELLECT to search databases on a regular basis. Several innovative
implementation ideas help to make INTELLECT successful. First, the parser
uses the contents of the database to parse queries; for example, the parser
can determine that a query containing Cleveland refers to city locations,
because Cleveland is an instance in the database. Second, the system

```
PLEASE ENTER YOUR FIRST REQUEST

WHAT'S IN THE DATABASE?
FIELDS IN THE FILE OF EMPLOYEES

NAME                  JOB          SALARY        SEX
AGE                   FAMILY       CITY          STATE
EMPLOYEE NUMBER

WHO WORKS IN NEW YORK CITY
PRINT THE JOB AND NAME OF ALL EMPLOYEES WITH CITY = NEW YORK

PROFESSIONAL                      NAME
OCCUPATION

MACHINIST                         ANGELIN
PHYSICIAN                         ANGUS

WHAT IS THE NUMBER OF ANGUS
COUNT THE EMPLOYEES WITH NAME = ANGUS

ANSWER:   1

WHAT IS THE EMPLOYEE NUMBER OF ALL EMPLOYEES WITH NAME = ANGUS
EMPLOYEE
NUMBER

0034

WHICH WOMEN WORK IN NEW YORK CITY
PRINT THE JOB OF ALL EMPLOYEES WITH SEX = FEMALE & CITY = NEW YORK

PROFESSIONAL
OCCUPATION

MACHINIST
ADMINISTRATOR
ELECTRICIAN

FEMALE EMPLOYEES IN NEW YORK CITY
PRINT THE NAME OF ALL EMPLOYEES WITH SEX = FEMALE & CITY = NEW YORK

NAME

ANGELIN
CANTEBURY
EDWARDS

HOW MANY NEW YORK CITY MEN ARE OVER 30 YEARS OLD
COUNT THE EMPLOYEES WITH CITY = NEW YORK & SEX = MALE & AGE>30

ANSWER:   9

PRINT THEM
PRINT THE NAME AND AGE OF ALL EMPLOYEES WITH CITY = NEW YORK &
      SEX = MALE & AGE>30

                YEARS
NAME             OF
                 AGE

ANGUS            43
ELEY             69
HILTON           44
```

Figure 4.10

Demonstration session with Intellect. User input is underscored. Intellect rephrases user input into a structured query language, which users often mimic as they become more knowledgeable. (AI Corp., Cambridge, MA.)

administrator can conveniently include guidance for handling domain-specific requests, by indicating fields related to who, what, where, when, how, etc. queries. Third, INTELLECT rephrases the user's query and displays a response, such as PRINT THE CHECK NUMBERS WITH PAYEE = GEORGE BUSH. This structured response serves as an educational aid, and users gravitate toward expressions that mimic the style. Eventually, as users become more knowledgeable, they often use concise, commandlike expressions that they believe will be parsed successfully. Even the promoters of INTELLECT recognize that novice users who are unfamiliar with the task domain will have a difficult time, and that the ideal user is a knowledgeable intermittent user.

A more successful product is Q & A from Symantec, which provides rapid, effective query interpretation and execution on IBM PCs (Figure 4.11). The package makes a very positive impression, but few data have been collected about actual usage. The designers cite many instances of happy NLQ users and find practical applications in their daily work, but the popularity of the package seems to be more closely tied to the fine word processor plus database, and the form fillin facilities. A further NLQ package is CLOUT, which is part of the Rbase package.

An innovative blend of NLQ and menus was developed under the name NLMENU (Tennant et al., 1983) and is distributed by Texas Instruments under the name NaturalLink. Natural-language phrases are shown as a series of menus. As phrases (for example, `FIND/COLOR/AND/NAME  OF PARTS/WHOSE  COLOR  IS`) are chosen by a pointing strategy, a query is formed in a command window. Users receive information from the menus, obviating the need for a query. For example, if the database of parts and suppliers contains only red, green, and blue parts, only these choices appear in the window containing the `PART COLOR` menu. Users can see the full range of possible queries and thereby can avoid the frustration of probing the boundaries of system functionality. With this strategy, typing is eliminated, and the user is guaranteed a semantically and syntactically correct query.

4.7.3   Text-database searching

Searching of textual databases is a growing application for natural-language enthusiasts who have developed filters and parsers for queries expressed in natural language. For example, in a legal application (`Find cases of tenants who have sued landlords for lack of heat`) the filter eliminates pronouns and other noise words, provides synonyms from a thesaurus (`renters`), deals with singulars versus plurals, and handles other problems such as misspellings or foreign terms. Then, the parser separates the query into standard components, such as `plaintiff, defendant`, and `cause`; the query can now be used to search a more structured database.

Another application with textual databases is to use natural-language parsing strategies to parse the stored text and to arrange it into more structured formats. The advantage here is that the parsing can be done once in advance to structure the entire database and to speed searches when users pose queries. Legal (Supreme Court decisions or state laws), medical (scientific journal articles or patient histories), and journalistic (Associated

```
┌──────────────────────────────────────────────────────────────┐
│                                                                │
│                                                                │
└──────────────────────────────────────────────────────────────┘

  Type your request in English in the box above, then press ¬.

  Examples:
  "List the average salary and average bonus from the forms on
  which sex is male and the department is sales."

  "Get the forms of the Administration employees, sorted by city."

            Press F1 for more information.
```

```
┌──────────────────────────────────────────────────────────────┐
│ WHERE ARE THE 3 MOST EXPENSIVE HOUSES WITH A FIREPLACE?        │
│                                                                │
└──────────────────────────────────────────────────────────────┘

                    Shall I do the following?

        Create a report showing
           the Address and
           the Neighborhood and
           the Cost and
           the Home Type
        from the forms on which
           the Home Type includes "HOUSE" and
           the Fireplace is YES and
           the Cost is maximum

        Yes - Continue            No - Cancel Request
```

Address	Neighborhood	Cost	Home Type
7924 Jones Street	Chevy Chase, MD	$411,950	House
4719 Dorset Ave.	Chevy Chase, MD	$678,235	House
1287 Highland Ct.	Potomac, MD	$782,125	House

Figure 4.11

Q&A supports a natural language front end for its database. Users can type questions in English and produce database search results. This figure shows the three stages: forming a query, verifying it, and receiving the results. (Q&A is a product of Symantec Corp., Cupertino, CA.)

Press news stories or Dow Jones reports) texts have been used. This application is promising because even a modest increase in suitable retrievals is appreciated by users, and incorrect retrievals are tolerated better than are errors in NLI.

4.7.4   Natural-language text generation

Although the artificial-intelligence community often frowns on *natural-language text generation* (NLTG) as a modest application, it does seem to be a worthy one (Fedder, 1990). It handles certain simple tasks, such as the preparation of structured weather reports (`80 percent chance of light rain in northern suburbs by late Sunday afternoon`) from complex mathematical models. These reports can be sent out automatically, or even can be used to generate spoken reports available over the telephone. More elaborate applications of NLTG include preparation of reports of medical laboratory or psychological tests. The computer generates not only readable reports (`White-blood-cell count is 12,000`), but also warnings (`This value exceeds the normal range of 3000 to 8000 by 50 percent`) or recommendations (`Further examination for systemic infection is recommended`). Still more involved NLTG scenarios involve the creation of legal wills, contracts, or business proposals.

On the artistic side, computer generation of poems and even novels is a regular discussion point in literary circles. Although computer-generated combinations of randomly selected phrases can be provocative, it is still the creative work of the person who chose the set of possible words and decided which of the outputs to publish. This position parallels the customary attitude of crediting the human photographer, rather than the camera or the subject matter of the photograph.

4.7.5   Adventure and educational games

A notable and widespread success of NLI techniques is in the variety of adventure games (Figure 4.12). Users may indicate directions of movement or type commands, such as `TAKE ALL OF THE KEYS`, `OPEN THE GATE`, or `DROP THE CAGE AND PICK UP THE SWORD`. Part of the attraction of NLI in this situation is that the system is unpredictable, and some exploration is necessary to discover the proper incantation.

4.8   Practitioner's Summary

Command languages can be attractive when frequent use of a system is anticipated, users are knowledgeable about the task domain and computer concepts, screen space is at a premium, response time and display rates are slow, and numerous functions that can be combined in many ways are supported. Users have to learn the semantics and syntax, but they can initiate rather than respond, rapidly specifying actions involving several

Figure 4.12

This adventure game is modeled on the Wizard of Oz story. The user types phrases such as open the door or take slippers or abbreviations such as s to move south. More complex phrases, such as put the hat on the scarecrow, are possible. (Courtesy of Spinnaker Software, Cambridge, MA.)

objects and options. Finally, complex sequences of commands can be easily specified and stored for future use as a macro.

Designers should begin with a careful task analysis to determine what functions should be provided. Hierarchical strategies and congruent structures facilitate learning, problem solving, and human retention over time. Laying out the full set of commands on a single sheet of paper helps to show the structure to the designer and to the learner. Meaningful specific names aid learning and retention. Compact abbreviations constructed according to a consistent rule facilitate retention and rapid performance for frequent users.

Innovative strategies, such as command menus, can be effective if rapid response to screen actions can be provided. Natural-language interaction can be implemented partially, but its advantage for widespread application has yet to be demonstrated.

4.9 Researcher's Agenda

Designers could be helped by development of strategies for task analysis, taxonomies of command-language designs, and criteria for using commands or other techniques. The benefits of structuring command languages based on such concepts as hierarchical structure, congruence, consistency, and mnemonicity have been demonstrated in specific cases, but replication in varied situations is important. Experimental testing should lead to a more comprehensive cognitive model of command language learning and use (Table 4.3).

A generator of command-language systems would be a useful tool for research and development of new command languages. The designer could provide a formal specification of the command language, and the system

Table 4.3

Command Language Guidelines
- Create an explicit model of objects and actions.
- Choose meaningful, specific, distinctive names.
- Implement a hierarchical structure where possible.
- Provide a consistent structure (hierarchy, argument order, action–object).
- Support consistent abbreviation rules (preferably truncation to one letter).
- Offer frequent users the capability to create macros.
- Use command menus on high-speed displays when appropriate.
- Limit the number of commands and the ways of accomplishing a task.

would generate an interpreter. With experience in using such a tool, design analyzers might be built to critique the design, to detect ambiguity, to check for consistency, to verify completeness, to predict error rates, or to suggest improvements. Even a simple but thorough checklist for command-language designers would be a useful contribution.

Novel input devices and high-speed, high-resolution displays offer new opportunities, such as command and pop-up menus, for breaking free from the traditional syntax of command languages. Natural-language interaction still holds promise in certain applications, and empirical tests offer us a good chance to identify the appropriate niches and design strategies.

References

Barnard, P. J. and Hammond, N. V., Cognitive contexts and interactive communication, IBM Hursley (U.K.) Human Factors Laboratory Report HF070 (December 1982).

Barnard, P., Hammond, N., MacLean, A., and Morton, J., Learning and remembering interactive commands, *Proc. Conference on Human Factors in Computer Systems*, available from ACM, Washington DC (1982), 2–7.

Barnard, P. J., Hammond, N. V., Morton, J., Long, J. B., and Clark, I. A., Consistency and compatibility in human–computer dialogue, *International Journal of Man–Machine Studies 15* (1981), 87–134.

Benbasat, Izak and Wand, Yair, Command abbreviation behavior in human–computer interaction, *Communications of the ACM 27*, 4 (April 1984), 376–383.

Black, J., and Moran, T., Learning and remembering command names, *Proc. Conference on Human Factors in Computer Systems*, available from ACM Washington, DC (1982), 8–11.

Carroll, John M., Learning, using and designing command paradigms, *Human Learning 1*, 1 (1982), 31–62.

Carroll, J. M., and Thomas, J., Metaphor and the cognitive representation of computing systems, *IEEE Transactions on Systems, Man, and Cybernetics, SMC-12*, 2 (March/April 1982), 107–115.

Ehrenreich, S. L., and Porcu, Theodora, Abbreviations for automated systems: Teaching operators and rules. In Badre, Al, and Shneiderman, Ben, (Editors), *Directions in Human–Computer Interaction*, Ablex, Norwood, NJ (1982), 111–136.

Fedder, Lee., Recent approaches to natural language generation. In Diaper, D., Gilmore, D., Cockton, G., and Shackel, B. (Editors), *Human–Computer Interaction: Interact '90*, North-Holland, Amsterdam, The Netherlands (1990), 801–805.

Ford, W. Randolph, *Natural Language Processing by Computer — A New Approach*, Ph. D. Dissertation, Department of Psychology, Johns Hopkins University, Baltimore, MD (1981).

Green, T. R. G. and Payne, S. J., Organization and learnability in computer languages, *International Journal of Man–Machine Studies 21* (1984), 7–18.

Grudin, Jonathan and Barnard, Phil, When does an abbreviation become a word and related questions, *Proc. CHI '85 Conference on Human Factors in Computer Systems*, ACM, New York (1985), 121–126.

Hanson, Stephen J., Kraut, Robert E., and Farber, James M., Interface design and multivariate analysis of UNIX command use, *ACM Transactions on Office Information Systems 2*, 1 (1984), 42–57.

Hauptmann, Alexander G. and Green, Bert F., A comparison of command, menu-selection and natural language computer programs, *Behaviour and Information Technology 2*, 2 (1983), 163–178.

Hayes-Roth, Frederick, The knowledge-based expert system: A tutorial, *IEEE Computer 17*, 9 (September 1984), 11–28.

Jarke, Matthias, Turner, Jon A., Stohr, Edward A., Vassiliou, Yannis, White, Norman H., and Michielsen, Ken, A field evaluation of natural language for data retrieval, *IEEE Transactions on Software Engineering SE-11*, 1 (January 1985), 97–113.

Kraut, Robert E., Hanson, Stephen J., and Farber, James, M., Command use and interface design, *Proc. CHI '83 Conference on Human Factors in Computing Systems*, ACM, New York (1983), 120–123.

Landauer, T. K., Calotti, K. M., and Hartwell, S., Natural command names and initial learning, *Communications of the ACM 26*, 7 (July 1983), 495–503.

Ledgard, H., Whiteside, J. A., Singer, A., and Seymour, W., The natural language of interactive systems, *Communications of the ACM 23* (1980), 556–563.

Napier, H. Albert, Lane, David, Batsell, Richard R., and Guadango, Norman S., Impact of a restricted natural language interface on ease of learning and productivity, *Communications of the ACM 32*, 10 (October 1989), 1190–1198.

Norman, Donald, The trouble with UNIX, *Datamation 27* (November 1981), 139–150.

Pausch, Randy and Leatherby, James H., An empirical study: Adding voice input to a graphical editor, *Journal of the American Voice Input/Output Society 9*, 2 (July 1991), 55–66.

Roberts, Terry, *Evaluation of Computer Text Editors*, Ph. D. dissertation, Department of Computer Science, Stanford University, Stanford, CA (1980).

Rosenberg, Jarrett, Evaluating the suggestiveness of command names, *Behaviour and Information Technology 1* (1982), 371–400.

Rosson, Mary Beth, Patterns of experience in text editing, *Proc. CHI '83 Conference on Human Factors in Computing Systems*, ACM, New York (1983), 171–175.

Scapin, Dominique L., Computer commands labelled by users versus imposed commands and the effect of structuring rules on recall, *Proc. Conference on Human Factors in Computer Systems*, available from ACM, Washington, DC (1982), 17–19.

Schneider, M. L., Ergonomic considerations in the design of text editors, In Vassiliou, Y. (Editor), *Human Factors and Interactive Computer Systems*, Ablex, Norwood, NJ (1984), 141–161.

Schneider, M. L., Hirsh-Pasek, K., and Nudelman, S., An experimental evaluation of delimiters in a command language syntax, *International Journal of Man–Machine Studies 20*, 6 (June 1984), 521–536.

Shneiderman, Ben, *Software Psychology: Human Factors in Computer and Information Systems*, Little, Brown, Boston (1980).

Small, Duane and Weldon, Linda, An experimental comparison of natural and structured query languages, *Human Factors 25* (1983), 253–263.

Tennant, Harry R., Ross, Kenneth M., and Thompson, Craig W., Usable natural language interfaces through menu-based natural language understanding, *Proc. CHI '83 Conference on Human Factors in Computing Systems*, ACM, New York (1983), 154–160.

CHAPTER 5

Direct Manipulation

Leibniz sought to make the form of a symbol reflect its content. "In signs," he wrote, "one sees an advantage for discovery that is greatest when they express the exact nature of a thing briefly and, as it were, picture it; then, indeed, the labor of thought is wonderfully diminished."

Frederick Kreiling, "Leibniz," *Scientific American,* **May 1968**

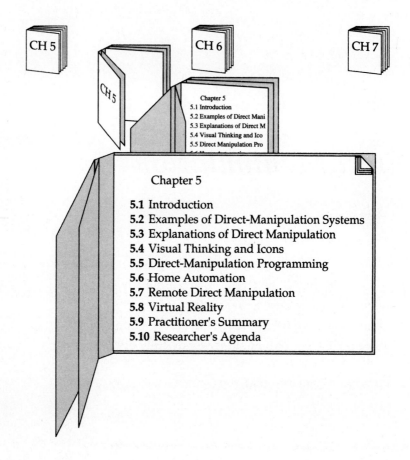

5.1   Introduction

Certain interactive systems generate a glowing enthusiasm among users that is in marked contrast with the more common reaction of grudging acceptance or outright hostility. The enthusiastic users' reports reflect the following positive feelings:

- Mastery of the system
- Competence in performing tasks
- Ease in learning the system originally and in assimilating advanced features
- Confidence in the capacity to retain mastery over time
- Enjoyment in using the system
- Eagerness to show the system off to novices
- Desire to explore more powerful aspects of the system

These feelings are not universal, but this amalgam is meant to convey an image of the truly pleased user. The central ideas seem to be visibility of the objects and actions of interest; rapid, reversible, incremental actions; and replacement of complex command-language syntax by direct manipulation of the object of interest—hence, the term *direct manipulation*. The SSOA model provides a sound foundation for understanding direct manipulation, since it steers the designer to represent the task domain objects and actions, while minimizing the computer concepts and the syntactic load.

5.2 Examples of Direct-Manipulation Systems

No single system has all the admirable attributes or design features—that may be impossible. Each of the following examples, however, has enough of them to win the enthusiastic support of many users.

My favorite example of direct manipulation is driving an automobile. The scene is directly visible through the front window, and performance of actions such as braking or steering has become common knowledge in our culture. To turn left, the driver simply rotates the steering wheel to the left. The response is immediate and the scene changes, providing feedback to refine the turn. Imagine trying to turn by issuing a command LEFT 30 DEGREES and then another command to see the new scene; but that is the level of operation of many office-automation tools of today! Another well-established example is air-traffic control in which users see a representation of the airspace with brief data blocks attached to each plane. Controllers move a trackball to point at specific planes and to perform actions.

5.2.1 Display editors and word processors

In the early 1980s, users of *full-page display editors* were great advocates of their systems, preferring these editors to the then-common *line-oriented text editors*. A typical comment was, "Once you've used a display editor, you will never want to go back to a line editor—you'll be spoiled." Similar comments came from users of stand-alone word processors such as the WANG system, early personal computer word processors such as WORDSTAR, FINALWORD, XYWRITE, and Microsoft WORD, or display editors such as EMACS on the MIT/Honeywell MULTICS system or vi (for visual editor) on the UNIX system. A beaming advocate called EMACS "the one true editor."

Roberts (1980) found overall performance times with line-oriented editors were twice as long as with display editors. Training time with display editors is also reduced, so there is evidence to support the enthusiasm of

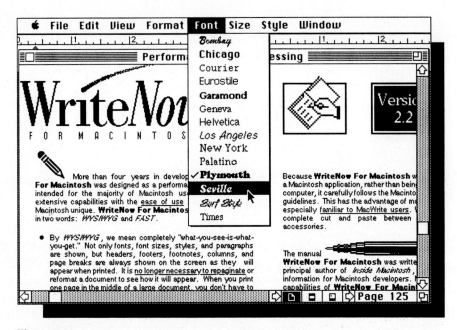

Figure 5.1

WriteNow, an example of a WYSIWYG ("What You See Is What You Get") editor. (Courtesy of T/Maker Company, Mountain View, CA.)

display-editor devotees. Furthermore, office-automation evaluations consistently favor full-page display editors for secretarial and executive use.

In the past decade, *what you see is what you get* (WYSIWYG) word processors have become standard. Claris MacWrite II and Microsoft Word 4.0 are popular on the Macintosh; Microsoft Word and Lotus Ami Pro are challenging WordPerfect's domination in the IBM PC and compatibles environment (Figure 5.1). An interesting combination of WYSIWYG display editors and command editing over structured documents shows two views simultaneously and permits editing on either view (Brooks, 1991). There are some advantages to command editing approaches, such as that history keeping is easier, more flexible markup languages are available (for example, SGML), macros tend to be more powerful, and some tasks are simpler to express (for example, `change all italics to bold`). The next generation of direct-manipulation display editors should accommodate many of these features. The advantages of display editors include

- *Display of a full page of text*: Showing 20 to 60 lines of text gives the reader a clearer sense of context for each sentence, while permitting simpler reading and scanning of the document. By contrast, working with the one-line-at-a-time view offered by some line editors is like seeing the world through a narrow cardboard tube. Some large displays can support two full pages of text, set side by side.

- *Display of the document in the form that it will appear when the final printing is done*: Eliminating the clutter of formatting commands also simplifies reading and scanning of the document. Tables, lists, page breaks, skipped lines, section headings, centered text, and figures can be viewed in their final form. The annoyance and delay of debugging the format commands are almost eliminated because the errors are apparent immediately.

- *Show cursor action that is visible to the user*: Seeing an arrow, underscore, or blinking box on the screen gives the operator a clear sense of where to focus attention and to apply action.

- *Control cursor motion through physically obvious and intuitively natural means*: Arrow keys or cursor-motion devices—such as a mouse, joystick, or graphic tablet—provide natural physical mechanisms for moving the cursor. This setup is in marked contrast to commands such as UP 6 that require an operator to convert the physical action into a correct syntactic form that may be difficult to learn and hard to recall, and thus may be a source of frustrating errors.

- *Use labeled buttons for actions*: Many workstations designed for use with display editors have buttons with actions etched onto them, such as INSERT, DELETE, CENTER, UNDERLINE, SUPERSCRIPT, BOLD, and SEARCH. These buttons act as a permanent menu-selection display to remind users of the features, so that users avoid memorization of a complex command-language syntax. On some editors, only 10 or 15 labeled buttons provide the basic functionality. A specially marked button may be the gateway to the world of advanced or infrequently used features that are offered on the screen in menu form.

- *Display of the results of an action immediately*: When a button is pressed to move the cursor or center text, the results are shown immediately on the screen. Deletions are immediately apparent; the character, word, or line is erased, and the remaining text is rearranged. Similarly, insertions or text movements are shown after each keystroke or function-key press. In contrast, with line editors, users must issue print or display commands to see the results of changes.

- *Provide rapid response and display*: Most display editors operate at high speed; a full page of text appears in a fraction of a second. This high display rate coupled with short response time produces a thrilling sense of power and speed. Cursors can be moved quickly, large amounts of text can be scanned rapidly, and the results of actions can be shown almost instantaneously. Rapid response also reduces the need for additional commands and thereby simplifies design and learning.

Line editors with slow display rates and long response times bog down the user. Speeding up line editors would add to their attractiveness, but they would still lack such features as direct overtyping, deletion, and insertion.

- *Offer easily reversible actions*: When users enter text, they repair an incorrect keystroke by merely backspacing and overstriking. They can make simple changes by moving the cursor to the problem area and overstriking, inserting, or deleting characters, words, or lines. A useful design strategy is to include natural inverse operations for each operation (Section 4.4.3). An alternative offered by many display editors is a simple UNDO command to return the text to its state before the previous action or action sequence. The easy reversibility reduces user anxiety about making a mistake or destroying the file.

Display editors are worth studying because the large market demand generates an active competition that propels the rapid evolutionary refinement of design. New directions for word processors include

- *Integration* of graphics, spreadsheets, animations, photographs, etc. in the body of a document. Advanced systems, such as Hewlett-Packard's NewWave, even permit "hot links" so that, if the graphic or spreadsheet is changed, the copy in the document also will be changed.

- *Desktop publication software* to produce sophisticated printed formats with multiple columns and output to high-resolution printers. Multiple fonts, gray scales, and color permit preparation of high-quality documents, newsletters, reports, newspapers, or books. Examples include Aldus PageMaker and Xerox Ventura.

- *Slide-presentation software* to produce text and color graphic slides for use as overhead transparencies or 35-millimeter slides, or directly from the computer with a large screen projector.

- *Hypermedia environments* with selectable buttons or embedded menu items to allow users to jump from one article to another. Links among documents, bookmarks, annotations, and tours can be added by readers.

- *Improved macro facilities* to enable users to construct, save, and edit sequences of frequently used actions. A related feature is a style sheet that allows users to specify and save a set of options for spacing, fonts, margins, etc.

- *Spelling checkers* have become standard on most full-feature word processors. Less common, but increasingly available, is an integrated thesaurus.

- *Grammar checkers*, such as RightWriter or Grammatik IV, offer users comments about potential problems in writing style, such as use of passive voice, excessive use of certain words, or lack of parallel construction. Some writers, both novices and professionals, appreciate the comments and know they can decide whether to apply the suggestions. Critics point out, however, that the advice is often inappropriate and therefore wastes time.

- *Document assemblers* to compose complex documents such as contracts or wills, from standard paragraphs using appropriate language for males or females, citizens or foreigners, high, medium, or low income earners, renters or home owners, etc.

5.2.2   VISICALC and its descendents

The first electronic spreadsheet, VISICALC, was the product of a Harvard Business School student, Bob Frankston, who was frustrated when trying to carry out repetitious calculations in a graduate business course. With a friend, Dan Bricklin, they built an "instantly calculating electronic worksheet" (as the user manual described it) that permits computation and display of results across 254 rows and 63 columns. The worksheet can be programmed so that column 4 displays the sum of columns 1 through 3; then, every time a value in the first three columns changes, the fourth column changes as well. Complex dependencies among manufacturing costs, distribution costs, sales revenue, commissions, and profits can be stored for several sales districts and months so that the effects of changes on profits can be seen immediately.

By simulating an accountant's spreadsheet or worksheet, VISICALC made it easy for novices to comprehend the objects and permissible actions. The display of 20 rows and up to nine columns, with the provision for multiple windows, gave the user sufficient visible display for easy scanning of information and comprehension of relationships among entries. The command language for setting up the worksheet was tricky for novices to learn and for infrequent users to remember, but most users needed to learn only the basic commands. The distributor of VISICALC attributed the system's appeal to the fact that "it jumps," referring to the user's delight in watching the propagation of changes across the screen.

VISICALC users could try out many alternate plans easily, and could see the effects on sales or profit rapidly. Changes to commissions or economic slowdowns could be added quickly to the worksheet. The current status of the worksheet could be saved for later review.

Competitors to VISICALC emerged quickly, and they made attractive improvements to the user interface and expanded the tasks that were supported. Among these, LOTUS 1-2-3 has come to dominate the market (Figure 5.2a), although there are many successful competitors, such as Excel and Quattro. They offer integration with graphics, three-dimensional repre-

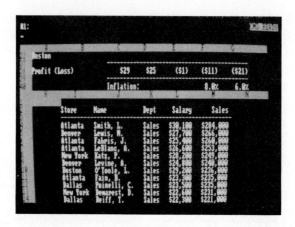

Figure 5.2(a)

Lotus spreadsheets. (Figure 5.2a and b: Printed with permission of Lotus Development Corporation, Cambridge, MA.) (a) Early version of Lotus 1-2-3, the dominant spreadsheet program.

sentations, multiple windows, and database features. The actions are invoked easily with command menus. Advanced systems such as Improv (Figure 5.2b) are attempting to win users with novel ways of showing and manipulating data items and graphs.

5.2.3   Spatial data management

In geographic applications, it seems natural to give a spatial representation in the form of a map that provides a familiar model of reality. The developers of the prototype spatial data-management system (Herot, 1980; 1984) attribute the basic idea to Nicholas Negroponte of MIT. In one early scenario, the user was seated before a color-graphics display of the world and could zoom in on the Pacific Ocean to see markers for convoys of military ships (Figure 5.3). By moving a joystick, the user caused the screen to be filled with silhouettes of individual ships that could be zoomed in on to display detailed data—such as, ultimately, a full-color picture of the captain.

In another scenario, icons representing such different aspects of a corporation as personnel, an organizational chart, travel information, production data, and schedules were shown on a screen. By moving the joystick and zooming in on objects of interest, the user was taken through complex "information spaces" or "I-spaces" to locate the item of interest. A building floorplan showing departments might be displayed; when a department was chosen, individual offices became visible. As the cursor was moved into a room, details of the occupant appeared on the screen. If users chose the wrong room, they merely backed out and tried another. The lost effort was

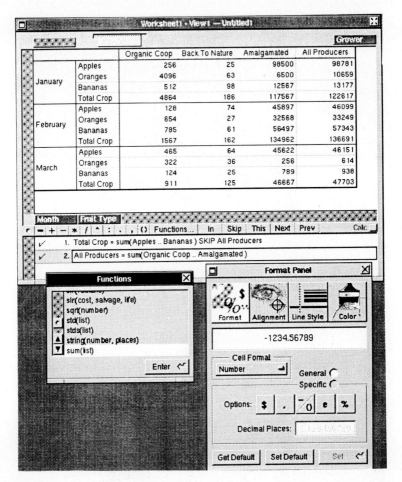

Figure 5.2(b)

Lotus's Improv, a spreadsheet program for the NeXT machine that has novel ways of showing and manipulating data. (Printed with permission of Lotus Development Corporation.)

minimal, and there was no stigma attached to error. The recent Xerox PARC Information Visualizer is an ensemble of tools that permit three-dimensional animated explorations of buildings, cone-shaped file directories, organization charts, a perspective wall that puts featured items up front and centered, and several two- and three-dimensional information layouts (Card et al., 1991).

The Voyager Data Exploration Software for Windows enables users to explore spatial and temporal databases visually. For example, if a map of the United States and an energy-use plot for the previous 30 years are shown on the screen, the user can select a year on the plot and can then see energy use

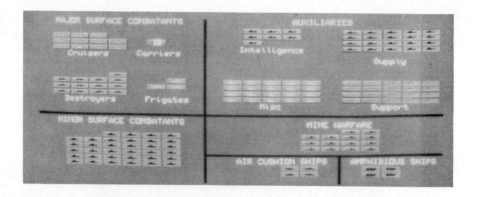

Figure 5.3

The Spatial Data Management System has three displays to show multiple levels of detail or related information. The user moves a joystick to traverse information spaces or to zoom in on a map to see more details about ship convoys. (Courtesy of the Computer Corporation of America, Cambridge, MA.)

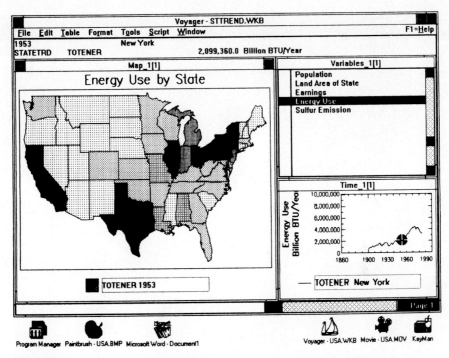

Figure 5.4

The Voyager Data Exploration Software with features for choosing a subset of data to show in detailed plots. Users can click on individual states to see energy use, or on the plot to select the year. (Courtesy of Husar, R. B., Oberman, T., and Hutchins, E. A., Environmental Informatics: Implementation Through the Voyager Data Exploration Software. *Air and Waste Management Association 83rd Annual Meeting*, June 24–29, 1990, Pittsburgh, PA.)

for every state in that year (Figure 5.4). Alternatively, users can retrieve facts about a specific state by pointing and clicking on the map.

The success of a spatial data-management system depends on the skill of the designers in choosing icons, graphical representations, and data layouts that are natural and comprehensible to the user. The joy of zooming in and out, or of gliding over data with a joystick, entices even anxious users, who quickly demand additional power and data.

5.2.4   Video games

For many people, the most exciting, well-engineered, and commercially successful application of these concepts lies in the world of video games (Crawford, 1984). The early but simple and popular game called PONG required the user to rotate a knob that moved a white rectangle on the screen. A white spot acted as a ping-pong ball that ricocheted off the wall

Figure 5.5(a)

Video games. (a) Home video games are enjoyable computer applications that have become extremely popular (©1991 Nintendo. Courtesy of Nintendo).

and had to be hit back by the movable white rectangle. Users developed speed and accuracy in placing the "paddle" to keep the increasingly speedy ball from getting by, while the speaker emitted a ponging sound when the ball bounced. Watching someone else play for 30 seconds is all the training needed to become a competent novice, but many hours of practice are required to become a skilled expert.

Later games, such as Missile Command, Donkey Kong, Pac Man, Tempest, TRON, Centipede, or Space Invaders, were much more sophisticated in their rules, color graphics, and sound effects. Recent games include video-disk images, two-person competition in tennis or karate, still higher resolution, and stereo sound (Figures 5.5a and b). The designers of these games provide stimulating entertainment, a challenge for novices and experts, and many intriguing lessons in the human factors of interface design—somehow, they have found a way to get people to put quarters in the sides of computers. Thirty-million Nintendo game players have penetrated to 70 percent of American households that include 8 to 12 year olds. Brisk sales of

Figure 5.5(b)

Video games employ direct manipulation principles to create a world of action and fantasy, such as a flight simulation of an old plane, *Red Baron*. (©1992 Dynamix, Inc.)

Super Mario Brothers and variations testify to the games' strong attraction, in marked contrast to the anxiety and resistance many users have for office automation equipment.

These games provide a field of action that is simple to understand since it is an abstraction of reality—learning is by analogy. The commands are physical actions, such as button presses, joystick motions, or knob rotations, whose results are shown immediately on the screen. There is no syntax to remember, and therefore there are no syntax-error messages. If users move their spaceships too far left, then they merely use the natural inverse operation of moving back to the right. Error messages are unnecessary because the results of actions are obvious and can be reversed easily. These principles can be applied to office automation, personal computing, or other interactive environments.

Most games continuously display a numeric score so that users can measure their progress and compete with their previous performance, with friends, or with the highest scorers. Typically, the 10 highest scorers get to store their initials in the game for regular display. This strategy provides one

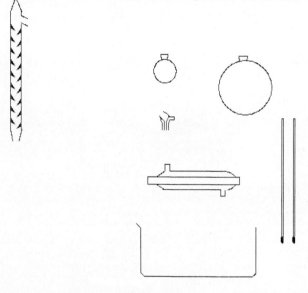

Here are the parts to a distillation apparatus.
Put the apparatus together by touching a piece
and then touching where it goes on the column.

For help press HELP

Figure 5.6(a)

Computer-based instruction can become more appealing with direct manipulation, instead of drill and practice. This early CDC PLATO lesson, written by Stan Smith of the Department of Chemistry at the University of Illinois, allows students to construct a distillation aparatus by using proper finger actions on a touch-sensitive screen. (Figure 5.6a and b: Courtesy of Stan Smith, University of Illinois.) (a) Once the student has assembled the apparatus and begun the experiment, the display shows an animation of the process with the graph of distillation temperature versus volume.

form of positive reinforcement that encourages mastery. Malone's (1981) and our studies with elementary-school children have shown that continuous display of scores is extremely valuable. Machine-generated feedback—such as "Very good" or "You're doing great!"—is not as effective, since the same score means different things to different people. Users prefer to make their own subjective judgments and perceive the machine-generated messages as an annoyance and a deception.

Many educational games use direct manipulation effectively. Elementary- or high-school students can learn about logic by using Rocky Boots, which shows logic circuits visually and lets students progress to more complex tasks by going through doors to enter a series of rooms.

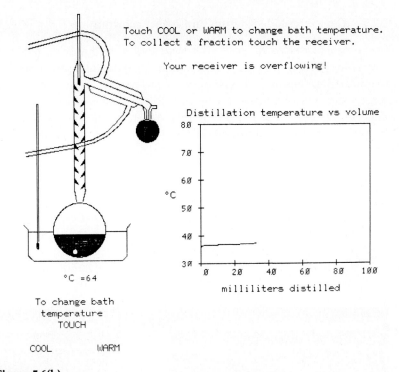

Figure 5.6(b)

The student experimenter has gotten into trouble.

Stan Smith's chemistry lessons on the PLATO system enabled college students to conduct laboratory experiments by touching beakers, pipettes, or burners to assemble and operate equipment (Figure 5.6). A Navy training simulator shows gauges, dials, and knobs that users can manipulate directly to gain experience with boilers, valves, and so on (Hollan et al., 1984). Several versions of the Music Construction Set offer users the possibility of constructing musical scores by selecting and moving notes onto a staff.

Carroll (1982) draws productive analogies between game-playing environments and applications-systems. However, game players are seeking entertainment and focus on the challenge of mastery, whereas applications-systems users focus on their task and may resent the intrusion of forced learning of system constraints. Furthermore, the random events that occur in most games are meant to challenge the user; in nongame designs, however, predictable system behavior is preferred. Game players are engaged in competition with the system, whereas applications-systems users apparently prefer a strong internal locus of control, which gives them the sense of being in charge.

5.2.5   Computer-aided design and manufacturing

Many *computer-aided design* (CAD) systems for automobiles, electronic circuitry, architecture, aircraft, or newspaper layout use principles of direct
manipulation (Figure 5.7). The operator may see a circuit schematic on the
screen and, with lightpen touches, be able to move resistors or capacitors
into or out of the proposed circuit. When the design is complete, the
computer can provide information about current, voltage drops, and fabrica-
tion costs, and warnings about inconsistencies or manufacturing problems.
Similarly, newspaper-layout artists or automobile-body designers can easily
try multiple designs in minutes, and can record promising approaches until
they find a better one.

The pleasures in using these systems stem from the capacity to manipulate the object of interest directly and to generate multiple alternatives
rapidly. Some systems have complex command languages; others have
moved to using cursor action and graphics-oriented commands.

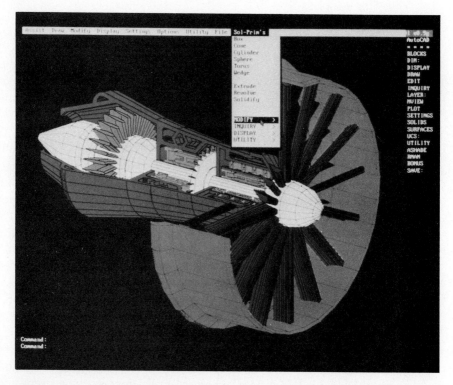

Figure 5.7

Many computer-aided design (CAD) systems use a direct-manipulation interaction
style. This design tool, AutoCAD, supports three-dimensional designs. (Courtesy
of AutoDesk, Inc., Sausalito, CA.)

Another related direction is the world of *computer-aided manufacturing* (CAM) and process control. Honeywell's process-control system provides the manager of an oil refinery, paper mill, or power-utility plant with a colored schematic view of the plant. The schematic may be on eight displays, with red lines indicating a sensor value that is out of normal range. By pressing a single, numbered button (there are no commands to learn or remember), the operator can get a more detailed view of the troubling component; with a second press, the operator can move down the tree structure to examine individual sensors or to reset valves and circuits.

A basic strategy for this design is to eliminate the need for complex commands that need to be recalled only in once-a-year emergency conditions. The schematic of the plant facilitates problem solving by analogy, since the linkage between real-world high temperatures or low pressures and screen representations is so close.

5.2.6   Office automation, databases, and directories

A large part of the success and appeal of the *Query-by-Example* (Zloof, 1975) approach to data manipulation is due to the direct representation of the relations on the screen (Figure 5.8). The user moves a cursor through the

```
Query:

SKI-RESORTS |  NAME  |  CITY  |  STATE  |  LIFTS  |  VERTICAL
-------------------------------------------------------------------
            |  P.    |  P.    |  NY     |         |  P. >1200
            |        |        |         |         |
```

```
Response:

SKI-RESORTS |  NAME         |  CITY         |  VERTICAL
-------------------------------------------------------------------
            |  BELLEAYRE    |  HIGHMOUNT    |  1340
            |  GORE         |  NORTH CREEK  |  2100
            |  HUNTER       |  HUNTER       |  1600
            |  SKI WINDHAM  |  WINDHAM      |  1550
            |  WHITEFACE    |  WIMLINGTON   |  3216
```

Figure 5.8

Zloof's Query-by-Example system shows users a relational-table skeleton and enables them to fill in literals (such as NY or 1200) and to specify fields to be printed (P.). Users can also specify variables to link between relations. In this example, the query produces the NAMEs of ski resorts in NY state that have a vertical drop of more than 1200 feet.

columns of the relational table and enters examples of how the result should look. There are just a few single-letter keywords to supplement the direct-manipulation style. Of course, expressing complex Booleans or mathematical operations requires knowledge of syntactic forms. Still, the basic ideas and facilities in this language can be learned within 1/2 hour by many nonprogrammers. Query-by-Example succeeds because novices can begin working with just a little training, yet there is ample power for the expert. Directly manipulating the cursor across the relation skeleton is simple, and showing the linking variable by giving an example is intuitively clear to someone who understands tabular data. Zloof (1982) expands his ideas into Office-by-Example, which smoothly integrates database search with word processing, electronic mail, business graphics, and menu creation. The OfficeVision line of products from IBM enables integration of OS/2 applications with networks of mainframe machines to support office work.

Other designers of advanced office-automation systems have made use of direct-manipulation principles. The pioneering Xerox Star (Smith et al., 1982) offered sophisticated text-formatting options, graphics, multiple fonts, and a high-resolution, cursor-based user interface (Figure 5.9). Users could move a document icon to a printer icon to generate a hard-copy printout. The Apple Lisa system elegantly applied many of the principles of direct manipulation and, although it was not a commercial success, it laid the groundwork for the successful Macintosh. The Macintosh designers drew from the Star and Lisa experience, but made many simplifying decisions while preserving adequate power for users (Figure 5.10). The hardware and software designs supported rapid and continuous graphical interaction for pull-down menus, window manipulation, editing of graphics and text, and dragging of icons. Variations on the Macintosh appeared soon afterward for other popular personal computers, such as the IBM PS/2 (Figure 5.11).

Studies of users of direct-manipulation interfaces have confirmed the advantages for at least some users and tasks. In a study of 30 novices, MS-DOS commands for creating, copying, renaming, and erasing files were contrasted with Macintosh direct-manipulation actions. After training and practice, average task times were 5.8 minutes versus 4.8 minutes, and average errors were 2.0 versus 0.8 (Margono and Shneiderman, 1987). Subjective preference also favored the direct-manipulation interface. In a study of a command-line versus a direct-manipulation database interface, 55 "computer naive but keyboard literate" users made more than twice as many errors with the command line format. No significant differences in time were found (Morgan et al., 1991). These users preferred the direct-manipulation interface overall, and rated it as more stimulating, easier, and more adequately powerful. Both reports caution about generalizing the results to more experienced users. A study with novices and experienced users was cosponsored by Microsoft and Zenith Data Systems (Temple,

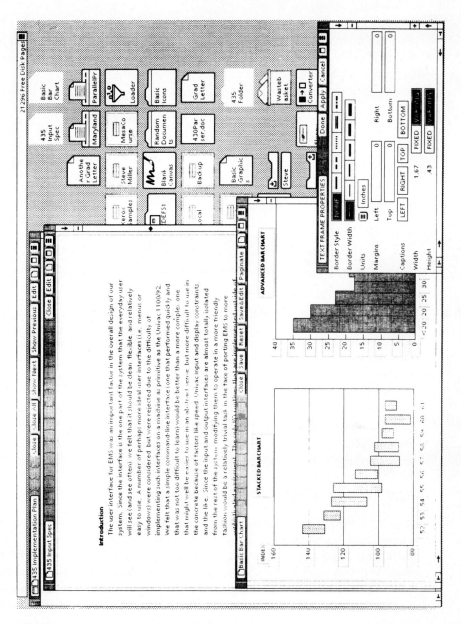

Figure 5.9

The Xerox Star 8010 with the ViewPoint system enables users to create documents with multiple fonts and graphics. This session shows the Text Frame Properties sheet over sample bar charts, with a document in the background and many desktop icons available for selection. (Prepared by Steve Miller, University of Maryland.)

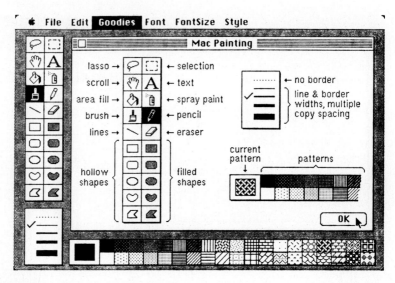

Figure 5.10

The original Apple Macintosh MacPaint program offers a command menu on the top, a menu of action icons on the left, a choice of line thicknesses on the lower left, and a palette of texture on the bottom. All actions can be accomplished with only the mouse. (Photo courtesy of Apple Computer, Inc.)

Barker, and Sloane, Inc., 1990). Although details about subjects, interfaces, and tasks were not reported, the results showed improved productivity and reduced fatigue for experienced users with a graphical user interface, as compared with a character-based user interface.

5.2.7   Further examples of direct manipulation

The trick in creating a direct-manipulation system is to come up with an appropriate representation or model of reality. Some designers may find it difficult to think about information problems in a visual form; with practice, however, they may find it more natural. With many applications, the jump to visual language may be difficult; later, however, users and designers can hardly imagine why anyone would want to use a complex syntactic notation to describe an essentially visual process.

Several designers applied direct manipulation to a stack of cards portraying a set of addresses, telephone numbers, events, and so on. Clicking on a card brings it to the front, and the stack of cards moves to preserve alphabetic ordering (see Figure 9.13). This simple card-deck metaphor, combined with other notions (Heckel, 1991) led to Bill Atkinson's innovative development of HyperCard stacks in 1987 (Section 11.4). Billed as a way to "create your own applications for gathering, organizing, presenting, search-

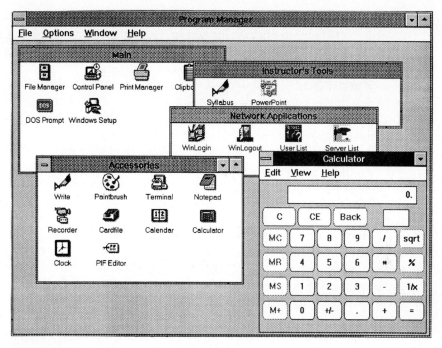

Figure 5.11

Microsoft Windows 3.0 and other systems on IBM's PS/2 offered variations on the direct-manipulation style popularized by the Macintosh. (Screen shot ©1985–1991 Microsoft Corporation. Reprinted with permission from Microsoft Corporation, Redmond, WA.)

ing, and customizing information," HyperCard quickly spawned variants such as SuperCard and ToolBook. Each has a scripting language to enable users to create appealing graphics applications.

Checkbook maintenance and searching can be done in a direct manipulation manner by displaying a checkbook register with labeled columns for check number, date, payee, and amount, as is done in the Quicken product from Intuit, Inc. Changes can be made in place, new entries can be made at the first blank line, and a check mark can be made to indicate verification against a monthly report or bank statement. Users can search for a particular payee by filling in a blank `payee` field and then typing a ?.

Bibliographic searching has more elaborate requirements, but a basic system could be built by first showing the user a wall of labeled catalog-index drawers. A cursor in the shape of a human hand might be moved over to the section labeled `Author Index` and to the drawer labeled `F-L`. Depressing the button on the joystick or mouse would cause the drawer to open, revealing an array of index cards with tabs offering a finer index. By moving the cursor-hand and depressing the selection button, the user would make the individual index cards appear. Depressing the button while holding a card would cause a copy of the card to be made in the user's notebook, also represented on the screen. Entries in the notebook might be edited to create a printed bibliography, or combined with other entries to perform set intersections or unions. Copies of entries could be stored on user files or transmitted to colleagues by electronic mail. It is easy to visualize many alternate approaches, so careful design and experimental testing would be necessary to sort out the successful comprehensible approaches from the idiosyncratic ones.

Why not do airline reservations by showing the user a map and prompting for cursor motion to the departing and arriving cities? Then, use a calendar to select the date, and a clock to indicate the time. Seat selection is done by showing the seating plan of the plane on the screen, with a diagonal line to indicate an already-reserved seat.

The term *direct manipulation* is accurately applied to describe the programming of some industrial robot tools. The operator holds the robot "hand" and guides it through a spray painting or welding task while the controlling computer records every action. The control computer can then operate the robot automatically and repeat the precise action as many times as necessary.

Why not teach students about polynomial equations by letting them move sliders to set values for the coefficients and watch how the graph changes, where the y-axis intercept occurs, or how the derivative equation reacts (Shneiderman, 1974). Similarly, direct manipulation of sliders for red, green, and blue is a satisfying way to explore color space. Slider-based dynamic queries are a powerful tool for information exploration (Section 11.8).

These ideas are sketches for real systems. Competent designers and implementers must complete the sketches and fill in the details. Direct manipulation has the power to attract users because it is comprehensible, natural, rapid, and even enjoyable. If actions are simple, reversibility ensured, and retention easy, then anxiety recedes and satisfaction flows in.

5.3   Explanations of Direct Manipulation

Several authors have attempted to describe the component principles of direct manipulation. An imaginative observer of interactive system designs, Ted Nelson (1980), perceives user excitement when the interface is constructed by what he calls the *principle of virtuality*—a representation of reality that can be manipulated. Rutkowski (1982) conveys a similar concept in his *principle of transparency*: "The user is able to apply intellect directly to the task; the tool itself seems to disappear."

Heckel (1991) laments that "Our instincts and training as engineers encourage us to think logically instead of visually, and this is counterproductive to friendly design." He suggests that thinking like a filmmaker can be helpful for interactive systems designers: "When I design a product, I think of my program as giving a performance for its user."

Hutchins et al. (1986) review the concepts of direct manipulation and offer a thoughtful decomposition of concerns. They describe the "feeling of involvement directly with a world of objects rather than of communicating with an intermediary," and clarify how direct manipulation breaches the *gulf of execution* and the *gulf of explanation*.

These writers and others (Ziegler and Fahnrich, 1988; Thimbleby, 1990; Phillips and Apperley, 1991) support the growing recognition that a new form of interactive system is emerging. Much credit also goes to the individual designers who have created systems that exemplify aspects of direct manipulation.

Another perspective on direct manipulation comes from the psychology literature on *problem-solving* and *learning research*. Suitable representations of problems have been clearly shown to be critical to solution finding and to learning. Polya (1957) suggests drawing a picture to represent mathematical problems. This approach is in harmony with Maria Montessori's teaching methods for children (Montessori, 1964). She proposed use of physical objects, such as beads or wooden sticks, to convey such mathematical principles as addition, multiplication, or size comparison. Bruner (1966) extended the physical-representation idea to cover polynomial factoring and other mathematical principles. Carroll, Thomas, and Malhotra (1980) found that subjects given spatial representation were faster and more successful in problem solving than were subjects given an isomorphic problem with a temporal representation. Similarly, Te'eni (1990) found that the feedback in direct-manipulation designs was effective in reducing users' logical errors in a task requiring statistical analysis of student grades. The advantage appears to stem from having the data entry and display combined in a single location on the display. Deeper understanding of the relationship between problem solving and visual perception can be obtained from Arnheim (1972) and McKim (1972).

Physical, spatial, or visual representations also appear to be easier to retain and manipulate than do textual or numeric representations. Wertheimer (1959) found that subjects who memorized the formula for the area of a parallelogram, $A = h \times b$, rapidly succeeded in doing such calculations. On the other hand, subjects who were given the structural understanding of cutting off a triangle from one end and placing it on the other end could more effectively retain the knowledge and generalize it to solve related problems. In plane-geometry theorem proving, spatial representation facilitates discovery of proof procedures over a strictly axiomatic representation of Euclidean geometry. The diagram provides heuristics that are difficult to extract from the axioms. Similarly, students are often encouraged to solve algebraic word problems by drawing a picture to represent that problem.

Papert's (1980) LOGO language creates a mathematical microworld in which the principles of geometry are visible. Based on the Swiss psychologist Jean Piaget's theory of child development, LOGO offers students the opportunity to create line drawings easily with an electronic turtle displayed on a screen. In this environment, users derive rapid feedback about their programs, can determine what has happened easily, can spot and repair errors quickly, and can gain satisfaction from creative production of drawings. These features are all characteristic of a direct-manipulation environment.

5.3.1   Problems with direct manipulation

Spatial or visual representations are not necessarily an improvement over text, because they may be too spread out, causing off-page connectors on paper or tedious scrolling on displays. In professional programming, use of high-level flowcharts and database-schema diagrams can be helpful for some tasks, but there is a danger that they will be confusing. Similarly, direct-manipulation designs may consume valuable screen space and thus force valuable information offscreen, requiring scrolling or multiple actions. Studies of flowchart usage in programming (Shneiderman, 1982) and in business graphics (Tullis, 1981) show that these visual representations can produce poorer performance than the equivalent program text or tabular presentation, probably because of the low density of information in the visual displays. For experienced users, a tabular textual display of 50 document names may be more appealing than only 10 document graphic icons with the names abbreviated to fit the icon size.

A second problem is that users must learn the meaning of components of the visual representation. A graphic icon may be meaningful to the designer, but may require as much or more learning time than a word. Some airports that serve multilingual communities use graphic icons extensively, but the meanings of these icons may not be obvious. Similarly, some computer terminals designed for international use have icons in place of names, but the meaning is not always clear.

A third problem is that the visual representation may be misleading. Users may grasp the analogical representation rapidly, but then draw incorrect conclusions about permissible actions. Ample testing must be carried out to refine the displayed objects and actions and to minimize negative side effects.

A fourth problem is that, for experienced typists, moving a mouse or raising a finger to point may sometimes be slower than typing. This problem is especially likely to occur if the user is familiar with a compact notation, such as arithmetic expressions, that is easy to enter from a keyboard, but may be more difficult with mouse-based selection. The keyboard remains the most effective direct-manipulation device for some tasks.

Choosing the right objects and actions is not an easy task. Simple metaphors, analogies, or models with a minimal set of concepts seem most appropriate to start. Mixing metaphors from two sources may add complexity that contributes to confusion. The emotional tone of the metaphor should be inviting rather than distasteful or inappropriate (Carroll and Thomas, 1982)—sewage-disposal systems are an inappropriate metaphor for electronic message systems. Since the users may not share the metaphor, analogy, or conceptual model with the designer, ample testing is required. For help in training, an explicit statement of the model, the assumptions, and the limitations is necessary.

5.3.2   The SSOA model explanation of direct manipulation

The attraction of direct manipulation is apparent in the enthusiasm of the users. The designers of the examples in Section 5.2 had an innovative inspiration and an intuitive grasp of what users would want. Each example has features that could be criticized, but it seems more productive to construct an integrated portrait of direct manipulation:

1. Continuous representation of the objects and actions of interest
2. Physical actions or presses of labeled buttons instead of complex syntax
3. Rapid incremental reversible operations whose effect on the object of interest is immediately visible

Using these three principles, it is possible to design systems that have these beneficial attributes:

- Novices can learn basic functionality quickly, usually through a demonstration by a more experienced user.
- Experts can work rapidly to carry out a wide range of tasks, even defining new functions and features.
- Knowledgeable intermittent users can retain operational concepts.
- Error messages are rarely needed.
- Users can immediately see if their actions are furthering their goals, and, if the actions are counterproductive, they can simply change the direction of their activity.
- Users experience less anxiety because the system is comprehensible and because actions can be reversed so easily.
- Users gain confidence and mastery because they are the initiators of action, they feel in control, and the system responses are predictable.

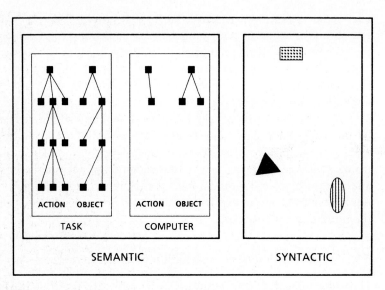

Figure 5.12

Users of direct-manipulation systems, may need to have substantial task-domain semantic knowledge. However, users must acquire only a modest amount of computer-related semantic knowledge and syntactic knowledge.

The success of direct manipulation is understandable in the context of the SSOA model. The object of interest is displayed so that actions are directly in the high-level task domain. There is little need for the mental decomposition of tasks into multiple commands with a complex syntactic form. On the contrary, each action produces a comprehensible result in the task domain that is visible immediately. The closeness of the task to the action syntax reduces operator problem-solving load and stress. This principle is related to the principle of stimulus–response compatibility in the human-factors literature.

The task semantics dominate the users' concerns, and the distraction of dealing with the computer semantics and the syntax is reduced (Figure 5.12).

Dealing with representations of objects may be more "natural" and closer to innate human capabilities: Action and visual skills emerged well before language in human evolution. Psychologists have long known that spatial relationships and actions are grasped more quickly with visual rather than linguistic representations. Furthermore, intuition and discovery are often promoted by suitable visual representations of formal mathematical systems.

The Swiss psychologist Jean Piaget described *four stages of development*: *sensorimotor* (from birth to approximately 2 years), *preoperational* (2 to 7 years), *concrete operational* (7 to 11 years), and *formal operations* (begins at approximately 11 years) (Copeland, 1979). According to this theory, physical actions on an object are comprehensible during the concrete operational stage, and children acquire the concept of conservation or invariance. At about age 11, children enter the formal-operations stage, in which they use symbol manipulation to represent actions on objects. Since mathematics and programming require abstract thinking, it is more difficult for children, and a greater effort must be made to link the symbolic representation to the actual object. Direct manipulation brings activity to the concrete-operational stage, thus making certain tasks easier for children and adults.

It is easy to envision use of direct manipulation in cases where the task is confined to a small number of objects and simple actions. In complex applications, it may be more difficult to design a direct-manipulation interface. On the other hand, display editors provide impressive functionality in a natural way. The limits of direct manipulation will be determined by the imagination and skill of the designer. With more examples and experience, researchers should be able to test competing theories about the most effective metaphor or analogy. Familiar visual analogies may be more appealing to users in the early stages of learning about the system; more specific, abstract models may be more useful during regular use.

5.4   Visual Thinking and Icons

The concepts of a *visual language* and of *visual thinking* were promoted by Arnheim (1972), and were embraced by commercial graphic designers (Verplank, 1988), semiotically oriented academics (*semiotics* is the study of signs and symbols), and data-visualization gurus. The computer provides a remarkable visual environment for revealing structure, showing relationship, and enabling interactivity that attracts users with artistic, right-brained, holistic, intuitive personalities. The increasingly visual nature of computer interfaces can sometimes challenge or even threaten the logical, linear, text-oriented, left-brained, compulsive, rational programmers who were the heart of the first generation of hackers. Although these stereotypes—or caricatures—will not stand up to scientific analysis, they do convey the dual paths that computing is following. The new visual directions are sometimes scorned by the traditionalists as *WIMP* (windows, icons, mouse, and pull-down menus) interfaces, whereas the command-line devotees are seen as inflexible, or even stubborn.

There is evidence that different people have different cognitive styles, and it is quite understandable that individual preferences may vary. Just as there are multiple ice-cream flavors or car models, so too there will be multiple interface styles. It may be that preferences will vary by user and by tasks. So

Figure 5.13

A small set of small, but effective, icons with no labels to convey the formatting actions of left, center, right, and dual justification, and a pair of action icons plus a label to convey printing orientation. (©Apple Computer, Inc., Cupertino, CA. Used with permission.)

Orientation

respect is due to each community, and the designer's goal is to provide the best of each style and the means to cross over when desired.

The conflict between text and graphics becomes most heated when the issue of *icons* is raised. Maybe it is not surprising the dictionary definitions of *icon* usually refer to religious images, but the central notion is that an icon is an image, picture, or symbol representing a concept (Gittins, 1986; Rogers, 1989). In the computer world, icons are usually small (approximately 1 inch square, or 64 by 64 pixels) representations of a file or program (an object or action; see Figures 5.13, 5.14, and 5.15). Smaller icons are often used to save space or to be integrated in other objects, such as a window border (see Chapter 9). It is not surprising that icons are often used in painting programs to represent the tools or actions (lasso or scissors to cut out an image, brush for painting, pencil for drawing, eraser to wipe clean), whereas word

Figure 5.14

Macintosh icon collection: folder with the manuscript for this book, applications MacWrite II and MacPaint, a MacPaint image. On the second line are four documents in different formats, as indicated by their varied styles. (Courtesy of Claris Corp. Microsoft Word: Screen shot ©1984–1990 Microsoft Corporation. Reprinted with permission from Microsoft Corporation, Redmond, WA.)

Figure 5.15

SAS uses icons with labels to the right to identify different applications. (Screens reprinted by permission. Copyright 1991 by SAS Institute Inc.)

processors usually have textual menus for their actions. This difference appears to reflect the differing cognitive styles of visually and textually oriented users, or at least differences in the tasks. Maybe, while you are working on visually oriented tasks, it is helpful to "stay visual" by using icons, whereas, while you are working on a text document, it is helpful to "stay textual" by using textual menus.

For situations where both a visual icon or a textual item are possible—for example, in a directory listing—designers have two interwoven issues: how to decide between icons and text and how to design icons. The well-established highway signs are a useful source of experience. Icons are unbeatable for showing things such as a road curve, but sometimes a phrase such as ONE WAY—DO NOT ENTER is more comprehensible than an icon. Of course, the smorgasbord approach is to have a little of each (as with, for example, the octagonal STOP sign) and there is evidence that icons plus words are effective in computing situations (Norman, 1991). So the answer to the first question (deciding between icons and text) depends not only on the users and the tasks, but also on the quality of the icons or the words that are proposed. Textual menu choices are covered in Chapter 3; many of the principles carry over. In addition, these icon-specific guidelines should be considered:

- Represent the object or action in a familiar and recognizable manner.
- Limit the number of different icons.
- Make the icon stand out from its background.
- Consider three-dimensional icons; they are eye-catching, but also can be distracting.
- Ensure that a single selected icon is clearly visible when surrounded by unselected icons.
- Make each icon distinctive from every other icon.
- Ensure the harmoniousness of each icon as a member of a family of icons.
- Design the movement animation: when dragging an icon, the user might move the whole icon, just a frame, possibly a grayed-out version, or a black box.
- Add detailed information, such as shading to show size of a file (larger shadow indicates larger file), thickness to show breadth of a directory folder (thicker means more files inside), color to show the age of a document (older might be yellower or grayer), or animation to show how much of a document has been printed (a document folder is absorbed progressively into the printer icon).
- Explore the use of combinations of icons to create new objects or actions—for example, dragging a document icon to a folder, trashcan, outbox, or printer icon has great utility. Can a document be appended or prepended to another document by pasting of adjacent icons? Can security levels be set by dragging a document or folder to a guard dog, police car, or vault icon? Can two database icons be intersected by overlapping of the icons?

Marcus (1992) applies semiotics as a guide to four levels of icon design:

1. *Lexical qualities*: Machine-generated marks—pixel shape, color, brightness, blinking
2. *Syntactics*: Appearance and movement—lines, patterns, modular parts, size, shape
3. *Semantics*: Objects represented—concrete, abstract, part–whole
4. *Pragmatics*: Overall legible, utility, identifiable, memorable, pleasing

He recommends starting by creating quick sketches, pushing for consistent style, designing a layout grid, simplifying appearance, and evaluating the designs by testing with users. We might consider a fifth level of icon design:

5. *Dynamics*: Receptivity to clicks—highlighting, dragging, combining

The dynamics of icons might also include a rich set of gestures with a mouse, touchscreen, or pen. The gestures might indicate copy (up and down), delete (a cross), edit (circle), etc. Icons might also have associated sounds. For example, if each document icon had a tone associated with it (the lower the tone, the bigger the document), then, when a directory was opened, each tone might be played simultaneously or sequentially. Users might get used to the symphony played by each directory and could detect certain features or anomalies.

Icon design becomes more interesting as computer hardware improves and as designers become more creative. Animated icons that demonstrate their function improve online help capabilities (see Chapter 12). Beyond simple icons, there have been increasing numbers of visual programming languages (Chang, 1990; Shu, 1988; Glinert et al., 1990) and specialized languages for mechanical engineering, circuit design, and database query (see Chapter 11).

5.5   Direct-Manipulation Programming

Performing tasks by direct manipulation is not the only goal. It should be possible to do programming by direct manipulation as well, for at least some problems. Robot programming is sometimes done by moving the robot arm through a sequence of steps that are later replayed, possibly at higher speed. This example seems to be a good candidate for generalization. How about moving a drill press or a surgical tool through a complex series of motions that are then repeated exactly? How about programming a car by driving it once through a maze and then having the car repeat the path? In fact, these direct-manipulation programming ideas are implemented in modest ways with automobile radios that the user presets by turning the frequency control knob and then pulling out a button. When the button is depressed, the radio tunes to the frequency. Some professional television-camera supports allow the operator to program a sequence of pans or zooms and then to replay it smoothly when required.

Programming of physical devices by direct manipulation seems quite natural, but an adequate visual representation of information may make direct-manipulation programming possible in other domains. Several word processors allow users to create macros by simply performing a sequence of commands that is stored for later reuse. WordPerfect enables the creation of macros that are sequences of text, special function keys such as TAB, and other WordPerfect commands (Figure 5.16). EMACS allows its rich set of functions, including regular expression searching to be recorded into macros. Macros can invoke each other, leading to complex programming possibilities. These and other systems allow users to create programs with

```
{DISPLAY OFF}
{Tab}{Tab}{Tab}{Tab}Ben-Shneiderman{Enter}
{Tab}{Tab}{Tab}{Tab}Department-of-Computer-Science{Enter}
{Enter}
{Tab}{Tab}{Tab}{Tab}May-25,-1992{Enter}
{Enter}
{Enter}
Dear--,{Enter}
{Enter}
{Enter}
{Enter}
{Tab}{Tab}{Tab}{Tab}Sincerely-yours,{Enter}
```

Figure 5.16

This WordPerfect macro produces a template of a letter.

nonvarying action sequences using direct manipulation, but strategies for including loops and conditionals vary. EMACS allows macros to be encased in a loop with simple repeat factors. By resorting to textual programming languages, EMACS and WordPerfect allow users to attach more general control structures.

Spreadsheet packages, such as LOTUS 1-2-3, Excel, and Quattro, have rich programming languages and allow users to create portions of programs by carrying out standard spreadsheet operations. The result of the operations is stored in another part of the spreadsheet and can be edited, printed, and stored in a textual form. Macro facilities in graphic user interfaces are more challenging to design than are macro facilities in traditional command interfaces, but MacroMaker and Tempo2 on the Macintosh, and the Hewlett-Packard NewWave Agent facility on the IBM PCs, are current standouts. The MACRO command of Direct Manipulation Disk Operating System (DMDOS) (Iseki and Shneiderman, 1986) was an early attempt to support a limited form of programming for file movement, copying, and directory commands.

A delightful children's program, Delta Drawing from Spinnaker, enables children to move a cursor and to draw on the screen by typing D to draw one unit, R to rotate right 30 degrees, and so on. The 40 commands provide rich possibilities for drawing various kinds of screen images. In addition, Delta Drawing allows users to save, edit, and then invoke programs. For example, a user can draw a circle by saving the program consisting of a D and a R. Invoking the program with the argument 12 then produces a rough 12-sided circle.

Smith (1977) inspired work in this area with his Pygmalion system that allowed arithmetic programs to be specified visually with icons. A number of research projects have attempted to create direct manipulation programming systems (Rubin et al., 1985). Halbert's Smallstar (1984) was a programming-by-example system to enable programming of Xerox Star actions. Maulsby and Witten (1989) developed a system that could induce or infer a program from examples, questioning the users to resolve ambiguities. Myers (1991) coined the phrase *demonstrational programming* to characterize these efforts as programming-by-example or programming-with-examples in which users can create macros by simply doing their tasks and letting the system construct the proper generalization automatically to form a macro. Cypher (1991) built and ran a usability test with seven subjects for his EAGER system that monitored user actions within HyperCard. When EAGER recognized two similar sequences, a small smiling cat appeared on the screen to offer the users help in carrying out further iterations. Cypher's success with two specific tasks is encouraging, but more work is needed to generalize this approach.

If designers are to create a general tool that works reliably in many situations, it they must meet the *five challenges of programming in the user interface* (PITUI) (Potter, 1992):

1. Sufficient computational generality (conditionals, iteration)

2. Access to the appropriate data structures (file structures for directories, structural representations of graphical objects) and operators (selectors, Booleans, specialized operators of applications)

3. Ease in programming (by example, by demonstration, modularity, argument passing) and editing programs

4. Simplicity in invocation and assignment of arguments (direct manipulation, simple library strategies with meaningful names or icons, in-context execution, and availability of result)

5. Low risk (high probability of bug-free programs, halt and resume facilities to permit partial executions, undo operations to enable repair of unanticipated damage)

The goal of PITUI is to allow users easily and reliably to repeat automatically the actions that they can perform manually in the user interface. Rather than depending on unpredictable inferencing, users will be able to indicate their intentions explicitly by manipulating objects and actions. The design of direct-manipulation systems will undoubtedly be influenced by the need to support PITUI. This influence will be a positive step that will also facilitate history keeping, undo, and online help.

5.6   Home Automation

Internationally, many companies have logically concluded that the next big market will be the inclusion of richer controls in homes. Simple ideas such as turning off all the lights with a single button or remote control of devices (either from one part of the home to another, from outside, or by programmed delays) are being extended in elaborate systems that channel audio and video throughout the house, schedule lawn watering as a function of ground moisture, offer video surveillance and burglar alarms, and provide multiple-zone environmental controls plus detailed maintenance records. Demonstrations such as the Smart House project in Upper Marlboro, Maryland, and installations such as those by Custom Command Systems, are a testing ground for the next generation.

Some futurists and marketing specialists promote voice controls and home robots, but the practical reality is more tied to traditional pushbuttons, remote controllers, telephone keypads, and especially touchscreens, with the latter proving to be the most popular. Installations with two to 10 touchscreens spread around the house should satisfy most homeowners. Providing direct-manipulation controls with rich feedback is vital in these applications. Users are willing to take training, but operation must be rapid and easy to remember even if used only once or twice a year (such as spring and fall adjustments for daylight-savings time).

Our studies (Plaisant et al., 1990; Plaisant and Shneiderman, 1991) explored four touchscreen designs, all based on direct-manipulation principles, for scheduling operations such as VCR recording or light switching:

1. A digital clock that the user sets by pressing step keys (similar to onscreen programming in current video-cassette players)
2. A 24-hour circular clock whose hands can be dragged with the fingers
3. A 12-hour circular clock (plus A.M.–P.M. toggle) whose hands can be dragged with the fingers (Figure 5.17)
4. A 24-hour time line in which ON–OFF flags can be placed to indicate start–stop times (Figure 5.18)

Our results indicated that the 24-hour time line was easiest to understand and use. Direct-manipulation principles were central to this design; users selected dates by touching a monthly calendar, and times by moving the ON or OFF flags on to the 24-hour time line. The flags were an effective way of representing the ON or OFF actions and of specifying times without use of a keyboard. The capacity to adjust the flag locations incrementally, and the ease of removing them, were additional benefits. We are extending the design to accommodate more complex tasks, such as scheduling and synchronization of multiple devices, searching through schedules to find dates with specific events, scheduling repeated events (close curtains every night at dusk, turn lights on every Friday night at 7 P.M., record status monthly), and long-duration events. A generalization of the flags-on-a-line idea was applied to heating control, where users specified upper and lower bounds by dragging flags on a thermometer.

Many interesting product suggestions have emerged during our trials—for example, an alarm clock that would ring only on weekdays, thus

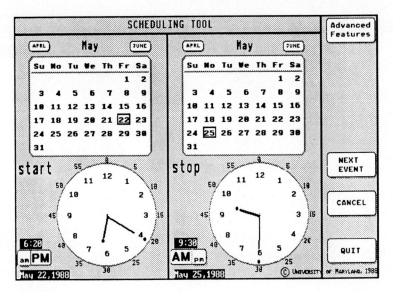

Figure 5.17

This scheduler shows two calendars for start and stop dates plus, two 12-hour
circular clocks with hands that can be dragged to set start and stop times.
(© University of Maryland, 1988.)

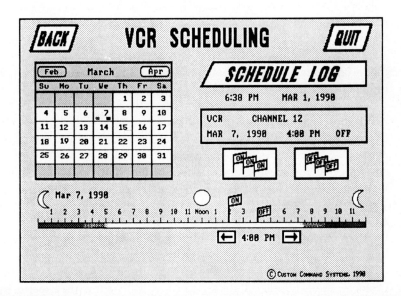

Figure 5.18

This 24-hour time line scheduler was most successful in our usability studies. The
users select a date by pointing to the calendar, and then drag ON and OFF flags to
the 24-hour time lines. The feedback is a red line on the calendar and the time
lines. (© 1990 Custom Command Systems, College Park, MD.)

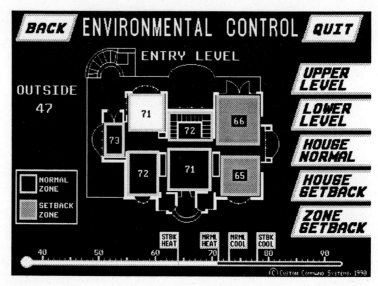

Figure 5.19

Direct-manipulation designs emphasize task-domain graphics, such as this floorplan of a private home used to set temperatures. (© 1990 Custom Command Systems, College Park, MD.)

avoiding the oversight that leads to a ruined Saturday morning when the alarm rings at 6 A.M. Other innovations include programming appliances such as washers, dryers, and ovens to run at night, when electricity costs might be lower. Utility companies are eager to see such devices installed to reduce peak loads.

Since so much of home control involves the room layouts and floorplans, many direct-manipulation actions take place on a display of the floorplan (Figure 5.19), with selectable icons for each status indicator (such as burglar alarm, heat sensor, or smoke detector), and for each activator (such as curtain or shade closing and opening motors, airconditioning or heating vent controllers, or audio and video speaker or screen). People could route sound from a compact-disc player located in the living room to the bedroom and kitchen by merely dragging the CD icon into those rooms. Sound volume control can be accomplished by having the user move a marker on a linear scale.

The simple act of turning a device ON or OFF proved to be an interesting problem. Wall-mounted light switches typically show their status by up for ON and down for OFF. Most people have learned this standard and can get what they want on the first try, if they know which switch to throw to turn on a specific light. Laying out the switches to reflect the floorplan does solve the problem quite nicely (Norman, 1988). Visitors may have problems

Figure 5.20

Varying designs for toggle buttons using three-dimensional graphic characteristics, designed by Catherine Plaisant.

because, in some countries, ON and OFF are reversed or the up–down switches have been replaced by push buttons. To explore possibilities, we constructed six kinds of touchscreen ON–OFF buttons with three-dimensional animation and sound (Figure 5.20). There were significant differences in user preferences, with high marks going to the simple button, rocker, and multiple push buttons. The multiple push buttons have a readily comprehensible visual presentation, and they generalize nicely to multiple state devices (OFF, LOW, MEDIUM, HIGH).

Controlling complex home equipment from a touchscreen by direct manipulation reshapes how we think of homes and their residents. New questions arise, such as whether residents will feel safer, be happier, save more money, or experience more relaxation. Are there new notations such as petri net variants or role–task diagrams for describing home automation and the social relations among residents? The benefits to users with disabilities and elderly users were often on our minds as we designed these systems, since these people may be substantial beneficiaries of this technology, even though initial implementations are for the healthy and wealthy.

5.7   Remote Direct Manipulation

There are great opportunities for the remote control of devices if acceptable user interfaces can be constructed. If designers can provide adequate feedback in sufficient time to permit effective decision making, then attractive applications in office automation, computer-supported collaborative work, education, and information services may become viable. Remote-controlled environments in medicine could enable specialists to provide consultations more rapidly, or allow surgeons to conduct more complex procedures during operations. Home-automation applications could extend remote operation of telephone-answering machines to security and access systems, energy control, and operation of appliances. Scientific applications in space, underwater, or in hostile environments can enable new research projects to be conducted economically and safely (Sheridan, 1987; Uttal, 1989).

In traditional direct-manipulation systems, the objects and actions of interest are shown continuously; users generally point, click, or drag, rather than type; and feedback, indicating change, is immediate. However, when the devices being operated are remote, these goals may not be realizable, and designers must expend additional effort to cope with slower response, incomplete feedback, increased likelihood of breakdowns, and more complex error recovery. The problems are strongly connected to the hardware, physical environment, network design, and the task domain.

5.7.1   The Corabi telepathology workstation

Telemedicine is the practice of medicine over communication links. The physician specialist being consulted and the patient's primary physician are in different locations. Corabi International Telemetrics developed the first telepathology system (Weinstein et al., 1989) that allows a pathologist to examine tissue samples or body fluids under a remotely located microscope. The transmitting workstation has a high-resolution camera mounted on a motorized light microscope. The image is transmitted via broadband satellite, microwave, or cable. The consulting pathologist at the receiving workstation can manipulate the microscope using a keypad, and can see a high-resolution image of the magnified sample. Both physicians talk by telephone to coordinate control and to request slides that are placed manually under the microscope (see Figure 5.21).

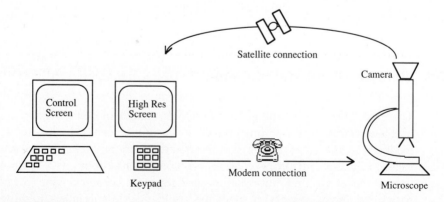

Figure 5.21

A simplified diagram of a telepathology system showing control actions sent by telephone, and images sent by satellite.

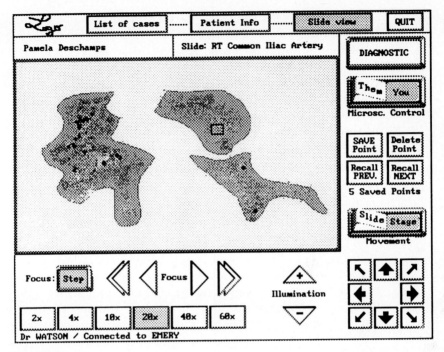

Figure 5.22

The control screen of a telepathology system showing the global view of the slide and the microscope stage position marked by a rectangle. Controls are for illumination, focus, magnification, and movement of the stage.

The pathologist uses a keypad (with arrows keys and function keys) and a large number of buttons and toggles to operate the microscope controls for

- Magnification (three or six objectives)
- Focus (coarse and fine bidirectional control)
- Illumination (bidirectional adjustment continuous or by step)
- Position (two-dimensional placement of the slide under the microscope objective)

A proposed improvement for the control screen consolidates the multiple controls (Figure 5.22).

5.7.2   Typical problems of remote direct manipulation

The architecture of remote environments introduces several complicating factors:

- *Time delays:* The network hardware and software cause delays in sending user actions and receiving feedback: *transmission delays,* the time it takes for the command to reach the microscope (in our case, transmitting the command through the modem), and *operation delays*, the time until the microscope responds (Van de Vegte et al., 1990). These delays in the system prevent the operator from knowing the current status of the system. For example, if a positioning command has been issued, it may take several seconds for the slide to start moving. As the feedback appears showing the motion, the users may recognize that they are going to overshoot their destination, but a few seconds will pass before the stopping command takes effect.

- *Incomplete feedback:* Devices originally designed for direct control may not have adequate sensors or status indicators. For instance, our microscope can report its current position, but it does so so slowly that it cannot be used continuously. Thus, it is not possible to indicate on the control screen the exact current position relative to the start and desired positions.

- *Feedback from multiple sources:* Incomplete feedback does not imply no feedback. The image received on the high-resolution screen is the main feedback to evaluate the result of an action. In addition, the microscope can occasionally report its exact position, allowing recalibration of the status display. It is also possible to indicate the estimated stage position during the execution of a movement. This estimated feedback can be used as a progress indicator whose accuracy depends on the variability of the time delays. To comply with the physical incompatibility between the high-resolution feedback (analog image) and the rest of the system (digital), the multiple feedbacks are spread over several screens. Thus, the pathologists are forced to switch back and forth between multiple sources of feedback, increasing their cognitive load.

- *Unanticipated interferences:* Since the devices operated are remote, and may be also operated by other persons in this or another remote location, unanticipated interferences are more likely to occur than in traditional direct-manipulation environments. For instance, if the slide under the microscope were moved (accidentally) by a local operator, the positions indicated might not be correct. A breakdown might also occur during the execution of a remote operation, without indicating this event properly to the remote site. Such breakdowns require increased status information for remote users and additional actions that allow for correction.

One solution to these problems is to make explicit the network delays and breakdowns as part of the system. The user sees a model of the starting state of the system, the action that has been issued, and the current state of the system as it carries out the action. It may be preferable to provide spatially parametrized positioning actions (for example, move of a distance $+x,+y$, or move to a fixed point (x,y) in a two-dimensional space), rather than providing temporal commands (for example, start moving right at a 36° angle from the horizontal). In other words, the users specify a destination (rather than a motion), and wait until the action is completed before readjusting the destination if necessary. In general, we try to turn the remote environment as much as possible into a direct-manipulation environment by applying the same basic principles.

5.7.3   The roots of a theory of remote direct manipulation

The theory of remote direct manipulation is rooted in two domains that, so far, have been independent. The first root of direct manipulation is in the context of personal computers and is often identified with the desktop metaphor and office automation. The second root is in process control where human operators control physical processes in complex environments. Typical tasks are operating power or chemical plants, controlling manufacturing, flying airplanes, or steering vehicles. If the physical processes take place in a remote location, we talk about *teleoperation* or *remote control*. To perform the control task, the human operator may interact with a computer, which may carry out some of the control tasks without any interference by the human operator. This idea is captured by the notion of *supervisory control* (Sheridan, 1988). Although supervisory control and direct manipulation stem from different problem domains and are usually applied to different system architectures, there is a strong resemblance.

Traditional direct manipulation can also be interpreted as a teleoperation, especially with high-speed networking that provides client–server environments. Files that appear on a screen may come from a remote computer, and the software may be distributed throughout the network. Messages and documents can be sent to or retrieved from remote machines, printers, or file servers. Even the letters on a display may be composed of font descriptions stored in a remote location from where the keystrokes are issued. Thus, the essential components of a teleoperation environment—such as sensors, displays, controls, remote effectors or tools, and communication links—are involved.

Remote direct manipulation (as well as supervisory control) cannot be taken as a design criterion that either is or is not fulfilled. One interface can be slightly more direct than another. Similarly, the control can be felt to be more or less remote. Thus, remote direct manipulation denotes a range of possible solutions rather than a binary variable. Direct manipulation is still an imprecise and subjective concept, although it has proved eminently useful in stimulating designers, revising existing systems, training designers, and comparing systems. The connection between direct manipulation and supervisory control seems promising.

5.8   Virtual Reality

Flight-simulator designers use many tricks to create the most realistic experience for fighter or airline pilots. The cockpit displays and controls are taken from the same production line as the real ones. Then, the windows are replaced by high-resolution computer displays, and sounds are choreographed to give the impression of engine start or reverse thrust. Finally, the vibration and tilting during climbing or turning are created by hydraulic jacks and intricate suspension systems. This elaborate virtual or artificial reality may cost almost $100 million, but it is a lot cheaper, safer, and more useful for training than the $400-million jet that it simulates. Of course, home videogame players have purchased millions of $30 flight simulators that run on their personal computers. Flying a plane is a complicated and specialized skill, but simulators are beginning to appear for more common—and for some surprising—tasks under the alluring name of *virtual reality* (VR).

Far above the office desktop, much beyond multimedia, and high above the hype of hypertext, the gurus and purveyors of virtuality are donning their EyePhones and DataGloves to explore the total-immersion experience. Whether soaring over Seattle, bending around bronchial tubes to find lung cancers, or grasping complex molecules, the cyberspace explorers (cybernauts, VR voyagers, or Chipster Columbuses) are playing Lewis and Clark to a grand Montana of the mind. The imagery and personalities involved in virtual reality are often colorful, and journalists have enjoyed the fun as much as the developers and promoters (Stewart, 1991; Rheingold, 1991). More sober researchers have tried to present a balanced view by conveying enthusiasm while reporting on problems (Brooks, 1988; Mercurio and Erickson, 1990).

The technology can be exotic and expensive. EyePhones comprise a pair of small color LCD computer displays (360 x 240 pixels) mounted in a soft swimmask (it weighs about 4 pounds). DataGloves are made of fiber optic sensors sewn to spandex that measure the degree of bending of each finger joint (Figure 5.23). Three-dimensional position and orientation information about the head and hand are captured by Polhemus trackers. However, clever researchers are quickly finding ways to bring down the cost (Pausch, 1991) and to apply VR ideas to existing applications.

Architects have been using computers to draw three-dimensional representations of building for more than a decade. Most of their design systems show the building on a standard or slightly larger display, but adding a large screen projector to create a wall-sized image gives prospective clients a more realistic impression. Now add animation that allows clients to see what

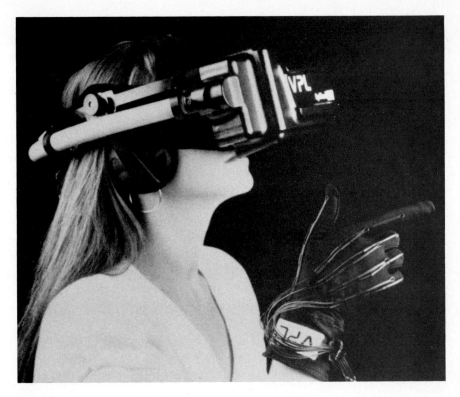

Figure 5.23

EyePhones and DataGlove from VPL Research are components of many virtual-reality (VR) systems. (EyePhones and DataGlove, VPL Research, Inc., Redwood City, CA.)

happens if they move left or right, or approach the image. Then enable clients to control the animation by walking on a treadmill (faster walking brings the building closer more quickly), and allow them to walk through the doors or up the stairs. Finally, replace the large-screen projector with EyePhones, and monitor head movement with Polhemus trackers. Each change takes users a bit farther along the range from "looking at" to "being in." Bumping into walls, falling down stairs, meeting other people, or having to wait for an elevator could be the next variations.

The architectural application is a persuasive argument for "being in" because we are used to "being in" buildings and moving around them. On the other hand, for many applications "looking at" is often more effective, which is why air-traffic–control workstations place the viewer above the situation display. Similarly, the large wraparound movie screens that put viewers "in" race cars or airplanes are special events compared to the more common "looking at" television experience. The Living Theater of the 1960s created an involving theatrical experience and "be-ins" were popular, but most theater goers prefer to take their "suspension of disbelief" experiences from the "looking at" perspective (Laurel, 1991).

It remains to be seen whether doctors, accustomed to "looking at" a patient, really want to crawl through the patient's lungs or "be in" the patient's brains. Modern surgical procedures and technology can benefit by "looking at" video images from inside a patient's heart taken through fiber-optic cameras and by remote direct-manipulation devices that minimize the invasive surgery. There are more mundane applications to such video and fiber-optic magic; imagine the benefits to household plumbers of being able to see lost wedding rings around the bends of a sink drain or to see and grasp the child's toy down the pipes of a clogged toilet.

Other concepts that were sources for the current VR excitement include artificial reality, pioneered by Myron Krueger (1980; 1991). His VideoPlace and VideoDesk installations with large-screen projectors and video recognition sensors combined full-body movement with projected images of light creatures that walked along a performer's arm or multicolored patterns and sounds generated by the performer's movement. Similarly, Vincent Vincent's demonstrations of the Mandala system carried performance art to a new level of sophistication and fantasy (Color Plate 4).

The telepresence perspective is, as Brenda Laurel of Telepresence Research says, "Be here there"—or is it "Be there here"? Either way, the message is to break the physical limitations of space and to act as though the user is somewhere else. Practical thinkers immediately grasp the connection to remote direct manipulation, remote control, and remote vision (Sheridan, 1987), but the fantasists quickly recognize the potential to escape current reality and to visit science-fiction worlds, cartoonlands, previous times in history, galaxies with different laws of physics, or unexplored emotional territories. And while telepresence trippers are changing the world around them, they can also change their own body features or personality.

Scientific analyses of VR user-interface issues may be too sober a process for those who are enjoying their silicon trips, but it may aid in choosing the appropriate applications and refining the technologies. The direct-manipulation principles and the SSOA model are helpful in designing VRs. Users should be able to select actions rapidly by pointing or gesturing, with incremental and reversible control, and display feedback should occur immediately to convey the sense of causality. Complex syntax should never be used, computer concepts should be minimized, and the users should be in the task domain as much as possible. The world of actions should contain visual representations of the objects *and* actions of interest; the surgeon's instruments should be readily available or easily called up by spoken command or gesture. Similarly, an architect walking through a house with a client should be able to pick up a window-stretching tool to try out a larger window, or a room-painting tool to change the wall colors while leaving the windows and furniture untouched. Since applications may require numerous tools, a menu-selection method or tool box is needed.

VR scenarios are such fun to get into, but the scientific analysis of components is a useful complement:

- *Visual display:* The normal computer display at a normal viewing distance (70 centimeters) subtends an angle of about 5 degrees, large screen displays can cover a 20- to 30-degree field, and the EyePhones cover 100 degrees horizontally and 60 degrees vertically. The EyePhones are mounted so as to block other images, so the effect is more dramatic, and head motion produces new images, so the users can get the impression of 360 degree coverage. Flight simulators also block extraneous images, but they do so without forcing the users to wear the sometimes-cumbersome EyePhones. Could a room with four walls of rear-projected displays and a black ceiling offer satisfying experiences? It seems interesting to consider the direct opposite of "being in": Palmtop computers or watch-sized computers exemplify the extreme of "looking at" because of their small displays. Are there personality correlates for users who want to "be in" versus those who prefer to "look at"?

  As hardware technology improves, it will be possible to provide more rapid and higher-resolution images. Most researchers agree that the displays must approach real time (probably under 100 millisecond delay) in presenting the images to the users. Low-resolution displays are acceptable while users or the objects are moving, but when users stop to stare, higher resolution is necessary to preserve the sense of "being in." Improved hardware and algorithms are needed to display rough shapes rapidly and then to fill in the details when the motion stops. A further requirement is that motion be smooth; both incremental changes and continuous display of the objects of interest are required.

  Graphics researchers have been perfecting image display to account for various lighting effects, textured surfaces, reflections, and shadows. All these phenomena need to be included in VR applications. Data structures and algorithms for zooming in or panning across an object rapidly and smoothly are still needed. Dealing with three-dimensional models to permit or prevent bumping into or going through are a good challenge for computer scientists interested in computational geometry. And why limit thinking to three dimensions? Four-dimensional realities may become more understandable after a

VR visit (Banchoff, 1990). And why stop at four dimensions? Multidimensional statistics problems are common in meteorology, sociology, and economics (Lewis et al., 1991). Feiner and Beshers (1990) built a six-dimensional financial data model that the user manipulated with a DataGlove and viewed with a StereoGraphics CrystalEyes LCD stereo system.

- *Head position sensing:* The EyePhones and other head-mounted displays (HMDs) can provide differing displays depending on head position. Look to the right, and you see a forest; look to the left, and the forest gives way to a city. The Polhemus tracker requires mounting on the user's head, but other devices embedded in a hat or eyeglasses are possible. Video recognition of head position is possible. Sensor precision should be high (within 1 degree) and rapid (within 100 milliseconds). Eye tracking to recognize the focus of attention might be useful, but it is difficult to accomplish while the user is moving and wearing EyePhones.

- *Hand-position sensing:* The DataGlove is a highly innovative invention; it surely will be refined and improved beyond its current low resolution. It may turn out that accurate measurement of finger position is required only for one or two fingers or for only one or two joints. Hand orientation is provided by a Polhemus tracker mounted on the glove or wrist. Sensors for other body parts such as knees, arms, or legs may yet find uses. The potential for sensors and tactile feedback on more erotic body parts has been referred to by more than one journalist.

- *Force feedback:* Hand-operated remote-control devices for performing experiments in chemistry laboratories or for handling nuclear materials provide force feedback that gives users a good sense of when they grasp an object or bump into one. Force feedback to car drivers and pilots is carefully configured to provide realistic and useful tactile information. Recreating such experiences from purely software sources is a novelty, but the University of North Carolina's success with force feedback to indicate docking of two complex molecules has stimulated several researchers (Brooks, 1988). It might be helpful for surgeons to receive force feedback as they perform novel procedures or practice difficult operations. Remote handshaking as part of a video conference has been suggested, but it is not clear that the experience could be as satisfying as the real thing.

- *Sound input and output:* Sound output adds realism to bouncing balls, beating hearts, or dropping vases, as videogame designers have found out long ago. Making convincing sounds at the correct moment with full stereo effect is possible, but it too is hard work. The digital sound hardware is adequate, but the software tools are still inadequate. Music output from virtual instruments is promising; early work simulates existing instruments such as a violin, but novel instruments seem likely to follow quickly. Speech recognition may complement hand gestures in some applications. Discrete spoken commands are useful to solve the "two-cursor problem" (Brooks, 1988): one cursor points at an object or a direction, while the other cursor selects an action from a menu. Two DataGloves could be used, but speech recognition plus one DataGlove seems a workable alternative.

- *Other sensations:* The tilting and vibration of flight simulators might provide other clues and experiences for VR designers. Could a tilting and vibrating virtual roller coaster become popular if users could travel at 60, 600, or 6000 miles per hour and crash through mountains or go into orbit? Other effects such as a throbbing disco sound and strobe lights could also amplify some VR experiences. Why should we not include real gusts of air, made hot or cold to convey the virtual weather? Finally, the power of smells to evoke strong reactions has been understood by writers from Proust to Gibson. Olfactory computing has been discussed, but appropriate and practical applications have yet to be found.

- *Cooperative and competitive virtual reality:* Computer-supported cooperative work (Chapter 10) is a lively research area, so why not cooperative VRs, or as one developer called it, "virtuality built for two." Two people at remote sites could work together in the same VR, seeing each other's actions and sharing the experience. Competitive games such as virtual racquetball have been built for two players. Software for training Army tank crews took on a much more compelling atmosphere when the designs shifted from playing against the computer to shooting at other tank crews and worrying about their attacks. The realistic sounds created such a sense of engagement that crews experienced elevated heart rates, more rapid breathing, and increased perspiration. Presumably, VRs could also bring relaxation and pleasant encounters with other people. VR is an inadequate substitute for being there, but children who appreciate telephone calls from their parents, might like a VR call from their parents while the parents are away on business.

VR's compelling attraction should be acknowledged, and its positive aspects applied. Cyberphilia is spreading rapidly on an international basis and will inevitably find its niches—whether only as an amusement, or instead as a widely applied technology, remains to be seen.

Table 5.1

Direct manipulation definition with benefits and concerns.

Direct Manipulation

Definition

- Visual representation (metaphor) of the world of action
    Objects and actions are shown
    Analogical reasoning is tapped
- Rapid, incremental, and reversible actions
- Typing replaced by pointing and selecting
- Results of actions visible immediately

Benefits

- Control and display compatibility
- Less syntax, resulting in reduced error rates
- More preventable errors
- Faster learning and higher retention
- Exploration encouraged

Concerns

- Increased system resources
- Cumbersome actions
- Weak macro techniques
- Difficult history and tracing
- Difficult for visually impaired users

5.9   Practitioner's Summary

Among interactive systems that provide equivalent functionality and reliability, some systems emerge to dominate the competition. Often, the most appealing systems have an enjoyable user interface that offers a natural representation of the task objects and actions—hence the term *direct manipulation* (Table 5.1). These systems are easy to learn, use, and retain over time. Novices can acquire a simple subset of the commands and then progress to more elaborate operations. Actions are rapid, incremental, and reversible, and can be performed with physical actions instead of complex syntactic forms. The results of operations are visible immediately, and error messages are needed less often.

Just because direct-manipulation principles have been used in a system does not ensure that system's success. A poor design, slow implementation, or inadequate functionality can undermine acceptance. For some applications, menu selection, form fillin, or command languages may be more appropriate. However, the potential for direct-manipulation programming, remote direct manipulation, and virtual reality is great. Many new products will certainly emerge. Iterative design (Section 13.2) is especially important in testing direct-manipulation systems, because the novelty of this approach may lead to unexpected problems for designers and users.

5.10   Researcher's Agenda

Research needs to be done to refine our understanding of the contribution of each feature of direct manipulation: analogical representation, incremental operation, reversibility, physical action instead of syntax, immediate visibility of results, graceful evolution, and graphic form. The relative merits of competing analogical or metaphorical representations could be better understood through experimental comparisons (Bewley et al., 1983). Reversibility is easily accomplished by a generic UNDO command, but designing natural inverses for each operation may be more attractive. Can complex actions always be represented with direct manipulation, or is there a point at which command syntax becomes appealing?

As the hardware improves, we can begin to realize the fantasies of user-interface researchers. Beyond the office desktops, the laptops, and the kitchen countertops, there is the allure of telepresence and virtual realities. The playful aspect should be pursued, but the challenge is to find the practical situations in which people need and want to be in and part of the application, not just to be observers.

If researchers and designers can free themselves to think visually, then the future of direct manipulation is promising. Tasks that could have been performed only with tedious command or programming languages may soon be accessible through lively, enjoyable interactive systems that reduce learning time, speed performance, and increase satisfaction.

References

Arnheim, Rudolf, *Visual Thinking*, University of California Press, Berkeley, CA (1972).

Banchoff, Thomas F., *Beyond the Third Dimension: Geometry, Computer Graphics, and Higher Dimensions*, Scientific American Library, New York (1990).

Bewley, William L., Roberts, Teresa L., Schroit, David, and Verplank, William L., Human factors testing in the design of Xerox's 8010 "Star" Office Workstation, *Proc. CHI '83 Conference—Human Factors in Computing Systems*, ACM, New York (1983), 72–77.

Brooks, Frederick, Grasping reality through illusion: Interactive graphics serving science, *Proc. CHI '88 Conference—Human Factors in Computing Systems*, ACM, New York (1988), 1–11.

Brooks, Kenneth P., Lilac: A two-view document editor, *IEEE Computer 24*, 6 (June 1991), 7–19.

Bruner, James, *Toward a Theory of Instruction*, Harvard University Press, Cambridge, MA (1966).

Card, Stuart K., Robertson, George G., and Mackinlay, Jock D., The Information Visualizer, an information workspace, *Proc. CHI '91 Conference—Human Factors in Computing Systems*, ACM, New York (1991), 181–188.

Carroll, J. M., The adventure of getting to know a computer, *IEEE Computer 15* (1982), 49–58.

Carroll, John M. and Thomas, John C., Metaphor and the cognitive representation of computing systems, *IEEE Transactions on Systems, Man, and Cybernetics, SMC-12*, 2 (March/April 1982), 107–116.

Carroll, J. M., Thomas, J. C., and Malhotra, A., Presentation and representation in design problem-solving, *British Journal of Psychology 71* (1980), 143–153.

Chang, Shi-Kuo (Editor), *Principles of Visual Programming*, Prentice-Hall, Englewood Cliffs, NJ (1990).

Copeland, Richard W., *How Children Learn Mathematics* (Third Edition), MacMillan, New York (1979).

Crawford, Chris, *The Art of Computer Game Design: Reflections of a Master Game Designer*, Osborne/McGraw-Hill, Berkeley, CA (1984).

Cypher, Allen, EAGER: Programming repetitive tasks by example, *Proc. CHI '91 Conference—Human Factors in Computing Systems*, ACM, New York (1991), 33–39.

Feiner, Steven and Beshers, Clifford, Worlds within worlds: Metaphors for exploring *n*-dimensional virtual worlds, *Proc. User Interface Software and Technology '90*, ACM, New York (1990), 76–83.

Gittins, David, Icon-based human–computer interaction, *International Journal for Man–Machine Studies 24* (1986), 519–543.

Glinert, Ephraim P., Kopache, Mark E., and McIntyre, David W., Exploring the general-purpose visual alternative, *Journal of Visual Languages and Computing 1* (1990), 3–39.

Halbert, Daniel, *Programming by Example*, Ph.D. dissertation, Department of Electrical Engineering and Computer Systems, University of California, Berkeley, CA; available as Xerox Report OSD-T8402, Xerox PARC, Palo Alto, CA (1984).

Heckel, Paul, *The Elements of Friendly Software Design: The New Edition*, SYBEX, San Francisco (1991).

Herot, Christopher F., Spatial management of data, *ACM Transactions on Database Systems 5*, 4, (December 1980), 493–513.

Herot, Christopher, Graphical user interfaces. In Vassiliou, Yannis (Editor), *Human Factors and Interactive Computer Systems*, Ablex, Norwood, NJ (1984), 83–104.

Hollan, J. D., Hutchins, E. L., and Weitzman, L., STEAMER: An interactive inspectable simulation-based training system, *AI Magazine* (Summer 1984), 15–27.

Hutchins, Edwin L., Hollan, James D., and Norman, Don A., Direct manipulation interfaces. In Norman, Don A. and Draper, Stephen W. (Editors), *User Centered*

System Design: New Perspectives on Human–Computer Interaction, Lawrence Erlbaum Associates, Hillsdale, NJ (1986), 87–124.

Iseki, Osamu and Shneiderman, Ben, Applying direct manipulation concepts: Direct Manipulation Disk Operating System (DMDOS), *Software Engineering Notes 11*, 2, (March 1986), 22–26.

Krueger, Myron, *Artificial Reality*, Addison-Wesley, Reading, MA (1980).

Krueger, Myron, *Artificial Reality II*, Addison-Wesley, Reading, MA (1991).

Laurel, Brenda, *Computers as Theater*, Addison-Wesley, Reading, MA (1991).

Lewis, J. Bryan, Koved, Lawrence, and Ling, Daniel T., Dialogue structures for virtual worlds, *Proc. CHI '91 Conference—Human Factors in Computing Systems*, ACM, New York (1991), 131–136.

McKim, Robert H., *Experiences in Visual Thinking*, Brooks/Cole, Monterey, CA (1972).

Malone, Thomas W., What makes computer games fun? *BYTE 6*, 12 (December 1981), 258–277.

Marcus, Aaron, *Graphic Design for Electronic Documents and User Interfaces*, ACM Press, New York (1992).

Margono, Sepeedeh and Shneiderman, Ben, A study of file manipulation by novices using commands versus direct manipulation, *Twenty-sixth Annual Technical Symposium*, ACM, Washington, DC (June 1987), 154–159.

Maulsby, David L. and Witten, Ian H., Inducing programs in a direct-manipulation environment, *Proc. CHI '89 Conference—Human Factors in Computing Systems*, ACM, New York (1989), 57–62.

Mercurio, Philip J. and Erickson, Thomas D., Interactive scientific visualization: An assessment of a virtual reality. In Diaper, D., Gilmore, D., Cockton, G., and Shackel, B. (Editors), *Human–Computer Interaction: Interact '90*, North-Holland, Amsterdam, The Netherlands (1990), 741–745.

Montessori, Maria, *The Montessori Method*, Schocken, New York (1964).

Morgan, K., Morris, R. L., and Gibbs, S., When does a mouse become a rat? or... Comparing performance and preferences in direct manipulation and command line environment, *The Computer Journal 34*, 3 (1991), 265–271.

Myers, Brad A., Demonstrational programming: A step beyond direct manipulation. In Diaper, Dan and Hammond, Nick (Editors), *People and Computers VI*, Cambridge University Press, Cambridge, England (1991), 11–30.

Nelson, Ted, Interactive systems and the design of virtuality, *Creative Computing 6*, 11, (November 1980), 56 ff., and 12 (December 1980), 94 ff.

Norman, Donald A., *The Psychology of Everyday Things*, Basic Books, New York (1988).

Norman, Kent, *The Psychology of Menu Selection: Designing Cognitive Control at the Human/Computer Interface*, Ablex, Norwood, NJ (1991).

Papert, Seymour, *Mindstorms: Children, Computers, and Powerful Ideas*, Basic Books, New York (1980).

Pausch, Randy, Virtual reality on five dollars a day, *Proc. CHI '91 Conference—Human Factors in Computing Systems*, ACM, New York (1991), 265–270.

Plaisant, Catherine and Shneiderman, Ben, Scheduling ON–OFF home control devices: Design issues and usability evaluation of four touchscreen interfaces, *International Journal for Man–Machine Studies* (in press).

Plaisant, C., Shneiderman, B., and Battaglia, J., Scheduling home-control devices: A case study of the transition from the research project to a product, *Human-Factors in Practice*, Computer Systems Technical Group, Human-Factors Society, Santa Monica, CA (December 1990), 7–12.

Polya, G., *How to Solve It*, Doubleday, New York, (1957).

Potter, Richard, Just in Time Programming: Long Overdue, Ph.D. Dissertation, Department of Computer Science, University of Maryland, College Park, MD (1992).

Rheingold, Howard, *Virtual Reality*, Simon and Schuster, New York (1991).

Roberts, Teresa L., Evaluation of Computer Text Editors, Ph.D. dissertation, Department of Computer Science, Stanford University. Available from University Microfilms, Ann Arbor, MI, Order Number AAD 80-11699. Stanford, CA (1980).

Rogers, Yvonne, Icons at the interface: Their usefulness, *Interacting with Computers 1*, 1 (1989), 105–117.

Rubin, Robert V., Golin, Eric J., and Reiss, Steven P., Thinkpad: A graphics system for programming by demonstrations, *IEEE Software 2*, 2 (March 1985), 73–79.

Rutkowski, Chris, An introduction to the Human Applications Standard Computer Interface, Part 1: Theory and principles, *BYTE 7*, 11 (October 1982), 291–310.

Sheridan, T. B., Teleoperation, telepresence, and telerobotics: Research needs for space. In Sheridan, T. B., Kruser, D. S., and Deutsch, S. (Editors), *Human Factors in Automated and Robotic Space Systems*, Proceedings, National Research Council, Washington, DC (1987), 279–291.

Sheridan, T. B., Task allocation and supervisory control. In Helander, M. (Editor), *Handbook of Human–Computer Interaction*, Elsevier Science Publishers, Amsterdam, The Netherlands (1988), 159–173.

Shneiderman, Ben, A computer graphics system for polynomials, *The Mathematics Teacher 67*, 2 (1974), 111–113.

Shneiderman, Ben, Control flow and data structure documentation: Two experiments, *Communications of the ACM. 25*, 1 (January 1982), 55–63.

Shu, Nan C., *Visual Programming*, Van Nostrand Reinhold, New York (1989).

Smith, David Canfield, *Pygmalion: A Computer Program to Model and Stimulate Creative Thought*, Birkhauser Verlag, Basel, Switzerland (1977).

Smith, D. Canfield, Irby, Charles, Kimball, Ralph, Verplank, Bill, and Harslem, Eric, Designing the Star user interface, *BYTE 7*, 4 (April 1982), 242–282.

Stewart, Doug, Through the looking glass into an artificial world—via computer, *Smithsonian*, (January 1991), 36–45.

Temple, Barker and Sloane, Inc., The benefits of the graphical user interface, *Multimedia Review* (Winter 1990), 10–17.

Thimbleby, Harold, *User Interface Design*, ACM Press, New York (1990).

Tullis, T. S., An evaluation of alphanumeric, graphic and color information displays, *Human Factors 23* (1981), 541–550.

Uttal, W. R., Teleoperators, *Scientific American 261*, 6 (December 1989), 124–129.

Van de Vegte, J. M. E., Milgram, P., Kwong, R. H., Teleoperator control models: Effects of time delay and imperfect system knowledge, *IEEE Transactions on Systems, Man, and Cybernetics 20*, 6 (November/December 1990), 1258–1272.

Verplank, William L., Graphic challenges in designing object-oriented user interfaces. In Helander, M. (Editor), *Handbook of Human–Computer Interaction*, Elsevier Science Publishers, Amsterdam, The Netherlands (1988), 365–376.

Weinstein, R., Bloom, K., Rozek, S., Telepathology: Long distance diagnosis, *American Journal of Clinical Pathology*, 91 (Suppl 1) (1989), S39–S42 .

Wertheimer, M., *Productive Thinking*, Harper and Row, New York (1959).

Ziegler, J. E. and Fähnrich, K.-P., Direct manipulation. In Helander, M. (Editor), *Handbook of Human–Computer Interaction*, Elsevier Science Publishers, Amsterdam, The Netherlands (1988), 123–133.

Zloof, M. M., Query-by-Example, *Proceedings of the National Computer Conference*, AFIPS Press, Montvale, NJ (1975), 431–438.

Zloof, M. M., Office-by-Example: A business language that unifies data and word processing and electronic mail, *IBM Systems Journal 21*, 3 (1982), 272–304.

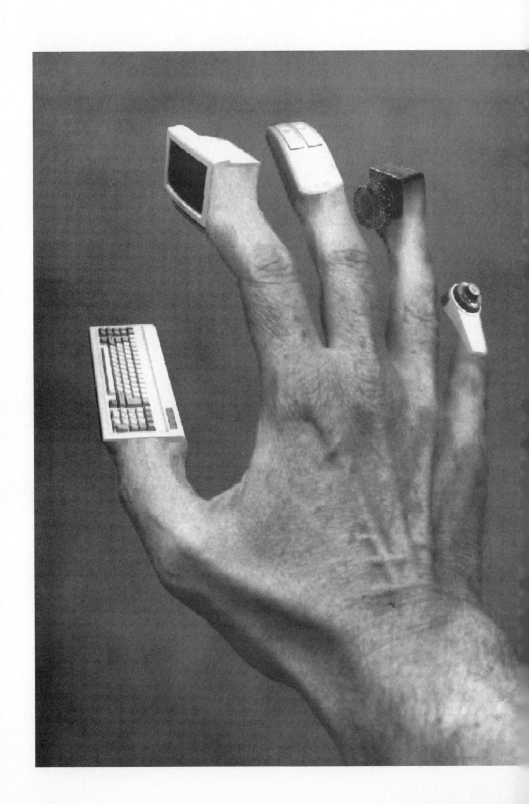

CHAPTER 6

Interaction Devices

The wheel is an extension of the foot,
the book is an extension of the eye,
clothing, an extension of the skin,
electric circuitry an extension of the central nervous system.

Marshall McLuhan and Quentin Fiore, *The Medium Is the*
Message, **1967**

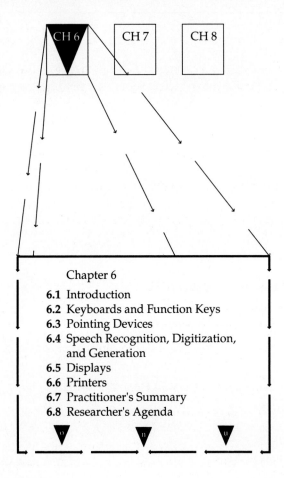

Chapter 6

6.1 Introduction
6.2 Keyboards and Function Keys
6.3 Pointing Devices
6.4 Speech Recognition, Digitization, and Generation
6.5 Displays
6.6 Printers
6.7 Practitioner's Summary
6.8 Researcher's Agenda

6.1 Introduction

The remarkable progress in computer-processor speeds and storage capabilities is now being matched by improvements in input–output devices. Ten-character-per-second Teletypes have been replaced by high-speed mega-pixel graphical displays for output, and the 100-year-old keyboard is giving way to rapid and high-precision pointing devices for input. Breaking away from previous strategies has proved to be more difficult than anticipated, but the advantages are growing daily. Although the common Sholes keyboard layout is likely to remain the primary device for text input, pointing devices increasingly free users from keyboards for many tasks. The future of computing is likely to include gestural input, three-dimensional pointing, more voice input–output, and whole-body involvement for input and output.

The increased concern for human factors has led to hundreds of new devices and variants on the old devices: novel keyboards; pointing devices such as the mouse, touchscreen, stylus, and trackball; speech recognizers and generators, eyetrackers, DataGloves, and force feedback. Output devices have increasingly favored color displays, but monochrome displays (especially flat-plate liquid-crystal panels) continue to proliferate in small and large formats. The lively controversy surrounding these devices is healthy, and empirical studies are now beginning to yield comparative evaluations as well as insights that lead to further innovations (Brown, 1988; Sherr, 1988; Greenstein and Arnaut, 1988; Foley et al., 1990; Card et al., 1990).

6.2   Keyboards and Function Keys

The primary mode of textual data entry is still the keyboard. This often-criticized device is quite impressive in its success. Hundreds of millions of people have managed to use keyboards with speeds of up to 15 keystrokes per second (approximately 150 words per minute), although rates for beginners are less than 1 keystroke per second, and rates for average office workers are 5 keystrokes per second (approximately 50 words per minute). Contemporary keyboards generally permit only one keypress at a time, although dual keypresses (SHIFT plus a letter) are used to produce capitals and special functions (CTRL plus a letter).

More rapid data entry can be accomplished by chord keyboards that allow several keys to be pressed simultaneously to represent several characters or a word. Courtroom recorders regularly use chord keyboards serenely to enter the full text of spoken arguments, reaching rates of up to 300 words per minute. This feat requires months of training and frequent use to retain the complex pattern of chord presses. The piano keyboard is an impressive data-entry device that allows several finger presses at once and is responsive to different pressures and durations. It seems that there is potential for higher rates of data entry than is possible with the current keyboards.

Keyboard size and packaging also influence user satisfaction and usability. Large keyboards with many keys give an impression of professionalism and complexity but may threaten novice users. Small keyboards seem lacking in power to some users, but their compact size is an attraction to others. A thin profile (30 to 45 millimeters thick) allows users to rest the keyboard on their laps easily and permits a comfortable hand position when the keyboard is on a desk. A moderate keyboard slope (10 to 25 degrees) appears to provide greatest comfort (Emmons and Hirsch, 1982).

6.2.1   Keyboard layouts

The Smithsonian Institution's National Museum of American History in Washington, D.C., has a remarkable exhibit on the development of the typewriter. During the middle of the nineteenth century, hundreds of attempts were made to build typewriters, with a stunning variety of positions for the paper, mechanisms for producing a character, and layouts for the keys. By the 1870s, Christopher Latham Sholes's design was becoming successful because of a good mechanical design and a clever placement of the letters that slowed down the users enough that key jamming was infrequent. This *QWERTY layout* put frequently used letter pairs far apart, thereby increasing finger travel distances.

Sholes's success led to such widespread standardization that, a century later, almost all English-language keyboards use the QWERTY layout (Figure 6.1). The development of electronic keyboards eliminated the mechanical problems and led many twentieth-century inventors to propose alternative layouts to reduce finger travel distances (Montgomery, 1982). The *Dvorak layout* (Figure 6.2), developed in the 1920s, supposedly reduces finger travel distances by at least one order of magnitude, thereby increasing the typing rate of expert typists from about 150 words per minute to more than 200 words per minute, while reducing errors (Kroemer, 1972; Martin, 1972; Potosnak, 1988).

Acceptance of the Dvorak design has been slow despite the dedicated efforts of some devotees. These people hope that the ease of switching keyboards on some machines may entice some users. Those who have tried report that it takes about 1 week of regular typing to make the switch, but most users have been unwilling to invest the effort. We are confronted with an interesting example of how even documented improvements are hard to disseminate be-

Figure 6.1

QWERTY keyboard from Macintosh with function keys, numeric keypad, separate cursor-control keys, and special functions.

Figure 6.2

Dvorak layout on IBM keyboard with function keys, separate cursor control keys, and special functions. The keycaps also show the APL character set.

cause the perceived benefit of change does not outweigh the effort.

A third keyboard layout of some interest is the *ABCDE style* that has the 26 letters of the alphabet laid out in alphabetical order. The rationale here is that nontypists will find it easier to locate the keys. Some data-entry terminals for numeric and alphabetic codes use this style (Figure 6.3). The

Figure 6.3

One approach to an ABCDE layout on the Texas Instruments Speak & Spell educational toy. The vowels are highlighted and special functions are included to fill the 4 by 10 array of membrane keys.

Figure 6.4

Early IBM PC keyboard with 10 function keys on the left, numeric keypad on the right and cursor-control keys embedded in the numeric keypad.

widespread availability of QWERTY keyboards has made typing a more common skill and has reduced the importance of the ABCDE style. Our study and those of other researchers have shown no advantage for the ABCDE style; users with little QWERTY experience are eager to acquire this expertise.

Beyond the letters, many debates rage about the placement of additional keys. The early IBM PC keyboard was widely criticized because of the placement of a few keys, such as a backslash key where most typists expected to find the SHIFT key, and the placement of several special characters near the ENTER key (Figure 6.4). Later versions relocated the offending keys, to the acclaim of critics. Other improvements included a larger ENTER key and LEDs to signal the status of the CAPSLOCK, NUMLOCK, and SCROLLLOCK keys. Even on laptop or notebook computers, keyboards are fullsize (Figure 6.5), but some pocket computers used a greatly reduced keyboard (Figure 6.6).

Number pads are another source of controversy. Telephones have the 1-2-3 keys on the top row, but calculators place the 7-8-9 keys on the top row. Studies have shown a slight advantage for the telephone layout, but most computer keyboards use the calculator layout.

Some researchers have recognized that the wrist and hand placement for standard keyboards is awkward. Redesigned keyboards that separated the keys for the left and right hands by 9.5 centimeters, had an opening angle of 25 degrees with an inclination of 10 degrees, and offered large areas for forearm–wrist support led to lower reported tension, better posture, and higher preference scores (Nakaseko et al., 1985).

Figure 6.5

Full-size keyboard on the IBM PS/2 portable.

Figure 6.6

Sharp's Wizard electronic organizer is a pocket-sized portable memo pad, calendar, appointment book, phone and address list. Users can enter text and perform searches using the small QWERTY keyboard. (Reproduced with permission of Sharp Electronics Corporation, Mahwah, NJ.)

6.2.2   Keys

Modern electronic keyboards use 1/2-inch-square keys with about a 1/4-inch space between keys. The design has been refined carefully and tested thoroughly in research laboratories and the marketplace. The keys have a slightly concave surface for good contact with fingertips, and a matte finish to reduce both reflective glare and the chance of finger slips. The keypresses require a 40- to 125-gram force and a displacement of 3 to 5 millimeters (IBM, 1984). The force and displacement have been shown to produce rapid typing with low error rates while providing suitable feedback to users. As user experience increases and the chance of a misplaced finger is reduced, the force and displacement can be lowered.

An important element in key design is the profile of force displacement. When the key has been depressed far enough to send a signal, the key gives way and emits a click. The tactile and audible feedback is extremely important in touch typing. For these reasons, membrane keyboards that use a nonmoving touch-sensitive surface are unacceptable for touch typing. However, they are durable and therefore effective for public installations at museums or amusement parks.

Certain keys, such as the space bar, ENTER key, SHIFT key, or CTRL key, should be larger than others to allow easy, reliable access. Other keys, such as the CAPSLOCK or NUMLOCK should have a clear indication of in what position they are set, such as by physical locking in a lowered position or by an embedded light. Key labels should be large enough to read, meaningful, and permanent. Discrete color coding of keys helps to make a pleasing, informative layout. A further design principle is that some of the home keys—F and J in the QWERTY layout—may have a deeper concavity or a small raised dot to reassure users that their fingers are placed properly.

6.2.3   Function keys

Many keyboards contain a set of additional *function keys* for special functions or programmed functions. These keys are often labeled F1...F10 or PF1...PF24. Users must remember the functions, learn about them from the screen, or consult an attachable plastic template. This strategy attempts to reduce user keystrokes by replacing a command name with a single keystroke. Most function-key strategies do not require pressing the ENTER key to invoke the function.

On the positive side, the function keys can reduce keystrokes and errors, thereby speeding work for novice users who are poor typists and for expert users who readily recall the purpose of each function key. On the negative side, the purpose of each function key may not be apparent to some users, and users must remove their fingers from the home position to use the function keys.

For function keys, there are several design decisions that affect users. The association of a function with a key is vital. Novices need a screen display or a template to remind them of the function. Many systems confuse users with inconsistent key use. For example, the HELP key varies from F1 to F9 to F12 on some systems. Consistent use is important.

The placement of function keys is important if the task requires users to go from typing to using function keys. The greater the distance of the function keys from the home position on the keyboard, the more severe the problem. Some users would rather type six or eight characters than remove their fingers from the home position. Key layout of function keys also influences ease of use. A 3 by 4 layout of 12 keys is helpful, because users quickly learn functions by their placement on the upper-left or lower-right. A 1 by 12 layout only has two anchors and leads to slower and more error-prone selection of middle keys. A small gap between the sixth and seventh keys could aid users by grouping keys. A 2 by 5 layout is a reasonable intermediate style.

Function keys are sometimes built in the display screen bezel so that they are close to displayed labels—a popular technique with bank machines. This position supports novices who need labels, but it still requires hands to stray from the home position. Lights can be built into and next to function keys to indicate availability or ON–OFF status.

If all work can be done with labeled function keys, as on some CAD systems, then the latter can be a benefit. WordPerfect became a worldwide success with all actions initiated by function keys (plus CTRL, ALT, and SHIFT) and refined by onscreen menus. If movement between the home position on the keyboard and the function keys is frequent, then function keys can be disruptive. An alternative strategy is to use CTRL plus a letter to invoke a function. This approach has some mnemonic value, keeps hands on the home keys, and reduces the need for extra keys.

6.2.4   Cursor movement keys

A special category of function keys is the *cursor-movement keys*. There are usually four keys—up, down, left, and right. Some keyboards have eight keys to simplify diagonal movements. The placement of the cursor-movement keys is important in facilitating rapid and error-free use. The best layouts place the keys in their natural positions (Figure 6.7a through d), but designers have attempted several variations (Figure 6.7e through g). The increasingly popular inverted-T arrangement (Figure 6.7a) allows users to place their middle three fingers in a way that reduces hand and finger movement. The cross-arrangement in Figure 6.7(b) was found to be faster for novice users than the linear arrangement in Figure 6.7(e) (Foley, 1983). The cross-arrangement was also found to be faster for novices, but not for frequent users, than the box arrangement in Figure 6.7(f) (Emmons, 1984).

Figure 6.7

These seven styles of key layout for arrow keys are only a subset of what is commercially available. (a–d) Key layouts that are compatible with the arrow directions. (e–g) Incompatible layouts that may result in slower performance and higher error rates.

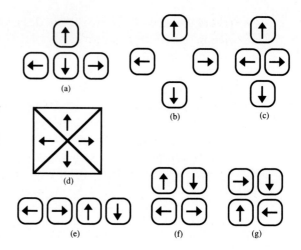

Cursor-movement keys often have a *typamatic (auto-repeat) feature;* that is, repetition occurs automatically with continued depression. This feature is widely appreciated and may improve performance, especially if users can control the rate to accommodate their preferences (important for users who are very young, elderly, or handicapped). Gould et al. (1985) found that cursor-speed treatments of 10, 14, and 33 characters per second did not show statistically significant differences in productivity in a text-editing task.

Cursor-movement keys have become more important with the increased use of form-fillin strategies, of word processing, and of direct manipulation. Additional cursor movements might be performed by the TAB key for larger jumps, a HOME key to go to the top-left or END key to go to the bottom-right of the display. Other accelerators are popular, such as CTRL with up, down, left, or right keypresses. Cursor-movement keys can be used to select items in a menu or on a display, but more rapid pointing at displays than can be provided by cursor-movement keys is often desired.

6.3   Pointing Devices

When a screen is used to display information—such as in air-traffic control, text editing, and CAD—it is often convenient to point at and thus to select an item. This direct-manipulation approach is attractive because the users can avoid learning commands, reduce the chance of typographic errors on a keyboard, and keep their attention on the display. The results are often faster performance, fewer errors, easier learning, and higher satisfaction (Foley et al., 1984; Buxton, 1985).

6.3.1 Pointing tasks

Pointing devices are applicable in six types of interaction tasks (Foley et al., 1984):

1. *Select*: The user chooses from a set of items. This technique is used for traditional menu selection, identification of a file in a directory, or marking of a part in an automobile design.

2. *Position*: The user chooses a point in a one-, two-, three-, or higher-dimensional space. Positioning may be used to create a drawing, to place a new window, or to drag a block of text in a figure.

3. *Orient*: The user chooses a direction in a two-, three-, or higher-dimensional space. The direction may simply rotate a symbol on the screen, indicate a direction of motion for a space ship, or control the operation of a robot arm.

4. *Path*: The user rapidly performs a series of position and orient operations. The path may be realized as a curving line in a drawing program, the instructions for a cloth cutting machine, or the route on a map.

5. *Quantify*: The user specifies a numeric value. The quantify task is usually a one-dimensional selection of integer or real values to set parameters, such as the page number in a document, the velocity of a ship, or the amplitude of a sound.

6. *Text*: The user enters, moves, and edits text in a two-dimensional space. The pointing device indicates the location of an insertion, deletion, or change. Beyond the simple manipulation of the text, there are more elaborate tasks, such as centering; margin setting; font sizes; highlighting, such as boldface or underscore; and page layout.

It is possible to perform all these tasks with a keyboard by typing: numbers or letters to select, integer coordinates to position, a number representing an angle to point, a number to quantify, and cursor control commands to move about text. In the past, the keyboard was used to perform all these tasks, but novel devices have been created that permit users to perform these tasks more rapidly and with fewer errors.

These devices can be grouped into those that offer (1) *direct control* on the screen surface, such as lightpen, touchscreen, and pen or stylus, and (2) *indirect control* away from the screen surface, such as mouse, trackball, joystick, graphics tablet, and touchpad. Within each category are many variations, and novel designs emerge frequently.

6.3.2 Direct pointing devices

The *lightpen* was an early device that enabled users to point to a spot on a screen and to perform a select, position, or other task (Figure 6.8). In fact, the

Figure 6.8

The lightpen allows direct control in pointing to a spot on the display. (Courtesy of Koala Technologies Corporation, San Jose, CA.)

lightpen could also be used to perform all six tasks. The lightpen was attractive because it allowed direct control by pointing to a spot on the display, as opposed to the indirect control provided by a graphics tablet, joystick, or mouse. Most lightpens incorporate a button for the user to press when the cursor is resting on the desired spot on the screen. Lightpens vary in thickness, length, weight, shape (the lightgun with a trigger is one variation), and position of buttons. Unfortunately, direct control on an upright screen can cause arm fatigue for some users. The lightpen has three further disadvantages: the users' hands obscures part of the screen, users must remove their hands from the keyboard, and users must reach to pick up the lightpen.

Some of these disadvantages are overcome by the *touchscreen* (Tyler, 1984), which does not require picking up some device, but instead allows direct control touches on the screen using a finger (Figure 6.9). Early touchscreen designs were rightly criticized for causing fatigue, hand-obscuring-the-screen, hand-off-keyboard, imprecise pointing, and the eventual smudging of the display. Some touchscreen implementations have a further problem: the software accepts the touch immediately (*land-on strategy*), denying the user the opportunity to verify the correctness of the selected spot, as is done with lightpens. These early designs were based on physical pressure, impact, or a grid of infrared beams

These early designs have been replaced by dramatically improved touchscreens that permit high precision (Sears and Shneiderman, 1991). The resistive, capacitive, or surface acoustic-wave hardware can provide 1024 x

Figure 6.9

With a touchscreen, the user needs only to point with a finger. High-precision touchscreens increase the range of possible applications, especially if the screens are mounted in a convenient position (30 to 45 degrees from the horizontal) for pointing and reading.

1024 sensitivity, and the *lift-off strategy* enables users to point at a single pixel. The lift-off strategy has three steps. The users touch the surface, and then see a cursor that they can drag around on the display; when the users are satisfied with the position, they lift their fingers off the display to activate. The availability of high-precision touchscreens has opened the doors to many applications (Sears et al., 1992b).

Refinements to touchscreens can be expected since touchscreens are in high demand for applications directed at novice users in which the keyboard can be eliminated and touch is the only interface mechanism. Touchscreens are valued by designers of public-access systems because there are no moving parts, durability in high use environments is good (touchscreens are the only input devices that have survived at EPCOT), and the price is relatively low. Touchscreens have also become popular for frequent users of home, building, process, or air-traffic control systems, medical instruments, or military systems. In these systems, space is at a premium, rugged design with no moving parts is appreciated, and users can be guided through a complex activity.

Touchscreen can produce varied displays to suit the task. Form-fillin or menu selection works naturally by touchscreen, as does typing on a touchscreen keyboard. In our studies with keyboards from 7 to 25 centimeters wide, users could, with some practice, type from 20 to 30 words per minute, respectively (Sears et al., in press).

Multiple-touch touchscreens will open up even more possibilities for drawing, music, typing, and so on. As touchscreens become integrated during the display-construction process, cost is likely to drop and parallax problems from an attached glass panel will decrease. A touchable surface on a flat-plate LCD would enable construction of many new devices from pocket-sized computers to museum placards that contain extensive information available by touch. Every car, refrigerator, camera, TV, or other appliance could have helpful explanations, information resources, or complete user manuals constantly available.

The advent of *notebook computers* has stimulated interest in penlike devices, such as the *lightpen*, for pointing, handwriting, gestural input, and drawing. The handheld notebooks make it natural to have pointing on the LCD surface, which is held in the hand, placed on a desk, or rested on the lap. Handwriting recognition, selections from a keyboard displayed on the surface, or selections from menus and forms permits simple and rapid data entry. The *stylus* is attractive to designers because it is familiar and comfortable for users, and because it permits high precision with good control to limit inadvertent selections. Users can rest their palms on the display surface and guide the pen tip to the desired location while keeping the critical sections of the display in view. These advantages over touchscreens are balanced against the need to pick up and put down a stylus. The early and bulky LINUS notebook was not a commercial success, but the higher-resolution and more compact machines from GO Corporation, NCR Corporation, SONY (see Figure 1.1), and others seem to be more viable. The market should be large if the price can be brought down. Although handwriting-recognition algorithms are steadily improving, keyboard selection may still be preferred in many situations.

6.3.3   Indirect pointing devices

Indirect pointing devices eliminate the hand-fatigue and hand-obscuring-the-screen problems but must overcome the problem of indirection. As with the lightpen, the off-keyboard hand position and pick-up problems remain. Also, indirect control devices require more cognitive processing and hand–eye coordination to bring the onscreen cursor to the desired target.

The *mouse* (Lu, 1984) is appealing because the hand rests in a comfortable position, buttons on the mouse are easily pressed, even long motions can be rapid, and positioning can be precise (Figure 6.10). However, the user must pick up the mouse to begin work, desk space is consumed, the mouse wire can be distracting, pickup and replace actions are necessary for long

Figure 6.10

Three versions of the mouse with one (Apple Macintosh), two (IBM PS/2), and three (Sun Microsystems) buttons.

motions, and some practice (5 to 50 minutes) is required to develop skill. The variety of mouse technologies (physical, optical, or acoustic), number of buttons, placement of the sensor, weight, and size indicate that designers and users have yet to settle on alternatives. Personal preferences and the variety of tasks leave room for lively competition.

The *trackball* has sometimes been described as an upside-down mouse (Figure 6.11). It is usually implemented as a rotating ball 2 to 6 inches in diameter that moves a cursor on the screen as it is moved. The trackball is firmly mounted in a desk or a solid box to allow the operators to hit the ball

Figure 6.11

The trackball moves the cursor through the rotating motion of the ball. (Courtesy of Microspeed Inc., Fremont, CA.)

Figure 6.12

The joystick makes it easy
to move around on the
screen.

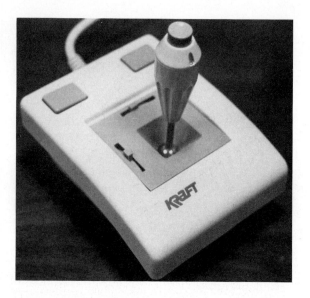

vigorously and to make it spin. The trackball has been the preferred device in the high-stress world of air-traffic control and in some video games. Small trackballs have also been employed as a pointing device in portable laptop computers.

The *joystick* has a long history that begins in automobile- and aircraft-control devices (Figure 6.12). There are dozens of computer versions, with varying stick lengths and thicknesses, displacement forces and distances, buttons or triggers, anchoring strategies for bases, and placement relative to the keyboard and screen. Joysticks are appealing for tracking purposes—that is, to follow a moving object on a screen—in part because of the relatively small displacements necessary to move a cursor, and the ease of direction changes.

The *graphics tablet* is a touch-sensitive surface separate from the screen, usually laid flat on the table (Figure 6.13) or in the user's lap (see Figure 10.8). This position allows for a comfortable hand position and keeps the users' hands off the screen. Furthermore, the graphics tablet permits a surface even larger than the screen to be covered with printing to indicate available choices, thereby providing guidance to novice users and pre-serving valuable screen space. Limited data entry can be done with the graphics tablet. The graphics tablet can be operated by placement of a finger, pencil, puck, or stylus, using acoustic, electronic, or contact position sensing.

A *touchpad* (3- by 4-inch touchable surface) attached near the keyboard offers the convenience of a touchscreen while keeping the user's hand off the display surface. Increased hand–eye coordination is needed, but this approach is a workable compromise.

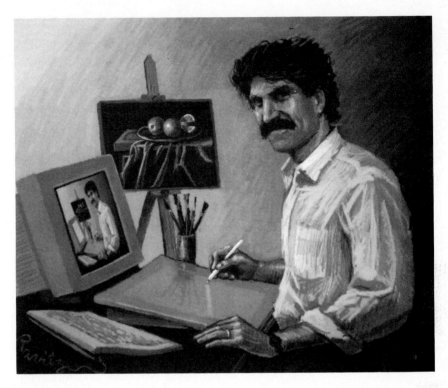

Figure 6.13

The WACOM stylus and graphics tablet allows precise pointing and accurate control necessary for artists. An all electronic painting using PhotoShop and a Wacom tablet, created by Larry Ravitz, shows him drawing with the WACOM stylus. (Photograph courtesy of Larry Ravitz, Takoma Park, MD.)

Among these indirect pointing devices, the mouse has been the success story of the past decade. Given the rapid high-precision pointing and a comfortable hand position, the modest training period is only a small impediment. Most new computer systems offer a mouse, and some require it.

6.3.4 Comparisons of pointing devices

Each pointing concept has its enthusiasts and detractors, motivated by commercial interests, personal preference, and increasingly by empirical evidence. Human-factors variables of interest are speed of motion for short and long distances, accuracy of positioning, error rates, learning time, and user satisfaction. Other variables are cost, durability, space requirements, weight, left- versus right-hand use, and compatibility with other systems.

In early studies, direct pointing devices, such as the lightpen or touchscreen, were often the fastest but the least accurate devices (Stammers and Bird, 1980; Albert, 1982; Haller et al., 1984). The speed appears to accrue from the directness of pointing, and the inaccuracy from problems with feedback, physical design, and use strategies. New strategies such as lift-off and greater precision in the devices have made it feasible to build high-precision touchscreens and pens.

Indirect pointing devices have been the cause of much controversy. The graphics tablet is appealing when the user can remain with the device for long periods without switching to a keyboard. Pens accompanying graphics tablets allow a high degree of control that is appreciated by artists using drawing programs. The Wacom tablet with its wireless pen and directional sensitivity allows freedom and control; and the "bat brush" gives 6 degrees of freedom for artistic effects (Ware and Baxter, 1989). The mouse was found to be faster than the joystick (English et al., 1967; Card et al., 1978). A trackball was found to be faster and more accurate than a joystick, and a graphics tablet was found to be slightly faster but slightly less accurate than the trackball (Albert, 1982). New graphics tablets have higher precision.

The usual wisdom is that pointing devices are faster than keyboard controls, such as cursor-movement keys (Goodwin, 1975; Card et al., 1978; Albert, 1982), but this result depends on the task. When a few (two to 10) targets are on the screen and the cursor can be made to jump from one target to the next, then the cursor jump keys can become faster than pointing devices (Figure 6.14) (Ewing et al., 1986). For tasks that mix typing and pointing, cursor keys have also been shown to be faster and more preferred than the mouse (Karat et al., 1984). Since muscular strain is low for cursor keys (Haider et al., 1982), they should be considered for this special case. This result is supported by Card et al. (1978), who reported that, for short distances, the cursor keys were faster than the mouse (Figure 6.15). The positioning time increases rapidly with distance for cursor keys, but only slightly for the mouse or trackball.

Figure 6.14

Path-completion time for arrow jump and mouse as a function of average target distance of the traversed path (Ewing et al., 1986). Long-distance targets were farther away from the start point than were short-distance targets. The arrow-jump strategy was faster, since a single keypress produced a jump to the target, whereas mouse users had to move the cursor across the screen.

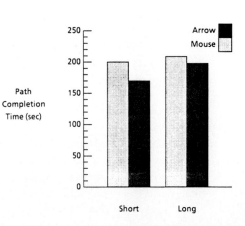

Figure 6.15

The effect of target distance on position time for arrow keys and mouse. The positioning time for arrow keys increased dramatically with distance because many keypresses were necessary to move the cursor to the target. The mouse time is quite independent of distance over these distances. With very short distances and a few character positions, the arrow keys had a shorter mean time. (Adapted from S. K. Card, W. K. English, and B. J. Burr, Evaluation of mouse, rate-controlled isometric joystick, step keys, and task keys for text selection on a CRT, *Ergonomics 17*, 6 (1965).)

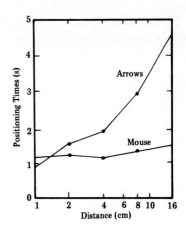

In summary, much work remains to sort out the task and individual differences with respect to pointing devices. However, some practical recommendations can be made before precise evidence emerges (Reinhart and Marken, 1985; Shinar et al., 1985). The touchscreen seems attractive when durability and public-access applications are required. The mouse and trackball are attractive when accurate pixel-level pointing is needed. Cursor jump keys are attractive when there is a small number of targets.

There is little evidence about use of graphics tablets, but the additional space they provide for options not listed on the screen is appealing, although the physical space requirements are a serious limitation in many applications.

Lightpens and styli have the advantage of familiarity and fewer inadvertent touches over touchscreens, but the requirement to pick up the lightpen is a disadvantage. The stylus is attractive, compared to the touchscreen, because users can rest their hands on the screen surface to gain precision, and the narrow stylus may obscure less of the screen. Joysticks are appealing to game or aircraft-cockpit designers, apparently because of the firm grip and easy movement, but they are slow and inaccurate in guiding a cursor to a fixed destination in office automation and personal computing. Indirect pointing devices require more learning than do direct control devices.

6.3.5 Fitts' Law

The major pointing devices depend on hand movement to control a cursor on the display. An effective predictive model of time to move a given distance, *D*, to a target of width, *W*, was developed by Paul Fitts (1954). He discovered that the pointing time is a function of the distance and the width; farther away and smaller targets take longer to point to. The *index of difficulty* is defined as

$$\textit{Index of difficulty} = \log_2 (2D \ / \ W)$$

and the time to perform the point action is

$$\textit{Time to point} = C_1 + C_2 \ (\textit{index of difficulty})$$

where C_1 and C_2 and constants that depend on the device. Once data have been collected for a given device, C_1 and C_2 can be computed, and then predictions can be made regarding the time for other tasks. For example, for a 1-inch-wide target at a distance of 8 inches, the Index of difficulty is $\log_2$ $(2*8/1) = \log_2(16) = 4$. If the device to be used has been tested, and $C_1 = 0.2$, $C_2 = 0.1$, then the *time to point* = 0.2 + 0.1 (4) = 0.6 seconds.

Welford (1968) found that, for short distances, a more effective equation is

$$\textit{Index of difficulty} = \log_2 (D \ / \ W + 0.5)$$

In our studies of high-precision touchscreen, we found that, in addition to the gross arm movement predicted by Fitts and Welford, there was also a fine-tuning motion of the fingers to move in on a small targets such as a single pixel. A three-component equation was thus more suited for the high-precision pointing task:

$$\textit{Time for precision pointing} = C_1 + C_2 \ (\textit{index of difficulty}) + C_3 \log_2 (C_4 \ / \ W)$$

The third term, time for fine tuning, increases as the target width, W, decreases. This extension to Fitts' law is quite understandable and simple; it suggests that the *time to point* at an object consists of a time for initiation of action, C_1, a time for gross movement, and time for fine adjustment. Fitts' studies focused on finger movement, but most current studies deal with specific devices such as a mouse, pen, or trackball. An open problem is to understand how to design devices that produce smaller constants for the predictive equation.

6.3.6   Novel pointing devices

The popularity of pointing devices and the quest for new ways to engage diverse users for diverse tasks has led to provocative innovations. Since a user's hands might be busy on the keyboard, several designers have explored other methods for selection and pointing. Foot controls are popular with rock music performers, dentists, medical-equipment users, car drivers, and pilots, so maybe computer users could benefit from them as well. A foot mouse was tested and found to take about twice as much time as a hand-operated mouse, but benefits in special applications may exist (Pearson and Weiser, 1986).

Eye-tracking, gaze-detecting controllers have been developed by several researchers and companies who make devices to assist the handicapped (Jacob, 1990). Nonintrusive and noncontact equipment using video-camera image recognition of pupil position can give 1- to 2-degree accuracy, and fixations of 200 to 600 milliseconds are used to make selections. Unfortunately, the "Midas touch problem" intrudes, since every gaze has the potential to activate an unintended command. For the moment, eye tracking remains a research tool and an aid for the handicapped.

The VPL DataGlove appeared in 1987 and has attracted serious researchers, technology explorers, game developers, cyberspace adventurers, and virtual-reality devotees (see Section 5.8). The DataGlove is made of sleek black spandex with attached fiber-optic sensors to measure finger position. The displayed feedback can show the placement of each finger; thus commands, such as a closed fist, open hand, index-finger pointing, and thumbs-up gesture, can be recognized. With a Polhemus tracker, complete three-dimensional placement and orientation can be recorded. Control over three-dimensional models seems natural, but comparisons with other strategies have not been published. Precision is low and response slow, but devotees claim that the naturalness of gestures will enable use by many keyboard- or mouse-fearing nonusers.

6.4 Speech Recognition, Digitization, and Generation

The dream of speaking to computers and having computers speak has lured many researchers and visionaries. Arthur C. Clarke's fantasy of the HAL 9000 computer in the book and movie *2001* has set the standard for future performance of computers in science fiction and for some advanced developers. The reality is more complex and sometimes more surprising than the dream. Hardware designers have made dramatic progress with speech and voice-manipulation devices, and current directions are diverging from the science-fiction fantasy (McCauley, 1984; Schmandt, 1985; Strathmeyer, 1990).

The vision of a computer that has a leisurely chat with the user seems more of a fantasy than a desired or believable reality. Instead, practical applications for specific tasks with specific devices are being designed to be more effective in serving the user's need to work rapidly with low error rates. The benefits to people with certain physical handicaps are rewarding to see, but the general users of office or personal computing are not rushing toward speech input and output. However, speech store-and-forward systems, speech-assisted instructional systems, and speech help systems are growing in popularity.

Speech technology has four components: discrete-word recognition, continuous-speech recognition, speech store and forward, and speech generation. A further topic is the use of audio tones, audiolization, and music. These components can be combined in creative ways: from simple systems that merely play back or generate a message, to complex interactions that accept speech commands, generate speech feedback, provide audiolizations of scientific data, and allow annotation plus editing of stored speech.

6.4.1   Discrete word recognition

Discrete-word recognition devices recognize individual words spoken by a specific person; they work with 90- to 98-percent reliability for vocabularies of from 50 to 150 words. *Speaker-dependent training*, in which the user repeats the full vocabulary once or twice, is a part of most systems. *Speaker-independent* systems are under development and are beginning to be reliable enough for certain commercial applications.

Applications for the physically handicapped have been successful in enabling bedridden, paralyzed, or otherwise disabled people to broaden the horizons of their life. They can control wheelchairs, operate equipment, or use personal computers for a variety of tasks.

Other applications have been successful when at least one of these conditions exist:

- Speaker's hands are busy
- Mobility is required
- Speaker's eyes are occupied
- Harsh (underwater or battlefield) or cramped (airplane-cockpit) conditions preclude use of a keyboard

Example applications include aircraft-engine inspectors who wear a wireless microphone as they walk around the engine opening coverplates or adjusting components. They can issue orders, read serial numbers, or retrieve previous maintenance records by using a 35-word vocabulary. Baggage handlers for a major airline speak the destination city names as they place bags on a moving conveyor belt, thereby routing the bag to the proper airplane loading gate. For this application, the speaker-dependent training produced *higher* recognition rates when done in the noisy, but more realistic, environment of the conveyor belt, rather than in the quiet conditions of a recording studio. Implementers should consider conducting the speaker-dependent training in the same environment as the task.

Many advanced development efforts have tested speech recognition in military aircraft, medical operating rooms, training laboratories, and office automation. The results reveal problems with recognition rates, even for speaker-dependent training systems, when background sounds change, when the user is ill or under stress, and when words in the vocabulary are similar (dime–time or Houston–Austin).

For common computing applications when a screen is used, speech input has not been beneficial. Studies of controlling cursor movement by voice (Murray et al., 1983) found that cursor-movement keys were twice as fast and were preferred by users. In a study with four 1-hour sessions, 10 typists and 10 nontypists used typed and spoken commands to correct online documents using the UNIX ed editor (Morrison et al., 1984). For both typed and spoken commands, the user still had to type parameter strings. Typists preferred to use the keyboard. Nontypists began with a preference for spoken commands, but switched to favor using the keyboard by the end of the four sessions. No significant differences were found for task-completion time or error rates.

In a study of 24 knowledgeable programmers, a voice editor led to a lower task-completion rate than did a keyboard editor. However, the keyboard entry produced a higher error rate (Leggett and Williams, 1984) (see Table 6.1). The authors suggest that further experience with voice systems, beyond the 90 minutes of this study, might lead to better performance. A speed advantage for voice entry over a menu-selection strategy was found in a study of two beginners and three advanced users of a CAD system (Shutoh et al., 1984). A study of eight MacDraw users drawing eight diagrams each showed that allowing users to select one of 19 commands by voice reduced performance times by an average of 21 percent (Pausch and Leatherby, 1991). The advantage seems to have been gained through avoidance of the time-consuming and distracting effort of moving the cursor repeatedly from the diagram to the tool palette and back.

Table 6.1

Average percentage scores for input and editing tasks using keyboard and voice editors. (Source: Data from Leggett, John and Williams, Glen, An empirical investigation of voice as an input modality for computer programming, *International Journal Man–Machine Studies 21* [1984], 493–520.)

	Key Editor	Voice Editor
Input task		
Input task completed	70.6	50.7
Erroneous input	11.0	3.8
Edit task		
Edit task completed	70.3	55.3
Erroneous commands	2.4	1.5
Erroneous input	14.3	1.2

Current research projects are devoted to improving the recognition rates in difficult conditions, eliminating the need for speaker-dependent training, and increasing the vocabularies handled to 10,000 and even 20,000 words.

Speech recognition for discrete words shows much promise for special-purpose applications, but not as a general interaction medium. Keyboards, function keys, and pointing devices with direct manipulation are often more rapid, and the actions or commands can be made visible for easy editing; error handling and appropriate feedback with voice input is difficult and slow, and the audio channel is reserved for human–human communication. Combinations of voice and direct manipulation may be useful, as in Pausch and Leatherby's study.

6.4.2   Continuous-speech recognition

HAL's ability to understand the astronauts' spoken words and even to read their lips was an appealing fantasy, but the reality is more sobering. Although many research projects have pursued *continuous-speech recognition*, most observers believe that a commercially successful product will not be forthcoming within the next decade or two. The difficulty revolves around recognizing the boundaries between spoken words. Normal speech patterns slur the boundaries.

The hope is that, with a continuous-speech recognition system, users could dictate letters, compose reports verbally for automatic transcription, and enable computers to scan long audio tapes, radio programs, or telephone calls for specific words or topics.

Continuous-speech recognition products are offered by manufacturers such as Verbex, which claims greater than 99.5-percent accuracy with speaker-dependent training with vocabularies of up to 10,000 words, and Speech Systems, which claims 95-percent accuracy for speaker-independent systems with 40,000 word vocabularies. Although progress has been made by the many companies and researchers still pursuing the dream, "comfortable and natural communication in a general setting (no constraints on what you can say and how you say it) is beyond us for now, posing a problem too difficult to solve" (Peacocke and Graf, 1990).

6.4.3   Speech store and forward

Less exciting, but probably more immediately useful, are the systems that enable the storing and forwarding of spoken messages. Stored messages are commonly used for weather, airline, and financial information, but personal messaging through the telephone network is growing more popular. After registering with the service, users can touch commands on a 12-key telephone to store spoken messages, and can have the messages sent to one or more people who are also registered with the service. Users can receive messages, replay messages, reply to the caller, forward messages to other users, delete messages, or archive messages. The messages are converted from the analog voice input to a digitized and usually compressed form for storage on magnetic media. Conversion from digital to analog for output is a standard technique, preserving the original tone quality quite well. Automatic elimination of silences and speedup by sound clipping are available.

This voice mail technology works reliably, is fairly low cost, and is generally liked by users. Problems focus mainly on the awkwardness of using the 12-key telephone pad for commands, the need to dialin to check whether messages have been left, and the potential for too many "junk" telephone messages because of the ease of broadcasting a message to many people.

Other applications of digitized speech are for instructional systems and online help and document annotation. Educational psychologists conjecture that, if several senses (sight, touch, hearing) are engaged, then learning can be facilitated. Adding a spoken voice to a computer-assisted instructional system or an online help system may improve the learning process. Adding voice annotation to a document may make it easier for teachers to comment on student papers or business executives to leave detailed responses or instructions. Editing the voice annotation is possible but still difficult.

6.4.4   Speech generation

Speech generation is an example of a successful technology that is used, but its applicability was overestimated by some developers. Inexpensive, compact, reliable speech-generation (also called synthesis) devices have been used in cameras ("too dark—use flash"), soft-drink vending machines ("insert correct change and make your selection," "thank you"), automobiles ("your door is ajar"), children's games (Figure 6.16), and utility-control rooms to warn of danger.

In some cases, the novelty wears off quickly and the application needs become dominant, leading to removal of the speech generation. Talking supermarket checkout machines that read products and prices were found to violate a sense of privacy about purchases and to be too noisy. Automobile speech-generation devices are now less widely used; a few tones and red-light indicators were found to be more acceptable. Spoken warnings in cockpits or control rooms were sometimes missed or were in competition with human–human communication.

Applications for the blind are an important success story (Songco et al., 1980). The Kurzweil Reader is used in hundreds of libraries. Patrons can place a book on a copierlike device that scans the text and does an acceptable job of reading the text one word at a time.

Figure 6.16

Speak & Spell (Texas Instruments) offers several word games, including a version of hangman and spelling drill. See Figure 6.3 for a closeup. Instructions are given by synthesized voice, and the user presses on the membrane keyboard.

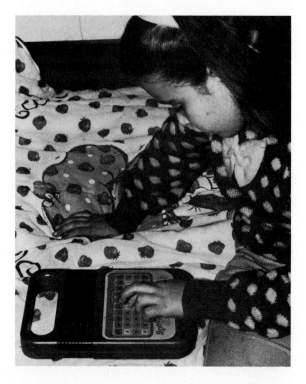

The quality of the sound can be very good when the words and pronunciation or digitized human speech can be stored in a dictionary. When algorithms are used to generate the sound, the quality is sometimes degraded. Digitized human speech for phrases or sentences is often a useful strategy, since human intonation provides more authentic sound. For some applications, a computerlike sound may be preferred. Apparently, the robotlike sound in the Atlanta airport subway drew more attention than did a tape recording of a human giving directions.

Michaelis and Wiggins (1982) suggest that speech generation is "frequently preferable" under these circumstances:

1. The message is simple.
2. The message is short.
3. The message will not be referred to later.
4. The message deals with events in time.
5. The message requires an immediate response.
6. The visual channels of communication are overloaded.
7. The environment is too brightly lit, too poorly lit (possibly to preserve dark adaptation), subject to severe vibration, or otherwise unsuitable for transmission of visual information.

8. The user must be free to move around.

9. The user is subjected to high G forces or anoxia (lack of oxygen, typically occurs at high altitudes). The magnitude of G forces or anoxia at which eyesight begins to be impaired is well below that needed to affect hearing.

These criteria apply to digitized human speech and to simple playbacks of tape recordings.

Digitized speech segments can be concatenated to form more complex phrases and sentences. Telephone-based voice information systems for banking (Fidelity Automated Service Telephone (FAST)), credit-card information (Citibank Customer Service), airline schedules (American Airlines Dial-AA-Flight), and so on have touchtone keying of codes and voice output of information.

In summary, speech generation is technologically feasible. Now, clever designers must find the situations in which it is superior to competing technologies. Novel applications may be by way of the telephone, as a supplement to the CRT, or through embedding in small consumer products.

6.4.5   Audio tones, audiolization, and music

In addition to speech, auditory machine outputs include individual *audio tones*, more complex information presentation by combinations of sound, or *audiolization*, and *music*. Early Teletypes did include a bell tone to alert users that a message was coming or that paper had run out. Later computer systems added a range of tones to indicate warnings or simply to acknowledge the completion of an action. Even keyboards were built with the intent to preserve sound feedback. As digital-signal-processing (DSP) chips to perform digital-to-analog (D-to-A) and analog-to-digital (A-to-D) conversions have become more powerful and cheaper, innovations have begun to appear. Gaver's SonicFinder (1989) added sound to the Macintosh interface by offering a dragging sound when a file was being dragged, a click when a window boundary was passed, and a thunk when the file was dropped into the trashcan for deletion. The effect for most users is a satisfying confirmation of actions; for visually impaired users, the sounds are vital. On the other hand, after a few hours, the sound can become a distraction rather than a contribution, especially in a room with several machines and users.

Auditory browsers for blind users or for telephonic usage have been proposed. Each file might have a sound whose frequency was related to its size and assigned an instrument (violin, flute, trumpet). Then, when the directory is opened, each file might play its sound simultaneously or sequentially (in alphabetical order?). Alternatively, files might have sounds associated with their file types so that users could hear whether there were only spreadsheet, graphic, or text files (Blattner et al., 1989).

More ambitious audiolizations have been proposed (Smith et al., 1990; Blattner et al., 1991) in which scientific data are presented as a series of stereo phonic sounds, rather than as images. Other explorations have included audio tones for mass-spectrograph output to hear the differences between a standard and a test sample, and quite appealing musical output to debug the execution of a computer with 16 parallel processors.

Adding traditional music to user interfaces seems to be an appropriate idea to heighten drama, to relax users, to draw attention, or to set a mood (patriotic marches, romantic sonatas, or gentle waltzes). These approaches have been used in video games and educational packages; but they might also be suitable for public access, home control, sales kiosks, bank machines, and other applications.

The potential for novel musical instruments seems especially attractive. With a touchscreen, it should be possible to offer appropriate feedback to give musicians an experience similar to a piano keyboard, a drum, a woodwind, or a stringed instrument. There is a possibility of inventing new instruments whose frequency, amplitude, and effect are governed by the placement of the touch, direction, speed, and even acceleration. Music composition using computers will certainly expand as powerful musical instrument digital interface (MIDI) hardware and software become widely available at reasonable prices, and user interfaces effectively combine piano and computer keyboards (Baggi, 1991).

6.5 Displays

The *visual display unit (VDU)* has become the primary source of feedback to the user from the computer (Cakir et al., 1980; Grandjean, 1987; Helander, 1987). The VDU has many important features, including these:

- *Rapid operation:* Thousands of characters per second or a full image in a few milliseconds
- *Reasonable size:* Typically 24 lines of 80 characters, but devices of at least 66 lines of 166 characters are available
- *Reasonable resolution:* Typically resolution is 640 by 480 pixels, but 1280 by 1024 is common
- *Quiet operation*
- *No paper waste*
- *Relatively low cost:* Displays can cost as little as $100
- *Reliability*
- *Highlighting:* Overwriting, windowing, and blinking are examples
- *Graphics and animation*

The widespread use of VDUs has led designers to develop a variety of technologies with hundreds of special-purpose features. International standards are beginning to appear, and costs continue to decrease, even as quality increases. Such health concerns as visual fatigue, stress, and radiation levels are being addressed by manufacturers and government agencies, but some concerns remain (Kleiner, 1985).

6.5.1   Monochrome displays

For many applications, *monochrome displays* are adequate, and even preferred, especially if the monochrome display has a higher resolution than does the color display. Monochrome displays are produced by several technologies (Foley et al., 1990; IBM, 1984):

- *Raster-scan cathode-ray tube (CRT):* This popular device is similar to a television monitor, with an electron beam sweeping out lines of dots to form letters. The refresh rates (the reciprocal of the time required to produce a full screen image) vary from 30 to 65 per second. Higher rates are preferred, because they reduce *flicker*. CRT displays are often green because the P39 green phosphor has a long decay time, permitting relatively stable images. The P38 orange–amber phosphor has an even longer decay time and is preferred by many users. Another important property of a phosphor is the low *bloom level*, allowing sharp images because the small granules of the phosphor do not spread the glow to nearby points. The maximum resolution of a CRT is about 100 lines per inch. Displays can have light letters against a dark background or dark letters against a light background. CRT sizes (measured diagonally) range from less than 2 inches to almost 30 inches; popular models are in the range of 9 to 15 inches.

- *Stroke character CRT:* Instead of a line of dots, characters are formed by movement of the electron beam to paint the character. This approach is effective when line-drawn images are the main display items, as in air traffic control or CAD.

- *Storage-tube CRT:* The interior surface of the display contains special phosphors that maintain the image created by the electron-beam sweep. This approach eliminates the need for rapid refreshing and the distraction of flicker, but the contrast is usually poorer.

- *Plasma panel:* Rows of horizontal wires are slightly separated from vertical wires by small glass-enclosed capsules of neon-based gases. When the horizontal and vertical wires on either side of the capsule receive a high voltage, the gas glows. Plasma displays are usually orange and flicker-free, but the size of the capsules limits the resolution. Plasma computer displays have been built to display up to 62 lines of 166 characters.

- *Liquid-crystal displays (LCDs):* Voltage changes influence the reflectivity of tiny capsules of liquid crystals, turning some spots darker when viewed by reflected light. LCDs are flicker-free; but again, the size of the capsules limits the resolution. Watches and calculators often use LCDs because of their small size, light weight, and low power consumption. Portable computers have been built with LCD displays having up to 24 lines by 80 characters.

- *Light-emitting diodes (LEDs):* Certain diodes emit light when a voltage is applied. Arrays of these small diodes can be assembled to display characters. Here again, the resolution is limited by manufacturing techniques.

- *Electroluminescent displays:* Instead of striking a phosphor by an electron beam, the electroluminescent displays operate with phosphors that emit light when a voltage is applied directly. The front panel conductor must be transparent to allow the user to see the phosphor. The manufacturing technology enables these displays to be of high resolution, in addition to having the attractive properties of thinness and light weight. Electroluminescent displays have been used for pocket-sized televisions but have yet to be widely used for computer displays because of the high cost of producing a large display.

The technology employed affects these variables:

- Size
- Refresh rate
- Capacity to show animation
- Resolution
- Surface flatness
- Surface glare from reflected light
- Contrast between characters and background
- Brightness
- Flicker
- Line sharpness
- Character formation
- Tolerance for vibration

Each display technology has advantages and disadvantages with respect to these variables. Further consideration should be given to the availability of these features:

- User control of contrast and brightness
- Software highlighting of characters by brightness
- Underscoring, reverse video, blinking (possibly at several rates)

- Character set (alphabetic, numeric, special and foreign characters)
- Multiple type styles (for example, italic, bold) and fonts
- Shape, size, and blinking rate of the cursor
- User control of cursor shape, blinking, and brightness
- Scrolling mechanism (smooth scrolling is preferred)
- User control of number of lines or characters per line displayed
- Support of negative and positive polarity (light on dark or dark on light)

Some frequent users place contrast-enhancement filters or masks in front of displays. Filters reduce reflected glare by using polarizers or a thin film of antireflective coating. Masks may be made of nylon mesh or simple matte surfaces. These devices are helpful to some users, but they can reduce resolution and are subject to smudging from fingerprints.

6.5.2   Color displays

Color displays can make videogames, educational simulations, CAD, and many other applications programs more attractive and effective for users, but there are real dangers in misusing color.

Color images are produced with several phosphors located on the display surface. The *RGB shadow-mask displays* have small dots of red, green, and blue phosphors packed closely, so that a full range of colors can be created by combinations of these dots. With all three dots illuminated, the users see white. This approach reduces the resolution when monochrome images or texts are displayed. A second, but increasingly rare, strategy is to have translucent layers of phosphors that glow in response to different electron-beam frequencies. In this *beam-penetration strategy*, combinations of beams cause several layers to glow, producing a range of colors while preserving high resolution.

Color images are attractive to the eye, and color coding of screen objects can lead to rapid recognition and identification (Christ, 1975; Robertson, 1980; IBM, 1984; Durrett, 1987; Thorell and Smith, 1990). Of course, excessive or inappropriate use of color can inhibit performance and confuse the user. See Chapter 8 for a discussion of color use in screen design.

Software for creating color graphics images is rapidly becoming more effective. Still, it may take several hours or weeks for users to generate a satisfactory image. Simple shapes, such as boxes, circles, or lines, are easy to draw, but designing an automobile engine part, creating a map, or laying out a building floorplan may take weeks. The great gift of computer graphics is that small changes to existing images usually can be made rapidly. Effective computer graphics systems are often application specific.

Dramatic progress in computer graphics has led to increasing use in motion pictures and television. Startling images have been created for movies, such as the Star Wars series (George Lucas's Industrial Light and Magic), TRON (Walt Disney Studios), and Terminator 2 (Industrial Light and Magic). Many television commercials, station-identification segments, and news-related graphics have been constructed by computer animation. Finally, videogames are another source of impressive computer graphics images. The ACM's SIGGRAPH (Special Interest Group on Graphics) has an exciting annual conference with exhibitions of novel graphics devices and applications. The conference proceedings and videotape digest are rich sources of information.

6.5.3   Television images, videodisks, and compact disks

Another approach to graphics is to use television technology to capture an image from an existing photograph, drawing, or map, or from the real world. This strategy provides a detailed image rapidly and allows modifications to be made relatively easily. These *television images* can be stored in digitized form on magnetic media, sent electronically, edited, and printed (see Section 11.5). Several computer-based video-conferencing systems allow users to send an image over normal telephone lines in compressed data formats in from 5 to 30 seconds. About 240 compressed images can be stored on a single 1.44-megabyte floppy disk. Printers for television images are beginning to appear commercially. Several companies offer an attachment that enables consumers to print images taken with home video-recording equipment.

In addition to video cameras as input devices, there are many digitizing packages that support input of maps or line drawings by having users mark coordinates for line beginnings and endings. An automatic scanner is available that turns a printer into a cheap input device for paper images. The paper image is placed in the printer, and the printer ribbon is replaced by a photoelectric scanner. As the printer head moves back and forth, the image is digitized and is entered into the computer's storage. High-resolution (300 dots per inch and greater) black-and-white or color scanners convert paper images into digitized formats that can be manipulated electronically.

Another emerging blend of image display and computers is the computer-controlled *videodisk*. Videodisks can store more than 100,000 images on a single 12-inch-diameter platter. Each image is directly addressable, and retrieval time is a maximum of eight seconds. The Library of Congress uses videodisks to store 100,000 publicity photographs from 6000 commercial films. After the user has selected a film from the menu-based index, successive images from that film appear within a fraction of a second after a single keypress. Another Library of Congress project provides online access to more than 1 million images of frequently used current magazines and old deteriorating books. The *optical disk jukebox* rotates to deliver the proper disk to the reading device within 15 seconds. Users perform searches using the standard SCORPIO system, and then receive the image on a high-resolution monitor or as hard copy from a laser printer.

Videodisks for art, photography, travel, consumer goods, and history appear regularly. The videodisk technology is read-only, and the cost of producing a videodisk is still a limitation to more widespread use.

Compact disks (often called *CD-ROMs*, for *compact disk with read-only memory*) with sound, text, or images have a promising future (see Section 11.5). Electronic encyclopedias, numerical databases, and maps are appearing with increasing frequency. A compact-disk player and a small display will enable automobile drivers to view highway or street maps. The potential for rapid access to indexed databases of images and text will attract many designers and users.

6.5.4   Multiple-display workstations

A single small display often limits what the user can accomplish. One remedy is to use a larger display, possibly with multiple windows; another, sometimes easier and less expensive approach is to use two or more screens. A computer graphics display and a videodisk display side by side can show computer-generated text and a television image simultaneously. The Spatial Data Management System installed on the aircraft carrier USS *Carl Vinson* by Computer Corporation of America has three displays for graphics, maps, reconnaissance photographs, and text.

Air-traffic controllers, satellite controllers at NASA, pilots, power-plant operators, stock-market traders, and computer- or telephone-network control-room workers may view three or more displays to perform their tasks. Screens may show related data from different sources or in different formats (graphics, text, or images).

6.5.5   Projectors, heads-up displays, helmet-mounted displays, and EyePhones

The desire to show and see computer-generated images has inspired several novel products. *Projector* television systems have been adapted to show the higher-resolution images from computers. These devices can generate 4- by 6-foot displays with good saturation, and larger displays with some loss of fidelity. An important variation is to use an LCD plate in connection with a common overhead projector to show good monochrome and color computer displays for meetings of 10 to 40 people. These devices are declining in price and increasing in quality.

Personal display technology involves small portable monitors, often made with LCD in monochrome or color. A *heads-up display* projects information on a partially silvered windscreen of an airplane or car, so that the pilots or drivers can keep their attention focused on the surroundings while receiving computer-generated information. An alternative, the helmet-mounted display, consists of a small partially silvered glass mounted on a helmet or hat so that users can see information even while turning their heads. In fact, the information they see may be varied as a function of the direction in which they are looking.

Virtual-reality researchers (see Section 5.8) have explored *EyePhones*, a pair of small monitors mounted in goggles that produces a full three-dimensional effect. LCD displays are needed to keep the weight and volume down, since users expect to be able to walk around and to move smoothly while wearing the eyephones. The Private Eye technology uses a line of 200 LEDs and a moving mirror to produce 720- by 200-pixel resolution images in a lightweight and small display that can be mounted on a pair of glasses.

Other attempts to produce three-dimensional displays include vibrating surfaces, holograms, polarized glasses, red–blue glasses, and synchronized shutter glasses.

6.6 Printers

Even with good-quality and high-speed displays, people still have a great desire for hardcopy printouts. Paper documents can be easily copied, mailed, marked, and stored. These are the important criteria for printers:

- Speed
- Print quality
- Cost
- Compactness
- Quiet operation
- Use of ordinary paper (fanfolded or single sheet)
- Character set
- Variety of typefaces, fonts, and sizes
- Highlighting techniques (boldface, underscore, and so on)
- Support for special forms (printed forms, different lengths, and so on)
- Reliability

Early computer printers worked at 10 characters per second and did not support graphics. Modern personal-computer *dot-matrix printers* print more than 200 characters per second, have multiple fonts, can print boldface, use variable width and size, and have graphics capabilities. *Daisy-wheel printers* generate 30 to 65 letter-quality characters per second. *Inkjet printers* offer quiet operation and high-quality output. *Thermal printers* offer quiet, compact, and inexpensive output on specially coated papers. This technology has led to cheap portable typewriters with storage for a few thousand characters of text and the capability to act as a terminal.

Printing systems on mainframe computers have *impact line printers* that operate at 1200 lines per minute and *laser printers* that operate at 30,000 lines per minute. The laser printers, now widely available for microcomputers, support graphics and produce high-quality images from Postscript, TrueType, or other page-description languages. Speeds vary from 4 to 40 pages per minute, resolution ranges from 200 to 400 points per inch. Software to permit publication-quality typesetting has opened the door to *desktop-publishing* ventures. Compact laser printers offer users the satisfaction of producing elegant business documents, scientific reports, novels, or personal correspondence. Users should consider output quality, speed, choice of faces and fonts, graphics capabilities, and special paper requirements. Users of laser printers must take care in choosing papers whose surface bonds well with the toner and can tolerate the high heat. Fortunately, recycled papers work especially well in such conditions.

Color printers allow users to produce hardcopy output of color graphics, usually by a dot-matrix or inkjet approach with three-color print heads or inks. The printed image is often of lower quality than the screen image and may not be faithful to the screen colors. Color laser printers bring the satisfaction of bright and sharp color images.

Plotters enable output of graphs, bar charts, line drawings, and maps on rolls of paper or sheets up to 36 by 50 inches. Plotters may have single pens or multiple pens for color output. Other design factors are the precision of small movements, the accuracy in placement of the pens, the speed of pen motion, the repeatability of drawings, and the software support.

Photographic printers allow the creation of 35-millimeter or larger slides (transparencies) and photographic prints. These printers are often designed as add-on devices in front of a display, but high-quality printing systems are independent devices. Computer output to microfilm devices is effective with high-volume applications. *Newspaper-* or *magazine-layout systems* allow electronic editing of images and text before generation of production-quality output for printing.

6.7 Practitioner's Summary

Choosing hardware always involves making a compromise between the ideal and the practical. The designer's vision of what an input or output device should be must be tempered by the realities of what is commercially available and within the project budget. Devices should be tested in the application domain to verify the manufacturer's claims, and testimonials or suggestions from other users should be obtained.

Attention should be paid to current trends for specific devices, such as the mouse, touchscreen, stylus, or voice recognizer, and service to the user's real needs also should be considered adequately. Since new devices and refinements to old devices appear regularly, device-independent architecture and software will permit easy integration of novel devices. Avoid being locked into one device; the hardware is often the softest part of the system. Also, remember that a successful idea can become even more successful if reimplementation on other devices is easy to achieve.

Keyboard entry is here to stay for a long time, but consider other forms of input when text entry is limited. Selecting rather than typing has many benefits for both novice and frequent users. Direct-pointing devices are faster and more convenient for novices than are indirect-pointing devices, and accurate pointing is now possible. Beware of the hand-off-the-keyboard problem for all pointing devices, and strive to reduce the number of shifts between the keyboard and the pointing device.

Speech input and output are commercially viable and should be applied where appropriate, but take care to ensure that performance is genuinely improved over other interaction strategies. Display technology is moving rapidly and user expectations are increasing. Higher-resolution, color, and larger displays will be sought by users. Even with sharp, rapid, and accurate color displays, users have a strong desire for high-quality hard-copy output.

6.8   Researcher's Agenda

Novel text-entry keyboards to speed input and to reduce error rates will have to provide significant benefits to displace the well-entrenched QWERTY design. For numerous applications not requiring extensive text entry, opportunities exist to create special-purpose devices or to redesign the task to permit direct-manipulation selection instead. Increasingly, input can be accomplished by copying of data from other online sources; for example, instead of the user keying in economic research data, the system might obtain the data from a commercial database system. Another input source is from optical character recognition of bar codes printed in magazines, on bank statements, in books, or on record albums.

Pointing devices will certainly play an increasing role. A clearer understanding of pointing tasks and the refinement of pointing devices to suit each task seem inevitable. Improvements can be made not only to the devices, but also to the software with which the devices are used. The same mouse hardware can be used in many ways to speed up movement, to provide better feedback to the user, and to reduce errors.

Research on speech systems can also be directed at improving the device and at redesigning the application to make more effective use of the speech input and output technology. Complete and accurate continuous-speech recognition does not seem attainable, but if users will modify their speaking style in specific applications, then more progress is possible. Another worthy direction is to increase rates of continuous-speech recognition for such tasks as finding a given phrase in a large body of recorded speech. Speech output to support training or to offer additional information to users is attractive.

Larger, higher-resolution displays seem attainable. Techniques such as antialiasing do improve text readability and graphics clarity. Thin, lightweight, durable, and inexpensive displays will spawn many applications, not only in portable computers, but also for embedding in briefcases, appliances, telephones, and automobiles. A battery-powered book-sized computer could contain the information from thousands of books, making that information rapidly available by simple finger touches on indexes or embedded menus. Small data cards or a built-in modem would expand the information without limitation.

Among the most exciting developments will be the increased facility for manipulating images. Improved graphics editors, faster image-processing hardware and algorithms, and cheaper image input, storage, and output devices will open up many possibilities. How will people search for images, integrate them with text, or modify them? What level of increased visual literacy will be expected? Can animation become a more common part of computer applications? Will computer displays become more like movies? Can the hardware or software evoke more emotional responses and broaden the spectrum of computer devotees?

References

Albert, Alan E., The effect of graphic input devices on performance in a cursor positioning task, *Proc. Human Factors Society—Twenty-sixth Annual Meeting* (1982), 54–58.

Baggi, Dennis L., Computer-generated music, *IEEE Computer 24*, 7 (July 1991), 6–9.

Blattner, Meera M., Greenberg, R. M., and Kamegai, M., Listening to turbulence: An example of scientific audiolization. In Blattner, M. and Dannenberg, R. B. (Editors), *Interactive Multimedia Computing*, ACM Press, New York (1991).

Blattner, Meera M., Sumikawa, Denise A., and Greenberg, R. M., Earcons and icons: Their structure and common design principles, *Human–Computer Interaction 4* (1989), 11–44.

Brown, C. Marlin, *Human–Computer Interface Design Guidelines*, Ablex, Norwood, NJ (1988).

Buxton, William, There's more to interaction than meets the eye: Some issues in manual input. In Norman, D. A., and Draper, S. W. (Editors), *User Centered System Design: New Perspectives on Human–Computer Interaction*, Lawrence Erlbaum Associates, Hillsdale, NJ (1985) 319–337.

Cakir, A., Hart, D. J., and Stewart, T. F. M., *The VDT Manual*, John Wiley and Sons, New York (1980).

Card, Stuart K., Mackinlay, Jock D., and Robertson, George G., The design space of input devices, *Proc. CHI '90 Conference: Human Factors in Computing Systems*, ACM, New York (1990), 117–124.

Card, S. K., English, W. K., and Burr, B. J., Evaluation of mouse, rate-controlled isometric joystick, step keys, and task keys for text selection on a CRT, *Ergonomics 21*, 8 (August 1978), 601–613.

Christ, Richard E., Review and analysis of color coding research for visual displays, *Human Factors 17*, 6 (1975), 542–570.

Dunsmore, H. E., Data entry. In Kantowitz, Barry H., and Sorkin, Robert D., *Human Factors: Understanding People–Systems Relationships*, John Wiley and Sons, New York (1983), 335–366.

Durrett, H. John (Editor), *Color and the Computer*, Academic Press, New York (1987).

Emmons, W. H., A comparison of cursor-key arrangements (box versus cross) for VDUs. In Grandjean, Etienne (Editor), *Ergonomics and Health in Modern Offices*, Taylor and Francis, London and Philadelphia (1984), 214–219.

Emmons, William H. and Hirsch, Richard, Thirty millimeter keyboards: How good are they?, *Proc. Human Factors Society—Twenty-sixth Annual Meeting* (1982), 425–429.

English, William K., Engelbart, Douglas C., and Berman, Melvyn L., Display-selection techniques for text manipulation, *IEEE Transactions on Human Factors in Electronics, HFE-8*, 1 (March 1967), 5–15.

Ewing, John, Mehrabanzad, Simin, Sheck, Scott, Ostroff, Dan, and Shneiderman, Ben, An experimental comparison of a mouse and arrow-jump keys for an interactive encyclopedia, *International Journal of Man–Machine Studies 23*, 1 (January 1986), 29–45.

Fitts, Paul M., The information capacity of the human motor system in controlling amplitude of movement, *Journal of Experimental Psychology 47* (1954), 381–391.

Foley, James D., Report of a student project, Department of Electrical Engineering and Computer Science, George Washington University, Washington, DC (1983).

Foley, James D., Van Dam, Andries, Feiner, Steven K., and Hughes, John F., *Computer Graphics: Principles and Practice* (Second Edition) Addison-Wesley, Reading, MA (1990).

Foley, James D., Wallace, Victor L., and Chan, Peggy, The human factors of computer graphics interaction techniques, *IEEE Computer Graphics and Applications 4*, 11 (November 1984), 13–48.

Gaver, William W., The SonicFinder: An interface that uses auditory icons, *Human–Computer Interaction 4*, 1 (1989), 67–94.

Goodwin, N. C., Cursor positioning on an electronic display using lightpen, lightgun, or keyboard for three basic tasks, *Human Factors 17*, 3 (June 1975), 289–295.

Gould, John D., Lewis, Clayton, and Barnes, Vincent, Effects of cursor speed on text-editing, *Proc. ACM CHI '85 Conference* (1985), 7–10.

Grandjean, E., Design of VDT workstations. In Salvendy, Gavriel (Editor), *Handbook of Human Factors*, John Wiley and Sons, New York (1987), 1359–1397.

Greenstein, Joel and Arnaut, Lynn, Input devices. In Helander, Martin, *Handbook of Human–Computer Interaction*, North-Holland, Amsterdam, The Netherlands (1988), 495–516.

Haider, E., Luczak, H., and Rohmert, W., Ergonomics investigations of workplaces in a police command-control centre equipped with TV displays, *Applied Ergonomics 13*, 3 (1982), 163–170.

Haller, R., Mutschler, H., and Voss, M., Comparison of input devices for correction of typing errors in office systems, *INTERACT 84* (1984), 218–223.

Helander, Martin G., Design of visual displays. In Salvendy, Gavriel (Editor), *Handbook of Human Factors*, John Wiley and Sons, New York (1987), 507–548.

IBM Corporation, *Human Factors of Workstations with Visual Displays*, IBM, San Jose, CA (April 1984).

Jacob, Robert J. K., What you look at is what you get: Eye movement-based interaction techniques, *Proc. CHI '90 Conference: Human Factors in Computing Systems*, ACM, New York (1990), 11–18.

Karat, John, McDonald, James, and Anderson, Matt, A comparison of selection techniques: Touch panel, mouse and keyboard, *INTERACT 84* (September 1984), 149–153.

Kleiner, Art (Editor), The health hazards of computers: A guide to worrying intelligently, *Whole Earth Review 48* (Fall 1985), 80–93.

Kroemer, K. H. E., Human engineering the keyboard, *Human Factors 14*, 1 (February 1972), 51–63.

Leggett, John, and Williams, Glen, An empirical investigation of voice as an input modality for computer programming, *International Journal of Man–Machine Studies 21* (1984), 493–520.

Lu, Cary, Computer pointing devices: Living with mice, *High Technology* (January 1984), 61–65.

McCauley, Michael E., Human factors in voice technology. In Muckler, Frederick A. (Editor), *Human Factors Review: 1984*, Human Factors Society, Santa Monica, CA (1984), 131–166.

Martin, A., A new keyboard layout, *Applied Ergonomics 3*, 1 (1972).

Michaelis, Paul Roller, and Wiggins, Richard H., A human factors engineer's introduction to speech synthesizers. In Badre, A. and Shneiderman, B. (Editors), *Directions in Human–Computer Interaction*, Ablex, Norwood, NJ (1982), 149–178.

Montgomery, Edward B., Bringing manual input into the twentieth century, *IEEE Computer 15*, 3 (March 1982), 11–18.

Morrison, D. L., Green, T. R. G., Shaw, A. C., and Payne, S. J., Speech-controlled text-editing: effects of input modality and of command structure, *International Journal of Man–Machine Studies 21*, 1 (1984), 49–63.

Murray, J. Thomas, Van Praag, John, and Gilfoil, David, Voice versus keyboard control of cursor motion, *Proc. Human Factors Society—Twenty-seventh Annual Meeting* (1983), 103.

Nakaseko, M., Grandjean, E., Hunting, W., and Gierer, R., Studies of ergonomically designed alphanumeric keyboards, *Human Factors 27*, 2 (1985), 175–187.

Pausch, Randy and Leatherby, James H., An empirical study: Adding voice input to a graphical editor, *Journal of the American Voice Input/Output Society 9*, 2 (July 1991), 55–66.

Peacocke, Richard D. and Graf, Daryl H., An introduction to speech and speaker recognition, *IEEE Computer 23*, 8 (August 1990), 26–33.

Pearson, Glenn and Weiser, Mark, Of moles and men: The design of foot controls for workstations, *Proc. ACM CHI '86: Human Factors in Computing Systems*, ACM, New York (1986), 333–339.

Potosnak, Kathleen M., Input devices. In Helander, Martin (Editor), *Handbook of Human–Computer Interaction*, North-Holland, Amsterdam, The Netherlands (1988), 475–494.

Reinhart, William and Marken, Richard, Control systems analysis of computer pointing devices, *Proc. Human Factors Society—Twenty-ninth Annual Meeting*, (1985) 119–121.

Robertson, P. J., *A Guide to Using Color on Alphanumeric Displays*, IBM Technical Report G320-6296-0, White Plains, NY (June 1980).

Schmandt, Christopher, Voice communication with computers. In Hartson, H. Rex (Editor), *Advances in Human–Computer Interaction*, Volume 1, Ablex, Norwood, NJ (1985), 133–159.

Sears, Andrew, Plaisant, Catherine, and Shneiderman, Ben, A new era for touchscreen applications: High-precision, dragging, and direct manipulation metaphors. In R. H. Hartson and D. Hix (Editors), *Advances in Human–Computer Interaction*, Volume 3, Ablex, Norwood, NJ (in press).

Sears, Andrew, Revis, Doreen, Swatski, Jean, Crittenden, Robert, and Shneiderman, Ben, Investigating touchscreen typing: The effect of keyboard size on typing speed, Technical Report, Department of Computer Science, University of Maryland, (in press).

Sears, Andrew and Shneiderman, Ben, High precision touchscreens: Design strategies and comparison with a mouse, *International Journal of Man–Machine Studies 34*, 4 (April 1991), 593–613.

Sherr, Sol (Editor), *Input Devices*, Academic Press, San Diego, CA (1988).

Shinar, David, Stern, Helman, I., Bubis, Gad, and Ingram, David, The relative effectiveness of alternate selection strategies in menu driven computer programs, *Proc. Human Factors Society—Twenty-ninth Annual Meeting* (1985), 645–649.

Shutoh, Tomoki, Tsuruta, Shichiro, Kawai, Ryuichi, and Shutoh, Masamichi, Voice operation in CAD system. In Hendrick, H. W., and Brown, O., Jr., (Editors), *Human Factors in Organizational Design and Management*, Elsevier Science Publishers B. V. (North-Holland), Amsterdam, The Netherlands (1984), 205–209.

Smith, Stuart, Bergeron, R. Daniel, and Grinstein, Georges, G., Stereophonic and surface sound generation for exploratory data analysis, *Proc. CHI '90: Conference: Human Factors in Computing Systems*, ACM, New York (1990), 125–132.

Songco, D. C., Allen, S. I., Plexico, P. S., and Morford, R. A., How computers talk to the blind, *IEEE Spectrum*, (May 1980), 34–38.

Stammers, R. B. and Bird, J. M., Controller evaluation of a touch input air traffic data system: An indelicate experiment, *Human Factors 22*, 5 (1980), 581–589.

Strathmeyer, Carl R., Voice in computing: An overview of available technologies, *IEEE Computer 23*, 8 (August 1990), 10–16.

Thorell, L. G. and Smith, W. J., *Using Computer Color Effectively*, Prentice-Hall, Englewood Cliffs, NJ (1990).

Tyler, Michael, Touchscreens: Big deal or no deal? *Datamation 30*, 1 (January 1984), 146–154.

Ware, Colin and Baxter, Curtis, Bat Brushes: On the uses of six position and orientation parameters in a paint program, *Proc. CHI '89 Conference: Human Factors in Computing Systems*, ACM, New York (1989), 155–160.

Welford, A. T., *Fundamentals of Skill*, Methuen, London, UK (1968).

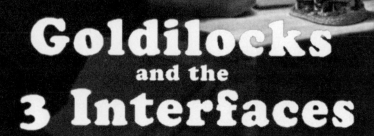

CHAPTER 7

Response Time and Display Rate

Stimulation is the indispensable requisite for pleasure in
an experience, and the feeling of bare time is the least
stimulating experience we can have.

William James, *Principles of Psychology*, Volume I, 1890

Nothing can be more useful to a man than a determination
not to be hurried.

Henry David Thoreau, *Journal*

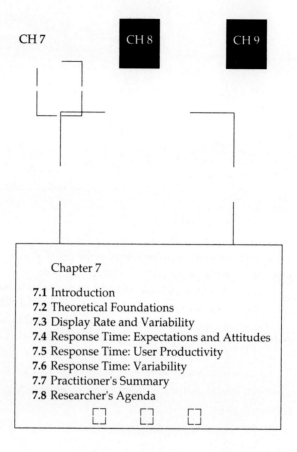

CH 7   CH 8   CH 9

Chapter 7

7.1 Introduction
7.2 Theoretical Foundations
7.3 Display Rate and Variability
7.4 Response Time: Expectations and Attitudes
7.5 Response Time: User Productivity
7.6 Response Time: Variability
7.7 Practitioner's Summary
7.8 Researcher's Agenda

7.1 Introduction

Time is precious. When unexpected delays impede the progress on a task, many people become frustrated, annoyed, and eventually angry. Lengthy system response times and slow display rates produce these reactions from computer users, leading to more frequent errors and lower satisfaction. Even if they simply accept the situation with a shrug of their shoulders, most users would prefer to work more quickly than the computer allows.

There is also, however, a danger in working too quickly. As users pick up the pace of a rapid interaction sequence, they may learn less, read with lower comprehension, make more ill-considered decisions, and commit more data-entry errors. Stress can build in this situation if errors are hard to recover from or if they destroy data, damage equipment, or imperil human life (for example, in air-traffic control or medical systems) (Emurian, 1989; Kuhman, 1989).

Figure 7.1

Simple model of system response time and user think time.

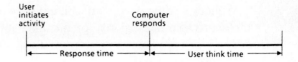

7.1.1 Definitions

The computer system's *response time* is the number of seconds it takes from the moment users initiate an activity (usually by pressing an ENTER key or mouse button) until the computer begins to present results on the display or printer (Figure 7.1). When the response is completely displayed, the user begins formulating the next command. The *user think time* is the number of seconds during which the user thinks before entering the next command. In this simple model, the user initiates, waits for the computer to respond, watches while the results appear, thinks for a while, and initiates again.

In a more realistic model (Figure 7.2), the user plans while reading results, while typing, and while the computer is generating a display of the results. Most people will use whatever time they have to plan ahead; thus, precise measurements of user think time are difficult to obtain. The computer's response is usually more precisely defined and measurable, but there are problems here as well. Some systems respond with distracting messages, informative feedback, or a simple prompt immediately after a command is initiated, but actual results may not appear for a few seconds.

7.1.2 Issues to raise

Designers who specify response times and display rates in human–computer interactions have to consider the complex interaction of technical feasibility, costs, task complexity, user expectations, speed of task performance, error rates, and error-handling procedures. These decisions are further complicated by the influence of personality differences, time of day, fatigue, familiarity with computers, experience with the task, and motivation (Carbonell et al., 1968; Shneiderman, 1980).

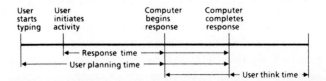

Figure 7.2

Model of system response time, user planning time, and user think time. This model is more realistic than is the one depicted in Figure 7.1.

Although some people are content with a slower system for some tasks, the overwhelming majority prefer rapid interactions. Overall productivity depends not only on the speed of the system, but also on the rate of human error and the ease of recovery from those errors. Lengthy response times (longer than 15 seconds) are generally detrimental to productivity, increasing error rates and decreasing satisfaction. More rapid interactions (less than 1 second) are generally preferred and can increase productivity, but may increase errors. The high cost of providing rapid response times or display rates and the loss from increased errors must be evaluated in choosing an optimum pace.

This review begins with a model of short-term human memory and the sources of human error (Section 7.2). Section 7.3 isolates the issue of display rate from response time. Section 7.4 focuses on the role of users' expectations and attitudes in shaping their subjective reactions to the computer-system response time. Section 7.5 concentrates on productivity as a function of response time; Section 7.6 reviews the research on the influence of variable response times.

7.2   Theoretical Foundations

A cognitive model of human performance that accounts for the experimental results in response time and display rates would be useful in making predictions, designing systems, and formulating management policies. A complete, predictive model that accounts for all the variables is currently inaccessible, but we are able to realize useful fragments of such a model.

Robert B. Miller's review (1968) presented a lucid analysis of response-time issues and a list of 17 situations in which preferred response times might differ. Much has changed since his paper was written, but the principles of closure, short-term–memory limitations, and chunking still apply.

7.2.1   Limitations of short-term and working memory

Any cognitive model must emerge from an understanding of human problem-solving abilities and information-processing capabilities. A central issue is the limitation of short-term memory capacity.

George Miller's classic 1956 paper, "The magical number seven—plus or minus two," identified the limited capacities people have for absorbing information (Miller, 1956). People can rapidly recognize approximately seven (this value was contested by later researchers, but serves as a good estimate) *chunks* of information at a time, and can hold them in short-term memory for 15 to 30 seconds. The size of a chunk of information depends on the person's familiarity with the material.

For example, most people could look at seven binary digits for a few seconds and then recall the digits correctly from memory within 15 seconds. A distracting task, such as reciting a poem, would erase the binary digits. Of course, if people concentrate on remembering the binary digits and succeed in transferring them to long-term memory, then they can retain the binary digits for much longer periods. Most Americans could also probably remember seven decimal digits, seven alphabetic characters, seven English words, or even seven familiar advertising slogans. Although these items have increasing complexity, they are still treated as single chunks. However, Americans might not succeed in remembering seven Russian letters, Chinese pictograms, or Polish sayings. Knowledge and experience govern the size of a chunk for each individual.

Short-term memory is used in conjunction with working memory for processing information and for problem solving. Short-term memory processes perceptual input, whereas working memory is used to generate and implement solutions. If many facts and decisions are necessary to solve a problem, then short-term and working memory may become overloaded. People learn to cope with complex problems by developing higher-level concepts that bring together several lower-level concepts into a single chunk. Novices at any task tend to work with smaller chunks until they can cluster concepts into larger chunks. Novices will break a complex task into a sequence of smaller tasks that they are confident about accomplishing.

This chunking phenomenon was demonstrated by Neal (1977), who required 15 experienced keypunch operators to type data records organized into numeric, alphanumeric, and English word fields. The median interkeystroke time was 0.2 seconds, but it rose to more than 0.3 seconds at field boundaries and 0.9 seconds at record boundaries.

Short-term and working memory are highly volatile; disruptions cause loss of memory, and delays can require that the memory be refreshed. Visual distractions or noisy environments also interfere with cognitive processing. Furthermore, anxiety apparently reduces the size of the available memory, since the person's attention is partially absorbed in concerns that are beyond the problem-solving task.

7.2.2 Sources of errors

If people are able to construct a solution to a problem in spite of possible interference, they must still record or implement the solution. If they can implement the solution immediately, they can proceed very quickly through their work. On the other hand, if they must record the solution in long-term memory, on paper, or on a complex device, the chances for error increase and the pace of work slows.

Multiplying two four-digit numbers in your head is difficult because the intermediate results cannot be maintained in working memory and must be transferred to long-term memory. Controlling a nuclear reactor or air traffic is a challenge, in part because these tasks often require integration of information (in short-term and working memory) from several sources, as well as maintenance of awareness of the complete situation. In attending to newly arriving information, operators may be distracted and may lose the contents of their short-term or working memory.

When using an interactive computer system, users may formulate plans and then have to wait while they execute each step in the plan. If a step produces an unexpected result or if the delays are long, then the user may forget part of the plan or be forced to review the plan continually.

Long (1976) studied delays of approximately 0.1 to 0.5 seconds in the time for a keystroke to produce a character on an impact printer. He found that unskilled and skilled typists worked more slowly and made more errors with longer response times. Even these brief delays were distracting in the rapid process of typing.

On the other hand, if users try to work too quickly, they may not allow sufficient time to formulate a solution plan correctly, and error rates may increase. As familiarity with the task increases, the user's capacity to work more quickly and with fewer errors should increase.

This model leads to the conjecture that, for a given user and task, there is a preferred response time. Long response times lead to wasted effort and more errors when a solution plan is reviewed continually. Shorter response times may generate a faster pace in which solution plans are prepared hastily and incompletely. More data from a variety of situations and users would help us to clarify these conjectures.

7.2.3   Conditions for optimum problem solving

As response times grow longer, users may become more anxious because the penalty for an error increases; also, users often slow down in their work. As the difficulty in handling an error increases, the anxiety level increases, further slowing performance and increasing errors. As response times grow shorter and display rates increase, users pick up the pace of the system and may fail to comprehend the presented material, may generate incorrect solution plans, and may make more execution errors. Wickelgren (1977) reviews speed–accuracy tradeoffs.

Car driving may offer a useful analogy. Although higher speed limits are attractive to many drivers and do produce faster completion of trips, they also lead to higher accident rates. Since automobile accidents have dreadful consequences, we accept speed limits. When incorrect use of computer systems can lead to damage to life, property, or data, should not speed limits be provided?

Rapid task performance, low error rates, and high satisfaction can occur if the following criteria are met:

- Users have adequate knowledge of the objects and actions necessary for the problem-solving task.
- The solution plan can be carried out without delays.
- Distractions are eliminated.
- User anxiety is low.
- There is feedback about progress toward solution.
- Errors can be avoided or, if they occur, can be handled easily.

These conditions for optimum problem solving, along with cost and technical feasibility, are the basic constraints on design. However, other conjectures may play a role in choosing the optimum interaction speed:

- Novices to a task exhibit better performance and prefer to work at slower speeds than knowledgeable frequent users.
- When there is little penalty for an error, users prefer to work more quickly.
- When the task is familiar and easily comprehended, users prefer more rapid action.
- If users have experienced rapid performance previously, they will expect it in future situations.

These informal conjectures need to be qualified and verified. Then, a more rigorous cognitive model needs to be developed to accommodate the great diversity in human work styles and in computer-use situations. Practitioners can conduct field tests to measure productivity, error rates, and satisfaction as a function of response times in their application areas.

The experiments described in the following sections are tiles in the mosaic of human performance with computers, but many more tiles are necessary before the fragments form a complete image. Some guidelines have emerged for designers and computer-center managers, but local testing and continuous monitoring of performance and satisfaction are useful. The remarkable adaptability of computer users means that researchers and practitioners will have to be alert to novel conditions that require revisions of these guidelines.

7.3 Display Rate and Variability

For alphanumeric hard-copy or display terminals, the *display rate* is the speed, in characters per second (cps), at which characters appear for the user to read. On hard-copy terminals, typical rates vary from 10 to 160 characters per second; faster rates are possible with line-printer devices. On display terminals, the rate may be limited by inexpensive modems to 30 cps (more typical is 1000 cps), or the display may fill instantaneously (typical for many personal computers and workstations).

Reading textual information from a screen or printer is a challenging cognitive and perceptual task—it is more difficult than reading from a book. If the display rate can be made so fast that the screen appears to fill instantly (beyond the speed at which someone might feel compelled to keep up), subjects seem to relax, to pace themselves, and to work productively. Many people find a slow display rate (30 cps) appealing because they can keep up with the output and comprehend the full text (Bevan, 1981; Tombaugh et al., 1985). As the display rate increases beyond human reading rates, compre-hension and satisfaction probably deteriorate. The pacing provided by the emergence of characters on the screen may be too rapid for many users, who, in their effort to keep up, have lower comprehension. One approach is to allow users to control the display rate to synchronize it with their reading speed.

If users only scan a display to pick out relevant material, then faster display rates will usually speed performance. Since many computer-related tasks do not require careful reading of the full screen, rapid filling of the screen seems preferable; it is pleasing and relieves the anxiety about delays in paging back and forth through multiple screens.

If the task is largely data entry, then rapid display of brief prompts is of little benefit to overall productivity. Variability in the display rate should be limited. Optimal display rates should be determined from performance and error data from subjects working on the specific task.

7.4   Response Time: Expectations and Attitudes

How long will users wait for the computer to respond before they become annoyed? This apparently simple question has provoked much discussion and several experiments. There is no simple answer to the question; more important, it may be the wrong question to ask.

Related design issues may clarify the question of acceptable response time. For example, how long should users have to wait before they hear a dial tone on a telephone or see a picture on their television? If the cost is not excessive, the frequently mentioned 2-second limit (Miller, 1968) seems appropriate for many tasks. In some situations, however, users expect responses within 0.1 second, such as when turning the wheel of a car; pressing a key on a typewriter, piano, or telephone; or changing channels on a television. Two-second delays in these cases might be unsettling because users have adapted a working style and expectation based on responses within a fraction of a second. In other situations, users are accustomed to longer response times, such as waiting 30 seconds for a red traffic light, 2 days for a letter to arrive, or 1 or more months for flowers to grow.

The first factor influencing acceptable response time is that people have established expectations based on their past experiences of the time required to complete a given task. If a task is completed more quickly than expected, people will be pleased; but if the task is completed much more quickly than expected, they may become concerned that something is wrong. Similarly, if a task is completed much more slowly than expected, users become concerned or frustrated. Even though people can detect 8-percent changes in a 2- or 4-second response time (Miller, 1968), users apparently do not become concerned until the change is much greater.

Two installers of time-shared computer systems have reported a problem concerning user expectations with new systems. The first users are delighted because the response is short with a light load. As the load builds, these first users become unhappy as the response time deteriorates. The users who have come on later may be satisfied with what they perceive as normal response times. Both installers devised a *response-time choke* by which they could slow down the system when the load was light, thus making the response time uniform over time and across users.

Computer-center managers have similar problems with varying response times as new equipment is added or as large projects begin or complete their work. The variation in response time can be disruptive to users who have developed expectations and working styles based on a specific response time. There are also periods within each day when the response time is short, such as at lunch time, or long, such as midmorning or late afternoon. Some users rush to complete a task when response times are short, and as a result they may make more errors. Some workers refuse to work when the response time is poor relative to their expectations.

There has also been a change in expectations during the recent years as people become more accustomed to using computers. The widespread dissemination of microcomputers will further raise expectations about how quickly computers should respond.

A second factor influencing response-time expectations is the individual's tolerance for delays. Novice computer users may be willing to wait much longer than are experienced users. In short, there are large variations in what individuals consider acceptable waiting time. These variations are influenced by many factors, such as the nature of the task, familiarity with the task, experience in performing the task, personality, costs, age, mood, cultural context, time of day, and by such environmental issues as noise and perceived pressure to complete work.

A third factor influencing response-time expectations is that people are highly adaptive and can change their working style to accommodate different response times. This factor, discussed in detail in Section 7.5, was found in early studies of batch-programming environments and in more recent studies of interactive system usage. Briefly, if delays are long, users will seek alternate strategies that reduce the number of interactions, whenever possible. They will fill in the long delays by performing other tasks, daydreaming, or planning ahead in their work. These long delays may or may not increase error rates when they are in the range of 3 to 15 seconds, but they probably will increase error rates when they are above 15 seconds if people must remain at the keyboard waiting for a response. Even if diversions are available, dissatisfaction grows with longer response times.

In summary, the three factors influencing response-time expectation are

1. Previous experiences are critical in shaping expectations.
2. There is enormous variation in response-time expectations across individuals and tasks.
3. People are highly adaptive; however, although they may be able to accommodate long and variable delays, their performance and satisfaction are likely to suffer.

Experimental results do show interesting patterns of behavior for specific tasks, individuals, times of day, and so on, but it is difficult to distill a simple set of conclusions. Several experiments attempted to identify acceptable waiting times by allowing subjects to press a key if they thought that the waiting time was too long. In some cases, the subjects received immediate response for that interaction; in other cases, subjects could shorten the response time in future interactions.

Youmans (1983) publicly reports on an IBM confidential study done in 1979 by Hogan and Youmans in which eight subjects were tested for 2 days while they performed text-entry and editing tasks at a display station. The system response time was varied, and subjective-satisfaction questionnaires were filled out after each of the 16 sessions. Results indicated that "subjective operator reaction to system response time changed from predominantly acceptable to predominantly unacceptable as the overall mean response time of the system increased from 1.8 to 2.5 seconds." Such findings support the conjecture of a 2-second limit for response time to simple commands.

C. M. Williams (1973) had 24 subjects working for 4 hours per day for 5 consecutive days on a 15-cps printing terminal. Subjects were divided into three groups that worked with 2-, 4-, or 8-second response times on four types of data-entry tasks. Each subject worked on all four tasks but stayed at the same response time. Subjects could get immediate response from the system if they pressed the "attention" key. The main results are summarized in Table 7.1.

The results for this task indicate that 2 seconds was generally an acceptable response time, since the attention key was pressed only 1.42 percent of the time. Eight seconds was generally unacceptable, since the attention key

Table 7.1

Results of study by C. M. Williams, 1973.

	Total Number of Trials	Average Delay (seconds)	Standard Deviation (seconds)	Percent of Trials Attention Key Pressed
Standard response time				
2 seconds	11,634	1.98	0.53	1.42
4 seconds	9,754	3.50	2.08	17.44
8 seconds	10,103	2.27	5.63	82.92

was pressed almost 83 percent of the time. A closer look at the data shows enormous individual differences, especially among the eight subjects in the 8-second group. One subject only occasionally pressed the attention key; all others pressed it almost every time.

The four tasks required brief and long requests for either an information retrieval or a calculation. Subjects tolerated longer response times only for the calculation when the standard response time was 8 seconds. One-half of the subjects received instructions that emphasized speed; the other half received instructions that emphasized accuracy. There was no difference between groups in the toleration of delay.

This study provides detailed and intriguing results, but the author makes too general a summary statement: "An absolute maximum response time interval of four seconds appears acceptable for a transaction-oriented system."

In another extensive study, Youmans (1981) allowed subjects to reduce the response time for each type of command by one-eighth by pressing a red button. Five subjects performed a variety of office-automation tasks over 4 days using a specially prepared keyboard and a display with 55 lines of 112 characters. Subjects were tolerant of longer delays during training; as they became proficient, however, they pressed the red button more frequently, driving the response time lower and lower. Subjects would remain at a certain response time for many invocations of a command, then return to pressing the red button to reduce the response time further. There were clear differences across subjects, commands, and times of day.

The data from the two least tolerant subjects were reported in a summary table. These subjects forced the response time to below 1 second for all commands (except one command that the system could not perform in less than 1 second). Such editing commands as inserting a line, deleting a line, or turning a page were forced into the 0.3- to 0.5-second range, and display and copy commands were forced into the 0.6- to 0.8-second range. These results suggest that, given the chance to choose a shorter response time, many users will take advantage of that feature as they become more experienced. It seems appealing to offer users a choice in the pace of the interaction.

In summary, there are so many variables governing response-time expectations and attitudes that it is difficult to arrange adequate experimental controls. Even if that were possible, the generalizability of the results would be in question.

In spite of these unsatisfying observations, we can make three conjectures:

1. People will work faster as they gain experience with a command, so it may be useful to allow people to set their own pace of interaction.
2. In the absence of such constraints as cost or technical feasibility, people will eventually force response time to well under 1 second.
3. Although people can adapt to working with slower response times, they are generally dissatisfied with rates longer than 2 seconds.

7.5   Response Time: User Productivity

Shorter system response times usually lead to higher productivity, but in some situations users who receive long system response times can find clever shortcuts or ways to do concurrent processing to reduce the effort and time to accomplish a task. Working too quickly may lead to errors that reduce productivity.

In computing, just as in driving, there is no general rule about whether the high-speed highway or the slower, clever shortcut is better. Each situation has to be surveyed carefully to make the optimal choice. The choice is not critical for the occasional excursion, but becomes worthy of investigation when the frequency is great. When computers are used in high-volume situations, more effort can be expended in discovering the proper response time for a given task and set of users. It should not be surprising that a new study must be conducted when the tasks and users change, just as a new evaluation must be done in each choice of highways.

Some tasks have been studied in controlled experimental conditions, with the general conclusion that response times do affect performance times, error rates, and user satisfaction. In general, with shorter response times, performance times are reduced, error rates are increased, and user satisfaction is increased. The frequent exceptions to these results depend on the nature of the task, the difficulty in repairing an error, the feedback from the system, the possibility of using different methods to solve the given problem, and the expectations of the users. Careful design of computer systems and highways can reduce errors so that higher speeds can be permitted safely.

7.5.1   Repetitive control tasks

The nature of the task has a strong influence on whether changes in response time alter user productivity. A repetitive control task involves monitoring a display and issuing commands in response to changes in the display. Although the operator may be trying to understand the underlying process, the basic activities are to respond to a change in the display, to issue commands, and then to see whether the commands produce the desired effect. When there is a choice among commands, the problem becomes more interesting and the operator tries to pick the optimal command in each situation. With shorter system response times, the operator picks up the pace of the system and works more quickly, but decisions on commands may be less than optimal. On the other hand, with short response times, the penalty for a poor choice may be small, because it is easy to try another command. In fact, operators may learn to use the system more quickly with short system response times because they can explore alternatives more easily.

Goodman and Spence (1978) studied a control task involving multiparameter optimization. The goal was to force "a displayed graph to lie wholly within a defined acceptance region." Operators could adjust five parameters by using lightpen touches, thus altering the shape of the graph. There were response times of 0.16, 0.72, or 1.49 seconds. Each of the 30 subjects worked at each of the three response times in this repeated-measures experiment. The total times to solution (just over 500 seconds) and the total user think time (around 300 seconds) were the same for the 0.16- and 0.72-second treatments. The 1.49-second treatment led to a 50-percent increase in solution time and a modest increase in user think time. In this case, reducing the response time to less than 1 second was beneficial in terms of human productivity. A pilot study of this task with six subjects provided further support for short response time, since a response time of 3 seconds drove the solution time up to more than 1200 seconds.

7.5.2   Problem-solving tasks

When complex problem solving is required and many approaches to the solution are possible, users will adapt their work style to the response time. A demonstration of this effect emerged from studies done in the late 1960s (Grossberg et al., 1976) using four experienced subjects in a complex computational problem-solving situation. The response times were variable, but the means were set at 1, 4, 16, and 64 seconds for commands that generated output or an error message. Nonoutput commands were simply accepted by the system. Each subject performed a total of 48 tasks of approximately 15-minutes duration each, distributed across the four response-time treatments.

The remarkable outcome of this study was that the time to solution was invariant with respect to response time! When working with 64-second delays, subjects used substantially fewer output commands and also fewer total commands. Apparently, with long response times, subjects thought carefully about the problem solution, since there were also longer intervals between commands. There were differences across subjects, but all subjects stayed within a limited range of solution times across the four system response times with which they worked.

Although the number of subjects was small, the results are very strong in support of the notion that, if possible, users will change their work habits as the response time changes. As the cost, in time, of an error or an unnecessary output command rose, subjects made fewer errors and issued fewer commands. These results were closely tied to the study's complex, intellectually demanding task, for which there were several ways to solve the problem.

Similar (but less dramatic) results appeared in a study of computer-based instruction in chemistry distillation (Weinberg, 1981). In a question-answering situation, 120 students worked at either 0.33- or 1.25-second response times. If they guessed wrong, the students received a hint about the correct answer. With 0.33 second response times, subjects averaged 11.1 errors; but when working at 1.25 seconds, the subjects considered their guesses more carefully and averaged only 4.7 errors. This performance result contrasted with another part of the study, in which subjects used repetitive control to keep the distillation running within prescribed bounds. The subjects violated the bounds only 28.4 times with the 0.33 delay, but 35.0 times with the longer delay. Shorter response times allowed more interventions within the fixed time of the lesson. Overall, subjects working at the shorter response time completed their lessons more quickly and had a more favorable attitude toward the system. There were clear indications that subjects tried to work more carefully and made fewer errors with the longer response time.

7.5.3   Programming tasks

Since programmers often use interactive systems, it is not surprising that several studies have been conducted to measure the affect of response-time changes on programmer productivity (Boies, 1974; Doherty and Kelisky, 1979; Smith, 1983). These studies tend to focus on the number of interactions per hour as measured by the system, rather than on specific task-completion times. The programmers performed a mixture of program and text editing, compilations, program testing, and debugging. These studies also tended to be field studies of actual work, rather than controlled experiments.

A preliminary study by Dannenbring (1983) focused on novices and experienced programmers debugging a 25-line BASIC program. Changing the response time from 0 to 5 to 10 seconds did not affect performance time or satisfaction for novices or experienced programmers, although there were significant differences between the scores of these two groups of program-mers. These results are surprising because experienced programmers gener-ally benefit from shorter response times. Programmers often have a sequence of commands that they are ready to apply, but they must maintain these plans in their short-term memory while they wait for the computer to complete the previous command. This additional memory burden prevents swift completion and may lead to higher error rates. The danger of a shorter response time is that programmers may make hasty decisions as they keep up the rapid pace of interaction. Can programmers learn the discipline of working carefully, even with short response times?

Thadhani (1981) found that, on one IBM MVS/TSO system, users went from 106 interactions per hour at 3-second response time up to 222 interac-tions per hour at 0.5-second response time. On another system, the users went from approximately 200 to 340 interactions per hour as the response time was reduced from 3 to 0.5 seconds. Similar results were reported with IBM programmers in England (Lambert, 1984), where the rate of interactions per hour went from 161 for the control group to 258 for the study group. The control group was given a mean response time of 2.2 seconds; the study group was given a mean response time of 0.8 seconds.

These results are strong, but they measure only interactions per hour, not productivity, and they do not reveal how work habits changed as the response time was changed. Thadhani (1984) offers further evidence that programmer interaction rates increase with short response times. He also refers to a study of engineers that showed no significant change in number of interactions to complete a task when the response time was varied from 0.25 to 2 seconds, but did show a doubling in the total task time. The task was not described, but Thadhani suggests that these results have relevance for programming tasks.

Several studies demonstrate that, as the system response time increases, so does the user think time. Boies (1974) found that as the response time increased from 1 to 10 seconds, the user think time increased from about 15 to 24 seconds. Thadhani (1981) found somewhat higher times on one system and somewhat lower times on another system (Figure 7.3).

We may conjecture that knowledgeable programmers build a plan and then seek to carry it out as rapidly as possible. They pick up the pace of the system, being more cautious with long response times and moving quickly with short response times. They are not afraid of making errors when working rapidly because they know that the system allows rapid error recovery.

7.5.4 Professionals at work

Programmers are a special community of users because of their familiarity with computers; other professional users also are affected by response-time

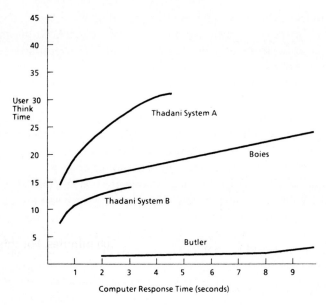

Figure 7.3

User think time as a function of computer response time from Boies (1974),
Thadhani (1981), and Butler (1983).

issues. Users of CAD systems tend to work at a rapid rate in making changes
to a displayed object. An IBM study (Smith, 1983) of circuit designers using
lightpens at a graphics workstation found dramatic improvements in interaction rates as the response time was reduced. The most skilled user went
from 800 interactions per hour with a 1.5-second response time up to 4300
interactions per hour with 0.4-second response time. A novice designer went
from 60 to 650 interactions per hour as the response time was reduced from
1.5 to 0.25 seconds. Error rates and user satisfaction were not presented in
this report.

Few tasks allow the high interaction rate provided by this graphics
system. Barber and Lucas (1983) studied 100 professional circuit-layout
clerks who assigned telephone equipment in response to service requests.
Ten or more interactions were needed to complete these complex tasks. Data
were collected about normal performance for 12 days, with an average
response time of 6 seconds. Then, 29 clerks were given response times
averaging 14 seconds for 4 days. When the response time was as short as 4
seconds, there were 49 errors out of 287 transactions. As the response time
increased to 12 seconds, the errors dropped to 16 of 222 transactions; and as
the response time increased further to 24 seconds, the errors increased to 70
of 151 transactions (Figure 7.4). The volume of transactions was recorded

Figure 7.4

Error rates as a function of reponse time for complex telephone circuit layout task by Barber and Lucas (1983). Although error rates were lowest with long response times (12 seconds), the productivity increased with shorter response times because the system could detect errors, and users could correct them rapidly.

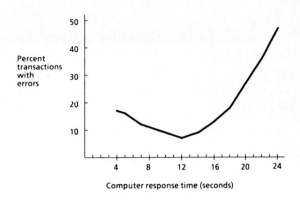

with an "active time" (session length) of 200 minutes. For this complex task, the data reveal that the lowest error rate occurred with a 12-second response time. With shorter response times, the workers made hasty decisions; with longer response times, the frustration of waiting burdened short-term memory. It is important to recognize that the number of productive transactions (total minus errors) increased almost linearly with reductions in response time. Apparently, reduced error rates were not sufficient to increase satisfaction, since subjective preference was consistently in favor of the shorter response time.

In a Bell Labs study with low complexity data entry tasks, J. D. Williams (1975) found no differences in error rates with 5-, 15-, 30-, or 45-second response times. With higher-complexity tasks such as data retrieval and correction, the 30- and 45-second conditions resulted in higher error rates. Typing speed during data entry deteriorated steadily as the response time increased.

Butler (1983), also at Bell Labs, studied simple data-entry tasks with computer-displayed prompts. The response times were 2, 4, 8, 16, and 32 seconds. Error rates remained unchanged over this range, but the user think time increased, contributing to an overall decrease in productivity.

7.5.5   Summary

It is clear that users pick up the pace of the system to work more quickly with shorter response times, and that they consistently prefer the faster pace. The profile of error rates at shorter response times varies across tasks. Not surprisingly, there appears to be an optimal pace for each user–task situation—response times that are shorter or longer than this pace lead to increased errors. The ease of error recovery and the damage caused by an error must be evaluated carefully by managers who are choosing the optimal pace of interaction. If higher throughput of work is desired, then attention must be paid to minimizing the cost and delay of error recovery. In short, the optimal response time may be longer than the minimum possible response time.

7.6   Response Time: Variability

People are willing to pay substantial amounts of money to reduce the variability in their life. The entire insurance industry is based on the reduction of present pleasures, through the payment of premiums, to reduce the severity of a future loss. Most people appreciate predictable behavior that lessens the anxiety of unpleasant surprises.

7.6.1   Range of variation

In using computers, the operator cannot see into the machine to gain reassurance that the commands are being executed properly, but the response time can provide some clue. If users come to expect a response time of 3 seconds for a common operation, they may become apprehensive if this operation takes 0.5 or 15 seconds. Such extreme variation is unsettling and should be prevented or acknowledged by the system, with a message for unusually fast response, and a progress report for an unusually slow response.

The more difficult issue is the effect of modest variations in response time. As discussed earlier, Miller (1968) raised this issue and reported that 75 percent of subjects tested could perceive 8-percent variations in time for time periods in the interval of 2 to 4 seconds. These results prompted some designers to suggest restrictive rules for variability of response time. For example, Gallaway (1981) proposed a variability of plus or minus 5 percent for response times in the 0- to 2-second range, and of plus or minus 10 percent for the 2- to 4-second range.

Since it may not be technically feasible to provide a fixed short response time (such as 1 second) for all commands, several authors have suggested that the time be fixed for classes of commands. Many commands could have a fixed response time of less than 1 second, other commands could take 4 seconds, and still other commands could take 12 seconds. Experimental results are beginning to shed light on the results of response-time variability. Although there are some effects, the influence of modest variations on performance has not proved to be severe. Users are apparently capable of adapting to varying situations, although some of them may become frustrated when performing certain tasks.

7.6.2   Experimental results

Goodman and Spence (1981) attempted to measure performance changes in a problem-solving situation (a similar situation was used in their earlier experiment described in Section 7.5.1). Subjects used lightpen touches to manipulate a displayed graph. The mean response time was set at 1.0 second with three levels of variation: quasinormal distributions with standard deviations of 0.2, 0.4, and 0.8 seconds. The minimum response time was 0.2 second, and the maximum response time was 1.8 seconds. Goodman and Spence found no significant performance changes as the variability was increased. The time to solution and the profile of command use were unchanged. As the variability increased, they did note that subjects took more advantage of fast responses by making their subsequent commands immediately, balancing the time lost in waiting for slower responses. In summary, this study found that, as the percentage of responses deviating from the mean grew, performance remained largely unchanged, within the range specified (0.2 to 1.8 seconds).

A closely related experiment (Goodman and Spence, 1982) found no significant direct effect of response variability. But a large and nearly significant interaction was found with time of day for the number of lightpen touches. Increased response-time variability led to slower performance in the morning and faster performance in the afternoon. The mean response interval and its variability tended to increase with increasing variability, with significance approaching the 10- and 5-percent levels, respectively.

Similar results were found using a mean response time of 10 seconds and three variations: standard deviations of 0.0, 2.5, and 7.5 seconds (Bergman et al., 1981). The authors conclude that an increase in variability of response time "does not have any negative influence on the subject's performance on a rather complicated problem-solving task."

A third failure to find variability effects emerged from a study of a repetitive control task (Weiss et al., 1982; described in Section 7.5.1). Variances of 0 and 0.33 seconds were applied to mean response times of 6 and 10 seconds. No significant main effects were found for the response time or the response-time variability. A significant two-way interaction of response time and response-time variability was intriguing. With a 10-second response time and high variability, errors, heart rate, and blood pressure were reduced. The authors conjecture that the occasional short response time was perceived as a positive opportunity. This conjecture fits with the belief that surprising short response times are much appreciated, even if the penalty is occasional unanticipated long response times.

Two studies detected modest increases in user think time as variability increased. Butler (1983) studied six subjects who worked for 2 hours at each of 10 response-time conditions: the means were 2, 4, 8, 16, and 32 seconds, each with low and high variability. Subjects performed simple data-entry tasks, but had to wait for the system response before they could proceed. Accuracy and rate of typing were unaffected by the duration or variability of response time. User think time increased with the duration and with variability of the computer's response time (Figure 7.3). Butler describes a second experiment with a more complex task whose results are quite similar.

Four videotex studies (Murray and Abrahamson, 1983) with novice users examined response time and response-time variability. No significant effects were found for response-time changes. The authors interpret this result as "a strong indication that inexperienced videotex users are relatively immune to a wide range of constant values of system delay." Of the three experiments that tested response-time variability, two showed significant effects that indicated that subjects who worked with higher-variability times took longer to respond.

The physiological effect of response-time variability was studied by Kuhman et al. (1987), who found no dramatic effects between constant and variable treatments for detection and correction tasks with 68 subjects. Constant response times of 2 and 8 seconds were compared with variable response times ranging over 0.5 to 5.75 seconds (mean 2 seconds) and 2.0 to 22.81 seconds (mean 8 seconds). Statistically significantly higher error rates, higher systolic blood pressure, and more pronounced pain symptoms were found with shorter response times. However, no significant differences were found for response-time variability at either the short or long response times. Similarly, Emurian (1991) compared an 8-second constant response time to a variable response time ranging from 1 to 30 seconds (mean 8 seconds). His 10 subjects solved 50 database queries with 45-second time limits. Although diastolic blood pressure and masseter (jaw-muscle) tension did increase when compared to resting baseline values, there were no significant differences in these physiological measures between constant and variable treatments.

7.6.3   Summary

In summary, modest variations in response time (plus or minus 50 percent of the mean) appear to be tolerable and to have little effect on performance. As the variability grows, there may be some decrease in performance speed. Frustration may emerge only if delays are unusually long—at least twice the anticipated time. Similarly, anxiety about an erroneous command may emerge only if the response time is unusually short—say, less than one-quarter of the anticipated time. But even with extreme changes, users appear to be adaptable enough to complete their tasks. Of course, these conjectures are task dependent and need further validation.

It may be useful to slow down unexpected fast responses to avoid surprising the user. This proposal is controversial, but would affect only a small fraction of user interactions. Certainly, a serious effort should be made to avoid extremely slow responses, or, if they must occur, the user should be given information to indicate progress toward the goal. One graphics system displays a large clock ticking backward; the output appears only when the clock has ticked down to zero. A document-formatting system displays the section numbers to indicate progress and to confirm that the computer is at work productively on the appropriate document.

7.7   Practitioner's Summary

Computer-system response time and display rate are important determinants of user productivity, error rates, working style, and satisfaction (Table 7.2). In most situations, shorter response times (less than 1 second) lead to higher productivity. For typed data entry, mouse actions, direct manipulation, and animation, even faster performance is necessary for each individual step. Satisfaction generally increases as the response time decreases, but there may be a danger from stress induced by a rapid pace. As users pick up the pace of the system, they may make more errors; if these errors are

Table 7.2

Response Time Guidelines

- Users prefer shorter response times.
- Longer response times (greater than 15 seconds) are disruptive.
- Users change usage profile with response time.
- Shorter response times lead to short user think times.
- A faster pace may increase productivity, but error rates also may increase.
- Error-recovery ease and time influence the optimal response time.
- Response time should be appropriate to the task:
    Typing, cursor motion, mouse selection: 50 to 150 milliseconds
    Simple frequent tasks: less than 1 second
    Common tasks: 2 to 4 seconds
    Complex tasks: 8 to 12 seconds
- Users should be advised of long delays.
- Modest variability in response time is acceptable.
- Unexpected delays may be disruptive.
- Empirical tests can help to set suitable response times.

detected and corrected easily, then productivity will generally increase. If errors are hard to detect or are excessively costly, then a moderate pace may be the most beneficial.

We can determine the optimal response time for a specific application and user community by measuring the productivity, cost of errors, and cost of providing short response times. Managers must be alert to changes in work style as the pace quickens; productivity is measured by correctly completed tasks, not by interactions per hour. Novices may prefer a slower pace of interaction. When technical feasibility or costs prevent response times of less than 1 second, each class of commands can be assigned to a response-time category—for example, 2 to 4 seconds, 4 to 8 seconds, 8 to 12 seconds, and more than 12 seconds. Modest variations around the mean response time are acceptable, but large variations (less than one-quarter of the mean or more than twice the mean) should be accompanied by an informative message. An alternative approach is to slow down overly rapid responses and thus to avoid the need for a message.

For tasks that require reading the full text, filling the display instantaneously is the preferred approach for most situations. When this approach cannot be implemented designers might consider a display rate that matches human reading speed (15 to 30 cps). For other tasks that do not require full text reading, faster display rates will speed performance but may lead to more errors. Keeping these important exceptions in mind, we can state that faster display rates are preferable.

7.8   Researcher's Agenda

In spite of the many experiments described here, many unanswered questions remain. The taxonomy of issues provides some framework for research, but a finer taxonomy of tasks, of relevant cognitive-style differences, and of work situations is necessary to specify adequate experimental controls. Next, a sound theory of problem-solving behavior with computers is necessary to generate useful hypotheses.

Doherty and Kelisky (1979) suggest that longer response times lead to slower work, more emotional upset, and more errors. This statement appears to be true with long response times of more than 15 seconds, but there is little evidence to support the claim that fewer errors are made with short response times of less than 1 second. Barber and Lucas (1983) found a U-shaped error curve, with the lowest error rate at a 12-second response time. It would be productive to study error rates as a function of response time for a range of tasks and users.

It is understandable that error rates vary with response times, but how else are users' work styles affected? Do users issue more commands as response times shorten? Grossberg et al. (1976) found this result for a complex task with extremely long response times of up to 64 seconds, but there is little evidence with more common tasks and speeds. Does the profile of commands shift to a smaller set of more familiar commands as the response time shortens? Does the session length increase or decrease with response time increases? Are workers more willing to pursue higher-quality results when they are given shorter response times that enable multiple quick changes?

Many other questions are worthy of investigation. When technical feasibility prevents short responses, can users be satisfied by diversionary tasks, or are progress reports sufficient? Do warnings of long responses relieve anxiety or further frustrate users?

Operating-systems designers can also contribute by providing better control over response time. It should be possible for a designer to specify upper and lower limits for response time for each command. It is still difficult on large time-shared computers to specify a response time, even on an experimental basis. With better control of response time, new approaches could be tried. For example, imagine that the response time is always 1.0 second but that keyboard lockout time is a function of command type. After you issue a quick, simple command, you can immediately enter the next command; however, after you issue a longer, more complex command, you will be forced to review your work and to consider the next step, because your terminal will be locked out for 12 seconds. Boehm et al. (1971) and others suggest that keyboard lockout may be less disruptive than anticipated and that lockout has several beneficial effects.

Program designers can contribute by actively pursuing algorithms that reduce response time, designing software to reduce the effects of long response times, and simplifying error recovery to reduce the problems of higher error rates with short response times.

References

Barber, Raymond E. and Lucas, H. C., System response time, operator productivity and job satisfaction, *Communications of the ACM 26*, 11 (November 1983), 972–986.

Bergman, Hans, Brinkman, Albert, and Koelega, Harry S., System response time and problem solving behavior, *Proc. of the Human Factors Society—Twenty-fifth Annual Meeting*, Rochester, NY (October 12–16, 1981), 749–753.

Bevan, Nigel, Is there an optimum speed for presenting text on a VDU?, *International of Journal Man–Machine Studies*, 14 (1981), 59–76.

Boehm, Barry W., Seven, M. J., and Watson, R. A., Interactive problem solving—An experimental study of "lockout" effects, *Proc. Spring Joint Computer Conference, 38*, (1971), 205–210.

Boies, S. J., User behavior on an interactive computer system, *IBM Systems Journal 13*, 1 (1974), 1–18.

Butler, T. W., Computer response time and user performance, *ACM SIGCHI'83 Proceedings: Human Factors in Computer Systems* (December 1983), 56–62.

Carbonell, J. R., Elkind, J. I., and Nickerson, R. S., On the psychological importance of time in a timesharing system, *Human Factors 10*, 2 (1968), 135–142.

Dannenbring, Gary L., The effect of computer response time on user preference and satisfaction: A preliminary investigation, *Behavioral Research Methods and Instrumentation 15* (1983), 213–216.

Doherty, W. J. and Kelisky, R. P., Managing VM/CMS systems for user effectiveness, *IBM Systems Journal 18*, 1, (1979) 143–163.

Emurian, Henry H., Physiological responses during data retrieval: Consideration of constant and variable system response times, *Computers and Human Behavior* (1991), 291–310.

Emurian, Henry H., Human–computer interactions: Are there adverse health consequences?, *Computers and Human Behavior 5* (1989), 265–275.

Gallaway, Glen R., *Response Times to User Activities in Interactive Man/Machine Computer Systems*, National Cash Register Corporation HFP 81–25, Dayton, OH (August 25, 1981).

Goodman, T. J. and Spence, Robert, The effect of computer system response time on interactive computer aided problem solving, *ACM SIGGRAPH 1978 Conference Proceedings* (1978), 100–104.

Goodman, T. J., and Spence, R., The effect of computer system response time variability on interactive graphical problem solving, *IEEE Transactions on Systems, Man and Cybernetics 11*, 3 (March 1981), 207–216.

Goodman, Tom and Spence, Robert, The effects of potentiometer dimensionality, system response time, and time of day on interactive graphical problem solving, *Human Factors 24*, 4 (1982), 437–456.

Grossberg, Mitchell, Wiesen, Raymond A., and Yntema, Douwe B., An experiment on problem solving with delayed computer responses, *IEEE Transactions on Systems, Man, and Cybernetics 6*, 3 (March 1976), 219–222.

Kuhmann, Werner, Experimental investigation of stress-inducing properties of system response times, *Ergonomics 32*, 3 (1989), 271–280.

Kuhmann, Werner, Boucsein, Wolfram, Schaefer, Florian, and Alexander, Johanna, Experimental investigation of psychophysiological stress-reactions induced by different system response times in human–computer interaction, *Ergonomics 30*, 6 (1987), 933–943.

Lambert, G. N., A comparative study of system response time on program developer productivity, *IBM System Journal 23*, 1 (1984), 36–43.

Long, John, Effects of delayed irregular feedback on unskilled and skilled keying performance, *Ergonomics 19*, 2 (1976), 183–202.

Miller, G. A., The magical number seven, plus or minus two: Some limits on our capability for processing information, *Psychological Science 63* (1956), 81–97.

Miller, Robert B., Response time in man–computer conversational transactions, *Proceedings Spring Joint Computer Conference 1968*, 33, AFIPS Press, Montvale, NJ (1968), 267–277.

Murray, Robert P. and Abrahamson, David, The effect of system response time delay variability on inexperienced videotex users, *Behaviour and Information Technology 2*, 3 (1983), 237–251.

Neal, Alan S., Time interval between keystrokes, records, and fields in data entry with skilled operators, *Human Factors 19*, 2 (1977), 163–170.

Shneiderman, Ben, *Software Psychology: Human Factors in Computer and Information Systems*, Little, Brown and Co., Boston, MA (1980).

Smith, Dick, Faster is better: A business case for subsecond response time, *Computerworld* (April 18, 1983), in-depth pages 1–11.

Thadhani, A. J., Interactive user productivity, *IBM Systems Journal 20*, 4 (1981), 407–423.

Thadhani, A. J., Factors affecting programmer productivity during application development, *IBM Systems Journal 23*, 1 (1984), 19–35.

Tombaugh, Jo W., Arkin, Michael D., and Dillon, Richard F., The effects of VDU text-presentation rate on reading comprehension and reading speed, *Proc. CHI'85— Human Factors in Computing Systems*, ACM, New York (1985), 1–6.

Weinberg, Sherry, Learning effectiveness: The impact of response time, Slides for presentation at May 1981 Conference, Control Data Corporation, Minneapolis, MN (May 1981).

Weiss, Stuart Martin, Boggs, George, Lehto, Mark, Shodja, Sogand, and Martin, David J., Computer system response time and psychophysiological stress II, *Proc. Human Factors Society—Twenty-sixth Annual Meeting*, Santa Monica, CA (1982), 698–702.

Wickelgren, Wayne A., Speed-accuracy tradeoff and information processing dynamics, *Acta Psychologica 41* (1977), 67–85.

Williams, C. M., System response time: A study of users' tolerance, IBM Advanced Systems Development Division Technical Report, 17–272, Yorktown Heights, NY (July 1973).

Williams, J. D., The effects of computer subsystem response time and response time variance on operator performance in an interactive computer system, unpublished manuscript, Bell Telephone Laboratories, Memorandum 75-9131-3, Human Performance Technology Center (1975).

Youmans, D. M., User requirements for future office workstations with emphasis on preferred response times, IBM United Kingdom Laboratories, Hursley Park (September 1981).

Youmans, D. M., The effects of system response time on users of interactive computer systems, IBM United Kingdom Laboratories, Hursley Park (January 1983).

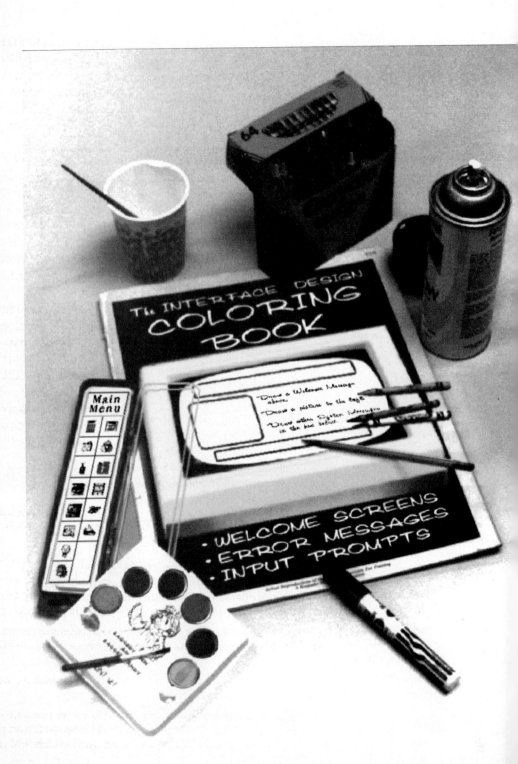

CHAPTER 8

System Messages, Screen Design, and Color

Words are sometimes sensitive instruments of precision
with which delicate operations may be performed and
swift, elusive truths may be touched.

Helen Merrell Lynd, *On Shame and the Search for Identity*

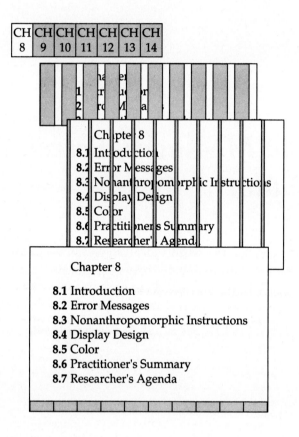

CH CH CH CH CH CH CH
8 9 10 11 12 13 14

Chapter 8

8.1 Introduction
8.2 Error Messages
8.3 Nonanthropomorphic Instructions
8.4 Display Design
8.5 Color
8.6 Practitioner's Summary
8.7 Researcher's Agenda

8.1 Introduction

User experiences with computer-system prompts, explanations, error diagnostics, and warnings play a critical role in influencing acceptance of software systems. The wording of messages is especially important in systems designed for novice users; experts also benefit from improved messages.

Another opportunity for design improvements is in the layout of information on a display. Densely packed displays may overwhelm even knowledgeable users; but with only modest effort, layouts can be substantially improved to reduce search time and increase subjective satisfaction. Large, rapid, multicolor, high-resolution displays offer new possibilities and challenges for designers. Designers and users are developing strategies to make good use of these opportunities.

8.2   Error Messages

Normal prompts, advisory messages, and system responses to commands may influence user perceptions, but the phrasing of error messages or diagnostic warnings is critical. Since errors occur because of lack of knowledge, incorrect understanding, or inadvertent slips, users are likely to be confused, to feel inadequate, and to be anxious. Error messages with an imperious tone that condemns users can heighten anxiety, making it more difficult to correct the error and increasing the chances of further errors. Messages that are too generic, such as `WHAT?` or `SYNTAX ERROR`, or too obscure, such as `FAC RJCT 004004400400` or `0C7`, offer little assistance to novices.

These concerns are especially important with respect to novices, whose lack of knowledge and confidence amplify the stress-related feedback that can lead to a sequence of failures. The discouraging effects of a bad experience in using a computer are not easily overcome by a few good experiences. In some cases, systems are remembered more for what happens when things go wrong than when things go right. Although these effects are most prominent with novice computer users, experienced users also suffer. Experts in one system or part of a system are still novices in many situations.

Producing a set of guidelines for writing system messages is not an easy task because of differences of opinion and the impossibility of being complete (Golden, 1980; Dwyer, 1981a, 1981b; Dean, 1982). However, explicit guidelines generate discussions and help less experienced designers to produce better systems. Improving the error messages is one of the easiest and most effective ways to improve an existing system. If the software can capture the frequency of errors then attention can be focused on the most important messages.

Error-frequency distributions also enable system designers and maintainers to revise error-handling procedures, to improve documentation and training manuals, to alter online help, or even to change the permissible actions or command-language syntax. The complete set of messages should be reviewed by peers and managers, tested empirically, and included in user manuals.

Specificity, constructive guidance, positive tone, user-centered style, and appropriate physical format are recommended (see Section 8.2.1) as the bases for preparing system messages. These guidelines are especially important when the users are novices, but they can benefit experts as well. The phrasing and contents of system messages can significantly affect user performance and satisfaction.

8.2.1   Specificity

Messages that are too general make it difficult for the novice to know what has gone wrong. Simple and condemning messages are frustrating because they provide neither enough information about what has gone wrong nor the knowledge to set things right. The right amount of specificity therefore is important.

Poor	Better
SYNTAX ERROR	Unmatched left parenthesis
ILLEGAL ENTRY	Type first letter: <u>S</u>end, <u>R</u>ead, or <u>D</u>rop
INVALID DATA	Days range from 1 to 31
BAD FILE NAME	File names must begin with a letter

Execution-time messages in programming languages should provide the user with specific information about where the problem arose, what objects were involved, and what values were improper. When division by zero occurs, some processors will terminate with a crude message, such as DOMAIN ERROR in APL, or SIZE ERROR in some COBOL compilers. Pascal specifies division by zero but may not include the line number or variables. Maintaining symbol-table and line-number information at execution time so that better messages can be generated is usually well worth the modest resource expenditure.

One system for hotel checkin required the desk clerk to enter a 40- to 45-character string containing the name, room number, credit-card information, and so on. If the clerk made a data-entry error, the only message was INVALID INPUT. YOU MUST RETYPE THE ENTIRE RECORD. This led to frustration for users and delays for irritated guests. Interactive systems should be designed to minimize input errors by proper form-fillin strategies (see Chapter 3); when an error occurs, the users should have to repair only the incorrect part.

Systems that offer an error-code number leading to a paragraph-long explanation in a manual are also annoying because the manual may not be available, or consulting it may be disruptive and time consuming. In most cases, system developers can no longer hide behind the claim that printing complete messages consumes too many system resources (Hahn and Athey, 1972; Heaps and Radhakrishnan, 1977).

8.2.2   Constructive guidance and positive tone

Rather than condemning users for what they have done wrong, messages should, where possible, indicate what users need to do to set things right:

Poor: DISASTROUS STRING OVERFLOW. JOB ABANDONED. (from a well-known compiler-compiler)

Better: String space consumed. Revise program to use shorter strings or expand string space

Poor: UNDEFINED LABELS (from a FORTRAN compiler)

Better: Define statement labels before use

Poor: ILLEGAL STA. WRN. (from a FORTRAN compiler)

Better: RETURN statement cannot be used in a FUNCTION subprogram.

Unnecessarily hostile messages using violent terminology can disturb nontechnical users. An interactive legal-citation–searching system uses this message: FATAL ERROR, RUN ABORTED. A popular operating-system threatens many users with CATASTROPHIC ERROR; LOGGED WITH OPERATOR. There is no excuse for these hostile messages; they can easily be rewritten to provide more information about what happened and what must be done to set things right. Such negative-tone words as ILLEGAL, ERROR, INVALID, or BAD should be eliminated or used only infrequently.

It may be difficult for the software writer to create a code that accurately determines what the user's intention was, so the advice that is intended to be constructive is often difficult to apply. Some designers argue for automatic error correction, but the disadvantage is that the user may fail to learn proper syntax and may become dependent on unpredictable alterations that the system makes. Another approach is to inform the user of the possible alternatives and to let the user decide. A preferred strategy is to prevent errors from occurring (Section 2.5).

8.2.3   User-centered phrasing

The term *user-centered* suggests that the user controls the system—initiating more than responding. Designers partially accomplish this scenario by avoiding the negative and condemning tone in messages and by being courteous to the user. Prompting messages should avoid such imperative forms as ENTER DATA, and should focus on such user control as READY FOR COMMAND or simply READY.

Brevity is a virtue, but the user should be allowed to control the kind of information provided. Possibly, the standard system message should be less than one line; but, by keying a ?, the user should be able to obtain a few lines of explanation. ?? might yield a set of examples, and ??? might produce explanations of the examples and a complete description. CONFER from the University of Michigan and EIES from the New Jersey Institute of Technology are two pioneering teleconferencing systems that provide appealing assistance similar to this. Many word-processing systems offer a special HELP button to provide explanations when the user needs assistance.

The designers of the Library of Congress's SCORPIO system (Woody et al., 1977) (see Figure 1.1) for bibliographic retrieval understood the importance of making the users feel that they are in control. In addition to using the properly subservient READY FOR NEXT COMMAND, the designers avoid the use of the words *error* or *invalid* in the text of system messages. Blame is never assigned to the user; instead, the system displays SCORPIO COULD NOT INTERPRET THE FOURTH PART OF THE COMMAND CONTENTS, WHICH IS SUPPOSED TO BE A 4-CHARACTER OPTION CODE. The message then goes on to define the proper format and to present an example of its use.

Some telephone companies long used to dealing with nontechnical users, offer this tolerant message: "We're sorry, but we were unable to complete your call as dialed. Please hang up, check your number, or consult the operator for assistance." They take the blame and offer constructive guidance for what to do. A thoughtless programmer might have generated a harsher message: "Illegal telephone number. Call aborted. Error number 583-2R6.9. Consult your user manual for further information."

8.2.4   Appropriate physical format

Although professional programmers have learned to read upper-case–only text, most users prefer and find it easier to read upper- and lower-case messages (Section 8.4). Upper-case–only messages should be reserved for brief, serious warnings. Messages that begin with a lengthy and mysterious code number serve only to remind the user that the designers were insensitive to the user's real needs. If code numbers are needed at all, they might be enclosed in parentheses at the end of a message.

There is some disagreement about the placement of messages in a program display. One school of thought argues that the messages should be placed at the point in the program where the problem has arisen. The second opinion is that the messages clutter the program; also, it is easier for the compiler-writer to place them all at the end! This issue is a good subject for experimental study; for now, a reasonable strategy is to place messages in the program body, provided that a blank line is left above and below the message to minimize interference with reading. Of course, certain messages must come at the end, and execution-time messages must appear in the output display.

Some application systems ring a bell or sound a tone when an error has occurred. This alarm can be useful if the operator could miss the error, but it is extremely embarrassing if other people are in the room and is potentially annoying even if the operator is alone. The use of audio signals should be under the control of the operator.

The early high-level language MAD (Michigan Algorithmic Decoder) printed out a full-page picture of Alfred E. Neuman if there were syntactic errors in the program. Novices enjoyed this playful approach, but after they had accumulated a drawer full of pictures, the portrait became an annoying embarrassment. Highlighting errors with rows of asterisks is a common but questionable approach. Designers must walk a narrow path between calling attention to a problem and avoiding embarrassment to the operator. Considering the wide range of experience and temperament in users, maybe the best solution is to offer the user control over the alternatives—this approaches coordinates well with the user-centered principle.

8.2.5   Development of effective messages

The designer's intuition can be supplemented by simple, fast, and inexpensive design studies with actual users and several alternative messages. If the project goal is to serve novice users, then ample effort must be dedicated to designing, testing, and implementing the user interface. This commitment must extend to the earliest design stages so that programming-language, command-language, or menu-selection approaches can be modified in a way that contributes to the production of specific error messages. Messages should be evaluated by several people and tested with suitable subjects (Isa et al., 1983). Messages should appear in user manuals and be given greater visibility. Records should be kept on the frequency of occurrence of each error. Frequent errors should lead to software modifications that provide better error handling, to improved training, and to revisions in user manuals.

Users may remember the one time when they had difficulties with a computer system, rather than the 20 times when everything went well. The strong reaction to problems in using computer systems comes in part from the anxiety and lack of knowledge that novice users have. This reaction may be exacerbated by a poorly designed, excessively complex system; from a poor manual or training experience; or from hostile, vague, or irritating system messages. Improving the messages will not turn a bad system into a good one, but it can play a significant role in improving the user's performance and attitude.

To explore the influence of error messages on users, we conducted five controlled experiments (Shneiderman, 1982). In one experiment, COBOL compiler syntactic error messages were modified, and undergraduate novice users were asked to repair the COBOL statement. Messages with increased specificity generated 28-percent higher repair scores.

Subjects using a text editor with only a ? for an error message made an average of 10.7 errors, but made only 6.1 errors when they switched to an editor offering brief explanatory messages. In another experiment, students corrected 4.1 out of 10 erroneous text-editor commands using the standard system messages. Using improved messages, the experimental group corrected 7.5 out of the 10 commands.

In a study of the comprehensibility of job-control–language error messages from two popular contemporary systems, students scored 2.9 and 3.8

out of 6, whereas students receiving improved messages scored 4.8. Subjective preferences also favored the improved messages.

Mosteller (1981) studied error patterns in IBM's MVS Job Entry Control Language by capturing actual runs in a commercial environment. Analysis of the 2073 errors resulted in specific suggestions for revisions to the error messages, parser, and command language. Remarkably, 513 of the errors were exact retries of the previous runs, confirming concerns over the persistence of errors when messages are poor. As improvements were made to the messages, Mosteller found lower error rates.

These initial experiments support the contentions that improving messages can upgrade performance and result in greater job satisfaction. They have led us to make the following recommendations for system developers (Table 8.1):

1. *Increase attention to message design*: The wording of messages displayed by a computer system should be considered carefully. Technical writers or copy editors should be consulted about the choice of words and phrasing to improve both clarity and consistency.

2. *Establish quality control*: Messages should be approved by an appropriate quality-control committee consisting of programmers, users, and human-

Table 8.1

Error-message guidelines for the product and for the development process. These guidelines come from practical experience and some empirical data.

Error-Message Guidelines

Product

- Be as specific and precise as possible.
- Be constructive: indicate what needs to be done.
- Use a positive tone: avoid condemnation.
- Choose user-centered phrasing.
- Consider multiple levels of messages.
- Keep consistent grammatical form, terminology, and abbreviations.
- Keep consistent visual format and placement.

Process

- Establish a message quality-control group.
- Include messages in the design phase.
- Place all messages in a file.
- Review messages during development.
- Attempt to eliminate the need for messages.
- Carry out acceptance tests.
- Collect frequency data for each message.
- Review and revise messages over time.

factors specialists. Changes or additions should be monitored and recorded.

3. *Develop guidelines*: Error messages should meet these criteria:

   - *Have a positive tone:* Indicate what must be done, rather than condemning the user for the error. Reduce or eliminate the use of such terms as ILLEGAL, INVALID, ERROR, or ILLEGAL PASSWORD. Try Your password did not match the stored password. Please try again.
   - *Be specific and address the problem in the user's terms:* Avoid the vague SYNTAX ERROR or obscure internal codes. Use variable names and concepts known to the user. Instead of INVALID DATA in an inventory application, try Dress sizes range from 5 to 16.
   - *Place the users in control of the situation:* Provide them with enough information to take action. Instead of INCORRECT COMMAND, try Permissible commands are: SAVE, LOAD, or EXPLAIN.
   - *Have a neat, consistent, and comprehensible format:* Avoid lengthy numeric codes, obscure mnemonics, and cluttered displays.

   Writing good messages—like writing good poems, essays, or advertisements—requires experience, practice, and a sensitivity to how the reader will react. It is a skill that can be acquired and refined by programmers and designers who are intent on serving the user. However, perfection is impossible and humility is the mark of the true professional.

4. *Carry out usability test*: System messages should be subjected to an usability test with an appropriate user community to determine whether they are comprehensible. The test could range from a rigorous experiment with realistic situations (for life-critical or high-reliability systems) to an informal reading and review by interested users (for personal computing or low-threat applications).

   Complex interactive systems that involve thousands of users are never really complete until they are obsolete. Under these conditions, the most effective designs facilitate evolutionary refinement (Chapter 13). If designers, maintainers, and operators of interactive systems are genuinely interested in building user-friendly systems, they must understand users' problems.

5. *Collect user performance data*: Frequency counts should be collected for each error condition on a regular basis. If possible, the user's command should be captured for a more detailed study. If you know where users run into difficulties, you can then revise the message, improve the training, modify the manual, or change the system. The error rate per thousand commands should be used as a metric of system quality and a gauge of how improvements affect performance. An error-counting option is useful for internal systems and can be a marketing feature for software products.

Improved messages will be of the greatest benefit to novice users, but regular users and experienced professionals will also profit. As examples of excellence proliferate, complex, obscure, and harsh systems will seem more and more out of place. The crude programming environments of the past will gradually be replaced by systems designed with the user in mind. Resistance to such a transition should not be allowed to impede progress toward the goal of serving the growing user community.

8.3   Nonanthropomorphic Instructions

There is a great temptation to have computers "talk" as though they were people. It is a primitive urge that designers often follow, and that children and many adults accept without hesitation. Children accept humanlike references and qualities for almost any object, from Humpty Dumpty to Tootle the Train. Adults reserve the *anthropomorphic* references for objects of special attraction, such as cars, ships, or computers.

Unfortunately, the words and phrases used in designing computer dialogs can make important differences in people's perceptions, emotional reactions, and motivations. Attributions of intelligence, independent activity, free will, or knowledge to computers can deceive, confuse, and mislead users. The suggestion that computers can think, know, or understand may give users an erroneous model of how computers work and what the machines' capacities are. Ultimately, the deception becomes apparent and users may feel poorly treated.

A second reason for using nonanthropomorphic phrasing stems from a personal belief that everyone benefits from a clear sense of how people are different from computers. Relationships with people are different from relationships with computers. Users learn to control computers, but they must respect the unique desires of individuals. Furthermore, users and designers must accept responsibility for misuse of computers, rather than blaming the machine for errors.

A third motivation is that, although an anthropomorphic interface may be attractive to some people, it can be anxiety producing for others. A large proportion of the population expresses anxiety about using computers and believes that computers "make you feel dumb." Presenting the computer through the specific functions it offers may be a stronger stimulus to user acceptance than the fantasy that the computer is a friend, parent, or partner. As users become engaged, the computer becomes transparent and they can concentrate on their writing, problem solving, or exploration.

Although children and some adults may be attracted by the anthropomorphic interface, they eventually prefer the sense of mastery, internal locus of control, competence, and accomplishment that can come from using a computer as a tool.

In an experimental test with 26 college students, the anthropomorphic design (HI THERE, JOHN! IT'S NICE TO MEET YOU, I SEE YOU ARE READY NOW) was seen as less honest than a mechanistic dialog (PRESS THE ENTER KEY TO BEGIN SESSION) (Quintanar et al., 1982). In this computer-assisted instruction task, subjects took longer with the anthropomorphic design, possibly contributing to the observed improved scores on a quiz, but they felt less responsible for their performance.

Evidence is sparse and individual differences will be important, but there may be an advantage to clearly distinguishing human abilities from computer powers. On the other hand, there are advocates of creating an anthropomorphic computer and of creating agents who are characters that are enacted by the computer (Laurel, 1990). Apple created a videotape in 1987, "The Knowledge Navigator," with a preppie bow-tied young male agent carrying out tasks for an environmental researcher. Some futurists celebrated this vision, but skeptics scorned the scenario as a deception; while most viewers seemed mildly amused.

In a study of 36 junior-high-school students conducted by Lori Gay and Diane Lindwarm under my direction, the style of interaction was varied. Students received a computer-assisted instruction session in one of three forms:

1. *I:* (HI! I AM THE COMPUTER. I AM GOING TO ASK YOU SOME QUESTIONS.)
2. *You:* (YOU WILL BE ANSWERING SOME QUESTIONS. YOU SHOULD....)
3. *Neutral:* (THIS IS A MULTIPLE CHOICE EXERCISE.)

Before and after the three sessions at the computer, subjects were asked to describe whether using a computer was "easy" or "hard." Most subjects thought using a computer was "hard" and did not change their opinion. Of the seven who changed their minds, the five who moved toward "hard" were all using the *I* or *neutral* interface. Both subjects who moved toward "easy" were using the *you* interface. Performance measures on the tasks were not significantly different, but anecdotal evidence and the positive shift for the group that used *you* messages warrant further study.

Software designers and evaluators should be alert to phrasing and to choice of words. The anthropomorphic interface that uses first-person pronouns may be counterproductive because it deceives, misleads, and confuses. It may seem cute on first encounter to be greeted by I AM SOPHIE, THE SOPHISTICATED TEACHER, AND I WILL TEACH YOU TO SPELL CORRECTLY. By the second session, however, this approach strikes people as uselessly repetitive; by the third session, it is an annoying distraction from the task.

The alternative for the software designer is to focus on the user and to use third-person singular pronouns or to avoid pronouns altogether; for example,

Poor: I will begin the lesson when you press RETURN.

Better: You can begin the lesson by pressing RETURN.

Better: To begin the lesson, press RETURN.

The *you* form seems preferable for introductory screens; once the session is underway, however, reducing the number of pronouns avoids distractions from the task.

An alternative for children is to have a fantasy character, such as a teddy bear or busy beaver, serve as a guide through a lesson. A cartoon character can be drawn on the screen and possibly animated, adding visual appeal. Another approach is to identify the human author of a lesson or other software package and to allow that person to speak to the reader, much as Carl Sagan or Jacob Bronowski speaks to the television viewer.

Similar arguments apply to the use of value judgments as reinforcement for correct answers. Our study with 24 third-grade students found that positive reinforcement with value-judgment phrases (EXCELLENT, THAT'S GOOD!, YOU'RE DOING GREAT, etc.) did not improve performance or satisfaction in an arithmetic drill and practice lesson. On the other hand, the presence of a simple numerical counter (6 CORRECT 2 INCORRECT) improved learning.

A study of 54 users of a medical history-taking program indicated higher preference for moderate use of encouraging and "chatty" phrases (Spiliotopoulos and Shackel, 1981). A high level of these nonfunctional phrases, however, led to increased scores on the measures *boring* and *awkward*.

Male and female styles of wording for instructions were tested on male and female undergraduates with varying levels of computer experience (Fulton, 1985). Potency ratings of the computer varied with the user's gender and experience. Further research is indicated to determine male versus female perceptions of acceptability and performance with differing wordings of instructions and feedback.

Instead of making the computer into a person, software designers may put their names on a title or credits page, just as authors do in a book. The credits are an acknowledgment for the work done, and they identify the people responsible for the contents if there are complaints. In software, there is the additional motivation of making it clear that people created the software and that the computer is merely the medium. Credits may encourage designers to work a bit harder, since they know their names will appear.

8.4   Display Design

For most interactive systems, the displays are a key component to successful designs, and are the source of many lively arguments. Dense or cluttered displays can provoke anger, and inconsistent formats can inhibit performance. The complexity of this issue is suggested by the 162 guidelines for data display offered by Smith and Mosier (1986). This diligent effort (see Table 8.2 for some examples) represents progress over the many useful, but sometimes vague, guidelines from earlier reviews (for example, Jones, 1978; Pakin and Wray, 1982). Hopes for an expert system to perform display

Table 8.2

Samples of the 162 data-display guidelines from Smith and Mosier (1986).

Data-Display Guidelines

- At any step in a transaction sequence, ensure that whatever data a user needs will be available for display.
- Display data to users in directly usable form; do not make users convert displayed data.
- For any particular type of data display, maintain consistent format from one display to another.
- Use short, simple sentences.
- Use affirmative statements rather than negative statements.
- Adopt some logical principle by which to order lists; where no other principle applies, order lists alphabetically.
- Ensure that labels are sufficiently close to be associated with their data fields but are separated from their data fields by at least one space.
- Left-justify columns of alphabetic data to permit rapid scanning.
- In multipaged displays, label each page to show its relation to the others.
- Begin every display with a title or header, describing briefly the contents or purpose of the display; leave at least one blank line between the title and the body of the display.
- For size coding, a larger symbol should be at least 1.5 times the height of the next smaller symbol.
- Consider color coding for applications in which users must distinguish rapidly among several categories of data, particularly when the data items are dispersed on the display.
- When blink coding is used, the blink rate should be 2 to 5 hertz, with a minimum duty cycle (ON interval) of 50 percent.
- For a large table that exceeds the capacity of one display frame, ensure that users can see column headings and row labels in all displayed sections of the table.
- When data-display requirements may change (which is often the case) provide some means for users (or a system administrator) to make necessary changes to display functions.

layout seem dim because the demands of each task and user community are so varied and are so difficult to measure. Display design will always have elements of art and require invention, but some principles are becoming clearer (Tullis, 1988a, 1988b; Galitz, 1989).

Designers should begin, as always, with a thorough knowledge of the users' tasks, free from the constraints of display size, response time, or available fonts. Effective display designs must provide all the necessary data in the proper sequence to carry out the task. To account for limited display sizes, designers can organize the displays into pages. Meaningful groupings of items (with labels suitable to the user's knowledge), consistent sequences of groups, and orderly formats all support task performance. Groups can be surrounded by blank spaces or a marker, such as a box. Alternatively, related items can be indicated by highlighting, reverse video, color, or special fonts. Within a group, orderly formats can be accomplished by left or right justification, alignment on decimal points for numbers, or markers to decompose lengthy fields.

8.4.1   Field layout

Exploration with a variety of layouts can be a helpful process. These design alternatives should be developed directly on a display screen. An employee record with information about a spouse and children could be displayed crudely as

Poor:

```
TAYLOR,SUSAN034787331WILLIAM TAYLOR
THOMAS102974
ANN082177
ALEXANDRA090872
```

This record may contain the necessary information for a task, but extracting the information will be slow and error-prone. As a first step at improving the format, blanks can separate fields:

Better:

```
TAYLOR, SUSAN  034787331      WILLIAM TAYLOR
THOMAS 102974
ANN 082177
ALEXANDRA 090872
```

The children's names can be listed in chronological order, with alignment of the dates. Familiar separators for the dates and the employee's social-security number also aid recognition:

Better:

```
TAYLOR, SUSAN   034-78-7331      WILLIAM TAYLOR

ALEXANDRA 09-08-72 THOMAS    10-29-74 ANN      08-21-77
```

The reversed order of "last name, first name" for the employee may be desired to highlight the lexicographic ordering in a long file. However, the "first name, last name" order for the spouse is usually more readable. Consistency seems important, so a compromise might be made to produce

Better:

```
SUSAN TAYLOR   034-78-7331      WILLIAM TAYLOR

ALEXANDRA 09-08-72 THOMAS    10-29-74 ANN      08-21-77
```

For frequent users, this format may be acceptable, since labels have a cluttering effect; but for most users, labels will be helpful:

Better:

```
Employee: SUSAN TAYLOR   Social Security Number: 034-78-7331
Spouse: WILLIAM TAYLOR

Children: Names       Birthdates

ALEXANDRA 09-08-72  THOMAS     10-29-74 ANN      08-21-77
```

Lower-case letters have been used for labels, but the coding might be switched. The lengthy label for social-security number might be abbreviated if the users are knowledgeable. Indenting the information about children might help to convey the grouping of these repeating fields:

Better:

```
EMPLOYEE: Susan Taylor   SSN: 034-78-7331

SPOUSE: William Taylor

CHILDREN:
  NAMES      BIRTHDATES
  Alexandra  09-08-72
  Thomas     10-29-74
  Ann        08-21-77
```

Even in this simple example, the possibilities are numerous. In more realistic situations, a variety of designs should be explored. Further improvements could be made with other coding strategies, such as highlighting, underscoring, color, and reverse video. An experienced graphic designer can be a great benefit. Pilot testing with actual users can yield subjective satisfaction scores and objective times to complete tasks plus error rates for a variety of proposed formats.

8.4.2   Empirical results

Empirical tests of alternative display designs have been conducted in some cases. A narrative form (Figure 8.1a), taken from a telephone-line–testing program, was replaced with a structured form (Figure 8.1b) (Tullis, 1981). The structured form eliminated unnecessary information, grouped related information, and emphasized the information relevant to the required tasks. After practice in reading these displays, Bell System employees were required to carry out typical tasks. The narrative form required an average of 8.3 seconds, whereas the structured form took only 5.0 seconds, resulting in an estimated saving of 79 person-years over the life of the system.

Central issues in displaying complex information are these: How much information should be placed on a display? When are multiple displays preferred? If data fields can be grouped so that tasks can be accomplished using only one display, this approach seems preferable. Crowded displays are more difficult to scan, especially for novice users. In a NASA study of space-shuttle displays, sparsely filled screens with approximately 70-percent blanks were searched in an average of 3.4 seconds, but more densely packed screens with approximately 30-percent blanks took an average of 5.0 seconds (Figure 8.2) (Dodson and Shields, 1978). This study also demonstrated that functionally grouped displays yielded shorter search times.

A study with improved shuttle displays demonstrated that improving the data labels, clustering related information, using appropriate indentation and underlining, aligning numeric values, and eliminating extraneous characters could improve performance (Burns et al., 1986). Task times were reduced by 31 percent and error rates by 28 percent for a population of 16 technical and clerical employees at NASA and Lockheed who were unfamiliar with either version. Sixteen experts with the existing system did not perform statistically significantly faster with the improved displays, but they did perform significantly more accurately.

Frequent expert users can deal with more dense displays and may prefer these displays because they are familiar with the format and because they must initiate fewer operations. Systems for stock-market data, air-traffic control, and airline reservations are examples of successful applications that have dense packing, limited labels, and highly coded fields.

In a study of 12 telephone operators, Springer (1987) found that suppressing the presentation of redundant family names in a directory-assistance listing reduced target location time by 0.8 seconds. She also found that, when the target was in the upper quarter of the display, users found it more quickly if the screen were only one-quarter full, as opposed to one-half full or com-

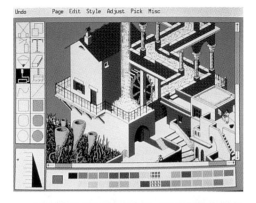

Plate 1: PC Paintbrush IV supports high-resolution color images (up to 256 colors) and a wide variety of painting tools. (Courtesy of ZSoft Corp., Marietta, GA.)

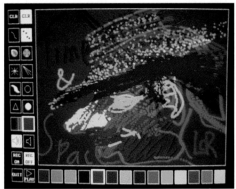

Plate 2: PenPlay II allows fingerpainting with a touch-screen or free-hand drawing with a mouse. Position, speed, and direction of motion affect the results and the accompanying sounds. (Created by Andrew Sears at the Human–Computer Interaction Laboratory at the University of Maryland.)

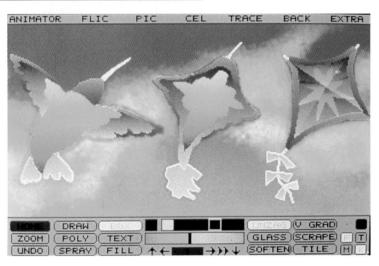

Plate 3: Animator program allows graphics editing and creation of animations. In this example the bird turns into a kite, with the in-between frames created automatically by the "tweening" feature. (Courtesy of Autodesk, Inc., Sausalito, CA.)

Plate 4: The Mandala System allows users to interact with electronic images, such as the cymbals, by merely moving their hands and body. A video camera superimposes the users' image on the large screen display, so no special attachments are needed. (Courtesy of The Vivid Group, Toronto, Ontario, Canada.)

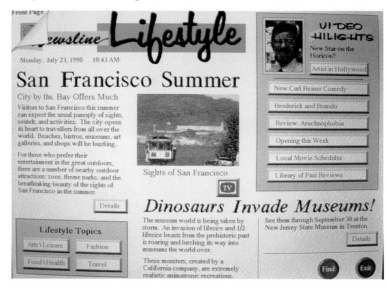

Plate 5: Hyperties 3.0 supports high-resolution images (768 x 1024 pixels with 256 colors), DVI or laserdisc full motion video, and touch-screen selection. (Produced by Cognetics Corporation, Princeton Junction, NJ, for AT&T Bell Laboratories, with permission of AT&T.)

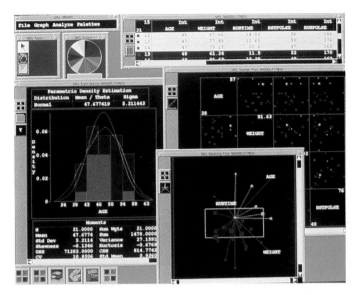

Plate 6: Multiple arbitrary overlapped windows support this information delivery software system. SAS/INSIGHT provides users with multiple views for statistics, exploratory data analysis, and visualization. (Screens reprinted by permission. Copyright 1991 by SAS Institute Inc., Cary, NC.)

Plate 7: H-P VUE offers users six workspaces, each with multiple windows, that are selectable from the control panel on the lower part of the display. The content of the large window is an image of the Hewlett-Packard palmtop computer. (Courtesy of Hewlett-Packard Company, Corvallis, OR.)

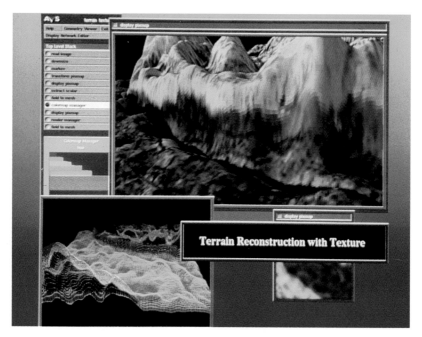

Plate 8: Scientific-visualization software shows three-dimensional analysis of terrain. (Courtesy of Kubota Pacific Computer, Inc., Reston, VA.)

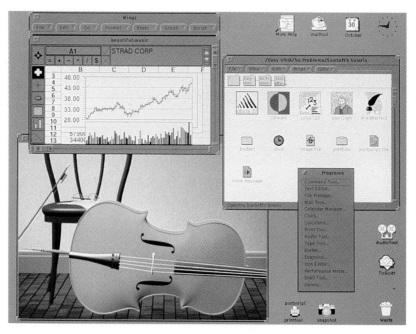

Plate 9: SunSoft's OPEN LOOK Graphical User Interface, as implemented in Open Windows V3. (Copyright 1991 by Sun Microsystems, Inc., Mountain View, CA.)

```
TEST RESULTS    SUMMARY: GROUND

GROUND, FAULT T-G
3 TERMINAL DC RESISTANCE
   >  3500.00 K OHMS T-R
   ■     14.21 K OHMS T-G
   >  3500.00 K OHMS R-G
3 TERMINAL DC VOLTAGE
   ■     0.00 VOLTS  T-G
   ■     0.00 VOLTS  R-G
VALID AC SIGNATURE
3 TERMINAL AC RESISTANCE
   ■     8.82 K OHMS T-R
   ■    14.17 K OHMS T-G
   ■   628.52 K OHMS R-G
LONGITUDINAL BALANCE POOR
   ■    39    DB
COULD NOT COUNT RINGERS DUE TO
  LOW RESISTANCE
VALID LINE CKT CONFIGURATION
CAN DRAW AND BREAK DIAL TONE
```

(a)

```
        ********************************
        *                              *
        *   TIP GROUND       14 K      *
        *                              *
        ********************************

DC RESISTANCE        DC VOLTAGE        AC SIGNATURE

3500 K T-R                                9 K T-R
  14 K T-G           0 V T-G             14 K T-G
3500 K R-G           0 V R-G            629 K R-G

 BALANCE                               CENTRAL OFFICE

 39 DB                                 VALID LINE CKT
                                       DIAL TONE OK
```

(b)

Figure 8.1

Two versions of screens in Bell Labs study (Tullis, 1981): (a) narrative format, (b) structured format.

```
AEP1 COMMANDS                    70 PERCENT DSPLY
1 EMERGENCY PARK=YES/NO      6  START=YES/NO
2 MOUNT CHECK=YES/NO         7  EDIT=YES/NO
3 SW CHECK=YES/NO            8  SELF DUMP=YES/NO
4 RUN=YES/NO          43:4   9  SW RELOAD=YES/NO
5 HALT=YES/NO                10 CALIBRATE=YES/NO
                  126:26:48     XRAY=ON
FO SEQUENCE 11 1A-774:12:36     15 2C-445:35:43
            12 1B-785:48:50     16 03-451:19:42
63 XLG2     13 2A-930:15:28     17 04-287:23:51
            14 2B-300:56:41     18 05-515:21:20
08-288:28:26        432:48:56 DELAYED
19 FW0=73    23 FOCUS=15        27 TRACK=YES/NO
20 FW1=83    24 CAM  HV=2       28 RAY=90
21 FW2=61    25 PCA  HV=9       29 MPD DELAY 88
22 FOV=14    26 EXP TIME=1      30 RESET=703



WHAT IS THE TIME VALUE OF 1A >
```

Figure 8.2(a)

Three versions of screen layouts used in study of density by Dodson and Shields (1978). (a) 70 percent characters.

pletely full. This result suggests that, if possible, screen densities should be kept low, and that extraneous information does slow performance.

8.4.3   Display-complexity metrics

Although a thorough knowledge of the users' tasks and abilities is the key to designing effective screen displays, an objective, automatable metric of screen complexity is an attractive aid. After a thorough review of the

```
CMDS
1 FAULT CK=YES/NO            5  SRT=YES/NO
2 VAL CK=YES/NO              7  FC=YES/NO
3 START=YES/NO               8  TEST SELF=YES/NO
4 CAL=YES/NO                 9  RESTART 1=YES/NO
5 STOP=YES/NO                10 POWER=YES/NO

FO SEQ      11 1A-870:16:14     14 2B-801:41:48
            12 1B-411:21:23     15 2C-958:46:50
            13 2A-582:49:10     16 03-391:35:21
08 675:48:58
19 PA0=28       23 AMPER=12     27 SIGNL=YES/NO
20 PB0=40       24 HI  VLT=2    28 FOV=7
21 PC0=26       25 LO  VLT=4    29 MSG RELAY=61
                26 HOLD OFF=1   30



WHAT IS THE VALUE OF ITEM 23 >
```

Figure 8.2(b)

50 percent.

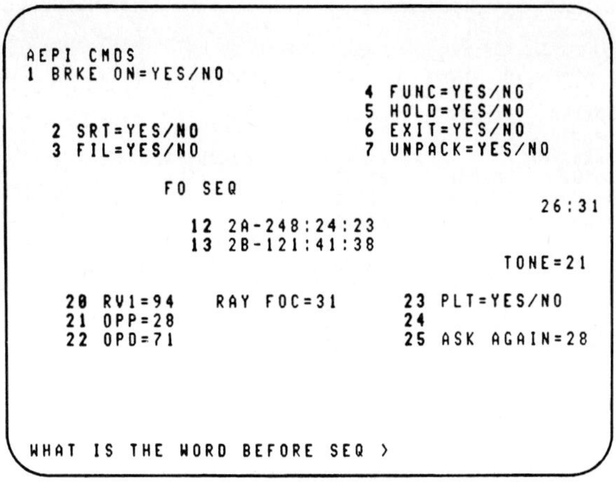

```
AEPI CMDS
1 BRKE ON=YES/NO
                                    4 FUNC=YES/NO
                                    5 HOLD=YES/NO
     2 SRT=YES/NO                   6 EXIT=YES/NO
     3 FIL=YES/NO                   7 UNPACK=YES/NO

          FO SEQ
                                                   26:31
              12 2A-248:24:23
              13 2B-121:41:38
                                            TONE=21

     20 RVI=94      RAY FOC=31     23 PLT=YES/NO
     21 OPP=28                     24
     22 OPD=71                     25 ASK AGAIN=28



   WHAT IS THE WORD BEFORE SEQ >
```

Figure 8.2(c)

30 percent.

literature, Tullis (1988a) developed four metrics for alphanumeric displays:

1. *Overall density:* Number of filled character spaces as a percentage of total spaces available

2. *Local density:* Average number of filled character spaces in a 5-degree visual angle around each character, expressed as a percentage of available spaces in the circle and weighted by distance from the character

3. *Grouping:* (1) Number of groups of "connected" characters, where a connection is any pair of characters separated by less than twice the mean of the distances between each character and its nearest neighbor; (2) average visual angle subtended by groups, and weighted by number of characters in the group

4. *Layout complexity:* Complexity, as defined in information theory, of the distribution of horizontal and vertical distances of each label and data item from a standard point on the display

The argument for local density emerges from studies of visual perception indicating that concentration is focused in a 5-degree visual angle. At normal viewing distances from displays, this area translates into a circle approximately 15 characters wide and seven characters high. Lower local and overall densities should yield easier-to-read displays. The grouping metric was designed to yield an objective, automatable value that assesses the number of clusters of fields on a display. Typically, clusters are formed by characters that are separated by no more than one intervening space horizontally and that are on adjacent lines. Layout complexity measures the variety of shapes that confront the user on a display. Neat blocks of fields

```
To: Atlanta, GA

    Departs    Arrives    Flight

Asheville, NC         First: $92.57    Coach: $66.85
    7:20a    8:05a      PI 299
   10:10a   10:55a      PI 203
    4:20p    5:00p      PI 259

Austin, TX            First: $263.00  Coach: $221.00
    8:15a   11:15a      EA 530
    8:40a   11:39a      DL 212
    2:00p    5:00p      DL 348
    7:15p   11:26p      DL 1654

Baltimore, MD         First: $209.00  Coach: $167.00
    7:00a    8:35a      DL 1767
    7:50a    9:32a      EA 631
    8:45a   10:20a      DL 1610
   11:15a   12:35p      EA 147
    1:35p    3:10p      DL 1731
    2:35p    4:16p      EA 141
```

(a)

```
To: Knoxville, TN
Atlanta, GA  Dp: 9:28a  Ar: 10:10a  Flt: DL 1704  1st: 97.00  Coach: 86.00
Atlanta, GA  Dp: 12:28p  Ar: 1:10p  Flt: DL 152  1st: 97.00  Coach: 86.00
Atlanta, GA  Dp: 4:58p  Ar: 5:40p  Flt: DL 418  1st: 97.00  Coach: 86.00
Atlanta, GA  Dp: 7:41p  Ar: 8:25p  Flt: DL 1126  1st: 97.00  Coach: 86.00
Chicago, Ill.  Dp: 1:45p  Ar: 5:39p  Flt: AL 58  1st: 190.00  Coach: 161.00
Chicago, Ill.  Dp: 6:30p  Ar: 9:35p  Flt: DL 675  1st: 190.00  Coach: 161.00
Chicago, Ill.  Dp: 6:50p  Ar: 9:55p  Flt: RC 398  1st: 190.00  Coach: 161.00
Cincinnati, OH  Dp: 12:05p  Ar: 1:10p  Flt: FW 453  1st: 118.00  Coach: 66.85
Cincinnati, OH  Dp: 5:25p  Ar: 6:30p  Flt: FW 455  1st: 118.00  Coach: 66.85
Dallas, TX  Dp: 5:55p  Ar: 9:56p  Flt: AL 360  1st: 365.00  Coach: 215.00
Dayton, OH  Dp: 11:20a  Ar: 1:10p  Flt: FW 453  1st: 189.00  Coach: 108.00
Dayton, OH  Dp: 4:40  Ar: 6:30p  Flt: FW 455  1st: 189.00  Coach: 108.00
Detroit, Mich.  Dp: 9:10a  Ar: 1:10p  Flt: FW 453  1st: 183.00  Coach: 106.00
Detroit, Mich.  Dp: 2:35p  Ar: 6:30p  Flt: FW 455  1st: 183.00  Coach: 106.00
```

(b)

Figure 8.3

Two versions of screens from the first experiment by Tullis (1984). (a) A structured format that leads to superior performance and preference, compared to version b. (b) The results led to predictive equations.

that start in the same column will have a lower layout complexity. These metrics do not account for coding techniques, upper- versus lower-case characters, continuous text, graphics, or multidisplay issues.

Ten Bell Laboratories employees did motel- and airline-information retrieval tasks on 520 different displays in a variety of formats (Figure 8.3). Performance times and subjective evaluations were collected to generate a predictive equation. The efficacy of the predictor equations for performance times and subjective ratings were validated in a second study. Fourteen Bell Laboratories employees did author- and book-information retrieval tasks on 150 displays using 15 different display formats (Figure 8.4). Correlations between predicted and actual values were 0.80 for search times and 0.79 for subjective ratings.

This impressive result is encouraging; unfortunately, however, the metrics require a computer program to do the computations and they do not include coding techniques, user-experience levels, or multidisplay considerations. Tullis is cautious in interpreting the results, and emphasizes that displays that optimize search times do not necessarily optimize subjective ratings. Grouping of items led to fast performance, but high subjective ratings were linked to low local density and low layout complexity. A simple interpretation of these results might be that effective display designs contain a middle number of groups (six to 15) that are neatly laid out, surrounded by blanks, and similarly structured. This conclusion is a satisfying confirmation of a principle that, when stated, seems intuitively obvious but has not emerged explicitly in the numerous guidelines documents. Further study of human visual search strategies would be helpful in preparing design guidelines (Shields, 1980; Treisman, 1982).

8.4.4   Multidisplay design

Little is known about *multidisplay design*, but every guideline document implores the designer to preserve consistent location, structure, and terminology across displays. Supportive evidence for consistent location comes from a study of 40 inexperienced computer users of a menu system (Teitelbaum and Granda, 1983). The position of the title, page number, topic heading, instruction line, and entry area were varied across displays for one-half of the subjects, whereas the other half saw constant positions. Mean response time to questions about these items for subjects in the varying condition was 2.54 seconds, but was only 1.47 seconds for those seeing constant positions.

Sequences of displays should be similar throughout the system for similar tasks, but exceptions will certainly occur. Within a sequence, users should be offered some sense of how far they have come and how far they have to go to reach the end. It should be possible to go backward in a sequence to correct errors, to review decisions, or to try alternatives.

```
Books

Author:         Aird, C
Author#:        33
Title:          Henrietta Who?
Price:          $5
Publisher:      Macmillan
#Pages:         253

Author:         Aird, C
Author#:        33
Title:          His Burial Too
Price:          $4
Publisher:      Macmillan
#Pages:         287

Author:         Aird, C
Author#:        33
Title:          Late Phoenix
Price:          $8
Publisher:      McGraw
#Pages:         362
```

(a)

```
Books

Silverberg,R    #112    Downward to the Earth    $8    McGraw      314p

Silverberg,R    #112    Dying Inside    $6    McGraw      284p

Silverberg,R    #112    Earth's Other Shadow    $4    Harper      295p

Silverberg,R    #112    Invaders from Earth    $3    McGraw      302p

Silverberg,R    #112    Lord Valentine's Castle    $12    Macmillan      354p

Silverberg,R    #112    Man in the Maze    $7    McGraw      322p

Springer, N     #204    Sable Moon    $3    Prentice      185p

Springer, N     #204    Silver Sun    $4    Norton      198p

Springer, N     #204    White Hart    $5    Prentice      215p

Stewart, M      #64     Crystal Cave    $11    McGraw      428p

Stewart, M      #64     Hollow Hills    $8    Macmillan      403p
```

(b)

Figure 8.4

Two versions of screens in the second experiment by Tullis (1984). Equations based on objective metrics accurately predicted performance and preference scores, indicating the superiority of version in (a) over that in (b).

8.5   Color

Color displays are attractive to users and can often improve task performance, but the danger of misuse is high. Color can

- Soothe or strike to the eye
- Add accents to an uninteresting display
- Facilitate subtle discriminations in complex displays
- Emphasize the logical organization of information
- Draw attention to warnings
- Evoke strong emotional reactions of joy, excitement, fear, or anger

The principles developed by graphic artists for using color in books, magazines, highway signs, and television are now being adapted for computer displays (Thorell and Smith, 1990; Marcus, 1992). Programmers and interactive systems designers are quickly learning how to create effective computer displays and to avoid the pitfalls (Weitzman, 1985; Brown, 1988; Galitz, 1989) (see Color Plates for examples).

There is no doubt that color makes videogames more attractive to users, conveys more information on power-plant or process-control diagrams, and is necessary for realistic images of people, scenery, or three-dimensional objects (Kron and Rosenfeld, 1983; Bobko, Bobko, and Davis, 1984; Foley et al., 1990). These applications require color. Greater controversy exists about the benefits of color for alphanumeric displays.

No simple set of rules governs use of color, but a number of guidelines can become the starting point for designers:

- *Use color conservatively:* Many programmers and novice designers are eager to use color to brighten up their displays, but the results are often counterproductive. One home information system had the seven letters in its name in large letters, each with a different color. At a distance, the display appeared inviting and eye-catching; up close, however, it was difficult to read.

   Instead of showing meaningful relationships, inappropriately colored fields mislead users into searching for relationships that do not exist. In one poorly designed display, white lettering was used for input fields and for explanations of PF keys, leading users to think that they had to type the letters PF3 or PF9.

   Using a different color for each of 12 items in a menu produces an overwhelming effect. Using four colors (such as red, blue, green, and yellow) for the 12 items will still mislead users into thinking that all the similarly colored items are related. An appropriate strategy would be to show all the menu items in one color, the title in a second color, the instructions in a third color, and error messages in a fourth color. Even this strategy can be overwhelming if the colors are too striking visually.

- *Limit the number of colors:* Many design guides suggest limiting the number of colors in a single alphanumeric display to four, with a limit of seven colors in the entire sequence of displays. Experienced users may be able to benefit from a larger number of color codes.

- *Recognize the power of color as a coding technique:* Color speeds recognition for many tasks, but it can inhibit performance of tasks that go against the grain of the coding scheme. For example, in an accounting application, if data lines with accounts overdue more than 30 days are coded in red, they will be readily visible among the nonoverdue accounts coded in green. In air-traffic control, high-flying planes might be coded differently from low-flying planes to facilitate recognition. In programming workstations, newly added programming-language statements might be coded differently from the old statements, to show progress in writing or maintaining programs.

- *Ensure that color coding supports the task:* If, in the accounting application with color coding by days overdue, the task is now to locate accounts with balances of more than $55, the coding by days overdue may inhibit performance on the second task. In the programming application, the coding of recent additions may make it more difficult to read the entire program. Designers should attempt to make a close linkage between the users' tasks and the color coding.

- *Have color coding appear with minimal user effort:* In general, the color coding should not have to be assigned by the users each time they perform a task, but should appear because they, for example, initiate the program to check for accounts overdue by more than 30 days. When the users perform the task of locating accounts with balances of more than $55, the new color coding should appear automatically.

- *Place color coding under user control:* When appropriate, the users should be able to turn off the color coding. For example, if a spelling checker color codes possibly misspelled words in red, then the user should be able to accept the spelling and to turn off the coding. The presence of the highly visible red coding is a distraction from reading the text for comprehension.

- *Design for monochrome first:* The primary goal of a display designer should be to lay out the contents in a logical pattern. Related fields can be shown by contiguity or by similar structural patterns; for example, successive employee records may have the same indentation pattern. Related fields can also be grouped by a box drawn around the group. Unrelated fields can be kept separate by blank space—at least one blank line vertically or three blank characters horizontally. Monochrome displays should be seriously considered as the primary format because approximately 8 percent of males in European and North American communities have some form of color blindness. It may be advantageous to design for monochrome because color displays may not be universally available. Monochrome designs may increase the consumer audience of a product or permit operation when a color monitor fails.

- *Use color to help in formatting:* In densely packed displays where space is at a premium, similar colors can be used to group related items. For example, in a police dispatcher's tabular display of assignments, the police cars on emergency calls might be coded in red and the police cars on routine calls might be coded in green. Then, when a new emergency arises, it will be relatively easy to identify the cars on routine calls and to assign one to the emergency. Dissimilar colors can be used to distinguish physically close but logically distinct fields. In a block-structured programming language, designers could show the nesting levels by coding the statements in a progression of colors—for example, dark green, light green, yellow, light orange, dark orange, red, and so on.

- *Be consistent in color coding:* Use the same color-coding rules throughout the system. If error messages are in red, then make sure that every error message appears in red; a change to yellow may be interpreted as a change in importance of the message. If colors are used differently by several designers of the same system, then users will hesitate as they attempt to assign meaning to the color changes. A set of color-coding standards should be written down for the benefit of every designer.

- *Be alert to common expectations about color codes:* The designer needs to speak to operators to determine what color codes are applied in the task domain. From automobile-driving experience, red is commonly considered to indicate stop or danger, yellow is a warning, and green is go. In investment circles, red is a financial loss and black is a gain. For chemical engineers, red is hot and blue is cold. For map makers, blue means water, green means forests, and yellow means deserts. These multiple conventions can cause problems for designers. A designer might consider using red to signal that an engine is warmed up and ready, but a user might understand the red coding as an indication of danger. A red light is often used to indicate power ON for electrical equipment, but some users are made anxious by this decision since red has a strong association with danger or stopping. When appropriate, indicate the color-code interpretations on the display or in a help panel.

- *Be alert to problems with color pairings:* If saturated (pure) red and blue appear on a display at the same time, it may be difficult for users to absorb the information. Red and blue are on the opposite ends of the spectrum, and the muscles surrounding the human eye will be strained by attempts to produce a sharp focus for both colors simultaneously. The blue will appear to recede and the red will appear to come forward. Blue text on a red background would present an especially difficult challenge for users to read. Similarly, other combinations will appear to be garish and difficult to read—for example, yellow on purple, magenta on green. Too little contrast also is a problem: Imagine yellow letters on a white background or brown letters on a black background. On each color monitor, the color appears differently, and careful tests with various text and background colors are necessary. Pace (1984) tested 24 color combinations on an Amdek monitor connected to an IBM PC, using 36 undergraduate subjects. He found errors rates ranged from approximately one to four errors per 1000 characters read. Black on blue and blue on white were two colors with low error rates in both tasks, and magenta on green and green on white were two colors with high error rates. Tests with other monitors and tasks are necessary to reach a general conclusion about the most effective color pairs.

- *Use color changes to indicate status changes:* If an automobile speedometer had a digital readout of the driving speed, it might be helpful to change from green numbers below the speed limit to red above the speed limit to act as a warning. Similarly, in an oil refinery, pressure indicators might change color as the value went above or below acceptable limits. In this way, color acts as an attention-getting method. This technique is potentially valuable when there are hundreds of values displayed continuously.

- *Use color in graphic displays for greater information density:* In graphs with multiple plots, color can be helpful in showing which line segments form the full graph. The usual strategies for differentiating lines in black-on-white graphs—such as dotted lines, thicker lines, and dashed lines—are not as effective as is using separate colors for each line. Architectural plans benefit from color coding of electrical, telephone, hot-water, cold-water, and natural-gas lines. Similarly, map makers can have greater information density when color coding is used.

- *Beware of the loss of resolution with color displays:* Many color displays have poorer resolution than do monochrome displays. The benefits of color coding must be weighed against the loss of resolution. Color displays may also be more costly, heavier, less reliable, hotter, and larger than monochrome displays.

Christ (1975) reports on 41 studies of the benefits of color, but few of these studies were conducted on CRTs. Tullis (1981, see Section 8.4.2) describes an experiment that used color in one of four versions of a CRT display. The color graphics display did not yield significantly improved performance, but user reactions were positive: "Color highlights important parts," "High speed and very clear," and "Color adds to what might otherwise be a boring task."

The complexity of using color was demonstrated in studies of decision-making tasks, rather than of simple location of information or recall, with management information systems (Benbasat et al., 1986). Although color coding was found to be beneficial and preferred, there was an interaction with personality factors. Further intricate relationships were found in a comparison of monochrome versus color-coded pie charts, bar charts, line graphs, and data tables in which color coding sped performance in all but the line graphs (Hoadley, 1990). Hoadley concludes that "uncritical addition of color may not be uniformly beneficial. Color is a subtle variable that can significantly enhance the decision maker's ability to extract information."

In summary, with color-display quality increasing and cost decreasing, designers are tempted to use color in system designs. There are undoubtedly benefits of increased user satisfaction and often increased performance; however, there are real dangers in misusing color. Care should be taken to make appropriate designs and to conduct thorough evaluations (Table 8.3).

8.6 Practitioner's Summary

The wording of system messages may have an effect on performance and attitudes of users, especially novices whose anxiety and lack of knowledge put them at a disadvantage. Designers might make improvements by merely using more specific diagnostic messages, offering constructive guidance rather than focusing on failures, employing user-centered phrasing, choosing a suitable physical format, and avoiding vague terminology or numeric codes.

When giving instructions, focus on the user and the user's tasks. Avoid anthropomorphic phrasing and use the *you* form to guide the novice user. Avoid judging the user. Simple statements of the status are more succinct and usually are more effective.

Pay careful attention to display design, and develop a local set of guidelines for all designers. Use spacing, indentation, columnar formats, and field labels to organize the display for users. Color can improve some displays and can lead to more rapid task performance with higher satisfaction; but improper use of color can mislead and slow users.

Organizations can benefit from careful study of display-design guidelines documents and from the creation of their own set of guidelines tailored to local needs (Section 13.3.1). This document should also include a list of local terminology and abbreviations. Consistency and thorough testing are critical.

Table 8.3

Guidelines highlight the complex potentials for benefits and dangers with color coding of alphanumeric displays.

Color Guidelines

Benefits

- Soothes or strikes the eye
- Accents an uninteresting display
- Facilitates subtle discriminations in complex displays
- Emphasizes the logical organization of information
- Draws attention to warnings
- Evokes more emotional reactions of joy, excitement, fear, or anger

Guidelines

- Use color conservatively: limit the number and amount of colors.
- Recognize the power of color to speed or slow tasks.
- Ensure color coding supports the task.
- Have color coding appear with minimal user effort.
- Place color coding under user control.
- Design for monochrome first.
- Use color to help in formatting.
- Be consistent in color coding.
- Be alert to common expectations about color codes.
- Use color changes to indicate status changes.
- Use color in graphic displays for greater information density.

Dangers

- Resolution may degrade with color displays.
- Color pairings may cause problems.
- Color fidelity may degrade on other hardware.
- Printing or conversion to other media may be a problem.

8.7   Researcher's Agenda

Experimental testing could refine the proposed error-message guidelines and identify the sources of user anxiety or confusion. Message placement, highlighting techniques, and multiple-level message strategies are candidates for exploration. Improved parsing strategies to provide better messages automatically would be useful.

There is a great need for testing to validate data-display and color-design guidelines. Basic understanding and cognitive models of visual perception of displays would be a dramatic contribution. Do users follow a scanning pattern from the top left? Do users whose natural language reads from right to left or users from different cultures scan displays differently? Does white space or boxing of items facilitate comprehension and speed interpretation? How does color coding reorganize the pattern of scanning? When is a single dense display preferable to two sparse displays?

Performance and preference data for multiple tasks and user communities would help to make the case for improved message, display, and color design. Such studies would be likely to yield clues to improved strategies.

References

Benbasat, I., Dexter, A. S., and Todd, P., The influence of color and graphical information presentation in a managerial decision simulation, *Human–Computer Interaction 2* (1986), 65–92.

Bobko, P., Bobko, D. J., and Davis, M. A., A multidimensional scaling of video games, *Human Factors 26* (1984), 477–482.

Brown, C. Marlin, *Human–Computer Interface Design Guidelines*, Ablex, Norwood, NJ (1988).

Burns, Michael J., Warren, Dianne L., and Rudisill, Marianne, Formatting space-related displays to optimize expert and nonexpert user performance, *Proc. ACM SIGCHI '86 Human Factors in Computing Systems*, ACM, New York (1986), 274–280.

Christ, R. E., Review and analysis of color coding research for visual displays, *Human Factors 17* (1975), 542–570.

Dean, M., How a computer should talk to people, *IBM Systems Journal 21*, 4 (1982), 424–453.

Dodson, D. W., and Shields, N. L., Jr., Development of user guidelines for ECAS display design, Volume 1, Report No. NASA-CR-150877, Essex Corp., Huntsville, AL (1978).

Dwyer, B., Programming for users: A bit of psychology, *Computers and People 30*, 1 and 2 (1981a), 11–14, 26.

Dwyer, B., A user friendly algorithm, *Communications of the ACM 24*, 9 (September 1981b), 556–561.

Foley, James D., van Dam, Andries, Feiner, Steven K., and Hughes, John F., *Computer Graphics: Principles and Practice* (Second Edition), Addison-Wesley, Reading, MA (1990).

Fulton, Margaret A., A research model for studying the gender/power aspects of human–computer interaction, *International Journal of Man–Machine Studies 23* (1985), 369–382.

Galitz, Wilbert O., *Handbook of Screen Format Design* (Third Edition), Q.E.D. Information Sciences, Wellesley, MA (1989).

Golden, D., A plea for friendly software, *Software Engineering Notes 5*, 4 (1980), 4–5.

Hahn, K. W., and Athey, J. G., Diagnostic messages, *Software—Practice and Experience 2* (1972), 347–352.

Heaps, H. S., and Radhakrishnan, T., Compaction of diagnostic messages for compilers, *Software—Practice and Experience 7* (1977), 139–144.

Hoadley, Ellen D., Investigating the effects of color, *Communications of the ACM 33*, 2 (February 1990), 120–139.

Isa, Barbara S., Boyle, James M., Neal, Alan S., and Simons, Roger M., A methodology for objectively evaluating error messages, *Proc. ACM SIGCHI '83 Human Factors in Computing Systems*, ACM, New York (1983), 68–71.

Jones, P. F., Four principles of man–computer dialog, *IEEE Transactions on Professional Communication PC-21*, 4 (December 1978), 154–159.

Kron, Hildegard, and Rosenfeld, Edward, *Computer Images: State of the Art*, Stewart, Tabori and Chang, New York (1983).

Laurel, Brenda, Interface agents: Metaphors with character. In Laurel, Brenda (Editor), *The Art of Human–Computer Interface Design*, Addison-Wesley, Reading, MA (1990), 355–365.

Marcus, Aaron, *Graphic design for Electronic Documents and User Interfaces*, ACM Press, New York (1992).

Mosteller, W., Job entry control language errors, *Proceedings of SHARE 57*, SHARE, Chicago (1981), 149–155.

Pace, Bruce J., Color combinations and contrast reversals on visual display units, *Proceedings of the Human Factors Society Twenty-Eighth Annual Meeting*, Santa Monica, CA (1984), 326–330.

Pakin, S. E., and Wray, P., Designing screens for people to use easily, *Data Management* (July 1982), 36–41.

Quintanar, Leo R., Crowell, Charles R., and Pryor, John B., Human–computer interaction: A preliminary social psychological analysis, *Behavior Research Methods and Instrumentation 14*, 2 (1982), 210–220.

Robertson, P. J., A guide to using color on alphanumeric displays, IBM Technical Report G320-6296, IBM White Plains, NY (1980).

Shields, Nicholas, Jr., Spacelab display design and command usage guidelines, NASA Report MSFC-PROC-711A, Huntsville, AL (April 1980).

Shneiderman, Ben, System message design: Guidelines and experimental results. In Badre, A., and Shneiderman, B. (Editors), *Directions in Human/Computer Interaction*, Ablex, Norwood, NJ (1982), 55–78.

Smith, Sid L. and Mosier, Jane N., *Guidelines for Designing User Interface Software*, Report ESD-TR-86-278, The MITRE Corporation, Bedford, MA (August 1986).

Spiliotopoulos, V. and Schackel, B., Towards a computer interview acceptable to the naive user, *International Journal of Man–Machine Studies 14* (1981), 77–90.

Springer, Carla J., Retrieval of information from complex alphanumeric displays: Screen formatting variables' effect on target identification time. In Salvendy, Gavriel (Editor), *Cognitive Engineering in the Design of Human–Computer Interaction and Expert Systems*, Elsevier, Amsterdam, The Netherlands (1987), 375–382.

Teitelbaum, Richard C., and Granda, Richard F., The effects of positional constancy on searching menus for information, *Proc. ACM CHI '83 Human Factors in Computing Systems*, ACM, New York (1983), 150–153.

Thorell, L. G., and Smith, W. J., *Using Computer Color Effectively*, Prentice-Hall, Englewood Cliffs, NJ (1990).

Treisman, Anne, Perceptual grouping and attention in visual search for features and for objects, *Journal of Experimental Psychology: Human Perception and Performance 8*, 2 (1982), 194–214.

Tullis, T. S., An evaluation of alphanumeric, graphic and color information displays, *Human Factors 23* (1981), 541–550.

Tullis, T. S., Screen design. In Helander, Martin (Editor), *Handbook of Human–Computer Interaction*, Elsevier Science Publishers, Amsterdam, The Netherlands (1988a), 377–411

Tullis, T. S., A system for evaluating screen formats: Research and application. In Hartson, H. Rex, and Hix, Hartson (Editors), *Advances in Human–Computer Interaction* (Volume 2), Ablex, Norwood, NJ (1988b), 214–286.

Weitzman, Donald O., Color coding re-viewed, *Proc. Human Factors Society—Twenty-ninth Annual Meeting*, Santa Monica, CA (1985), 1079–1083.

Woody, C. A., Fitzgerald, M. P., Scott, F. J., and Power, D. L., A Subject-Content-Retriever-for-Processing-Information-On-Line (SCORPIO), *AFIPS Conference Proceedings 46* (1977).

CHAPTER 9

Multiple-Window Strategies

Through even the smallest window the eye can reach the
most distant horizon.

A. Bergman, *Visual Realities,* **1992**

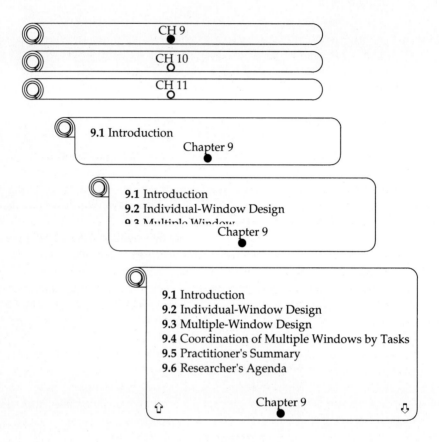

9.1 Introduction

The output of early computers was printed by Teletype on an ever growing scroll of paper. As designers switched to high-speed displays, the need to go back was sometimes supported by electronic scrolling of the session. This technique is useful, but designers became aware of similar situations in which users have to jump around to related text or graphics. Programmers have to jump from procedural code to data declarations, or from procedure invocations to procedure definitions. Authors of scientific papers jump from writing the text to adding a bibliographic reference to reviewing empirical data to creating figures to reading previous papers. Airline reservationists jump from working on a client itinerary to reviewing schedules to choosing seat assignments. Office workers jump from writing a document to revising a spreadsheet to checking electronic mail. The problem is still greater because users must also compare output to input files, consult online help, cope with error messages relating to lengthy programs, and use accessories such as calculators or calendars. Further motivation stems from the frequent need to jump among unrelated materials. Quick shifts of attention may be required from authoring new documents, to consulting old databases to satisfying requests from superiors, or to revising spreadsheets based on information received in electronic-mail messages. All these situations led designers to develop varied strategies for managing multiple windows with related information easily accessible.

The general problem for many computer users is the need to consult multiple sources rapidly, while minimally disrupting their concentration on their task. With large desk- or wall-sized displays, a large number of related documents could be displayed simultaneously, but visibility and eye–head movement might be a problem. With small displays, windows are usually too small to provide adequate information or context. In the middle ground, with 9- to 27-inch displays (approximately 640 x 480 to 2048 x 2048 pixels), it becomes a design challenge to offer users sufficient information and flexibility to accomplish their tasks while reducing window housekeeping actions, distracting clutter, and eye–head movement. The animation characteristics, three-dimensional appearance, and graphic design play key roles in efficacy and acceptance (Gait, 1985; Kobara, 1991; Marcus, 1992).

If users' tasks are well understood and regular, then there is a good chance that an effective *multiple-window display* strategy can be developed. The airline reservationist might start a `client-itinerary` window and, as flight segments are selected from a `schedule` window, have them be entered automatically in the `itinerary` window. Windows labeled `seat selection` or `food preferences` might appear as needed, and then the `charge-card information` window would appear to complete the transaction. When the sequence is varied and unpredictable, users will need to have more control of the layout and will need more training.

Window housekeeping is an activity related to the computer domain and not directly related to the user's task. If window-housekeeping actions can be reduced, then users can complete their tasks more rapidly. In an empirical test with eight experienced users, the windowed version of a system produced longer task-completion times than did the nonwindowed (full-screen) environment (Bury et al., 1985). Multiple smaller windows led to more time arranging information on the display and more scrolling activity to bring necessary information into view. However, after the time to arrange the display was eliminated, the task-solution times were shorter for the windowed environment. Fewer errors were made in the windowed environment. These results suggest that there are advantages to using windows, but these advantages may be compromised unless automatic window arrangement is provided.

On small displays with poor resolution, opportunities for using multiple windows are limited unless the user can tolerate frequent and annoying horizontal and vertical scrolling. With medium-resolution displays and careful design, multiple windows can be practical and esthetically pleasing. Window-border decorations can be made to be informative, useful, and attractive. On larger, high-resolution displays, windows become still more attractive, but the manipulation of windows can remain as a distraction from the user's task (Lu and Ader, 1989). Opening windows, moving them around, changing their size, or closing them are the most common operations supported (Card et al., 1984; Myers, 1988).

The visual nature of window use has led many designers to apply a direct-manipulation strategy (see Chapter 5) to window actions. Instead of typing a command to stretch, move, and scroll a window, users can point at appropriate icons on the window border and simply click on the mouse button (Billingsley, 1988; Kobara, 1991; Marcus 1992). Since the dynamics of windows have a strong effect on user perceptions, the animations for transitions (zooming boxes, sequencing of repainting when a window is opened or closed, blinking outlines, or highlighting during dragging) must be designed carefully.

It is hard to trace the first explicit description of windows (Hopgood et al., 1985), although several sources credit Doug Engelbart with the invention of the mouse, windows, outlining, collaborative work, and hypertext as part of his pioneering NLS system at the Stanford Research Institute during the mid-1960s (Engelbart, 1988). Movable, overlapping windows appeared in the Smalltalk graphical environment (Figure 9.1) as it evolved in the 1970s at

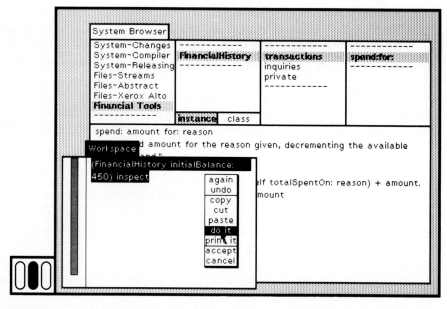

Figure 9.1

Many versions of Smalltalk were created in the 1970s, but the user interface is remembered for overlapping windows, a multipane hierarchical browser, window titles that stick out like tabs, pop-up menus for window actions, and an unorthodox scroll bar. This display from Smalltalk-80 illustrates all these features. (Courtesy of Parc Place Systems, Mountain View, CA.)

Figure 9.2

The Xerox 8010 Star played a leading role in popularizing high-resolution, what-you-see-is-what-you-get editing for document preparation in office environments. The Xerox 8010 Star system pioneered the concept of the display screen as an electronic desktop as well as introducing such user-friendly interfaces as the "mouse" pointing device, symbolic icons, multiple display windows, and a bit-mapped display that showed graphics in very fine detail. (Caption and photograph courtesy of Xerox Corp., Rochester, NY.)

Xerox PARC, with contributions from Alan Kay, Larry Tesler (1981), Daniel Ingalls, and many others. In 1981, the highly graphical Xerox Star (Figure 9.2) (Smith et al., 1982, Johnson et al., 1990) allowed up to six nonoverlapping windows (with limited size control, movement, but no dragging of windows or icons) to cover the desktop plus multiple property sheets to overlay temporarily parts of the windows or desktop. Soon after, the Apple Lisa and, in 1984, the Apple Macintosh (Figure 9.3) made popular their style of graphical user interface with overlapping windows (Apple, 1987).

IBM's Topview and VisiCorp's Visi On (Seybold, 1983), were bold but commercially unsuccessful attempts at window management in character-

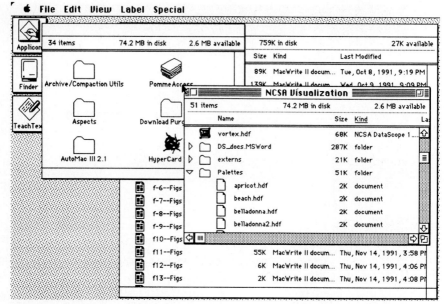

Figure 9.3

Macintosh System 7 windows overlap with the active window showing stripes in the title bar. Windows can be dragged partially off the display to the left, right, and bottom. (Various System 7.0 graphic illustrations, and icons © Apple Computer, Inc., Cupertino, CA. Used with permission.)

based environments. Microsoft followed with the graphical MS Windows 1.0, 2.03, and 3.0 (in 1990) (Figure 9.4a–c) for IBM PCs (IBM's OS/2 Presentation Manager and OfficeVision/2, Hewlett-Packard NewWave 3.0, Tandy DeskMate, Digital Research GEM/3 Desktop, and Quarterdeck DESQview offer interesting variations). Other important windowing systems include NeXT Step (Figure 9.5) (Webster, 1989), OSF/Motif (Kobara, 1991), Sun NeWS and OPEN LOOK (Color Plate 9) (Sun Microsystems, 1989), DECwindows, Andrew (Morris et al., 1986), and the X family (twm, uwm) (Quercia and O'Reilly, 1990).

The notion of collections of windows assembled into *rooms* is an important step forward in matching window strategies to users' tasks (Henderson and Card, 1986; Card and Henderson, 1987). Users can open and leave a set of windows in one room for reading electronic mail, while another room might have a set of windows for composing an article or a program. Rooms can be seen as a form of window macro that enables users to specify actions on several windows at a time. Hewlett-Packard's HP-VUE implements the rooms idea as a set of six workspaces users can visit (Color Plate 7). Much progress has been made, but there is still an opportunity to reduce dramati-

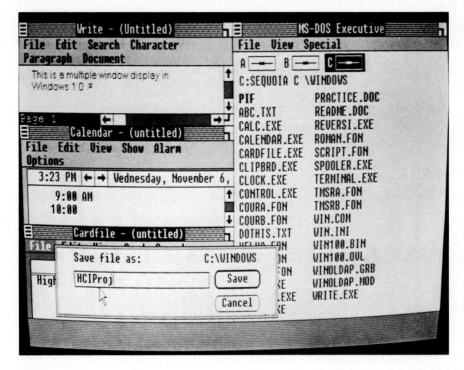

Figure 9.4(a)

Microsoft Windows 1.0 display with variable size/place/number and space-filling tiling only. (Figure 9.4a–c: Screen shot ©1985–1991 Microsoft Corporation. Reprinted with permission from Microsoft Corporation, Redmond, WA.)

cally the housekeeping chores with individual windows and to provide task-related multiple-window coordination. Innovative features, inventive borders or color combinations, individual tailoring, programmable actions, and cultural variations should be expected. An effective overview of windowing strategies is available in videotape form (Myers, 1990).

9.2 Individual-Window Design

The *MS Windows 3.0 User's Guide* (1990) identifies a window as: "A rectangular area that contains a software application, or a document file. Windows can be opened and closed, resized and moved. You can open several of them on the desktop at the same time and you can shrink windows to icons or enlarge them to fill the entire desktop." Although some people might disagree with aspects of this definition (for example, windows are not always rectangular, other window actions are possible), it is a useful

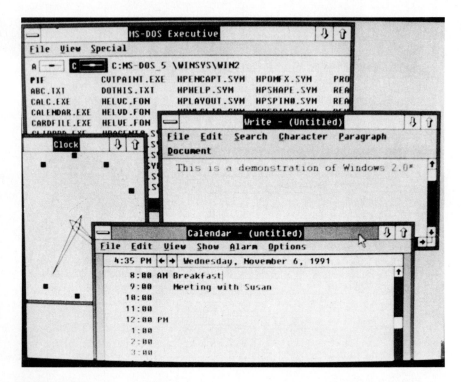

Figure 9.4(b)

Microsoft Windows 2.0 display with arbitrary overlapping windows.

description. Window components include

- *Titles*: Most windows have an identifying title at the top-center, top-left, or bottom-center, or on a tab that extends from the window (Figure 9.6). Tabbed window titles can be helpful in locating a window on a cluttered desktop. To save window space, designers create some windows with no title. Title bars may change shading or color to show which window is the currently active window (the window that receives keystrokes from the keyboard). When a window is closed, it may be represented as an icon and it may show a title to its right, below it and centered, or below it and left-justified. Other approaches show the titles in a pop-up menu list or as a tab sticking out of a pile of windows.

- *Borders or frames*: The window border or frame may be 1 pixel thick or much thicker to accommodate selection or to distinguish each window. Thin borders conserve display space for window contents. Several systems use three-dimensional lighting models and may show a

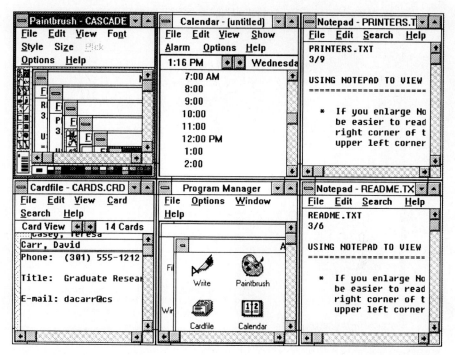

Figure 9.4(c)

Microsoft Windows 3.0 display with six windows arranged in a space-filling tiled form. A cascade version of these six windows appears in Figure 9.13. Other displays of Microsoft Windows 3.0 are shown in Figures 5.11 and 9.14.

shadow below each window. Three-dimensional buttons and icons on the borders have become popular. This three-dimensional effect is attractive to many users (although some may find it distracting), but it may also use precious pixels that could be devoted to window contents. Borders may be colored with user-selected palettes. Border thickness or color changes can be used to show which window is the currently active one.

- *Scroll bars:* Since a window may be small compared to its contents, some method for moving the window over the contents or moving the contents under the window is needed. The basic operation of a scroll bar is to move up or down and left or right, but many variations have been implemented. Small and large motions must be supported, incremental and destination actions are appreciated, and feedback is necessary to help users formulate their plans (Figure 9.7a). Most scroll bars have some form of up and down arrows on which the user can click to produce a small motion, such as a single-line scroll. An important

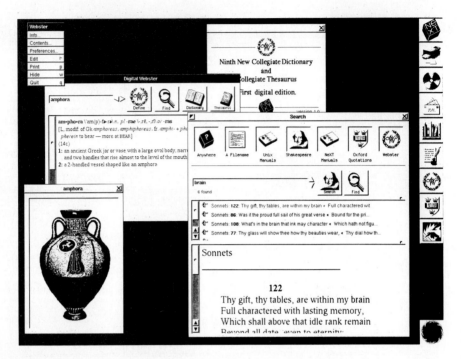

Figure 9.5

NeXTstep user interface shows three overlapping windows related to the
dictionary, and a single window with several coordinated panes for doing string
search in Shakespeare's sonnets. (Figure courtesy of Merriam-Webster Inc.,
Springfield, MA; computer screen shot courtesy of NeXT Computer, Inc.)

feature is to permit repeated smooth scrolling when the up or down
arrow is selected continuously (for example, when the user holds down
the mouse button). This strategy is preferable to repeated mouse clicks,
which distract the user from reading the contents. Scrolling by a full
window or page turning is often supported by clicks above or below
the scroll box. Users can get to a specific destination in a document,
such as the end, by dragging the scroll box to the desired destination.

Feedback in scroll bars is important for ensuring confidence and
correct operations. An important approach uses proportional scroll
boxes that indicate what portion of the document is visible currently.
Another appreciated feature displays a page number inside the scroll
box, so that, as users drag the scroll box, they can see where they are in
a document (Figure 9.7b). If the scroll bar is used on a list such as
alphabetically organized document names, then the scroll box could
show the first letter of the names.

There is room for improvement of scroll bars. For example, it might
be nice to mark a particular position and see a small triangle on the

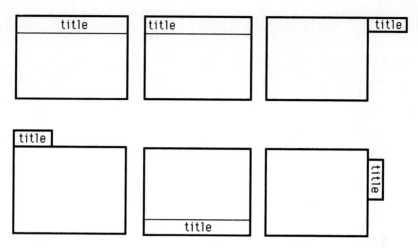

Figure 9.6

Titles may be inside the window in various locations, or protruding from it in various positions.

scroll bar (Figure 9.7c). Then, merely clicking on the triangle would cause the scroll bar and the window's contents to jump to that location. Another addition might be to turn the scroll bars into *value bars*, showing document attributes such as the location of section boundaries (Figure 9.7d).

Scroll-bar arrows usually indicate the direction for movement of the window, but they could also represent the direction of movement of the contents. An early study (Bury et al., 1982) showed that a majority of users thought that a down arrow meant that the window moved down to show later portions of a document, but many users are still confused and make errors. Recovery of errors is rapid, but creative

Figure 9.7

Scroll bars showing existing and proposed features: (a) page number in scroll box, (b) proportional scroll box, (c) selectable position markers, (d) value bar showing sections.

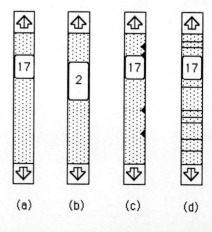

designers might still pursue visual cues to give users a better indication of which motion will occur.

Window actions include

- *Open action*: A window may be opened from its icon or test-menu list onto the display by a typed command, a menu selection, a voice command, or a double click. The icons can be of varying size (1/4 to 2 square inches) and labels can be in varying locations.

Feedback during opening could vary from simply having the window appear after the full display repaints, to blanking or blackening of the window destination followed by appearance of the window border and then the contents. Visually appealing animations such as zoom boxes (animated series of growing boxes emanating from the icon growing into the window), zoom lines (streaks, dots, etc. of light going to the corners of the window), window-shade opening (the window appears to pull down like a window shade), or three-dimensional flips or spins from the icon to the full window (Silicon Graphics Iris). Open actions may have accompanying sounds. Each chapter opener graphic shows a different possible strategy for icons opening into windows.

- *Open place and size*: A key determinant of the usability of window systems is the choice of where the window opens. Some windows systems always have a window open in the same designer-designed place and size, thus supporting predictability but at the expense of users often having to move and resize each window. Others window systems support the most-recently-used place and size approach, which has a better chance to satisfy user needs but is still often suboptimal. Another strategy is to use a computed approach in which the place and size are determined as a function of which windows are currently on the display. I believe the computed approach has the potential to reduce housekeeping overhead substantially, while preserving predictability. Often the most effective solution is to open the new window close to the current focus (icon, menu item, field, etc.) to limit eye motion, but far enough away to avoid obscuring the current focus. For example, if a control-panel icon is selected, then the control panel should appear just below the icon. If a word in a document is selected for a dictionary definition or thesaurus entry, the resulting window should be just below (or above or to the right of) the word. Similarly, if a fill-in field for a form is selected with a help action, the help window should appear to the side, but should not obscure the field in question. A final example is the automatic placement of a message window; it should not obscure the objects of interest, forcing the user to move the message window to see the message at the same time as the objects of interest.

- *Close action*: Windows may have a small icon (typically in the upper-left or upper-right corners) to close the window to its iconic or list form. Alternatively, there may be a special window control menu with a close action or the window may contain a CLOSE, CANCEL, or OK button. Feedback during closing varies from none (can be a problem for users to know where the icon is located) to zoom boxes (animated series of shrinking boxes moving toward where the window rests on the desktop as an icon), zoom lines (streaks, dots, etc. of light closing in on the icon), window shade closing (window appears to close up to just the title bar), or three-dimensional flips or spins of the window as it shrinks to an icon. Most systems close windows smoothly and rapidly; in slower systems, however, awkward sequences of display painting can be unsettling—for example, if the window is cleared in strips that break up the window frame or the contents.

- *Resize action*: There is great diversity in approaches to resizing a window. The Macintosh permits sizing only from a size box on the lower-right corner, whereas the NeXT machines have small sizing handles on the lower-left and lower-right. MS Windows, OSF/Motif, OS/2, and many other systems permit sizing by all four corners and by each of the four sides. Another class of systems, such as NeWS and many Smalltalk versions, offer a size menu item that gives users the chance to select the upper-left and lower-right corners of the redrawn window. Some systems will resize adjacent windows automatically. An interesting question is whether or not resizing the window causes reformatting of text (reflowing of documents or changing fontsize), graphics (size changes to ensure that the full object is seen no matter what the window size) or icon layouts (icons are moved to ensure that they remain visible in a smaller window). Another way in which window systems vary is on size limits. Some systems allow windows to be made very small (for example, 1 x 2 centimeter); other systems require windows to be above a certain minimum (for example, 4 x 6 centimeter, or big enough to show the contents). Most window systems have upper bounds on window size that are as large as the display, but some have upper bounds that are larger than the display.

- *Move action*: There is also great diversity in approaches to moving a window. The Xerox STAR and MS Windows 1.0 had a `move` menu item, which users selected and then clicked on the destination, but the results were sometimes surprising because of the complex layout strategies. The Macintosh designers use the entire title bar as a handle, and have the users drag an outline of the window until they are satisfied with the placement. A variety of visual feedbacks have been created. As display rates have become faster, some systems now support displays of the full window as it is dragged. Other system designers, such as those of X-uwm, require users to select a menu item—then, the entire window becomes a handle. Some systems require that the full window be visible on the display, whereas others permit portions of a window to be off the display in three (typically left, right, or bottom), or in all four, directions. Some systems constrain a window (the child) to be contained within another window (the parent).

- *Bring forward or activation*: When overlapping windows are used, there is a need for some mechanism to bring forward and make active a window that is totally or partially obscured by other windows. Approaches to bringing a window forward include typing a command such as `Front` on the keyboard, clicking on a menu list of open windows to select one, selecting an action such as `Top` from a pop-up menu associated with each window, clicking in any part of a window (or a restricted part, such as the title bar), or simply moving the cursor into a window. Variations include the possibility that all windows are active with text flowing into the window that contains the cursor, and that a window is made active but is not brought to the top. Activation may be shown by changes to the border (color or thickness changes), title (color or stripes are added), or text background (brightness increases). An important part of activation is the smoothness and sequence of the painting process. Although some systems are so rapid that the entire window and its contents appear instantaneously (in less than 100 milliseconds), many systems may clear the area first, then paint the border, and finally fill the window top to bottom. Awkward paintings—such as painting different colored parts of a frame, or filling the window from the bottom to the top—can be unsettling.

These basic window components and actions are shared by many systems, but there are numerous variations and extensions. An interesting extension is to use spoken commands and speech-recognition technology (Section 6.4) to control window actions (Schmandt et al., 1990). An initial version of an X Window System implementation, called Xspeak, was tested by four users to explore useful features. The authors conclude that "navigation in a window can be handled with speech input" but, in the current implementation they "found the use of voice in navigation an incomplete substitute for the mouse."

9.3   Multiple-Window Design

The challenge of providing access to multiple sources of information has stimulated many solutions:

- *Multiple monitors*: stock-market traders or process-control plants sometimes use multiple physical monitors because that is the only way to see all the information needed with the hardware available. Experience suggests that a smaller number of higher-resolution monitors with multiple windows is superior in most cases, because the distraction of eye motion across the 3- to 4-inch gaps between monitors slows work.

- *Rapid display flipping:* Another alternative is rapid alternation or flipping among displays, automatically or by user control. This strategy can be helpful, but it too has been shown to place greater burdens on users to recognize where they are, to know the commands, to formulate a plan to reach the desired display, and to execute the plan. User-controlled rapid display flipping can be usefully applied with knowledgeable users to supplement windowing. Automatic page flipping can be useful in public-access information systems, but airport designers have recognized that, if budget and space permit, having a bank of six or eight displays for departures and another six or eight displays for arrivals is superior to using an automatic page-flipping strategy on one display.

- *Split displays:* Many early word processors enabled users to split their display to show two (or more) parts of a document, or two (or more) documents. Split displays are available in text-oriented systems such as EMACS, WordPerfect (two windows), MS Word on IBM-PCs (eight windows), and many other word processors. Splits could be made horizontally (to create two full-width windows) or vertically (to allow side-by-side comparisons—but this was effective for only those files with narrow lists). A split display is a simplified approach to multiple windows, with fewer features than window systems.

- *Fixed number, size, and place, and space-filling tiling:* Simple display splits are often described as being *tiled*, since the display space is often covered completely with rectangular sections resembling the ceramic tiles on a floor. Tiling usually is meant to convey space filling and no overlapping, but there are many variations. Making a simple dichotomy between tiling and overlapping ignores many interesting variations. The simplest case is a fixed number of fixed-sizes and fixed-placement tiles—for example, two, four, six, or eight rectangles filling the display—with the possible exception of some control or icon region. Some displays, such as the IBM 3290 Plasma Display, have four tiles built into the hardware with interesting function-key operations for copying or saving window contents.

- *Variable size, place, and number, and space-filling tiling:* A common strategy is to start with a single large window and, when a second window is opened, to cut the first one in half horizontally or vertically to make space for the second. Microsoft Windows 1.0 used this tiling strategy with splits occurring when a document or application icon was dragged to the horizontal or vertical borders to cause a vertical or horizontal splits, respectively. Moving a window was possible, but the results were often surprising to users. Similarly, closing a window in a variable-number space-filling tiled layout could produce unexpected results, such as other windows growing to use the space, windows moving, or simply blank space appearing. Resizing of a window forces neighbors to be resized, and zooming allows a single window to fill the entire screen temporarily. Dialog boxes might still popup over the tiled windows, much as in the overlapped-windows strategy, but dialog boxes are not the same as a normal window.

- *Non–space-filling tiling:* Variations emerged that did not require the entire display to be covered. The RTL system (Figure 9.8) allowed gaps between tiles anywhere on the display, but allowed no overlaps (Cohen et al., 1986, 1988). The Andrew system at Carnegie Mellon University had a tiling window manager that allowed blank spaces on only the bottom of the display, and the Xerox Star allowed blank space on the right half of the two-column display. In the original Xerox Star, the first window to open would be a full-page size on the left side of the display; then, the second window would cause the left side of the display to be shared by upper and lower halves. The third window would result in each window getting one-third of the left side of the display. The fourth through sixth (a maximum of six was allowed) windows would fill the right side of the display. This strategy avoided narrow windows that require annoying and frequent horizontal scrolling.

- *Piles-of-tiles:* Variations on the basic tiling strategy, include the piles-of-tiles strategy, in which windows are stacked on top of one another (complete overlap), so that tiles can be popped to reveal previously used windows (Figure 9.9). Typically piles-of-tiles are of fixed size and

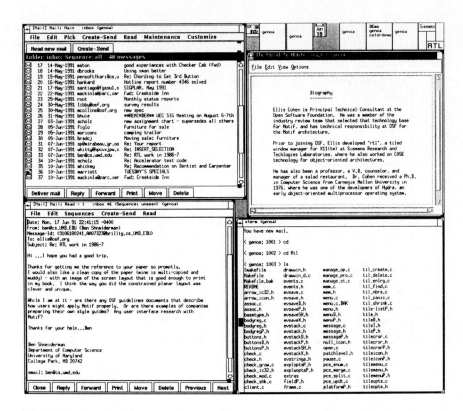

Figure 9.8

The RTL system kept the windows arranged in a single plane, preventing overlaps but possibly leaving some gaps between windows (Cohen, 1987). (RTL was developed at Siemens Corporate Research, Inc., Princeton, NJ, Copyright 1988, all rights reserved.)

fixed position to simplify usage. The Rational Ada environment initializes by dividing a large portrait-format display into three equal-sized piles-of-tiles. Subsequent windows are placed on the least recently used pile. Users can alter the size and placement strategy. The PenPoint interface (Figure 9.10) for notebook computers uses a display filling pile-of-tiles with tabs protruding to the right to allow selection.

- *Automatic panning:* A simple approach to managing multiple windows is to specify panning from bottom to top. The new window appears at the bottom of the display and forces the previous bottom window upward. The topmost window moves off the display (Figure 9.11). More complex panning can be arranged with four, six, or more windows open at a time.

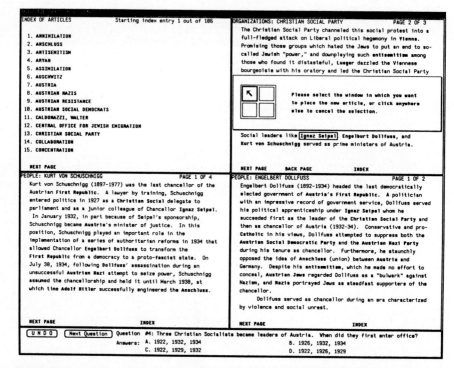

Figure 9.9

These four piles-of-tiles cover the display completely. Each pile can have different numbers of windows, and the top window in the pile can be removed. (Lifshitz and Shneiderman, 1991.)

- *Window zooming:* Since users often need to expand a window temporarily, some systems offer a convenient feature to enlarge a window—even to full display size—and then to shrink it back to the previous size. This technique is often used in the context of showing many tiled windows on the display at once. A variant of this strategy appears in HyperCard; it makes available the 42 most recent cards, and users can select any one by simple clicking on the postage-stamp–sized images (Figure 9.12). The selected card pops up full sized.

- *Arbitrary overlaps:* There is a great appeal to seeing multiple windows on a display with the appearance of partial and arbitrary overlaps. With this now popular strategy, windows can be moved to any point on the display, and portions of the window may be off the display, clipped by the display boundary. This approach has been called two-and-one-half dimensional programming to characterize the appearance of multiple windows overlapping as if they were floating one above the other. This

Figure 9.10

These piles-of-tiles in the PenPoint interface each cover the full screen and signal their presence by the tab at the right side of the display. (Courtesy of GO Corp., Foster City, CA.)

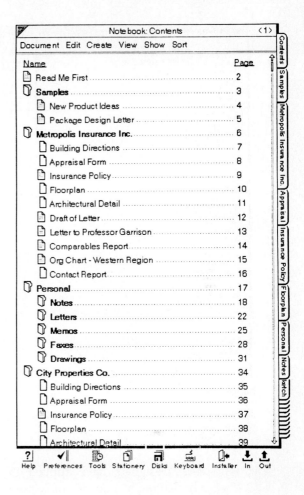

strategy was used in Smalltalk, the Apple Lisa, the innovative but ill-fated VisiCorp Visi On (Seybold, 1983), the Apple Macintosh, MS Windows 2.03, and many later window systems (Color Plates 7 and 9). Arbitrary overlapping windows can be advantageous if independent tasks are being carried out. For example, in the middle of using a word processor, users can decide to send a piece of electronic mail, to use a calculator, to check a calendar, or to consult a personal schedule. The user can pop up a new window, take care of the task, and return to the main task without losing context or restarting the work. However, overlapping windows have the potential to obscure relevant material and to increase the housekeeping load. Arbitrary overlaps can be useful in providing a variety of personal services rapidly and conveniently; for example, Borland's Sidekick 2.0 offers calculator, notepad, calendar, telephone and address book, etc.

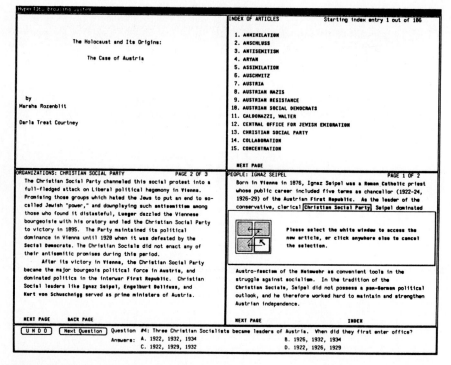

Figure 9.11

Automatic panning across the four windows is in a zigzag pattern. (Lifshitz and Shneiderman, 1991.)

- *Cascades:* Designers have applied the familiar deck-of-cards metaphor by having a sequence of windows from the upper-left down to the lower-right (or from the lower-left up to the upper-right). Successive windows are offset below (or above) and to the right to allow a window title to remain visible (Figure 9.13). Some systems automatically lay out successively opened windows in the cascade. Other systems allow users to select a cascade action from a menu, which places the currently open windows in a cascade, but newly opened windows appear elsewhere on the display. Tombaugh et al. (1987) demonstrated that, with sufficient practice, users could answer questions more rapidly from a multiple-window cascade representing chapters of a book than they could from a paged single window.

There are certainly other approaches to multiple windows, and a theory is still needed to guide designers. A theory might emerge from computational

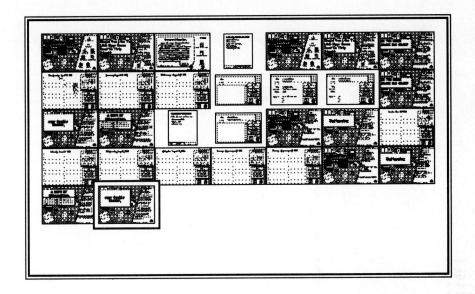

Figure 9.12

HyperCard `Recent` feature shows up to 42 postage-stamp–sized images of previously visited cards. (Courtesy of Claris Corp., Santa Clara, CA.)

geometry, from mathematical analyses of window placement and visibility (Matsuoka et al., 1989), or from a more task-related model, such as the working-set model (Card, 1989).

Empirical studies are beginning to clarify the issues and to establish methods for measuring performance and ability in windowing environments. Enthusiasts of the greater flexibility of arbitrary overlaps may have been disappointed by an empirical comparison with a tiled approach of the early Xerox Star (Bly and Rosenberg, 1986). Tasks requiring little window manipulation were carried out more quickly with the tiled strategy, but other tasks were carried more quickly with the overlapping strategy by some users. Overlapping window manipulation appeared to require more experience to use effectively, and overall the authors suggest that, possibly, for users with a higher level of expertise, tiled windows are better.

Program browsing with a multiwindow hypertext environment using a tiled approach was implemented using automatic window placement plus zooming (Seabrook and Shneiderman, 1989). Typical program-exploration tasks were shown, by keystroke counts and a small thinking-aloud usability study, to be performed more rapidly than with a standard single-window editor.

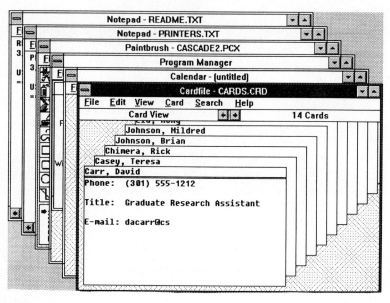

Figure 9.13

Users can produce automatically a cascade of six windows from upper-left to lower-right in MS Windows 3.0 by invoking an action from a pull-down menu. The active window (in front) shows a cascade from lower-left to upper-right within the Cardfile program. See Figure 9.4c also. (Screen shot ©1985–1991 Microsoft Corporation. Reprinted with permission from Microsoft Corporation, Redmond, WA.)

Four fixed-size piles-of-tiles (Figure 9.9) using user-controlled placement versus automatic panning window strategies were compared in a study with 23 knowledgeable computer users (Lifshitz and Shneiderman, 1991). They could select any of the four piles-of-tiles as the destination for the next window, or they could pop the top window tile to reveal the previous window. In the automatic panning version (Figure 9.11), the new window always appeared on the lower-right, with the previous window holding that position moving to the lower-left. The lower-left window moved to the upper-right, the upper-right window moved to the upper-left, and the upper-left window moved off the display. The automatic-panning strategy is convenient because no placement decision is required and reversibility is simple, but users cannot control window placement. There was no significant difference in speed in answering factual questions, but a significant difference in subjective preference favored the user-controlled placement, even though that strategy required extra decision-making effort.

9.4   Coordination of Multiple Windows by Tasks

Designers may gain an advantage by developing coordinated windows, in which windows appear, change contents, and close as a direct result of user activity in the task domain (Norman et al., 1986; Shneiderman et al., 1986). For example, in medical insurance-claims processing, when the agent retrieves information about a client, such fields as the address, telephone numbers, and membership numbers should appear on the display. Simultaneously, and with no additional effort, the medical history might appear in a second window, and the record of previous claims might appear in a third window. A fourth window might contain a form for the agent to complete to indicate payment or exceptions. Scrolling the medical-history window might produce a synchronized scroll of the previous claims window to show related information. When the claim is completed, all window contents are saved and the windows are closed. Such sequences of activity can be established by designers and implementers, or by users with end-user programming tools such as the Agent facility in NewWave.

A careful study of user tasks can lead to task-specific coordinations based on sequences of actions, but there are some typical classes of coordination that might be supported by developers.

- *Synchronized scrolling*: A simple coordination is synchronized scrolling, in which the scroll bar of one window might be linked to another scroll bar, and motion on one scroll bar would cause the other to scroll its window contents. This technique is useful for comparing two versions of a program or document. Synchronization might be on a line-for-line basis, on a proportional basis, or keyed to matching tokens in the two windows. Another way to do synchronization might be as an option on an open action that would specify two window to open side by side with a single scroll bar between them.

- *Hierarchical browsing*: Coordinated windows can be used to support hierarchical browsing (Figure 9.14). If one window contains the table of contents of a document or a list of program modules, selection of an item by a pointing device should lead to display, in an adjoining window, of the chapter or module contents. A finer-grained approach would be to have each level of a table of contents in a separate window (Figure 9.15).

- *Direct selection*: Another coordination might be direct selection, in which pointing at an icon, a word in the text, or a variable name in a

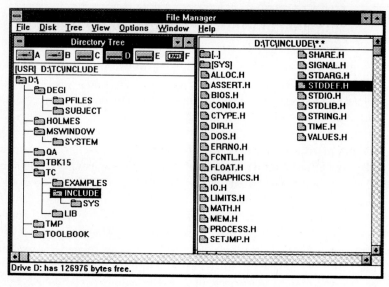

Figure 9.14

Hierarchical browsing in Windows 3.0 shows the tree structure on the left and the file names on the right. (Screen shot ©1985–1991 Microsoft Corporation. Reprinted with permission from Microsoft Corporation, Redmond, WA.)

Figure 9.15

Multiple coordinated windows make for a convenient browsing environment. Clicking in the top window automatically fills the lower windows. (Chimera and Shneiderman, 1991.)

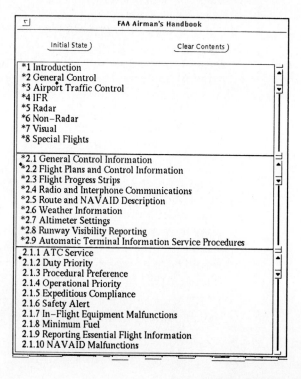

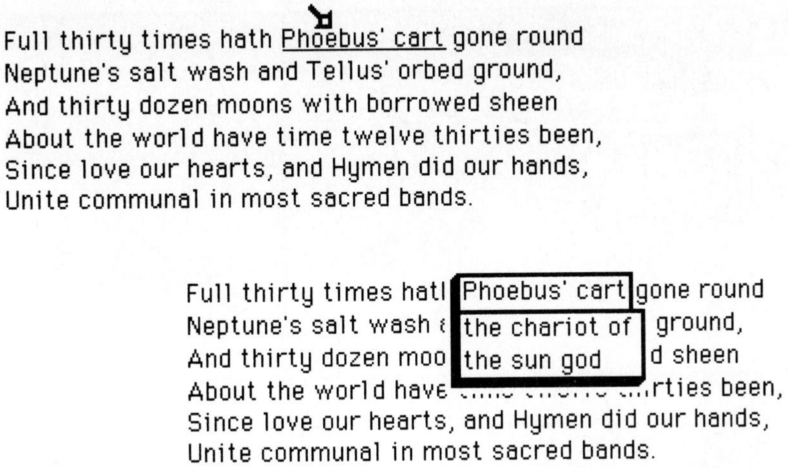

Full thirty times hath <u>Phoebus' cart</u> gone round
Neptune's salt wash and Tellus' orbed ground,
And thirty dozen moons with borrowed sheen
About the world have time twelve thirties been,
Since love our hearts, and Hymen did our hands,
Unite communal in most sacred bands.

Full thirty times hatl Phoebus' cart gone round
Neptune's salt wash & the chariot of ground,
And thirty dozen moo the sun god d sheen
About the world have ~~time twelve thirties~~ been,
Since love our hearts, and Hymen did our hands,
Unite communal in most sacred bands.

Figure 9.16

Direct selection of the phrase Phoebus' cart in this sample of Shakespeare produces an explanation immediately in place. This technique is effective in showing data definitions for program variables.

program pops up an adjoining window with the details of the icon, word definition, or the variable declaration (Figure 9.16).

- *Two-dimensional browsing*: This two-dimensional cousin of hierarchical browsing shows a high-level view of a map, graphic, photograph, or other image in one corner, and the details in a larger surrounding window (Figure 9.17). Users can move a locator rectangle in the high-level view to adjust the larger window's content. Multiple strategies are possible; design refinements plus an understanding of when to use each strategy are useful research topics.

- *Dependent-windows opening*: An option on opening a window might be to open dependent windows in a nearby and convenient location. For example, when users are browsing a program, when they open a main procedure, the dependent set of procedures could open up (Figure 9.18).

- *Dependent-windows closing*: An option on closing a window would be to close all the dependent windows. This option might be applied to closing dialog, message, and help windows with a single action. For example, in filling in a form, users might receive a dialog box with a choice of preferences. That dialog box might have led the user to activate a pop-up or error-message window, which in turn might have

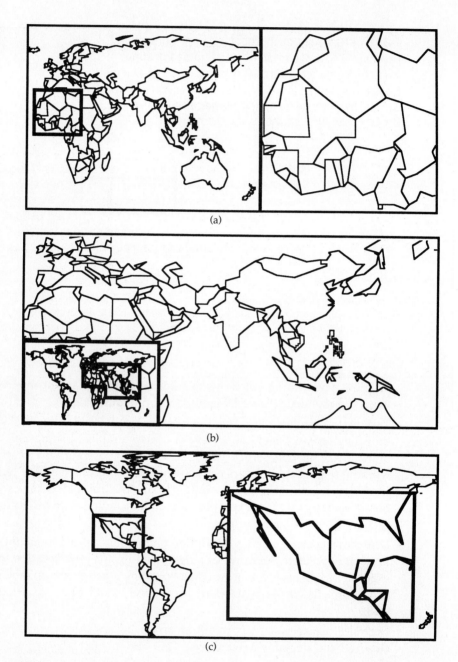

Figure 9.17

Two-dimensional browser strategies enable users to select a small region for magnification elsewhere on the display. These strategies can be applied recursively: (a) marked rectangle is magnified on the right side, (b) inset shows irregularly shaped marked region that fills the entire display, (c) marked rectangle is magnified on top of the entire display. (Prepared by Brian Johnson.)

Figure 9.18

Dependent windows opening
might cause several windows to
open automatically. In this
example, the main procedure of
a program has been opened, and
the dependent procedures 1, 2,
and 3 have been opened and
placed at a convenient location.
Connecting lines, shading, or
decoration on the frame might
indicate the parent and child
relationships.

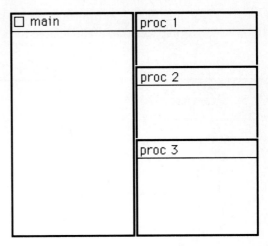

led to an invocation of the help window. After the user indicates the
desired choice in the dialog box, it would be convenient to double click
on the dialog box `close` icon (or to select from a menu) and to have all
three or four windows close (Figure 9.19).

- *Save or open window state*: A natural extension of saving a document or
  a set of preferences is to save the current state of the display with all the
  windows and their contents. This feature might be implemented by a
  simple addition of a `Save By...` menu item to the `File` menu of actions.
  This action would create a new icon representing the current state; it
  could be opened to reproduce that state. This feature is a simple version

Figure 9.19

Dependent windows
closing might cause all
four windows to be closed
automatically when the
parent window `form` is
closed. Lines, shading, or
decoration on the border
might indicate families of
windows with special
marks for parents and
children.

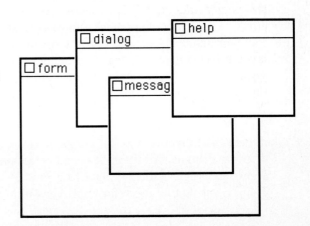

of the rooms approach (Henderson and Card, 1986), or of the six workspaces that are available in H-P VUE (Color Plate 7).

9.5   Practitioner's Summary

Multiple windows are an accepted feature of contemporary computers. Window-frame designs are distinctive and graphic-design style is important, as are features such as title bars, action menus, and scroll bars. Users expect to perform typical actions such as opening, closing, moving, and sizing rapidly, conveniently, and comprehensibly. The popular style of overlapping windows has an appealing three-dimensional (some say two-and-one-half–dimensional) look and serves some purpose, but it can produce clutter and be inefficient. Approaches that limit the overlap can be helpful in many situations. They include tiling, piles-of-tiles, automatic panning, and zooming. Organizing strategies such as cascades can also reduce the housekeeping effort required of window users. Coordination strategies based on user tasks can bring further benefits by automating multiple window actions, bringing windows close to where they are needed, reducing the housekeeping burden, and avoiding unwanted overlaps. Scrolls bars are applied widely and are usually successful, but there is some room for improvement.

9.6   Researcher's Agenda

Windows provide visually appealing possibilities and intriguing opportunities for designers, but advantages and disadvantages of design features are still poorly understood. Eye-motion studies might begin to provide data for effective design, but basic task analysis can still be productive in classifying the information needs and action sequences of users. A theory of window layouts, based on psychological principles, task analysis, and computational geometry, would be a significant contribution. Even without a deeper theory, there seems to be much room for innovation in multiple-window layouts and strategies, and for aesthetic refinements by graphic designers. As higher-resolution displays appear and color is used widely, novel three-dimensional layouts may be possible with dramatic animations and eye-catching designs. Addition of coordinated windows and window macros seems accessible and may lead to a new generation of window systems. There is substantial room for improvement in window strategies.

References

Apple Human Interface Guidelines: The Apple Desktop Interface, Addison-Wesley, Reading, MA (1987).

Billingsley, Patricia A., Taking panes: Issues in the design of windowing systems. In Helander, M. (Editor), *Handbook of Human–Computer Interaction*, Elsevier Science Publishers B.V., Amsterdam, The Netherlands (1988), 413–436.

Bly, Sara and Rosenberg, Jarrett, A comparison of tiled and overlapping windows, *Proc. CHI '86 Conference—Human Factors in Computing Systems*, ACM, New York (1986), 101–106.

Bury, K. F., Boyle, J. M., Evey, R. J., and Neal, A. S., Windowing versus scrolling on a visual display terminal, *Human Factors 24*, 4 (1982), 385–394.

Bury, Kevin F., Davies, Susan E., and Darnell, Michael J., Window management: A review of issues and some results from user testing, IBM Human Factors Center Report HFC-53, San Jose, CA (June 1985).

Card, Stuart K., Theory-driven design research. In McMillan, Grant R., Beevis, David, Salas, Eduardo, Strub, Michael H., Sutton, Robert, and Van Breda, Leo (Editors), *Applications of Human Performance Models to System Design*, Plenum Press, New York (1989), 501–509.

Card, Stuart K., Pavel, M., and Farrell, J. E., Window-based computer dialogues, *INTERACT '84, First IFIP Conference on Human–Computer Interaction*, London (1984), 355–359.

Card, Stuart K. and Henderson, Austin, A multiple virtual-workspace interface to support task switching, *Proc. CHI '87 Conference—Human Factors in Computing Systems*, ACM, New York (1987), 53–59.

Cohen, E. S., Smith, E. T., and Iverson, L. A., Constraint-based tiled windows, *IEEE Computer Graphics and Applications 6*, 5 (May 1986).

Cohen, Ellis S., Berman, A. Michael, Biggers, Mark R., Camaratta, Joseph C., and Kelly, Kevin M., Automatic strategies in the Siemens RTL tiled window manager, *Proc. IEEE Second International Conference on Computer Workstations*, IEEE, Piscataway, NJ (1988), 111–119.

Engelbart, Douglas C. and English, William K., A research center for augmenting human intellect. In Greif, I. (Editor), *Computer-Supported Cooperative Work: A Book of Readings*, Morgan Kaufmann, Palo Alto, CA (1988), 81–105.

Gait, Jason, An aspect of aesthetics in human–computer communications: Pretty windows, *IEEE Transactions on Software Engineering SE-11*, 8 (August 1985), 714–717.

Henderson, Austin and Card, Stuart K., Rooms: The use of multiple virtual workspaces to reduce space contention in a window-based graphical user interface, *ACM Transactions on Graphics 5*, 3 (1986), 211–243.

Hopgood, F. R. A., Duce D. A., Fielding, E. V. C., Robinson, K., and Williams, A. S. (Editors), *Methodology of Window Management*, Springer-Verlag, Berlin (April 1985).

Johnson, Jeff, Roberts, Teresa L., Verplank, William, Smith, David C., Irby, Charles H., Beard, Marian, and Mackey, Kevin, The Xerox Star: A Retrospective, *IEEE Computer 22*, 9 (September 1989), 11–29.

Kobara, Shiz, *Visual Design with OSF/Motif*, Addison-Wesley, Reading, MA (1991).

Lifshitz, J. and Shneiderman, B., Multi-window browsing strategies for hypertext traversal, *Proc. Thirtieth Annual Technical Symposium of the Washington, DC Chapter of the ACM* (June 1991), 121–131.

Lu, Gang and Ader, Martin, A knowledge-based solution to the messy screen problem, *Proc. Colloque sur l'ingeniere des Interfaces Homme–Machine*, Sophia-Antipolis, France (May 1989), 236–244.

Marcus, Aaron, *Graphic Design for Electronic Documents and User Interfaces*, ACM Press, New York (1992).

Matsuoka, Satoshi, Kamada, Tomihisa, and Kawai, Satoru, Asymptotic evaluation of window visibility, *Information Processing Letters 31* (1989), 119–126.

Morris, James H., Satyanarayanan, Mahadev, Conner, Michael H., Howard, John H., Rosenthal, David S., and Smith, F. D., Andrew: A distributed personal computing environment, *Communications of the ACM 29*, 3 (March 1986), 184–201.

Myers, Brad, Window interfaces: A taxonomy of window manager user interfaces, *IEEE Computer Graphics and Applications 8*, 5 (September 1988), 65–84.

Myers, Brad, *All the Widgets*, SIGGRAPH Video Review #57, ACM, New York (1990).

Norman, Kent L., Weldon, Linda J., and Shneiderman, Ben, Cognitive layouts of windows and multiple screens for user interfaces, *International Journal of Man–Machine Studies 25* (1986), 229–248.

Quercia, Valerie and O'Reilly Tim, *X Window System User's Guide,* Volume 3, O'Reilly and Associates, Inc. Sebastapol, CA (May 1990).

Schmandt, Chris, Ackerman, Mark S., and Hindus, Debby, Augmenting a window system with speech input, *IEEE Computer 23*, 8 (August 1990), 50–56.

Seabrook, Richard and Shneiderman, Ben, The user interface in a hypertext, multi-window browser, *Interacting with Computers 1*, 3 (1989), 299–337.

Seybold, Patricia B., VisiCorp's Visi On: A Professional Computing Environment, *The Seybold Report on Professional Computing 2*, 3 (November 21, 1983).

Shneiderman, Ben, Shafer, Phil, Simon, Roland, and Weldon, Linda, Display strategies for program browsing: Concepts and experiment, *IEEE Software 3*, 3 (May 1986), 7–15.

Smith, D. C., Irby, C., Kimball, R., and Verplank, W. L., Designing the Star user interface, *Byte 7*, 4 (April 1982), 242–282.

Sun Microsystems, *OPEN LOOK Graphical User Interface: Functional Specifications*, Addison-Wesley, Reading MA (1989).

Sun Microsystems, *OPEN LOOK Graphical User Interface: Application Style Guidelines*, Addison-Wesley, Reading, MA (1989).

Tesler, Larry, The Smalltalk Environment, *Byte* 6 (August 1981), 90–147.

Tombaugh, J., Lickorish, A., and Wright P., Multi-window displays for readers of lengthy texts, *International Journal of Man–Machine Studies* 26 (1987), 597–615.

Webster, Bruce F., *The NeXT Book*, Addison-Wesley, Reading, MA (1989).

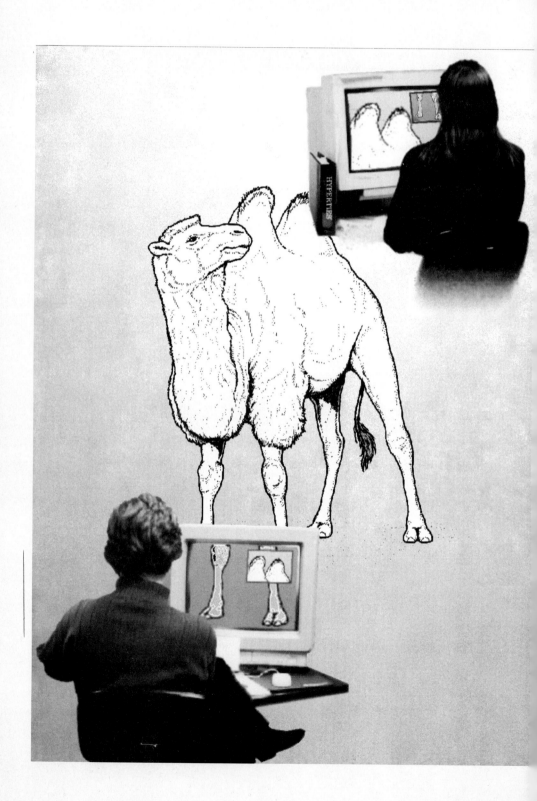

CHAPTER 10

Computer-Supported Cooperative Work

Three helping one another will do as much as six working singly.

Spanish proverb

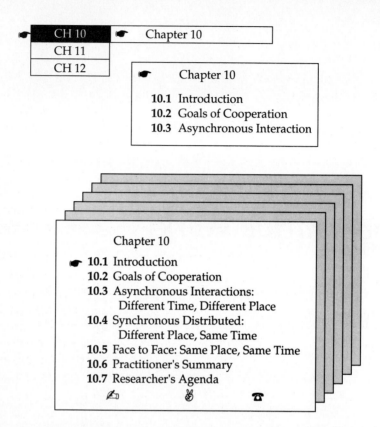

10.1 Introduction

The introversion and isolation of early computer use has given way to lively online communities of busily interacting dyads, triads, and bustling crowds of chatty users. The desire for email (electronic mail), the urge to socialize, and the pursuit of human connections have prompted many users to fill bboards (bulletin-boards systems) with useful information, helpful responses, outrageous humor, and pornographic graffiti. Inventive hackers have found clever ways to personalize even the lowest-bandwidth text-only messages.

More goal-directed personalities quickly recognized the benefits of electronic cooperation and the potential to live in the immediacy of the networked global village. The distance to colleagues is no longer measured in miles but in intellectual compatibility and responsiveness; a close friend is someone who responds from 3000 miles away within 3 minutes with the necessary reference to finish a paper at 3 A.M.

The good news is that computing, once seen as alienating and antihuman, is becoming a socially respectable and interpersonally positive force. Enthusiasts hail cooperative technologies, groupware, team processes, coordination science, and other communal utopias, but there may be a dark side to the force. Even 9600 baud is not enough to express a sigh, to send a handshake, or to look a colleague in the eye. Do human relationships suffer from a lack of intimacy when mediated by the remoteness in time and physical space? Can laughter and tears mean the same thing for electronic-dialog partners as for face-to-face partners? Can cooperative systems be used as an oppressive tool? When will competitive or confrontive applications appear?

New terminology and metaphors are appearing rapidly. Although the conferences on *computer-supported cooperative work* have established *CSCW* as a new acronym, even the organizers debated about whether it meant *cooperative* or *collaborative* systems. The implementers and marketeers quickly gravitated to *groupware* as a term to describe the products. For researchers, new research paradigms and fresh ideas are flowing from industrial, organizational, and social psychologists, sociologists, and anthropologists, as well as from business and management researchers (Vaske and Grantham, 1990).

10.2   Goals of Cooperation

People cooperate because doing so is satisfying or productive. Communication can have purely emotionally rewarding purposes or specific task-related goals. Communication can be sought individually or imposed managerially. Relationships can be one-time encounters or enduring. The analysis of cooperative systems is governed by the goals and tasks of the participants:

- *Complementary partners:* One user has a question and the other user has the answer. One person is the sender and the other is the receiver. Complementary partners can use email, voice mail, telephone, video mail, etc. No history is required. Online user assistance, product ordering, airline reservations, etc. are stereotypic exchanges.

- *Lecture or demo:* One person shares information with many users at remote sites. Time is scheduled for all, questions may be asked by the recipients. No history is required, but a replay may be possible at a later time.

- *Necessary partners:* Cooperations between two users who need each other to complete a task: joint authors of a technical report, two pathologists consulting about a cancer patient, programmers trying to debug a program together, or astronaut and ground-controller trying to repair a faulty satellite. Often, there is some electronic document or image to "conference over."

- *Conference:* Group participation at the same time or spread out over time, but distributed in space. Many-to-many messaging may be used, with a record of previous conversations: a scientific-meeting program committee might discuss the plans for an upcoming event, or a group of students might discuss the most recent class examination.

- *Directed conference:* A leader has a goal and supervises the online discussion: a teacher runs a virtual classroom, a project leader coordinates the completion of a report, or a manager directs a team of salespeople.

- *Structured work process:* A set of people with distinct roles cooperates on some task: a scientific-journal editor arranges online submission, reviewing, revisions, and publication; a health-insurance agency receives, reviews, and reimburses or rejects medical bills; or a university admissions committee registers, reviews, chooses, and informs high-school applicants.

- *Electronic classroom or meeting room:* A face-to-face meeting with each user working at a computer and making simultaneous contributions. Shared and private windows, plus large-screen projector, enable simultaneous shared comments that may be anonymous. Anonymity not only encourages shy participants to speak up, but also allows forceful leaders to accept novel suggestions without ego conflicts.

There are undoubtedly other cooperative situations, but this list gives some indication of the diversity of situations. Within each situation, there are numerous variations, and the potential for innovative software products is large. However, designing for cooperation is a challenge because of the numerous and subtle questions of etiquette, dominance, ego, anxiety, posturing, etc. These situations are all serious and business-related, but each could also become the basis for multiperson games, contests, or other social encounters.

The traditional way (Ellis et al., 1991) to decompose cooperative systems is by a time–space matrix:

	Same Time	**Different Times**
Same place	face to face (classrooms, meeting rooms)	asynchronous interaction (project scheduling, coordination tools)
Different places	synchronous distributed (shared editors, video windows)	asynchronous distributed (email, bboards, conferences)

This decomposition focuses on two critical dimensions, and thus guides designers and evaluators.

Cooperative systems are a challenge for designers because they are so new, and therefore there are few examples to follow. Grudin (1990) outlines some of the causes of groupware failures: threats to existing political power structures, violation of social taboos, rigidity that counters common practice or prevents exception handling, and additional work by people who perceive little benefit.

Research in cooperative systems is still more difficult than in single-user interfaces. The multiplicity of users makes it nearly impossible to conduct controlled experiments, and the flood of data from multiple users defies orderly analysis. Small-group psychology, industrial and organization behavior, sociology, and anthropology provide useful research paradigms, but many researchers must invent their own methodologies. Subjective reports, case studies, and users' eagerness to continue using the groupware tools are the strongest indicators of success.

10.3   Asynchronous Interactions: Different Time, Different Place

For many users, email is only a starting point for cooperation. Email requires that the message creator know the recipient's address, or at least the group address to which a public message is broadcast. Email also has the potential of being too loosely structured (endless chatting with no process or leader to reach a goal or to make a decision), too overwhelming (hundreds of messages per day can be difficult to absorb effectively), and transient (lack of storage organization may make it difficult to locate relevant messages, and late joiners in a discussion have no means to catch up on earlier comments). To remedy these problems, a variety of structured methods for ongoing group discussions has been created (Hiltz and Turoff, 1978; Hiltz, 1984; Glossbrenner, 1990).

10.3.1   Electronic Mail

The atomic unit of cooperation is the message; the FROM party sends a message to the TO party. *Email systems* exist on many networks in varied systems such as CompuServe, PRODIGY, PROFS, Internet, Bitnet, and MCI Mail (Figure 10.1). They share the notion that an individual can send a message to another individual or a list of individuals. Messages within

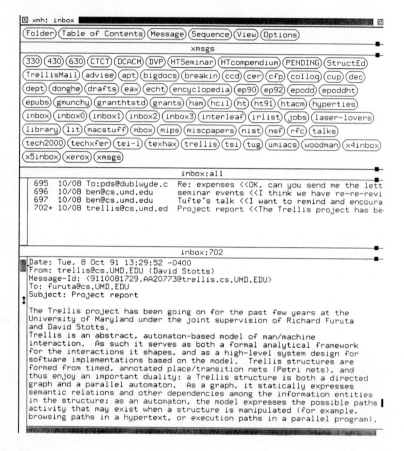

Figure 10.1

This X Windows mail handler shows a set of pull-down menus on the top row, followed by a large collection of topical directories for archiving mail. Then the scrollable inbox listing shows the dates, sender, and subject. If a mail message is selected its contents appears in the bottom window. (Courtesy of Richard Furuta.)

one system are delivered in seconds or minutes and a reply is easy and rapid.

Email messages typically contain text only, but increasingly graphics, spreadsheets, images, sounds, animations, executable programs, videos, or other structured objects can be included. The quest for more flexibility and instantaneous distribution is persistent. Sending graphics or spreadsheets is becoming more common as standard formats and effective conversions emerge. Embedding these multiple structured objects in documents is increasingly common. Still rare is the availability of video email or the inclusion of still images, but these should spread during the next decade.

Those users who have been able to add video comments to their email say they like this feature and use it regularly—it does seem to have the capacity to add a more personal touch. Problems of standardization across systems and the need for good user interfaces are apparent in the reports from early projects (Borenstein, 1991; Hoffert and Gretsch, 1991). *Voice mail* is effectively sent by the normal telephone networks, but the inclusion of a voice annotation in an email message will certainly become a more widespread possibility. The success of *FAX machines* is an indictment of the failure to create convenient email with graphics.

Most mail systems provide at least TO (list of recipients), FROM (sender), CC (list of copy recipients), DATE, and SUBJECT fields. Malone et al. (1987) showed the surprising benefit of semistructured messages in their Information Lens. If messages were identified as being a lecture announcement, then they would indicate the time, date, place, speaker, title, and host, in addition to the talk abstract and possibly other free-form text. The semistructured portions of the message enabled more automatic filtering of incoming messages or automatic routing and replies. Users could specify that they did not want to receive lecture announcements for speeches after 5 P.M. or on weekends. Alternatively, users could specify that copies of certain messages would be sent to colleagues, to the secretarial staff, or to their assistants. This feature provides a basis for dealing with the dangers of information overload as users begin to receive dozens or hundreds of messages per day.

A still more structured version of email was developed as the commercial product called The Coordinator (Flores et al., 1988). It was based on a speech-acts theory of requests and commitments that compelled users to be explicit about their expectations for responses when a message was sent. The additional requirement for specifying expectations was intended to clarify the communication process and to lead to more effective team coordination; however, many users found this approach oppressive and too rigid. An interesting and successful product is Lotus Notes, which was sold only in 200 unit lots to large corporations; more than 75 sites with over 50,000 licences were using Notes after its first year on the market. This product provided IBM PC support to integrate email, bboards, telephone-call tracking, status reporting, text database searching, document sharing, meeting scheduling, and other cooperation tools. Some large multinational corporations have recognized Notes as providing a competitive advantage because widely distributed communities of employees can conveniently share information, make decisions, and carry out complex action plans.

Email is here to stay and is growing at a steady pace. It is constrained by several problems, whose solution might lead to a dramatic increase in use. The incompatibility of the dozens of systems is slowly being overcome, in part by the efforts of the Electronic Mail Association, by pressure from users, and by commercial realities that force cooperation. The possibility of including materials richer than text is an attraction for some new users who still prefer FAX machines because even poor graphics are better than no graphics. Online directories would be a great facilitator, since it is still necessary to know a person's email address before sending a message. Such online directories would also include group lists and the capacity to create new group lists conveniently, so that whole communities could be reached easily. Finally, improved archiving and retrieval systems would enable users to find old email messages conveniently and rapidly. The dangers of junk email remain, and even noble ideas of cooperation can be undermined by annoying users who fail to be polite, nuisances who persistently disrupt, electronic snoopers who do not respect privacy, or calculating opportunists who abuse their privileges.

10.3.2   Bulletin boards and conferences

Thousands of bboards have emerged around the world, administered by devoted *system operators* who maintain the software and hardware, keep the discussion moving, filter malicious or unsavory messages, and act as the Gertude Steins of the modern electronic salons. The basic bboard feature are notes or items posted in chronological order by users; the note may contain a question, an offer to buy or sell, interesting news, a joke, or a "flame" (abusive criticism) (Fischer and Stevens, 1991). Each item has a short one-line heading and an arbitrarily long body (Figure 10.2). The items remain available for weeks or months, and replies are linked to each item so that everyone can follow a thread in the discussion. When users log on they are customarily informed about new items that have appeared since the last time they signed on.

The user interfaces tend to be simple to accommodate even low-speed dial-in access. Choices are few; the intrigue lies in the complexity of the conversations, especially in lively replies and debates. As usage increases, the systems operator (often known as the SYSOP) must decide about splitting topics into more focused topics to avoid the overwhelming experience of finding thousands of new messages. Ensuring that the groups remain interesting is a challenge; if a bboard used by advanced programmers to discuss esoteric details is invaded by novices asking beginner-level questions, the experts will want to split off to form their own discussion. Discussion groups can be found about most computer-related issues, but other topics—such as movies, kayaking, rap music, folk dancing, and restaurants—are popular. Practical information exchange by bboards is common for diverse groups such as cancer researchers, NASA scientists,

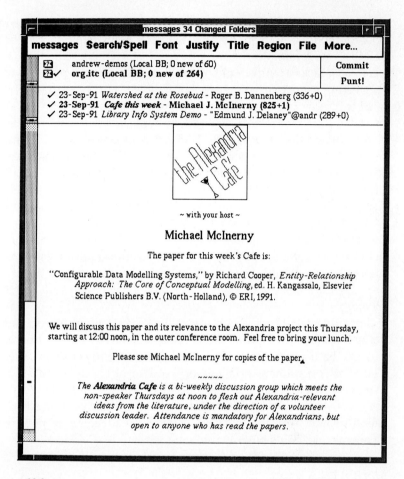

Figure 10.2

This bulletin board system on the Andrew system shows a set of pull-down menus on the top row, followed by a list of bulletin boards by topic (for example, `org.itc` is selected, indicating organizational information about the Information Technology Center at CMU). Then there are three dated items, and `Cafe this week` has been selected, producing the large display on the bottom.

handicapped users, and human-factors researchers. Within corporations, universities, or government agencies, specialized bboards may be established for topics such as corporate policy, medical-insurance information, or product updates.

Filtering the hundreds of items that may be added per week is usually a manual task, although string search on heading or the body are common. Filtering programs can be run automatically and will inform users only if there is a match on specified topics. Another form of filtering is to have a bboard moderator, who decides whether new items should be posted. Effective moderators can keep a discussion well focused, eliminate hostile personal attacks or unpleasant obscenity, and prevent repetitious discussion by steering users to existing items of interest.

Bboard advocates usually focus on open access to all, but the alternative model of a conference is designed to provide access to a known community (Hiltz, 1984; Hiltz and Turoff, 1985). A conference is usually moderated, meaning that a conference leader invites participants, poses an issue or theme, and keeps the discussion going if a question is unanswered or if some participants fail to read new notes in a timely manner. Conferences are more likely to have voting features to allow consensus formation or decision making. Votes may be required within 48 hours, with results posted by the moderator. Thoughtful discussions within a conference are encouraged because participants can consider their position judiciously, consult other materials, and phrase their contributions carefully, without the pressure for an immediate comment that is inherent a telephone call or face-to-face meeting.

Bboards have become controversial. When federal government agents confiscated bboard equipment alleging that illegal information was being posted, the hacker community joined forces to protect the accused people. The First Amendment principle of freedom of speech should certainly be extended to electronic speech, but there are certainly dangers of illegal activities. Other bboards have been criticized for spreading hateful racist literature and software, but here again the challenge is to preserve valued freedoms and rights without allowing harm.

10.3.3   File-transfer programs

Getting something for nothing is an attraction to many people; getting data, programs, text, images, or technical reports electronically is a thrill for file-transfer–program users, sometimes called *FTPers*. Instead of a conversation, many computer-network users are eager to scour remote databases for useful materials to *download* (load onto their personal computers). Creators of programs, images, databases, etc. often seek to publish their materials electronically, or *upload*, for people who can put these products to use. Some services provide informative listings of available materials, but more could be done to provide effective library resources. The creator will often use other means, such as email or printed newsletters, to announce availability by *file transfer*. Enthusiasts delight in the free exchange of *shareware*, *freeware*, and *public-access software*. A slight variation is the honor system that offers a notice requesting a modest fee ($10 to $100) to become a registered user who might receive notices of changes or a printed user manual. Commercial services such as CompuServe are heavily used for file transfers, and many software companies may have specialized software available for downloading.

10.3.4   Structured processes

A variety of more specific asynchronous exchange mechanisms have been attempted. The gIBIS system (graphical Issue Based Information System) enables participants to add *issues, positions,* or *arguments* to a growing tree-structured discussion accessible in a hypertext form. A typical application allows designers to debate a variety of features offering pros and cons and leading to a decision (Yakemovic and Conklin, 1990). Having a record of the reasons for design decisions is seen as an advantage. During an 18-month trial period with five users, approximately 16,000 text lines in 8000 nodes on 2260 issues were generated. The positive evaluation indicates that "the IBIS *paid for itself* by helping the project team to detect design elements that had 'fallen through the cracks', even though both high and low level design reviews were held."

A semistructured message system turned out to be surprisingly helpful since many messages had simple and useful structures such as meeting announcements or information requests (Malone et al., 1987). Semi-structured messages have additional fields such as time of meeting, name of speaker, location, date, and time that enable easy filtering or ordering. Nonprogrammers could specify their own filter procedures to ensure that they saw only messages that were relevant.

Coordination of larger groups for longer periods of time characterizes software for project management or specifically for computer-assisted software engineering (CASE). These tools enable a manager to specify a complex procedure for many people to coordinate creation, review, correction, dissemination, and maintenance. Ideally, designs are created, reviewed, and approved before programming begins. Documentation is required and test cases are completed before testing is permitted. These coordinated steps and approvals have the potential to speed work and to improve quality, but assessment is difficult, and social and political issues can undermine the orderly process.

Coordination of students in a *virtual classroom* is an even more complex process but it can enable a stimulating educational experience for people who cannot travel to a regular classroom (Hiltz, 1992). Multiple trials with sociology, computer science, and philosophy courses demonstrated the efficacy of a conference format for college courses, complete with homework assignments, projects, tests, and final examinations. Instructors found the constant flow of messages to be a rewarding challenge, and students were generally satisfied with the experience:

> The essence of the Virtual Classroom is an environment to facilitate collaborative learning. For distance education students, the increased ability to be in constant communication with other learners is obvious. But even for campus-based courses the technology provides a means for a rich, collaborative learning environment which exceeds the traditional classroom in its ability to 'connect' students and course materials on a round-the-clock basis. (Hiltz, 1992)

Other forms of asynchronous coordination are possible. Some networks enable the distribution of a document for review by multiple readers whose annotations are collected and can be viewed in order by section. A research system called Quilt was built at Bellcore (Leland et al., 1988), and an IBM PC-based product, For Comment, has been produced by Broderbund.

10.4 Synchronous Distributed: Different Place, Same Time

The dream of being in two places at once becomes realizable with modern technologies such as telephone and television, but the possibility of being in 10 places at once is now possible through *synchronous distributed applications* such as *group editing*. For example, in the GROVE system (GRoup Outline Viewing Editor), developed at the Microelectronics and Computing Technology Corporation (MCC), multiple users can view and edit the same document simultaneously (Ellis et al, 1991). Coordination is accomplished by voice communication. The default mode in GROVE is to allow every user to type simultaneously—there is no locking. Although the authors report collisions are surprisingly infrequent, since users tend to work on different parts of a document, locking by sentence or paragraph would seem to be a necessary option for some situations. Both GROVE and a follow-on system, rIBIS (Rein et al., 1991) included small images of current users (Figure 10.3). Important features in the development of ShrEdit (for shared editor) at the University of Michigan were the mixture of private and public workspaces, identity of participants, location of actions, and care with updating (Olson et al., 1990).

Shared-editor sessions or shared spreadsheets seem to be simple yet potentially popular applications. IBM's CVIEW demonstrated the benefits of shared screens for customer assistance. Users with problems could call the customer engineer, and both could see the same screens as the customer

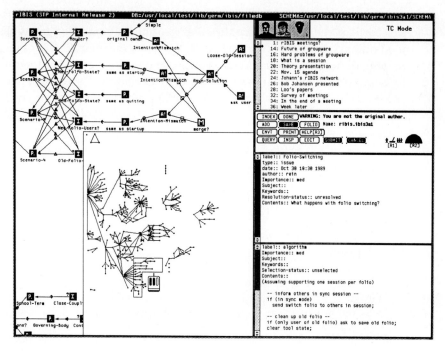

Figure 10.3

This rIBIS display shows a large two-dimensional browser on the left that contains the network of Issues, Positions, and Arguments. On the top right are small images of the three participants who are interacting in tightly coupled mode. The mouse cursor on the left is controlled by the person on the far right (his image is highlighted by a larger gray square). The numbered list of nodes is below the images, followed by a control window and two node viewing windows. Users can signal that they are done using the mouse by putting it back in the semicircular mouse hole, so that others can take mouse. Alternatively, users can grab the mouse. (Rein and Ellis, 1991.) (Courtesy of Academic Press Ltd., London.)

walked through the problem. Demonstrations of new software have been given at multiple sites by having the presenter show screens to dozens of people while talking on a conference call. Another potential application is to allow sharing of information for applications such as airlines reservations. When the agent has located a selection of possible flights, it would be convenient to be able to *show* the customer the list, rather than to read it. The customer could then make the selection and have an electronic copy to save, print, or include in other documents. An innovative commercial project is the development of an interactive game network that permits two or more people to participate simultaneously in games such as poker, checkers, or in complex fantasies.

Even simple exchanges of text messages in systems such as CHAT, PARTI (for participate), or TALK produce lively social clubhouses on many distributed online information services. Participants may be genuinely caring and helpful, or maybe wisecracking "flamers" more intent on a putdown with a tendency to violent or obscene language. Sometimes users take on new personalities with lively names such as Gypsy, Larry Lightning, or Really Rosie. The social chatter can be light, provocative, or intimidating, but it is almost always interesting.

The hardware, network, and software architectures to support synchronous applications with multimedia capabilities are being developed at many sites (Crowley et al., 1990; Patterson et al., 1990); each project is dealing with the problems of delays, locking, sharing, and synchronization.

Innovative attempts to use video to bridge distance have been made. A simple approach is to have two video cameras and displays so that you can have an informal chat:

> Imagine sitting in your work place lounge having coffee with some colleagues. Now imagine that you and your colleagues are still in the same room, but are separated by a large sheet of glass that does not interfere with your ability to carry on a clear, two-way conversation. Finally imagine that you have split the room into two parts and moved one part 50 miles down the road, without impairing the quality of your interaction with your friends. That scenario illustrates the goal of the VideoWindow project: to extend a shared space over considerable distance without impairing the quality of the interactions among users or requiring any special actions to establish a conversation. (Fish et al., 1990)

Another approach to video conferencing is to have individuals hold real-time conferences with video images of one another and voice contact (Watabe, 1990; Mantei et al., 1991). In these systems users can be at their own desks using their normal computer systems while seeing one or more other participants in the video conference. In the University of Toronto's CAVECAT (Computer Audio Video Enhanced Collaboration and Telepresence) system, up to four sites can be viewed on a single monitor (Figure 10.4). Identified problems include slow response time for entering or leaving a session, distracting background audio that exacerbated the difficulty of determining who was speaking, inappropriate lighting, difficulty in making eye contact since participants would look at their monitors rather than into the cameras, changed social status, small image size, and potential invasion of privacy. In spite of the difficulties, CAVECAT is reported to be used extensively for communicating about software development.

Controlled experimentation on performance with different media (Chapanis, 1975) is guiding designers in shaping effective systems.

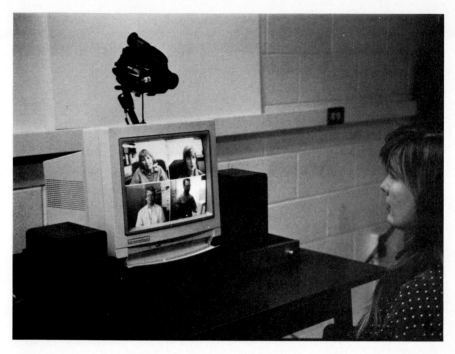

Figure 10.4

The CAVECAT system at the University of Toronto allows researchers casually to observe what is going on in several rooms, or to have conversations among distributed groups. Video camera and microphone are above the display and speakers are on the side. (Courtesy of Marilyn Mantei.)

Chapanis' series of studies and recent work confirm that a voice channel is an important component for discussion of what participants see on a shared display. In one comparison, a shared workspace on a computer display was used without supplements, with audio, and with audio and video (Gale, 1990). One group of four performed three tasks five times in each media format. Significant differences were found for the meeting-scheduling task, which took almost twice as long with the workspace-alone treatment as it did with the two other treatments. This result reinforces the importance of having a voice channel for coordination while users are looking at the objects of interest.

The promise of video windows, walls, tunnels, spaces, tables, etc. is that they enable an enriched form of communication compared to a telephone conference or email, with less disruption than a trip. They enable participants to have the resources of their office environments while affording a greater chance for successful communication and emotional contact. However, picturephones and videoconferences have met with only modest success, so advocates will need to understand and find the situations that are most well matched to these new media.

10.5   Face to Face: Same Place, Same Time

Teams of people often work together and use complex shared technology. Pilot and copilot cooperation in airplanes has been designed carefully with shared instruments and displays. Coordination among air-traffic controllers has a long history that has been studied thoroughly (Weiner and Nagel, 1988). Stock-market trading rooms and commodity markets are other existing applications of face-to-face teamwork or negotiations that are computer mediated.

Newer applications in office and classroom environments are attracting more attention because of the large numbers of potential users and the potential for innovative approaches to work and to learning. These applications include

- *Shared display from lecturer workstation*: In this simple form of group computing, a professor or lecturer may use the computer with a large-screen projector to demonstrate a computing application, to show a set of slides with business graphics, to retrieve videodisk images, or to run an animation. Everyone sees the same images, and only the lecturer can control the computer. The University of Delaware's Fred Hofstetter (1989) developed multimedia lectureware consisting of a videodisk database that allowed instructors to compose illustrated lectures using slides, computer graphics, animations, videos, and audio sequences.

- *Audience response units*: IBM has promoted Advanced Technology Classrooms for its training courses, in which students can answer multiple-choice questions by selecting from a number pad at their desks. Individual and summary results can be shown to the full class on a large display. Similar units have been used by advertising researchers who ask test audiences to respond to commercials shown on a large screen. Promoters claim that this simple technology is easy to learn, is acceptable to most people, is nonthreatening, and heightens attention because of the participatory experience. The National Geographic interactive exhibit gallery in Washington, DC, has five-button response units that allow visitors to try their hand at multiple-choice questions such as What percentage of the earth is covered by water? The set of answers is shown on the shared display, but the presentation sequence is unaffected by the audience's selections.

- *Text-submission workstations*: By giving each participant a keyboard and simple software, it is possible to create a lively atmosphere for conversation or brainstorming. Batson (1992) at Gallaudet University constructed a highly successful networking program that allows each participant to type a line of text that is immediately shown with the author's name on every participant's display. With 10 people typing, new comments appear a few times per second, and lively conversations ensue. Batson's goal was to overcome his frustrated efforts at teaching college-level English writing, and his English Natural Form Instruction (ENFI) network software was spectacularly successful:

> It seems slightly ironic that the computer, which for twenty-five years has been perceived as anti-human, a tool of control and suppression of human instinct and intuition, has really humanized my job. For the first time in a long time, I have real hope that we might make some progress…. Freed of having to be the cardboard figure at the front of the classroom, I became a person again, with foibles, feelings and fantasies. As a group, we were more democratic and open with each other than any other writing class I'd had. (Batson, 1992).

The clatter of the keyboards adds to the lively atmosphere of laughter, groans, cheers, and grimaces.

- *Brainstorming, voting, and ranking*: Beyond talking, structured social processes can produce dramatic educational discussions and highly productive business meetings. The University of Arizona was a pioneer in developing the social process, the physical environment, and the software tools (Valacich et al., 1991) to "reduce or eliminate the dysfunctions of the group interaction so that a group reaches or exceeds its task potential" (Figure 10.5). By allowing anonymous submission of suggestions and ranking of proposals, they introduced a wider range of possibilities; also ideas were valued on their merits, independently of the originator (Figure 10.6a–c). Because ego investments and conflicts were reduced, groups seemed to be more open to novel suggestions. IBM has built 19 Decision Center rooms based on the Arizona model for its internal use, and another 20 for rental to users under the TeamFocus name. Well-trained facilitators with back-

Figure 10.5

Semi-circular classroom with 24 personal computers built into the desks at the University of Arizona. (Nunamaker et al., 1991.) (Photo by Steven Meckler, Tucson, AZ. Courtesy of the University of Arizona.)

grounds in social dynamics consult with the team leader to plan the decision session and to write the problem statement. In a typical task, 45 minutes of brainstorming by 15 to 20 people can produce hundreds of lines of suggestions for questions such as, How can we increase sales? Or, What are the key issues in technological support for group work? Then items can be filtered out, clustered into similar groups, and presented to participants for refinement and ranking. Afterward, a printout and electronic-file version of the entire session is immediately available. Numerous studies of electronic meeting systems with thousands of users have demonstrated and explored the benefits (Nunamaker et al., 1991):

- Parallel communication promotes broader input into the meeting process and reduces the chance that a few people dominate the meeting;

Electronic Brainstorming

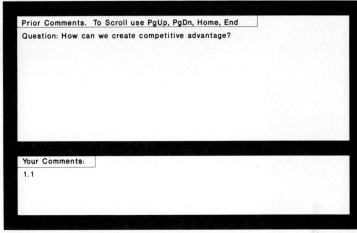

Figure 10.6(a)

Sample screens from Electronic Meeting System at the University of Arizona (Figure 10.6a–c: Valacich et al., 1991, Courtesy of the University of Arizona): (a) Electronic brainstorming.

Idea Organizing

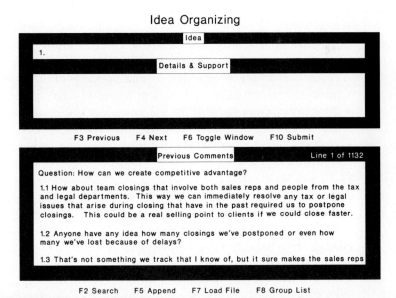

Figure 10.6(b)

Idea organizing.

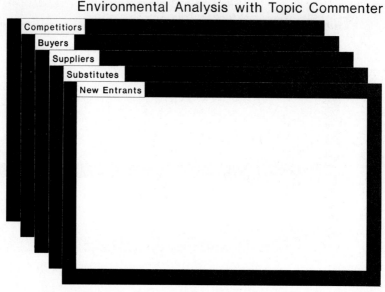

Figure 10.6(c)

Environmental analysis with topic commenter.

- Anonymity mitigates evaluation apprehension and conformance pressure, so that issues are discussed more candidly;
- The group memory constructed by participants enables them to pause and reflect on information and opinions of others during the meeting and serves as a permanent record of what occurred;
- Process structure helps focus the group on key issues and discourages irrelevant digressions and unproductive behaviors; and
- Task support and structure provides information and approaches to analyze it.

The University of Arizona system is marketed under the name GroupSystems, but a competing product called VisionQuest (Collaborative Technologies Corporation, Austin, TX) has appeared.

Both systems are oriented toward business meetings and decision making, but projects at the University of Maryland are directed at supporting teaching using VisionQuest. The specially constructed room at the University of Maryland supports 20 or 40 students working at 20 AT&T 386 personal computers with high-resolution monitors and large-screen projectors, plus a host of audio visual aids (Figure 10.7). The displays were built down in custom desks to preserve sightlines,

Figure 10.7

AT&T Teaching Theater at the University of Maryland has 20 high-resolution displays built into custom desks with seats for 40 students. The AT&T 386 computers are connected by a Novell network, and two large screen displays support 768 x 1024 resolution.

and the computers were housed in a nearby room to reduce noise, heat, volume, and damage. In addition to the brainstorming, ranking, and voting facilities of VisionQuest, the instructor can show the entire class the instructor's or any of the students' displays, can share files with all students, or can receive files. The networked computers are also connected to the campus network, so access to assorted databases and software is provided.

- *File sharing*: A simple but powerful use of networked computers in a classroom or meeting room is to share files. Participants may arrive with homework assignments or sales reports that can be shared with other people in the room rapidly. Alternatively, the teachers or group leaders may have class notes, slides, bibliographies, schedules, budgets, etc. that they wish to publish, or broadcast, to all the participants, who may then annotate or extract notes from the file. The files may contain text, programs, spreadsheets, databases, graphics, animations, sound, X-ray images, or video. Presumably distribution can go beyond the meeting room to allow participants to access the files from their offices and homes.

- *Shared workspace*: The complement to each person receiving a personal copy of a file is to have a shared view of a workspace that every user can access. The Capture Lab at Electronic Data Systems contained an oval desk with eight Macintoshs built down into the desk to preserve the business-meeting atmosphere (Mantei, 1988). The large display in front of the desk is visible to all attendees, who can all grab the large screen by pressing a button on their machine. At Xerox PARC's Colab, each user can see the current list of topics, agenda, or proposals, and can point to, edit, move, or add to it under the policy sometimes called WYSIWIS (What you see is what I see) (Stefik et al., 1987). There is a danger of contention when two or more users wish to edit the same item, but these "cursor wars" can be resolved by proper social processes (agreed-on turn taking) or by technological means (first user to access an item causes lockout of others). The advantage of a shared workspace is that everyone sees the same display and can work communally to produce a joint and recorded result (Figure 10.8) (Weiser, 1991).

- *Group activities*: With the proper networking software between workstations, users can be assigned a problem, and those needing assistance can "raise their hands" to show their display on a large shared display or on the group leader's display. Then, the group leader or other participants can issue commands to resolve the problem. Similarly, if participants have a particularly nice result, graphic, or comment, they can share it with the group either on the large shared display or on individual workstations.

10.6   Practitioner's Summary

Computing has become social. The dedicated networks and public telephone lines have opened up possibilities for cooperation. Email has made it easy to reach out and touch someone, or thousands of someones. Bboards, electronic conferences, and file transfer have enabled users to be woven together closely. Coordination within projects or between organizations is facilitated by text, graphic, and even video exchanges. Even face-to-face meetings are getting a facelift with new tools for electronic meetings and teaching theaters. The introspective and isolated style of the past computer use is giving way to a lively social environment where training has to include *netiquette* (network etiquette). These collaboration tools are begin-

Figure 10.8

Team cooperation with a large common board and multiple personal pads (Weiser, 1991.) (Photograph by Matthew Mulbry. Permission of *Scientific American*, appeared in September 1991, page 95.)

Table 10.1

The novelty and diversity of CSCW means that clear guidelines have not emerged, but these sobering questions might help to guide designers and managers.

Computer-Supported Cooperative Work (CSCW) Questions

What ways do people work together in the organization?
How would facilitating communication improve or harm teamwork?
Where does the community of users stand on centralization versus decentralization?
What pressures exist for conformity versus individuality?
How is privacy compromised or protected?
What are the sources of friction among participants?
Is there protection from hostile, aggressive, or malicious behavior?
Will there be sufficient equipment to support equal access for all participants?
What network delays are expected and tolerable?
What is the level of technological sophistication or resistance?
Who is most likely to be threatened by CSCW?
Whose status will rise or fall?
How will high-level management participate?
Which jobs may have to be redefined?
What are the additional costs or projected savings?
Is there an adequate phase-in plan with sufficient training?
Will there be consultants and adequate assistance in the early phases?
Is there enough flexibility to handle exceptional cases and special needs (disabilities)?
What international, national, organizational standards, and practices must be
  considered?
How will success be evaluated?

ning to have a visible effect; it seems that their success will spread rapidly. However, like all new technologies, there will be failures, because our intuitions about the design of groupware are based on shallow experience (Table 10.1). Thorough testing of new applications is necessary before widespread dissemination.

10.7   Researcher's Agenda

The opportunities for new products and refinements of existing products seem great. Even basic products such as email could be dramatically improved by inclusion of online directories and archiving tools. Conferencing methods and cooperative document production will change quickly as bandwidth increases and video is added. The most dramatic projects seem to be the ambitious electronic-meeting systems and teaching theaters. These are costly, but are so attractive that many organizations are likely to spend heavily on this new technology during the next decade. Although user-interface design of applications will be a necessary component, the larger and more difficult research problems lie in studying the social processes. The excitement for researchers in computer-supported cooperative work stems from the vast uncharted territory: theories are sparse, measurement is informal, data analysis is overwhelming, and predictive models are nonexistent.

References

Bruce, Bertram, Peyton, Joy, and Batson, Trent, *Network-Based Classrooms*, Cambridge University Press, Cambridge, U.K. (1992).

Borenstein, Nathaniel S., Multimedia electronic mail: Will the dream become a reality? *Communications of the ACM 34*, 4 (April 1991), 117–119.

Chapanis, Alphonse, Interactive human communication, *Scientific American 232*, 3 (March 1975), 36–42.

Conklin, J. and Begeman, M., gIBIS: A hypertext tool for exploratory policy discussion, *Proc. Second Conference on Computer-Supported Cooperative Work*, ACM, New York (1988), 140–152.

Crowley, Terrence, Milazzo, Paul, Baker, Ellie, Forsdick, Harry, and Tomlinson, Raymond, MMConf: An infrastructure for building shared multimedia applications, *Proc. Third Conference on Computer-Supported Cooperative Work*, ACM, New York (1990), 329–355.

Ellis, C. A., Gibbs, S. J., and Rein, G. L., Groupware: Some issues and experiences, *Communications of the ACM 34*, 1 (January 1991), 680–689.

Fischer, Gerhard and Stevens, Curt, Information access in complex, poorly structured information spaces, *Proc. ACM SIGCHI '91 Human Factors in Computing Systems*, ACM, New York (1991), 63–70.

Fish, Robert S., Kraut, Robert E., and Chalfonte, Barbara, The VideoWindow System in informal communications, *Proc. Third Conference on Computer-Supported Cooperative Work*, ACM, New York (1990), 1–11.

Flores F., Graves, M., Hartfield, B., and Winograd, T. Computer systems and the design of organizational interaction, *ACM Transactions on Office Information Systems 6*, 2 (April 1988), 153–172.

Gale, Stephen, Human aspects of interactive multimedia communication, *Interacting with Computers 2*, 2 (1990), 175–189.

Glossbrenner, Alfred, *The Complete Handbook of Personal Computer Communications* (Third Edition), St. Martin's Press, New York (1990).

Grudin, Jonathan, Groupware and cooperative work: Problems and prospects. In Laurel, Brenda (Editor), *The Art of Human–Computer Interface Design*, Addison-Wesley, Reading, MA (1990), 171–185.

Hiltz, S. R., *Online Communities: A Case Study of the Office of the Future*, Ablex, Norwood, NJ (1984).

Hiltz, S. R., *The Virtual Classroom*, Ablex, Norwood, NJ (1992).

Hiltz, S. R. and Turoff, M., *The Network Nation: Human Communication via Computer*. Addison-Wesley, Reading, MA (1978).

Hiltz, S. R., and Turoff, M., Structuring computer-mediated communication systems to avoid information overload, *Communications of the ACM 28*, 7 (July 1985), 680–689.

Hoffert, Eric M. and Gretsch, Greg, The digital news system at EDUCOM: A convergence of interactive computing, newspapers, television and high-speed networks, *Communications of the ACM 34*, 4 (April 1991), 113–116.

Hofstetter, Fred T., PODIUM: Presentation overlay display for interactive uses of media, *Academic Computing 4*, 3 (November 1989), 10–12, 48–50.

Leland, M. D. P., Fish, R. S., and Kraut, R. W., Collaborative document production using Quilt, *Proc. Second Conference on Computer-Supported Cooperative Work*, ACM, New York (1988), 206–215.

Malone, T., and Crowston, K. What is coordination theory and how can it help design cooperative work systems? In *Proc. Third Conference on Computer-Supported Cooperative Work*, ACM, New York (1990), 357–370.

Malone, T. W., Grant, K. R., Turbak, F. A., Brobst, S. A., and Cohen, M. D., Intelligent information-sharing systems, *Communications of the ACM 30* (1987), 390–402.

Mantei, M., Capturing the capture lab concepts: A case study in the design of computer supported meeting environments, *Proc. Second Conference on Computer-supported Cooperative Work*, ACM, New York (1988), 257–270.

Mantei, Marilyn M., Baecker, Ronald S., Sellen, Abigail J., Buxton, William A. S., and Milligan, Thomas, Experiences in the use of a media space, *Proc. ACM SIGCHI '91 Human Factors in Computing Systems*, ACM, New York (1991), 203–208.

Nunamaker, J. F., Dennis, Alan R., Valacich, Joseph S., Vogel, Douglas R., and George, Joey F., Electronic meeting systems to support group work, *Communications of the ACM 34*, 7 (July 1991), 40–61.

Olson, Judith S., Olson, Gary M., Mack, Lisbeth A., and Wellner, Pierre, Concurrent editing: The group's interface. In Diaper, D., Gilmore, D., Cockton, G., and Shackel, B. (Editors), *Human–Computer Interaction—INTERACT'90*, Elsevier Science Publishers, Amsterdam, The Netherlands (1990), 835–840.

Patterson, John F., Hill, Ralph D., and Rohall, Steven L., Rendezvous: An architecture for synchronous multi-user applications, *Proc. Third Conference on Computer-Supported Cooperative Work*, ACM, New York (1990), 317–328.

Rein, Gail L. and Ellis, Clarence A., rIBIS: a real-time group hypertext system, *International Journal of Man–Machine Studies 34*, 3 (1991), 349–367.

Stefik, M., Bobrow, D. G., Foster, G., Lanning, S., and Tartar, D., WYSIWIS revised: Early experiences with multiuser interfaces, *ACM Transactions on Office Information Systems 5*, 2 (April 1987), 147–186.

Valacich, J. S., Dennis, A. R., and Nunamaker, Jr., J. F., Electronic meeting support: The GroupSystems concept, *International Journal of Man–Machine Studies 34*, 2 (1991), 261–282.

Vaske, Jerry and Grantham, Charles, *Socializing the Human–Computer Environment*, Ablex, Norwood, NJ (1990).

Yakemovic, K. C. Burgess and Conklin, E. Jeffrey, Report on a development project use of an issue-based information system, *Proc. Third Conference on Computer-Supported Cooperative Work*, ACM, New York (1990), 105–118.

Watabe, Kazuo, Sakata, Shiro, Maeno, Kazutoshi, Fukuoka, Hideyuki, and Ohmori, Toyoko, Distributed multiparty desktop conferencing system: MERMAID, *Proc. Third Conference on Computer-Supported Cooperative Work*, ACM, New York (1990), 27–28.

Weiser, Mark, The computer for the twenty-first century, *Scientific American*, *265*, 3 (September 1991), 94–104.

Wiener, Earl L. and Nagel, David C. (Editors), *Human Factors in Aviation*, Academic Press, New York (1988).

CHAPTER 11

Information Exploration Tools

Gradually I began to feel that we were growing something
almost organic in a new kind of reality, in cyberspace,
growing it out of information . . . a pulsing tree of data
that I loved to climb around in, scanning for new growth.

Mickey Hart, *Drumming at the Edge of Magic: A Journey into
the Spirit of Percussion,* **1990**

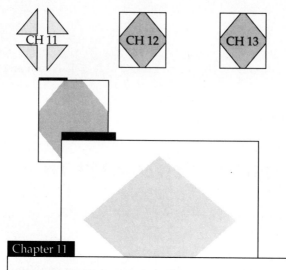

11.1 Introduction

Information exploration and discovery should be a joyous experience, but commentators often talk of information overload and anxiety (Wurman, 1989). The deluge of information is likely to continue growing, but methods for converting the flood into irrigation on the field of ideas are beginning to mature. The next generation of systems for database management, computer-directory browsing, information retrieval, hypermedia, scientific data management, and libraries will enable convenient exploration of growing information spaces by a wider range of users. User-interface designers can provide more powerful search techniques, more comprehensible query facilities, better presentation methods, and smoother integration of technology with task.

Exploring information resources becomes increasingly difficult as the volume grows. A page of information is easy to explore, but when the information becomes the size of a book, or library, or even larger, it may be difficult to locate desired information or to browse to gain an overview. The strategies to focus and narrow are well understood by librarians and information-search specialists, and now these strategies are beginning to be implemented for widespread use. The computer is a powerful tool for searching, but current user interfaces may be a hurdle for novice users (complex commands, Boolean operators, unwieldy concepts) and an inadequate tool for experts (difficulty in repeating searches across multiple databases, weak methods for narrowing broad searches, poor integration with other tools) (Borgman, 1986; Humphrey and Melloni, 1986). This chapter suggests some novel possibilities for first time or occasional versus frequent computer users, and also for task-domain novices versus experts. Some improvements on traditional text searching seem possible, hypermedia solutions are becoming well understood, and a new generation of visualization ideas for query formulation and data presentation is emerging. There will certainly be other inventions and refinements, but this presentation should enable other researchers and developers to create still more effective variants.

The SSOA model helps us to separate the level of task domain knowledge into low and high, and the level of computer-syntax knowledge into low and high. First-time users of an information-exploration system (whether they have little or much task-domain knowledge) are struggling to understand what they see on the display while keeping in mind their information requests. They would be distracted if they had to learn complex command languages, and therefore they need the low syntactic burdens of menu and direct-manipulation designs offering a small number of meaningful choices with online help. As users gain experience with the system, they can request additional features in a level-structured manner through selections on a control panel. Knowledgeable and frequent users want a wide range of search tools with many options, and may prefer a command language that allows them to compose, study, store, replay, and revise increasingly elaborate command sequences.

Information might be organized into *documents* (containing text, graphics, images, etc.) grouped into *collections*, with accompanying tools such as indexes (by author, title, controlled vocabularies of keywords, etc.), concordances (uncontrolled vocabularies of all words with pointers to the specific lines in which each word appears), thesauri (synonyms, narrower or broader terms), and tables of contents. The user's tasks range from specific (fact finding) to general (browsing) (Marchionini and Shneiderman, 1988):

- To locate the documents in the collection that are relevant to their specific fact finding needs; for example, get the document on corn production in Iowa in 1977, or find the document with the birthdate of Louis Daguerre.

- To gain a general overview by browsing the collection; for example, Would this database help in writing an article on Babe Ruth's child-hood? or Are there more documents related to architecture than there are ones related to musicology? or Are these scientific-journal abstracts or popular-magazine articles? or What percentage of the oncology documents deal with air pollutants?

The users might range from high-school students wanting an introduction to French history, to expert historians wanting to find every primary source on Madame de Stael's salons and as many of her contemporaries as possible. Of course, readers could start at the beginning and simply work their way through the entire document collection, but the time required makes this approach unrealistic for large collections.

11.2   String Search, Database Query, and Indexes

Developing computer-based *filters* to reduce the set of documents that needs to be examined is a primary goal of researchers in computer and information science. The broad range of users and tasks makes the designers' role difficult, but computer-based search interfaces do provide useful and powerful tools:

- *Full-text string search:* Users type a word, and the system locates the next occurrence of the word in a document, or returns the complete list of documents that contain the word. For example, `(human OR person OR man) AND (computer OR machine)`. Many variants of string search exist:

  - *Word stemming* (plurals and other variants are retrieved)
  - *Word proximity* (two words (for example, "human" and "factors") adjacent, in the same sentence, or in the same paragraph)
  - *Boolean combinations* (AND, OR, NOT, and parentheses)
  - *Online thesaurus*, used to add synonyms, or broader or narrower terms
  - *Word-list input* with relevance feedback indicating strength of relationship between the search terms and the documents
  - *More-like-this document retrieval*, where users indicate which documents are relevant, and the system provides more documents with similar terms

  String search is effective and is used widely, although it has the serious problems of overloading the user with too many "hits" and failing to retrieve by concepts (Salton, 1989; Egan et al., 1989). String search may be implemented to require searching through the entire database; in many systems, however, the database has been preprocessed and an internal index of all words or hash-coding methods, such as signature files, are used to perform the search rapidly (Faloutsos, 1991).

- *Formatted field search:* Users write queries in a database query language (Reisner, 1988; Jarke and Vassiliou, 1986) and specify matches on specific field values, such as `author`, `date of publication`, `language`, or `publisher`. Each document has values for the formatted fields, and database-management methods enable rapid retrieval even with millions of documents. For example, a SQL-like command might be

```
SELECT DOCUMENT#
FROM JOURNAL-DB
WHERE    (DATE > 1986 AND DATE < 1990)
   AND   (LANGUAGE = ENGLISH OR FRENCH)
   AND   (PUBLISHER = ASIS OR HFS OR ACM).
```

SQL has powerful features, but it requires training (2 to 20 hours) and even then users make frequent errors for many classes of queries (Welty, 1985). Alternatives such as *query-by-example* can help in simpler queries, such as English-language ASIS articles after 1986:

```
JOURNAL | DOCUMENT# | DATE  | AUTHOR | LANGUAGE | PUBLISHER
------------------------------------------------------------
        |   P._X     | >1986 |        | ENGLISH  | ASIS
        |            |       |        |          |
```

The full set of Boolean expressions, however, is difficult to express except inside a special *condition box*. *Form-fillin queries* can substantially simplify many queries, and, if the user interface permits some Boolean combinations, can be easy to express:

```
JOURNAL DATABASE
   DOCUMENT#:
        DATE: 1987..1989
      AUTHOR:
    LANGUAGE: ENGLISH, FRENCH
   PUBLISHER: ASIS, HFS, ACM
```

Information-retrieval systems, such as DIALOG and LEXIS/NEXIS, also require users to learn keywords and syntactic forms that are not easily acquired by many communities of users.

- *Controlled-vocabulary index search:* Rather than supplying a string for searching in the full text, users explore a hierarchical index of subject terms that has been created by the document-collection owner. They can retrieve all the documents that have been indexed under that subject term (Soergel, 1985). With a rapid display, it may be possible to browse productively through the subject index and to learn its structure. Index terms may be organized alphabetically, as in the Library of Congress Subject Headings, or organized meaningfully, as in the Dewey Decimal System. Other indexes may be organized geographically, chronologically (by publication date or by historical contents), etc.

Controlled-vocabulary indexes defined by subject specialist have the advantage that the terms are selected carefully, synonyms are cross-referenced, and hierarchic structures help by clustering related documents. By contrast, automatically generated keyword indexes with terms extracted from a document (except for a stop list of commonly used words) are easier to construct, but tend to be larger, more chaotic, and more ambiguous. Controlled-vocabulary indexes take time to develop, and each document must be classified manually by a subject specialist, whereas automatically generated indexes are created rapidly. Software to classify documents automatically by word frequencies is improving.

- *Back-of-the-book index and table-of-contents search:* A back-of-the-book index is often created by the author and lists important topics with clusters of related topics and cross-references. A table of contents usually is generated by the author and usually is much shorter than an index, but is sequential by topic (rather than alphabetical). Tables of contents or back-of-the-book indexes have the advantage that they can be scanned to get an overall impression of scope of coverage.

- *Concordance and key-word-in-context (KWIC):* By contrast, a concordance or a key-word-in-context (KWIC) is an automatically generated index on all words (except for a filter list of commonly used words); it is too large to use for browsing or to gain an overview.

Of course, combinations of these approaches exist and are used widely. Index terms may be combined with full-text string search, or a table of contents may be used to limit the range of a string search. The most effective strategy or combination of strategies will depend on the tasks, document-collection structure, and experience of the users. In our studies in museums, walk-up users rarely used indexes, but preferred to browse actual documents, whereas in controlled studies on specific-fact retrieval with graduate library students, 95 percent went immediately to the index screen. String search is helpful for specific-fact retrieval, whereas tables of contents are preferred for gaining an overview.

Refinements of the user interface can make a powerful difference. For example, the Library of Congress's SCORPIO system is an effective query language that has been in use since 1975 by thousands of Capitol Hill staffers and library visitors (see Figure 1.2). However, users need at least some training and practical experience to gain even basic proficiency (Stevens and Shneiderman, 1981). The first-time user will need the assistance of a librarian acting as an intermediary. SCORPIO supports controlled-vocabulary index searching (for authors, titles, and subjects) and formatted field search (for dates of publication, national language, etc.). Boolean combinations can be specified, but only one operator at a time can be applied to a numbered set of already-selected documents (for example COMBINE 3 AND 5). Full-text string search is not supported, and neither is hypertext traversal. The recent development of a touchscreen interface has made life easier for first-time users, and shortcuts to permit easier link following are being implemented.

Continuing research on improving the user interface for these search methods is needed because novice and first-time users have great difficulty in learning new systems and because even expert users often fail to find relevant information efficiently. As the flood of available information increases in online databases, electronic mail, bulletin-board systems, and other automated media, improved interfaces can help users to cope successfully.

11.3 Flexible Search

Recent advances in computer algorithms will enable greater flexibility in locating information. Existing search paradigms are quite structured and rigid. Many users wish for the perfect search paradigm that retrieves all and only all of the desired items. This goal is unattainable, but there is the potential for important incremental improvements and some exciting products that are a bit more flexible.

- *Rainbow search:* First, for searches within a document, there is the chance to enable *rainbow* searching. Most search facilities treat text as though it had only a single style, but most word processors already support a range of colorful features such as multiple faces, sizes, styles (*italic*, **bold**, underscore), and text attributes (footnotes, references, titles, headers, footers). It might be useful to allow users to locate the next bold-faced occurrence of **George Washington** or to search through only the footnotes. This option is fairly easy to implement, and there are some limited facilities available (such as MacWrite II, Figure 11.1), but user-interface improvements are possible to permit Boolean ORs and NOTs, and wildcard characters.
- *Search expansion:* For searches across documents, increased ability to specify search within a component—such as the title, abstract, or

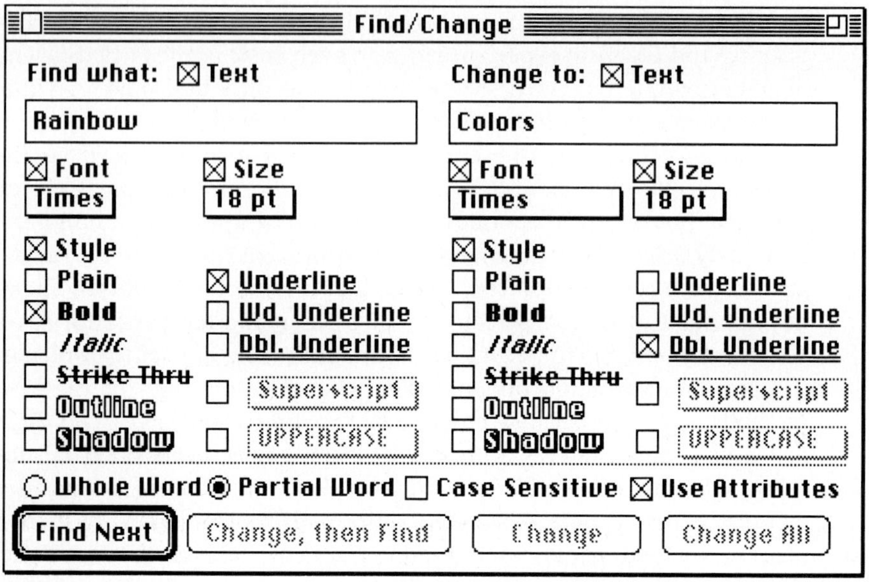

Figure 11.1

MacWrite `Find/Change` dialog box that allows limited rainbow searching on attributes of the text. Selected attributes are ANDed together. (Courtesy of Claris Corp., Santa Clara, CA.)

conclusion—might be helpful in some situations. *Search expansions* would also facilitate solution of some problems; for example, if users desire to locate documents dealing with New England, the system thesaurus would inform them that the search could be expanded to include Connecticut, Rhode Island, Massachusetts, Vermont, New Hampshire, and Maine. Search expansions might provide more specific terms (as in this example), more general terms, synonyms, or related terms from a thesaurus or data dictionary.

- *Sound search:* Search concepts are increasingly important for nontext databases. For example, imagine a music database that would enable users to hum a few notes and would produce a list of symphonies that contain that string of notes. Then, with a single touch, users could bring up the full symphony. Implementing this idea in the unstructured world of analog or even digitally encoded music is very difficult, but imagine that the score sheets of symphonies were stored with the music and that string search over the score sheets was possible. Then, the application becomes easier to conceive. Identifying the users' hummed input may not be reliable, but if visual feedback were provided or if users entered the notes on a staff, as in the Deluxe Music Construction Kit on the Macintosh, then the fantasy would become feasible.

- *Picture search:* Other nontext applications are also appealing. Imagine a database of Adobe Illustrator pictures. It would be nice to be able to find all the pictures with a circle inside a square, or maybe a green square to the left of a yellow oval. If the data representation were searchable, then these tasks would be relatively simple, although there are some interesting user-interface problems to be solved. Imagine a CAD/CAM database that could be searched to find electrical circuits that used components in a certain relationship, or an automobile-engine database that could be searched to find designs in which valves were within 3 centimeters of each other. Imagine weather map databases that could be searched to find regions with more than 30-mile-per-hour gusts at the boundary of a low-pressure system. In all these cases, there is some representation of the contents that is more easily searched than are the bit patterns. When computer-image analysis programs can be applied effectively—for example, identifying defective red blood cells or light bulbs—then the results of such analyses could also be used in search algorithms.

- *Photograph libraries:* Current photograph libraries are organized according to date, photographer, geographic regions, or topic, but indexing is sometimes inaccurate and cross-referencing incomplete. A powerful *faceted* index that dealt with all these topics and still others would be a great benefit. If digitally photographed images could contain encoded information on the date, photographer, place, personalities, and topical references, then some of the burden of indexing could be lightened and a flexible photograph or video library could be built. We are still a long way from systems that could automatically identify images that contain a handshake, ribboncutting, or other event, but when there is some representation of the contents (constructed by human experts), then a flexible search paradigm can enhance the user's power.

11.4 Hypertext and Hypermedia

In July 1945, Vannevar Bush, President Franklin Roosevelt's Science Adviser, wrote a provocative article (Bush, 1945) offering his vision of science projects that might become feasible in the post-World War II period. He wisely identified the information-overload problem and sought to make cross-references within and across documents easy to create and traverse. His desktop information-exploration tool, *memex*, was based on microfilm and eye-tracking technology. Memex would enable readers to follow cross-references by merely staring at them:

> Wholly new forms of encyclopedias will appear, ready-made with a mesh of associative trails running through them, ready to be dropped into the memex and there amplified. The lawyer has at his touch the associated opinions and decisions of his whole experience, and of the experience of friends and authorities…. There is a new profession of trail blazers, those who find delight in establishing useful trails through the enormous mass of the common record. The inheritance from the master becomes, not only his addition to the world's record, but for his disciples the entire scaffolding by which they were erected. (Bush, 1945)

It has taken nearly 50 years to create effective—although somewhat revised—models of Bush's vision. Now the technology is beginning to make possible a useful reading, browsing, linking, and annotating environment to support communal nonlinear writing and reading. The name *hypertext*, or *hypermedia*, has been applied to networks of nodes (also called articles, documents, files, cards, pages, frames, screens) containing information (in text, graphics, video, sound, etc.) that are connected by links (also called cross-references, citations). Hypertext is more commonly applied to text-only applications, whereas hypermedia is used to convey the inclusion of other media, especially sound and video.

Ted Nelson coined the term *hypertext* in the 1960s as he was writing about his universal library and *docuverse* with *stretch text* that expands when selected. Nelson's enthusiasm and imagination infected many who shared his *computopian* hopes. Using less psychedelic terms, Douglas Engelbart created his Human Augmentation system at Stanford Research Institute during the 1960s with hypertext point-and-click features, expanding outline processors, multiple windows, remote collaboration, and the mouse (Engelbart, 1984). In parallel, Andries van Dam developed early electronic books at Brown University under the warm colorful sunshine of dynamic graphics and three-dimensional animation (Yankelovich et al., 1985; van Dam, 1988).

By the mid-1980s, many research and commercial packages offered hypertext features to enable convenient jumps among articles (Conklin, 1987; Halasz, 1988; Shneiderman and Kearsely, 1989; Nielsen, 1990). In 1987, Apple provided Bill Atkinson's HyperCard system free with every Macintosh. Although the brochures referred to Vannevar Bush's vision, Apple refrained from using the term *hypertext* in describing HyperCard (Figure 11.2a–d). Building on the metaphor of cards arranged in stacks, Apple claimed in the software online help that "you can use HyperCard to create your own applications for gathering, organizing, presenting, searching and customizing information."

Figure 11.2(a)

HyperCard displays from the original 1987 version (Figure 11.2a–d: Courtesy of Claris Corp., Santa Clara, CA.) (a) Welcome to HyperCard stack.

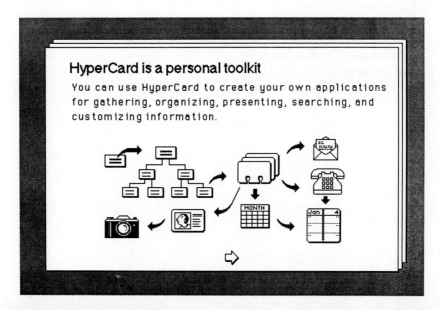

Figure 11.2(b)

What is HyperCard explanation.

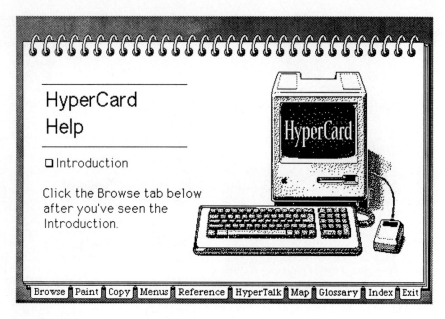

Figure 11.2(c)

`HyperCard Help` spiral notebook with selectable tabs for sections.

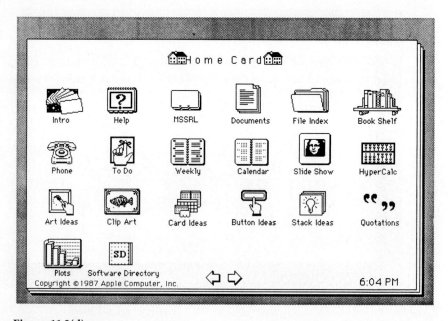

Figure 11.2(d)

`HomeCard` to provide an iconic index of HyperCard stacks.

Other pioneering hypertext systems include NoteCards developed at Xerox PARC, KMS from Knowledge Systems, Inc., Guide from OWL International, and our Hyperties system, now marketed and expanded by Cognetics Corp. (Shneiderman, 1989) (Figure 11.3a–e and Color Plate 5). In Hyperties, we chose to make a strong separation between the browser tool for reading documents, and the author tool for creating documents. Our model was a publication system with thousands of readers for each writer. We chose a simple metaphor of a book made of a collection of titled articles. Links are embedded in the text, and a simple click with a mouse, a touch on a touchscreen, or a few presses of arrow keys produces the related article. Our experiences with hundreds of experimental subjects and thousands of museum patrons led us to strategies that novice and first-time users could master. The browser has no error messages, and every action is reversible. A meaningfully organized author-generated table of contents and an alpha-betical automatically generated list of articles are supplemented by a history-keeping mechanism that enables backtracking and by a full-text string-searching feature.

The Hyperties author tool helps authors to manage the index and development process, allowing links to be made even before the articles were created. The Hyperties 3.0 author tool supports a powerful automatic

Figure 11.3(a)

Hyperties displays from the *1988 Guide to Opportunities in Volunteer Archaeology* (GOVA) was installed in two public access touchscreen kiosks in a six-city Smithsonian Institution Traveling Exhibit entitled "King Herod's Dream" (Plaisant, 1991). (a) Title display.

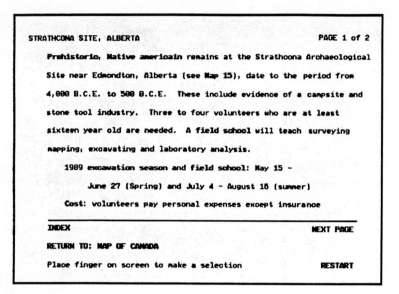

Figure 11.3(b)

Article describing Strathcona Site, Alberta.

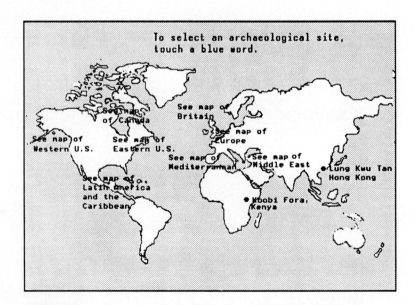

Figure 11.3(c)

World map to select regional maps.

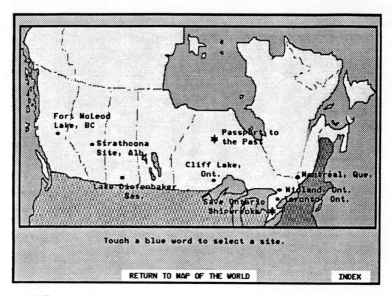

Figure 11.3(d)

Canada regional map to select dig sites.

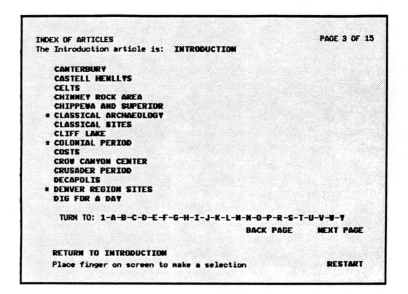

Figure 11.3(e)

Alphabetical index of articles shows asterisks next to articles that have been viewed.

Table 11.1

Candidate list for hypertext and hypermedia applications.

Hypertext and Hypermedia Applications

Business

- Product catalogs and advertisements
- Organizational charts and policy manuals
- Annual reports and orientation guides
- Resumes and biographies
- Treaties, contracts, and wills
- Newsletters and news magazines
- Software documentation and code

Information resources

- Encyclopedias, glossaries, and dictionaries
- Medical and legal reference books
- Religious and literary annotations
- College catalogs and departmental guides
- Travel and restaurant guides
- Scientific journals, abstracts, and indexes

Personal learning

- Instruction and exploration
- Repair and maintenance manuals
- Time lines and geographical maps
- Online help and technical documentation
- Cookbooks and home-repair manuals
- Mysteries, fantasies, and jokebooks
- Hypernovels and hyperpoems

importation tool that enables construction of large hypertexts (articles and links) from existing electronic files.

The intrigue of hypertext is the replacement of the simple linearity of traditional written text with the opportunity for jumping to a variety of successor articles or cards. Convenient backtracking, various clickable indexes and tables of contents, string searching, and other navigation tools profoundly alter the reader's experience. For some purposes, hypertext can be a welcome improvement over linear paper documents (Table 11.l), but there is a real danger that jumping around can also lead to hyperchaos. To reduce confusion, hypertext authors need to choose appropriate projects, to organize their documents suitably, and to adjust their writing style to make the best use of this new medium. The first step in creating effective hypertexts is to choose projects that adhere to the *Golden Rules of Hypertext* (Shneiderman, 1989):

- There is a large body of information organized into numerous fragments.

- The fragments relate to one another.
- The user needs only a small fraction of the fragments at any time.

The dual dangers are that hypertext may be inappropriate for some projects and that the design of the hypertext may be poor (for example, too many links, confusing structure). Inappropriate applications would violate the Golden Rules of Hypertext. For example, a traditional novel is written as a linear form and the reader is expected to read the entire text from beginning to middle to end. Most poems, fairy tales, newspaper articles, and even the chapters of this book are written in a linear form. Of course, hypernovels, hyperpoems, hyper–fairy tales, hypernewspapers, and hyperbooks are possible, but they would require rethinking of the traditional forms so that they could satisfy the Golden Rules of Hypertext.

Poor design of hypertext is the more common problem: Too many links are overwhelming, too many long articles makes reading dull and noninteractive, long chains of links to reach required articles can be disorienting, and inadequate tables of contents or overviews make it difficult for users to determine what is contained in the hypertext. Just because a text has been broken into fragments and linked does not ensure that it will be effective or attractive. Successful hypertext, just like any successful writing project, depends on good design of the contents. The hypertext author who creates a new work, or the hypertext editor who takes existing materials and puts them into hypertext form must take great care to produce an excellent document. Just as turning a theater production into a movie requires learning new techniques of zooming, panning, closeups, cuts, fades, etc., creating successful hypertext requires learning to use the features of the new medium (Table 11.2).

11.4.1   Author-system features

Enthusiasts of hypertext systems often dwell on nonlinear reading, yet there is also a great sense of novelty and adventure in *writing* nonlinear hypertexts. Primitive authoring tools from the world of computer-assisted instruction were employed to create early hypertext documents, but the recent crop of hypertext systems contains a variety of features to meet the demands of this new environment. To analyze the authoring features, we can begin with this tableau of actions and objects:

Actions	Objects
importation	an article or node
editing	a link
exportation	collections of articles or nodes, or webs of links
printing	entire database

Table 11.2

User-interface features to consider in choosing a hypertext system.

User Interface Features

Content

- Nodes (text, graphics, video, sound)
- Links (typed versus single type)
- Formatting, margins, fonts, spacing
- Screen resolution, size, and color
- Window size and management

Interaction

- Selection mechanism (touch, mouse, keys)
- Response time and display rate
- Video and animation control panels
- Invocation of external programs and databases

Navigation

- Structure of graph
- Multiple tables of contents
- Graphic versus tabular overviews
- Indexing versus keyword search
- Position and size indicators

Recording

- Path history and bookmarks
- Annotation
- Exportation
- Save status and search results

Hypertext systems should be compared by their ability to support importation of articles, links, collections of articles or webs of links, or entire databases. There is great variation across systems. Most systems enable each of the actions to be applied to a single node or article from or to an ASCII file, but not much more. For example, most systems enable the author to edit one article at a time, but few systems enable the author to make a global change to all articles with one command. Researchers are developing strategies for exporting entire databases in book formats with links indicated by bold-face type and a page number. In constructing *Hypertext Hands-On!* (Shneiderman and Kearsley, 1989), we had to build the book version of the hypertext database one step at a time, indicating page numbers by hand. Automation of this process is a natural next step.

There are two key issues in the authoring process. The first is the management of nodes. If the hypertext system provides an index of all the nodes or articles that have been referenced or created, that will be of great benefit. The second issue is the indication of links. This process should be simple and easy to manipulate. Marking a phrase or a region can usually be accomplished easily, but then it should also be easy to indicate the link destination. Furthermore, if the same phrase appears many times, it should be possible to resolve the link more easily the second time. Automatic facilities for marking and linking every occurrence of a link are attractive, but can lead to an excessive number of links, which clutters the screen and distract the reader. One problem that occurs in some hypertext systems is that the link buttons on phrases are marked by regions of the screen, so when the text is edited, the link buttons must all be moved. For text articles, the link buttons should move with the words.

Other features to consider in an authoring tool are

- Range of editing functions available (for example, copying, moving, insertion, deletion, global change within an article)
- Availability of lists of link names, index terms, synonyms, etc.
- Range of display-formatting commands
- Availability of search-and-replace functions for making global changes across multiple nodes
- Control of color (text, background); color can make the text look attractive, but it can also be distracting; since users have different preferences and tasks, it should be possible to reset color-usage parameters.
- Capability to switch easily between author and browser modes to test ideas
- Access to CD-ROM, videodisk, or other devices, new devices are emerging regularly with remarkable storage capabilities; it should be possible to access information on a variety of devices
- Capability to export files to other systems
- Capability to operate on a local-area network
- Availability of multiuser, network, and distributed databases
- Ability to store old versions of an article
- Availability of graphics and video facilities; embedded graphics editors and mechanisms for exploring the videodisk
- Possibility of collaboration; more than one person should be able to edit the database at one time; different people should be able to author components of the database, which are then merged
- Data compression; compression algorithms can reduce the size of the database and facilitate distribution of disks or dissemination by electronic networks
- Security control; password control can restrict access to the database or parts of it
- Encryption; sensitive-nodes encryption enhances security

- Reliability; bug-free performance with no loss of data
- Possibility of integration with other software or hardware
- Import and export of standard interchange formats, such as SGML
- *Browser distribution*; every user of the hypertext may have to acquire a copy of the full system; alternatively, the browsing part can be included with the database

There are undoubtedly more items to add, but this list—which emerged from our own experience—is a start. Not one of the currently available systems provides the full set of desirable features.

11.4.2   Authoring or editing hypertext

For at least the last 3000 years, authors and editors have explored ways to structure knowledge to suit the linear medium of the written word. When appropriate, authors have developed strategies for linking related fragments of text and graphics even in the linear format. Now, hypertext encourages nonlinear interconnecting links among nodes.

Restructuring knowledge to suit this new medium is a fascinating experience. The first challenge is to structure the knowledge such that an overview can be presented to the reader in the root document or introductory article. The overview should identify the key subsidiary ideas and the breadth of coverage. A paper book presents a clear vision of its boundaries, so readers can know when they have read it all, but in the hypertext world other mechanisms must be created to give the reader a sense of scope and closure. The overall structure of articles must make sense to readers so that they can form a mental image of the topics covered. This facilitates traversal and reduces disorientation. Just as important is the reader's understanding of what is not in the database. Readers may become terribly frustrated if they think that something of interest may be in the database, but they can neither find it nor convince themselves that it is not there.

In writing articles, the hypertext author is free (and encouraged) to use high-level concepts and terminology. Novices can select terms to learn about; knowledgeable readers can move ahead to more complex topics. For example, in a historical database, key events, people, or places can be mentioned without description, and novices can follow the links to read the articles in related nodes if they need background material. The database on "Austria and the Holocaust" was based on people, places, events, organizations, and social organizations. These could be mentioned freely throughout the text and readers could follow the links to find more information. Names of people or places that were not in the database were mentioned only when necessary, and with a brief description.

Hypertext is conducive to the inclusion of appendices, glossaries, examples, background information, original sources, and bibliographic references. Interested readers can pursue the details; casual readers can ignore them.

Creating documents for a hypertext database introduces some additional considerations beyond the usual concerns of good writing. No list can be complete, but here again this list, derived from our experience, may be useful to other people:

- *Know the users and their tasks:* Users are a vital source of ideas and feedback; use them throughout the development process to test your designs. Realize that you are not a good judge of your own design because you know too much. Study the target population of users carefully to make certain you know how the system really will be used. Create demonstrations and prototypes early in the project; do not wait for the full technology to be ready.

- *Ensure that meaningful structure comes first:* Build the project around the structuring and presentation of information, not around the technology. Develop a *high concept* for the body of information you are organizing. Avoid fuzzy thinking when creating the information structure.

- *Apply diverse skills:* Make certain that the project team includes information specialists (trainers, psychologists), content specialists (users, marketers), and technologists (systems analysts, programmers), and that the team members can communicate.

- *Respect chunking:* The information to be presented needs to be organized into small "chunks" that deal with one topic, theme, or idea. Chunks may be 100 words or 1000 words—but when a chunk reaches 10,000 words, the author should consider restructuring into multiple smaller chunks. Screens are still usually small and hard to read, so lengthy linear texts are not as pleasant for users. Each chunk represents a node or document in the database.

- *Show interrelationships:* Each document should contain links to other documents. The more links contained in the documents, the richer the connectivity of the hypertext. Too few links means that the medium of hypertext may be inappropriate; too many links can overwhelm and distract the reader. Author preferences range from those who like to put in a maximum of one or two links per screen, to the more common range of two to eight links per screen, to the extreme of dozens of selectable links per screen.

- *Be consistent in creating document names:* It is important to keep a list of names given to documents as they are created; otherwise, it becomes difficult to identify links properly. Synonyms can be used, but misleading synonyms can be confusing.

- *Work from a master reference list:* Create a master reference list as you go to ensure correct citations, and prevent redundant or missing citations. Some hypertext systems construct this list for you automatically.

- *Ensure simplicity in traversal:* Authors should design the link structure so that navigation is simple, intuitive, and consistent throughout the system. Movement through the system should be effortless and should require a minimum of conscious thought. Find simple, comprehensible, and global structures that the readers can use as a cognitive map. Be sensitive to the possibility that the user will get "lost in hyperspace" and develop the system to make recovery simple.

- *Design each screen carefully:* Screens should be designed so they can be grasped easily. The focus of attention should be clear, headings should guide the reader, links should be useful guides that do not overwhelm the reader. Visual layout is extremely important in screen design.

- *Require low cognitive load:* Minimize the burden on the user's short-term memory. Do not require the user to remember terms or ideas from one screen to another. The goal is to enable users to concentrate on their tasks and on the contents while the computer vanishes.

11.4.3 Creating the introduction

Key design issues are how to organize the network, and how to convey that order to the reader. Some documents begin with an "Executive Overview" that summarizes and provides pointers to sections. Some reference books have a main table of contents that points to tables of contents for each section or volume. Most books start with a hierarchical table of contents. These models can be a guide to authoring strategies for creating the root or starting document:

- *Glossary strategy:* Make the root document an overview that contains links to all major concepts in the database.

- *Top-down strategy:* Adopt a hierarchical approach in which the links in the root document are major categories.

- *Menu strategy:* Organize the root article as a list or table of contents of the major concepts in the database.

- *Search strategy:* Make string search easily available as a possible first step. The search should be rapid in generating a full list of articles.

The suitability of the different authoring strategies will depend on the purposes and anticipated uses of the database.

A major concern to authors of hypertext databases is determining the optimal length for documents. Research suggests that many short documents are preferable to a smaller number of long documents.

An experiment was performed at the University of Maryland using the Hyperties system in which the same database was created as 46 short articles (four to 83 lines) and as five long articles (104 to 150 lines). Participants in the study were given 30 minutes to locate the answers to a series of questions by using the database. The 16 participants who worked with the short articles answered more questions correctly and took less time to answer the questions.

The optimal article length may be affected by such variables as screen size, nature of task, session duration, and experience of user. One problem with databases consisting of many small articles is that the reader must perform excessive navigation.

11.4.4   Converting existing documents and files

Converting existing documents into hypertext form is a major concern of hypertext developers. Thousands of large online databases already exist and are available via information-retrieval systems such as DIALOG, BRS, or Nexis/Lexis. Organizing these databases in a hypertext format would be a monumental task. Links would need to be placed in each record (document), and browsing capabilities would have to be added to these databases. If links were to be established across databases, they would need to have comparable structures.

It seems likely that many existing databases will be converted to hypertext form (for example the Oxford English Dictionary and the AIRS Bible projects). In some cases, only new records added to databases will contain coded links suitable for hypertext.

In the personal-computer domain, text conversion is much more feasible, since most personal-computer–based hypertext systems accept standard ASCII files as input. Most existing documents can be converted to ASCII format. There remains the task of identifying links using the authoring capabilities of the hypertext program.

Many documents to be converted contain various kinds of graphics. The conversion of graphics to hypertext format is problematic. Graphics file formats differ widely across systems. Modern digitizing technology makes it possible to convert most graphic images from paper to electronic form so that they can be incorporated into hypertext databases. However, the degree of manipulation possible with the graphic once in electronic form (for example, resizing, rotation, or cropping) depends on the graphic editor available.

There is good reason to hope that processes for automatic conversion will be developed and will become widely available. We have already succeeded in converting databases with explicit and consistent structure that are contained in document-formatting commands. The process involves writing a grammar and parser for the input and a generator to output the articles and the links.

11.5 Multimedia: Videodisk, DVI, CD-ROM, and Beyond

What is multimedia? Artists think that any work executed on more than one medium (oil, collage, watercolor, wood sculpture, neon, etc.) is a multimedia work. In computing circles, *multimedia* suggests the use of more than text-only applications, especially sound and video. But is multimedia a subset or superset of hypermedia? *Hypermedia* suggests the node-and-link world with user-controlled traversal. *Multimedia* is more vague and would probably include starting and stopping a video shown inside a window on a computer display. Multimedia seems to be defined by the hardware required (video-display hardware) rather than by the user's experience.

The first generation of multimedia applications was based on static video-disk sources provided by producers who have access to interesting visual re-sources. Producers such as National Geographic (GEO), the Library of Congress (American Memory), ABC News (Election of 1988, Middle East history), Voyager (National Gallery of Art), and many others generated video-disks with tens of thousands of still images or hundreds of motion video segments. Each package had its own access software, and the thrill was to view the treasured images on command. Success often depended more on content than on design. The Interactive Media Industry Association initiated Tech 2000, a gallery of multimedia computing in Washington, DC. Visitors can see approximately 75 applications in this Disney World–like demo heaven.

The 12-inch videodisks can store up to 54,000 still images per side or 30 minutes of motion video. Access time has been reduced steadily; on new players, it is under 1 second. Videodisk databases are a major application in museums (paintings, photos, etc.), travel (previews of hotels, tourist attrac-tions, etc.), education (microbiology slides, environmental awareness, cur-rent events, etc.), industrial training (truck drivers, financial sales, power-plant control, etc.), and sales (shoes, sports equipment, real estate, etc.). User-interface issues revolve around access to indexes, searching methods, action sets (start, pause, replay, stop, fast forward or backward), branching capability to allow individual exploration, capacity to extract and export, annotation, and synchronization with other activities.

Abbe Don, a multimedia artist who created "We Make Memories," used a HyperCard stack and videodisk to display family history as told by herself, her sister, her mother, and her grandmother. In this electronic version of a

Figure 11.4

SONY's Data Discman was released in Spring 1990 in Japan, in an all-Japanese version, and later in English versions that include graphics as well as text. (Courtesy of SONY Corp., Tokyo, Japan.)

family photo album, events take on universal themes, and the emotional engagement foretells future applications that deal more with the heart than the head.

An alternative to videodisk that is gaining popularity is the 120-millimeter (5-inch) CD-ROM that can provide up to 600 megabytes of textual or numeric data, or approximately 6000 graphic images, 1 hour of music, or 6 to 72 minutes (depending on effectiveness of compression and the resolution of the images) of motion video. CD-ROMs are relatively cheap, are small (60-millimeter disks are also available), and have smaller reading devices than videodisks. CD-ROMs are restructuring libraries and offices as they acquire more electronic reference sources and the computers to search them.

An interactive standard, called CD-I (compact disk—interactive), combining data with programs, has the potential to reach millions of consumers during the coming decade. Players for under $1000 will connect to computers or to TVs and use remote controllers to enable users to select information and entertainment applications.

SONY's Data Discman (Figure 11.4) was released in fall 1990 in Japan; and 100,000 were sold within 6 months, exceeding the early popularity of the Walkman. Forty 3-inch discs were available, containing reference and booklike resources that could be string searched and displayed in the 10-line LCD display.

Second-generation multimedia capabilities, in which users can create and store their own images and videos and send them to other people have already begun to spice the pot of computing applications (Phillips, 1991).

The pace seems likely to accelerate as hardware becomes more standardized, more widely available, and cheaper. Writeable CDs, or magnetic storage devices, are being developed to handle the high volume of image data that can consume 1 to 20 megabytes per image. Applications include video email, video bboards, video conferences, medical image processing (X-ray images, sonograms, nuclear magnetic-resonant images, computerized axial tomography (CAT), scans, etc.), remote control with video feedback, personal image databases, video tutorials, and video online help.

Personal photography is likely to become a major market for multimedia technologies. Electronic photography has become widespread in the news media and photographic agencies, where rapid electronic editing and dissemination is paramount. Many suppliers offer specialized cameras or addons for existing cameras (such as Kodak's attachment for Nikon cameras) that can take 100 images on a portable battery-driven hard-disk drive. By contrast, amateur photographers have been cool to the digital cameras offered since 1989 by Canon (XapShot) and SONY (Mavica). The nonstandard 2-inch magnetic diskettes hold 50 images that can be viewed on any television or copied onto a videocassette. Hard copies are obtainable only with specialized printers, and conversion to standard personal computers requires special boards. The community of interested amateur photographers might be enlarged with Kodak's CD-ROMs produced from standard 35-millimeter negatives at the same time as prints are made. The higher resolution and better integration with personal computers may allow this product greater success. If users can copy images, edit the images, integrate them into documents, print them, and send them electronically, digital photography may become attractive.

Electronically generated music played through MIDI interfaces has become standard fare in professional music circles. High-quality sound systems can process music from electronic keyboards or other instruments, and composers have unusual freedom to manipulate the sounds. Digital recording and playback allow high-quality sound reproduction that does not degrade with copying or with time.

Since video or sound storage can consume many megabytes of storage, efficient and rapid compression and decompression techniques become vital. The Digital Video Interactive (DVI) approach, originally developed by the David Sarnoff Laboratories and acquired by Intel, has the potential to replace videodisks. DVI hardware can compress 1 second of full-motion video into approximately 150 kilobytes—approximately 5 kilobytes per frame. DVI algorithms attempt to store only differences across frames, so that stable images are compressed more than active or panning sequences. DVI enables up to 72 minutes to be stored on a CD-ROM, and at least a few seconds to be stored on a floppy disk. The elimination of special videodisk players and the capacity for recording video with standard computers (that have the DVI boards) makes DVI attractive.

User-interface issues for these multimedia environments are just beginning to be explored. For retrieval-oriented applications, the key question is how to find the desired images. The methods mentioned in Section 11.2 have been applied to visual and sound databases, and the hypertext approaches of Section 11.3 are becoming more and more common. Speed of retrieval remains an issue, and management of multiple images in multiple windows is still being explored. A physician may want to examine the five of the forty images in a full body CAT scan at once, and may want to compare this week's CAT scan to last week's. Images of 512 by 512 pixels shown with four to 12 gray levels are common; the pressure is for higher resolution. Only by putting together eight to 10 of today's high-resolution displays is it possible to match the image quality and speed of comparing multiple images that doctors expect. Similarly, film editors, graphic artists, or photographic researchers are demanding higher resolution and faster displays. Search algorithms on indexes and structured representations of contents is a further challenge for the next decades. How does a museum curator index a photograph library with 1 million images, or a video library with 100,000 segments, so that future researchers can find all segments with Senator Gephardt's campaign speeches on health-care issues, or all nineteenth-century West African percussion instruments with Sun god carvings.

Still more innovative approaches to multimedia come from performance artists such as Vincent Vincent, whose Mandala system is a three-dimensional environment for theatrical exploration. Performers or amateur users touch images of harps, bells, drums, or cymbals, and the instruments respond (Color Plate 4). Myron Krueger's artificial realities contain friendly video-projected cartoonlike creatures who playfully crawl on your arm or approach your outstretched hand. In both of these environments, input is from video cameras or body sensors that do not require the user–performers to wear special equipment. Such environments invite participation, and the serious research aspects fade as joyful exploration takes over and you step inside the computer.

11.6 Visual Approaches for Information Exploration

Visualization is a method of computing. It transforms the symbolic into the geometric, enabling researchers to observe their simulations and computations. Visualization offers a method for seeing the unseen. It enriches the process of scientific discovery and fosters profound and unexpected insights. In many fields it is already revolutionizing the way scientists do science. **(McCormick et al., 1987)**

The success of direct-manipulation interfaces is indicative of the power of using computers in a more visual or graphic manner. A picture is often cited to be worth a thousand words and, for some (but not all) tasks, it is clear that a visual presentation—such as a map or photograph—is dramatically easier to use than is a textual description or a spoken report (Color Plate 8). As computer speed and display resolution increase, scientific visualization and graphical interfaces are likely to have an expanding role. If a map of the United States is displayed, then it should be possible to point rapidly at one of 1000 cities to get tourist information. Of course, a foreigner who knows a city's name (for example, New Orleans), but not its location, may do better with a scrolling alphabetical list. Visual displays become even more attractive to provide orientation or context, to enable selection of regions, and to provide dynamic feedback for identifying changes (for example, a weather map). Scientific visualization has the power to make atomic, cosmic, or statistical worlds visible and comprehensible. These approaches to computing might be called "visual reality" in contrast with virtual reality (Section 5.8).

Overall, the bandwidth of information presentation seems potentially higher in the visual domain than for media reaching any of the other senses. Users can scan, recognize, and remember images rapidly, and can detect changes in size, color, shape, movement, or texture. They can point to a single pixel, even in a megapixel display, and can drag one object to another to perform an action. User interfaces have been largely text-oriented, so it seems likely that, as visual approaches are explored, some new opportunities will emerge.

There have been many attempts to describe graphical query formulation (Wong and Kuo, 1982; Jarke and Vassiliou, 1986; Kim et al., 1988) but the focus has often been on specifying linkages across relations, between components of an entity–relationship diagram, or between components of a binary relationship diagram (Senko, 1977; Mark, 1989). Graphical selection of attribute values and graphical specification of Boolean operations (Michard, 1982) are likely to be worthy directions for expansion.

There have been fewer efforts to create graphical displays of database-search results, although the potential seems strong (Roussopoulos and Leifker, 1984). There is a growing movement among researchers in user interfaces for Geographic Information Systems that have a graphic query and output (Egenhofer, 1990). The attraction of visual displays, when compared to textual displays, is that the representation may be closer to the more familiar three-dimensional world in which we were raised and in which we live. Within visual displays, there are opportunities for showing relationships by proximity, by containment, by connected lines, or by color coding. Highlighting techniques (for example, bold-face text or brightening, inverse video, blinking, underscoring, or boxing) can be used to draw attention to certain items in a field of thousands of items. Pointing to a visual display can allow rapid selection, and feedback is apparent. The eye, the hand, and the mind seem to work smoothly and rapidly as users perform actions on visual displays.

11.7 Graphical Boolean Expressions

Commercial information-retrieval systems, such as DIALOG or BRS, permit complex *Boolean expressions* with parentheses, but widespread adoption has been inhibited by the difficulty of using them. Numerous proposals have been put forward to reduce the burden of specifying complex Boolean expressions (Reisner, 1988). Part of the confusion stems from informal English usage where a query such as `List all employees who live in New York and Boston` would result in an empty list because the "and" would be interpreted as an intersection; only employees who live in *both* cities would qualify! In English, "and" usually expands the options; in Boolean expressions, AND is used to narrow a set to the intersection of two others. Similarly, in the English "I'd like Russian or Italian salad dressing," the "or" is exclusive, indicating that you want one or the other but not both; in Boolean expressions, an OR is inclusive, and is used to expand a set.

This section describes two research projects to develop more graphical visualizations of Boolean expressions. One of the advantages of direct-manipulation interfaces is that users are reminded of attribute names and values and merely select from the list provided by the designer. This approach works well for lists up to a few hundred values, because recognition is easier than recall, typographic errors are eliminated, keystrokes are reduced, and fast scrolling can be accomplished on modern displays.

Imaginative designers have discovered that they do not need to limit the lists to scrolling columns of words; two-dimensional graphical selectors can be very attractive. For example, a graphical selector for states in the United States might be a map on which the users click on as many of the states as they wish. Numeric values are represented nicely with some form of a slider in which the user can specify (Figure 11.5), for example,

- A point (for example, 5.1)
- A range that is less than a given value (for example, 10.2)
- A range that is greater than a given value
- Upper and lower bounds for values

For example, to search for books published between 1968 and 1975, or to locate patients with white-blood-cell counts in the range of 5.1 to 10.2, users simply adjust the markers. When the list of numbers or names for selection grows very long or high precision is required, a higher-precision scale, keyboard entry, or some hierarchical menu approach can be used.

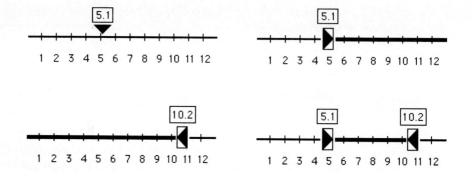

Figure 11.5

Four sliders to allow selection of points or ranges.

11.7.1   Boolean expressions based on aggregation and generalization hierarchies

Our hypermedia kiosk for the Guide to Opportunities in Volunteer Archaeology (GOVA) was installed in the Smithsonian Institution's National Museum of Natural History in March 1988 (Figure 11.3). It allowed visitors to explore possible dig sites by following links or using an index (Shneiderman et al., 1989; Plaisant, 1991). Users could touch a region on a world map and then see a close-up map with dig sites labeled in blue letters that users could touch to get an article about the dig site. Other articles discussed periods of history or special projects such as underwater archaeological explorations. This low-cognitive-load approach and the touchscreen interface, coupled with complete reversibility of actions, made for a low-risk and easy-to-browse environment.

It would, however, be difficult and time consuming to satisfy queries such as, Give me all the Hellenistic or Roman dig sites in the Middle East that accept volunteers in May or June, since dozens of relevant articles would have to be located and read. Responding to this need, an alternate query facility was implemented.

A linear keyword-oriented search language is a typical solution, but it hardly seemed possible to teach museum visitors the use of such a language. Our approach was to turn the map items into set selectors (instead of merely links), so that the users could select several world regions and get the union of the possibilities, without ever thinking of the OR operator or typing field names and values (Figure 11.6). Similarly, the 12 months of the year were laid out as a sequence of buttons and the users could select as many as they wished. The months selected were ORed together, then were ANDed with the world regions. Periods of history were specified by a scrolling list, and the cost was shown by a vertical bar on which users could select ranges (for

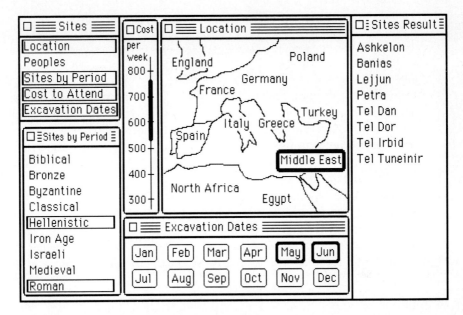

Figure 11.6

Graphical query for GOVA found eight dig sites that were Hellenistic or Roman in the Middle East during May or June, for $530 to $760 per week. (Based on Weiland and Shneiderman, 1991.)

example $400 to $600 per week). As each selection was made, the list of matching dig sites was immediately shown on the display. This progressive-refinement approach was much appreciated by users, since they could immediately see the effect of adding or deleting a selected value. Since the permitted combinations were conjuncts of disjuncts (ANDing over ORed groups), some queries could not be constructed (for example, Select dig sites in the Mediterranean region in July <u>or</u> in the Middle East in August).

Empirical testing was conducted with 16 subjects in a counterbalanced-ordering within-subjects design that compared this graphical approach to a linear keyword approach (Weiland and Shneiderman, 1991). The novice users had more problems than anticipated with the graphical approach because of inadequate experience with the mouse and scrolling menus, and because of an unwieldy window manager. Still, error rates with the graphical interface were approximately one-tenth of what they were with the linear keyword interface, although significant time differences did not emerge. Graphical selection of attribute values, progressive refinement of queries, and immediate recomputation and redisplay of the results appears to contribute many benefits. Subjective comments favored the graphical interface. Improved window management should enable shorter training and more rapid performance.

11.7.2   Filter–flow representation of Boolean expressions

The desire for *full Boolean expressions*, including nested parentheses and NOT operators, led us toward novel metaphors for query specification. *Venn diagrams* (Michard, 1982) and *decision tables* (Greene et al., 1990) have been used, but these both become clumsy as query complexity increases. We sought to support arbitrarily complex Boolean expressions with a graphical specification. Our approach was to apply the metaphor of water flowing from left to right through a series of pipes and filters, where each filter lets through only the appropriate documents, and the pipe layout indicates relationships of AND or OR.

In this filter–flow model, ANDs are shown as a linear sequence of filters, suggesting the successive application of required criteria (Figure 11.7a). As the flow passes through each filter, it is reduced, and the visual feedback shows a narrower bluish stream of water. ORs are shown two ways: within an attribute, multiple values can be selected in a single filter; and across

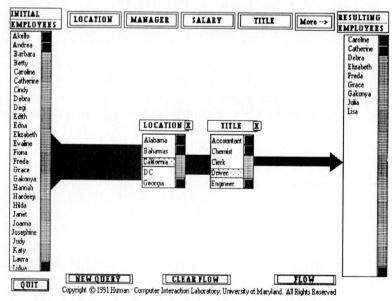

Find the Californian drivers.

Figure 11.7(a)

Filter-flow model allows full Boolean expressions (Figure 11.7a–d: Prepared by Degi Young.) (a) AND is expressed by a sequence of selector boxes which each filter out some items.

multiple attributes, filters are arranged in parallel paths (Figure 11.7b). When the parallel paths converge, the width of the flow reflects the size of the union of the document sets.

Negation was handled by a NOT operator that, when selected, inverts all currently selected items in a filter (Figure 11.7c). For example, if `California` and `Georgia` were selected and then the NOT operator was chosen, those two states would become deselected and all the other states would become selected. Finally, clusters of filters and pipes can be made into a single labeled filter (Figure 11.7d). This facility ensures that the full query can be shown on the display at once, and allows clusters to be saved in a library for later reuse.

We believe that this approach can help novices and intermittent users to specify complex Boolean expressions and to learn Boolean concepts. A usability study was conducted with 20 subjects with little experience using Boolean algebra. The prototype filter–flow interface was preferred over textual interface by all 20 subjects and statistically significant advantages emerged with comprehension and composition tasks.

UNION OPERATOR

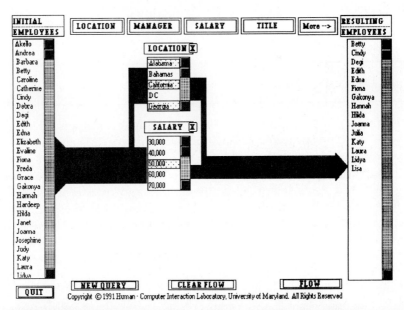

Find the employees who live in either Alabama, California, or Georgia or the employees who earn 50,000.

Figure 11.7(b)

OR is expressed as parallel flows.

NEGATION OPERATOR

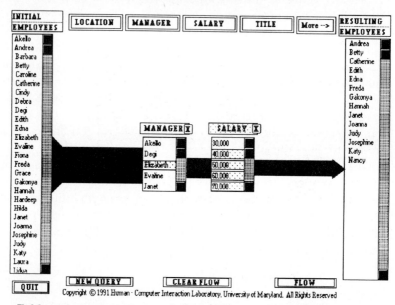

Find the employees who are managed by Elizabeth who don't earn exactly 30,000

Figure 11.7(c)

NOT is a process which reverses the selections within a box.

11.8   Dynamic Queries

The results of the graphical Boolean query methods described in Section 11.7 are merely lists of items. This traditional approach is appropriate in many problem-solving tasks, but we found that displaying the results in a graphical manner was an advantage in some situations. For example, in GOVA, if users select `July or August` and costs of `less than $600 per week`, it would be nice to show the set of dig sites by bright yellow spots on the world map. Then, users could click on the yellow spots to get the full information on the dig site. If there were only a few dig sites that satisfied this query, users would discover this fact immediately, and could move the slider to a slightly higher cost, producing more yellow spots in the desired geographic regions.

Other geographic applications emerge naturally. A college-selection tool could be built based on sliders for location, size, cost, and male-to-female ratios. A system for real-estate brokers and their clients could locate homes by price, number of bedrooms, maintenance costs, quality of schools, etc. (Figure 11.8). Another geographic application would highlight states of the

COMBINATION OF INTERSECTION AND UNION OPERATORS

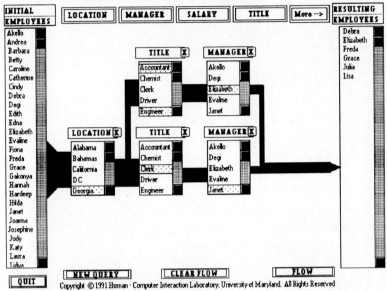

Find the Georgian accountants or engineers who are managed by Elizabeth or the Georgian clerks who are managed by Janet

Figure 11.7(d)

Complex cluster of filters and flows is shown (which can be replaced by a single box to preserve screen space).

United States that satisfy values such as per capita income, air quality, employment, or housing costs, to help users choose a potential state in which to live (Figure 11.9).

Other applications also seem attractive when there is a natural two-dimensional background to show search results: calendars, building layouts, circuit diagrams, or airplane seating. Imagine a chemical table of elements with a set of sliders for melting point, specific heat, ionization energy, or other properties (Figure 11.10). As the sliders are moved, the appropriate chemicals are highlighted, and students can refine their intuitions about the relationships among these properties and the atomic number or position in the table. Concert-seat selection might be done by dynamic query: after indicating the number of adjacent seats you need, you could move the price slider to see how spending more would bring you closer to the stage. Scientific applications seem abundant: Imagine a star map with sliders for attributes of the stars, or DNA chains with selectors for specific sequences. Exploration of sociological data would highlight individuals satisfying a range of attributes, such as economic status, family size, education level, and age.

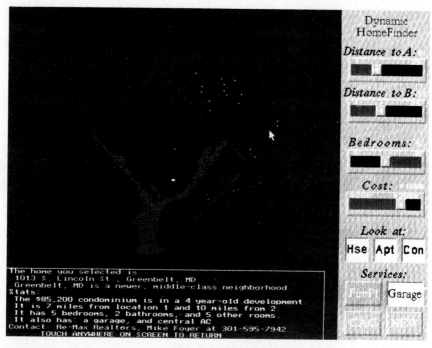

The home you selected is
1013 S. Lincoln St., Greenbelt, MD
Greenbelt, MD is a newer, middle-class neighborhood.
Stats:
The $85,200 condominium is in a 4 year-old development.
It is 7 miles from location 1 and 10 miles from 2.
It has 5 bedrooms, 2 bathrooms, and 5 other rooms.
It also has: a garage, and central AC
Contact: Re-Max Realtors, Mike Foyer at 301-595-7942
        TOUCH ANYWHERE ON SCREEN TO RETURN

Figure 11.8

Dynamic query applied to real-estate brokerage. To find appropriate homes in the Washington, D.C. area, users move the sliders for location, number of bedrooms, and price. Selected homes are shown by a bright point of light. (Courtesy of Christopher Williamson, University of Maryland.)

In addition to conveying a sense of power and fun in dragging the sliders, dynamic queries offer a unique capacity for finding cutpoints in the data when the number of satisfying records moves from a few to many. For example, in the real-estate database, it is useful to discover that moving from $180,000 to $185,000 might double the number of available homes, but that moving up to $190,000 hardly makes any difference. Another cutpoint-exploration benefit is to find that the minimum price for three-bedroom houses is $165,000. Outliers are also located easily with dynamic queries; users can see that all low-priced houses are located in suburban neighborhoods, but then discover that there are one or two bargains in the downtown sections.

Dynamic queries might be called *direct-manipulation queries*, since they share the same concepts of visual display of actions (the sliders or buttons) and objects (the query results in the task-domain display); the use of rapid, incremental, and reversible actions (sliders); and the immediate display of feedback. The benefits of no error messages and the encouragement of exploration are common to both concepts.

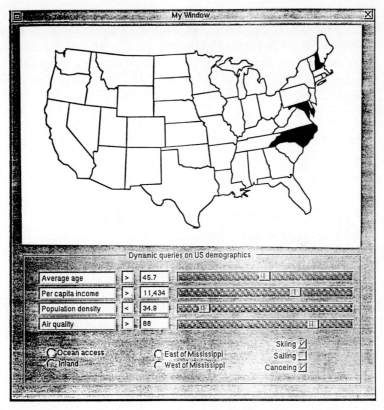

Figure 11.9

Dynamic query of U.S. demographics allows selection of states by sliders on the average age, per-capita income, population density, and air quality. Implemented using the NeXT User Interface Builder.

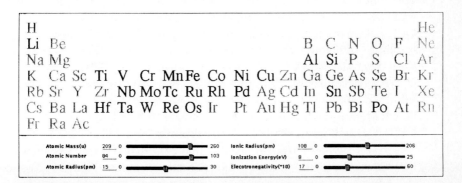

Figure 11.10

Dynamic query of chemical table of elements shows element labels changing color as sliders are moved for the atomic mass, atomic radius, etc. (Ahlberg et al., 1992).

Dynamic queries can reveal global properties as well as assist users in answering specific questions. As the database grows, it will be more difficult to update the display fast enough, and specialized data structures or parallel computation may be required. Dynamic queries have been attracting attention in our laboratory, although many user-interface problems remain; for example, we need to discover how to perform these tasks:

- Select a set of sliders from a large set of attributes
- Specify greater than, less than, or greater than and less than
- Deal with Boolean combinations of slider settings
- Choose among highlighting by color, points or light, regions, blinking, etc.
- Cope with thousands of points by zooming
- Permit weighting of criteria

The dynamic-query approach to the chemical table of elements was tested in an empirical comparison with a form-fillin query interface. The counterbalanced-ordering within-subjects design with 18 chemistry students showed strong advantages for the dynamic queries in terms of faster performance and lower error rates (Ahlberg et al., 1991).

11.9   Tree-Maps

In exploring visual presentations for common information, designers often have to deal with hierarchical structures such as tables of contents, menu structures, organization charts, the Dewey Decimal System, stock portfolios, or computer programs. A variety of tree-diagram formats has been developed, and there are numerous algorithms for displaying partial diagrams that have traversal mechanisms to show remaining portions of the diagram. Our goal was to show the entire tree structure on the display at one time (no scrolling) by using every pixel as part of a space-filling representation of trees (Shneiderman, 1992; Johnson and Shneiderman, 1991).

We were confronted with the problem of an 80-megabyte computer disk filling up, and we had to find large files as candidates for deletion. With 14 user folders at the root directory and a total of 3200 files in 400 folders at six levels, this task was a challenging one. This problem led to the development of a novel two-dimensional space-filling representation of tree structures that shows files with an area proportional to their size. Figure 11.11 shows five approaches to representing hierarchies; Figure 11.12 shows a large disk directory as a *tree-map*. With a few moments of observation, users can identify files and directories; by moving the cursor to these files, users can display a pop-up window that reveals the file and path name plus other

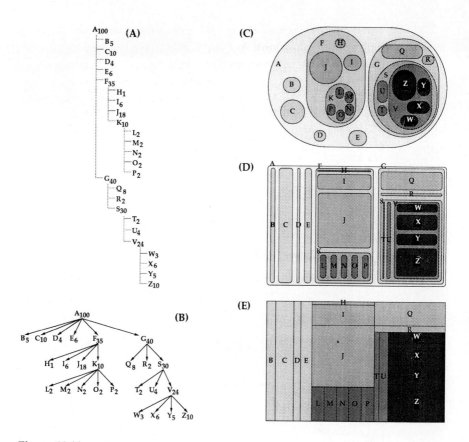

Figure 11.11

Tree-maps are shown as a natural evolution from more traditional hierarchical structure representations (a) and (b). Venn diagram style in (c) shows proportional sizes, but layout is done by hand and space is wasted. In (d), a space-filling approach with directories still visible is shown; (e) has full space utilization for files only. (Courtesy of Brian Johnson.)

attributes. Area can be used to show size, and color can be used to show other file properties, such as date of creation, security status, or file type.

Tree-maps are attractive for applications such as stock-portfolio analysis, where industry groups are decomposed into specific stocks, and then specific purchases. Area could indicate amount of money invested, and color might indicate whether the owner was in the black (making a profit) or in the red (suffering a loss). Similarly, tree-maps might be used to show library holdings organized by Dewey Decimal numbers to cluster books in biology, chemistry, physics, etc. Area could indicate the number of books on each topic, and color might indicate frequency of use.

It takes a few minutes for new users to understand the tree-map layout; once they do, however, they have unusual powers to cruise rapidly from one

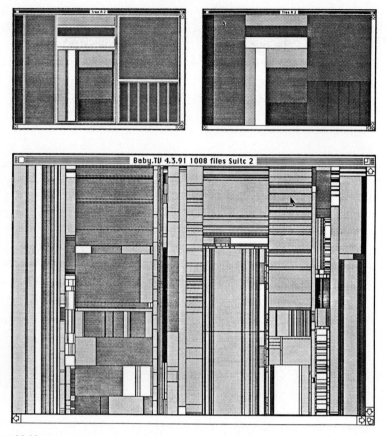

Figure 11.12

A complete tree-map of more than 1000 files is shown. Root-directory files are on the left, followed by the directories in alphabetical order. Notice the three copies of a directory in the center. The details about each file appear in a small pop-up window when the cursor is moved. (Courtesy of Brian Johnson.)

subtree to another, crossing many levels of the hierarchy. Our usability tests are with experienced UNIX users browsing a large multilevel hierarchy of files, and show strong advantages for tree-maps for global search tasks and for discovery of usage patterns.

11.10   Practitioner's Summary

Improved user interfaces to traditional string search, database query, and index search will be beneficial because of the great power of these methods. Flexible queries against complex text, sound, graphics, and image databases are emerging. Hypertext, hypermedia, and multimedia are overlapping notions describing the world of linked nodes of information in text, graphics, image, sound, animation, and video formats. These technologies are now becoming commercially viable as designers gain experience in choosing and creating appropriate projects.

Novel graphical and direct-manipulation approaches to query formulation and information presentation and manipulation are now possible. These approaches include a graphical approach to restricted Boolean query formulation based on generalization and aggregation hierarchies, a filter–flow metaphor for complete Boolean expressions, dynamic query methods with continuous visual presentation of results as the query is changed (possibly employing parallel computation), and color-coded two-dimensional space-filling tree-maps to show multiple-level hierarchies in a single display (hundreds of directories and more than 1000 files can be seen at once). These ideas are attractive because they present more information rapidly and allow for more rapid exploration. If they are to be fully effective, some of these approaches require novel data structures, high-resolution color displays, fast data retrieval, specialized data structures, parallel computation, and some user training.

11.11 Researcher's Agenda

Although the computer contributes to the information explosion, it is potentially the magic lens for finding, sorting, filtering, and presenting the relevant items. String search for textual databases can still be refined to give more precise searches with simpler specifications. Moving to complex structured documents, graphics, images, sound, or video presents grand opportunities for the design of user interfaces and search engines to find the needle in the haystack. Hypertext, hypermedia, and multimedia are all in the Model T stage of development. Hardware is catching up to the user-interface concepts, but progress is still possible in many aspects. Strategies for blending text, sound, images, and video are poorly understood and effective rhetorics for hypermedia are only now being created. Who will be the first to write the Great American Hypernovel or Hypermystery? The novel-information exploration tools—such as graphical Boolean queries, dynamic queries, and tree-maps—are but a few of the inventions that will have to be tamed by user-interface researchers.

References

Ahlberg, Christopher, Williamson, Christopher, and Shneiderman, Ben, Dynamic queries for information exploration: An implementation and evaluation, *Proc. CH192 Conference: Human Factors in Computing Systems*, ACM, New York (1992).

Borgman, Christine, L., Why are online catalogs hard to use? Lessons learned from information-retrieval studies, *Journal of the American Society for Information Science 37*, 6 (1986), 387–400.

Bush, Vannevar, As we may think, *Atlantic Monthly 76*, 1 (July 1945), 101–108.

Conklin, Jeff, Hypertext: A survey and introduction, *IEEE Computer 20*, 9 (September 1987), 17–41.

Egan, Dennis E., Remde, Joel R., Gomez, Louis M., Landauer, Thomas K., Eberhardt, Jennifer, and Lochbum, Carol C., Formative design-evaluation of SuperBook, *ACM Transactions on Information Systems 7*, 1 (January 1989), 30–57.

Egenhofer, Max, Manipulating the graphical representation of query results in Geographic Information Systems, *1990 IEEE Workshop on Visual Languages*, IEEE Computer Society Press, Los Alamitos, CA (1990) 119–124.

Engelbart, Douglas, Authorship provisions in AUGMENT, *Proc. IEEE CompCon Conference*, (1984), 465–472.

Faloutsos, C., Lee, R., Plaisant, C., and Shneiderman, B., Incorporating string search in a hypertext system: User interface and signature file design issues, *Hypermedia 2*, 3 (1991), 183–200.

Greene, S. L., Devlin, S. J., Cannata, P. E., and Gomez, L. M., No IFs, ANDs, or ORs: A study of database querying, *International Journal of Man–Machine Studies 32* (March 1990), 303–326.

Halasz, Frank, Reflections on NoteCards: Seven issues for the next generation of hypermedia systems, *Communications of the ACM 31*, 7 (July 1988), 836–852.

Humphrey, Susanne M. and Melloni, Biagio John, *Databases: A Primer for Retrieving Information by Computer*, Prentice-Hall, Englewood Cliffs, NJ (1986).

Jarke, M., and Vassiliou, Y., A framework for choosing a database query language, *ACM Computing Surveys 11*, 3 (1986), 313–340.

Johnson, Brian, and Shneiderman, Ben, Tree-maps: A space-filling approach to the visualization of hierarchical information structures, *Proc. IEEE Visualization'91*, IEEE, Piscataway, NJ (1991), 284–291.

Kim, H. J., Korth, H. F., and Silberschatz, A., PICASSO: A graphical query language, *Software: Practice and Experience 18*, 3 (1988), 169–203.

Marchionini, Gary and Shneiderman, Ben, Finding facts and browsing knowledge in hypertext systems, *IEEE Computer 21*, 1 (January 1988), 70–80.

Mark, Leo, A graphical query language for the binary relationship model, *Information Systems 14*, 3 (1989), 231–246.

McCormick, B., DeFanti,T., and Brown, R. (Editors), Visualization in scientific computing and computer graphics, *ACM SIGGRAPH 21*, 6 (November 1987).

Michard, A., A new database query language for non-professional users: Design principles and ergonomic evaluation, *Behavioral and Information Technology 1*, 3 (July–September 1982), 279–288.

Nielsen, Jakob, *Hypertext and Hypermedia*, Academic Press, New York (1990).

Phillips, Richard L., MediaView: A general multimedia digital publication systems, *Communications of the ACM 34*, 7 (July 1991), 74–83.

Plaisant, Catherine, Guide to Opportunities in Volunteer Archaeology: Case study of the use of a hypertext system in a museum exhibit. In Berk, Emily and Devlin, Joseph, (Editors), *Hypertext/Hypermedia Handbook*, McGraw-Hill, New York (1991), 498–505.

Reisner, Phyllis, Query languages. In Helander, Martin (Editor), *Handbook of Human–Computer Interaction*, North-Holland, Amsterdam, The Netherlands (1988), 257–280.

Roussopoulos, N. and Leifker, D., An introduction to PSQL: A Pictorial Structured Query Language, *1984 IEEE Workshop on Visual Languages*, IEEE Computer Society Press, Washington, DC (1984).

Salton, G., *Automatic Text Processing: The Transformation, Analysis, and Retrieval of Information by Computer*, Addison-Wesley, Reading, MA (1989).

Senko, M. E., DIAM II and FORAL LP: Making pointed queries with light pen, *Proc. IFIP Congress 77*, North-Holland, Amsterdam, The Netherlands (1977), 635–640.

Shneiderman, Ben, Reflections on authoring, editing, and managing hypertext. In Barrett, E. (Editor), *The Society of Text*, MIT Press, Cambridge, MA (1989), 115–131.

Shneiderman, Ben, Tree visualization with tree-maps: A 2-d space-filling approach, *ACM Transactions on Graphics*, (1992).

Shneiderman, Ben, Brethauer, Dorothy, Plaisant, Catherine and Potter, Richard, Three evaluations of museum installations of a hypertext system, *Journal of the American Society for Information Science*, 40, 3 (May 1989), 172–182.

Shneiderman, Ben and Kearsley, Greg, *Hypertext Hands-On! An Introduction to a New Way of Organizing and Accessing Information*, Addison-Wesley, Reading, MA (1989).

Soergel, Dagobert, *Organizing Information: Principles of Data Base and Retrieval Systems*, Academic Press, Orlando, FL (1985).

Stevens, Pat and Shneiderman, Ben, Exploratory research on training aids for naive users of interactive systems, *Proc. American Society for Information Science* (1981), 65–67.

van Dam, Andries, Hypertext 87: Keynote Address, *Communications of the ACM 31*, 7 (July 1988), 887–895.

Welty, C., Correcting user errors in SQL, *International Journal of Man–Machine Studies* 22 (1985), 463–477.

Weiland, William J. and Shneiderman, Ben, A graphical query interface based on aggregation/generalization hierarchies, Technical Report CS-TR-2702, Department of Computer Science, University of Maryland, College Park, MD (1991).

Wong, H. K. T. and I. Kuo, GUIDE: Graphical user interface for database exploration, *Proceedings of the Eighth Very Large Databases Conference* (1982).

Yankelovich, Nicole, Meyrowitz, Norm, and van Dam, Andries, Reading and writing the electronic book, *IEEE Computer 18*, 10 (October 1985), 15–30.

Wurman, Richard Saul, *Information Anxiety*, Doubleday, New York (1989).

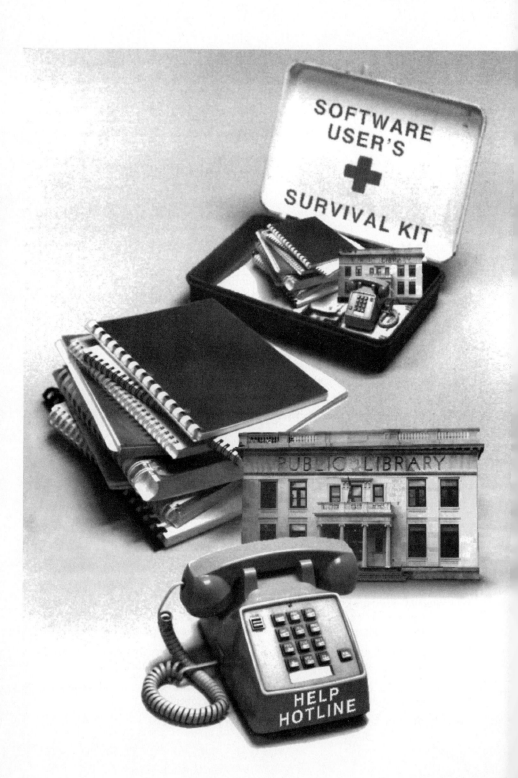

CHAPTER 12

Printed Manuals, Online Help, and Tutorials

What is really important in education is . . . that the mind
is matured, that energy is aroused.

Soren Kierkegaard, *Either/Or,* **Volume II**

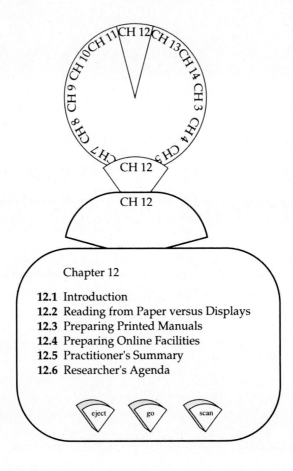

Chapter 12

12.1 Introduction
12.2 Reading from Paper versus Displays
12.3 Preparing Printed Manuals
12.4 Preparing Online Facilities
12.5 Practitioner's Summary
12.6 Researcher's Agenda

12.1 Introduction

All users of interactive computer systems require some training. Many users can learn from another person who knows the system, but training materials are often necessary. Traditional printed manuals are sometimes poorly written, but this medium can be effective and convenient if prepared properly (Price, 1984; Brockman, 1990). Online help, manuals, and tutorials that use the same interactive system to provide training, reference, and reminders about specific features and syntax have become expected components of most systems. In fact, as display devices appear in cars, cameras, VCRs, etc., ubiquitous help should be the norm.

Learning anything new is a challenge. Although challenge is usually joyous and satisfying, when it comes to learning about computer systems, many people experience anxiety, frustration, and disappointment. Much of the difficulty flows directly from the poor design of the commands, menus, display formats, or prompts that lead to error conditions, or simply from the inability of users to know what to do next.

Even though increasing attention is being paid to improving user-interface design, there will always be a need for supplemental materials that aid users, in both paper and online form. Materials of the first type are traditional paper user manuals—documents that describe the system features. There are many variations on this theme:

- *Alphabetic listing* and description of the commands
- *Quick reference card* with a concise presentation of the syntax
- *Brief getting-started notes* to enable eager users to try out features
- *Novice user introduction* or tutorial
- *Conversion manual* that teaches the features of the current system to users who are knowledgeable about some other system
- *Detailed reference manual* with all features covered

There is also a variety of online materials:

- *Online user manual*: An electronic version of the traditional user manual. The simple conversion to electronic form may make the text more readily available but more difficult to read and absorb.
- *Online help facility*: The most common form of online help is the hierarchical presentation of keywords in the command language, akin to the index of a traditional manual. The user selects or types in a keyword and is presented with one or more screens of text about the command.
- *Online tutorial*: This potentially appealing and innovative approach uses the electronic medium to teach the novice user by showing simulations of the working system, by displaying attractive animations, and by engaging the user in interactive sessions.
- *Online demonstration*: Potential users who want an overview of the software can benefit from an online demonstration that walks them through the use of the software.

Duffy et al. (1992) make an interesting classification of paper and online materials:

User's Goal	Medium of Delivery	
	Paper	*Online*
I want to *buy* it	sales brochure fact sheet	demonstration program
I want to *learn* it	tutorial manual	guided tour
I want to *use* it	user's manual	online help online document

Other forms of instruction or information acquisition include classroom instruction, personal training and assistance, telephone consultation, videotapes, instructional films, and audio tapes (Francas et al., 1982). These forms are not discussed here, but many of the same instructional design principles apply.

12.2 Reading from Paper versus Displays

The technology of printing text on paper has been evolving for more than 500 years. The paper surface and color, the type face and font, character width, letter sharpness, text contrast with the paper, width of the text column, size of margins, spacing between lines, and even room lighting all have been explored to produce the most appealing and readable format.

In the last 30 years, the *cathode ray tube* (CRT), often called the *visual display unit* or *tube* (VDU or VDT), has emerged as an alternate medium for presenting text, but researchers have only begun the long process of optimization (Cakir et al., 1980; Shurtleff, 1980; Grandjean and Vigliani, 1982; Heines, 1984; Helander, 1987; Hansen and Haas, 1988; Oborne and Holton, 1988; Creed and Newstead, 1988; Horton, 1990) to meet user needs. Serious concerns about radiation or other health hazards have lessened as manufacturers, labor unions, and government agencies have applied major efforts in this area. Suffolk County, New York, and San Francisco, California, were leaders in enacting laws to protect employees who use computers. The widespread reports about visual fatigue and stress have been confirmed, but these conditions respond well to rest, frequent breaks, and task diversity. But even before users are aware of visual fatigue or stress, their capacity to work with CRTs may be below their capacity to work with printed materials.

Approximately 10 studies during the 1980s found 15- to 30-percent slower task times for comprehension or proofreading of text on computer displays, compared to on paper. The potential disadvantages to reading from displays include:

- Poor fonts, especially on low resolution displays. The dots composing the letters are so large that each is visible and it takes effort to recognize the character. Monospace fonts, lack of appropriate kerning (for example, adjustments to bring "V" and "A" closer together), inappropriate inter-letter and inter-line spacing, and white letters on a black background may be unfamiliar.
- *Low contrast* between the characters and the background, and *fuzzy character boundaries.*

- *Emitted light* from displays may be more difficult to read by than reflected light from paper; glare may be greater, *flicker* can be a problem, and the *curved display surface* may be confusing.

- *Small displays* require more frequent *page turning*; issuing the page-turning actions is disruptive, and the page turns are unsettling especially if they are slow and visually distracting.

- *Reading distance* can be greater than for paper, displays are *fixed* in place, and display *placement* may be too high for comfortable reading (optometrists suggest reading be done with the eyes in a downward-looking direction); the "near quintad" are the five ways eyes accommodate to seeing close items: *accommodation* (lens-shape change), *convergence* (looking toward the center), *mioisis* (pupillary contraction), *excyclotorsion* (rotation), and *depression-of-gaze* (Grant, 1990).

- *Layout and formatting* problems, such as improper margins, inappropriate line width (35 to 55 characters is recommended), or awkward justification (left justification and ragged right is recommended).

- *Reduced hand and body motion* with displays as compared to paper, and *rigid posture* for displays, both of which may be fatiguing.

- *Unfamiliarity of displays* and the *anxiety* that the image may disappear can increase *stress*.

Hansen et al. (1978) found that seven students who were asked to take examinations on paper and on PLATO terminals took almost twice as long online. Much of the increased time could be attributed to system delays, poor software design, and slower output rates, but the authors could not thus account for 37 percent of the longer time on PLATO. They conjecture that this additional time could be attributed to uncertainty about how to control the medium, what the system would do, and what the system had done.

Wright and Lickorish (1983) studied proofreading of 134-line texts that contained 39 errors (typographical errors, spelling errors, missing words, and repeated words). Thirty-two subjects read from an Apple II using an 80-column display on a 12-inch black-and-white display screen or from hardcopy generated from a dot-matrix printer. There was a modest, but significant, increase in detected errors with the printed text. There was also a 30 to 40 percent advantage in speed with the printed text.

Gould and Grischkowsky (1984) studied proofreading for typographic errors on IBM 3277 displays and output from an APS5 computer-controlled photocomposer. Both the displays and the hardcopy texts had 23 lines per page with about nine words per line. Twenty-four subjects spent 8 hours reading in each format. The reading rate was significantly faster on hardcopy (200 words per minute) than on the screens (155 words per minute). Accuracy was slightly, but reliably, higher on hardcopy. The subjective ratings of readability were similar for both forms. A later series of studies with improved displays led to much smaller differences and even to the elimination of differences (Gould et al., 1987a, 1987b).

Recent results demonstrate no difference between reading text on displays versus paper when researchers control for enough of the variables. Bender et al. (1987) found that, using antialiased characters (pixels could be gray to create visually acceptable curves in letters), there was no difference in proofreading speed on displays versus good-quality printed output. Oborne and Holton (1988) believe that earlier studies may have been flawed by lack of control and comparing low-resolution displays to high-quality print. In their comprehension studies using a within-subjects design with approximately 380-word passages, there were no statistically significant differences between displays and photographs of displays, using dark on light and light on dark. They controlled for position, distance to retina, line length, layout, and illumination. Research in this area is further complicated by variations in reading skill, task type, motivation, familiarity, and even time-of-day effects (Koubek and Janardan, 1985).

Other evidence lends support to the conjecture that higher-resolution displays and antialiasing techniques can produce sharper characters that improve readability. Large high-resolution displays are recommended if users are to read lengthy texts online.

12.3   Preparing Printed Manuals

Traditionally, training and reference materials for computer systems were printed manuals. Writing these manuals was often left to the most junior member of the development team as a 5-percent effort at the end of the project. As a result, the manuals were often poorly written, were not suited to the background of the users, were delayed or incomplete, and were tested inadequately.

There is a growing awareness that users are not like designers, that system developers might not be good writers, that it takes time and skill to write an effective manual, that testing and revisions must be done before widespread dissemination, and that system success is closely coupled to documentation quality (Sohr, 1983).

In one experiment, Foss, Rosson, and Smith (1982) modified a standard text-editor manual. The standard manual presented all the details about a command; the modified manual offered a progressive, or *spiral*, approach to the material by presenting subsets of the concepts. The standard manual used an abstract formal notation to describe the syntax of the commands; the modified manual showed numerous examples. Finally, the standard manual

Table 12.1

Results of a study comparing use of a standard manual with use of a modified manual (spiral approach, numerous examples, more readable explanations) (Foss et al., 1982).

Variable Measured	Standard Manual	Modified Manual
Tasks completed	7.4	8.8
Average minutes/task	26.6	16.0
Average edit errors/task	1.4	0.3
Average commands/task	23.6	13.0
Average requests for verbal help	5.5	2.6

used terse technical prose; the modified manual included readable explanations with fewer technical terms.

During the experiment, subjects took 15 to 30 minutes to study the manuals, and were then asked to complete nine complex text-editing or creation tasks within a 3-hour period. On all five dependent measures, the subjects with the modified manual had superior performance (Table 12.1). The results make a strong case for the effect of the manual on the success of the user with the system.

The iterative process of refining a text-editor manual and evaluating its effectiveness is described by Sullivan and Chapanis (1983). They rewrote a manual for a widely used text editor, conducted a walk-through test with colleagues, and performed a more elaborate test with five temporary secretaries. Subjective and objective metrics showed substantial benefits from the rewriting.

12.3.1   Using the SSOA model to design manuals

The SSOA model offers insight to the learning process, providing guidance to instructional-materials designers. If the reader knows the task, such as letter writing, but not the computer-related concepts in text editing and syntactic details (Figure 12.1), then instructional materials should start from familiar concepts and tasks in letter writing, link these concepts to the computer-related concepts, and then show the syntax needed to accomplish each task (Morariu, 1985). If the reader is knowledgeable about letter writing and computer-based text editing but must learn a new text editor, then all that is needed is a brief presentation of the relationship between the syntax and the computer-related semantics (Figure 12.2). Finally, if the reader knows letter writing, computer-based text editing, and most of the syntax on this text editor, then all that is needed is a concise syntax reminder.

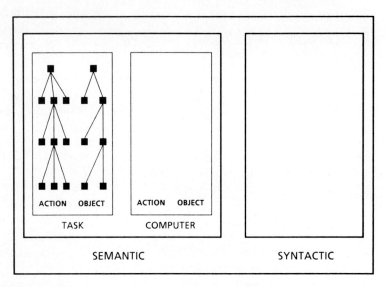

Figure 12.1

A representation of a user who knows the task domain but not the computer domain or syntactic details. Educational materials for this community should start with the task domain, explain the computer concepts, and then show the syntax. If the system represents the task domain conveniently, then learning can be simplified.

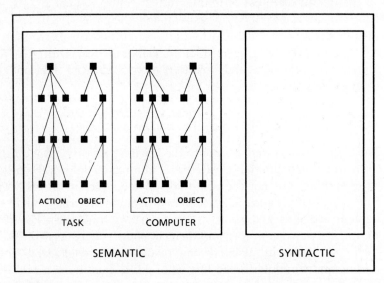

Figure 12.2

Users who are knowledgeable about the task and computer domains need to learn the syntax of only this specific system. For example, someone who knows about writing scientific articles and is familiar with at least one word processor will find it relatively easy to acquire the syntax of another word processor.

These three scenarios demonstrate the three most popular forms of printed materials: the *introductory tutorial*, the *command reference*, and the *quick review* (or "cheat sheet"). The *A CMS Primer* from IBM was a welcome tutorial for the many users who had to struggle through the *CMS User's Guide* with its detailed, highly technical descriptions of each command. Many Apple Macintosh manuals are appealing because of their graphic layout, use of color and photographs, ample illustrations, and task orientation.

The SSOA model can also help researchers to map the current levels of knowledge in learning systems. For example, a user who is learning about database-management systems for Congressional voting patterns might have some knowledge about the database and its manipulation, the query-language concepts, and the syntax needed. This user would benefit from seeing typical queries that would demonstrate the syntax and serve as templates for other queries. In fact, complete *sample sessions* are extremely helpful in giving a portrait of the system features and interaction style (Figure 12.3). Many users will work through these sessions to verify their understanding, to gain a sense of competence in using the system, and to see whether the system and the manual match.

Another helpful guide to using a system is an overall *flow diagram* of activity from logon to logoff (Figure 12.4). This high-level representation provides a map that orients users by presenting a visual representation of transitions from one activity to another. Similarly, if the system uses a complex model of data objects, a diagram may help users sort out the details.

12.3.2   Organization and writing style

Designing instructional materials is a challenging endeavor. The author must be knowledgeable about the technical content; sensitive to the background, reading level, and intellectual ability of the reader; and skilled in writing lucid prose. Assuming that the author has acquired the technical content, the primary job in creating a manual is to understand the readers and the tasks they must perform.

A precise statement of the *educational objectives* (Mager, 1962) is an invaluable guide to the author and the reader. The sequencing of the instructional contents is governed by the reader's current knowledge and ultimate objectives. Precise rules are hard to identify, but the author should attempt to present concepts in a logical sequence with increasing order of difficulty, to ensure that each concept is used in subsequent sections, to avoid forward references, and to construct sections with approximately equal amounts of new material. In addition to these structural requirements, the manual should have sufficient *examples* and complete *sample sessions*.

Within a section that presents a concept, the author should begin with the reason for the concept, describe the concept in task-domain semantic terms,

TASK 1
RETRIEVE DOCUMENTS CONTAINING A WORD OR ACRONYM;
VIEW FULL TEXT

Retrieve FSD Management Instructions (MIs) that reference subcontracting; page
through the retrieved MIs, viewing the words in context.

You can substitute another query for **subcontract$,** a different manual for "MGTI".
To retrieve all FSD instructions and procedures that reference subcontracting, use
the manual named "OMIR".

USER		RESPONSE
• Type **QPROC** □		WELCOME TO STAIRS
• Type option number ==> 1 manual name ==> * □		List of manuals
• Move cursor next to "MGTI", Type **s** □		MGTI LOGO
• □		SEARCH mode, ready for first query
• Type **subcontract$**		Words starting with "subcontract", Number of times each word appears; Number of MIs retrieved
• Type **..brw** □	(PF4)	First page of first MI
• □		Next page
• Type **p*** □	(PF11)	Next page containing a word starting with "subcontract"
• Type **doc+1** □	(PF8)	First page of next MI
• Type **..search** □	(PF2)	SEARCH mode, ready for next query
• Type **..end** □	(PF3)	WELCOME TO STAIRS
• Return to PROFS	(PF4)	PROFS menu

□ = press ENTER

Figure 12.3

A sample session is often a convenient way to show system usage. Many users try
the sample session and then make variations to suit their needs. This sample
session shows the use of a text-retrieval system meant for nontechnical users.
(Published with the permission of the International Business Machines
Corporation.)

GETTING STARTED WITH STAIRS/CMS

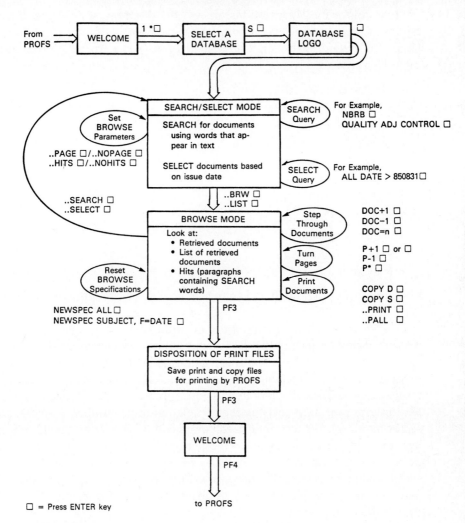

□ = Press ENTER key

Figure 12.4

A transition diagram can be a helpful aid for users. This diagram shows user
actions on the arrows and computer responses in the boxes, for the same system as
that in Figure 9.3. (Courtesy of Barbara Young, International Business Machines,
Inc., Federal Systems Division, Bethesda, MD.)

then show the computer-related semantic concepts, and, finally, offer the
syntax.

The choice of words and their phrasing is as important as the overall structure. A poorly written sentence mars a well-designed manual, just as an incorrect note mars a beautifully composed sonata. The classic book on writing, *The*

Elements of Style (Strunk and White, 1979) is a valuable resource. Another classic is the article by Chapanis (1965) titled "Words, words, words."

Style guides for organizations are worthy attempts at ensuring consistency and high quality (see *Documentation Style Manual* from General Electric (1981) for a good example). The *Ease-of-Use Reference* from IBM (undated) offers this advice:

- *Make information easy to find:*
  - Include entry points
  - Arrange information to be found
- *Make information easy to understand*:
  - Keep it simple
  - Be concrete
  - Put it naturally
- *Make information task-sufficient*:
  - Include all that is needed
  - Make sure it is correct
  - Exclude what is not needed

Of course, no set of guidelines can turn a mediocre writer into a great writer. Writing is a highly creative act; effective writers are national treasures.

One study focused on the effect of authors' writing style and users' reading ability on users learning to work on a computer terminal (Roemer and Chapanis, 1982). A tutorial was written at the fifth-, tenth-, and fifteenth-grade levels. Then, 54 technical and nontechnical subjects were divided into groups with low, middle, and high reading ability. Increased reading ability led to significant differences in the completion time, number of errors, and scores on a concepts test. Increased complexity of the writing style did not lead to significant differences on the performance variables, but subjective preferences significantly favored the fifth-grade version. For this task, subjects could overcome the complex writing style, but the authors conclude that "the most sensible approach in designing computer dialogue is to use the simplest language."

Thinking-aloud studies (see Section 13.2.3) of subjects who were learning word processors revealed the enormous difficulties that most novices have and the strategies they adopt to overcome those difficulties (Carroll and Mack, 1984). Learners are actively engaged in trying to make the system work, to read portions of the manual, to understand the screen displays, to explore the function of keys, and to overcome the many problems they encounter. Learners apparently prefer trying out actions on the computer rather than reading lengthy manuals. They want to perform meaningful, familiar tasks immediately, and to see the results for themselves. They apply real-world knowledge, experience with other computer systems, and frequent guesswork, unlike the stereotypic image of the new user patiently reading through and absorbing the contents of a manual.

These observations led to the design of *minimal manuals* that drastically cut verbiage, encouraged active involvement with hands-on experiences, supported error recovery, focused on realistic tasks, and promoted *guided exploration* of system features (Carroll, 1984). Results of field trials and empirical studies are encouraging; they suggest that learning time can be reduced substantially and user satisfaction increased.

Visual aspects are important, especially with highly visual direct-manipulation and graphic user interfaces. Showing numerous screen prints that demonstrate typical uses enables users to develop an understanding and a *predictive model* of the system. Often, users will mimic the examples in the manual during their first trials of the software. Figures containing complex data structures, transition diagrams, and menu maps (Parton et al., 1985) can improve performance dramatically by giving users access to fundamental structures created by designers.

Of course, every good manual should have a *table of contents* and an *index*. *Glossaries* can be helpful for clarifying technical terms. *Appendices* with error messages are recommended.

Whether to give *credit* to authors and designers is a lively and frequently debated issue. Advocates, including me, encourage giving credit in the manuals to honor good work, to encourage contributor responsibility for doing an excellent job, and to build the users's trust. Responsibility and trust are increased because the contributors were willing to have their names listed publicly. Having names in the manual makes software fit in with other creative human endeavors, such as books, films, and music, in which contributors are acknowledged, even if there are dozens of them. Opponents say that it is difficult to identify each contribution or that unwelcome telephone calls might be received by contributors.

12.3.3 Nonanthropomorphic descriptions

The metaphors used in describing computer systems can influence the user's reactions. Some writers are attracted to an anthropomorphic style that suggests that the computer is close to human in its powers. This suggestion can anger some users; more likely, it is seen as cute the first time, silly the second, and annoyingly distracting the third time.

Many designers prefer to focus attention on the users and on the tasks that the users must accomplish. In introductory sections of user manuals and online help, use of the second person singular pronoun ("you") seems appropriate. Then, in later sections, simple descriptive sentences place the emphasis on the user's tasks.

In a transportation-network system, the user might have to establish the input conditions on the screen and then invoke the program to perform an analysis.

Poor: `The expert system will discover the solution when the F1 key is pressed.`

Better: `You can get the solution by pressing F1.`

Better: `To solve, press F1.`

The first description emphasizes the computer's role, the second focuses on the user and might be used in an introduction to the system. In later sections, the briefer third version is less distracting from the task.

In discussing computers, writers might be well advised to avoid such verbs as these:

Poor: `know, think, understand, have memory`

In their place, use more mechanical terms, such as

Better: `process, print, compute, sort, store, search, retrieve`

When describing what a user does with a computer, avoid such verbs as

Poor: `ask, tell, speak to, communicate with`

In their place, use such terms as

Better: `use, direct, operate, program, control`

Still better is to eliminate the reference to the computer and to concentrate instead on what the user is doing, such as writing, solving a problem, finding an answer, learning a concept, or adding up a list of numbers:

Poor: `The computer can teach you some Spanish words.`

Better: `You can use the computer to learn some Spanish words.`

Make the user the subject of the sentence:

Poor: `The computer will give you a printed list of employees.`

Poor: `Ask the computer to print a list of employees.`

Better: `You can get the computer to print a list of employees.`

Better: `You can print a list of employees.`

The last sentence puts the emphasis on the user and eliminates the computer.

Poor: `The computer needs to have the disk in the disk drive to boot the system.`

Better: `Put the disk labeled A2 in the disk drive before starting the computer.`

Better: `To begin writing, put the Word Processor disk in the drive.`

The last form emphasizes the function or activity that the user is about to perform.

Poor: `The computer knows how to do arithmetic.`

Better: `You can use the computer to do arithmetic.`

Focus on the user's initiative, process, goals, and accomplishments.

12.3.4 Development process

Recognizing the difference between a good and a bad manual is necessary to produce a successful manual on time and within a reasonable budget. *Manual writing*, like any project, must be managed properly, staffed with suitable personnel, and monitored with appropriate milestones (Table 12.2).

Getting started early is invaluable. If the manual-writing process begins before the implementation, then there is adequate time for review, testing,

Table 12.2

User manual guidelines based on practice and on empirical studies.

User-Manual Guidelines

Product

- Let user's tasks guide organization (outside in)
- Let user's learning process shapes sequencing
- Present semantics before syntax
- Keep writing style clean and simple
- Show numerous examples
- Offer meaningful and complete sample sessions
- Draw transition diagrams
- Use advance organizers and summaries
- Provide table of contents, index, and glossary
- Include list of error messages
- Give credits to all project participants

Process

- Seek professional writers and copy editors
- Prepare user manuals early (before implementation)
- Review drafts thoroughly
- Field test early editions
- Provide a feedback mechanism for readers
- Revise to reflect changes regularly

and refinement. Furthermore, the user's manual can act as an alternate that is sometimes more complete and comprehensible to the formal specification for the software. Implementers may miss or misunderstand some of the design requirements when reading a formal specification, but a well-written user manual may clarify the design. The manual writer becomes an effective critic, reviewer, or question asker who can stimulate the implementation team. Early development of the manual enables pilot testing of the software's learnability, even before the system is built. In the months before the software is completed, the manual may be the best way to convey the designers' intentions to potential customers and users, as well as to system implementers and project managers.

Ample lead time in the development of the manual allows for reviews and suggestions by designers, other technical writers, potential customers, intended users, copy editors, graphic artists, lawyers, marketing personnel, instructors, telephone consultants, and product testers (Wagner, 1980; Brockman, 1990).

Beyond informal reviews by people with different backgrounds, there are other strategies for evaluating the manual. Checklists of features have been developed by many organizations based on experience with previous manuals. Automated metrics of reading level or difficulty are available to help users isolate complex sections of text. Computer-based style evaluations and spelling checkers are useful tools in refining any document.

Informal walkthroughs with users are usually an enlightening experience for software designers and manual writers. Potential users are asked to read through the manual and to describe aloud what they are seeing and learning. More controlled experiments with groups of users may help authors to make design decisions about the manual. In such studies, subjects are assigned tasks, and their time to completion, error rates, and subjective satisfaction are the dependent variables.

Field trials with moderate numbers of users are a further process for identifying problems with the user manual and the software. Field trials can range from a 1/2 hour with a half-dozen people to several months with thousands of users. One effective and simple strategy is for field-trial users to mark up the manual while they are using it. They can rapidly indicate typos, misleading information, and confusing sections.

Software and the accompanying manuals are rarely completed. Rather, they go into a continuous process of evolutionary refinement. Each version eliminates errors, adds refinements, and extends the functionality. If the users can communicate with the manual writers, then there is a greater chance of rapid improvement. Most manuals offer a tear-out sheet for users to indicate comments for the manual writers. This device can be effective, but other routes should also be explored: electronic mail, interviews with users, debriefing of consultants and instructors, written surveys, group discussions, and further controlled experiments or field studies.

Brockman (1990) offers a nine-step process for writing user documentation:

1. Develop the document specifications:

   Use task orientation
   Use minimalist design
   Handle diverse audiences
   State the purpose
   Organize information and develop visualizations
   Consider layout and color

2. Prototype

3. Draft

4. Edit

5. Review

6. Field test

7. Publish

8. Perform postproject review

9. Maintain

12.4 Preparing Online Facilities

There is a great attraction to making technical manuals available on the computer. The positive reasons for doing so are these:

- Information is available whenever the computer is available. There is no need to locate the correct manual—which could cause a minor disruption if the proper manual is close by, or a major disruption if the manual must be retrieved from another building or person.

- Users do not need to allocate work space to opening up manuals. Paper manuals can be clumsy to use and can clutter a workspace.

- Information can be electronically updated rapidly and at low cost. Electronic dissemination of revisions ensures that out-of-date material cannot be retrieved inadvertently.

- Specific information necessary for a task can be located rapidly if the online manual offers electronic indexing or text searching. Searching for one page in a million can usually be done more quickly on a computer than with printed material.

- Authors can use graphics, sound, color, and animations that may be helpful in explaining complex actions and creating an engaging experience.

However, these positive attributes can be compromised by several potentially serious negative side effects:

- Displays may not be as readable as printed materials (Section 12.2).
- Displays may contain substantially less information than a sheet of paper, and the rate of paging is slow compared to the rate of paging through a manual. The display resolution is lower than that for paper, which is especially important when pictures or graphics are used.
- The command language of displays may be novel and confusing to novices. By contrast, most people are thoroughly familiar with the "command language" of paper manuals. The extra mental effort required for navigating through displays may interfere with concentration and learning.
- If the display is used for other work, it becomes a severe burden on the user's short-term memory if users have to switch between the work and the online manual. Users lose their context of work and have difficulty remembering what they read in the online manual. Multiple displays or windows provide a potential resolution for this problem.

Still, the online environment opens the door to a variety of helpful facilities that might not be practical in printed form. Relles and Price (1981) offer this list:

- Successively more detailed explanations of a displayed error message
- Successively more detailed explanations of a displayed question or prompt
- Successive examples of correct input or valid commands
- Explanation or definition of a specified term
- A description of the format of a specified command
- A list of allowable commands
- A display of specified sections of documentation
- A description of the current value of various system parameters
- Instruction on the use of the system
- News of interest to users of the system
- A list of available user aids

Houghton (1984) reviews online help facilities and points out the great difficulty in helping the novice user get started, as well as helping the expert user who needs one specific piece of information. Kearsley (1988) offers examples, empirical data about online help systems, and these guidelines:

- Make the help system easy to access and easy to return from.
- Make helps as specific as possible.
- Collect data to determine what helps are needed.

- Give users as much control over the help system as possible.
- Supply different helps for different types of users.
- Make help messages accurate and complete.
- Do not use helps to compensate for poor interface design.

12.4.1   Online manuals

Developers of traditional paper manuals are often proud of their work, and may be tempted to load the text automatically to make it available online. This course is attractive, but the results are likely to be less than optimal. Page layouts for paper may not be convertible to a useful online format, and dealing with the figures automatically is risky. The automatic conversion to online text is most attractive if the users have a display large enough to show a full page of text; then precise images of the printed text can be scanned in with text, figures, photographs, page numbers, etc. A close match between printed and online manuals can be useful, but if the quality of the displayed image is significantly lower than that of the printed version, users may prefer the paper.

Online manuals can be enhanced by availability of string search, multiple indices, tables of contents, tables of figures, electronic bookmarks, annotation, hypertext traversal, and automatic history keeping (Figure 12.5). The designers will be most effective if they can redesign the manuals to fit the electronic medium and to take advantage of multiple windows, text highlighting, color, sound, animation, and especially string search with relevance feedback.

Several workstation manufacturers have attempted to put their user manuals online. Symbolics was an early success, with 4000 pages online in such a convenient browser that many purchasers never removed the shrinkwrap plastic from their printed manuals (Walker, 1987). The growing availability of CD-ROM players has encouraged hardware suppliers such as Sun Microsystems to produce browsers for online manuals that were exact images of the printed manuals (Figure 12.6). Apple put its six-volume *Inside Macintosh* series for developers onto a single CD with scanned images and hypertext links. This HyperCard effort took only 1 month of intense effort (Bechtel, 1990). A vital feature for online manuals is a properly designed table of contents that can remain visible to the side of the page of text. Selection of a chapter or other entry in the table of contents should immediately produce the appropriate page on the display. Expanding or contracting tables of contents (Egan et al., 1989) or multiple panes to show several levels at once are beneficial (Chimera and Shneiderman, 1991).

A more primitive approach to online manuals is the UNIX man facility, which has textual descriptions of each command and its options. Users must know the command names to find the material, but a clever and simple system called apropos helps substantially. The apropos file contains the name

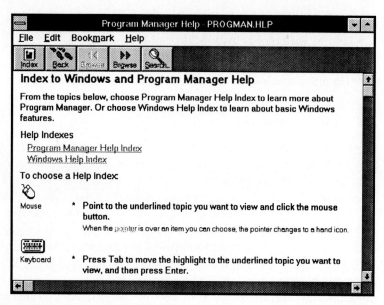

Figure 12.5

Microsoft Windows 3.0 has an elaborate online help with an index, bookmarks, definition buttons, and other features to assist navigation. (Screen shot ©1985–1991 Microsoft Corporation. Reprinted with permission from Microsoft Corporation, Redmond, WA.)

of each UNIX command with a carefully written one line description. Users can type `apropos sort` to get this listing and then display the manual pages:

```
sortm                    - sort messages
comm                     - select, reject lines common to
                           two sorted files
look                     - find lines in a sorted file
qsort                    - quick sort
scandir, alphasort       - scan a directory
sort                     - sort or merge files
sortbib                  - sort bibliographic database
tsort                    - topological sort
```

This approach can work some of the time, but seems to be more effective for experienced than for novice users.

Searching through the full text of online manuals is increasingly rapid, and the user-interface strategies are being refined steadily. An expanding and contracting table of contents was combined with string search and relevance feedback indicating number of "hits" on the table of contents listing (Egan et

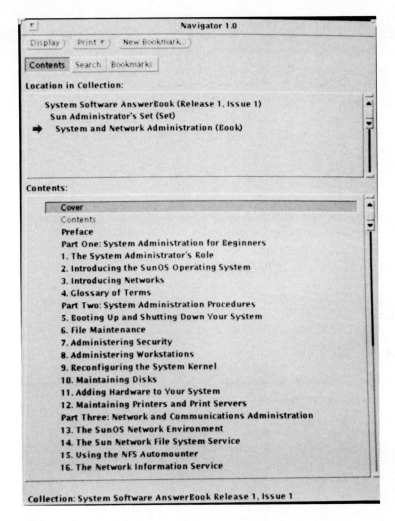

Figure 12.6

Sun Microsystems online CD-ROM Answerbook contains 16,000 exact images of printed manual pages. The powerful Navigator tool allows users to type in free-form sentences or lists of keywords, and returns a set of relevance ranked documents. This figure shows the table of contents viewer that allows users to click on the chapter or section to produce the full page of text and diagrams. Cross-references in the text can be clicked on to jump to the related document. (Copyright 1991 Sun Microsystems, Inc. Reprinted with permission of Sun Microsystems, Inc., Billerica, MA.)

al., 1989). A series of three empirical studies showed the effects of several improvements and the advantage over print versions of the same document. The electronic version was advantageous, especially when the search questions contained words that were in the document headings or text.

12.4.2   Keyword and keystroke lists

Online help that offers concise descriptions of the command syntax and semantics is probably most effective for intermittent knowledgeable users, but is likely to be difficult for novices who have more need for tutorial training. The traditional approach is to have the user type or select a help menu item, and to display six or 60 or 600 alphabetically arranged command names for which there is a paragraph or more of help that the user can retrieve by typing help followed by the command name. This method can also work, but it is often frustrating for the users who are not sure of the correct name for the task they wish to accomplish; for example, the name might be search, query, select, browse, find, reveal, display, info, or view. They may see several familiar terms but not know which one to select to accomplish their task. Worse still, there may not be a single command that accomplishes the task, and there is usually little information about how to assemble commands to perform tasks.

Designers can improve *keyword lists* by clustering keywords into meaningful categories, and indicating a starter set of commands for novices. Users may also be able to set the level of detail and the kind of information (for example, descriptions with or without options, examples, complete syntax) they obtain about each command.

Two other useful lists might be of *keystrokes* or *menu items*. Each might have an accompanying feature description, such as the first few lines from WordPerfect's help list:

```
Key            Feature                        Key Name
Ctrl-F5        Add Password                   Text In/out,2
Shft-F7        Additional Printers            Print,S
Shft-F8        Advance Up, Down or Line       Format,4
Ctrl-PgUp      Advanced Macros                Macro Commands
Ctrl-F10       Advanced Macros, Help on       Macro Definition
Shft-F8        Align/Decimal Character        Format,4
```

12.4.3   Context-sensitive help

Many designers recognized that the keyword lists were overwhelming and that users probably wanted to have local information about the task that they were performing. They developed *context-sensitive help*, in which users get different messages from the help processor, depending on where they are in the software. Help inside a dialog box produces a window with information about that dialog box, preferably in a nearby pop-up window.

Another approach to context-sensitive help in form-fillin or menu systems is to have the user position the cursor and then press F1 or a help key to produce information about the item on which the cursor is resting. A subtle variation is to use a mouse to click on a help button or a ? to turn the cursor into a question mark. Then, the cursor is dropped on a field, icon, or menu item, and a pop-up window describes that item. In an accelerated version of this technique, the user simply drags the cursor over items, and the items reply by popping up small windows with their explanations. This strategy is the idea behind Apple's System 7.0 Balloon help (Figure 12.7).

A variant of Balloon help is to turn on all the balloons at once, so that the user can see all the explanations simultaneously. A mode switch might change from the balloons to a set of marks that indicate which parts of the display are clickable, double-clickable, draggable, etc.

12.4.4   Online tutorials, demonstrations, and animations

First-time users of a software package need an interactive tutorial environment in which the computer instructs the user to carry out commands right on the system. One introductory tutorial for the Lotus 1-2-3 package displays the exact keystrokes the user must type and then carries out the commands.

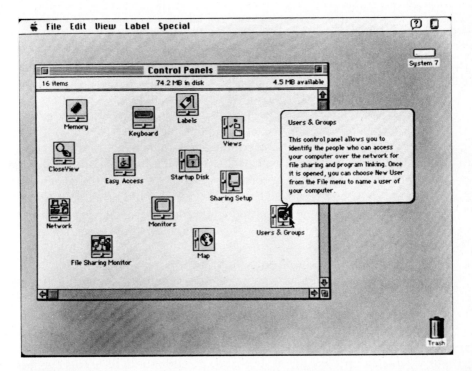

Figure 12.7

Apple's System 7.0 balloon help pops up a single balloon with an explanation of the item on which the cursor is resting. Users can turn off the balloon help. (Various System 7.0 graphic illustrations, and icons Copyright Apple Computer, Inc., used with permission. Cupertino, CA.)

The user can type the exact keystrokes or just keep pressing the space bar to speed through the demonstration. Some users find this technique attractive; others are put off by the restrictive sequencing that prevents errors and exploration.

Online tutorials can be effective because the user (Al-Awar et al., 1981)

- Does not have to keep shifting attention between the terminal and the instructional material
- Practices the skills needed to use the system
- Can work alone at an individual pace and without the embarrassment of mistakes made before a human instructor or fellow students

Creators of interactive tutorials must address the usual questions of instructional design and also with the novelty of the computer environment. Repeated testing and refinement is highly recommended (Al-Awar et al., 1981).

Demonstration (demo) disks have become a modern high-tech art form. Someday soon, someone should start a museum of demo disks to preserve these innovative, flashy, and slick byproducts of the computer era. Demo disks are designed to attract potential users of software or hardware by showing off system features using the best animations, color graphics, sound, and information presentation that advertising agencies can produce. The technical requirement to fit on a single diskette makes it a still greater challenge. Animated text (words zooming, flipping, or spinning), varied transitions (fades, wipes, mosaics, or dissolves), sound effects, bright graphics, and finally an address or telephone number to use for ordering the software are typical. The user-interface requirements are to capture and maintain the users's interest, while conveying information and building a positive product image. Automatic pacing or manual control satisfies hands-off or hands-on users, respectively. Sessions should be alterable to suit the user who wants a 3-minute introduction and the user who wants a 1-hour in-depth treatment. Additional control to be able to stop, replay, or skip parts adds to the acceptability.

Animations as part of online help are still rare, but improved hardware and increased competition are promoting attempts. A simple and ingenious approach is to animate the action icons in a display to give a quick demonstration of usage (Baecker et al., 1991). An artist created brief animations for the 18 icons in the HyperCard tool menu (paint brush, lasso, eraser, etc.) that ran within each icon's 20- by 22-pixel box. A usability test was conducted to refine the designs and to demonstrate their effectiveness: "In every case in which static icons were not understood, the dynamic icons were successful in conveying the purpose of the tool." Another approach to animated help showed sequences of menu or icon selections that performed a complex task, such as moving a block of text (Sukaviriya and Foley, 1990).

This project had a further goal of generating the animations automatically from task descriptions.

12.4.5   Helpful guides

Sometimes, users need more than just a machine to guide their learning. A friendly helper, such as the marketing manager for the software, or a famous personality, or a cartoon character, can guide users through some body of knowledge. Introductions to online services such as CompuServe and Prodigy typically welcomes new users and offers guidance about which features to begin using.

In designing a museum database, we planned to have a major international authority lead the users through the database, just as the audio cassettes of J. Carter Brown leads visitors through the National Gallery of Art in Washington, DC. A similar pioneering effort was the GUIDES 3.0 project, in which a Native American chief, a settler wife, or a cavalry man appear as small photographs on the display to guide readers through the materials by offering their points of view on the settling of the American west (Oren et al., 1990). When selected, the guides tell their stories through video sequences from laser disk. In addition, a modern woman is available in TV format to help guide the readers through using the system. This approach does not anthropomorphize the computer, but rather makes the computer a medium of communication, much like a book enables the author to speak to readers by way of the printed page.

12.4.6   Natural-language and intelligent help

Natural-language dialog was proposed for interactive learning about an operating-system command language (Shapiro and Kwasny, 1975). The prototype was engaging and occasionally successful in helping users, but this strategy has not yet been refined sufficiently for widespread use. Various attempts to develop intelligent advisors have been made over the years (Wilensky et al., 1984), but this interaction style has not yet been successful in communicating effectively with users. An optimistic discussion of advice-giving expert systems (Carroll and McKendree, 1987) laments the lack of behavioral research and focuses on issues such as these: In what ways do people voluntarily restrict their use of natural language when interacting with a recognition facility? Can user models that incorporate learning transitions and trajectories (as well as end states) be developed? A simulated "intelligent help" system was tested with eight users doing business tasks, such as printing a mailing list (Carroll and Aaronson, 1988). The researchers prepared messages for expected error conditions, but they found that "people are incredibly creative in generating errors and misconceptions, and incredibly fast." The results, even with a simulated system, were mixed; the authors concluded that "development of intelligent help systems faces serious usability challenges."

12.4.7   Experimental results

The contrast between novice and expert users was demonstrated in an early study (Relles, 1979) with a simple bank-account management system that had a 37-page paper user manual. In a pilot study, six computer-naive subjects were each given 30 minutes to read the manual. The subjects then had to carry out a set of tasks using the command language. Half the subjects were given access to online help, or aides, but this group had "exceptionally poor performance" as compared to the group that had access to only the printed manual. Apparently, the group using the online help had difficulty using them, and the existence of the help was a distraction from the task. Relles wrote: "The provision of online aides did have an adverse effect on user performance, and subjects who used the aides had significantly less confidence in their ability to use the system without a manual."

After redesigning the online help, Relles ran his main experiment by testing 30 subjects who had had interactive computer experience. After all subjects read the manual for 20 minutes, they carried out a set of tasks. Those with only the paper manual took 42 minutes; those with carefully designed online help took only 30 minutes. The availability of online help significantly increased users' confidence that they could use the system without a manual.

Dunsmore (1980) also found that novice users had difficulty with online help. Apparently, the printed version could be accessed more quickly, whereas the online version interrupted and delayed problem solving in this menu-searching environment.

More positive results demonstrating the efficacy of online help facilities come from a study with 72 novice users of a text editor (Cohill and Williges, 1982). A control group receiving no online help facilities was compared with groups in eight experimental conditions formed from all combinations of initiation (user versus computer causes the help session to begin), presentation (printed manual versus online), and selection of topics (user versus computer selects which material is displayed). The control group with no online facilities performed significantly less well than the experimental groups (Table 12.3). Of the eight experimental groups, the best performance was achieved by the user-initiated, user-selected, and printed-manual group.

A well-designed help facility is more beneficial than a poorly designed help facility. Magers (1983) revised an online help facility to offer context-sensitive help instead of keyword-indexed help, wrote tutorial screens in addition to the reference material, reduced computer jargon, used examples instead of a mathematical notation, provided an online dictionary of command synonyms, and wrote task-oriented rather than computer-oriented

Table 12.3

Results from a study comparing nine configurations of online help facilities (Cohill and Williges, 1982).

Initiation	Presentation	Selection	Time in Subtask	Errors per Subtask	Commands /Subtask	Subtasks Completed
user	manual	user	293.1	0.4	8.4	5.0
user	manual	system	442.2	2.0	17.7	4.9
user	online	user	350.9	1.1	13.5	5.0
user	online	system	382.2	1.8	17.6	4.9
system	manual	user	367.9	1.3	13.1	4.8
system	manual	system	399.1	0.9	13.8	4.9
system	online	user	425.9	2.8	15.1	5.0
system	online	system	351.5	1.2	13.7	4.9
Control: No help available			679.1	5.0	20.2	3.4

help screens. Thirty computer novices were split into two groups; half received the original and half the modified help facility. The subjects with the revised help achieved a task score of 90.6, compared with 43.0 for the other subjects. Time was reduced from 75.6 to 52.0 minutes with the improved help facility. Subjective-satisfaction scores also strongly favored the revised help facility.

Borenstein (1985) studied 16 novices and 12 expert computer users performing 22 tasks that required online help. The standard UNIX man system for manual reading was compared with improved texts delivered by Borenstein's ACRONYM system, a hybrid using man texts delivered by ACRONYM, a simulated natural-language system, and an everpresent human tutor. The human tutor led to significantly faster times, and the content of the texts appeared to be a more important factor than the format of the delivery system. The standard man system produced the poorest performance.

In summary, the experiments reveal that online help is not always more useful than hardcopy manuals; in fact, it may be less useful. Paper manuals are more familiar, can be examined without disrupting computer use, are faster to use, and do not require learning of additional commands. A second display or window may be necessary to make online help attractive when compared with paper manuals. Still, the advantage of helpful online information is considerable when no paper manual is available. Since users may not have access to printed manuals, some online facility is strongly recommended. Contemporary software without some form of online help will be seen as deficient by most reviewers. The form and content of the online help facility make a profound difference. Good writing, task-orientation, context sensitivity, and command examples may all contribute to improved online help.

12.5 Practitioner's Summary

Paper manuals, online help, and tutorials play an important role in the success or failure of a software or hardware product. Sufficient personnel, money, and time should be assigned to these support materials. A user manual should be developed before the implementation. Online manuals and help are attractive, but the poor readability, small size, and slow display rate of most displays are serious limitations. As technology matures and designers develop effective methods, online manuals and help are likely to become standard. Online help should be written with a specific user community in mind to accomplish specific goals (offering task concepts, computer concepts, or syntactic knowledge), while avoiding the difficulties of using online help (too many extra commands to learn, losing the context of work, requiring memorization of information from the help screen, flooding with irrelevant information, etc.). However, even excellent manuals or tutorials cannot be relied on to overcome the problems of a poorly designed user interface. Online help should be written lucidly, access should be offered conveniently, and contents should be reviewed and tested carefully. High-quality manuals, online help, and tutorials have a profound effect on users' success and on users' impressions of most interactive systems.

12.6 Researcher's Agenda

One important problem in human factors of computer systems is under-standing why displays are more difficult to read than are paper documents. Higher-resolution and larger, faster displays have definitely improved readability. Some designers may even dream of making displays more readable than paper. The main advantage of online materials is the poten-tial for rapid retrieval and traversal of large databases, but little is known about how to offer this advantage conveniently without overwhelming the user. The cognitive model of turning pages in a book is too simple, but users can easily get lost if more elaborate networks or multiple-level trees are used. Writing styles have a profound effect on comprehension, and a better understanding of when each style is most effective would be helpful. Multiple windows can help users by allowing the users to see the problem and the online help or tutorial at the same time, but the strategies are only beginning to be explored. Cognitive models of how people learn to use computer systems could aid designers of tutorials, manuals, and online help.

References

Al-Awar, J., Chapanis, A., and Ford, W. R., Tutorials for the first-time computer user, *IEEE Transactions on Professional Communication PC-24* (1981), 30–37.

Baecker, Ronald, Small, Ian, and Mander, Richard, Bringing icons to life, *Proc. CHI'91 Human Factors in Computer Systems*, ACM, New York (1991), 1–6.

Bechtel, Brian, Inside Macintosh as hypertext. In Rizk, A., Streitz, N., and Andre, J. (Editors), *Hypertext: Concepts, Systems and Applications*, Cambridge University Press, Cambridge, U.K. (1990).

Bender, W., Crespo, R. A., Kennedy, P. J., and Oakley, R., CRT typeface design and evaluation, *Proc. Human Factors Society Thirty-First Annual Meeting*, Human Factors Society, Santa Monica, CA (1987), 1311–1314.

Borenstein, Nathaniel S., *The Design and Evaluation of On-Line Help Systems*, Ph.D. dissertation, Department of Computer Science, Carnegie–Mellon University, Pittsburgh, PA (1985).

Brockman, R. John, *Writing Better Computer User Documentation: From Paper to Hypertext: Version 2.0*, John Wiley and Sons, New York (1990).

Cakir, A., Hart, D. J., and Stewart, T. F. M., *Visual Display Terminals: A Manual Covering Ergonomics, Workplace Design, Health and Safety, Task Organization*, John Wiley and Sons, New York (1980).

Carroll, J. M., Minimalist training, *Datamation 30*, 18 (1984), 125–136.

Carroll, J. M. and Aaronson, Amy P., Learning by doing with simulated intelligent help, *Communications of the ACM 31*, 9 (September 1988), 1064–1079.

Carroll, J. M. and Mack, R. L., Learning to use a word processor: By doing, by thinking, and by knowing. In Thomas, J. C., and Schneider, M. (Editors), *Human Factors in Computing Systems*, Ablex, Norwood, NJ (1984), 13–51.

Carroll, J. M. and McKendree, Jean, Interface design issues for advice-giving expert systems, *Communications of the ACM 30*, 1 (January 1987), 14–31.

Chapanis, Alphonse, Words, words, words, *Human Factors 7* (1965), 1–17.

Chimera, Richard and Shneiderman, Ben, Evaluating three interfaces for browsing tables of contents, Department of Computer Science, University of Maryland (unpublished manuscript).

Cohill, A. M. and Williges, Robert C., Computer-augmented retrieval of HELP information for novice users, *Proc. Human Factors Society—Twenty-Sixth Annual Meeting* (1982), 79–82.

Creed, A., Dennis, I., and Newstead, S., Effects of display format on proof-reading on VDUs, *Behaviour and Information Technology 7*, 4 (1988), 467–478.

Duffy, Thomas, Palmer, James, and Mehlenbacher, Brad, *Online Help Systems: Theory and Practice*, Ablex, Norwood, NJ (1992).

Dunsmore, H. E., Designing an interactive facility for non-programmers, *Proc. ACM National Conference* (1980), 475–483.

Egan, Dennis E., Remde, Joel R., Gomez, Louis M., Landauer, Thomas K., Eberhardt, Jennifer, and Lochbum, Carol C., Formative design-evaluation of SuperBook, *ACM Transactions on Information Systems 7*, 1 (January 1989), 30–57.

Foss, D., Rosson, M. B., and Smith, P., Reducing manual labor: An experimental analysis of learning aids for a text editor, *Proc. Human Factors in Computer Systems*, ACM, Washington, DC (March 1982).

Francas, M., Goodman, D., and Dickinson, J., Command-set and presentation method in the training of Telidon operators, *Proc. Human Factors Society—Twenty-Sixth Annual Meeting*, Human Factors Society, Santa Monica, CA (1982), 752–755.

General Electric Information Services Company, *Documentation Style Manual* (December 1981).

Gould, John, and Grischkowsky, Nancy, Doing the same work with hardcopy and with cathode ray tube (CRT) terminals, *Human Factors 26* (1984), 323–337.

Gould, J., Alfaro, L., Barnes, V., Finn, R., Grischkowsky, N., and Minuto, A., Reading is slower from CRT displays than from paper: Attempts to isolate a single-variable explanation, *Human Factors 29*, 3 (1987a), 269–299.

Gould, J., Alfaro, L., Finn, R., Haupt, B., and Minuto, A., Reading from CRT displays can be as fast as reading from paper, *Human Factors 29*, 5 (1987b), 497–517.

Grandjean, E. and Vigliani, E. (Editors), *Ergonomic Aspects of Visual Display Terminals*, Taylor and Francis, Ltd., London (1982).

Grant, Allan, Homo quintadus, computers and ROOMS (repetitive ocular orthopedic motion stress), *Optometry and Vision Science 67*, 4 (1990), 297–305.

Hansen, Wilfred J., Doring, Richard, and Whitlock, Lawrence R., Why an examination was slower on-line than on paper, *International Journal of Man–Machine Studies 10* (1978), 507–519.

Hansen, Wilfred J. and Haas, Christine, Reading and writing with computers: a framework for explaining differences in performance, *Communications of the ACM 31*, 9 (1988), 1080–1089.

Heines, Jesse M., *Screen Design Strategies for Computer-Assisted Instruction*, Digital Press, Bedford, MA (1984).

Helander, Martin G., Design of visual displays. In Salvendy, Gavriel (Editor), *Handbook of Human Factors*, John Wiley and Sons, New York (1987), 507–548.

Horton, William K., *Designing and Writing Online Documentation: Help Files to Hypertext*, John Wiley and Sons, New York (1990).

Houghton, Raymond C., Online help systems: A conspectus, *Communications of the ACM 27*, 2 (February 1984), 126–133.

IBM Santa Teresa Laboratory, *Ease-of-Use Reference*, Santa Teresa, CA (undated).

Kearsley, Greg, *Online Help Systems: Design and Implementation*, Ablex, Norwood, NJ (1988).

Koubek, Richard J. and Janardan, Chaya Garg, A basis for explaining the conflicting results in performance on CRT and paper displays, *Proc. Human Factors Society— Twenty-Ninth Annual Meeting*, Human Factors Society, Santa Monica, CA (1985), 1102–1105.

Mager, Robert F., *Preparing Instructional Objectives*, Fearon, Palo Alto, CA (1962).

Magers, Celeste S., An experimental evaluation of on-line HELP for non-programmers, *Proc. CHI'83 Conference: Human Factors in Computing Systems*, ACM, New York (1983), 277–281.

Morariu, Janis, Human factors for design and evaluation of software, *ASIS Bulletin*, 11 (October–November 1985), 18–19.

Oborne, David J. and Holton, Doreen, Reading from screen versus paper: There is no difference, *International Journal of Man–Machine Studies 28* (1988), 1–9.

Oren, Tim, Salomon, Gitta, Kreitman, Kristee, and Don, Abbe, Guides: Characterizing the interface. In Laurel, Brenda (Editor), *The Art of Human–Computer Interface Design*, Addison Wesley, Reading, MA (1990), 367–381.

Parton, Diana, Huffman, Keith, Pridgen, Patty, Norman, Kent, and Shneiderman, Ben, Learning a menu selection tree: Training methods compared, *Behaviour and Information Technology 4*, 2 (1985), 81–91.

Price, Jonathan, and staff, *How to Write a Computer Manual*, Benjamin/Cummings, Addison-Wesley, Reading, MA (1984).

Relles, Nathan, *The Design and Implementation of User-Oriented Systems*, Ph.D. dissertation, Technical Report 357, Department of Computer Science, University of Wisconsin, Madison, WI (July 1979).

Relles, Nathan and Price, Lynne A., A user interface for online assistance, *Proc. Fifth International Conference on Software Engineering*, IEEE, Silver Spring, MD (1981).

Relles, N., Sondheimer, N., and Ingargiola, G., A unified approach to online assistance, *Proc. AFIPS National Computer Conference 50*, AFIPS Press, Arlington, VA (1981), 383–388.

Roemer, Joan M. and Chapanis, Alphonse, Learning performance and attitudes as a function of the reading grade level of a computer-presented tutorial, *Proc. Human Factors in Computer Systems*, ACM, Washington, DC (1982), 239–244.

Shapiro, Stuart C. and Kwasny, Stanley C., Interactive consulting via natural language, *Communications of the ACM 18*, 8 (August 1975), 459–462.

Shurtleff, D. A., *How to Make Displays Legible*, Human Interface Design, La Mirada, CA (1980).

Sohr, Dana, Better software manuals, *BYTE Magazine 8* (May 1983), 286–294.

Strunk, William, Jr. and White, E. B., *The Elements of Style* (Third Edition), Macmillan, New York (1979).

Sukaviriya, Piyawadee "Noi" and Foley, James D., Coupling a UI framework with automatic generation of context-sensitive animated help, *Proc. User Interface Software and Technology 3*, ACM, New York (1990), 152–166.

Sullivan, Marc A. and Chapanis, Alphonse, Human factoring a text editor manual, *Behaviour and Information Technology 2*, 2 (1983), 113–125.

Wagner, Carl B., Quality control methods for IBM computer manuals, *Journal of Technical Writing and Communication 10*, 2 (1980), 93–102.

Walker, Janet, Issues and strategies for online documentation, *IEEE Transactions on Professional Communication PC 30* (1987), 235–248.

Wilensky, R., Arens, Y., and Chin, D., Talking to UNIX in English: An overview of UC, *Communications of the ACM 27*, 6 (June 1984), 574–593.

Wright, P. and Lickorish, A., Proof-reading texts on screen and paper, *Behaviour and Information Technology 2*, 3 (1983), 227–235.

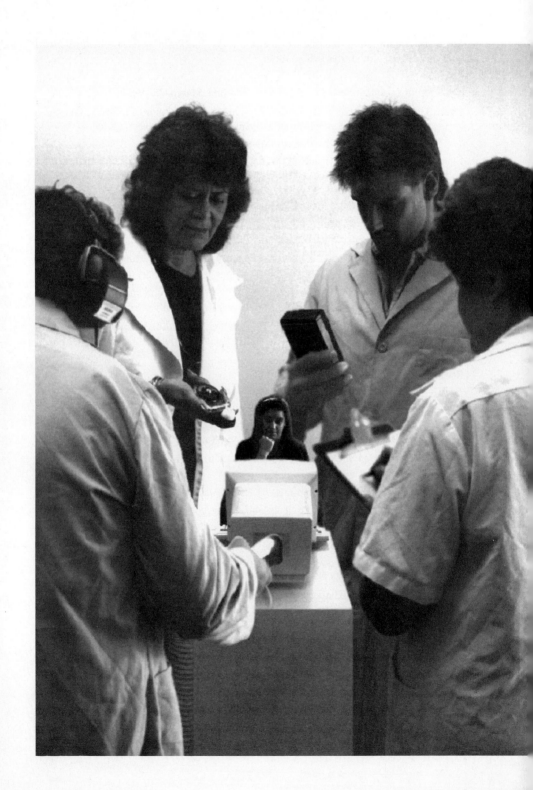

CHAPTER 13

Iterative Design, Testing, and Evaluation

Just as we can assert that no product has ever been created in a single moment of inspiration . . . nobody has ever produced a set of requirements for any product in a similarly miraculous manner. These requirements may well begin with an inspirational moment but, almost certainly, the emergent bright idea will be developed by iterative processes of evaluation until it is thought to be worth starting to put pencil to paper. Especially when the product is entirely new, the development of a set of requirements may well depend upon testing initial ideas in some depth.

Mayall, W. H., *Principles in Design*, 1979

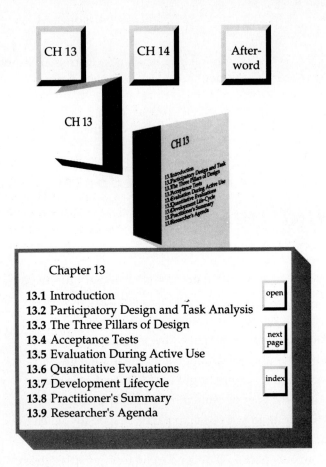

13.1   Introduction

In the first decades of computer software development, senior programmers designed text editors, operating-system control languages, programming languages, and applications packages for themselves and their peers. Now, the user population for control rooms, office automation, home and personal computing, and point-of-sales terminals is so vastly different that senior programmers' experience may be irrelevant, and their intuitions may be inappropriate. Designs must be validated through prototype, usability, and acceptance tests, which can also provide a finer understanding of user performance and capabilities.

The egocentric style of the past must yield to humility and a genuine desire to accommodate to the user's skills, wishes, and orientation. Designers must seek more direct interaction with the users during the design phase, during the development process, and throughout the system lifecycle.

Iterative design methods that allow early testing of prototypes, revisions based on feedback from users, and incremental refinements suggested by test administrators are necessary to arrive at a successful system.

Corporate marketing departments are aware of these issues and are a source of constructive encouragement. When more than 200 suppliers provide similar word-processing packages, human engineering is vital for product acceptance. Many organizations have created usability laboratories to conduct videotaped tests of products during development. Typical users are brought in to try out the system, to perform benchmark tasks, and to suggest improvements (Hirsch, 1981; Good et al., 1984; Whiteside et al., 1988; Klemmer, 1989).

Many organizations maintain a human-factors group or a usability laboratory that is a source of experience and expertise in testing techniques (Thomas, 1984; Gould et al., 1991). In some cases, this resource is not used because the group members are not familiar with the application area, are seen as outsiders, or must be paid as though they were external consultants. Development projects might be better served if a human-factors role were assigned to a project team member, or to several members if the project is large. The *user-interface architect* for a project would develop the necessary skills for the project, manage the work of other people, prepare budgets and schedules, and coordinate with internal and external human-factors professionals when further expertise, references to the literature, or experimental tests were required. This dual strategy balances the needs for centralized expertise and decentralized application. It enables professional growth in the user-interface area and in the application domain (for example geographic information, medical laboratory instruments, or legal systems).

As projects grow in complexity, size, and importance, role specialization will emerge, as it has in architecture, aerospace, and book design. Eventually, individuals will become highly skilled in such specific problems as user-interface management systems, graphic display algorithms, voice and audio tone design, and message, menu, or online tutorial writing. Consultation with graphic artists, book designers, advertising copy writers, instructional text-book authors, or film-animation creators may be useful. Perceptive system developers will recognize and employ psychologists for experimental testing, sociologists for evaluating organizational impact, educational psychologists for refining training procedures, and social workers for guiding user consultants or customer-service personnel.

13.2   Participatory Design and Task Analysis

Many authors have urged participatory design strategies (Olson and Ives, 1981; Mumford, 1983; Ives and Olson, 1984; Gould and Lewis, 1985; Gould et al., 1991), but the concept is controversial. The arguments in favor suggest that more user involvement brings more accurate information about tasks, an opportunity to argue over design decisions, the sense of participation that builds ego investment in successful implementation, and the potential for increased user acceptance of the final system (Baroudi et al., 1986).

On the other hand, extensive user involvement may be costly and may lengthen the implementation period, build antagonism with people who are not involved or whose suggestions are rejected, force designers to compromise their design to satisfy incompetent participants, and simply build opposition to implementation (Ives and Olson, 1984).

The social and political environment surrounding the implementation of a complex information system is not amenable to study by controlled experimentation. Social and industrial psychologists are interested in these issues, but dependable strategies may never emerge. The sensitive project leader must judge each case on its merits and decide on the right level of user involvement. The personalities of the design team and the users are such critical determinants that experts in group dynamics and social psychology may be useful as consultants.

The experienced user-interface architect knows that organizational politics and the preferences of individuals may be more important than the technical issues in governing the success of an interactive system. The warehouse managers who see their position threatened by an interactive system that provides senior managers with up-to-date information through the latter's terminals will ensure that the system fails by delaying data entry or by being less than diligent in guaranteeing data accuracy. The system designer should take into account the effect on users, and should solicit their participation to ensure that all concerns are made explicit early enough to avoid "counterimplementation" (Keen, 1981).

Collecting information from potential users about the range and frequency of tasks is still more of an art learned through experience than a science that can be made into a predictable process. Often, the range of tasks is specified by an existing manual or computer-based system for which some improvements are proposed. A table of users and tasks, and of the relative frequency with which each user performs each task, can be helpful. Another analysis tool is a table of task sequences, indicating which tasks follow other tasks. Often, a flowchart or transition diagram helps people to record and convey the sequences of possible actions. In less well-defined projects, we have found day-in-the-life scenarios helpful to characterize what happens when typical users perform typical tasks. During the early design stages, data about current performance should be collected to provide a baseline. Information about similar systems can be gathered, and interviews can be conducted with interested parties, such as users and managers.

Design is inherently creative and unpredictable. Interactive system designers must blend a thorough knowledge of technical feasibility with a mystical esthetic sense of what attracts users. Carroll and Rosson (1985) characterize design in this way:

- Design is a *process*; it is not a state and it cannot be adequately represented statically.
- The design process is *nonhierarchical*; it is neither strictly bottom-up nor strictly top-down.
- The process is *radically transformational*; it involves the development of partial and interim solutions that may ultimately play no role in the final design.
- Design intrinsically involves the *discovery of new goals*.

These characterizations of design convey the dynamic nature of the process. But in every creative domain, there can also be discipline, refined techniques, wrong and right methods, and measures of success. Once the early data collection and preliminary requirements are established, more detailed design and early development can begin. Fortunately, these stages are well understood, and reliable practices can be employed. The techniques described in the next section are meant to help designers to structure and channel the design process.

13.3   The Three Pillars of Design

The three pillars described in this section can help user-interface architects to turn good ideas into a successful system (Figure 13.1). They are not guaranteed to work, but experience has shown that each pillar can produce an order-of-magnitude speedup in the process and can facilitate the creation of excellent systems.

13.3.1   Guidelines documents

Early in the design process, the user-interface architect should generate, or require other people to generate, a set of working guidelines. This might be two people working for 1 week to produce a 10-page document, or a dozen people working for 2 years to produce a 300-page document. One component of Apple's success with the Macintosh was its early and readable guidelines document that provided a clear set of principles for the many applications developers to follow so as to ensure a harmony in design across products. IBM's *System Application Architecture (SAA) Common User Access (CUA)* documents appeared later, and it will take many years for applications developers to adhere to those guidelines. These and other guidelines

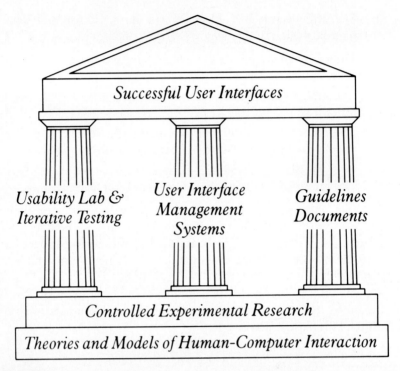

Figure 13.1

Three pillars of successful user-interface development (usability laboratories for iterative testing, User Interface Management Systems, and guidelines documents) rest on a foundation of theories and experimental research.

documents are referenced and are described briefly in the general reference section at the end of Chapter 1.

Each project has different needs, but guidelines should be considered for

- Screen-layout issues
  - Menu selection, form fillin, and dialog-box formats
  - Wording of prompts, feedback, and error messages
  - Data entry and display formats for items and lists
  - Terminology, abbreviations, capitalization, and justification
  - Character set, faces, fonts, icons, markers, line thickness, and white space
  - Use of color, highlighting, blinking, and inverse video
- Input and output devices
  - Keyboard, display, cursor control, and pointing devices
  - Audible sounds, touch input, and other special devices
  - Screen layout and use of multiple windows
  - Response times and display rates

- Action sequences
  - Direct-manipulation clicking, dragging, and gestures
  - Command syntax, semantics, and sequences
  - Programmed function keys
  - Recovery procedures
- Training
  - Online help and tutorials
  - Training and reference materials

Controversial guidelines can be reviewed by colleagues or tested empirically. Procedures must be established to distribute the guidelines, to ensure enforcement, to allow exceptions, and to permit enhancements. A three-level approach of rigid standards, accepted practices, and flexible guidelines may be useful to clarify which items are firmer and which items are easier to change.

The creation of a guidelines document (Table 13.1) at the beginning of an implementation project focuses attention on the interface design and provides an opportunity for discussion of controversial issues. When the guideline is adopted by the development team, the implementation proceeds quickly and with fewer design changes.

13.3.2   User-interface management systems and rapid prototyping tools

One difficulty in designing interactive systems is that the customer and the user may not have a clear idea of what the system will look like when it is

Table 13.1

Recommendations for guidelines documents.

Guidelines Documents
- Provide social process for developers
- Record decisions for all parties to see
- Promote consistency and completeness
- Facilitate automation of design
- Present philosophy
- Provide examples of
  Screen-layout issues
  Input–output devices
  Action sequences
  Training
- Multiple levels are possible:
  Rigid standards
  Accepted practices
  Flexible guidelines
- Enforcement, exemption, and enhancement policies

done. Since interactive systems are novel in many situations, the users may not realize the implications of design decisions. Unfortunately, it is difficult, costly, and time consuming to make major changes to systems once they have been implemented.

Even though this problem has no complete solution, some of the more serious difficulties can be avoided if, at an early stage, the customers and users can be given a realistic impression of what the final system will look like (Clark, 1981; Savage et al., 1982; Gould and Lewis, 1985). A printed version of the proposed displays is helpful for pilot tests, but an onscreen display with an active keyboard is more realistic. For some applications, a word-processor–generated display may be sufficient; in other situations, it may be useful to have the software drive a series of displays. The simulation or prototype of a menu system may only have one or two paths active instead of the thousands of paths in the final system. For a command-language system, the simulation may support the command for a minute fraction of the available options.

An imaginative approach that was first used in testing a speech-input device was to create a mockup of the system with a person simulating the hoped-for computer performance (Gould et al., 1983). This *Wizard of Oz approach* (in the Frank L. Baum story and movie, the Wizard was created by a charlatan operating from behind a curtain) has been used to test advanced concepts such as automatic macro creation, natural-language interaction, and help systems.

Since rapid prototyping is increasingly recognized as a valuable approach, there is a growing number of software support tools available (see Chapter 14). In some cases, the framework built for the prototype can become the basis for the actual implementation. *User-interface management systems* (UIMS) that permit quick implementations are increasingly available.

13.3.3   Usability laboratories and iterative testing

Theatrical producers know that extensive rehearsals are necessary to ensure a successful opening night. Early rehearsals may require only one or two performers wearing street clothes; but, as opening night approaches, dress rehearsals with the full cast, props, and lighting are expected. Aircraft designers carry out wind-tunnel tests, build plywood mockups of the cabin layout, construct complete simulations of the cockpit, and thoroughly flight test the first prototype. Similarly, interactive system designers are now recognizing that they must carry out many small and some large pilot tests of system components before release to customers (Dumas and Redish, in press). A professional society of *usability-laboratory* staff is being formed.

Procedures vary greatly depending on the goals of the usability study, the number of expected users, the dangers of errors, and the level of investment.

Subjects should be chosen to represent the intended user communities, with attention to background in computing, experience with the task, motivation, education, and ability with the natural language used in the interface. Investigators also must control for physical concerns, such as eyesight, left versus right handedness, age, and gender—and for other experimental conditions such as time of day, day of week, physical surroundings, noise, room temperature, and level of distractions.

Subjects should always be treated with respect and should be informed that it is not *they* who are being tested, but rather it is the software and user interface that are under study. They should be informed about what they will be doing (for example, typing text into a computer, creating a drawing using a mouse, or getting information from a touchscreen-based kiosk) and how long they will be expected to stay. Participation should always be voluntary, and *informed consent* should be obtained. We ask all subjects to read and sign this statement:

- I have freely volunteered to participate in this experiment.
- I have been informed in advance what my task(s) will be and what procedures will be followed.
- I have been given the opportunity to ask questions, and have had my questions answered to my satisfaction.
- I am aware that I have the right to withdraw consent and to discontinue participation at any time, without prejudice to my future treatment.
- My signature below may be taken as affirmation of all the above statements; it was given prior to my participation in this study.

Psychology undergraduates are frequent participants in experiments. When we were testing a touchscreen cash-register design, however, we solicited and paid local cashiers; when we were testing a home automation system, we solicited volunteer retirees.

Early pilot studies can be conducted using typewritten versions of screen displays to assess user reactions to wording, layout, and sequencing. A test administrator plays the role of the computer by flipping the pages while asking a potential user to carry out a set of carefully chosen tasks. This informal testing is inexpensive and rapid, and usually is productive.

Pilot tests can be run to compare design alternatives, to contrast the new system with current manual procedures, or to evaluate competitive products. Data can be collected informally, or more precisely (with stopwatch or computer recording of times down to the millisecond), to suit circumstances.

Instructional materials and command-language designs can be evaluated with paper-and-pencil tests run on typical users. As prototype versions become available, testing can be more elaborate. These preliminary tests help to build designers' confidence that the stringent acceptance test can be passed when the implementation is complete.

An effective technique during prototype testing is to invite users to perform a few well-chosen tasks and to *think aloud* about what they are doing (Lewis, 1982). The designer or tester should be supportive of the user, not taking over or giving instructions, but prompting and listening for clues about how the user is dealing with the system. After a suitable time period—possibly 1 or 2 hours—the user can be invited to make general comments or suggestions, or to respond to specific questions. The informal atmosphere of a thinking-aloud session is pleasant for both parties, and often leads to many suggestions for improvements. As the system is refined, more ambitious tests can be conducted with users who are doing real work. In their efforts to encourage thinking aloud, some usability laboratories found that having two users working together produced more talking, as one user explained procedures and decisions to the other.

Videotaping users performing tasks is often valuable for later review and for showing designers or managers the problems that users encounter (Lund, 1985). Review of videotapes is a tedious job, but sometimes designers can go back and spot the source and moment of user's confusion. The reactions of designers to seeing users failing with their system is sometimes powerful, and may be highly motivating. Videotape equipment can be costly and time consuming, so careful logging during the test is vital to reduce the time spent trying to find specific incidents. Most usability laboratories have acquired or developed software to facilitate logging of user activities by observers with automatic time stamping.

At each stage, the design can be refined iteratively (Carroll and Rosson, 1985), and the improved version can be put to the test. It is important to fix quickly even small flaws, such as of spelling errors or inconsistent layout, since they influence user expectations.

Usability-laboratory testing is effective because real users perform real tasks under the eye of experienced observers. Another reason for its success may be that designers and programmers may increase their diligence if they know that a usability test will be conducted (Gould, 1988).

Support for the iterative development of interactive systems comes from a project to develop a natural-language interaction for a personal calendar system (Kelley, 1984). As subjects used the system, the word dictionary was increased from about 50 to more than 200 terms, reflecting the diverse usage patterns. A similar strategy, termed *user-derived interface*, was used to develop a command language for an electronic-mail facility (Good et al., 1984). Users were encouraged to guess at possible commands, and their terms and structures were used to refine the system. As the number of parser rules and words increased from 120 to 330, the percentage of user-invented commands accepted by the system increased from almost 0 to more than 90. It seems appealing to try to use commands that users invent; but other evidence suggests that users do not always invent the best strategy. Especially as the command sets grow large, there may be an advantage to providing a more structured facility to start with, and then adding refinements to deal with problems.

Game designers pioneered the *can-you-break-this* approach to testing by providing energetic teen-agers with the challenge of trying to beat new games. This destructive testing approach, in which the users try to find fatal flaws in the system, or otherwise to destroy it, has been used in other projects and should be considered seriously. Software purchasers have little patience with flawed products and the cost of sending out tens of thousands of replacement disks is one that few companies can bear.

Another form of usability testing is to have expert reviewers use the system. There is a growing community of designers in each application area, and it may be useful to supplement user testing with expert reviewers. Experts have experience that enables them to recognize problems, to estimate what will happen with longer-term usage, to spot incompatibilities with other equipment, and to suggest innovative enhancements.

13.4 Acceptance Tests

For large implementation projects, the customer or manager usually sets objective and measurable goals for hardware and software performance. Many authors of requirements documents are even so bold as to specify mean time between failures and mean time to repair for hardware and, in some cases, for software. More typically, a set of test cases is specified for the software, with possible response-time requirements for the hardware–software combination. If the completed product fails to meet these acceptance criteria, the system must be reworked until success is demonstrated.

Now, these notions can be extended to the human interface. Explicit acceptance criteria should be established when the requirements document is written or when a contract is offered. Measurable criteria for the human interface can be established for the following:

- Time to learn specific functions
- Speed of task performance
- Rate of errors
- Subjective user satisfaction
- Human retention of commands over time

An acceptance test might specify that:

Thirty typical users will be trained in using the system for 45 minutes. These users will be given 15 minutes to carry out the enclosed benchmark set of tasks. The average completion rate must be above 80 percent, and the average number of errors must be below 3.

In a modest-sized system, there may be eight or 10 such tests to carry out on different components of the system and with different user communities. An important test might be for speed of performance of typical tasks after 1 week of regular use. Other issues, such as subjective satisfaction or retention of commands after 1 week, may also be tested.

If they establish precise acceptance criteria, both the customer and the system developer can benefit. Arguments about the user friendliness of the system are avoided, and contractual fulfillment can be demonstrated objectively.

Once acceptance testing has been successful, there may be a period of field testing before national distribution. In addition to further refining the user interface, field tests can improve training methods, tutorial materials, telephone help-desk procedures, marketing methods, and publicity strategies.

The goal of early pilot studies, prototypes, acceptance testing, and field testing is to force as much of the evolutionary development as possible into the prerelease phase, when change is relatively easy and inexpensive to accomplish.

13.5   Evaluation During Active Use

A carefully designed and thoroughly tested system is a wonderful asset, but successful active use requires constant attention from dedicated managers, user-services personnel, and maintenance staff. Everyone involved in supporting the user community can contribute to system refinements that provide ever higher levels of service. You cannot please all of the users all of the time, but earnest effort will be rewarded by the appreciation of a grateful user community. Perfection is not attainable, but percentage improvements are possible and are worth pursuing.

Gradual system dissemination is useful so that problems can be repaired with minimal disruption. As more and more people use the system, further changes should be limited to an annual or semiannual system revision that is announced adequately. If system users can anticipate the change, then resistance will be reduced, especially if they have positive expectations of improvement.

13.5.1   Surveys

There are many productive avenues for assessing user performance and attitudes (Hiltz, 1983). Written user surveys are an inexpensive and generally acceptable approach with both management and users. A *survey form* should be prepared, reviewed among colleagues, and tested with a small sample of users before a large-scale survey is conducted.

Online surveys avoid the cost of printing and the extra effort needed for distribution and collection of paper forms. Many people prefer to answer a brief survey displayed on a screen, instead of filling in and returning a printed form. So that costs are kept low, the survey might be administered to only a fraction of the user community.

In one survey, users were asked to respond to eight questions according to the following scale:

1 — strongly agree

2 — agree

3 — neutral

4 — disagree

5 — strongly disagree

The items in the survey were these:

1. I find the system commands easy to use.
2. I feel competent with and knowledgeable about the system commands.
3. When writing a set of system commands for a new application, I am confident that they will be correct on the first run.
4. When I get an error message, I find that it is helpful in identifying the problem.
5. I think that there are too many options and special cases.
6. I believe that the commands could be substantially simplified.
7. I have trouble remembering the commands and options, and must consult the manual frequently.
8. When a problem arises, I ask for assistance from someone who really knows the system.

This list of questions can help designers to identify problems users are having, and to demonstrate improvement to the interface as changes are made in training, online assistance, command structures, and so on; progress is demonstrated by improved scores on subsequent surveys.

In a study of error messages in text-editor usage, we asked users to rate the messages on 1-to-7 scales:

Hostile	1 2 3 4 5 6 7	Friendly
Vague	1 2 3 4 5 6 7	Specific
Misleading	1 2 3 4 5 6 7	Beneficial
Discouraging	1 2 3 4 5 6 7	Encouraging

If precise, as opposed to general, questions are used in surveys, then there is a greater chance that the results will provide useful guidance for taking action (Lyons, 1980; Root and Draper, 1983).

Coleman and Williges (1985) developed a set of bipolar semantically anchored items (pleasing versus irritating, simple versus complicated, concise versus redundant) that asked users to describe their reactions to using a word processor. Another approach is to ask users to evaluate aspects of the interface design, such as the readability of characters, the meaningfulness of command names, or the helpfulness of error messages. If users rate as poor one aspect of the interactive system, the designers have a clear indication of what needs to be redone.

The *Questionnaire for User Interface Satisfaction* (QUIS) was developed by me and was refined by Dr. Kent Norman. It has proved useful in demonstrating the benefits of improvements to a videodisk-retrieval program, in comparing two Pascal programming environments, in assessing word processors, and in setting requirements for redesign of an online public-access library catalog (Chin et al., 1988). Many researchers use only parts of QUIS, or add domain-specific items.

Table 13.2 contains the short form of a generic user-evaluation questionnaire for interactive systems. The long form shown in Table 13.3 was designed to have two levels of questions: general and detailed. If participants are willing to respond to every item, then the long-form questionnaire can be used. If participants are not likely to be patient, then only the general questions in the short form need to be asked.

13.5.2   Interviews and group discussions

Interviews with individual users can be productive because the interviewer can pursue specific issues of concern. After a series of individual discussions, *group discussions* are valuable to ascertain the universality of comments. Interviewing can be costly and time consuming, so usually only small fractions of the user community are involved. On the other hand, direct contact with users often leads to specific, constructive suggestions (Lieff and Allwood, 1985).

A large corporation conducted 45-minute interviews with 66 of the 4300 users of an internal message system. The interviews revealed that the users were happy with some aspects of the functionality, such as the capacity to pick up messages at any site, legible printed messages, and the convenience of after-hours access. However, the interviews also revealed that 23.6 percent of the users had concerns about reliability, 20.2 percent thought that using the system was confusing, and 18.2 percent said convenience and accessibility could be improved, whereas only 16.0 percent expressed no concerns. Later questions in the interview explored specific features. As a result of this interview effort, a set of 42 enhancements to the system was proposed and implemented. The designers of the system had earlier proposed a set of enhancements, but the results of the interviews led to a changed set of priorities that more closely reflected the users' needs.

Table 13.2

The short form of a generic user-evaluation questionnaire for interactive systems. (Copyright © 1988, 1989, 1991 Human–Computer Interaction Laboratory, University of Maryland. All Rights Reserved.) (This QUIS is available for license in paper, IBM PC, and Macintosh forms from the University of Maryland's Office of Technology Liaison.)

Questionnaire for User-Interaction Satisfaction 5.0 - S

Identification number: _____

Age: _____

Sex: __ male __ female

PART 1: Type of System to be Rated

1.1 Name of hardware: _____

1.2 Name of software: _____

1.3 How long have you worked on this system?

__ less than 1 hour	__ 6 months to less than 1 year
__ 1 hour to less than 1 day	__ 1 year to less than 2 years
__ 1 day to less than 1 week	__ 2 years to less than 3 years
__ 1 week to less than 1 month	__ 3 years or more
__ 1 month to less than 6 months	

1.4 On the average, how much time do you spend per week on this system?

__ less than one hour	__ 4 to less than 10 hours
__ one to less than 4 hours	__ over 10 hours

PART 2: Past Experience

2.1 How many different types of computer systems, including mainframes and personal computers, have you worked with (e.g., Macintosh, DEC VAX)?

__ none	__ 3-4
__ 1	__ 5-6
__ 2	__ more than 6

2.2 Of the following devices, software, and systems, check those that you have personally used and are familiar with:

__ keyboard	__ text editor	__ color monitor
__ numeric key pad	__ word processor	__ time-share system
__ mouse	__ file manager	__ workstation
__ light pen	__ electronic spreadsheet	__ personal computer
__ touch screen	__ electronic mail	__ floppy drive
__ track ball	__ graphics software	__ hard drive
__ joy stick	__ computer games	__ compact disk drive

Table 13.2

(Con't.)

PART 3: Overall User Reactions

Please circle the numbers which most appropriately reflect your impressions about using this computer system. Not Applicable = NA. There is room on the last page for your written comments.

3.1 Overall reactions to the system: terrible   wonderful
                                                       1 2 3 4 5 6 7 8 9   NA

3.2   frustrating   satisfying
                                                       1 2 3 4 5 6 7 8 9   NA

3.3   dull   stimulating
                                                       1 2 3 4 5 6 7 8 9   NA

3.4   difficult   easy
                                                       1 2 3 4 5 6 7 8 9   NA

3.5   inadequate power   adequate power
                                                       1 2 3 4 5 6 7 8 9   NA

3.6   rigid   flexible
                                                       1 2 3 4 5 6 7 8 9   NA

PART 4: Screen

4.1 Characters on the computer screen   hard to read   easy to read
                                                       1 2 3 4 5 6 7 8 9   NA

4.2 Was the highlighting on the screen helpful? not at all   very much
                                                       1 2 3 4 5 6 7 8 9   NA

4.3 Were the screen layouts helpful?   not at all   very helpful
                                                       1 2 3 4 5 6 7 8 9   NA

4.4 Sequence of screens   confusing   clear
                                                       1 2 3 4 5 6 7 8 9   NA

PART 5: Terminology and System Information

5.1 Use of terms throughout system   inconsistent   consistent
                                                       1 2 3 4 5 6 7 8 9   NA

5.2 Does the terminology relate well to the work unrelated   well related
     you are doing?   1 2 3 4 5 6 7 8 9   NA

5.3 Messages which appear on screen   inconsistent   consistent
                                                       1 2 3 4 5 6 7 8 9   NA

5.4 Messages which appear on screen   confusing   clear
                                                       1 2 3 4 5 6 7 8 9   NA

5.5 Does the computer keep you informed about never   always
     what it is doing?   1 2 3 4 5 6 7 8 9   NA

5.6 Error messages   unhelpful   helpful
                                                       1 2 3 4 5 6 7 8 9   NA

Table 13.2

(Con't.)

PART 6: Learning

6.1 Learning to operate the system   difficult   easy

                    1 2 3 4 5 6 7 8 9 NA

6.2 Exploration of features by trial and error discouraging   encouraging

                    1 2 3 4 5 6 7 8 9 NA

6.3 Remembering names and use of commands difficult   easy

                    1 2 3 4 5 6 7 8 9 NA

6.4 Can tasks be performed in a straight-forward never   always
manner?   1 2 3 4 5 6 7 8 9 NA

6.5 Help messages on the screen   confusing   clear

                    1 2 3 4 5 6 7 8 9 NA

6.6 Supplemental reference materials   confusing   clear

                    1 2 3 4 5 6 7 8 9 NA

PART 7: System Capabilities

7.1 System speed   too slow   fast enough

                    1 2 3 4 5 6 7 8 9 NA

7.2 How reliable is the system?   very unreliable very reliable

                    1 2 3 4 5 6 7 8 9 NA

7.3 System tends to be   noisy   quiet

                    1 2 3 4 5 6 7 8 9 NA

7.4 Correcting your mistakes   difficult   easy

                    1 2 3 4 5 6 7 8 9 NA

7.5 Are the needs of both experienced and never   always
inexperienced users taken into consideration? 1 2 3 4 5 6 7 8 9 NA

PART 8: User's Comments

Please write any comments you have in the space below.

_____

_____

_____

_____

_____

_____

_____

Table 13.3

The long form of a generic user-evaluation questionnaire for interactive systems. (Copyright © 1988–1991 Human–Computer Interaction Laboratory, University of Maryland. All Rights Reserved.) (This QUIS is available for license in paper, IBM PC, and Macintosh forms from the University of Maryland's Office of Technology Liaison.)

Questionnaire for User-Interaction Satisfaction 5.0 - L

Identification number: _____

Age: _____

Sex: __ male __ female

PART 1: Type of System to be Rated

1.1 Name of hardware: _____

1.2 Name of software: _____

1.3 How long have you worked on this system?

    __ less than 1 hour   __ 6 months to less than 1 year

    __ 1 hour to less than 1 day   __ 1 year to less than 2 years

    __ 1 day to less than 1 week   __ 2 years to less than 3 years

    __ 1 week to less than 1 month   __ 3 years or more

    __ 1 month to less than 6 months

1.4 On the average, how much time do you spend per week on this system?

    __ less than one hour   __ 4 to less than 10 hours

    __ one to less than 4 hours   __ over 10 hours

PART 2: Past Experience

2.1 How many different types of computer systems (e. g., main frames and personal computers) have you worked with?

    __ none   __ 3-4

    __ 1   __ 5-6

    __ 2   __ more than 6

2.2 Of the following devices, software, and systems, check those that you have personally used and are familiar with:

__ keyboard	__ text editor	__ color monitor
__ numeric key pad	__ word processor	__ time-share system
__ mouse	__ file manager	__ workstation
__ light pen	__ electronic spreadsheet	__ personal computer
__ touch screen	__ electronic mail	__ floppy drive
__ track ball	__ graphics software	__ hard drive
__ joy stick	__ computer games	__ compact disk drive

Table 13.3

(Con't.)

PART 3: Overall User Reactions

Please circle the numbers which most appropriately reflect your impressions about using this computer system. Not Applicable = NA. There is room on the last page for your written comments.

3.1 Overall reactions to the system:

terrible   wonderful
1 2 3 4 5 6 7 8 9   NA

3.2

frustrating   satisfying
1 2 3 4 5 6 7 8 9   NA

3.3

dull   stimulating
1 2 3 4 5 6 7 8 9   NA

3.4

difficult   easy
1 2 3 4 5 6 7 8 9   NA

3.5

inadequate power   adequate power
1 2 3 4 5 6 7 8 9   NA

3.6

rigid   flexible
1 2 3 4 5 6 7 8 9   NA

PART 4: Screen

4.1 Characters on the computer screen

hard to read   easy to read
1 2 3 4 5 6 7 8 9   NA

   4.1.1 Image of characters

fuzzy   sharp
1 2 3 4 5 6 7 8 9   NA

   4.1.2 Character shapes (fonts)

barely legible   very legible
1 2 3 4 5 6 7 8 9   NA

4.2 Was the highlighting on the screen helpful?

not at all   very much
1 2 3 4 5 6 7 8 9   NA

   4.2.1 Use of reverse video

unhelpful   helpful
1 2 3 4 5 6 7 8 9   NA

   4.2.2 Use of blinking

unhelpful   helpful
1 2 3 4 5 6 7 8 9   NA

4.3 Were the screen layouts helpful?

never   always
1 2 3 4 5 6 7 8 9   NA

   4.3.1 Amount of information that can be displayed on screen

inadequate   adequate
1 2 3 4 5 6 7 8 9   NA

   4.3.2 Arrangement of information on screen

illogical   logical
1 2 3 4 5 6 7 8 9   NA

4.4 Sequence of screens

confusing   clear
1 2 3 4 5 6 7 8 9   NA

   4.4.1 Next screen in a sequence

unpredictable   predictable
1 2 3 4 5 6 7 8 9   NA

Table 13.3

(Con't.)

4.4.2	Going back to the previous screen	impossible	easy
		1 2 3 4 5 6 7 8 9 NA	
4.4.3	Beginning, middle and end of tasks	confusing	clearly marked
		1 2 3 4 5 6 7 8 9 NA	

PART 5: Terminology and System Information

5.1 Use of terms throughout system

inconsistent   consistent

1 2 3 4 5 6 7 8 9   NA

    5.1.2 Task terms

inconsistent   consistent

1 2 3 4 5 6 7 8 9   NA

    5.2.3 Computer terms

inconsistent   consistent

1 2 3 4 5 6 7 8 9   NA

5.2 Does the terminology relate well to the work
you are doing?

unrelated   well related

1 2 3 4 5 6 7 8 9   NA

    5.2.1 Computer terminology is used

too frequently   appropriately

1 2 3 4 5 6 7 8 9   NA

    5.2.2 Terms on the screen

ambiguous   precise

1 2 3 4 5 6 7 8 9   NA

5.3 Messages which appear on screen

inconsistent   consistent

1 2 3 4 5 6 7 8 9   NA

    5.3.1 Position of instructions on the screen

inconsistent   consistent

1 2 3 4 5 6 7 8 9   NA

5.4 Messages which appear on screen

confusing   clear

1 2 3 4 5 6 7 8 9   NA

    5.4.1 Instructions for commands or choices

confusing   clear

1 2 3 4 5 6 7 8 9   NA

    5.4.2 Instructions for correcting errors

confusing   clear

1 2 3 4 5 6 7 8 9   NA

5.5 Does the computer keep you informed about
what it is doing?

never   always

1 2 3 4 5 6 7 8 9   NA

    5.5.1 Performing an operation leads to a
predictable result

never   always

1 2 3 4 5 6 7 8 9   NA

    5.5.2 User can control amount of feedback

never   always

1 2 3 4 5 6 7 8 9   NA

5.6 Error messages

unhelpful   helpful

1 2 3 4 5 6 7 8 9   NA

    5.6.1 Error messages clarify the problem

never   always

1 2 3 4 5 6 7 8 9   NA

    5.6.2 Phrasing of error messages

unpleasant   pleasant

1 2 3 4 5 6 7 8 9   NA

Table 13.3

(Con't.)

PART 6: Learning

6.1 Learning to operate the system
difficult   easy
1 2 3 4 5 6 7 8 9   NA

    6.1.1 Getting started
difficult   easy
1 2 3 4 5 6 7 8 9   NA

    6.1.2 Learning advanced features
difficult   easy
1 2 3 4 5 6 7 8 9   NA

    6.1.3 Time to learn to use the system
slow   fast
1 2 3 4 5 6 7 8 9   NA

6.2 Exploration of features by trial and error
discouraging   encouraging
1 2 3 4 5 6 7 8 9   NA

    6.2.1 Exploration of features
risky   safe
1 2 3 4 5 6 7 8 9   NA

    6.2.2 Discovering new features
difficult   easy
1 2 3 4 5 6 7 8 9   NA

6.3 Remembering names and use of commands
difficult   easy
1 2 3 4 5 6 7 8 9   NA

    6.3.1 Remembering specific rules about entering commands
difficult   easy
1 2 3 4 5 6 7 8 9   NA

6.4 Can tasks be performed in a straight-forward manner?
never   always
1 2 3 4 5 6 7 8 9   NA

    6.4.1 Number of steps per task
too many   just right
1 2 3 4 5 6 7 8 9   NA

    6.4.2 Steps to complete a task follow a logical sequence
rarely   always
1 2 3 4 5 6 7 8 9   NA

    6.4.3 Completion of sequence of steps
unclear   clear
1 2 3 4 5 6 7 8 9   NA

6.5 Help messages on the screen
confusing   clear
1 2 3 4 5 6 7 8 9   NA

    6.5.1 Accessing help messages
difficult   easy
1 2 3 4 5 6 7 8 9   NA

    6.5.2 Content of help messages
confusing   clear
1 2 3 4 5 6 7 8 9   NA

    6.5.3 Amount of help
inadequate   adequate
1 2 3 4 5 6 7 8 9   NA

6.6 Supplemental reference materials
confusing   clear
1 2 3 4 5 6 7 8 9   NA

    6.6.1 Tutorials for beginners
confusing   clear
1 2 3 4 5 6 7 8 9   NA

Table 13.3

(Con't.)

6.6.2 Reference manuals	confusing		clear
	1 2 3 4 5 6 7 8 9		NA

PART 7: System Capabilities

7.1 System speed — too slow fast enough
1 2 3 4 5 6 7 8 9   NA

    7.1.1 Response time for most operations — too slow fast enough
1 2 3 4 5 6 7 8 9   NA

    7.1.2 Rate information is displayed — too slow fast enough
1 2 3 4 5 6 7 8 9   NA

7.2 How reliable is the system? — unreliable reliable
1 2 3 4 5 6 7 8 9   NA

    7.2.1 Operations are — undependable dependable
1 2 3 4 5 6 7 8 9   NA

    7.2.2 System failures occur — frequently seldom
1 2 3 4 5 6 7 8 9   NA

    7.2.3 System warns the user about potential problems — never always
1 2 3 4 5 6 7 8 9   NA

7.3 System tends to be — noisy quiet
1 2 3 4 5 6 7 8 9   NA

    7.3.1 Mechanical devices such as fans, disks, and printers — noisy quiet
1 2 3 4 5 6 7 8 9   NA

    7.3.2 Computer tones, beeps, clicks, etc. — annoying pleasant
1 2 3 4 5 6 7 8 9   NA

7.4 Correcting your mistakes — difficult easy
1 2 3 4 5 6 7 8 9   NA

    7.4.1 Correcting typos or mistakes — complex simple
1 2 3 4 5 6 7 8 9   NA

    7.4.2 Ability to undo operations — inadequate adequate
1 2 3 4 5 6 7 8 9   NA

7.5 Are the needs of both experienced and inexperienced users taken into consideration? — never always
1 2 3 4 5 6 7 8 9   NA

    7.5.1 Novices can accomplish tasks knowing only a few commands — with difficulty easily
1 2 3 4 5 6 7 8 9   NA

    7.5.2 Experts can use features/shortcuts — with difficulty easily
1 2 3 4 5 6 7 8 9   NA

Table 13.3

(Con't.)

PART 8: User's Comments

Please write any comments you have in the space below.

_____

_____

_____

_____

_____

_____

_____

_____

13.5.3 Online or telephone consultants

Online or *telephone consultants* are an extremely effective way to provide assistance to users who are experiencing difficulties. Many users feel reassured if they know there is a human being to whom they can turn when problems arise. The consultants are an excellent source of information about problems users are having, suggestions for improvement, and potential extensions.

Several systems offer a toll-free 800 number by which the users can reach a knowledgeable consultant. On some network systems, the consultants can monitor the user's terminal and see the same displays that the user sees while maintaining telephone voice contact. This service can be extremely reassuring; the users know that someone can walk them through the correct sequence of screens to complete their tasks.

The Electronic Information Exchange System (EIES) allows users to send a message to a designated mailbox, called HELP, and to receive a response within a few minutes in most cases (Hiltz and Turoff, 1981). The Dartmouth College Kiewit Computer Center, known for its attempts to provide good service to the university community, used to offer these instructions:

```
Typing JOIN CONSULT will connect you with Kiewit's Public
Room Assistant, who is on duty 8 A.M. to midnight Monday
through Saturday and noon to midnight Sunday. You can carry
on a conversation with the assistant; you type in your
questions and the assistant's responses are printed at your
terminal.
```

```
Type /OLD SUGGEST***/RUN if you do not need an immediate
response. Your questions will be recorded and, in the morn-
ing of the next working day, answers will be supplied in a
file in your user number.
```

13.5.4   Online suggestion box or trouble reporting

Electronic mail can be employed to allow users to send messages to the maintainers or designers. Such an online suggestion box encourages some users to make productive comments, since writing a letter may be seen as requiring too much effort.

At the University of Maryland Computer Science Center, users can type the command GRIPE and receive a prompt for a comment to be sent to the systems-programming staff. A typical comment is this:

```
**** Message from user ****
I am having trouble with the editor when using a 132 charac-
ter display. I occasionally lose the character typed in the
last position.
     Gwen User


**** Response from User Services ****
Several users have reported this erratic problem that has
been traced to a bug in the new communications interface. It
has been fixed as of October 29-please let us know if you
are still encountering this problem.
     Sharon Staff
```

A large corporation installed a full-screen fill-in-the-blanks form for user problem reports, and received 90 comments on a new internal system within 3 months. The user's identification number and name were entered automatically, and the user moved a cursor to indicate which subsystem was causing a problem and what the problem's seriousness was (showstopper, annoyance, improvement, other). Each problem received a dated and signed response that was stored on a file for public reading.

13.5.5   Online bulletin board

Some users may have a question about the suitability of a software package for their application, or may be seeking someone with experience using a system feature. They do not have any individual in mind, so electronic mail does not serve their needs. Many systems designers offer users an *electronic bulletin board* (see Section 10.2) to permit posting of open messages and invitations. Many bulletin boards cover such technical topics as programming languages or hardware problems; others deal with tennis advice or film reviews.

Some professional societies offer bulletin boards by way of networks such as Prodigy, Internet, CompuServe, or through inexpensive one-user-at-a-time microcomputers with a modem to permit dial-up access. These bulletin boards may offer information services or permit downloading of software by way of the telephone.

Bulletin-board software systems usually offer a list of item headlines, allowing users the opportunity to select items for display. New items can be added by anyone, but usually someone monitors the bulletin board to ensure that offensive, useless, or repetitious items are removed.

13.5.6   User newsletters and conferences

When there is a substantial number of users who are geographically dispersed, managers may have to work harder to create a sense of community. *Newsletters* that provide information about novel system facilities, suggestions for improved productivity, requests for assistance, case studies of successful applications, or stories about individual users can promote user satisfaction and greater knowledge. Printed newsletters are more traditional and have the advantage that they can be carried away from the terminal workstation. A printed newsletter has an appealing air of respectability. Online newsletters may be less expensive and more rapidly disseminated.

Personal relationships established by face-to-face meetings also increase the sense of community among users. Conferences allow workers to exchange experiences with colleagues, promote novel approaches, stimulate greater dedication, encourage higher productivity, and develop a deeper relationship of trust. Ultimately, it is the people who matter, and human needs for social interaction should be satisfied. Every technical system is also a social system that needs to be encouraged and nurtured.

By soliciting user feedback in any of these ways, the system managers can gauge user attitudes and elicit useful suggestions. Furthermore, users may have a more positive attitude toward the system if they see that the system managers genuinely desire comments and suggestions.

13.6   Quantitative Evaluations

Scientific and engineering progress is often stimulated by improved techniques for precise measurement. Rapid progress in the designs of interactive systems will occur as soon as researchers and practitioners evolve suitable human-performance measures and techniques. We have come to expect that automobiles will have miles-per-gallon reports pasted to the window, appliances will have energy-efficiency ratings, and textbooks will be given grade-level designations; soon, we will expect software packages to show learning-time estimates and user-satisfaction indices from appropriate evaluation sources.

13.6.1   Controlled psychologically oriented experimentation

Academic and industrial researchers are discovering that the power of the traditional scientific method can be fruitfully employed in studying interactive systems. They are conducting numerous experiments that are uncovering basic design principles. The outline of the scientific method as applied to human–computer interaction might comprise these tasks:

- Deal with a practical problem and consider the theoretical framework
- State a lucid and testable hypothesis
- Identify a small number of independent variables that are to be altered
- Carefully choose the dependent variables that will be measured
- Judiciously select subjects and carefully or randomly assign subjects to groups
- Control for biasing factors
- Apply statistical methods to data analysis.
- Resolve the practical problem, refine the theory, and give advice to future researchers

The classic experimental methods of psychology are being enhanced to deal with the complex cognitive tasks of human performance with information and computer systems. The transformation from Aristotelian introspection to Galilean experimentation that took two millennia in physics is being accomplished in two decades in the study of human–computer interaction.

The reductionist approach required for controlled experimentation yields small but reliable results. Through multiple replications with similar tasks, subjects, and experimental conditions, reliability and validity can be enhanced. Each small experimental result acts like a tile in the mosaic of human performance with computer-based information systems.

Managers of actively used systems are also coming to recognize the power of controlled experiments in fine tuning the human–computer interface. As proposals are made for new command syntax, different menu-tree structures, novel cursor-control devices, and reorganized display formats, a carefully controlled experiment can provide data to support a management decision. Fractions of the user population could be given proposed improvements for a limited time, and then performance could be compared with the control group. Dependent measures could include performance times, user-subjective satisfaction, error rates, and user retention over time.

Experimental design and statistical analysis are complex topics (Hays, 1988; Cozby, 1989; Runyon and Haber, 1991; Winer et al., 1991.) Novice experimenters would be well advised to collaborate with experienced social scientists.

13.6.2   Continuous user-performance data collection

The software architecture should make it easy for system managers to collect data about the patterns of system usage, speed of user performance, rate of errors, or frequency of request for online assistance. Specific data provide guidance in the acquisition of new hardware, changes in operating procedures, improvements to training, plans for system expansion, and so on (Good, 1985).

For example, if the frequency of each error message is recorded, then the highest-frequency error is a candidate for attention. The message might be rewritten, training materials could be revised, the software could be changed to provide more specific information, or the command syntax might be simplified. Without specific data, the system-maintenance staff has no way of knowing which of the many hundreds of error-message situations is the biggest problem for users. Similarly, messages that never appear should be examined to see whether there is an error in the code or whether users are avoiding use of some facility.

If usage data for each command, each help screen, and each database record are available, then changes to the human–computer interface can be made to simplify access to frequently used features. Managers also should examine unused or rarely used facilities to understand why users are avoiding those features. A major benefit of usage-frequency data is the guidance they provide to system maintainers in optimizing performance and reducing costs for all participants. This latter argument may yield the clearest advantage to a cost-conscious manager, the increased quality of the human–computer interface is an attraction to the service-oriented manager.

13.7   Development Lifecycle

Designers, implementers, and managers want to build a high-quality system, but they may not have a clear vision of what steps to take. The following *lifecycle for interactive-systems development* is a framework that can be adapted to meet the widely varying needs of specific projects (Rouse, 1984; Chapanis and Budurka, 1990). Each project has special needs, and this framework is offered as a starting point for project management. The lifecycle is presented in an orderly step-by-step manner, but the reality is often iterative, requiring a return to earlier stages for some parts of the system design.

1. Collect information

Organize the design team.
Obtain management and customer participation.
Conduct interviews with users.
Submit written questionnaires to users.
Perform detailed task and task-frequency analysis.
Read professional and academic literature.
Speak with designers and users of similar systems.
Estimate development, training, usage, and maintenance costs.
Prepare a schedule with observable milestones and reviews.
Design the testing strategy with the usability laboratory.

2. Define requirements and semantics

Define high-level goals and middle-level requirements.
Consider alternatives in task-flow sequencing.
Organize tasks into transaction units.
Create task objects and actions.
Create computer objects and actions.
Determine reliability and availability needs.
Specify security, privacy, and integrity constraints.
Create guidelines document and process for enforcement.
Obtain manager and customer agreement on goals, requirements, and semantic design.

3. Design syntax and support facilities

Compare alternative display formats.
Create syntax for actions.
Design informative feedback for each action.
Develop error messages and error handling.
Specify system response times and display rates.
Plan user aids, online help, and tutorials.
Write user and reference manuals.
Review, evaluate, and revise design specifications.
Carry out paper-and-pencil pilot tests or field studies with an online mockup or prototype.

4. Specify physical devices

Choose hard- or soft-copy devices.
Consider color, screen size, and resolution.
Specify keyboard layout.
Specify pointing devices.
Select audio, graphics, or peripheral devices.
Establish requirements for communications lines.
Consider work environment, such as noise level, lighting, and table space.
Carry out further pilot tests and revise design.

5. Develop software

Use user-interface management systems.
Produce top-down modular design.
Emphasize modifiability and maintainability.
Ensure reliability and security.
Enable monitoring of user and system performance.
Provide adequate system documentation.
Conduct thorough software tests with realistic usage load.

6. Integrate system and disseminate to users

Ensure user involvement at every stage.
Conduct acceptance tests and fine tune the system.
Field test printed manuals, online help, and tutorials.
Implement a training subsystem or simulator.
Provide adequate training and consultation for users.
Follow phased approach to dissemination, and provide time and re-
   sources to make modest revisions in response to user feedback.

7. Nurture the user community

Provide on-site or telephone consultants.
Offer online consultant.
Develop online suggestion box.
Conduct interviews and focus groups with users.
Make user news and bulletin boards available online.
Publish newsletter for users.
Organize group meetings.
Respond to user suggestions for improvements.
Conduct subjective and objective evaluations of the current system and of
   proposed improvements.
Monitor usage frequencies and patterns (actions, help, other features).
Track user-error frequencies.

8. Prepare evolutionary plan

Design for easy repair and refinement.
Reserve staff time for enhancements.
Measure user performance regularly.
Improve error handling.
Carry out experiments to assess suggested changes.
Sample feedback from users by questionnaires and interviews.
Schedule revisions regularly, and inform users in advance.

It is easy to build an ordinary system, but to build an excellent interactive system requires substantial effort during the design phase. The investments in time and money during design can dramatically reduce the development time and cost. Well-designed systems have lower lifetime costs, enable rapid user-task performance, substantially reduce user-error rates, shorten user-learning times, and bring satisfaction to the user community. Users who experience the competence of mastery, the confidence to explore novel features, the satisfaction of being able to perform their work, and the joyous sense of accomplishment will celebrate the role of the system designers, maintainers, and managers.

13.8   Practitioner's Summary

Basic research in industrial and academic centers is beginning to yield guidelines for interactive systems designers. Industrial and governmental system developers employ empirical techniques by conducting informal pilot studies, evaluations of early prototypes, more careful studies of system components, rigorous acceptance tests, and continuous performance evaluation during the system's active use. If you are not measuring, you are not doing human factors!

Successful system managers understand that they must work hard to establish a relationship of trust with the user community. In addition to providing a properly functioning system, computer-center managers and information-systems directors recognize the need to create social mechanisms for feedback, such as online surveys, interviews, discussions, consultants, suggestion boxes, bulletin boards, newsletters, and conferences.

13.9   Researcher's Agenda

Human-interface guidelines are often based on best-guess judgments, rather than on experimental data. More experimentation could lead to refined standards that are more complete and dependable, and to more precise knowledge of how much improvement can be expected from a design change. It will take several decades to establish a stable and complete set of guidelines, but the benefits will be enormous in terms of the reliability and quality of the human interface.

Researchers can also contribute their experience with experimentation to developing techniques of system evaluation. Guidance in conducting pilot studies, acceptance tests, surveys, interviews, and discussions would benefit commercial development groups. Experts in constructing psychological tests would be extremely helpful in preparing a validated and reliable test instrument for subjective evaluation of interactive systems. Such a standardized test would allow independent groups to compare the acceptability of their systems.

Clinical psychologists, psychotherapists, and social workers could contribute to training online or as telephone consultants—after all, helping troubled users is a human-relationship issue. Finally, more input from experimental, cognitive, and clinical psychologists would help computer specialists to recognize the importance of the human aspects of computer use.

References

Baroudi, Jack J., Olson, Margrethe H., Ives, Blake, An empirical study of the impact of user involvement on system usage and information satisfaction, *Communications of the ACM 29*, 3 (March 1986), 232–238.

Carroll, John M., and Rosson, Mary Beth, Usability specifications as a tool in iterative development. In Hartson, H. Rex (Editor), *Advances in Human–Computer Interaction 1*, Ablex, Norwood, NJ (1985), 1–28.

Chapanis, Alphonse and Budurka, William J., Specifying human–computer interface requirements, *Behaviour and Information Technology 9*, 6 (1990), 479–492.

Chin, John P., Diehl, Virginia A., and Norman, Kent L., Development of an instrument measuring user satisfaction of the human–computer interface, *Proc. CHI'88—Human Factors in Computing Systems*, ACM, New York (1988), 213–218.

Clark, I. A., Software simulation as a tool for usable product design, *IBM Systems Journal 20*, 3 (1981), 272–293.

Coleman, William D. and Williges, Robert C., Collecting detailed user evaluations of software interfaces, *Proc. Human Factors Society—Twenty-Ninth Annual Meeting*, Santa Monica, CA (1985), 204–244.

Cozby, Paul C., *Methods in Behavioral Research* (Fourth Edition), Mayfield, Mountain View, CA (1989).

Dumas, Joseph and Redish, Jane, *Usability Testing*, Ablex, Norwood, NJ (in press).

Good, Michael, The use of logging data in the design of a new text editor, *Proc. CHI'85—Human Factors in Computing Systems*, ACM, New York (1985), 93–97.

Good, Michael D., Whiteside, John A., Wixon, Dennis R., and Jones, Sandra J., Building a user-derived interface, *Communications of the ACM 27*, 10 (October 1984), 1032–1043.

Gould, John, How to design usable systems. In Helander, Martin (Editor), *Handbook of Human–Computer Interaction*, North-Holland, Amsterdam, The Netherlands (1988), 757–789.

Gould, John D., Conti, J., and Hovanyecz, T., Composing letters with a simulated listening typewriter, *Communications of the ACM 26*, 4 (1983), 295–308.

Gould, John D., and Lewis, Clayton, Designing for usability: Key principles and what designers think, *Communications of the ACM 28*, 3 (March 1985), 300–311.

Gould, John D., Boies, Stephen J., and Lewis, Clayton, Making usable, useful productivity-enhancing computer applications, *Communications of the ACM 34*, 1 (January 1991), 75–85.

Hays, William L., *Statistics* (Fourth Edition), Holt, Rinehart and Winston, New York (1988).

Hiltz, Starr Roxanne, *Online Communities: A Case Study in the Office of the Future*, Ablex, Norwood, NJ (1983).

Hiltz, Starr Roxanne, and Turoff, Murray, The evolution of user behavior in a computer conferencing system, *Communications of the ACM 24*, 11 (November 1981), 739–751.

Hirsch, Richard S., Procedures of the Human Factors Center at San Jose, *IBM Systems Journal 20*, 2 (1981), 123–171.

Ives, Blake, and Olson, Margrethe H., User involvement and MIS success: A review of research, *Management Science 30*, 5 (May 1984), 586–603.

Keen, Peter G. W., Information systems and organizational change, *Communications of the ACM 24*, 1 (January 1981), 24–33.

Kelley, J. F., An iterative design methodology for user-friendly natural language office information applications, *ACM Transactions on Office Information Systems 2*, 1 (March 1984), 26–41.

Klemmer, Edmund T. (Editor), *Ergonomics: Harness the Power of Human Factors in Your Business*, Ablex, Norwood, NJ (1989).

Lewis, Clayton, Using the "thinking aloud" method in cognitive interface design, IBM Research Report RC-9265, Yorktown Heights, NY (1982).

Lieff, Ed and Allwood, Carl-Martin, Empirical methods in the Better Terminal Use project. In Agrawal, Jagdish C., and Zunde, Pranas (Editors), *Empirical Foundations of Information and Software Science*, Plenum Press, New York and London (1985), 157–168.

Lund, Michelle A., Evaluating the user interfaces: The candid camera approach, *Proc. CHI'85—Human Factors in Computing Systems*, ACM, Baltimore, MD (1985), 93–97.

Lyons, Michael, Measuring user satisfaction: The semantic differential technique, *Proceedings of the Seventeenth Annual Computer Personnel Research Conference*, ACM SIGCPR (1980), 79–87.

Mumford, Enid, *Designing Participatively*, Manchester Business School, U.K. (1983).

Olson, Margrethe H. and Ives, Blake, User involvement in system design: An empirical test of alternative approaches, *Information and Management 4* (1981), 183–195.

Root, Robert W. and Draper, Steve, Questionnaires as a software evaluation tool, *Proc. ACM CHI'83 Human Factors in Computing Systems*, ACM, New York (1983), 83–87.

Rouse, William B., Design and evaluation of computer-based decision support systems. In Salvendy, G. (Editor), *Human–Computer Interaction, Proceedings of the First USA–Japan Conference on Human–Computer Interaction*, Elsevier Science Publishers, B. V. Amsterdam, The Netherlands (1984), 229–246.

Runyon, Richard P. and Haber, Audrey, *Fundamentals of Behavioral Statistics*, (Seventh Edition), McGraw-Hill, New York (1991).

Savage, Ricky E., Habinek, James K., and Barnhart, Thomas W., The design, simulation, and evaluation of a menu driven user interface, *Proc. Human Factors in Computer Systems Conference*, Gaithersburg, MD (March 1982), 36–40.

Thomas, John C., Organizing for human factors. In Vassiliou, Y. (Editor), *Human Factors in Interactive Computer Systems*, Ablex, Norwood, NJ (1984), 29–46.

Whiteside, John, Bennett, John, and Holtzblatt, Karen, Usability engineering: Our experience and evolution. In Helander, Martin (Editor), *Handbook of Human–Computer Interaction*, North-Holland, Amsterdam, The Netherlands (1988), 791–817.

Winer, B. J., Brown, Donald R., and Michels, Kenneth M., *Statistical Principles in Experimental Design*, McGraw-Hill, New York (1991).

User-Interface Development Environments

If standardization can be humanized and made flexible in
design and the economics brought to the home owner, the
greatest service will be rendered to our modern way of
life. It may be really born—this democracy, I mean.

Frank Lloyd Wright, *The Natural House,* **1954**

The Plan is the generator.   Without a plan, you have lack
of order and willfulness. The Plan holds in itself the
essence of sensation.

Le Corbusier, *Towards a New Architecture,* **1931**

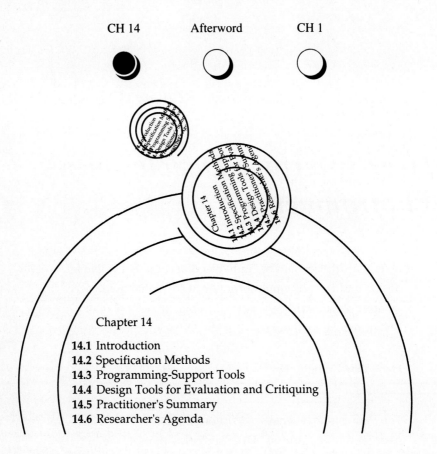

CH 14 Afterword CH 1

Chapter 14

14.1 Introduction
14.2 Specification Methods
14.3 Programming-Support Tools
14.4 Design Tools for Evaluation and Critiquing
14.5 Practitioner's Summary
14.6 Researcher's Agenda

14.1 Introduction

Log cabins were often built by settlers for personal housing on the American frontier, just as early user interfaces were built by programmers for their own use. As housing needs changed, windows and rooms were added in a process of iterative refinement, and dirt floors gave way to finished wood. Log cabins are still being built according to personal taste by rugged individualists, but modern private homes, apartment buildings, schools, hospitals, and offices require specialist training and more careful planning.

The emergence of user-interface architects, design and specification methods, standard components, and automated tools for construction are indicators of the maturation of our field. There will always be room for the innovator and the eccentric, but the demands of modern life are that we build reliable, standard, safe, inexpensive, effective, and widely acceptable user interfaces on a predictable schedule (Carey, 1988).

Like the architect, we must have simple and quick methods of sketching an interface to give the clients some way of identifying their needs. Then, we need more precise methods for working out the details with the clients (detailed floorplans become transition diagrams, screen layouts, and menu trees), coordinating with our more specialized colleagues (plumbers and electricians become graphic designers and technical writers), and for telling the builders what to do.

Like building architects, successful user-interface architects know it makes good sense to complete the design before we start building, even though we know that in the process of construction some changes will have to be made. With large projects, multiple designers (structural engineers for the steel framework, interior designers for space planning, and decorators for the esthetics) will be necessary. The size and importance of each project will determine the level of design effort and the number of participants. Just as their are specialists for airports, hospitals, and schools, there will be user interfaces specialists for air-traffic control, medical, and educational applications.

This chapter begins with user-interface specification methods, covers design notations and prototyping tools, then moves to the construction tools such as programmer toolkits and UIMSs. Although construction tools for well-accepted interface styles (menus, forms, command languages) are quite good, the tools for newer direct-manipulation and graphical user interfaces are still emerging. Like barefoot shoemaker's children, user-interface implementers often have to get by with crude interfaces that they would be embarrassed to give to their customers. Even as the power tools for established styles improve and gain acceptance, programmers will always have to hand-craft novel interface styles.

14.2   Specification Methods

The first asset in making designs is a good notation to record and discuss alternate possibilities. The default language for specifications in any field is the designer's natural language, such as English. But *natural-language specifications* tend to be lengthy, vague, and ambiguous, and therefore often are difficult to prove correct, consistent, or complete. *Formal* and *semiformal languages* have proved their value in many areas such as mathematics, physics, circuit design, music, and even knitting. Formal languages have a specified grammar, and effective procedures exist to determine whether a string adheres to the language's grammar. Grammars for command languages and multiparty grammars (Shneiderman, 1982) for interactions are fundamental methods in describing user interfaces.

Menu-tree structures are popular, and therefore specifying menu trees by simply drawing the tree and showing the menu layouts deserves attention. The more general method of *transition diagrams* has wide applicability in user-interface design. Improvements such as *statecharts* have features that are attuned to the needs of interactive systems. New approaches such as the *User Action Notation* (Hartson, 1990) are sure to proliferate.

14.2.1   Multiparty grammars

In computer programming, Backus–Naur form (also called *Backus normal form* or simply *BNF*) is often used to describe programming languages. High-level components are described by nonterminals, and specific strings are terminals. In this example of a telephone-book entry, the nonterminals describe a person's name (composed of a last name followed by a comma and a first name) and a telephone number (composed of an area code, exchange, and local number). Names consist of strings of characters. The telephone number has three components: a three-digit area code, a three-digit exchange, and a four-digit local number.

```
<Telephone book entry> ::= <Name> <Telephone number>
<Name> ::= <Last name>, <First name>
<Last name> ::= <string>
<First name> ::= <string>
<string> ::= <character>|<character><string>
<character> ::=
  A|B|C|D|E|F|G|H|I|J|K|L|M|N|O|P|Q|R|S|T|U|V|W|X|Y|Z

<Telephone number> ::= (<area code>) <exchange>-<local number>
<area code> ::= <digit><digit><digit>
<exchange> ::= <digit><digit><digit>
<local number> ::= <digit><digit><digit><digit>
<digit> ::= 0|1|2|3|4|5|6|7|8|9
```

The left-hand side of each specification line is a nonterminal (within angle brackets) that is defined by the right-hand side. Vertical bars indicate alternatives for nonterminals and terminals. Acceptable telephone-book entries include:

```
WASHINGTON, GEORGE (301) 555-1234
BEEF, STU (726) 768-7878
A, Z (999) 111-1111
```

The BNF notation is used widely, even though it is incomplete and must be supplemented by ad hoc techniques for specifying the semantics, such as permissible names or area codes. The benefit is that some aspects can be written down precisely and that software tools can be employed to verify some aspects of completeness and correctness of the grammar and of strings in the language. Command languages are nicely specified by BNF-like grammars as in the task–action grammar (Section 2.2.4). Reisner (1981) expanded the idea of BNF to sequences of actions, such as pushing a button, selecting a color, or drawing.

To accommodate the richness of interactive software, multiparty grammars (Shneiderman, 1982) have nonterminals that are labeled by the party that produces the string (typically the user, U, or the computer, C). Nonterminals acquire values during parsing for use by other parties, and therefore error-handling rules can be included easily. This grammar describes the opening steps in a log-in process:

```
<Session> ::= <U: Opening> <C: Responding>
<U: Opening> ::= LOGIN <U: Name>
<U: Name> ::= <U: string>
<C: Responding> ::= HELLO [<U: Name>]
```

Here square brackets indicate that value of the user's name should be produced by the computer in responding to the log-in command.

Multiparty grammars are quite effective for text-oriented command sequences that have repeated exchanges, such as a bank terminal. One of the attractions of multiparty grammars is that they can be used with compiler-compilers to generate quickly a prototype and a working system. Unfortunately, two-dimensional styles such as form fillin or direct manipulation and graphical layouts are more difficult to describe with multiparty grammars. Menu selection can be described by multiparty grammars, but the central aspect of tree structure and traversal is not shown conveniently in a grammar-based approach.

14.2.2   Menu trees

For many applications a *menu-selection tree* is an excellent selection style because of the simple structure that guides designers and users alike. Guidelines for the contents of the menu trees are covered in Chapter 2. Specification methods include online tools to help in the construction of menu trees and simple drawing tools that enable designers and users to see the entire tree at one time. For example, command menu tree for Lotus 1-2-3 is conveniently displayed in two pages from the user manual, as shown in Figure 14.1.

Menu trees are powerful as a specification tool since they show users, managers, implementers, and other interested parties the complete and

File Commands

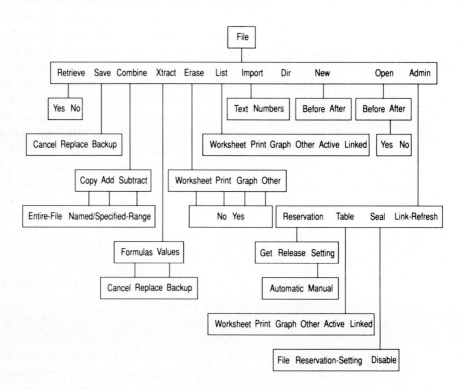

Figure 14.1

Partial menu tree from Lotus 1-2-3 showing four levels. (Printed with permission of Lotus Development Corporation, Cambridge, MA.)

detailed coverage of the system. Like any map, a menu tree shows high-level relationships and low-level details. With large systems, the menu tree may have to be laid out on a large wall or floor, but it is important to be able to see the entire structure at once to check easily for consistency, completeness, and lack of ambiguity or redundancy.

14.2.3   Transition diagrams

Menu trees are incomplete because they do not show the entire structure of possible user actions, such as returns to the previous menu, jumps to the starting menu, or detours to error handling or to help screens. However, adding all these transitions would clutter the clean structure of a menu tree.

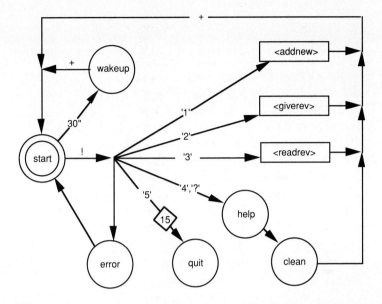

Figure 14.2

Transition diagram for a simple menu system. (Wasserman and Shewmake, 1985. Reprinted with permission of Ablex Publishing Corporation, Norwood, NJ.)

For some aspects of the design process, more precise specification of every possible transition is required. Also for many nonmenu interaction styles, there is a set of possible states and permissible transitions among the states that may not form a tree structure. For these and other circumstances, a more general design notation known as *transition diagrams* has been used widely.

Typically, the transition diagram has a set of *nodes* that represents system states and a set of *links* between the nodes that represents possible transitions. The links are labeled with the user action that selects that link and possible computer responses. The simple transition diagram in Figure 14.2 (Wasserman and Shewmake, 1985) represents a numbered menu-selection system for restaurant reviews that shows what happens if the user selects numbered choices 1 (add a restaurant to the list), 2 (provide a review of a restaurant), 3 (read a review), 4 (get help, also accessed by a ?), 5 (quit), or anything else (error message). The script that matches the transition diagram (Figure 14.3) provides additional information, but the overview of the diagram is of great assistance in comprehending the system. Figure 14.4 shows another form of transition diagram; Figure 14.5 shows its text form (Jacob, 1985).

Many forms of transition diagrams have been created with special notations to fit needs of application areas such as air-traffic control or word processing. Tools, such as MacBubbles (StarSys), for creating and maintaining transition diagrams on computer graphic displays have proliferated.

```
node start
    cs, r2, rv, c_' Interactive Restaurant Guide', sv,
    r6, c5, 'Please make a choice: ',
    r+2, c10, '1: Add new restaurant to database',
    r+2, c10, '2: Give review of a restaurant ',
    r+2, c10, '3: Read reviews for a given restaurant',
    r+2, c10, '4: Help', r+2, c10, '5: Quit', r+3,c5, 'Your choice: ', mark_A

node help
    cs, r5, c0, 'This program stores and retrieves information on',
    r+1, c0, 'restaurants, with emphasis on San Francisco.',
    r+1, c0, 'You can add or update information about restaurants',
    r+1, c0, 'already in the database, or obtain information about',
    r+1, c0, 'restaurants, including the reviews of others.',
    r+2, c0, 'To continue, type RETURN.'

node error
    r$-1, rv, 'Illegal command.', sv, 'Please type a number from 1 to 5.',
    r$, 'Press RETURN to continue.'
node clean
    r$-1, cl,r$,cl
node wakeup
    r$,cl,rv,'Please make a choice',sv, tomark_A
node quit
    cs, 'Thank you very much. Please try this program again',
    nl,'and continue to add information on restaurants.'
arc start single_key
    on '1' to <addnew>
    on '2' to <giverev>
    on '3' to <readrev>
    on '4', '?' to help
    on '5' to quit
    alarm 30 to wakeup
    else to error
arc error
    else to start
arc help
    skip to clean
arc clean
    else to start
arc <addnew>
    skip to start
arc <readrev>
    skip to start
arc <giverev>
    skip to start
```

Figure 14.3

Text form of Figure 14.2, with additional information in comment lines. (Wasserman and Shewmake, 1985. Reprinted with permission of Ablex Publishing Corporation, Norwood, NJ.)

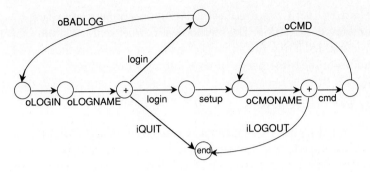

Figure 14.4

Transition diagram for simple messaging system. (Jacob, 1985. Reprinted with permission of Ablex Publishing Corporation, Norwood, NJ.)

Often, they are included as part of *computer-assisted software engineering* (CASE) environments, such as the Visible Analyst Workbench (Visible Systems). In most systems, the diagram is created by direct-manipulation actions, but designers can get a text form of the transition diagram as well. The transition diagram then acts as a generator for the system or at least for a mockup to be evaluated in a usability-laboratory test. This approach was taken at Virginia Polytechnic Institute and State University, where the SUPERvisory Methodology And Notation (SUPERMAN) (Yunten and

```
mms'end

st:            oLOGIN 'promptlog

promptlog:        oLOGNAME 'getlog

+getlog:       login '(setup,badlog)
+getlog:       iQUIT 'end

badlog:        oBADLOG 'st

setup:         setup 'promptcmd

promptcmd:     oCMDNAME 'getcmd

+getcmd:       cmd 'ready
+getcmd:       iLOGOUT 'end

ready:         oCMD 'promptcmd
;
```

Figure 14.5

Text form of Figure 14.4. (Jacob,1985. Reprinted with permission of Ablex Publishing Corporation, Norwood, NJ.)

Hartson, 1985) was used as the basis for a holistic approach to specification and implementation. The method uses direct-manipulation tools for creating and manipulating the enhanced transition diagrams that include specialized nodes to meet the needs of user-interface designers.

14.2.4   Statecharts

Although transition diagrams are effective for following flow or action and for keeping track of the current state plus current options, they can rapidly become large and confusing. Modularity is possible if nodes are included with subgraphs, but this strategy works well with only orderly, one-in, one-out graphs. Transition diagrams also become confusing when each node must show links to a help state, jumps back to the previous or start state, and a quit state. Concurrency is poorly represented by transition diagrams, although the addition of petri-net markers helps. An appealing alternative is *statecharts* (Harel, 1988) which have several virtues in specifying interfaces. Because a grouping feature is offered through nested roundtangles (Figure 14.6), repeated transitions can be factored out to the surrounding roundtangle. Extensions to statecharts such as concurrency, external interrupt events, and user actions are represented in Statemaster, which is a UIMS based on statecharts (Wellner, 1989).

14.2.5   User Action Notation (UAN)

The grammar or diagram approaches to specification are suited for menus, commands, or form fillin, but with direct-manipulation interfaces they are

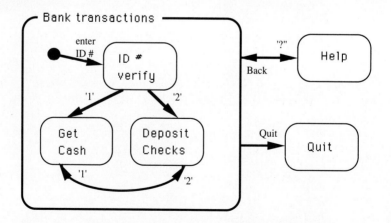

Figure 14.6

Statechart of a simplified bank-transaction system showing grouping of states.

clumsy because they cannot cope conveniently with the variety of permissible actions and visual feedback that the system must provide. In addition, direct-manipulation interfaces depend heavily on context to determine the meaning of an input. For example, a mouse-button click can mean select a file, open a window, or start an application, depending on where the cursor is when the click is applied. Similarly, it is difficult to characterize the results of dragging an icon, since it will depend on where the icon is dropped.

To cope with the rich world of direct-manipulation interfaces, high-level notations that focus on the users' tasks, that deal with pointing, dragging, and clicking, and that describe the interface feedback seem more likely to be helpful. For example, to select an icon, the user must move the cursor to the icon location and click down and release on the mouse button. The movement to an icon is represented by a ~[icon] and the mouse-button motion is represented by Mv (mouse-button depress) followed by M^ (mouse-button release). The system response, which is to highlight the icon, is represented by icon! The sequencing is shown by a complete *User Action Notation* (UAN) description (Hartson et al., 1990):

TASK: select an icon

User Actions	Interface Feedback
~[icon] Mv	icon!
M^	

A more complex task might be to delete a file, which requires user actions of dragging a file icon around the display to a trash icon while holding down the mouse button. The interface feedback is to highlight the file that is selected and to dehighlight (file-! indicates dehighlight the file) other files, then to drag an outline of the file icon to the trash icon (outline(file) > ~ means that the outline is dragged by the cursor). Then, the user drops the file-icon outline on the trash icon, the file icon is erased, and the trash icon blinks. The selected file is shown in the interface-state column:

TASK: select an icon

User Actions	Interface Feedback	Interface State
~[file] Mv	file!, forall(file!): file-!	selected = file
~[x,y]*	outline(file) > ~	
~[trash]	outline(file) > ~, trash!	
M^	erase(file), trash!!	selected = null

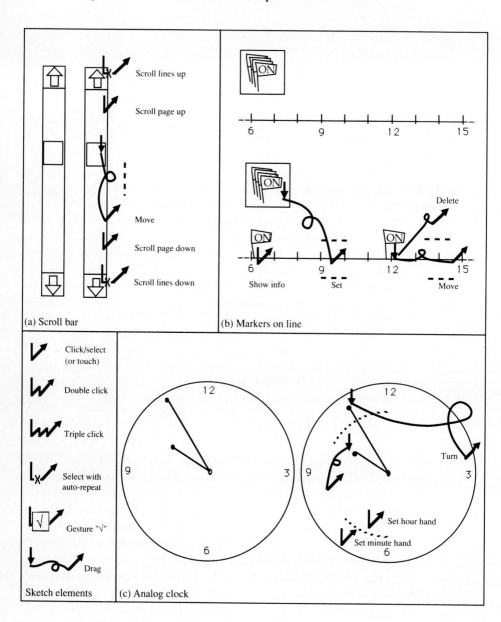

(a) Scroll bar

Scroll lines up

Scroll page up

Move

Scroll page down

Scroll lines down

(b) Markers on line

Delete

Show info   Set   Move

Sketch elements

Click/select
(or touch)

Double click

Triple click

Select with
auto-repeat

Gesture "√"

Drag

(c) Analog clock

Set hour hand

Set minute hand

Turn

The UAN has interface-specific symbols for actions such as moving the cursor, pressing a button, entering a string, or setting a value, and for concurrency, interrupts, and feedback such as highlighting, blinking, dragging, rubberbanding, and erasing. The symbols were chosen to mimic the actions—such as v for button depress, ^ for button release, and ~ for cursor movement—but it still takes a while to get used to this novel notation.

◄ **Figure 14.7**

DMsketch (Direct Manipulation Sketch, a paper version of a 20-second demo) is not a specification language, but rather is a technique to help designers exchange and record ideas. The sketches could also be used as a first level of help, each sketch being associated with a more complete description. Each figure shows a user-interface component next to the same component overlayed with DMsketches showing possible actions. Screen dumps can be a background layer with color sketches drawn on them or on transparent foils. The scroll bar DMsketch (a) shows actions for move (drag the elevator box), scroll page up–down (clicks), and scroll lines up–down (select with auto-repeat). The "markers on line" (b) shows that the flags can be used to set a time (drag to time line), can be moved along the line, or deleted (drag away from the line). The dashed lines mark the existence of a region of applicability. The "analog clock" sketch (c) shows that users can turn or set hands directly to the intended time. The drag element shows that the user control point can go outside the clock face once the hand has been grabbed. The dotted lines show the existence of a virtual inner circle, allowing the differentiation between the two hands when they are close to each other. (Developed jointly with Catherine Plaisant.)

However, the UAN is a compact, powerful, and high-level approach to specifying system behavior and describing user actions.

The UAN is a textual language, but visual languages for describing actions are being explored (Figure 14.7).

14.3 Programming-Support Tools

Specification tools are important for the early design phases when consideration of multiple alternatives is helpful, but eventually the system must be built to run in a software and hardware environment. Some specification tools can be analyzed by software tools to check for some aspects of consistency, completeness, complexity, and lack of ambiguity. In the ideal case, the specifications can also be used to generate portions of the application program automatically.

Most current programming-support tools are only weakly linked to any formal specification method. Rather, they provide designers an environment for bringing a user interface to life on the display so that further design and testing can be accomplished in the intended software and hardware platforms. Often, the prototyping tools are used as a specification method. The benefits from using these programming support tools are great (Table 14.1), and it seems likely that these tools will spread widely as they are improved. The central advantage stems from the notion of *user-interface independence*— decoupling the user-interface design from the complexities of programming. This decoupling allows the designers to lay out displays and sequences of

Table 14.1

User-Interface Management Systems

User-interface (Dialog) independence

- Separate interface design from internals.
- Enable multiple user-interface strategies.
- Establish role of user-interface architect.
- Enforce standards.

Methodology and notation

- Develop design procedures.
- Find ways to talk about design.
- Create project management.

Rapid prototyping

- Try out ideas very early.
- Test and revise repeatedly.
- Engage end users, managers, and other concerned people.

Software support

- Increase productivity.
- Offer constraint and consistency checks.
- Facilitate team approaches.
- Ease maintenance.

---

displays in just a few hours, to make revisions or alternative versions in minutes, and to support the usability-testing process. The programming effort to complete the underlying system can be applied once the user-interface design has been stabilized.

14.3.1   Screen mockup and prototyping tools

Building and user-interface architects recognize that creating quick sketches and three-dimensional models is important during the early stages of design to explore multiple alternatives, to allow communication within the design team, and to explain to clients what the product will look like. User-interface mockups can be created with paper and pencil, word processors, business slide-show presentation software (Aldus Persuasion or Microsoft Powerpoint), or specialized prototyping tools. Resourceful designers have also built user-interface prototypes with computer-assisted instruction software such as Authology, Courseware, or Pilot, and with multimedia construction tools such as MacroMind Director, VideoWorks Interactive, or AutoDesk Animator.

In the simplest case, the designers create a slide show of still images, which are turned at a user-controlled pace. The tools to support more effective prototyping are increasingly available. Dan Bricklin's Demo II Program or Proteus enable IBM PC users to design sequences of character-based (with bit-map backgrounds) displays that can contain selectable menus so that jumping among displays is easy. Cursor motion and keyboard entry is supported so that menu selection and form-fillin interaction styles can be built quickly and modified to explore alternative layouts and colors. HyperCard or Toolbook allows designers to create button-oriented prototypes quickly.

Prototyping tools usually permit designers to lay out displays with cursor movements or mouse clicks, and to mark regions for selection, highlighting, or data entry. Then, they can specify which display should be shown next, to simulate activities, to invoke online help, to produce error messages, or to display dialog boxes. Prototyping tools are excellent aides to design discussions and are effective in winning contracts because clients can be given a rough idea of what the finished system will be like. However, software packages that support only prototyping require the implementers to start from scratch when creating the application program. You can imagine the frustration of the implementers when they consider writing code to produce the 1000 screens that were built in a few months by the design team.

14.3.2 Programming toolkits

Experienced programmers have built user interfaces with low-level assembly languages, high-level programming languages (C, Pascal, BASIC, COBOL, Ada, etc.), user-interface program libraries, and more advanced programming toolkits. Programming languages with accompanying libraries of functions are familiar to experienced programmers and afford great flexibility. However, the effort to build user interfaces with toolkits is great, potential for errors or lack of standardization is high, revisions are time consuming, and maintenance is difficult. Advanced *programming toolkits* are designed to provide programmers with specially designed routines that handle standard *widgets* such as windows, scroll bars, pull-down or pop-up menus, data-entry fields, buttons, and dialog boxes.

Toolkits can become complex, and the programming environments for those such as Microsoft Windows 3.0 Developer's Toolkit, Apple Macintosh MacApp, and UNIX X-Windows toolkit (Xtk) require months of learning for programmers to gain proficiency. Even then the burden in creating applications is great, and maintenance is difficult. The advantage is that the programmer has extensive control and great flexibility in creating the interface. Toolkits have become popular with programmers, but they provide only partial support for consistency, and designers and managers must still depend heavily on experienced programmers. The Motif example in Figure 14.8 conveys the challenge of programming user interfaces in X.

```
X/* Written by Dan Heller.  Copyright 1991, O'Reilly & Associates.
X * This program is freely distributable without licensing fees and
X * is provided without guarantee or warrantee expressed or implied.
X * This program is -not- in the public domain.
X */
========================================================
X    /* main window contains a MenuBar and a Label displaying a pixmap */
X    main_w = XtVaCreateManagedWidget("main_window",
X        xmMainWindowWidgetClass,   toplevel,
X        XmNscrollBarDisplayPolicy, XmAS_NEEDED,
X        XmNscrollingPolicy,        XmAUTOMATIC,
X        NULL);
X
X    /* Create a simple MenuBar that contains three menus */
X    file = XmStringCreateSimple("File");
X    edit = XmStringCreateSimple("Edit");
X    help = XmStringCreateSimple("Help");
X    menubar = XmVaCreateSimpleMenuBar(main_w, "menubar",
X        XmVaCASCADEBUTTON, file, 'F',
X        XmVaCASCADEBUTTON, edit, 'E',
X        XmVaCASCADEBUTTON, help, 'H',
X        NULL);
X    XmStringFree(file);
X    XmStringFree(edit);
X    /* don't free "help" compound string yet -- reuse it for later */
X
X    /* Tell the menubar which button is the help menu  */
X    if (widget = XtNameToWidget(menubar, "button_2"))
X        XtVaSetValues(menubar, XmNmenuHelpWidget, widget, NULL);
```

Figure 14.8

The challenge of programming user interfaces, using Motif.

Simplified programming languages with powerful features for user-interface construction have also become popular. Apple's HyperCard (Figure 11.2) allows designers to do some user-interface design merely by selecting buttons and other fields with simple semantics provided automatically (for example, clicking on a back-arrow would take the user to the previous card). For more complex requirements, the innovative HyperTalk language enables many users to create interesting interfaces with only moderate training. Programs can often be written with easy-to-understand terms:

```
on mouseUp
        play "boing"
        wait for 3 seconds
        visual effect wipe left very fast to black
        click at 150,100
        type "goodbye"
end mouseUp
```

Figure 14.9

Prograph 2.5 on the
Macintosh has visual
programming tools to
support user interface and
program development.
(Courtesy of TGS Systems,
Halifax, Nova Scotia,
Canada.)

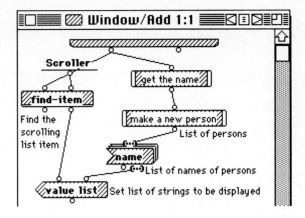

Of course, programming in such languages can often become exceedingly complex.

HyperCard's success spawned many variations, such as SuperCard on the Macintosh and Toolbook (Asymetrix) or Visual Basic (Microsoft) on the IBM PC. Features vary widely (availability of multiple windows, color, high-resolution displays, touchscreen support, string search, printing, rapid execution, storage management, invocation of external programs, etc.) and improvements are being made continuously. *Visual programming tools* with direct manipulation, such as Prograph 2.5 (TGS Systems) on the Macintosh, are an increasingly popular direction. Prograph 2.5 allows users to edit, execute, debug, and make changes during execution, with visual programming tools (Figure 14.9).

Combinations of prototyping tools and programming toolkits are available to support rapid application-system development by programmers. For example, C-scape can take the information from Dan Bricklin's Demo II program and create C language code for the user interface. Then the programmers can quickly move on to creating the supporting software. Skylights allows direct-manipulation user interfaces to be created on the IBM PC, and then provides a framework for application development. Similarly, the Smethers–Barnes Prototyper allows elaborate prototypes to be built rapidly on the Macintosh. Its capacity to generate C or Pascal source code and its advanced features have raised it to the level of being an *interface builder*.

Although it is difficult to find sharp boundaries to distinguish the growing variety of tools for interface developers, there are two important distinctions: how smoothly the tool leads to a running system and how much programming in traditional languages is necessary. As programmer-oriented toolkits are given improved interfaces (form fillin is commonly used to specify attributes of widgets) and are promoted to the level of interface builder, a larger community of people will be able to participate in the development process. Interface builders tailored for specific application domains (banking, scientific instruments, publishing, etc.) or hardware requirements (touchscreen, videodisc, music, etc.) are emerging rapidly.

14.3.3   User-interface management systems (UIMSs)

The term *user-interface management system* (UIMS) is used to describe software tools that enable designers to create a complete and working user interface without having to program in a traditional programming language. The users may have to use a programming language to implement additional functions such as database search, network communication, or scientific computation, but the user interface can be created, revised, and maintained in a high-level language, often with menus, forms, and direct-manipulation actions (Olsen, 1987; Myers, 1988, 1989).

The key idea in UIMSs is *user-interface independence* (or dialog independence), paralleling the idea of *data independence* in database-management systems (DBMSs). In both cases, the goal is to separate the logical design or user interface from the underlying implementation aspects "so that modifications in either tend not to cause changes in the other" (Hartson and Hix, 1989). In DBMSs, information designers do not need to know the physical file-manipulation operations (index management, hash-coding algorithms and collision resolution, pointer manipulation, deletion marking, etc.) to create information systems. Changes to the physical file organization, optimization algorithms, security, backup, and other computer-related aspects should not affect the information designer. Information designers can make certain changes to the information presentation without tampering with the internal storage, and transformations are handled automatically.

Similar independence of action is attained with UIMSs; user-interface architects can be insulated from the menu-traversal algorithms, error handling routines, or help-text storage strategies, and can concentrate on design issues. Some changes to internal algorithms can be done without effecting the user interface, and some changes to user interfaces can be done without recompiling programs. The major advantage of UIMSs is that the process of development becomes more open: It is more visible and comprehensible by a wider range of people, making changes easier as a result of usability testing. At the same time, the UIMS approach helps to ensure greater consistency in design because standard widgets are used, layouts can be made uniform, and terminology can be controlled. Instructional text, online help, and error messages are likely to get more attention in the UIMS context. From a management perspective, demonstrations are possible early, usability testing is facilitated, and the development process is more predictable. It is true that UIMSs are still new and therefore are prone to being "buggy," poorly documented, and frequently updated and enhanced. Also, there is some resistance on the part of programmers, since they are reluctant to learn to use yet another tool, but these impediments parallel the experience with DBMSs. Within a few years, most user interfaces will be built with UIMSs, and the convenience of these tools will greatly expand the number of people who create novel interfaces.

Some UIMSs support only text interfaces to create menus and forms. For many applications, these tools are not only adequate, but also excellent and appropriate. IBM's ISPF 3 has evolved over many years and many thousands of applications to be a powerful and rich environment to create user interfaces for mainframe-connected information systems, such as reservations, banking, inventory, order entry, or personnel management. Similarly DEC's Forms Management System (FMS) or Hewlett-Packard's VPLUS provide excellent support for these interfaces styles.

Hartson and Hix (1989) provide a thorough and thoughtful historical review of early academic and commercial systems, such as the George Washington University's GWUIMS (Sibert et al., 1988), which led to SUIMS and UIDE (Foley et al., 1990); Virginia Tech's Dialogue Management System (Roach et al., 1985); TRW's FLAIR II, Computer Technology Associate's Rapid Intelligent Prototyping Laboratory (RIPL); Interactive Development Environment's RAPID/USE (Wasserman and Shewmake, 1985); Boeing's TIGER, which matured into Electronic Data Systems' OASIS (Kasik et al., 1990); and Apollo's Domain/Dialogue (which is now H-P/Apollo's Open Dialogue). The current direction in applications and in UIMS tools is certainly toward graphics user interfaces with direct manipulation (Myers, 1988). Modern UIMSs for workstations include NeXT's User Interface Builder (Webster, 1990), Sun Microsystems' Developer's Guide (Sun Microsystems, 1990), and NASA's Transportable Applications Executive (TAE) Plus (Szczur, 1990).

The NeXT User Interface Builder's (Webster, 1989) palette of *controls* (widgets) includes sliders, radio buttons, check boxes, text entry fields, labels, scrolling lists, and buttons (Figure 14.10). Once the controls have been selected and dragged into place, the designer can choose attributes (properties) for each control from an `Inspector panel` (Figure 14.11). The simple actions for sizing, moving, and copying controls enables many kinds of complex user interfaces to be built quickly, such as the mockup for a dynamic query (Figure 11.9). Some linkages between controls can be specified by direct manipulation, but usually code must be written in Objective-C to complete the system.

A similar approach is used in Sun Microsystems developer's guide (Graphic User Interface Design Editor), called *DevGuide* (Sun Microsystems, 1990). It enables designers to select *glyphs* (widgets) from a palette (Figure 14.12), and to drag them to the appropriate position on a window or dialog

Figure 14.10

NeXT User Interface
Builder palette of controls
(widgets) that can be
dragged to create user-
interface elements.
(Webster, 1990. Reprinted
with permission of
Addison-Wesley Publ.
Co., Reading, MA).

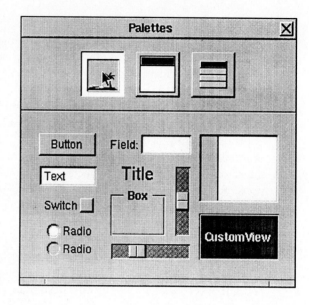

box, and then to specify the properties such as labels, location, size, orientation, etc. (Figure 14.13 shows a property window for sliders). When the designer has created the desired interface by moving the widgets to their desired
location, it is possible to test some aspects of the user interface immediately.
Simple interfaces can be built in a few minutes, but other projects with hundreds of displays may take months to design. Once the design is complete,
DevGuide can produce the code that forms the basis (software procedure
stubs) for the completed system. The architecture of the software allows revisions to the interface while preserving the linkage to the code.

The innovative Simple User Interface Toolkit (SUIT) (Pausch, 1991), built
for educational purposes, allows user-interface design students to create
interfaces that will run on Macintosh, IBM PC, and Sun workstations
(Figure 14.14).

A more elaborate approach to user-interface development is IBM's research and development project called ITS (Wiecha et al., 1990). UIMSs
typically make a separation between the user-interface design facilities and
the application programming facilities, but ITS has four layers: *actions* to
read or write values, *dialog* specification of control flow among logical
frames, *style rules* to ensure consistent usage of widgets, and *style programs* to
indicate layout of widgets for a specific display. Although this layering does
make designing more complex, the modularity can be an advantage for
organizations with multiple large projects, where four roles might be
assigned: application programmer to create actions, application expert
familiar with the problem domain to specify the dialog requirements, style

Figure 14.11

NeXT User Interface Builder inspector panel to set attributes of user-interface elements. (Webster, 1990. Reprinted with permission of Addison-Wesley Publ. Co., Reading, MA.)

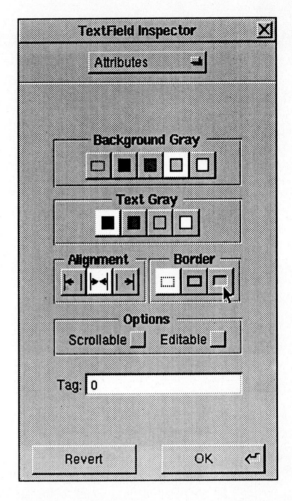

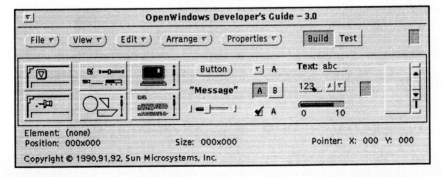

Figure 14.12

Sun Microsystem's Developer's Guide palette of glyphs (widgets) that can be dragged to create user-interface elements. (Copyright 1991 by Sun Microsystems, Inc., Mountain View, CA.)

Figure 14.13

Sun Microsystem's Developer's Guide property window to select and set properties of a slider. (Copyright 1991 by Sun Microsystems, Inc., Mountain View, CA.)

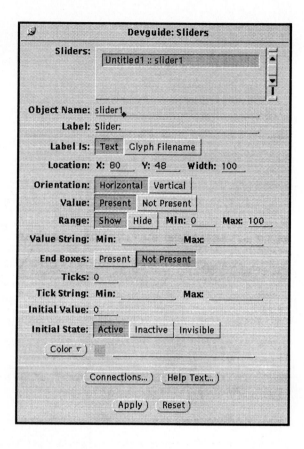

expert with graphic design and human-factors skills to coordinate look and feel across multiple applications, and style programmer to allocate space on different-sized displays, to manage input clicks, and to determine what happens in cases such as when users resize windows at run time.

Although ITS may be a step forward in its advanced architecture, the notation for specifying dialogs or style rules is still closer to a traditional command language. The dialog for an initial display in an airline-reservations system might be:

```
:frame id=main
    :choice purpose=overview, messages="Select an item to"
        :ci message="View today's flights",activate=check_today
        :ci message="View future flights",activate=check_future
        :ci message="Make reservation",activate=reserve
    :echoice
:eframe
```

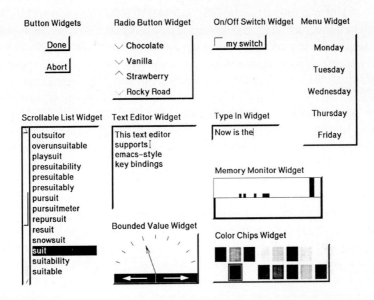

Figure 14.14

Simple User Interface Toolkit (SUIT) widget set includes radio buttons, menus, text entry, scrolling lists, color selector, and a graphic value selector that currently appears as a gauge but can become a scroll bar, thermometer, etc. (Pausch, 1991. Permission of Randy Pausch.)

The style rules to create help and quit buttons horizontally might be:

```
:conditions source=frame
   :unit type=VertGroup
      :unit type=Title
      :eunit
      :unit type=HorzGroup
          Frame contents arranged horizontally here
          :unit replicate=all
          :eunit
      :eunit
   :content
      :choice purpose=useraction
         :ci message=Help,activate=AppHelp
         :ci message=Quit,action=shutdown
      :echoice
   :econtent
   :eunit
:econditions
```

An important part of the ITS concept is that the system provides an environment for including emerging results from empirical studies of layout and interface design. As new guidelines are developed and verified, they can influence the style rules and lead to improvements in a whole family of applications with minimal effort. ITS promises greater flexibility than other systems in accommodating new hardware and changes to the application requirements.

Advanced methods for creating user interfaces seem likely to emerge in the future. Specification-by-example and programming-by-example allow designers to create a layout by direct manipulation of graphical objects. When there are ambiguities, the system prompts the designer to make choices. This approach to construction, pioneered in Peridot and refined in Garnet (Myers, 1988; Myers et al., 1989), allows high-level constraint specification by nonprogrammers. The advantages are great because, after the user indicates that data-entry fields should be aligned or that titles should be centered, the system can revise the layout even when changes are made to the screen size or new fields are added (Hudson and Mohamed, 1990).

14.4   Design Tools for Evaluation and Critiquing

The UIMS and ITS approaches are natural environments in which to add software to evaluate or critique the user interface. First, simple metrics that report numbers of displays, widgets, links between displays, etc. are likely to appear merely to capture the size of a user-interface project. But it does seem appropriate to suggest the inclusion of more sophisticated *evaluation packages* that can assess whether a menu tree is too deep or contains redundancies, widget labels have been used consistently, all buttons have proper transitions associated with them, etc. (Olsen and Halversen, 1988).

A second set of tools is *run-time logging software* to capture the users' patterns of activity. Simple reports, such as on the frequency of each error message, menu-item selection, dialog-box appearance, help invocation, form-field usage, etc., are of great benefit to maintenance personnel and to revisers of the initial design. Experimental researchers can also capture performance data for alternative designs to guide their decision making. Software to analyze and summarize the performance data will be welcome.

A good model for future developers is Tullis's Display Analysis Program, Version 4.0, which takes alphanumeric screen designs (no color, highlighting, separator lines, or graphics) and produces Tullis's display-complexity metrics plus some advice, such as this (Tullis, 1988):

```
Upper-case letters: 77% The percentage of upper-case letters
is high.
        Consider using more lower-case letters, since text
        printed in normal upper- and lower-case letters is
```

```
         read about 13% faster than text in all upper case.
         Reserve all upper-case for items that need to attract
         attention.

   Maximum local density = 89.9% at row 9, column 8.
   Average local density = 67.0%
         The area with the highest local density is
         identified...you can reduce local density by distrib-
         uting the characters as evenly as feasible over the
         entire screen.

   Total layout complexity = 8.02 bits
   Layout complexity is high.
         This means that the display items (labels and data)
         are not well aligned with each other...Horizontal
         complexity can be reduced by starting items in fewer
         different columns on the screen (that is, by aligning
         them vertically).
```

Analyzers for graphic displays, color, menu trees, error messages, online help, transition diagrams, etc. seem like worthy goals. As UIMSs become more widely used, analyzers will become attractive to determine whether widget placement and display sequences are well matched with the sequences of actions required for frequent tasks.

14.5   Practitioner's Summary

There will always be a need to write user interfaces with traditional programming tools, but the advantages of advanced toolkits, prototyping tools, and UIMSs will be increasingly attractive as the software improves and becomes widely known. The benefits include an order-of-magnitude increase in productivity, shorter development schedules, support for usability testing, ease in making changes and ensuring consistency, better management control, and reduced training necessary for designers.

The profusion of current tools and the promises of improved tools requires that managers, designers, and programmers stay informed and make fresh choices for each project. This educational process can be enlightening, since the benefits of improved and appropriate tools are enormous if the right tools are selected (Hix and Schulman, 1991) (Table 14.2).

From the toolmaker's viewpoint, there are still great opportunities to create effective tools that handle more user-interface situations, that produce output for multiple software and hardware platforms, that are easier to learn, that are more powerful, and that provide better evaluation. Existing CASE tools could be expanded to include UIMS features.

Table 14.2

Issues in choosing among UIMS and other software tools.

Issues in Choosing Software Tools

Widgets supported

- Windows and dialog boxes
- Pull-down or pop-up menus
- Buttons (rectangles, roundtangles, etc.)
- Radio buttons and switches
- Scroll bars (horizontal and vertical)
- Data-entry fields
- Field labels
- Boxes and separator lines
- Sliders, guages, meters

Interface features

- Color, graphics, images, animation, video
- Varying display size (low to high resolution)
- Sounds, music, voice input and output
- Mouse, arrow keys, touchscreen, stylus

Software architecture

- Prototype only, prototype plus application-programming support, UIMS
- Specification method (command language, menu, form fillin, or direct manipulation)
- Levels and strength of user-interface independence
- Programming language (specialized, standard (C, Pascal), visual)
- Evaluation and documentation tools
- Interface with database, graphics, networking, spreadsheets, etc.
- Logging during testing and use

Management issues

- Number of satisfied users of the tool
- Supplier reliability and stability
- Cost
- Documentation, training, and technical support
- Project-management support

14.6   Researcher's Agenda

Formal models of user interfaces and specification languages are at only the Model T stage of development. Much of the knowledge from software engineering and computer-science theory can be applied to UIMS development. Innovative methods of specification involving graphical constraints or visual programming seem to be a natural match for creating graphical user interfaces. Improved software architectures are needed to ease the burden during revision and maintenance of user interfaces. Structured editors, hypertext, and cooperative computing may provide a sound basis for developing more powerful authoring tools that enable multiple designers to work together effectively on large projects. Other opportunities exist to create tools for designers of interfaces in novel environments using sound, animation, video, and virtual reality, and manipulating physical devices as in flexible manufacturing systems or home automation. Other challenges are to specify dynamic processes (gestural input), to handle continuous input (data streams from a sensor), and to synchronize activities (pop up a reminder box for 10 seconds, if a file has not been saved after 30 minutes of editing). As new interfaces styles emerge, there will always be a need to develop new tools to facilitate their construction.

References

Carey, Tom, The gift of good design tools. In Hartson, H. R. and Hix, D. (Editors), *Advances in Human–Computer Interaction*, Volume II, Ablex, Norwood, NJ (1988), 175–213.

Foley, James, Kim, Wong Chul, Kovacevic, Srdjan, and Murray, Kevin, Defining interfaces at a high level of abstraction, *IEEE Software 6*, 1 (January 1989), 25–32.

Harel, David, On visual formalisms, *Communications of the ACM 31*, 5 (May 1988), 514–530.

Hartson, H. Rex and Hix, Deborah, Human–computer interface development: Concepts and systems for its management, *ACM Computing Surveys 21*, 1 (March 1989), 5–93.

Hartson, H. Rex, Siochi, Antonio C., and Hix, Deborah, The UAN: User-oriented representation for direct manipulation interface designs, *ACM Transactions on Information Systems 8*, 3 (July 1990), 181–203.

Hix, Deborah and Schulman, Robert S., Human–computer interface development tools: A methodology for their evaluation, *Communications of the ACM 34*, 3 (March 1991), 74–87

Hudson, Scott E. and Mohamed, Shamim P., Interactive specification of flexible user interface displays, *ACM Transactions on Information Systems 8*, 3 (July 1990), 269–288.

Jacob, Robert J. K., An executable specification technique for describing human–computer interaction. In Hartson, H. Rex (Editor), *Advances in Human–Computer Interaction 1*, Ablex, Norwood, NJ (1985), 211–242.

Jacob, Robert J. K., A state transition diagram language for visual programming, *IEEE Computer 18*, 8 (1985), 51–59.

Kasik, David J., Lund, Michelle A., and Ramsey, Henry W., Reflections on using a UIMS for complex applications, *IEEE Software 6*, 1 (January 1989), 54–61.

Myers, Brad A., *Creating User Interfaces by Demonstration*, Academic Press, Boston, MA (1988).

Myers, Brad, User interface tools: Introduction and survey, *IEEE Software 6*, 1 (January 1989), 15–23.

Myers, Brad, Vander Zanden, Brad, and Dannenberg, Roger, Creating graphical interactive application objects by demonstration, *Proc. ACM SIGGRAPH Symposium on User Interface Software and Technology* (1989), 95–104.

Olsen, Jr., Dan R. (Editor), ACM SIGGRAPH workshop on software tools for user interface management, *Computer Graphics 21*, 2 (April 1987), 71–147.

Olsen, Jr., Dan R. and Halversen, Bradley W., Interface usage measurement in a User Interface Management System, *Proc. ACM SIGGRAPH Symposium on User Interface Software and Technology* (1988), 102–108.

Pausch, Randy, Young III, Nathaniel, and DeLine, Robert, Simple user interface toolkit (SUIT): The Pascal of user interface toolkits, *Proc. ACM Symposium on User Interface Software and Technology 4* (1991), 117–125.

Reisner, Phyllis, Formal grammar and design of an interactive system, *IEEE Transactions on Software Engineering SE-5* (1981), 229–240.

Roach, J., Hartson, H. R., Ehrich, R., Yunten, T., and Johnson, D., DMS: A comprehensive system for managing human–computer dialogues, *Proc. Human Factors in Computer Systems Conference*, Gaithersburg, MD (March 1982), 102–105.

Shneiderman, Ben, Multi-party grammars and related features for defining interactive systems, *IEEE Systems, Man, and Cybernetics SMC-12*, 2 (March–April 1982), 148–154.

Sibert, J. L., Hurley, W. D., and Bleser, T. W., Design and implementation of an object-oriented user interface management system. In Hartson, H. R. and Hix, D. (Editors), *Advances in Human–Computer Interaction: Volume II*, Ablex, Norwood, NJ (1988), 175–213.

Sun Microsystems, *Open Windows Developer's Guide 1.1: User's Guide,* Mountain View, CA (1990).

Szczur, Martha, A user interface development tool for space science systems, *Proc. AIAA/NASA Symposium on Space Information Systems*, NASA Goddard, Greenbelt, MD (1990).

Tullis, Thomas, A system for evaluating screen formats: research and application. In Hartson, H. Rex and Hix, D. (Editors), *Advances in Human–Computer Interaction Vol. II*, Ablex, Norwood, NJ (1988), 214–286.

Wasserman, Anthony I., Extending state transition diagrams for the specification of human–computer interaction, *IEEE Transactions on Software Engineering 11*, 8 (August 1985), 699–713.

Wasserman, Anthony I., and Shewmake, David T., The role of prototypes in the User Software Engineering (USE) methodology. In Hartson, Rex (Editor), *Advances in Human–Computer Interaction 1*, Ablex, Norwood, NJ (1985), 191–210.

Webster, Bruce F., *The NeXT Book*, Addison-Wesley, Reading, MA (1989).

Wellner, Pierre D., Statemaster: A UIMS based on statecharts for prototyping and target implementation, *Proc. CHI '89 Conference—Human Factors in Computing Systems*, ACM, New York (1989), 177–182.

Wiecha, Charles, Bennett, William, Boies, Stephen, Gould John, and Greene, Sharon, ITS: A tool for rapidly developing interactive applications, *ACM Transactions on Information Systems 8*, 3 (July 1990), 204–236.

Yunten, Tamer, and Hartson, H. Rex, A SUPERvisory Methodology And Notation (SUPERMAN) for human–computer system development. In Hartson, Rex (Editor), *Advances in Human–Computer Interaction 1*, Ablex, Norwood, NJ (1985), 243–282.

Social and Individual Impact of User Interfaces

People who are so fascinated by the computer's lifelike feats—it plays chess! it writes poetry!—that they would turn it into the voice of omniscience, betray how little understanding they have of either themselves, their mechanical-electrical agents or the potentialities of life.

Lewis Mumford, *The Myth of the Machine,* **1970**

The machine itself makes no demands and holds out no promises: it is the human spirit that makes demands and keeps promises. In order to reconquer the machine and subdue it to human purposes, one must first understand it and assimilate it. So far we have embraced the machine without fully understanding it.

Lewis Mumford, *Technics and Civilization,* **1934**

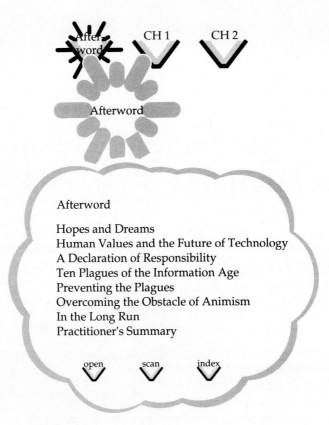

Hopes and Dreams

Why are many people enthusiastic about computers? For some, there is immediate gratification in using new technology and gadgets. For others, the opportunity for financial success or professional advancement must be appealing. Other motives are the sense of power computers offer to users and the feeling of godlike creation they convey (Turkle, 1984). These strong forces generate intense engagement for some people.

Beyond these motivations, what benefits to individuals and society might accrue from the widespread use of computers (Birnbaum, 1985)? Each person forms an individual answer, but here is a starting list of personal motivations to use computers.

- *Productivity enhancement*: The most natural way to promote computers in organizations and also for individuals is to suggest that the users will become more productive. Enthusiasts claim that time and cost to complete tasks can be reduced by employment of computers. For well-defined tasks in which information processing is prominent, there is little doubt that computers can produce benefits. Accounting, inventory, reservations, mathematical computations, library information retrieval, insurance claims, banking, student registration, and factory automation are only some of the areas in which successful applications of computers increase productivity. More difficult questions are: Who are the beneficiaries of the productivity gains? How are these gains distributed?

- *Quality improvement*: Since productivity is improved and the tedious parts of some work can be reduced by use of computers, there is an opportunity to improve quality of work. Word-processor users can take the time to ensure that consistent terminology is used, that spelling is correct, that complete references are included in scientific articles, and that comments from colleagues are taken into account. Hotel- or airline-reservations systems can help to ensure that individual physical or dietary needs are accommodated and that the lowest rate is offered. Automated factories can deliver custom-designed and thoroughly tested products.

- *Individual opportunity*: In the 1960s, the popular phrase was "[computer] power to the people"; in the 1970s, many people talked about "self-actualization." The 1980s were devoted to individual growth or opportunity. Indeed, in the 1960s, computers were available primarily to big business and big government, creating an imbalance. By the 1980s, personal computers had become widely—although not universally—available, thus offering many people the chance to be entrepreneurs and to develop a business or other interest of their own. The power of the computer enables individuals more easily to publish newsletters, to provide investment or accounting services, to develop educational materials, to write novels, to run mail-order businesses, or to develop a consulting company. Other information-intensive tasks that can be aided by personal computers include doing political campaigning, handling community organizing, maintaining family histories, and managing religious groups, parent–teacher associations, performing-arts troupes, or museums. Personal applications—such as home finance, tax preparation, automobile maintenance, health records, or vacation planning—are certain to expand.

- *Exploration*: Easy access to computing can encourage exploration of new ideas and individual self-expression. The chemist can easily try new mathematical models, the political scientist can conveniently trace voting patterns, the corporate planner can rapidly generate multiple business strategies, and the artist can experiment with a new medium for visual, aural, or tactile compositions.

- *Learning*: Computer facilitation of learning is still in its early stages. The familiar computer-assisted instruction systems with drill-and-practice strategies are simple, first applications of computers for rote memorization or forced learning. Some educational games offer role-playing fantasies that attempt to portray realistic situations, such as emergency-room decision making or a pioneer's wagon trip across the plains in the 1800s. Lively environments for learning are emerging in which the learner sets goals, encounters problems, formulates plans, measures progress, searches databases, performs computations, interacts with other people, and derives satisfaction from accomplishments (Bork, 1981; 1985).

- *Entertainment*: Never underestimate the importance of entertainment, sports, and leisure-time activities as potential applications of computers. The videogame phenomenon is well reported; computers also allow sports enthusiasts to manage Little League schedules; enable collectors to maintain stamp, music, or book collections; and permit students to explore mathematical puzzles.

- *Cooperation*: Increasingly, computers and communication networks offer the possibility of cooperation among people. Network facilities allow electronic mail among individuals, computer conferencing within organizations, interactive game playing, group decision making, and information sharing.

Human Values and the Future of Technology

We must learn to balance the material wonders of technology with the spiritual demands of our human nature.   **John Naisbitt, 1982**

Beyond the personal motivations, I believe that most designers desire to shape the future by ensuring that computers "serve human needs" (Mumford, 1934). An explicit list of enduring values can be a helpful guide for designers and developers for the next decade, century, and thereafter. After setting our goals, we can pursue the components and seek the process for fulfilling them.

Those who believe that they can change the future will change the future. This optimistic view is an extreme statement, but it does contain an important, useful, and action-oriented message. If commentators give up cursing the darkness of fatalism and light a candle of hope, they can guide us to a positive image of the future. Even with a positive attitude, however, inventing the future is not easy.

As scientists and technologists, we must begin with a belief that we can influence the future of technology (Florman, 1976). This goal seems realistic, since every day corporations and government agencies choose which technologies to support, and thereby shape the future. The lively debates about space exploration, the strategic defense initiative (star wars), heart transplants, high-definition television, recombinant DNA, birth control, etc. are powerful testimony that social forces are at work to shape the future of technology.

Similarly, I argue that decision makers in government, corporations, universities, etc. can and must take responsibility for shaping the future of people who use computers. My concern is on how users are empowered by new technologies, how they apply their growing power, and what choices researchers and developers make to influence user interfaces. I believe that we can choose to build a future in which computer users experience competence, clarity, control, comfort, and feelings of mastery and accomplishment. At the end of the day, these users can take pride in a job done well, and can appreciate the designers who created the technology.

A Declaration of Responsibility

I firmly believe that any organization, in order to survive and achieve success,
must have a sound set of beliefs on which it premises all its policies and
actions...the basic philosophy, spirit, and drive of an organization have far more to
do with its relative achievements than do technological or economic resources....
Tom Watson, Jr., 1962, cited by Jin, 1991

Earlier in this century, physicists recognized their responsibility in dealing with atomic energy and vigorously debated the issues. I believe that we in the computing professions must also recognize our responsibilities and set an example of moral leadership by inspiring discussion and influencing colleagues in other fields of science or in engineering, social sciences, medicine, law, etc. I believe that computer technology is pivotal in shaping the future, since it influences daily life in every office, store, farm, school, factory, and home (Zuboff, 1988). We have a unique responsibility to consider the influence of our technology and to guide it to produce the maximum benefits with minimum harm.

Therefore, I propose a *Declaration of Responsibility*:

1. We, the researchers, designers, managers, implementers, testers, and
   trainers of user interfaces and information systems, recognize the power-

ful influence of our science and technology. Therefore, we commit ourselves to studying ways to enable users to accomplish their personal and organizational goals while pursuing higher societal goals and serving human needs.

2. We agree to prepare a social-impact statement (patterned on the environmental-impact statement) at the start of every human–computer interaction project. The social-impact statement will identify user communities, establish training requirements, specify potential negative side effects (health, safety, privacy, financial, etc.), and indicate monitoring procedures to be used for the project's lifetime.

3. Our professional societies will prepare an agenda of vital, specific, and realizable goals for the next decade (with some thought to the next century and thereafter). These goals will be ambitious and inspirational for our profession and for others.

4. We recognize that each researcher, designer, manager, implementer, tester, and trainer of user interfaces and information systems has the right to reject the use of computers or destructive purposes, and has the responsibility to criticize potentially harmful applications.

Philosophers and ethicists can help us to refine the higher-level goals; entrepreneurs and marketeers can inform us of the practical realities. Project managers and experienced government regulators can help us to shape the social-impact statement so that it helps designers to meet their goals while reducing costs, saving time, and increasing quality. For people directly involved in creating the scientific theories and designing working systems, the following sections are a starting point for new ways of thinking.

Ten Plagues of the Information Age

The real question before us lies here: do these instruments further life and enhance its values, or not? **Mumford, 1934**

It would be naive to assume that widespread use of computers brings only benefits. There are legitimate reasons to worry that increased dissemination of computers might lead to a variety of oppressions—personal, organizational, political, or social. People who fear computers have good reason for their concerns. Computer-system designers have an opportunity and a responsibility to be alert to the dangers and to make thoughtful decisions about reducing the dangers they perceive. Here, then, is a personal list of potential and real dangers from use of computer systems:

- *Anxiety*: Many people avoid the computer or use it with great anxiety; they suffer from *computer shock, terminal terror,* or *network neurosis.* Their anxieties include the fear of breaking the machine, worry over losing control to the computer, trepidation about appearing foolish or incompetent ("computers make you feel so dumb"), or the common concern about facing something new. These anxieties are real, should be acknowledged rather than dismissed, and can often be overcome with positive experiences. Can we build improved user interfaces and systems that will reduce or eliminate the current high level of anxiety experienced by many users? In fact, can we not set our goal to make use of computers appealing, engaging, relaxing, and satisfying?

- *Alienation*: As people spend more time using computers, they may become less connected to other people (Sheridan, 1980). Computer users as a group are more introverted than are other people, and increased time with the computer may increase their isolation. One psychologist (Brod, 1984) fears that computer users come to expect rapid performance, yes–no or true–false responses, and a high degree of control not only from their machines but also from their friends, spouses, and children. The dedicated video-game player who rarely communicates with another person is an extreme case, but what happens to the emotional relationships of a person who spends 2 hours per day dealing with electronic mail rather than chatting with colleagues? Studies of households with personal computers reveal that family time watching television is reduced and that individuals spend more time using the computer or doing other projects alone (Vitalari et al., 1985). Can we build user interfaces that encourage more constructive human social interaction?

- *Information-poor minority*: Although some utopian visionaries believe that computers will eliminate the distinctions between rich and poor or right social injustices, often computers are just another way in which the disadvantaged are disadvantaged. Those people without computer skills may have a new reason for not succeeding in school or not getting a job. Already great disparity exists in the distribution of educational computers. The high-income school districts are more likely to have computer facilities than are the poorer school districts. Access to information resources is also disproportionately in the hands of the wealthy and established social communities. Can we build systems that empower low-skilled workers to perform at the level of experts? Can we arrange training and education for every able member of society?

- *Impotence of the individual*: Large organizations can become impersonal because the cost of handling special cases is great. Individuals who are frustrated in trying to receive personal treatment and attention may vent their anger at the organization, the personnel they encounter, or the technology that limits rather than enables. People who have tried to find out the current status of their social-security accounts or tried to have banks explain accounting discrepancies are aware of the problems, especially if they have language, or hearing deficits, or other physical handicaps. Interactive computer systems can be used to increase the influence of individuals or provide special treatment, but this application requires alert committed designers and sympathetic managers. How can we design so that individuals will feel more empowered and self-actualized?

- *Bewildering complexity and speed*: The tax, welfare, and insurance regulations developed by computer-based bureaucracies are so complex and fast changing that it is extremely difficult for individuals to keep up and to make informed choices. Even knowledgeable computer users are often overwhelmed by the torrent of software packages, each with hundreds of features and options. The presence of computers and other technologies can mislead managers into believing that they can deal with the complexities they are creating. Rapid computer systems become valued, speed dominates, and more features seem "better." This situation is apparent in nuclear-reactor control rooms, where hundreds of brightly lit annunciators overwhelm operators when indicating failures. Simplicity is a simple, but too often ignored, principle. Stern adherence to basic principles may be the only path to a safer, saner, simpler, and slower world where human concerns predominate.

- *Organizational fragility*: As organizations come to depend on more complex technology, they can become fragile. When breakdowns occur, they can propagate rapidly and halt the work of many people. With computer-based airline ticketing, telephone switching, or department-store sales, computer failures can mean immediate shutdowns of service. A more subtle example is that computer-based inventory control may eliminate or dramatically reduce stock on hand so that disruptions spread rapidly. For example, a strike in a ball-bearing plant can force the closure of a distant automobile assembly line within a few days. Computers can cause concentration of expertise, and then a small number of people can disrupt a large organization. Can developers anticipate the dangers and produce robust designs?

- *Invasion of privacy*: This widely reported threat is worrisome because the concentration of information and the existence of powerful retrieval systems make it possible to violate the privacy of many people easily and rapidly. Of course, well-designed computer systems have the potential of becoming more secure than paper systems if managers are dedicated to privacy protection. Airline, telephone, bank, and employment records can reveal much about an individual if confidentiality is compromised. Can managers seek policies and systems that increase rather than reduce the protection of privacy in a computer-based organization?

- *Unemployment and displacement*: As automation spreads, productivity and overall employment may increase, but some jobs may become less valued or eliminated. Retraining can help some employees, but others will have difficulty changing lifetime patterns of work. Displacement may happen to low-paid clerks or highly paid typesetters whose work is automated, as well as to the bank vice-president whose mortgage-loan decisions are now made by an expert system. Can employers develop labor policies that ensure retraining and guarantee jobs?

- *Lack of professional responsibility*: Faceless organizations may respond impersonally and deny responsibility for problems. The complexity of technology and organizations provides ample opportunities for employees to pass the blame on to others or to the computer: "Sorry, the computer won't let us accept the library book without the machine-readable card." Will users of medical diagnostic or defense-related systems be able to escape responsibility for decisions? Will computer printouts become more trusted than a person's word or a professional's judgment? Complex and confusing systems enable users and designers to blame the machine, but with improved designs, responsibility and credit will be given, and will be accepted by the users and designers.

- *Deteriorating image of people*: With the presence of *intelligent terminals*, *smart machines*, and *expert systems*, it seems that the machines have indeed taken over human abilities. These misleading phrases not only generate anxiety about computers, but also may undermine the image we have of people and their abilities. Some behavioral psychologists suggest that we are little more than machines; some AI workers believe that the automation of many human abilities is within reach. The rich diversity of human skills, the generative or creative nature of daily life, the emotional or passionate side of human endeavor, and the idiosyncratic imagination of each child seem lost or undervalued (Rosenbrock, 1982). Rather than be impressed by smart machines, accept the misguided pursuit of the Turing test, or focus on computational skills in people, I believe that we should recognize that designs that empower users will increase users' appreciation of the richness and diversity of unique human abilities.

Undoubtedly, more plagues and problems exist. Each situation is a small warning for the designer. Each design is an opportunity to apply computers in positive, constructive ways that avoid these dangers.

Preventing the Plagues

Before large-scale action can be taken, however, there must be public awareness, public debate, and a decision to take action as a society. We are not naive enough to think that this can take place overnight, but we do know that major transformations have already come about rapidly.   **Ornstein and Ehrlich, 1989**

There is no set formula for preventing these plagues. Even well-intentioned designers can inadvertently spread them, but alert, dedicated designers whose consciousness is raised can reduce the dangers. The strategies for preventing the plagues and reducing their effects include

- *Human-centered design*: Concentrate attention on the users and on the tasks they must accomplish. Make users the center of attention and build feelings of competence, mastery, clarity, and predictability. Construct well-organized menu trees, provide meaningful structure in command languages, present specific and constructive instructions and messages, develop uncluttered displays, offer informative feedback, enable easy error handling, ensure appropriate display rates and response time, and produce comprehensible learning materials.

- *Organizational support*: Beyond the software design, the organization must also support the user. Explore strategies for participatory design and elicit frequent evaluation and feedback from users. Techniques include personal interviews, focus groups, online surveys, paper questionnaires, and online consultants or suggestion boxes. A robust user community can be supported by meetings, newsletters, and an impartial ombudsman (Kling, 1980).

- *Job design*: European labor unions have been active in setting rules for terminal users to prevent the exhaustion, stress, or burnout caused by an *electronic sweatshop*. Rules might be set to limit hours of use, to guarantee rest periods, to facilitate job rotation, and to support education. Similarly, negotiated measures of productivity or error rates can help to reward exemplary workers and to guide training. Monitoring or metering of work must be done cautiously, but both managers and employees can be beneficiaries of a thoughtful plan. Responsibility for failures and for success should be shared explicitly among designers, users, and managers.

- *Education*: The complexity of modern life and computer systems makes education critical. Schools and colleges, as well as employers, all play a role in training. Special attention should be paid to continuing education, on-the-job training, and teacher education.

- *Feedback and rewards*: User groups can be more than passive participants. They can ensure that system failures are reported, that design improvements are conveyed to managers and designers, and that manuals and online aids are reviewed. Similarly, excellence should be acknowledged by awards within organizations and through public presentations. Professional societies in computing might promote awards, similar to the awards of the American Institute of Architects, the Pulitzer Prize Committee, or the Academy of Motion Picture Producers.

- *Public consciousness raising*: Informed consumers of personal computers and users of commercial systems can benefit the entire community. Professional societies such as the Association for Computing Machinery or the IEEE, and user groups such as the Washington Apple Pi or the Capitol IBM PC User's Group, can play a key role through public relations, consumer education, and professional standards of ethics.

- *Legislation*: Much progress has been made with legislation concerning privacy, right of access to information, and computer crime, but more work remains. Cautious steps toward regulation, work rules, and standardization can be highly beneficial. Dangers of restrictive legislation do exist, but thoughtful legal protection will stimulate development and prevent abuses.

- *Advanced research*: Individuals, organizations, and governments can support research to develop novel ideas, to minimize the dangers, and to spread the advantages of interactive systems. Theories of user-cognitive behavior, individual differences, acquisition of skills, visual perception, and organizational change would be helpful in guiding designers and implementers.

Overcoming the Obstacle of Animism

Unlike machines, human minds can create ideas. We need ideas to guide us to progress, as well as tools to implement them.... Computers don't contain "brains" any more than stereos contain musical instruments.... Machines only manipulate numbers; people connect them to meaning.   **Penzias, 1989**

The emergence of computers is one of the fundamental historical changes. Alvin Toffler (1980) describes this *third wave* as the successor to the agricultural and then the industrial revolutions. Such upheavals are neither all good nor all bad, but rather are an amalgam of many individual decisions about how a technology is applied. Each designer plays a role in shaping the direction. The computer revolution has passed its infancy, but there is still tremendous opportunity for change.

The metaphors, images, and names chosen for systems play a key role in the designers' and the users' perceptions. It is not surprising that many computer-system designers still derive their inspiration by mimicking human or animal forms. The first attempts at flight were to imitate birds, and the first designs for microphones followed the shape of the human ear. Eventually, human needs and the underlying technology shape products to maximize service and to reduce cost. Such primitive visions may be useful starting points, but success comes most rapidly to people who move beyond these fantasies and apply scientific analyses. Except for amusement, the goal is never to mimic human form, but rather is to provide effective service to the users in accomplishing their tasks.

Lewis Mumford, in his classic book, *Technics and Civilization* (1934), characterized the problem of "dissociation of the animate and the mechanical" as the "obstacle of animism." He describes Leonardo da Vinci's attempt to reproduce the motion of birds' wings, then Ader's batlike airplane (as late as 1897), and Branca's steam engine in the form of a human head and torso. Mumford wrote: "The most ineffective kind of machine is the realistic mechanical imitation of a man or another animal...for thousands of years animism has stood in the way of...development."

Choosing human or animal forms as the inspiration for some projects is understandable, but significant advances will come more quickly if we recognize the goals that serve human needs and the inherent attributes of the technology that is employed. Hand-held calculators do not follow human forms but serve effectively for doing arithmetic. Designers of championship chess-playing programs no longer imitate human strategies. Vision-systems researchers realized the advantages of radar or sonar range finders and retreated from using humanlike stereo depth-perception cues.

Robots provide an informative case study. Beyond stone idols and voodoo dolls, we can trace modern robots back to the devices built by Pierre Jacquet-Droz, a Swiss watchmaker, from 1768 to 1774. The first child-sized mechanical robot, called The Scribe, could be programmed to write any message up to 40 characters long. It had commands to change lines, to skip a space, or to dip the quill in the inkwell. The second, called The Draughtsman, had a repertoire of four pencil sketches: a boy, a dog, Louis XV of France, and a pair of portraits. The third robot, The Musician, performed five songs on a working pipe organ and could operate for 1.5 hours on one winding. These robots made their creators famous and wealthy since they were in great demand at the court of the kings and in public showings. Printing presses became more effective than The Scribe and The Draughtsman, and tape players and phonographs were superior to The Musician.

Robots of the 1950s included electronic components and a metallic skin, but their designs were also strongly influenced by the human form. Robot arms were of the same dimension as human arms and the hands had five fingers. Designers of modern robots have finally overcome the obstacle of animism and now construct arms whose dimensions are appropriate for the steel and plastic technology. Two fingers are more common than five on robot hands, and the hands can often rotate more than 270 degrees. Where appropriate, fingers have been replaced by rubber suction cups with vacuum pumps to pick up parts.

In spite of these improvements, the metaphor and terminology of human form can still mislead the designers and users of robots. Programmers of one industrial robot were so disturbed by the labels "upper arm" and "lower arm" on the control panel that they scratched out the words. They thought that the anthropomorphic term misled their intuitions about how to program the robot (McDaniel and Gong, 1982). The terms *programmable manipulators* and the broader *flexible manufacturing systems* are less exciting, but describe more accurately the newer generation of robotic systems.

The banking machine offers a simple example of the evolution from anthropomorphic imagery to a service orientation. Early systems had such names as Tillie the Teller or Harvey Wallbanker and were programmed with such phrases as "How can I help you?" These deceptive images rapidly gave way to a focus on the computer technology with such names as The Electronic Teller, CompuCash, Cashmatic, or CompuBank. Over time, the emphasis moves toward the service provided to the user: CashFlow, Money Exchange, 24-Hour Money Machine, All-Night Banker, and Money Mover.

The computer revolution will be judged not by the complexity or power of technology, but rather by the service to human needs. By focusing on users, researchers and designers will generate powerful yet simple systems that permit users to accomplish their tasks. These tools will enable short learning times, rapid performance, and low error rates. Putting users' needs first will lead to more appropriate choices of system features, a greater sense of mastery and control, and the satisfaction of achievement. At the same time, users will feel increased responsibility and may be more motivated to learn about the tasks and the interactive system.

Sharpening the boundaries between people and computers will lead to a clearer recognition of computer powers and human reasoning (Weizenbaum, 1976; Winograd and Flores, 1986). Rapid progress will occur when designers accept that human–human communication is a poor model for human–computer interaction. People are different from computers, and human operation of computers is vastly different from human relationships. Vital factors that distinguish human behavior include the diversity of skills and background across individuals; the creativity, imagination, and inventiveness incorporated in daily actions; the emotional involvement in every act; the desire for social contact; and the power of intention.

Ignoring these primitive but enduring aspects of humanity leads to inappropriate technology and to hollow experiences. Embracing these aspects can bring about powerful tools, joy in learning, the capacity to realize goals, a sense of accomplishment, and increased social interaction.

Although designers may be attracted to the goal of making impressive and autonomous machines that perform tasks as well as humans do, this is not what most users want. I believe that users want to have sense of their own accomplishment, rather than to admire a magically smart, intelligent, or expert system. Users want to be empowered by technology to be able to apply their knowledge and experience to make judgments that lead to improved job performance and greater personal satisfaction. Sometimes, predefined objective criteria can be applied to a task, but often human values must be applied and flexibility in decision making is a necessity (Weizenbaum, 1976). With increased automation, it is often beneficial to reconsider the balance between high-tech and high-touch (Naisbitt, 1982).

Some examples may help us to clarify this issue. Doctors do not want a machine that does medical diagnosis, but rather a machine that enables them to do a more accurate, reliable diagnosis, to obtain relevant references to scientific papers or clinical trials, to gather consultative support more rapidly, and to record that support more accurately. Similarly, air-traffic or manufacturing controllers do not want a machine that automatically does their job, but rather one that increases their productivity, reduces their error rates, and enables them to handle special cases or emergencies effectively. I believe that an increase in personal responsibility will result in improved service.

In the Long Run

Successful interactive systems will bring ample rewards to the designers, but widespread use of effective tools is only the means to reach higher goals. A computer system is more than a technological artifact: interactive systems, especially when linked by computer networks, create human social systems. As Marshall McLuhan pointed out, "the medium is the message," and therefore each interactive system is a message from the designer to the user. That message has often been a harsh one, with the underlying implication that the designer does not care about the user. Nasty error messages are obvious manifestations; complex commands, cluttered screens, and confusing sequences of operations are also part of the harsh message.

Most designers want to send a more kind and caring message. Designers, implementers, and researchers are learning to send warmer greetings to the users with effective and well-tested systems. The message of quality is compelling to the recipients and can instill good feelings, appreciation for the designer, and the desire to excel in one's own work. The capacity for excellent systems to instill compassion and connection was noted by Sterling (1974) at the end of his guidelines for information systems:

> In the long run what may be important is the *texture* of a system. By texture we mean the *quality* the system has to evoke in users and participants a feeling that the system increases the kinship among people.

At first, it may seem remarkable that computer systems can instill a kinship among people, but every technology has the potential to engage people in cooperative efforts. The same message emerges from Robert Pirsig's *Zen and the Art of Motorcycle Maintenance* (1974). Each act of quality is noticed and spreads like waves on the water. Each designer can play a role— not only that of fighting for the user, but also that of nurturing, serving, and caring for users.

Practitioner's Summary

High-level goals might include world peace, excellent health care, adequate nutrition, accessible education, communication, freedom of expression, support for creative exploration, safety, and socially constructive entertainment. Computer technology can help us to attain these high-level goals if we clearly state measurable objectives, obtain participation of professionals, and design effective human–computer interfaces. Design considerations include adequate attention to individual differences among users; support of social and organizational structures; design for reliability and safety; provision of access by the elderly, handicapped, or illiterate; and appropriate user-controlled adaptation. With suitable theories and empirical research we can achieve ease of learning, rapid performance, low error rates, and good retention over time, while preserving high subjective satisfaction.

References

Birnbaum, Joel S., Toward the domestication of microelectronics, *IEEE Computer 18*, 11 (November 1985), 128–140.

Bork, Alfred, *Learning with Computers*, Digital Press, Bedford, MA (1981).

Bork, Alfred, *Personal Computers for Education*, Harper and Row, New York (1985).

Brod, Craig, *Technostress: The Human Cost of the Computer Revolution*, Addison-Wesley, Reading, MA (1984).

Eisler, Riane, *The Chalice and the Blade: Our History, Our Future*, Harper and Row, San Francisco, CA (1987).

Florman, Samuel, *The Existential Pleasures of Engineering*, St. Martin's Press, New York (1976).

Jin, Gregory K., On a positive MIS idealogy. In Carey, Jane, *Human Factors in Information Systems: An Organizational Perspective*, Ablex, Norwood, NJ (1991), 195–216.

Kling, Rob, Social analyses of computing: Theoretical perspectives in recent empirical research, *ACM Computing Surveys 12*, 1 (March 1980), 61–110.

McDaniel, Ellen, and Gong, Gwendolyn, The language of robotics: Use and abuse of personification, *IEEE Transactions on Professional Communications PC-25*, 4 (December 1982), 178–181.

Mumford, Lewis, *Technics and Civilization*, Harcourt Brace and World, New York (1934).

Naisbitt, John, *Megatrends: Ten New Directions Transforming Our Lives*, Warner Books, New York (1982).

Norman, Don, *The Psychology of Everyday Things*, Basic Books, New York (1988).

Ornstein, Robert and Ehrlich, Paul, *New World New Mind: Moving Towards Conscious Evolution*, A Touchstone Book, Simon and Schuster, New York (1989).

Penzias, Arno, *Ideas and Information*, Simon and Schuster, New York (1989).

Pirsig, Robert, *Zen and the Art of Motorcycle Maintenance*, Morrow, New York (1974).

Rosenbrock, H. H., Robots and people, *Measurement and Control 15* (March 1982), 105–112.

Sheridan, Thomas B., Computer control and human alienation, *Technology Review 83*, 1 (October 1980), 51–73.

Sterling, T. D., Guidelines for humanizing computerized information systems: A report from Stanley House, *Communications of the ACM 17*, 11 (November 1974), 609–613.

Toffler, Alvin, *The Third Wave*, Morrow, New York (1980).

Turkle, Sherry, *The Second Self*, Simon and Schuster, New York (1984).

Vitalari, Nicholas P., Venkatesh, Alladi, and Gronhaug, Kjell, Computing in the home: Shifts in the time allocation patterns of households, *Communications of the ACM 28*, 5 (May 1985), 512–522.

Weizenbaum, Joseph, *Computer Power and Human Reason*, W. H. Freeman, San Francisco, CA (1976).

Winograd, Terry and Flores, Fernando, *Understanding Computers and Cognition: A New Foundation for Design*, Ablex, Norwood, NJ (1986).

Zuboff, Shoshanna, *In the Age of the Smart Machine: The Future of Work and Power*, Basic Books, New York (1988).

Name Index

Subject Index